Using This Guide

Overview Box Each city has an overview box that contains LGBT information. The overview also includes general tourist info: the city's major airport and directions to the most populated area of gay-friendly businesses; phone numbers for public transit and taxis; weather; tourist spots; local food favorites and day-trip suggestions.

Overview Map The overview map covers the city and its surrounding areas. This map highlights tourist landmarks, freeways, and main streets.

Detail Map The detail map focuses on the area where most LGBT businesses are located. All bars, accommodations, and LGBT bookstores that fall within this map are indicated by both a number and a symbol from the map legend (see **Legend to Maps** ==============>)

LEGEND TO MAPS

▲ Accommodations	➋ Bars & Nightclubs
③ LGBT Bookstores	▼ LGBT Centers

HIGHWAY MARKERS

(167) (70)	U S Highways
(630) (30)	Interstates
(367) (5)	State Highways
🍁	Trans Canada

GEOGRAPHIC

— · — · —	State Line
N ↑	North Orientation

PLACES

■	Points of Interest
✕	Airports
H	Hospitals
▦	Parks/Cemeteries
❶	Tourist Information

TRANSPORTATION

Ⓜ ◯	Metro/Subway Stop
	Transit Lines
- - - -	Ferries
▦▦▦▦	Railroads
▭ ▮	Tunnels
▬▬▬▬	Highways
← ↓ → ↑	Traffic Direction

Call first! Not because we haven't (in fact, we call several times a year!), but because every element of a listing, from hours to area codes, may have changed since we've hung up the phone.

Accommodations Most accommodations (especially B&Bs) require advance reservations. It's a good idea to request a brochure ahead of time, and to be clear about deposit and cancellation policies when making reservations.

Bars & Nightclubs Many codes apply only a few nights a week, especially when we've noted "theme nights." You should call the bar or club to verify what is scheduled for which nights. Bars coded BW (beer/wine) might not serve both. Nightclubs in particular tend to change their opening times and theme nights regularly. Be sure to call ahead! And remember, bars for women or with women's nights have their names printed in red.

Restaurants All restaurants listed are gay-friendly; those with mostly gay/lesbian clientele are coded MW. "Cont'l" means European or French fare. "American" menus range from steak & seafood to homestyle or hamburgers. If a variety of vegetarian entrees is offered, "plenty veggie" is noted.

Cafes are casual hangouts serving coffee and pastries, but usually not full menus.

Entertainment & Recreation Something touristy, maybe a little kitschy, definitely unusual or commonly overlooked, that even your friends who've lived there all their lives won't mind doing. Anything from a walking tour to a queer beach, as well as LGBT theaters and TV & radio shows.

Publications If you want to know what's new, get one when you get to town. They're usually free and distributed in many of the locations we list. Your best bet, however, is to go right to the local LGBT or alternative bookstore to get the latest issue.

Gyms are workout facilities, not bathhouses. They're mostly straight, unless coded MW or MO.

Unconfirmed means we called, several times, but no one answered. The phone still works but everything else may be different. Definitely call first.

TABLE OF CONTENTS

UNITED STATES

TABLE OF CONTENTS

ALABAMA

Birmingham

ACCOMMODATIONS

The Tutwiler Wyndham [GF,WI,WC] 205/322-2100 ■ 2021 Park Pl N (at 21st St N) ■ *upscale, also restaurant & lounge* ■ www.wyndham.com

BARS

1   **The Garage Cafe** [GF,F,E] 205/322-3220 ■ 2304 10th Terrace S ■ *11am-close, from 3pm Sun-Mon, great sandwiches, live music*

The Phoenix [MW,NH,K,DS] 205/595-5120 ■ 5120 5th Ave S ■ *[CW] dancing & lessons Wed, [L] party monthly, [F] Sun* ■ www.phoenixbham.com

NIGHTCLUBS

2   **22nd Street Jazz Cafe** [GF,D,MR,F,E] 205/252-0407 ■ 710 22nd St S (at 7th Ave S) ■ *4pm-midnight, till 2am Fri-Sat, live music* ■ www.22jazz.com

3   **Al's Lakeview Yacht Club** [MW,D,DS] 205/322-1682 ■ 2627 7th Ave S ■ *3pm-close* ■ LakeviewYachtClu@bell-south.net

4   **The Quest Club** [M,D,DS,PC,WC,$] 205/251-4313 ■ 416 24th St S (at 5th Ave S) ■ *24hrs, [19+] Wed-Sun, patio* ■ www.quest-club.com

5   **The U** [GF,D] 205/323-4266 ■ 2300 1st Ave N (at 23rd St) ■ *7pm-2am Th-Sat only* ■ www.firstand23rd.com

CAFES

Chez Lulu 205/870-7011 ■ 1909 Cahaba Rd ■ *lunch & dinner Tue-Sun, Sun brunch, clsd Mon, plenty veggie* ■ www.birminghammenus.com/chezlulu

Safari Cup [F] 205/326-0019 ■ 300 Richard Arrington Jr Blvd ■ *6am-6pm, independent movies 6pm Th, full menu, plenty veggie* ■ www.safaricup.com

RESTAURANTS

Bottega Cafe & Restaurant [WC] 205/939-1000 ■ 2240 Highland Ave S (btwn 22nd & 23rd) ■ *5:30pm-10pm, clsd Sun, full bar* ■ www.bottegarestaurant.com

Highlands Bar & Grill [WC] 205/939-1400 ■ 2011 11th Ave S (at 20th St) ■ *5:30pm-10pm, clsd Sun-Mon* ■ www.highlandsbarandgrill.com

BIRMINGHAM

Day Trips: Cheaha State Park

Located about 80 miles east of Birmingham, this park is home to the highest point in Alabama. At 2,407 feet and surrounded by the Talladega National Forest, the view from Mt. Cheaha is spectacular! The park currently has 10 miles (and growing) of bike trails, but rock-climbers, hikers, wildflower- and foliage-enthusiasts, and fisher-persons will also find plenty to do. Camping, cabins, and hotel accommodations are available if one day is not enough!

Tourist Info

AIRPORT DIRECTIONS

Birmingham Int'l. From Airport Blvd: take I-20 West to the 22nd St exit. 22nd runs one way south.

PUBLIC TRANSIT & TAXIS

Americas United Cab Co 205/969-7177.
Birmingham Transit Authority 205/521-0101, web: www.bjcta.org.

TOURIST SPOTS & INFO

Alabama Jazz Hall of Fame 205/254-2731, web: www.jazzhall.com.
Birmingham Zoo & Botanical Gardens 205/879-0409, web: www.birminghamzoo.com.
Civil Rights Museum 205/328-9696, web: www.bcri.org.
Vulcan Statue at 20th St S & Valley Ave, atop Red Mountain.
Sloss Furnaces Nat'l Historic Landmark 205/324-1911, web: www.slossfurnaces.com.
Visitor's Center: 800/458-8085 or 205/458-8000, web: www.birminghamal.org.

Weather

Hot and humid in the 80°s and 90°s during the summer, mild in the 50°s to low 40°s during the winter.

Best Views

Overlook Park.

City Calendar

LGBT PRIDE

June. web: www.centralalabamapride.org.

ANNUAL EVENTS

April - Birmingham Shout: Gay & Lesbian Film Festival of Alabama 205/324-0888, web: www.bhamshout.com.
April/May - Birmingham International Festival 202/252-7652, web: www.bifsalutes.org.
June - City Stages 205/251-1272, web: www.citystages.org.
June - Alabama Shakespeare Festival 800/841-4273, web: www.asf.net.

Queer Resources

COMMUNITY INFO

Live and Let Live LGBT AA 205/599-3363 (church #), web: www.birminghamaa.com. 6pm Wed, Fri & Sun at 5117 1st Ave N (Covenant Community Church).

AIDS Outreach 205/322-4197, web: www.birminghamaidsoutreach.org.

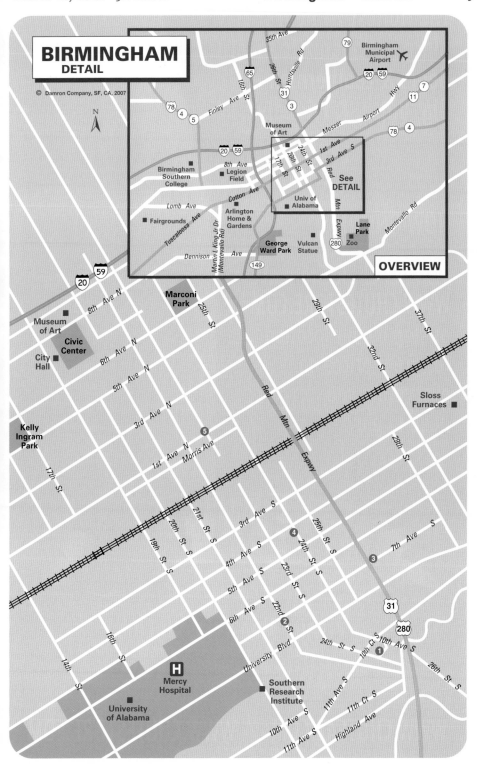

John's [WC] 205/322-6014 ■ 112 21st St N (btwn 1st & 2nd Ave N) ■ lunch weekdays & dinner Mon-Sat, clsd Sun, seafood & steak, full bar

Rojo 205/328-4733 ■ 2921 Highland Ave S ■ 11am-10pm, clsd Mon, wknd brunch, Latin & American cuisine ■ www.birminghammenus.com/rojo

Silvertron Cafe 205/591-3707 ■ 3813 Clairmont Ave S (at 39th St S) ■ 11am-10pm, till 9pm Sun, also full bar, more gay Mon

ENTERTAINMENT & RECREATION

Terrific New Theater 205/328-0868 ■ 2821 2nd Ave S (in Dr Pepper Design Complex)

EROTICA

Alabama Adult Books 205/322-7323 ■ 801 3rd Ave N (at 8th) ■ 24hrs, super-arcade

Birmingham Adult Books [★] 205/836-1580 ■ 7610 1st Ave N (at 76th St) ■ 24hrs, booths

The Downtown Bookstore 205/328-5525 ■ 2731 8th Ave N (at 28th St) ■ arcade, booths

Pleasure Books 205/836-7379 ■ 7606 1st Ave N (at 76th St) ■ arcade, booths

Screening Room 205/251-1025 ■ 2130 Second Ave S (at 22nd St S) ■ theater

ARIZONA

Phoenix

ACCOMMODATIONS

1 ▶Arizona Royal Villa Complex [MO,SW,N,NS,WI,GO] 602/266-6883, 888/266-6884 ■ 4312 N 12th St ■ hot tub ■ www.RoyalVilla.com

2 Arizona Sunburst Inn [MO,R,SW,N,NS,GO] 602/274-1474, 800/974-1474 ■ 6245 N 12th Pl (at Rose Ln) ■ hot tub ■ www.azsunburst.com

3 Cantera Fountains [GF,SW,NS,WI,GO] 480/266-9008, 602/445-6274 ■ 2228 E Campbell Ave ■ condo, fully equipped kitchen, hot tub ■ rbanks44@cox.net

4 Claremont House B&B [MW,SW,N,NS,WC,GO] 602/249-2974 ■ 502 W Claremont Ave (btwn Maryland & Bethany Home, enter 7th Ave) ■ full brkfst, hot tub ■ www.claremonthousephoenix.com

5 Clarendon Hotel & Suites [GS,SW,WI,WC,GO] 602/252-7363 ■ 401 W Clarendon Ave (at 3rd Ave) ■ modern boutique hotel in midtown ■ www.theclaren-don.net

6 Hotel San Carlos [GF,F,SW,WI] 602/253-4121, 866/253-4121 ■ 202 N Central Ave ■ boutique hotel, rooftop pool, restaurant, downtown ■ www.hotelsancar-los.com

39 Ivy Cottage Home Stay [GF,GO] 602/955-5157 ■ 2315 N 42nd St ■ B&B in historic home, heated Roman pool, full brkfst ■ alplusart@dcsinter.net

8 Maricopa Manor B&B Inn [GS,SW,WI,WC,GO] 602/274-6302, 800/292-6403 ■ 15 W Pasadena Ave ■ in heart of N Central Phoenix, hot tub ■ www.maricopa-manor.com

39 Yum Yum Tree Guest House [GS,SW,GO] 602/265-2590, 877/986-8733 ■ 90 W Virginia Ave #1 (at 3rd Ave) ■ suites in historic neighborhood, courtyard ■ www.yytguesthouse.com

BARS

10 Amsterdam [MW,F,E,K] 602/258-6122 ■ 718 N Central Ave (btwn Roosevelt & Fillmore) ■ 4pm-2am, till 4am wknds, upscale bar, also Club Miami [D] ■ www.amsterdambar.com

11 Apollo's [M,NH,K,S,WI] 602/277-9373 ■ 5749 N 7th St (S of Bethany Home) ■ 11am-1am, till 2am wknds, Sun brunch, diverse crowd ■ www.apollos.com

12 The Bunkhouse Saloon [M,NH,K] 602/200-9154 ■ 4428 N 7th Ave (at Indian School) ■ 8am-2am, from 10am Sun, patio ■ www.bunkhousesaloon.com

13 Burger Betty's [MW,F,K,GO] 602/240-6969 ■ 5111 N 7th St (N of Camelback) ■ 10am-1am, Sun brunch, full menu, 18+ karaoke & movie Wed ■ www.burgerbettys.com

14 Cash Inn Country [W,D,CW,K,WC] 602/244-9943 ■ 2140 E McDowell Rd (at 22nd St) ■ 2pm-close, from noon wknds ■ www.cashinncountry.net

15 Charlie's [M,D,CW,WC] 602/265-0224 ■ 727 W Camelback Rd (at 7th Ave) ■ 2pm-2am, noon-4am Fri-Sat, Sun BBQ ■ www.charliesphoenix.com

9 Club Vibe [MW,D,MR,E,K,DS,WC] 602/224-9977 ■ 3031 E Indian School #7 (at 32nd St) ■ 8pm-2am, clsd Mon-Wed ■ www.clubvibe602.com

16 Cruisin' 7th [M,WC] 602/212-9888 ■ 3702 N 7th St (near Indian School) ■ 6am-1am, from 10am Sun

17 Dick's Cabaret [M,D,S] 602/274-3425 ■ 3613 E Van Buren (at 37th St) ■ 7pm-1am, till 3am Fri-Sat, "all male nude review," no alcohol ■ www.dickscabaret.com

18 Friends [M,NH,B,F,K,GO] 602/277-7729 ■ 1028 E Indian School Rd (at N 10th Pl) ■ 11am-2am, from 10am Sun ■ www.friendsaz.com

19 Fuel Bar & Grill [MW,NH,E] 602/494-3835 ■ 2827 E Bell Rd ■ 3pm-2am, from 10am Th-Sun, motorcycle crowd, patio ■ www.fuelbarandgrill.com

20 Harley's 2303 [M,D,L] 602/956-2885 ■ 2303 E Indian School Rd ■ noon-close

21 Homme [MW,NH,D,K] 602/234-3023 ■ 138 W Camelback Rd (btwn 3rd & Central Aves) ■ 4pm-2am, from 6pm Fri-Sat ■ www.phoenixhomme.com

22 Incognito Lounge [MW,D,S,WC] 602/955-9805 ■ 2424 E Thomas Rd (at 24th St) ■ 8pm-1am, till 3am Fri-Sat, clsd Mon-Wed

23   **Kobalt** [MW,E] 602/264-5307 ■ 3110 N Central Ave ■ www.kobaltbarphoenix.com

24   <u>**The Locker Room**</u> [W,NH,K] 602/267-8707 ■ 3108 E McDowell Rd (at 32nd St) ■ 3pm-2:30am, from noon Sun, sports bar

25   **Marlys' Pub** [MW,NH] 602/867-2463 ■ 15615 N Cave Creek Rd (btwn Greenway Pkwy & Greenway Rd) ■ 3pm-1am, till 2am Fri-Sat

27   **Nu Towne Saloon** [★M,NH,WC] 602/267-9959 ■ 5002 E Van Buren (at 48th St) ■ noon-2am, patio, cruisy ■ www.nutowne.com

28   **Oz** [MW,NH] 602/242-5114 ■ 1805 W Bethany Home Rd (at 19th) ■ noon-2am

29   **Paco Paco's** [M,D,MR-L,TG,DS] 602/263-8424 ■ 3045 N 16th St (at Thomas) ■ 7pm-1am, clsd Mon-Tue

30   **Padlock** [M,L] 602/266-5640 ■ 998 E Indian School Rd (at 10th St) ■ 3pm-2am, special events ■ www.padlockaz.com

31   **Phoenix Eagle** [M,D,L] 602/493-0355 ■ 3114 E Cactus Rd ■ 4pm-2am, from 2pm Sun ■ www.phxeagle.com

32   **Plazma** [MW,NH,E,V] 602/266-0477 ■ 1560 E Osborn Rd (at N 16th St) ■ 4pm-2am

33   **Pumphouse II** [M,NH,K,S,V] 602/275-3509 ■ 4132 E McDowell Rd (at 41st St) ■ noon-2am ■ www.pumphousell.com

34   **The Rock/ La Roca** [M,NH,D,K] 602/248-8559 ■ 4129 N 7th Ave (at Indian School) ■ noon-2am ■ www.phxthe-rocklaroca.com

35   **Roscoe's on 7th** [MW,F] 602/285-0833 ■ 4531 N 7th St (at Minnezona) ■ 11am-1am, sports bar ■ www.roscoe-son7.com

     Wild Card [MW,NH,D,K,DS,V] 480/857-3088 ■ 801 N Arizona Ave, Chandler ■ 2pm-2am

36   **Z Girl Club** [W,D,MR,E,K,WC] 602/265-3233 ■ 4301 N 7th Ave (at Indian School Rd) ■ noon-2am, from 10am Th-Sun ■ www.zgirlclub.com

Nightclubs

37   <u>**E-Lounge**</u> [W,D] 602/279-0388 ■ 4343 N 7th Ave (btwn Camelback & Indian School Rd) ■ 7pm-2am Wed-Sun ■ www.eloungephx.com

10   <u>**Girl Bar Phoenix**</u> [W,D,MR] 702 Central Ave ■ 8pm 2nd Th only ■ www.girlbar.com

38   <u>**Karamba**</u> [★M,D,WC] 602/254-0231 ■ 1724 E McDowell (at 16th St) ■ 4pm-close, clsd Mon-Wed, Latin wknds ■ www.karambanightclub.com

Restaurants

     Alexi's [WC] 602/279-0982 ■ 3550 N Central (in Valley Bank Bldg at Osborn) ■ lunch & dinner, dinner only Sat, clsd Sun, int'l, full bar, patio

     Barrio Cafe [E] 602/636-0240 ■ 2814 N 16th St ■ lunch Mon-Fri, dinner Mon-Sun, Sun brunch, clsd Mon, Mexican, live music ■ www.barriocafe.com

     Circa 1900 602/256-0223 ■ 628 E Adams St ■ 5pm-10pm Tue-Sat, clsd Sun-Mon, upscale American

     Coronado Cafe 602/258-5149 ■ 2201 N 7th St ■ lunch & dinner, clsd Sun-Mon ■ www.coronadocafe.com

     Durant's 602/264-5967 ■ 2611 N Central Ave ■ lunch Mon-Fri, dinner nightly, American ■ www.durantsfine-foods.com

     Élevé 602/952-0733 ■ 3118 E Camelback ■ 5:30pm-10pm, contemporary American ■ www.azeats.com/eleve

     Harley's Bistro [MW] 602/234-0333 ■ 4221 N 7th Ave ■ lunch Sun-Fri, dinner nightly, Italian ■ harleysbistro@cox.net

     Katz's Deli 602/277-8814 ■ 5144 N Central (at Camelback) ■ 6:30am-2:30pm, from 7:30am Sat-Sun, kosher-style deli

     Los Dos Molinos 602/243-9113 ■ 8646 S Central Ave ■ lunch & dinner, clsd Sun-Mon, homecooking

     Mi Patio 602/277-4831 ■ 3347 N 7th Ave ■ 10am-10pm, till 9pm Sun, Mexican ■ www.mipatioaz.com

     My Florist Cafe [P] 602/254-0333 ■ 534 W McDowell Rd ■ 7am-midnight, salads & sandwiches, full bar ■ www.myfloristcafe.com

     Persian Garden Cafe 602/263-1915 ■ 1335 W Thomas Rd (at N 15th Ave) ■ lunch & dinner, clsd Sun, plenty veggie ■ www.persiangardencafe.com

     Portland's 602/795-7480 ■ 105 W Portland St (at Central Ave) ■ lunch Mon-Fri, dinner Mon-Sat, clsd Sun, also wine bar ■ www.portlandsphoenix.com

     Ticoz 602/200-0160 ■ 5114 N 7th St ■ 11am-11pm, till midnight Fri-Sat, Latin cuisine, full bar ■ www.ticozofari-zona.com

     Vincent's on Camelback [WC] 602/224-0225 ■ 3930 E Camelback Rd (at 40th St) ■ lunch Tue-Fri, dinner Tue-Sat, clsd Sun-Mon, Southwestern, some veggie ■ www.vincentsoncamelback.com

     Wild Thaiger 602/241-8995 ■ 2631 N Central Ave ■ lunch & dinner, Thai ■ www.wildthaiger.com

     Z Pizza 602/234-3289 ■ 53 W Thomas Rd ■ 11am-9pm, till 9:30pm Fri-Sat, healthy pizza ■ www.zpizza.com

Entertainment & Recreation

     <u>**Arizona Roller Derby**</u> 11420 N 19th Ave (at Castle Sports Club) ■ Arizona's female roller derby league, check web for upcoming events ■ www.azrollerderby.com

     <u>**Phoenix Mercury**</u> 480/784-4444 (Ticketmaster) ■ check out the Women's National Basketball Association while you're in Phoenix ■ www.wnba.com/mercury

Retail Shops

     EXPOSED Studio & Gallery [WC,GO] 602/248-8030 ■ 3302 N 3rd St (1 blk S of Osborn) ■ 11am-5pm, till 4pm Sat, clsd Sun, "new & established artists of all mediums" ■ www.exposedgallery.com

     Movies on Central [WC] 602/274-0994 ■ 4700 N Central #121 (at Highland) ■ 11am-10pm, till 11pm Fri-Sat, LGBT video rentals & sales

     Root Seller Gallery 602/712-9338 ■ 1605 N 7th Ave (at McDowell Rd) ■ 10am-7pm, 11am-5pm Sun, LGBT books & gifts ■ therootseller@aol.com

     <u>**Tomcat**</u> [GO] 602/314-4385 ■ 5835 N 16th St, Ste E (at Bethany Home Rd) ■ clothing, accessories & gifts for the lesbian community ■ www.tomcatthreads.com

35   <u>**Unique on Central**</u> [WC] 602/279-9691, 800/269-4840 (mail order) ■ 4700 N Central Ave #205 (at Highland) ■ 9am-9pm, 10am-7pm Sun, cards & gifts ■ www.uniqueoncentral.com

Publications

     Echo Magazine 602/266-0550, 888/324-6624 ■ bi-weekly LGBT newsmagazine ■ www.echomag.com

     Flavaz 602/460-2346 ■ 320 E Willetta Ste 3 (at McDowell & 3rd St) ■ first gay English/ Spanish magazine in AZ ■ www.flavazmag.com

     Ion Arizona Magazine 602/308-4662 x4 ■ entertainment guide ■ www.ionaz.com

     'N Touch Magazine 602/308-4662 x5 ■ LGBTQS newsmagazine ■ www.ionaz.com

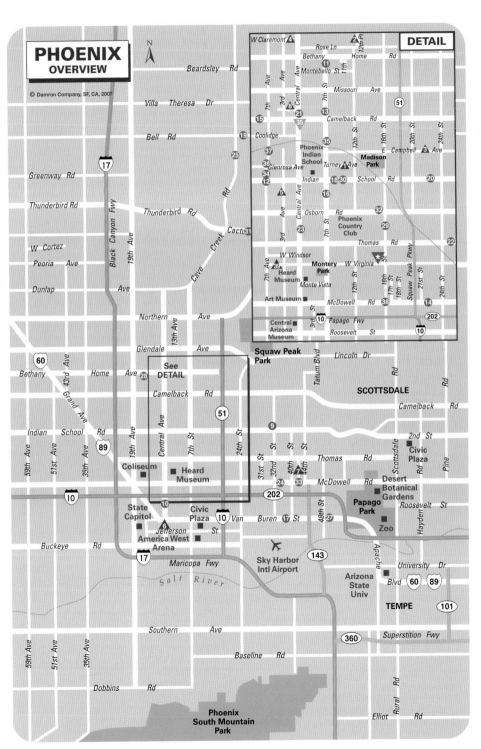

Red Magazine 602/308-8310 ■ *monthly gay nightlife & lifestyle magazine* ■ www.rednightlife.com

X-Factor 602/266-0550, 888/324-6614 ■ *adult video reviews, classified ads, bar & club listings* ■ www.xfactor.com

GYMS & HEALTH CLUBS

Alternatives Health & Wellness Center [GF,MR,TG,GO] 602/266-0801 ■ 4314 N 7th Ave (at Indian School Rd) ■ *11am-9pm, emphasizes spirituality* ■ alternatives@care2.com

MEN'S CLUBS

►**Chute** [MO,B,L,V,18+] 602/234-1654, 877/245-1094 ■ 1440 E Indian School Rd ■ *24hrs, private rooms, gym, steam room* ■ www.chuteaz.com

Flex Complex [SW,PC] 602/271-9011 ■ 1517 S Black Canyon Hwy (btwn 19th Ave & I-17) ■ *24hrs* ■ www.flexbaths.com

EROTICA

Adult Shoppe 602/306-1130 ■ 111 S 24th St (at Jefferson) ■ *24hrs; also 5021 W Indian School Rd (at 51st Ave), 623/245-3008 & 2345 W Holly St, 602/253-7126*

Castle Megastore 602/266-3348 ■ 300 E Camelback (at Central) ■ *24hrs; also 5501 E Washington, 602/231-9837; 8802 N Black Canyon Fwy, 602/995-1641; 8315 E Apache Tr, 480/986-6114* ■ www.castlemegastore.com

International Bookstore 602/955-2000 ■ 3640 E Thomas Rd (at 36th St)

Pleasure World/ Bookcellar [V] 602/275-0015 ■ 4029 E Washington (at 40th St) ■ *also 1838 NW Grand Ave, 602/252-6446 & 6327 N 59th Ave, 623/939-3411*

Tuff Stuff 602/254-9651, 877/875-4167 ■ 1716 E McDowell Rd (at 17th St) ■ *10am-6pm, till 4pm Sat, clsd Sun-Mon, custom leather shop* ■ www.tuffstuffleather.com

PHOENIX

Day Trips: Red Rock State Park/ Oak Creek Canyon

Roughly a 2-hour drive from Phoenix and located in the town of Sedona, this magical country is the most visited area in Arizona after the Grand Canyon. Once revered by the Native Americans as sacred land, Red Rocks is, by legend, one of the world's "power spots." The park contains 5 miles of different looped trails that wind through lush Oak Creek, to red-rock vistas and woodlands. You can hike the trails by yourself or take advantage of one of the free, guided bird, nature, or moonlight walks. Visit www.azparks.gov/Parks/parkhtml/redrock.html for more info.

Tourist Info

AIRPORT DIRECTIONS

Sky Harbor International (enter via 24th St or 44th St). Go north on 24th or 44th to McDowell Rd, then take a left. Turn right onto 7th Ave and go past Indian School Rd.

PUBLIC TRANSIT & TAXIS

Yellow Cab 602/252-5252.
Super Shuttle 602/244-9000.
Phoenix Transit 602/253-5000,
www.valleymetro.org.

TOURIST SPOTS & INFO

Arizona Golf Association 602/944-3035, web: www.azgolf.org.
Castles & Coasters Park on Black Canyon Fwy & Peoria 602/997-7575, web: www.castlesncoast-ers.com.
Heard Museum 602/252-8848, web: www.heard.org.
Phoenix Zoo 602/273-1341, web: www.phoenix-zoo.org.
Desert Botanical Garden in Papago Park 480/941-1225, web: www.dbg.org.
Hiking trails in Papago Park, Squaw Peak & Camelback Mtns.
Visitor's Center: Arizona Office of Tourism 602/364-3700 or 866/275-5816, web: www.arizonaguide.com.
Greater Phoenix Convention & Visitors Bureau 602/254-6500, web: www.phoenixcvb.com.

Weather

Beautifully mild and comfortable (60°s-80°s) October through March or April. Hot (90°s-100°s) in summer. August brings the rainy season (severe monsoon storms) with flash flooding.

Best Views

South Mountain Park at sunset, watching the city lights come on.

City Calendar

LGBT PRIDE

April. 602/277-7433, web: www.azpride.org.

ANNUAL EVENTS

February - OutFar! LGBT film Festival 602/410-1074, web: www.outfar.org.
October - Rainbows Festival 602/770-8241, web: www.rainbowsfestival.com.

Queer Resources

COMMUNITY INFO

1N10, 602/475-7456, community center & switchboard, web: www.1n10.org.
AA 602/264-1341. 2622 N 16th St, call for meeting times. Lambda Club.
Body Positive 602/307-5330, web: www.phoenix-bodypositive.org.

ARKANSAS

Little Rock

ACCOMMODATIONS

1 **Legacy Hotel & Suites** [★GF,WI,WC] 501/374-0100, 888/456-3669 ■ 625 W Capitol Ave (at Gaines) ■ *nat'l historic property in downtown area* ■ www.legacyhotel.com

BARS

2 **Backstreet** [MW,D,K,DS,S,V,PC,WC] 501/664-2744 ■ 1021 Jessie Rd (btwn Cantrell & Riverfront) ■ *9pm-5am, clsd Mon-Th, [18+] Sun & Fri* ■ www.backstreetdanceclub.com

3 **Easy Street Piano Bar** [GF,MR,C,P,GO] 501/372-3530 ■ 307 W 7th St (at Center St) ■ *5pm-2am* ■ www.easystreetpianobar.com

4 **The Factory** [GS,NH,D,F,K,DS,WC,GO] 501/372-3070 ■ 412 S Louisiana St (btwn 4th & Center) ■ *5:30pm-2am, 8pm-1am Sat, clsd Sun-Mon* ■ thefactorybar@aol.com

5 **Sidetracks** [M,NH,CW,B,L,OC,WI,WC] 501/244-0444 ■ 415 Main St, North Little Rock ■ *5pm-2am, also restaurant* ■ www.sidetracksnlr.com

NIGHTCLUBS

6 **UBU** [MW,D,MR,TG,E,K,DS,PC,WC,GO] 501/375-8580 ■ 824 W Capitol (at Izard) ■ *8pm-2am Fri, from 9pm Sat, clsd Sun-Th, lesbian-owned* ■ www.u-b-u.com

RESTAURANTS

Juanita's [E,R] 501/374-3271 ■ 1300 S Main ■ *11am-close, clsd Sun, live music* ■ www.juanitas.com

Lilly's Dim Sum, Then Some [GO] 501/716-2700 ■ 11121 N Rodney Parham Rd ■ *11am-9pm, till 10pm Fri-Sat, noon-9pm Sun, contemporary Asian, plenty veggie, lesbian-owned* ■ www.lillysdimsum.com

LITTLE ROCK

Day Trips: Hot Springs, AR

About an hour southeast of Little Rock, Hot Springs National Park is known as "America's first resort" and is the oldest park in the national park system. People have come for centuries to immerse themselves in the soothing waters. Tour the Fordyce Bathhouse and Visitors Center to learn more about the history of the healing thermal waters. Pamper yourself with a treatment in one of the upscale spas, or visit one of the public bathing facilities on Bathhouse Row. You'll find that Hot Springs has a thriving artist community and world-class antique shopping. It's also home to one LGBT nightclub: Jesters, 1010 E Grand Ave, 501/624-5455, web: www.jestershotsprings.net. For more info, visit www.hotsprings.org. 501-321-2835 or 1-800-SPA-CITY.

Tourist Info

AIRPORT DIRECTIONS
Little Rock National. Follow the signs to downtown, along 440 West, 30 East, then 630 West to Center St.

PUBLIC TRANSIT & TAXIS
Greater Little Rock Transportation 501/374-0333. Central Arkansas Transit 501/375-6717, web: www.cat.org.

TOURIST SPOTS & INFO
Check out Bill & Hillary's old digs at 18th & Center Sts. Central High Museum & Visitors Center 501/374-1957, web: www.nps.gov/chsc. Clinton Presidential Library 501/374-4242, web: www.clintonlibrary.gov. Arkansas Arts Center 501/372-4000, web: www.arkarts.com. Historical Quapaw Quarter. Visitor's Center: Arkansas Dept of Tourism 800/NATURAL, web: www.arkansas.com. Little Rock Convention & Visitors Bureau 800/844-4781, web: www.littlerock.com.

Weather
When it comes to natural precipitation, Arkansas is far from being a dry state. Be prepared for the occasional severe thunderstorm or ice storm. Summers are hot and humid (mid 90°s). Winters can be cold (30°s) with some snow and ice. Spring and fall are the best times to come and be awed by Mother Nature.

Best Views
Quapaw Quarter (in the heart of the city).

City Calendar
LGBT PRIDE
June, web: www.littlerockcapitalpride.org.

ANNUAL EVENTS
October - State Fair 501/372-8341, web: www.arkansasstatefair.com.

Queer Resources
COMMUNITY INFO
Women's Project 501/372-5113, 2224 Main St, 9am-5pm Mon-Fri, bookstore & feminist resource, web: www.womens-project.org. Arkansas AIDS Foundation 501/376-6299, web: www.araidsfoundation.org.

Vino's Pizza [BW] 501/375-8466 ■ 923 W 7th St (at Chester) ■ 11am-close, from 11:30am Sat, from noon Sun ■ www.vinosbrewpub.com

ENTERTAINMENT & RECREATION
The Weekend Theater [GO] 501/374-3761 ■ 1001 W 7th St (at Chester) ■ plays & musicals on wknds ■ www.weekendtheater.org

BOOKSTORES
7   **Women's Project** 501/372-5113, 501/372-6853 (TDD) ■ 2224 Main St (at 23rd) ■ 9am-5pm Mon-Fri, feminist resource, call for info ■ www.womens-project.org

8   **Wordsworth Books & Co** 501/663-9198 ■ 5920 R St ■ 9am-7pm, till 6pm Fri-Sat, noon-5pm Sun, independent

RETAIL SHOPS
A Twisted Gift Shop 501/376-7723 ■ 1007 W 7th St (at Chester) ■ noon-midnight, gift shop ■ atwistedgiftshop@aol.com

Wild Card 501/223-9071 ■ 400 N Bowman (at Maralynn) ■ 10am-6pm, noon-5pm Sun, novelties & gifts

EROTICA
Adult Video 501/562-9628 ■ 2923 W 65th St (off I-30 W) ■ 24hrs, arcade

Cupids 501/565-2020 ■ 3920 W 65th St (off I-30, exit 135) ■ 24hrs, arcade

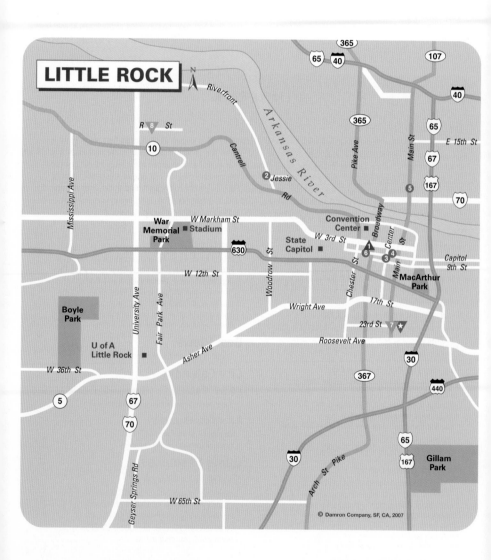

CALIFORNIA

Long Beach

ACCOMMODATIONS

1   **Beachrunners' Inn** [GS,NS] 562/856-0202, 866/221-0001 ■ 231 Kennebec Ave (at Junipero & Broadway) ■ B&B, close to beach, hot tub ■ www.beachrunnersinn.com

2   **The Coast Long Beach Hotel** [GF,SW,WI] 562/435-7676 ■ 700 Queensway Dr ■ full brkfst, gym ■ www.coasthotels.com

3   **Queen Mary** [GF,WC] 562/435-3511 ■ 1126 Queens Hwy ■ historic ocean liner ■ queenmary.com

21 **Turret House B&B** [GS,GO] 562/624-1991, 888/488-7738 ■ 556 Chestnut Ave (at Sixth St) ■ restored Victorian ■ www.turrethouse.com

BARS

4   **The Brit** [M,NH,WC] 562/432-9742 ■ 1744 E Broadway (at Cherry) ■ 10am-2am, patio

5   **The Broadway** [MW,NH,K,WC] 562/432-3646 ■ 1100 E Broadway (at Cerritos) ■ 10am-2am, [K] Fri-Sat

6   **CasaVino** [GF,F] 562/216-1590 ■ 15 S Pine Ave ■ 5pm-close, clsd Mon, some LGBT events, also art gallery, woman-owned ■ www.casavinowinebar.com

7   **Club Broadway** [W,NH,V,WC] 562/438-7700 ■ 3348 E Broadway (at Redondo) ■ 11am-2am

8   **The Crest** [M,L] 562/423-6650 ■ 5935 Cherry Ave (at South) ■ 2pm-2am ■ thecrestbar@aol.com

9   **The Falcon** [M,NH,WC] 562/432-4146 ■ 1435 E Broadway (at Falcon) ■ 7am-2am ■ www.thefalcon.us

10 **Flux** [MW,NH,WI] 562/633-6394 ■ 17817 Lakewood Blvd (at Artesia), Bellflower ■ noon-2am, patio, theme nights ■ www.fluxgaybar.com

11 **Liquid Lounge** [MW,NH,F,E,K] 562/494-7564 ■ 3522 E Anaheim St ■ 11am-1am, till 2am Fri-Sat, [K] Fri-Sat, patio ■ www.liquidloungelongbeach.com

12 **Mineshaft** [★M,B] 562/436-2433 ■ 1720 E Broadway (btwn Gaviota & Hermosa) ■ 10am-2am ■ www.mineshaftlb.com

12 **Paradise Piano Bar & Restaurant** [MW,NH,F,E,P] 562/590-8773 ■ 1800 E Broadway Blvd (at Hermosa) ■ 3pm-1am, from 10am Sat-Sun ■ www.paradiselb.com

13 **Pistons** [M,B,L] 562/422-1928 ■ 2020 E Artesia (at Cherry) ■ 6pm-2am, till midnight Mon, till 3am Fri-Sat, from 3pm Sun, patio, Leather Night Fri ■ www.pistonsbar.com

14 **Que Será** [GS,D,A,E] 562/599-6170 ■ 1923 E 7th St (at Cherry) ■ 4pm-2am Tue, from 5pm Wed-Sat, from 3pm Sun, clsd Mon, theme nights, [$] after 9pm ■ www.thequesera.com

15 **Silver Fox** [M,K,V,WC] 562/439-6343 ■ 411 Redondo (at 4th) ■ 4pm-2am, from noon wknds, popular happy hour, [K] Wed & Sun ■ www.silverfoxlongbeach.com

16 **Sweetwater Saloon** [M,NH,WC] 562/432-7044 ■ 1201 E Broadway (at Orange) ■ 10am-2am, popular days, cruisy

NIGHTCLUBS

17 **Boy's Room** [M,D,E,S,WC] 562/597-3884 ■ 3428 E Pacific Coast Hwy (at Redondo, at the Executive Suite) ■ 8pm-close Fri only ■ www.clubboysroom.com

18 **Club Flaunt** [W,D,E] 562/983-7002 ■ 740 E Broadway (at Mick & Mack's) ■ 8pm-2am 2nd Sat only ■ www.clubflaunt.com

19 **Club Ripples** [★M,D,MR,F,E,K,DS,S,V,YC] 562/433-0357 ■ 5101 E Ocean (at Granada) ■ noon-2am, patio, theme nights, more women Fri for Debra's @ the Beach, T-dance Sun, Bear Bar every 2nd Sat, Arriba Arriba every 3rd Sat ■ www.clubripples.com

19 **Debra's @ the Beach** [★W,D,MR,F,E,K,S,V,YC] 562/433-0357 ■ 5101 E Ocean (at Granada, at Ripples) ■ 7pm-2am Fri, 3 bars on 2 levels, go-go girls, patio ■ www.clubripples.com

17 **Executive Suite** [★MW,D,E,WC] 562/572-4810, 310/547-4730 ■ 3428 E Pacific Coast Hwy (at Redondo) ■ 8pm-close Th-Sat, Latin night Th, Boy's Bar Fri [M,YC], women Sat, 2 levels ■ www.executivesuitelb.com

CAFES

Coffee Haven [M] 562/437-3785 ■ 1708 E Broadway (at Gaviota) ■ 7am-midnight, from 7:30am Sun, sandwiches & desserts, internet access ■ www.coffeehaven.net

Hot Java [WI] 562/433-0688 ■ 2101 E Broadway Ave ■ 6am-11pm, till midnight Fri-Sat, also soups, sandwiches, salads ■ www.HotJavaLB.com

The Library [WI] 562/433-2393 ■ 3418 E Broadway ■ 6am-midnight, till 1am Fri-Sat, from 7am wknds

Phoenix Coffee House [WI,GO] 562/424-4774 ■ 539 E Bixby Rd (at Atlantic) ■ 6am-11pm, till midnight Fri-Sat

RESTAURANTS

Egg Heaven 562/433-9277 ■ 4358 E 4th St ■ 7am-2pm, till 3pm wknds, some veggie

➤**Four Olives Cafe** [E] 562/595-1131 ■ 4276 Atlantic Ave (at Burlinghall) ■ lunch & dinner, wknd brunch, clsd Mon, upscale bistro, live music Wed-Th ■ www.fourolivescafe.com

The House of Madame JoJo [★MW,BW,WC] 562/439-3672 ■ 2941 E Broadway (btwn Temple & Redondo) ■ 4:30pm-close, from 5:30pm wknds, clsd Mon, cont'l, some veggie ■ www.houseofmadamejojo.com

Margarita Grille 562/437-4583 ■ 70 Atlantic Ave (btwn 1st & Ocean) ■ 8am-9pm, till 10pm Fri-Sat, till 8:30pm Sun, full bar, theme nights ■ www.margaritagrille.net

Mick & Mack's [MW,D] 562/983-7001 ■ 740 E Broadway (at Alamitos) ■ 11am-2am, full bar w/ theme nights ■ www.mickandmacks.com

Omelette Inn 562/437–5625 ■ 108 W 3rd St (at Pine)
■ 7am-2:30pm ■ www.omeletteinn.com
Original Park Pantry [WC] 562/434–0451 ■ 2104 E
Broadway (at Junipero) ■ 6am-10pm, till 11pm Fri-Sat, some
veggie

ENTERTAINMENT & RECREATION
International City Theatre 562/495–4595 ■ 300 E Ocean
Blvd ■ Long Beach's resident professional theatre, some LGBT
events ■ www.ictlongbeach.org

BOOKSTORES
20 **Open** 562/499–6736 ■ 2226 E 4th St (btwn Cherry &
Junipero, in heart of Retro Row) ■ 11am-8pm, noon-6pm
Sun, clsd Mon, cool general bookstore w/ books, magazines,
films, art & a variety of events ■ www.accessopen.com

RETAIL SHOPS
Hot Stuff [GO] 562/433–0692 ■ 2121 E Broadway (at
Junipero) ■ 11am-7pm, 10am-6pm Sat, noon-5pm Sun, cards,
gifts & adult novelties, serving community since 1980 ■
www.hotstuffgifts.net
So Cal Tattoo 310/519–8282 ■ 339 W 6th St, San Pedro
■ woman-owned tattoo & piercing shop, reservations
recommended ■ www.socaltattoo.com
Toto's Revenge [GO] 562/434–2777, 877/688–8686
■ 2947 E Broadway (at Orizaba) ■ 10am-9pm, unique cards &
gifts, dog-friendly, also mail order ■ www.totosrevenge.com

LONG BEACH

Day Trips: Catalina Island
You've seen it as a backdrop in such wonderfully campy films as *The Glass Bottom Boat* with Doris Day or *Billy's Hollywood Screen Kiss* with *Will & Grace*'s Sean Hayes. So when you've had enough of Southern California's freeways, why not put yourself center stage and escape to Catalina Island for the day. All manner of aquatic adventure awaits you...boating, fishing, parasailing, and kayaking, not to mention more grounded pursuits such as golf, hiking, biking, and tennis. Scheduled tours for all levels of activity cover every inch of the island. You can get there easily by ferry, or if you're feeling decadent, by helicopter. Contact Catalina Express, 800/481-3470 (www.catalina-express.com), for a ferry from Long Beach. Visit www.catalina.com or www.catalinachamber.org for more info.

Tourist Info
AIRPORT DIRECTIONS
Long Beach Airport. From airport exit: turn right on Lakewood, then right on Spring St. Take a left on Redondo Ave. Some bars are on Redondo, while Broadway is a gay mecca. Bus 111 goes from the airport to Redondo and Broadway.

PUBLIC TRANSIT & TAXIS
Long Beach Taxi Co-op 562/435-6111.
Long Beach Transit & Runabout (free downtown shuttle) 562/591-2301. web: www.lbtransit.com.

TOURIST SPOTS & INFO
Belmont Shores area on 2nd St, south of Pacific Coast Highway—lots of restaurants & shopping, only blocks from the beach.
Long Beach Downtown Marketplace, 10am-4pm Fri.
The Queen Mary 562/435-3511, web: www.queen-mary.com.
"Planet Ocean" mural at 300 E Ocean Blvd.
Visitor's Center: 800/452-7829, web: www.visit-longbeach.com.

Weather
Quite temperate: highs in the mid-80°s July through September, and cooling down at night. In the winter, January to March, highs are in the upper 60°s, and lows in the upper 40°s.

Best Views
On the deck of the Queen Mary, docked overlooking most of Long Beach. Or Signal Hill, off 405. Take the Cherry exit.

City Calendar
LGBT PRIDE
3rd wknd in May. 562/987-9191, web: www.longbeachpride.com.

ANNUAL EVENTS
June - AIDS Walk, web: www.aidswalklb.org.
Aug - Long Beach Jazz Festival, web: www.longbeachjazzfestival.com.
October - Out Loud LGBT art & film festival, web: www.centerlb.org.

Queer Resources
COMMUNITY INFO
Gay & Lesbian Community Center & Switchboard 562/434-4455, web: www.centerlb.org. 2017 E 4th St (at Cherry), 9am-9pm, by appt Sat.
South Bay Center 310/328-6550, web: www.southbaycenter.org. 2235 W Sepulveda Blvd, Torrance, drop-in 7:30pm-10pm Wed.
AA Gay/Lesbian (Atlantic Alano Club) 562/432-7476. At 1403 E 4th St, call for mtg times.
Long Beach Department of Health and Human Services 562/570-4317.

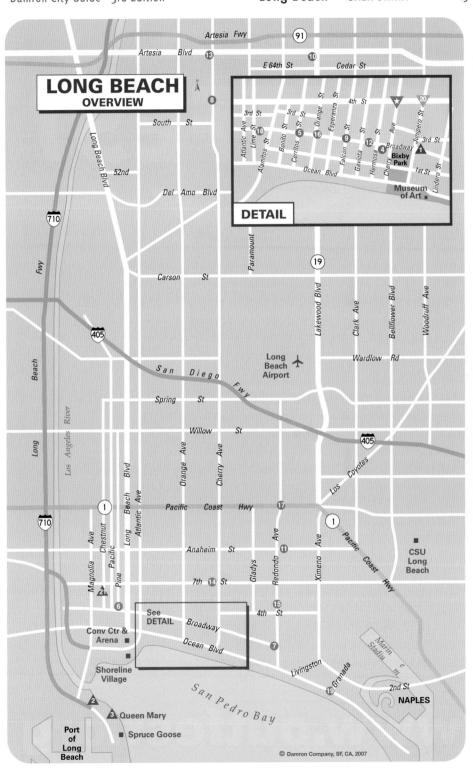

LONG BEACH
OVERVIEW

DETAIL

© Damron Company, SF, CA, 2007

Outfest: The Los Angeles Gay and Lesbian Film Festival
The oldest continuous film festival in Los Angeles.
Outfest 2007: July 12-23
Outfest 2008: July 10-21

Outfest Wednesdays Screening Series
The oldest LGBT screening series in the country.
Year-Round at the Egyptian Theatre, Hollywood

Fusion: The Los Angeles LGBT People of Color Film Festival
The only multi-racial, gender-inclusive LGBT People of Color film festival.

Legacy Project for LGBT Film Preservation
The first film preservation program in the world dedicated to saving and
protecting LGBT films.

Access LA
Forging connections between filmmakers and established industry professionals.

Outfest Screenwriting Lab
Nurturing emerging screenwriters and outstanding LGBT-themed screenplays.

www.outfest.org

PUBLICATIONS

Dot 562/435-6898 ■ *LGBT newsmagazine for S CA* ■ www.dotnewsmagazine.com

Lesbian News (LN) 310/787-8658, 800/458-9888 ■ *nat'l w/ strong coverage of southern CA* ■ www.LesbianNews.com

MEN'S CLUBS

1350 Club [18+] 310/830-4784 ■ 510 W Anaheim St (at Neptune), Wilmington ■ *24hrs* ■ www.midtowne.com

EROTICA

The Crypt on Broadway 562/983-6560 ■ 1712 E Broadway (btwn Cherry & Falcon) ■ *10am-11pm, till midnight Tue & Fri-Sat, from 11am Sun, leather, toys*

Front Door Theatre 562/423-9844 ■ 5832 Atlantic Ave ■ *shows adult movies*

The RubberTree 562/434-0027 ■ 5018 E 2nd St (at Granada) ■ *11am-9pm, till 10pm Fri-Sat, noon-7pm Sun, gifts for lovers, women-owned* ■ www.therubbertree.com

Los Angeles

Los Angeles is divided into 8 geographical areas:
- LA—Overview
- LA—West Hollywood
- LA—Hollywood
- LA—West LA & Santa Monica
- LA—Silverlake
- LA—Midtown
- LA—Valley
- LA—East LA & South Central

LA—Overview

ENTERTAINMENT & RECREATION

The Celebration Theatre 323/957-1884 ■ 7051 Santa Monica Blvd (at La Brea) ■ *LGBT theater, call for more info* ■ www.celebrationtheatre.com

The Ellen DeGeneres Show ■ *C'mon. You know you want to dance with Ellen! Check the website for ticket info.* ■ ellen.warnerbros.com

The Gay Mafia Comedy Company [MW,GO] 323/634-2820 ■ *improv/ sketch comedy* ■ www.thegay-mafia.net

Gay Men's Chorus 323/467-9741, 800/MEN-SING ■ www.gmcla.org

The Getty Center 310/440-7300 ■ 1200 Getty Center Dr, Brentwood ■ *10am-6pm, till 9pm Fri-Sat, clsd Mon, LA's shining city on a hill & world-class museum; of course, it's still in LA so you'll need to make reservations for parking (!)* ■ www.getty.edu

Highways 310/315-1459 (reservation line) ■ 1651 18th St (at the 18th Street Arts Center), Santa Monica ■ *"full-service performance center"* ■ www.highwaysperformance.org

IMRU Gay Radio KPFK LA 90.7 FM ■ *7pm Mon* ■ www.imru.org

LA Sparks 877/447-7275 (LA area only), 310/426-6033 ■ *check out the Women's National Basketball Association while you're in Los Angeles* ■ www.wnba.com/sparks

➤Outfest 213/480-7088 ■ *LGBT media arts foundation that sponsors the annual LGBT film festival each July, also screens LGBT films Wed at the Egyptian Theater in Hollywood* ■ www.outfest.org

Purple Circuit Hotline 818/953-5072 ■ *LGBT theater listings* ■ www.buddybuddy.com/pc.html

SoCalGirlGolf.com [WO,GO] 714/391-3615 ■ *women's golf organization, lesbian-owned* ■ www.socalgirlgolf.com

Vox Femina 310/922-0025 ■ *women's chorus* ■ www.voxfeminala.org

PUBLICATIONS

Adelante Magazine 323/256-6639 ■ *bilingual LGBT magazine* ■ www.adelantemagazine.com

Dot 562/438-6898 ■ *LGBT newsmagazine for Southern CA* ■ www.dotnewsmagazine.com

Frontiers Newsmagazine 323/930-3220 ■ *huge LGBT newsmagazine w/ listings for everything* ■ www.frontier-spublishing.com

Gloss Magazine 510/451-2090 ■ *CA arts/ entertainment magazine, bi-weekly* ■ www.sfgloss.com

Gorgeous Magazine 323/436-7546 ■ 11684 Ventura Blvd #531, Studio City 91604 ■ *bi-monthly* ■ gorgeousmag@aol.com

IN Los Angeles 323/848-2200 ■ *gay news & entertainment magazine for LA* ■ www.inmagla.com

Lesbian News (LN) 310/787-8658, 800/458-9888 ■ *nat'l w/ strong coverage of southern CA* ■ www.LesbianNews.com

MetroSource 323/933-2300 ■ 7250 Beverly Blvd ■ *LGBT lifestyle magazine & resource directory for LA & Southern CA* ■ www.metrosource.com

Odyssey Magazine 323/874-8788 ■ *dish on LA's club scene* ■ www.odysseymagazine.net

The Pink Pages 310/550-0368, 877/769-7465 ■ *LGBT business directory & lifestyle magazine* ■ www.lesgaypinkpages.com

LA—West Hollywood

ACCOMMODATIONS

1 **Chamberlain** [★GS,SW,WC] 310/657-7400, 800/201-9652 ■ 1000 Westmount Dr (near Holloway) ■ *boutique hotel, rooftop pool, restaurant & lounge* ■ www.chamberlainwesthollywood.com

2 **Élan Hotel Modern** [GS,NS,WI,WC,GO] 323/658-6663, 888/611-0398 ■ 8435 Beverly Blvd (at Croft) ■ *hip & trendy, fitness room, kids ok* ■ www.elanhotel.com

3 **The Grafton on Sunset** [GS,SW,WC] 323/654-4600, 800/821-3660 ■ 8462 W Sunset Blvd (at La Cienega) ■ *sundeck, panoramic views, located in heart of Sunset Strip* ■ www.graftononsunset.com

4 **The Grove Guesthouse** [MW,SW,WI,GO] 323/876-7778, 888/524-7683 ■ *1-bdrm villa, hot tub* ■ www.groveguesthouse.com

5 **Holloway Motel** [GS,NS] 323/654-2454, 888/654-6400 ■ 8465 Santa Monica Blvd (at La Cienega) ■ *centrally located* ■ www.hollowaymotel.com

6 **Hyatt West Hollywood** [GS,SW,NS,WI,WC] 323/656-1234, 800/233-1234 ■ 8401 Sunset Blvd (at Kings Rd) ■ *on the Sunset Strip, rooftop pool* ■ westhollywood.hyatt.com/hyatt/hotels/index.jsp

7 **Le Parc Suite Hotel** [★GF,F,SW,WC] 310/855-8888, 800/578-4837 ■ 733 N West Knoll Dr (at Melrose) ■ *deluxe-class all-suite hotel, tennis courts, also restaurant* ■ www.leparcsuites.com

3 **Mondrian** [GF] 323/650-8999, 800/525-8029 ■ 8440 Sunset Blvd ■ *home of trendy Skybar & Asia de Cuba restaurant* ■ www.mondrianhotel.com

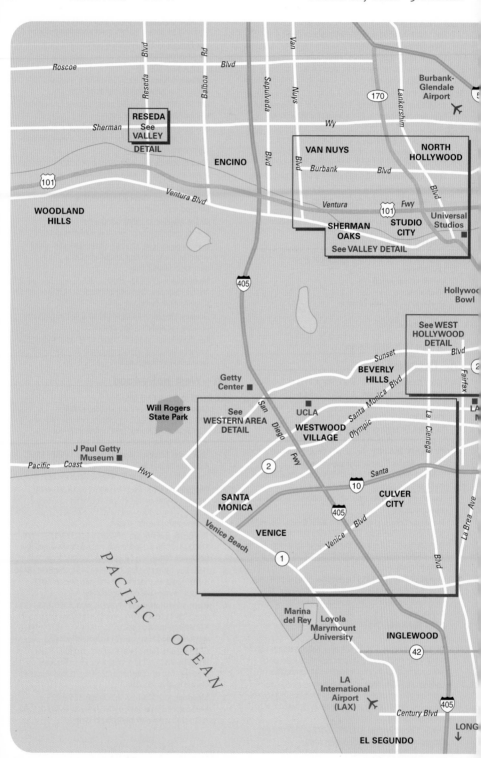

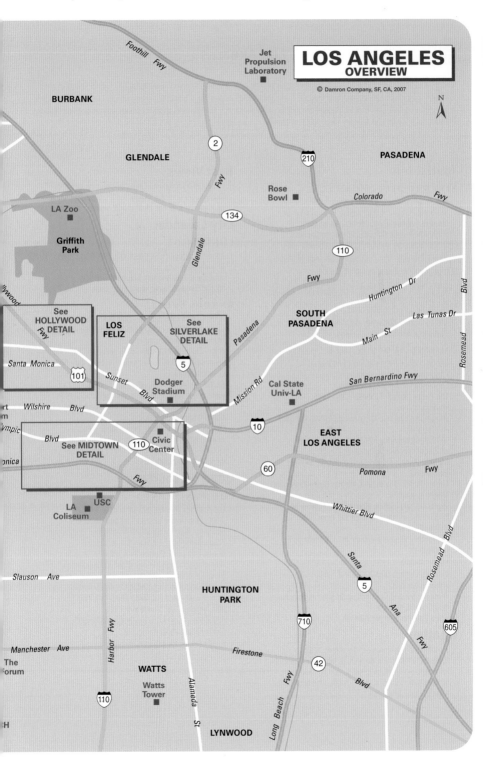

Foothill Fwy

BURBANK

Jet
Propulsion
Laboratory ■

LOS ANGELES
OVERVIEW

© Damron Company, SF, CA, 2007

N

GLENDALE

2

210

PASADENA

Fwy

Rose
Bowl ■

Colorado   Fwy

LA Zoo ■

134

Griffith
Park

Glendale

110

Fwy

Huntington Dr

Rosemead Blvd

See
HOLLYWOOD
DETAIL

Fwy

LOS
FELIZ

See
SILVERLAKE
DETAIL

SOUTH
PASADENA

Las Tunas Dr

Main   St

Santa Monica

101

Sunset

5

Pasadena

Mission Rd

San Bernardino Fwy

Blvd

Dodger
Stadium ■

Cal State
Univ-LA ■

rt
m   Wilshire   Blvd

10

EAST
LOS ANGELES

Olympic

Blvd

See MIDTOWN
DETAIL

110   Civic
Center ■

onica

Fwy

60

Pomona   Fwy

LA
Coliseum ■   USC ■

Whittier Blvd

Rosemead Blvd

Slauson   Ave

Santa

5

HUNTINGTON
PARK

Ana

605

Harbor Fwy

710

Fwy

Manchester   Ave

Firestone

42

The
orum

WATTS

Long Beach Fwy

Blvd

H

110

Watts
Tower ■

Alameda St

LYNWOOD

Los Angeles

Day Trips: Head up to the Angeles National Forest, in the San Gabriel Mountains. You'll find skiing in the winter, hiking year-round, and the Angeles Crest Hwy (SR2) makes for a beautiful scenic drive. Even during those few months when Los Angeles is swamped in fog and smog, the San Gabriel mountaintops soar above the clouds, offering blue skies and a new perspective on this sprawling city.

Tourist Info

AIRPORT DIRECTIONS

Los Angeles International LAX near West LA, Burbank Airport in the Valley, John Wayne in Orange County. To get from LAX to West Hollywood, take the airport exit to the 405 Freeway North. Get off, going northeast onto Santa Monica. Take Santa Monica past Melrose.

PUBLIC TRANSIT & TAXIS

Taxi Co-op 877/733-3305.

LA Express 800/427-7483.

Super Shuttle 310/782-6600.

Metro Transit Authority 800/266-6883, web: www.mta.net. Includes subway.

TOURIST SPOTS & INFO

3rd St outdoor mall in Santa Monica.
Chinatown, near downtown.
City Walk in Universal Studios.
The Getty Center 310/440-7300, web: www.getty.edu.
Grauman's Chinese Theatre on Hollywood Blvd 323/464-8111.
Griffith Observatory 213/473-0800, web: www.griffithobservatory.org.
Melrose Ave, hip commercial district in West Hollywood.
Theme Parks: Disneyland, Knotts Berry Farm, or Magic Mountain.
Watts Towers (Simon Rodia State Historical Park), 1765 E 107th St (not far from LAX), 213/847-4646.
Westwood Village premiere movie theaters & restaurants.
Venice Beach.
Visitor's Center: 800/228-2452, web: www.lacvb.com.
West Hollywood Convention & Visitors Bureau, 800/368-6020, web: www.visitwesthollywood.com.

Weather

Summers are hot, dry, and smoggy with temperatures in the 80°s-90°s. LA's weather is at its finest — sunny, blue skies, and moderate temperatures (mid 70°s) — during the months of March, April, and May.

Best Views

Drive up Mulholland Drive, in the hills between Hollywood and the Valley, for a panoramic view of the city, and the Hollywood sign.

City Calendar

LGBT PRIDE

June. Christopher St West 323/969-8302, web: www.lapride.org.
June-July. Los Angeles Black LGBT Pride 323/293-4285, web: www.atbla.com.

ANNUAL EVENTS

June - AIDS LifeCycle 866/BIKE-4AIDS, web: www.aidslifecycle.org. AIDS benefit bike ride from San Francisco to LA.
July - Outfest 213/480-7088, web: www.outfest.org. Los Angeles' lesbian/ gay film & video festival.
August - Sunset Junction Fair 323/661-7771, web: www.sunsetjunction.org. Carnival, arts & information fair on Sunset Blvd in Silverlake to benefit Sunset Junction Youth Center.
October - Gay Days at Disneyland, web: www.gayday2.com.
October - AIDS Walk-a-thon 213/201-9255, web: www.aidswalk.net.

Queer Resources

COMMUNITY INFO

Los Angeles Gay & Lesbian Center 323/993-7400, web: www.lagaycenter.org. 1625 N Schrader Blvd (1 blk W of Wilcox, see Hollywood map), 9am-9pm, till 1pm Sat, clsd Sun.
South Bay LGBT Center 310/328-6550, web: www.southbaycenter.org. 2235 W Sepulveda Blvd, Torrance.
The Village (Gay & Lesbian Center extension, see Hollywood map) 323/860-7302. 1125 N McCadden Pl (at Santa Monica).
Alcoholics Together Center 323/663-8882. 1773 Griffith Park Blvd, Silverlake.
AIDS Project LA 213/201-1600.

8   **Ramada Plaza Hotel—West Hollywood** [GF,F,SW,WC] 310/652-6400, 800/845-8585 ■ 8585 Santa Monica Blvd (at La Cienega) ■ art deco hotel & suites, poolside WiFi ■ www.ramadaweho.com

9   **San Vicente Inn-Resort** [M,SW,N,GO] 310/854-6915, 800/577-6915 ■ 845 N San Vicente Blvd (at Santa Monica) ■ cottages & suites, hot tub, steam room ■ www.gayresort.com

10   **Sunset Marquis Hotel & Villas** [GS,SW,WI,WC] 310/657-1333, 800/858-9758 ■ 1200 Alta Loma Rd (1/2 block S of Sunset Blvd) ■ full brkfst, sauna, hot tub, kids ok ■ www.sunsetmarquishotel.com

11   **Valadon Hotel** [GF,SW,WC] 310/854-1114, 800/835-7997 ■ 8822 Cynthia St (at Larrabee) ■ all-suite hotel, hot tub ■ www.valadonhotel.com

BARS

12   **Comedy Store** [GF] 323/650-6268 ■ 8433 Sunset Blvd (at La Cienega) ■ 8pm-2am, legendary stand-up club ■ www.comedystore.com

13   **East/ West Lounge** [★GS] 310/360-6186, 877/395-6864 ■ 8851 Santa Monica Blvd (at San Vicente) ■ 4:30pm-2am, clsd Mon, très hip lounge that blends the best of both East & West Coasts, [K] Tue ■ www.eastwest-lounge.com

14   **Fubar** [★M,D,K,S] 323/654-0396 ■ 7994 Santa Monica Blvd (at Crescent Hts) ■ 4pm-2am, theme nights, [K] Mon-Tue, [D,$] Fri-Sun, go-go boys Sat ■ www.fubarla.com

15   **Fuse** [★W,D] 310/360-8455 ■ 696 N Robertson Blvd (at Santa Monica, at Here Lounge) ■ Th only, swank cocktail gathering ■ www.fuse-events.com

16   **Gold Coast** [★M,NH,WC] 323/656-4879 ■ 8228 Santa Monica Blvd (at La Jolla) ■ 11am-2am, from 10am wknds ■ gcoastbar@aol.com

15   **Here Lounge** [MW,P] 310/360-8455 ■ 696 N Robertson Blvd (at Santa Monica) ■ 4pm-2am, swanky & stylish, DJ nightly, [W] Th for Fuse & Fri for Truck Stop, also juice bar ■ www.herelounge.com

17   **I Candy** [GS] 323/656-4000 ■ 7929 Santa Monica Blvd ■ 6pm-2am, clsd Sun, hip lounge, popular Wed for Mix, ■ www.icandylounge.com

18 **Improvisation** [GF,F] 323/651-2583 ■ 8162 Melrose Ave (at Crescent Heights) ■ *stand-up comedy, also restaurant* ■ www.improvclubs.com

13 **Micky's** [★M,D,F,V,YC,GO] 310/657-1176 ■ 8857 Santa Monica Blvd (at San Vicente) ■ *noon-2am, after-hours wknds, lunch on patio Mon-Fri* ■ www.mickys.com

19 **Mother Lode** [★M,NH,K,WC] 310/659-9700 ■ 8944 Santa Monica Blvd (at Robertson) ■ *3pm-2am, beer bust Sun*

20 **The Normandie Room** [GS,NH,WC] 310/659-6204 ■ 8737 Santa Monica Blvd (at Hancock) ■ *5pm-2am, "No homophobes, no heterophobes, no assholes," great cosmopolitans* ■ www.thenormandieroom.com

21 **Numbers** [★M,NH,F,WC,GO] 310/652-7700 ■ 8741 Santa Monica Blvd (at Hancock, 2nd flr) ■ *5pm-2am, restaurant/ bar, upscale cont'l menu* ■ www.numbersrestaurant.com

22 **The Palms on Las Olas** [★W,NH,D,MR,K,WC] 310/652-6188 ■ 8572 Santa Monica Blvd (at La Cienega) ■ *8pm-2am, from 4pm wknds, after-hours Fri-Sat, beer bust Sun, theme nights: [K] Mon; [A] Tue; go-go dancers Wed & Fri-Sat* ■ www.thepalmsbar.com

23 **Smack** [M] 323/822-3300 (O-Bar #), 323/654-0650 ■ 8279 Santa Monica Blvd (at Sweetzer, at O-Bar) ■ *9pm Th only, "world's fastest open bar": serves as many free cocktails in 5 minutes as possible at 9:15pm, 11:15pm & 12:15pm* ■ www.tomwhitmanpresents.com/events.smack.html

24 **Tempest** [GS,D,E,$] 323/850-5115 ■ 7323 Santa Monica Blvd (E of Fuller Ave) ■ *8:30pm-close, supper club w/ theme nights, patio*

25 **Trunks** [M,NH,V,YC] 310/652-1015 ■ 8809 Santa Monica Blvd (at Larrabee) ■ *1pm-2am*

26 **Viper Room** [GF,D,E,$] 310/358-1880, 310/358-1881 (ticketing) ■ 8852 Sunset Blvd (btwn San Vicente & Larrabee) ■ *doors open btwn 7pm-8pm nightly, live bands* ■ www.viperroom.com

NIGHTCLUBS

27 **7969** [GS,D,TG,DS,S,18+] 323/654-0280 ■ 7969 Santa Monica Blvd (at Fairfax) ■ *10pm-2am, theme nights: Illusions [DS] Mon & Fri, live bands Fri, strippers Sat*

28 **Area** [GF,D] 310/652-2012 ■ 643 N La Cienega Blvd ■ *10pm-2am Th-Sat, more gay last Sun for Sundays*

29 **Beige** [★MW,D,F] 323/850-5350 (Falcon #) ■ 7213 Sunset Blvd (btwn Poinsettia & Formosa, at Falcon restaurant & bar) ■ *Tue only* ■ www.falconslair.com

30 **Celebrity** [M,D,V,18+,YC] 310/652-7055 ■ 8911 Santa Monica Blvd (at Rage) ■ *9pm-2am Th only* ■ celebrity.boyu.com

31 **The Factory** [★M,D,V,$] 310/659-4551 ■ 652 N La Peer Dr (at Santa Monica, at the Factory) ■ *9pm-2am Fri-Sat, theme nights, PopStarZ Fri* ■ www.factorynightclub.com

32 **Girl Bar** [W,D] 310/659-4551, 877/447-5252 ■ 661 N Robertson Blvd (at Santa Monica, at Ultra Suede) ■ *9pm-2:30am Fri only* ■ www.girlbar.com

33 **La Plaza** [M,D,MR-L,DS,$] 323/939-0703 ■ 739 N La Brea Ave (at Melrose) ■ *9pm-2am, from 8pm Fri-Sat, clsd Tue, shows nightly at 10:15pm & midnight*

30 **Rage** [★M,D,F,DS,V,18+,YC,WC] 310/652-7055 ■ 8911 Santa Monica Blvd (at San Vicente) ■ *noon-2am* ■ www.ragewesthollywood.com

34 **The Ruby** [GF,D,A,18+,$] 323/467-7070 ■ 7070 Hollywood Blvd (at Sycamore) ■ *10pm-3am, theme nights: including '70s & '80s night, hip-hop, goth, electronica, house, patio*

32 **Ultra Suede** [GS,D,A,E] 310/659-4551 ■ 661 N Robertson Blvd (at Santa Monica) ■ *10pm-2am Wed-Sat, theme nights, [W] for Girlbar Fri* ■ www.factorynightclub.com/ultra-suede.htm

CAFES

Buzz Coffee [F] 323/656-7460 ■ 8000 W Sunset Blvd (at Laurel Canyon Blvd) ■ *7am-11pm, till midnight Fri-Sat, 8am-11pm Sun, stargaze while you drink your coffee, also sandwiches & pastries*

Cafe Marco [WI] 323/650-7742 ■ 8200 Santa Monica (at Crescent Hts) ■ *6:30am-10pm, till 11pm Fri-Sat, coffeehouse* ■ www.cafemarco.net

Champagne French Bakery & Cafe [F] 310/657-4051 ■ 8917-9 Santa Monica Blvd ■ *6:30am-10pm, till 11pm Fri-Sat, coffees & pastries as well as brkfst, lunch & dinner, some outdoor seating* ■ www.champagnebakery.com

Mäni's Bakery [F,WC] 323/938-8800 ■ 519 S Fairfax Ave (at Maryland Dr) ■ *6:30am-midnight, till 1am Fri, 7am-1am Sat, 7:30am-midnight Sun, also cafe & restaurant from 8am* ■ www.manisbakery.com

Urth Caffe [F] 310/659-0628 ■ 8565 Melrose Ave (btwn Robertson & La Cienega) ■ *6:30am-11:30pm, organic coffees & teas & treats, plenty veggie & vegan, patio* ■ urthcaffe.com

Who's On Third Cafe 323/651-2928 ■ 8369 W 3rd St (at Orlando) ■ *8am-5pm*

RESTAURANTS

15 **The Abbey** [★MW,WC] 310/289-8410 ■ 692 N Robertson Blvd (at Santa Monica) ■ *8am-2am, American/ cont'l, full bar, patio* ■ www.abbeyfoodandbar.com

African Restaurant Row Fairfax btwn Olympic & Pico ■ *many Ethiopian, Nigerian & other African restaurants to choose from on this block; Damron recommends Nyala, 1076 S Fairfax Ave, 323/936-5918*

AOC 323/653-6359 ■ 8022 W Third St (at Crescent Heights Blvd) ■ *dinner nightly, wine bar, eclectic, upscale* ■ www.aocwinebar.com

Benvenuto Caffe [WC] 310/659-8635 ■ 8512 Santa Monica Blvd (at La Cienega) ■ *lunch Tue-Fri, dinner nightly, Italian, full bar, patio* ■ www.benvenuto-caffe.com

Bossa Nova [BW,WC] 310/657-5070 ■ 685 N Robertson Blvd (at Santa Monica) ■ *11am-midnight, Brazilian, patio* ■ www.bossafood.com

Cafe D'Etoile 310/278-1011 ■ 8941 1/2 Santa Monica Blvd ■ *11am-11pm, till midnight Fri-Sat, cont'l*

Cafe La Boheme [WC] 323/848-2360 ■ 8400 Santa Monica Blvd (btwn Benecia Ave & Fox Hills Dr) ■ *5:30pm-1am Fri-Sat, till midnight Sun-Th, eclectic Californian, full bar, patio* ■ www.cafe-laboheme.com

Canter's Deli [WC] 323/651-2030 ■ 419 N Fairfax (btwn Melrose & Beverly) ■ *24hrs, hip after-hours, Jewish/ American, some veggie, full bar* ■ www.cantersdeli.com

Cut [R] 310/276-8500 ■ 9500 Wilshire Blvd (in Regent Beverly Wilshire), Beverly Hills ■ *5:30pm-10pm, till 10:30pm Fri-Sat, also sidebar 5pm-1:30am nightly, steak house by Wolfgang Puck* ■ www.wolfgangpuck.com

Doug Arango's 310/278-3684 ■ 8826 Melrose Ave ■ *noon-2:30pm Mon-Fri & 6pm-close Mon-Sat, clsd Sun, California cuisine* ■ www.dougarangos.com

Eat-Well [★] 323/656-1383 ■ 8252 Santa Monica Blvd (at La Jolla) ■ *7am-9:30pm, 8am-3pm wknds, comfort food diner*

Falcon [GS] 323/850-5350 ■ 7213 Sunset Blvd (btwn Poinsettia & Formosa) ■ *dinner, California/ cont'l fusion, hosts Beige [MW] Tue* ■ www.falconslair.com

Fiesta Cantina [★M] 310/652-8865 ■ 8865 Santa Monica Blvd (at San Vicente) ■ *4pm-2am, from noon Fri-Sun, Mexican, sidewalk patio & rooftop bar*

Fogo de Chao 310/289-7755 ■ 133 N La Cienega Blvd, Beverly Hills ■ *lunch Mon-Fri, dinner nightly, Brazilian churrascaria* ■ www.fogodechao.com

Hamburger Mary's Bar & Grill [MW,TG,E,K,DS,S,V,GO] 323/654-3800 ■ 8288 Santa Monica Blvd ■ *11am-midnight, till 1am Fri-Sat, from 10am wknds, full bar, ladies night Mon, theme nights* ■ www.hamburgermarysweho.com

Hedley's 310/659-2009 ■ 640 N Robertson Blvd ■ *lunch & dinner, also wknd brunch, clsd Sun night & Mon*

Il Pastaio 310/205-5444 ■ 400 N Canon Dr (at Brighton Wy), Beverly Hills ■ *lunch & dinner, dinner only Sun, homemade pasta, full bar* ■ www.giacominodrago.com

Il Piccolino Trattoria [WC] 310/659-2220 ■ 350 N Robertson Blvd (btwn Melrose & Beverly) ■ *lunch & dinner, clsd Sun, full bar, patio*

Joey's Cafe 323/822-0671 ■ 8301 Santa Monica Blvd ■ *8am-10pm, a little bit coffeehouse, a little bit diner, popular at lunch*

Kokomo Cafe 323/933-0773 ■ 6333 W 3rd St #120 ■ *diner*

Koo Koo Roo [BW,WC] 323/657-3300 ■ 8520 Santa Monica Blvd (at La Cienega Blvd) ■ *11am-11pm, till 10pm Sun, lots of healthy chicken dishes* ■ www.kookooroo.com

Louise's Trattoria [BW] 323/651-3880 ■ 7505 Melrose Ave (at Gardner) ■ *11am-10pm, till 11pm Fri-Sat, noon-10pm Sun, Italian, great foccacia bread, patio* ■ www.louises.com

Lucques [WC] 323/655-6277 ■ 8474 Melrose Ave (at La Cienega) ■ *lunch Tue-Sat, dinner nightly, French, full bar, patio* ■ www.lucques.com

Marco's Trattoria [WC] 323/650-2771 ■ 8136 Santa Monica (at Crescent Hts) ■ *9am-10pm, from 8am Fri-Sun* ■ www.marcoswesthollywood.com

Marix Tex Mex [MW,WC] 323/656-8800 ■ 1108 N Flores (btwn La Cienega & Fairfax) ■ *11:30am-11pm, from 11am wknds, great margaritas, patio* ■ marixtexmex.com

Mark's Restaurant [★] 310/652-5252 ■ 861 N La Cienega Blvd (at Santa Monica) ■ *7pm-10pm, Sun brunch from 11am, full bar* ■ www.marksrestaurant.com

Mason Jar Cafe 310/659-9111 ■ 8928 Santa Monica Blvd (at Robertson Blvd) ■ *9am-10pm, organic sandwiches, salads & smoothies, additive-free, plenty veggie*

Murakami 310/854-6212 ■ 8730 Santa Monica Blvd #F (at San Vicente) ■ *lunch Tue-Fri, dinner Tue-Sun, clsd Mon, sushi, popular w/ lesbians*

O-Bar [GS] 323/822-3300 ■ 8279 Santa Monica Blvd (at Sweetzer) ■ *6pm-2am, full bar, hosts Smack Th [M] for "boys who like boys who like blazers"* ■ www.obarrestaurant.com

Oasis [E] 323/939-8900 ■ 611 N La Brea (at Melrose) ■ *6pm-2am, clsd Sun-Mon, Moroccan, belly dancing Fri-Sat, patio* ■ oasislosangeles.com

Real Food Daily [★BW,WC] 310/289-9910 ■ 414 N La Cienega (btwn Beverly & Melrose) ■ *11:30am-10pm, till 11pm Fri-Sat, Sun brunch 10am-3pm, organic vegan, patio* ■ www.realfood.com

Sante Libre 323/857-0412 ■ 345 N La Brea (btwn Melrose & Beverly) ■ *9am-10pm, pastas, salads & wraps, plenty veggie* ■ santecuisine.com

Skewers [BW] 310/271-0555 ■ 8939 Santa Monica Blvd (at Robertson) ■ *11am-11pm, Middle Eastern, lowfat grill* ■ www.skewersbistro.com

Tango Grill [MW,BW,WC] 323/659-3663 ■ 8807 Santa Monica Blvd (at San Vicente) ■ *11:30am-11:30pm, Argentinian, some veggie*

Tart 323/556-2608, 800/334-1658 ■ 115 S Fairfax Ave ■ *7am-midnight, Southern* ■ www.farmersdaughterhotel.com

Trocadero [WC] 323/656-7161 ■ 8280 Sunset Blvd (at Sweetzer) ■ *6pm-2am, eclectic American, patio, full bar*

Yukon Mining Co [★BW,WC] 323/851-8833 ■ 7328 Santa Monica Blvd (at Fuller) ■ *24hrs, champagne brunch Sat-Sun*

BOOKSTORES

13 **A Different Light** [★] 310/854-6601 ■ 8853 Santa Monica Blvd (btwn San Vicente & Larrabee) ■ *10am-11pm, LGBT, readings* ■ www.adlbooks.com

35 **Book Soup** 310/659-3110, 800/764-2665 ■ 8818 W Sunset Blvd (at Larrabee) ■ *9am-10pm, till 7pm Sun, LGBT section* ■ www.booksoup.com

RETAIL SHOPS

665 Leather 310/854-7276 ■ 8722 Santa Monica Blvd (at Huntley Dr) ■ *noon-8pm, till 10pm Fri-Sat, custom leather & neoprene, also accessories & toys* ■ www.665leather.com

Dogspunk/ West Hollywood Tattoo [GO] 213/422-4801 ■ 8206 Santa Monica Blvd (2nd floor, above 20/20 Video) ■ *tattoo studio featuring Dave Davenport (aka "Dogspunk"), named best gay tattoo artist by Frontiers magazine* ■ www.dogspunk.com

Dorothy's Surrender 323/650-4111 ■ 7985 Santa Monica Blvd #111 (at Laurel, in French Market) ■ *10am-11pm, cards, periodicals, T-shirts, gifts*

Flight 001 323/966-0001, 877/354-4481 ■ 8235 W 3rd St (at S Harper Ave) ■ *11am-7pm, till 6pm Sun, way cool travel gear* ■ www.flight001.com

Perfect Beat 310/273-3337 ■ 8941 Santa Monica Blvd ■ *11am-midnight, club music* ■ www.perfectbeat.com

Syren 323/936-6693 ■ 7225 Beverly Blvd ■ *1pm-7pm, till 9pm Fri-Sat, clsd Sun-Mon, leather & latex* ■ www.syren.com

GYMS & HEALTH CLUBS

The Easton Gym [GF] 323/651-3636 ■ 8053 Beverly Blvd (at Crescent Hts) ■ eastongym.com

The Fitness Factory [★] 310/358-1838 ■ 650 N La Peer Dr (at Santa Monica) ■ *6am-9pm, till 8pm Fri, 7am-5pm Sat, 8am-1pm Sun* ■ www.fitnessfactoryla.com

MEN'S CLUBS

Melrose Spa [★18+,PC] 323/937-2122 ■ 7269 Melrose Ave (at Poinsettia) ■ *24hrs* ■ www.midtowne.com

Slammer [18+,PC] 213/388-8040 ■ 3688 Beverly Blvd (2 blocks E of Vermont) ■ *8pm-4am, from 2pm wknds* ■ www.slammerclub.com

EROTICA

Babeland 323/634-9480 ■ 7007 Melrose Ave (btwn La Brea & Sycamore) ■ noon-8pm, till 6pm Sun, women-run sex-toy shop ■ www.babeland.com

Circus of Books 323/656-6533 ■ 8230 Santa Monica Blvd (at La Jolla) ■ 6am-2am ■ www.circusofbooks.com

Drake's 310/289-8932 ■ 8932 Santa Monica Blvd (at San Vicente) ■ 10am-2am; also 7566 Melrose Ave, 323/651-5600, 24hrs

Hustler Hollywood 310/860-9009 ■ 8920 Sunset Blvd (at San Vicente) ■ 10am-2am, chic erotic department store, also cafe ■ www.hustlerhollywood.com

Pleasure Chest 323/650-1022 ■ 7733 Santa Monica Blvd (at Genesee) ■ 10am-midnight, till 1am Th, till 2am Fri-Sat ■ www.thepleasurechest.com

Unicorn Bookstore 310/652-6253 ■ 8940 Santa Monica Blvd ■ 9am-2am

LA—Hollywood

ACCOMMODATIONS

1 **Coral Sands Hotel** [M,SW] 323/467-5141, 800/367-7263 (CA) & 800/421-3650 (US) ■ 1730 N Western Ave (at Hollywood Blvd) ■ hot tub, sauna, cruisy for party & play crowd ■ www.coralsands-la.com

2 **Holiday Inn Hollywood** [GF,F,SW,WI,WC] 323/876-8600 ■ 2005 N Highland (at Franklin) ■ exercise room, jacuzzi ■ hollywoodholidayinn@sunstonehotels.com

3 **Hollywood Celebrity Hotel** [GF] 323/850-6464, 800/222-7017 ■ 1775 Orchid Ave (btwn Hollywood & Franklin) ■ 1930s art deco hotel ■ www.hotelcelebrity.com

4 **Hollywood Hotel** [GF,SW,NS,WI,WC] 323/315-1800, 800/800-9733 ■ 1160 N Vermont Ave (at Santa Monica) ■ www.hollywoodhotel.net

5 **Hollywood Metropolitan Hotel** [GF,NS,WC] 323/962-5800, 800/962-5800 ■ 5825 Sunset Blvd (btwn Bronson & Van Ness) ■ also restaurant ■ www.metropolitanhotel.com

BARS

6 **Boardner's** [GS,D,F,K] 323/462-9621 ■ 1652 N Cherokee Ave ■ 4pm-2am, "A Hollywood legend & best-kept secret since 1942" ■ www.boardners.com

7 **Faultline** [★M,B,LV] 323/660-0889 ■ 4216 Melrose Ave (at Vermont) ■ 5pm-2am, from 2pm wknds, clsd Mon-Tue, patio, occasional women's events ■ www.faultlinebar.com

7 **Machine** [★M,D,A,LV,$] 323/969-2596 ■ 4216 Melrose Ave (at Faultline) ■ 9pm-2am 3rd Sat, cruisy, patio ■ www.djpaulv.com

8 **Spotlight** [M,NH,WC] 323/467-2425 ■ 1601 N Cahuenga (at Hollywood) ■ 6am-2am

NIGHTCLUBS

9 **Arena/ Circus Disco** [★M,D,MR-L,S,V] 323/462-1291 ■ 6655 Santa Monica Blvd (at Seward, Circus behind Arena) ■ 9pm-2am Tue & Fri-Sat, theme nights ■ www.circus-disco.com

9 **Club Papi Los Angeles** [M,D,MR-L] 323/692-9573 ■ 6655 Santa Monica Blvd (at Seward, at Circus Disco) ■ 9pm-4am, monthly party, call for dates ■ www.clubpapi.com

10 **Miss Kitty's** [GS,D,A,E,C,S,$] 323/466-6111 (club #) ■ 6510 Santa Monica Blvd (at Wilcox, at Dragonfly) ■ 9pm Fri only, fetish/ goth/ rock 'n' roll dance club w/ "electro cabaret" ■ www.misskittysparlour.com

11 **Tempo** [M,D,MR-L,E,S] 323/466-1094 ■ 5520 Santa Monica Blvd (at Western) ■ 9pm-2am, 7pm-3am Th-Sat, from 2pm Sun, live bands Sat, beer bust Sun ■ www.clubtempo.com

9 **TigerHeat** [M,D,TG,E,DS,V,18+,$] 323/462-1291 ■ 6655 Sunset Blvd (E of Highland, at Arena nightclub) ■ 9:30pm-2am Th only ■ www.clubtigerheat.com

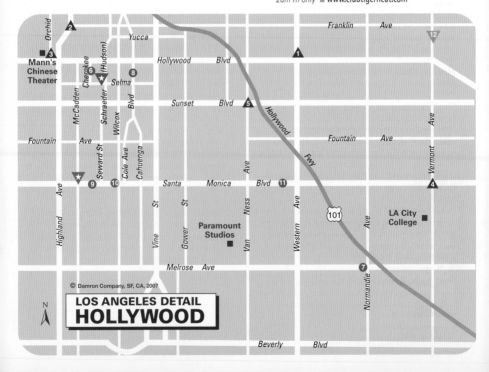

© Damron Company, SF, CA, 2007

LOS ANGELES DETAIL
HOLLYWOOD

RESTAURANTS

Cinespace [GS,F,E,R] 323/817-3456 ■ 6356 Hollywood Blvd (2nd floor) ■ 6pm-2am Th-Sat only, "Dinner and a Movie" at 8pm ■ www.cinespace.info

Hollywood Canteen 323/465-0961 ■ 1006 N Seward St (at Santa Monica) ■ 5pm-11pm, till 2am Th, 6pm-2am Fri-Sat, clsd Sun, classic, full bar ■ www.hollywoodcanteenla.com

La Poubelle [WC] 323/465-0807 ■ 5907 Franklin Ave (at Bronson) ■ 5:30pm-1am, French/ Italian, some veggie, full bar

Lucy's Cafe El Adobe 323/462-9421 ■ 5536 Melrose Ave (near Gower St) ■ 11:30am-11pm, clsd Sun, Mexican, patio

Musso & Frank Grill 323/467-7788, 323/467-5123 ■ 6667 Hollywood Blvd (near Las Palmas) ■ 11am-11pm, clsd Sun-Mon, the grand-dame diner/ steak house of Hollywood: great pancakes, potpies & martinis!

Off Vine [BW] 323/962-1900 ■ 6263 Leland Wy (at Vine) ■ lunch & dinner, wknd brunch ■ www.offvine.com

Prado [WC] 323/467-3871 ■ 244 N Larchmont Blvd (at Beverly) ■ lunch & dinner, dinner only Sun, Caribbean, some veggie ■ www.pradola.com

Quality [WC] 323/658-5959 ■ 8030 W 3rd St (at Laurel) ■ 8am-3:30pm, homestyle brkfst, some veggie

Roscoe's House of Chicken & Waffles 323/466-7453 ■ 1514 N Gower (at Sunset) ■ 8:30am-midnight

Sushi Hiroba 323/962-7237 ■ 776 N Vine St ■ lunch Mon-Fri, dinner nightly ■ www.sushihirobausa.com

BOOKSTORES

12 **Skylight Books** [★] 323/660-1175 ■ 1818 N Vermont Ave (at Melbourne Ave) ■ 10am-10pm, way cool independent in Los Feliz, great fiction & alt-lit sections ■ www.skylight-books.com

RETAIL SHOPS

Mondo Video-A-Go-Go 323/953-8896 ■ 4328 Melrose Ave (at Vermont) ■ noon-10pm, vintage clothes, cult & LGBT videos ■ mondofamilyfilms@mailcity.com

Mr S Leather & Fetters USA Los Angeles 323/663-7765, 800/746-7677 (orders) ■ 4232 Melrose Ave (at New Hampshire) ■ 2pm-10pm, till 8pm Sun, clsd Mon-Tue, erotic goods, custom leather & latex ■ www.mr-s-leather.com

Panpipes Magickal Marketplace 323/462-7078 ■ 1641 N Cahuenga Blvd ■ noon-7pm, clsd Mon, "nation's oldest occult store" w/ custom spells & classes ■ www.panpipes.com

Videoactive [WC] 323/669-8544 ■ 2522 Hyperion Ave (at Griffith Park Blvd) ■ 10am-11pm, till midnight Fri-Sat, LGBT section, adult videos

Y-Que Trading Post 323/664-0021 ■ 1770 N Vermont Ave ■ noon-8pm, kitsch boutique that's home to the "Free Wynona" & "Free Martha" T-shirts ■ www.yque.com

GYMS & HEALTH CLUBS

Gold's Gym [GF] 323/462-7012 ■ 1016 N Cole Ave (near Santa Monica & Vine) ■ 5am-midnight, 7am-9pm Sat-Sun ■ www.goldsgym.com/hollywoodca

MEN'S CLUBS

Flex [SW] 323/663-7786 ■ 4424 Melrose Ave (btwn Normandie & Vermont) ■ 24hrs, patio, steam ■ www.flexbaths.com

➤ **Hollywood Spa** [★PC] 323/463-5169, 800/772-2582 ■ 1650 N Ivar (near Hollywood & Vine) ■ 24hrs ■ www.hollywoodspa.com

The Zone [PC] 323/464-8881 ■ 1037 N Sycamore Ave (at Santa Monica) ■ 8pm-dawn, from 2pm Sun ■ www.thezoneLA.com

EROTICA

Romantix Adult Superstore [AYOR] 323/464-9435 ■ 6315-1/2 Hollywood Blvd (at Vine) ■ also arcade ■ www.romantixonline.com

X Spot 323/463-0295 ■ 6775 Santa Monica Blvd (at Highland) ■ 24hrs

LA—West LA & Santa Monica

ACCOMMODATIONS

1 **The Georgian Hotel** [GF,F,WI,WC] 310/395-9945, 800/538-8147 ■ 1415 Ocean Ave (btwn Santa Monica & Broadway), Santa Monica ■ great location ■ www.georgianhotel.com

2 **Hotel Angeleno** [GS,SW,NS,WI] 310/476-6411, 866/264-3536 ■ 170 N Church Ln (at Hwy 405) ■ boutique hotel w/ landmark circular shape, gym ■ www.hotelangeleno.com

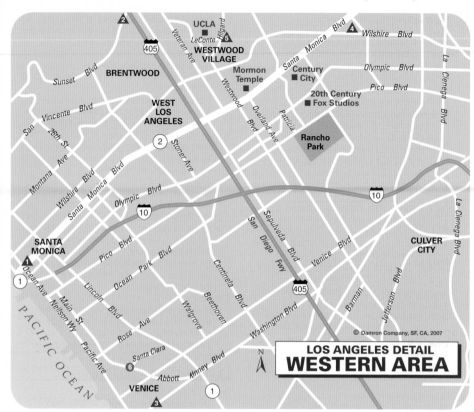

3   **The Inn at Venice Beach** [GF,WI,WC] 310/821-2557,
     800/828-0688 ■ 327 Washington Blvd (at Via Dolce),
     Marina Del Rey ■ *European-style inn, kids ok* ■
     www.innatvenicebeach.com

     The Linnington [MW,GO] 310/422-8825 ■ *B&B, jacuzzi,
     kids ok, lesbian-owned* ■ TheLinnington@aol.com

4   **The Mosaic Hotel** [GF,SW,NS,WC] 310/278-0303,
     800/463-4466 ■ 125 Spalding Dr (at Wilshire Blvd), Beverly
     Hills ■ *boutique hotel w/ restaurant & lounge, kids ok* ■
     www.mosaichotel.com

     Sea View Inn at the Beach [GF,SW,WI] 310/545-1504
     ■ 3400 Highland Ave (at Rosecrans), Manhattan Beach ■
     1 block from beach ■ www.seaview-inn.com

5   **W Los Angeles** [GF,F,SW] 310/208-8765, 800/421-2317
     ■ 930 Hilgard Ave (at Le Conte) ■ *suites, gym, day spa* ■
     www.starwoodhotels.com/whotels/index.html

BARS

     The Dolphin [MW,NH,K,WC] 310/318-3339 ■ 1995 Artesia
     Blvd (at Green Ln), Redondo Beach ■ *4pm-2am, from 2pm
     wknds, patio, [D] Tue & Fri-Sat, [K] Sun*

6   **Roosterfish** [★M,NH] 310/392-2123 ■ 1302 Abbot Kinney
     Blvd (at Cadiz), Venice ■ *11am-2am, patio* ■
     www.RoosterfishBar.com

CAFES

     The Novel Cafe 310/396-8566 ■ 212 Pier Ave, Santa
     Monica ■ *7am-1am, from 8am Sat, 8am-midnight Sun,
     coffeehouse that doubles as used bookstore* ■ www.novel-
     cafe.com

RESTAURANTS

     12 Washington 310/822-5566 ■ 12 Washington Blvd (at
     Pacific), Venice ■ *5pm-10pm, till 11pm Fri-Sun, cont'l* ■
     www.12-washington.com

     Baja Cantina 310/821-2252 ■ 311 Washington Blvd (at
     Sanborn), Venice ■ *10:30am-2am, also brunch wknds, full bar*
     ■ www.bajacantinavenice.com

Border Grill [★] 310/451-1655 ■ 1445 4th St (at Broadway), Santa Monica ■ *lunch & dinner, wknd brunch* ■ www.bordergrill.com/BGSM/bgsm.htm

➤**Cantalini's Salerno Beach Restaurant** [BW,E] 310/821-0018 ■ 193 Culver Blvd (at Vista del Mar), Playa del Rey ■ *lunch 11:30am-3pm Tue-Fri, dinner 4pm-10:30pm Tue-Sun, clsd Mon, Italian, homemade pastas, live music Sun nights* ■ www.salernobeach.com

Drago [WC] 310/828-1585 ■ 2628 Wilshire Blvd (btwn 26th & Princeton), Santa Monica ■ *lunch Mon-Sat, dinner nightly, Sicilian Italian* ■ www.celestinodrago.com

Golden Bull [GS] 310/230-0402 ■ 170 W Channel Rd (at Pacific Coast Hwy), Santa Monica ■ *4:30pm-10pm, till 11pm wknds, Sun brunch, American, full bar* ■ www.GoldenBull.us

Hamburger Habit [★] 310/478-5000 ■ 11223 National Blvd (at Sepulveda) ■ *10am-11pm, till midnight Fri-Sat, hamburgers, hot dogs, shakes* ■ www.hamburger-habit.com

Joe's 310/399-5811 ■ 1023 Abbot Kinney Blvd, Venice ■ *lunch Tue-Fri, dinner nightly, wknd brunch, clsd Mon, French/ Californian* ■ joesrestaurant.com

Real Food Daily [BW,WC] 310/451-7544 ■ 514 Santa Monica Blvd (btwn 5th & 6th), Santa Monica ■ *11:30am-10pm, organic vegan* ■ www.realfood.com

Wokcano 323/653-1998 ■ 8408 W 3rd St ■ *11am-12:30am, till 1:30am Fri-Sat, sushi bar & Chinese cafe* ■ www.wokcanocafe.com

BOOKSTORES

Diesel, A Bookstore 310/456-9961 ■ 3890 Cross Creek Rd, Malibu ■ *10am-7pm, till 9pm Fri-Sat, till 6pm Sun, independent* ■ www.dieselbookstore.com

RETAIL SHOPS

David Aden Gallery 310/396-2949 ■ 361 Vernon #8 (at 4th Ave), Venice Beach ■ *9am-5pm or by appt, large collection of male fine-art photography* ■ www.FotoFactory.com

MEN'S CLUBS

Roman Holiday 310/391-0200 ■ 12814 Venice Blvd (at Beethoven) ■ *24hrs* ■ www.clubromanholiday.com

EROTICA

The Love Boutique 310/453-3459 ■ 2924 Wilshire Blvd (W of Bundy), Santa Monica ■ *11am-7pm, till 9pm Th, noon-6pm Sun, toys, books for women* ■ www.loveboutiqueparty.com

Pleasure Island 310/793-9477 ■ 18426 Hawthorne Blvd (btwn Artesia & 190th), Torrance ■ *11am-midnight, till 2am Fri-Sat* ■ xxxpleasureisland.com

LA—Silverlake

ACCOMMODATIONS

1   **Hollywood Gay Guest House** [M,NS,GO] 323/661-1566 ■ 1300 Micheltorena St ■ *hilltop views, clothing-optional hot tub* ■ www.hollywoodgayguesthouse.com

2   **Sanborn GuestHouse** [GS,NS,WI,GO] 323/666-3947 ■ 1005 1/2 Sanborn Ave (near Sunset) ■ *private unit w/ kitchen* ■ www.sanbornhouse.com

BARS

3   **AKBar** [★GS,NH,D,WC] 323/665-6810 ■ 4356 W Sunset Blvd (at Fountain) ■ *7pm-2am, hip Silverlake hangout* ■ akbarsilverlake.com

4   **Bigfoot Lodge** [GS,D,K] 323/662-9227 ■ 3172 Los Feliz Blvd ■ *5pm-2am, "LA's only log cabin lounge," more women Wed for Mixtape* ■ www.bigfootlodge.com

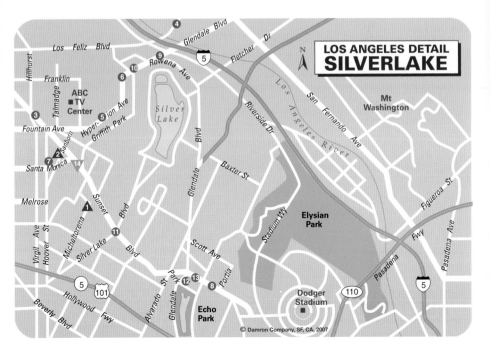

5 **Cavern Club Celebrity Theater** 323/969-2530, 323/662-4255 (restaurant #) ■ 1920 Hyperion Ave (at Casita Del Campo) ■ *wide variety of shows, Wed-Sat nights* ■ www.cavernclubtheater.com

6 **Cha Cha Lounge** [GF,NH,GO] 323/660-7595 ■ 2375 Glendale Blvd (at Silverlake) ■ *5pm-2am, hipster lounge*

7 **Eagle LA** [★M,L,WC] 323/669-9472 ■ 4219 Santa Monica Blvd (at Hoover) ■ *4pm-2am, from 3pm Sat, from 2pm Sun, uniform bar, cruisy, women's night Wed* ■ www.EagleLA.com

8 **Little Joy** [GS,NH,MR-L] 213/250-3417 ■ 1477 W Sunset Blvd (at Portia) ■ *4pm-2am, from 1pm wknds*

9 **MJ's** [★M,NH,D,B,L,WC] 323/660-1503 ■ 2810 Hyperion Ave (at Rowena) ■ *4pm-2am, from 2pm Sun, theme nights, including Rim Job [S] Tue, Anthem [$] Sat* ■ www.MJsbar.com

10 **The Other Side** [M,NH,E,P,OC] 323/661-4233, 323/661-0618 ■ 2538 Hyperion Ave (at Griffith Park) ■ *noon-2am* ■ www.flyingleapcafe.com/tos/tos/tos.html

11 **Silverlake Lounge** 323/663-9636 ■ 2906 Sunset Blvd (at Silver Lake Blvd) ■ *3pm-2am, rock 'n' roll club [GS,E] w/ live bands till Fri-Sun when more gay [M,MR-L,DS]*

NIGHTCLUBS

Club Cafe Con Leche [W,D,MR-L] 626/282-0330 (club info) ■ 700 S Almansor St (at The Almansor Court), Alhambra ■ *9pm-2am 2nd Fri only, live bands* ■ www.DelBarPresents.com

12 **Dragstrip 66** [★GS,D,A,DS,$] 323/969-2596 ■ 1151 Glendale Blvd (off Park Ave, at Sunset Blvd, at the Echo) ■ *9pm-2am 2nd Sat, trashy pansexual rock 'n' roll club* ■ www.dragstrip66.com

13 **The Echo** [GS,D,DS] 213/413-8200 ■ 1822 W Sunset Blvd (at Glendale Blvd) ■ *more gay 2nd Sat for Dragstrip 66* ■ www.attheecho.com

CAFES

The Coffee Table 323/644-8111 ■ 2930 Rowena Ave ■ *7am-11pm, patio, fab mosaic magic*

RESTAURANTS

Asia Los Feliz 323/906-9498 ■ 3179 Los Feliz Blvd ■ *lunch & dinner, Cal-Asian* ■ www.asialosfeliz.com

Casita Del Campo [★] 323/662-4255 ■ 1920 Hyperion Ave ■ *11am-midnight, till 2am Fri-Sat, Mexican, patio* ■ www.casitadelcampo.com

Cha Cha Cha [MW,WC] 323/664-7723 ■ 656 N Virgil Ave (at Melrose) ■ *8am-10pm, till 11pm Fri-Sat, Caribbean, plenty veggie* ■ theoriginalchachacha.com

Da Giannino [BW] 323/664-7979 ■ 2630 Hyperion Ave (at Griffith Park Blvd) ■ *5pm-close, clsd Mon, patio*

Eat Well Coffeeshop 323/664-1624 ■ 3916 Sunset Blvd (at Hyperion) ■ *8am-3pm, comfort food, some veggie*

El Conquistador [BW] 323/666-5136 ■ 3701 W Sunset Blvd (at Lucille) ■ *lunch Tue-Sun, dinner nightly, Mexican, patio* ■ www.elconquistadorrestaurant.com

The Flying Leap Cafe 323/661-0618 ■ 2538 Hyperion Ave (below The Other Side bar) ■ *dinner Tue-Sun, Sun brunch, cont'l, full bar, also Mary's Metro Station* ■ www.flyingleap-cafe.com

The Good Microbrew & Grill 323/660-3645 ■ 3725 Sunset Blvd (at Lucille) ■ *11am-10pm, till 11pm Fri, 9am-10pm wknds, Greek diner*

The Kitchen [GO] 323/664-3663 ■ 4348 Fountain Ave (at Sunset Blvd) ■ *5pm-midnight, till 1am Fri, 11am-1pm Sat, 11am-10pm Sun, cozy diner* ■ www.thekitchen-silverlake.com

Michelangelo Pizzeria Ristorante 323/660-4843 ■ 1637 Silverlake Blvd ■ *11:30am-2pm & 5:30pm-10:30pm, clsd Sun* ■ www.michelangelopizzeriaristorante.com

Zen Restaurant 323/665-2929 ■ 2609 Hyperion Ave (at Griffith Park Blvd) ■ *6pm-2am, Japanese, full bar [E,K]*

ENTERTAINMENT & RECREATION

Drama Queen Theater [GF,TG,F,C,DS,BW,WC,GO] 310/949-9255 ■ 1911 Sunset Blvd ■ *"come out for a great evening of fun, fine dining, drinks, entertainment, mystery & drag"* ■ www.dqtheater.com

BOOKSTORES

14 **Serifos** 323/660-7467 ■ 3814 W Sunset Blvd ■ *independent* ■ www.serifosonline.com

RETAIL SHOPS

Rough Trade 323/660-7956 ■ 3915 Sunset Blvd ■ *noon-10pm, 10am-midnight Fri-Sat, till 8pm Sun, toys, leather, gifts*

GYMS & HEALTH CLUBS

Body Builders [GF] 323/668-0802 ■ 2516 Hyperion Ave (at Tracy) ■ www.bodybuildersgym.com

EROTICA

Circus of Books 323/666-1304 ■ 4001 Sunset Blvd (at Sanborn) ■ *6am-2am* ■ www.circusofbooks.com

Romantix Adult Superstore 323/258-2867 ■ 3147 San Fernando Rd ■ *24hrs* ■ www.romantixonline.com

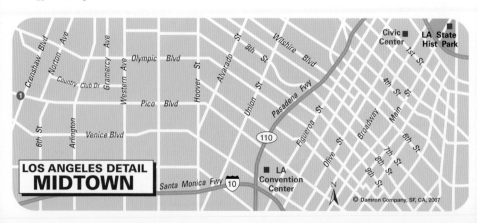

LOS ANGELES DETAIL
MIDTOWN

© Damron Company, SF, CA, 2007

LA—Midtown

BARS

Cafe Club Fais Do-Do [GF,F,E] 323/954-8080 ■ 5257 W Adams Blvd (btwn Fairfax & La Brea) ■ 8pm-2am, live music, also Cajun restaurant ■ www.faisdodo.com

NIGHTCLUBS

Coco Bongo [MW,D,MR-L,DS,S,18+] 213/748-2682 ■ 3311 S Main St ■ 9pm-2am, clsd Mon-Wed ■ www.cocobongola.com/A_LosAngeles.htm

1 **Jewel's Catch One Disco** [★GS,D,A,MR-AF,K,WC] 323/734-8849 (hotline), 323/737-1159 ■ 4067 W Pico Blvd (2 blocks E of Crenshaw) ■ 7:30pm-2am, from 8pm Th, 10pm-3am Fri, 10pm-4am Sat, clsd Tue-Wed, theme nights ■ www.jewelscatchone.com

RESTAURANTS

Cassell's 213/480-8668 ■ 3266 W 6th St (at Vermont) ■ 10:30am-4pm, clsd Sun, great burgers

Opus 213/738-1600 ■ 3760 Wilshire Blvd (at S Western) ■ 5pm-midnight, till 1am Fri-Sat, upscale contemporary, full bar ■ www.opusrestaurant.net

MEN'S CLUBS

Klyt [MR-L] 213/972-9145 ■ 132 E 4th St ■ 24hrs, steam room & dry sauna

Midtowne Spa—Los Angeles [SW] 213/680-1838 ■ 615 S Kohler (at Central) ■ 24hrs, 5 flrs ■ www.midtowne.com

LA—Valley

includes San Fernando & San Gabriel Valleys

ACCOMMODATIONS

The Graciela Burbank [★GF,NS,WI,WC] 818/842-8887, 888/956-1900 ■ 322 N Pass Ave, Burbank ■ luxury boutique hotel, lounge, rooftop sundeck & hot tub ■ www.thegraciela.com

BARS

1 **The Bullet** [M,L,WC] 818/762-8890 ■ 10522 Burbank Blvd (at Cahuenga), North Hollywood ■ noon-2am, patio ■ thebulletbar@aol.com

2 **Clear** [GS,D] 818/980-4811 ■ 11916 Ventura Blvd (btwn Laurel Canyon & Colfax), Studio City ■ 8pm-2am, clsd Mon, hip cocktail lounge, patio ■ www.clearlounge.net

3 **Club Fuel** [★M,D,TG,K,S,WC] 818/506-0404 ■ 11608 Ventura Blvd (at Laurel Canyon), Studio City ■ 3pm-2am, theme nights, go-go dancers Fri-Sun, Latin T-dance 4pm Sun, patio ■ www.clubfuel.us

4 **Club Olé Olé** [★M,D,MR-L,DS,S,WC] 818/760-9798, 818/261-5086 ■ 10937 Burbank Blvd (1 block E of Vineland, at Cobra), North Hollywood ■ 9pm-2am Fri-Sat, [S] Fri, [DS] Sat

4 **Cobra** [★M,D,CW,MR-L,WC] 818/760-9798 ■ 10937 Burbank Blvd (1 block E of Vineland), North Hollywood ■ 7pm-midnight Wed, 8pm-2am Th-Sat, from 3pm Sun, clsd Mon-Tue, Latin Fri-Sat, beer bust & CW dance lessons Sun ■ www.clubcobrala.com

6 **Liquid Lounge Too** [MW,BW,WI] 818/509-1938 ■ 12518 Burbank Blvd (at Whitsett), North Hollywood ■ 4pm-close, from 2pm Th-Fri, from noon Sat, from 10am Sun ■ www.liquidloungelongbeach.com

7 **MoonShadow** [★W,NH,D,E,K,WC] 818/508-7008 ■ 10437 Burbank Blvd (2 blocks E of Cahuenga), North Hollywood ■ 3pm-1:30am, from 1pm Fri-Sun ■ www.moonshadownightclub.com

8 **Oxwood Inn** [W,NH,D,K] 818/997-9666 (pay phone) ■ 13713 Oxnard (at Woodman), Van Nuys ■ 3pm-2am, from 2pm Sat, from 1pm Sun, from 5pm Mon-Tue, patio, one of the oldest lesbian bars in US ■ www.oxwoodinn.com

9 **Silver Rail** [MW,NH] 818/980-8310 ■ 11518 Burbank Blvd (btwn Colfax & Lankershim) ■ 4pm-2am, from noon wknds ■ www.silverrail.net

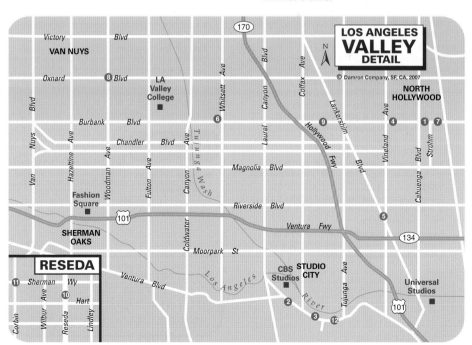

LOS ANGELES VALLEY DETAIL
© Damron Company, SF, CA, 2007

NIGHTCLUBS

10   **C Frenz** [★MW,NH,D,MR,K,C,S,WC,GO] 818/996-2976
■ 7026 Reseda Blvd (at Sherman Way), Reseda ■ *3pm-2am,
till 3am Sat, patio, theme nights: [S] Wed, [K] Th, Azucar Fri
(Latin & hip-hop), beer bust Sun* ■ www.cfrenz.com

11   **Club Coco Bongo** [MW,D,MR-L,DS,S,18+] 818/998-8464
■ 19655 Sherman Wy (at Corbin Ave), Reseda ■ *9pm-2am,
clsd Mon-Wed* ■ www.cocobongola.com/R_Reseda.htm

12   **Oil Can Harry's** [M,D,CW,S] 818/760-9749 ■ 11502
Ventura Blvd (at Tujunga & Colfax), Studio City ■ *7:30pm-
2am, from 9pm Fri, from 8pm Sat, clsd Sun-Mon & Wed,
dance lessons Tue & Th, classic disco Sat* ■ www.oilcanhar-
rysla.com

CAFES

Aroma 818/508-6505, 818/508-7377 (delivery) ■
4360 Tujunga Ave, Studio City ■ *6am-11pm, from 7am Sun,
coffeehouse w/ small bookstore*

Coffee Junction [E] 818/342-3405 ■ 19221 Ventura Blvd
(E of Tampa), Tarzana ■ *6:30am-9pm, till 11pm Fri, 7:30am-
11pm Sat, 7:30pm-2pm Sun* ■ www.thecoffeejunction.com

RESTAURANTS

Du-Par's 818/766-4437 ■ 12036 Ventura Blvd (at Laurel
Canyon), Studio City ■ *24hrs, plush diner schmoozing* ■
www.dupars.com

Du-Par's 805/373-8785 ■ 75 W Thousand Oaks Blvd,
Thousand Oaks ■ *6am-10:30pm, till 11:30pm Fri-Sat, plush
diner schmoozing*

Gourmet 88 818/848-8688 ■ 230 N San Fernando Blvd,
Burbank ■ *11:30am-10pm, till 11pm Fri-Sat, Mandarin* ■
www.gourmet88.com

GYMS & HEALTH CLUBS

Gold's Gym 818/506-4600 ■ 6233 N Laurel Canyon Blvd
(at Oxnard), North Hollywood ■
www.goldsgym.com/northhollywoodca

MEN'S CLUBS

The North Hollywood Spa [V] 818/760-6969,
800/772-2582 ■ 5636 Vineland (at Burbank) ■ *24hrs, no
membership req'd* ■ www.hollywoodspa.com

EROTICA

Eros Station 818/994-6100 ■ 15164 Oxnard St, Van Nuys
■ *10am-1am, videos & toys, also playspace w/ female
"fantasy guides"* ■ www.erosstation.com

The Love Boutique 818/342-2400 ■ 18637 Ventura Blvd,
Tarzana ■ *11am-8pm, 10am-9pm Fri-Sat, noon-6pm Sun,
toys, books for women* ■ www.loveboutiqueparty.com

Romantix Adult Superstore [AYOR] 818/760-9352
■ 12323 Ventura Blvd (at Laurelgrove Ave), Studio City
■ *24hrs* ■ www.romantixonline.com

Romantix Adult Superstore 818/992-9801 ■ 21625
Sherman Wy (at Nelson), Canoga Park ■ www.romantixon-
line.com

Romantix Adult Superstore 818/501-9609 ■ 4539 Van
Nuys Blvd (at Ventura), Sherman Oaks ■ *24hrs* ■
www.romantixonline.com

Romantix Adult Superstore 818/760-9529 ■ 4877
Lankershim Blvd (at Houston), North Hollywood ■ *24hrs, also
arcade* ■ www.romantixonline.com

LA—East LA & South Central

BARS

Annex [M,NH,MR-AF,K,WC] 310/671-7323 ■ 835 S La Brea
(at Arbor Vitae), Inglewood ■ *4pm-2am, from 2pm Fri, [K]
Mon & Sat-Sun*

Chico Bar [★M,D,MR-L,S] 323/721-3403 ■ 2915 W Beverly
Blvd (at Garfield), Montebello ■ *6pm-2am, theme nights* ■
www.clubchico.com

EROTICA

Joe's Adult Books 310/419-9064 ■ 4535 W Century Blvd,
Inglewood ■ *also arcade*

Palm Springs

ACCOMMODATIONS

1   **The 550** [★M,B,V,SW,N,GO] 760/323-7505,
800/798-8781 ■ 550 Warm Sands Dr (at Ramon) ■ *hot tub,
kitchens, bears welcome* ■ www.allworldsresort.com

2   **All Worlds Resort** [★M,SW,N,WI,GO] 760/323-7505,
800/798-8781 ■ 526 Warm Sands Dr (at Ramon) ■ *4 pools
& 4 spas & large steam room* ■ www.allworldsresort.com

2   **Another World** [M,SW,N,WI,GO] 760/323-7505,
800/798-8781 ■ 526 Warm Sands ■ *luxury clothing-
optional resort* ■ www.anotherworldresort.com

3   **Bacchanal Resort** [★M,SW,N,NS,WI,GO] 760/323-0760,
800/806-9059 ■ 589 S Grenfall Rd (at Parocela) ■ *kitchens,
9-man hot tub, private patios, mist system* ■ www.baccha-
nal.net

4   **Ballantines Hotel** [GF,SW,WI] 760/320-1178,
800/485-2808 ■ 1420 N Indian Canyon Dr ■ *'50s chic* ■
www.ballantinesoriginalhotel.com

5   **BauHouse in the Desert** [GS,SW,NS,WC] 760/320-6800
■ 2470 S Yosemite Dr (at Camino Real & Hwy 111) ■ *rental
home, jacuzzi* ■ jfmeagher@aol.com

6   **Caliente Tropics Resort** [GS,F,SW,NS,WC,GO]
760/327-1391, 888/277-0999 ■ 411 E Palm Canyon Dr
■ *pet-friendly motor hotel, jacuzzi, kids ok* ■ www.calien-
tetropics.com

7   **Calla Lily Inn** [GF,SW,NS,WI] 760/323-3654,
888/888-5787 ■ 350 S Belardo Rd (at Baristo) ■ *"a tranquil
oasis"* ■ www.callalilypalmsprings.com

8 ► **Camp Palm Springs** [★M,SW,N,WI,GO] 760/322-2267, 800/793-0063 or 747-7969 (CA only) ■ 1466 N Palm Canyon Dr (at Monte Vista) ■ *kitchens, sauna* ■ www.camp-palm-springs.com

6 **Canyon Club Hotel** [★M,SW,N,WI,GO] 760/778-8042, 877/258-2887 ■ 960 N Palm Canyon Dr (btwn Tachevah & El Alameda) ■ *clothing-optional, kitchens, hot tub & patios* ■ www.canyonclubhotel.com

9 **Casa Ocotillo** [M,SW,NS,WI,GO] 760/327-6110, 800/996-4108 ■ 240 E Ocotillo Ave ■ *intimate & elegant resort-style accommodations in a 1934 Mexican hacienda— "the ultimate get-away for the discriminating traveler"* ■ www.casaocotillo.com

10 <u>**Casitas Laquita**</u> [WO,SW,NS,WI,WC,GO] 760/416-9999, 877/203-3410 ■ 450 E Palm Canyon Dr (near Camino Real) ■ *lesbian resort, small pets ok* ■ www.casitaslaquita.com

11 ► **CCBC Resort Hotel** [★M,SW,N,WC,GO] 760/324-1350, 800/472-0836 ■ 68-369 Sunair Rd (btwn Melrose & Palo Verde), Cathedral City ■ *hot tub, steam room* ■ www.ccbc-gay-resort.com

12 **Century Palm Springs** [★M,SW,N,WI] 760/323-9966, 800/475-5188 ■ 598 Grenfall Rd (btwn Ramon & Sunny Dunes) ■ *'50s guesthouse w/ sleek retro style* ■ www.centurypalmsprings.com

13 **Chaps Inn** [M,SW,WI,WC,GO] 760/327-8222, 800/445-8916 (also TTY) ■ 312 E Camino Monte Vista ■ *exclusively gay men, catering to leather & bears mostly, hot tub, steam room, kitchens* ■ www.chapsinn.com

14 **Chestnutz** [M,SW,N,NS,WI,GO] 760/325-5269, 800/621-6973 ■ 641 San Lorenzo Rd (at Random) ■ *full brkfst, hot tub, private patios* ■ www.chestnutz.com

15 **Columns Resort** [M,SW,N,WI,WC,GO] 760/325-0655, 800/798-0655 ■ 537 Grenfall Rd (at Ramon) ■ *studios, hot tub* ■ www.pscolumns.com

17 <u>**Desert Hearts Inn**</u> [W,SW,GO] 760/322-5793, 888/275-9903 ■ Avenida Olancha (across from Queen of Hearts) ■ *full kitchens, lesbian-owned* ■ www.queenofheartsps.com/dhearts.html

PALM SPRINGS

Day Trips: Joshua Tree National Park

About an hour's drive northeast on Hwy 62, you will find one of the state's most unusual and amazing landscapes. Rugged granite monoliths jut out from the desert floor, creating an almost other-worldly effect. Two deserts, the Colorado and the Mojave, come together in this huge park (794,000 acres), illustrating the dramatic differences between high and low desert environments. For more info, visit www.nps.gov/jotr.

Tourist Info

AIRPORT DIRECTIONS

Palm Springs International Airport. Tahquitz Canyon Dr runs from the airport to the main drag—Palm Canyon Dr. This curves to become E Palm Canyon.

PUBLIC TRANSIT & TAXIS

City Cab 760/416-2594.
Classic Cab 760/322-3111.
Desert Valley Shuttle 800/413-3999.
Sun Line Transit Agency 760/343-3451 or 800/347-8628, web: www.sunline.org.

TOURIST SPOTS & INFO

Joshua Tree National Park, web: www.nps.gov/jotr.
Palm Springs Aerial Tramway to the top of Mt San Jacinto, on Tramway Rd, web: www.pstramway.com.
Palm Springs Art Museum 760/325-7186, web: www.psmuseum.org.
Visitor's Center: Palm Springs Visitors Bureau 760/778-8418 or 800/347-7746, web: www.palm-springs.org.

Weather

Palm Springs is sunny and warm in the winter, with temperatures in the 70°s. Summers are scorching (100°+).

Best Views

Top of Mt San Jacinto. Driving through the surrounding desert, you can see great views of the mountains. Be careful in the summer—always carry water in your vehicle, and be sure to check all fluids in your car before you leave and frequently during your trip.

City Calendar

LGBT PRIDE

November, web: www.pspride.org.

ANNUAL EVENTS

Spring - Kraft Nabisco Golf Tournament (aka "Dinah Shore") 760/324-4546, web: www.kncgolf.com. One of the biggest gatherings of lesbians on the continent. If you're more interested in the party than the golf, get the info at www.dinahshoreweekend.com.
White Party, web: www.jeffreysanker.com. Popular circuit party/fundraiser.

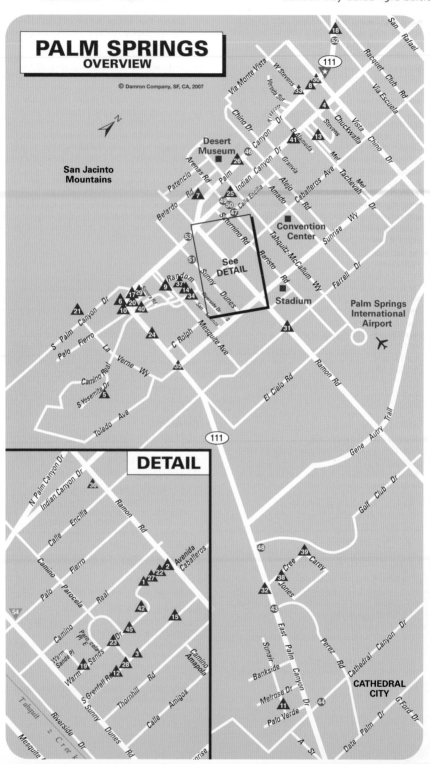

PALM SPRINGS
OVERVIEW

© Damron Company, SF, CA, 2007

San Jacinto
Mountains

Desert
Museum

See
DETAIL

Convention
Center

Stadium

Palm Springs
International
Airport

DETAIL

CATHEDRAL
CITY

18 **Desert Moon Resort & Spa** [M,SW,N,NS,WI,WC,GO]
760/325-8038, 800/506-1899 ■ 2150 N Palm Canyon Dr
(at Via Escuela) ■ *citrus-lined courtyard, hot tub* ■
www.desertmoonresort.com

19 **Desert Paradise Resort Hotel** [★M,SW,N,NS,WI,GO]
760/320-5650, 800/342-7635 ■ 615 Warm Sands Dr (at
Parocela) ■ *jacuzzi, firepit, outdoor shower, clothing-optional
throughout* ■ www.desertparadise.com

20 **Desert Star Bungalows** [GF,SW,NS,WI] 760/778-1047,
800/399-1006 ■ 1611 Calle Palo Fierro ■ *boutique hotel
made up of bungalows w/ fully equipped kitchen* ■
www.desertstarhotel.com

21 **The East Canyon Hotel & Spa** [★M,SW,NS,WI,GO]
760/320-1928, 877/324-6835 ■ 288 E Camino Monte
Vista ■ *boutique hotel for men, day spa on-site, winner of Out
& About's 5 Palm Award* ■ www.eastcanyonps.com

22 **El Mirasol Villas** [★M,SW,N,NS,WI,GO] 760/327-5913,
800/327-2985 ■ 525 Warm Sands Dr (at Ramon) ■ *newly
renovated bungalows in a garden setting, steam room &
jacuzzi* ■ www.elmirasol.com

23 ► **The Hacienda at Warm Sands** [★M,V,SW,N,NS,WI,WC,GO]
760/327-8111, 800/359-2007 ■ 586 Warm Sands Dr (at
Parocela) ■ *2 pools & hot tub* ■ www.thehacienda.com

24 **The Horizon Hotel** [GF,SW,WI] 760/323-1858,
800/377-7855 ■ 1050 E Palm Canyon Dr ■ *jacuzzi* ■
www.thehorizonhotel.com

25 **Hotel Zoso** [GF,SW,WI] 760/325-9676 ■ 150 S Indian
Canyon Dr ■ *4-acre resort, restaurant & bar, spa* ■
www.hotelzoso.com

26 **Hyatt Regency Suites Palm Springs** [GF,SW,WI]
760/322-9000, 800/554-9288 ■ 285 N Palm Canyon Dr
■ *also restaurant & bar* ■ www.palmsprings.hyatt.com

27 **Inn Exile** [★M,F,SW,N,WI,GO] 760/327-6413,
800/962-0186 ■ 545 Warm Sands Dr (at Ramon) ■ *resort,
hot tub, gym, steam, also Skivvies Cafe, 6pm-10pm, pizzas &
snacks* ■ www.innexile.com

28 ► **INNdulge Palm Springs** [★M,SW,N,NS,WI,GO]
760/327-1408, 800/833-5675 ■ 601 Grenfall Rd (at
Parocela) ■ *hot tub, Out & About-rated 5 Palms* ■
www.inndulge.com

La Casa Contenta [GS,SW,NS,WC] 760/322-2500,
800/777-4606 ■ *prestigious 5-bdrm estate property w/ lush
gardens, lots of privacy* ■ www.psvacation.net

29 **La Dolce Vita Resort** [M,SW,N,NS,WI,WC,GO]
760/325-2686, 877/644-4111 ■ 1491 S Via Soledad (at
Sonora & S Palm Canyon) ■ *full brkfst, jacuzzi, Out &
About-rated 4 Palms* ■ www.ladolcevitaresort.com

30 **Las Palmas Hotel** [M,SW,NS,WI,GO] 760/327-6883,
866/552-7272 ■ 1404 N Palm Canyon Dr ■ *resort, pets ok*
■ www.laspalmas-hotel.com

Mojave [GF,SW,NS,WC] 760/346-6121, 866/846-8358
■ 73721 Shadow Mountain Dr, Palm Desert ■ *boutique hotel*
■ www.hotelmojave.com

31 **Mountain View Villa** [GS,SW,NS] 305/294-1525 ■ on
Farrell Dr ■ *vacation rental at Mesquite Country Club* ■
www.vacationdepot.com/palmspringsmesquiterentals.htm

32 **Ozz Resort** [MW,SW,NS,WI,GO] 760/324-3000,
866/247-7443 ■ 67-580 Hwy 111 (at Gene Autry Tr),
Cathedral City ■ *also nightclub & restaurant* ■ www.ozzre-
sort.com

Parocela Villas at Warm Sands [M,SW] 760/322-7961,
877/322-7961 ■ *4 rental villas in the heart of Warm Sands*
■ www.parocelavillas.com

17 **Queen of Hearts Resort** [W,SW,GO] 760/322-5793,
888/275-9903 ■ 435 E Avenida Olancha ■ *full kitchens,
lesbian-owned* ■ www.queenofheartsps.com

33 **Ruby Montana's Coral Sands Inn** [GS,SW,WC,GO]
760/325-4900, 866/820-8302 ■ 210 W Stevens Rd (at N
Palm Canyon) ■ *resort, kids/ pets ok, kitschy 1950s chic* ■
www.coralsandspalmsprings.com

34 **Santiago Resort** [M,SW,N,NS,WI] 760/322-1300,
800/710-7729 ■ 650 San Lorenzo Rd (at Mesquite)
■ *clothing-optional, hot tub, sauna & shower garden, brkfst &
lunch included* ■ www.santiagoresort.com

Sun & Fun Vacation Rentals [GS,SW,NS,GO]
760/322-7961 ■ *rental houses & condos* ■
www.sandfvr.com

35 **Terrazzo Resort** [M,SW,NS,WI,WC,GO] 760/778-5883,
866/837-7996 ■ 1600 E Palm Canyon Dr (btwn Calle
Marcus & Sunrise) ■ *resort, full brkfst* ■ www.terrazzo-
ps.com

36 **The Three Thirty Three B&B** [GS,NS,GO] 760/320-7744
(9am-8pm PST) ■ 333 E Ramon Rd ■ *intimate 3-bdrm B&B,
hot tub [N]* ■ www.333bnb.com

34 **Tortuga del Sol** [M,SW,N,NS,WI,GO] 760/416-3111,
888/541-3777 ■ 715 San Lorenzo ■ *resort, jacuzzi* ■
www.tortugadelsol.com

37 **Triangle Inn Palm Springs** [★M,SW,N,GO] 760/322-7993,
800/732-7555 ■ 555 San Lorenzo Rd (at Random Rd)
■ *hot tub, 2 sundecks* ■ www.triangle-inn.com

Two Bunches Palm Resort & Spa [GF,SW,NS,WI]
760/329-8791, 800/472-4334 ■ 67425 Two Bunches
Palm Trail (at Palm Canyon Dr), Desert Hot Springs ■
www.twobunchpalms.com

38 **Villa Mykonos** [MW,SW,WI] 800/471-4753 ■ 67-590 Jones
Rd (at Cree), Cathedral City ■ *timeshare condos & rental
units* ■ www.villamykonos.com

39 **The Villa Resort Palm Springs** [★M,F,SW,WI,GO]
760/328-7211, 877/778-4552 ■ 67-670 Carey Rd (at
Cree), Cathedral City ■ *bungalows, also 2 restaurants & bars*
■ www.thevilla.com

40 **Villa Royale** [★GF,SW] 760/327-2314, 800/245-2314
■ 1620 Indian Trail ■ *jacuzzi, also Europa Restaurant, "named
one of the five best small inns in Southern California by
Sunset Magazine"* ■ www.villaroyale.com

41 **The Village Inn** [GS,NS,SW] 760/320-8622, 866/320-8622 ■ 855 N Indian Canyon Dr ■ *hotel, hot tub, kids/ pets ok* ■ www.palmspringsvillageinn.com

42 **Warm Sands Villas** [★M,SW,N,NS,WI,GO] 760/323-3005, 800/357-5695 ■ 555 Warm Sands Dr (at Ramon) ■ *hot tub* ■ warmsandsvillas.com

Bars

43 **The Barracks** [M,L] 760/321-9688 ■ 67-625 E Palm Canyon (at Canyon Plaza), Cathedral City ■ *2pm-2am, cruisy, also LeatherSmiths leather store* ■ www.thebarracksbar.com

44 **Club Whatever** [MW,NH,K] 760/321-0031 ■ 36-737 Cathedral Canyon Dr (at Commercial), Cathedral City ■ *9am-2am, patio, wknds [C,DS]* ■ www.club-whatever.com

45 **Delilah's** [W,D] 760/770-1210 ■ 67-555 Hwy 111 (across from Target Shopping Center), Cathedral City ■ *4pm-midnight, till 2am Fri-Sat, clsd Wed* ■ www.delilahspalmsprings.com

32 **Dorothy's Other Kansas (DOK)** [MW] 760/324-3000 ■ 67-580 Hwy 111 (at Ozz Resort), Cathedral City ■ *11am-3pm, clsd Mon* ■ www.ozzresort.com

46 **Georgie's Alibi** [MW,NH,V] 760/325-5533 ■ 369 N Palm Canyon Dr ■ *also restaurant* ■ www.georgiesalibi.com/palmsprings.htm

47 **Hunter's Video Bar** [★M,D,V] 760/323-0700 ■ 302 E Arenas Rd (at Calle Encilia) ■ *10am-2am, go-go boys Fri* ■ www.huntersnightclubs.com

32 **Ozz Patio & Palapa Bar** [★MW,F] 760/324-3000, 866/247-7443 ■ 67-580 Hwy 111 (at Ozz Resort), Cathedral City ■ *10am-close, also restaurant & nightclub [MW,D]* ■ www.ozzresort.com

48 **Sidewinders** [M,CW,L] 760/328-9919 ■ 67-555 E Palm Canyon Dr (at E Eagle Canyon Way), Cathedral City ■ *noon-2am* ■ www.sidewindersbar.com

49 **SpurLine** [M,NH,K,V] 760/778-4326 ■ 200 S Indian Canyon Dr (at Arenas) ■ *10am-2am, lounge, [K] Th, beer bust Sun*

50 **Streetbar** [★M,NH,E,K,WC] 760/320-1266 ■ 224 E Arenas Rd (at Indian) ■ *10am-2am, patio* ■ www.streetbarps.com

51 **Tool Shed** [M,NH,L] 760/320-3299 ■ 600 E Sunny Dunes Rd (at Palm Canyon) ■ *7am-2am, till 4am Fri-Sat, call for events, also leather shop* ■ www.toolshed-ps.com

52 **Toucan's Tiki Lounge** [MW,D,E,DS,S] 760/416-7584 ■ 2100 N Palm Canyon Dr (at Via Escuela) ■ *noon-2am, [E] Mon, [DS] Wed & Sun, go-go dancers wknds* ■ www.toucanstikilounge.com

39 **The Villa Palm Springs–Butterfield's** [MW] 760/328-7211 ■ 67-670 Carey Rd (at The Villa resort), Cathedral City ■ *10am-10pm, brunch daily, poolside bar, patio, also cafe w/ lunch & dinner* ■ www.thevilla.com

Nightclubs

53 **Oasis** [MW,D,S,V,$] 760/416-0950 ■ 611 S Palm Canyon Dr (in the Sun Center) ■ *9pm-2am Th [D,S], 8pm-4am Fri-Sat [D], clsd Sun-Wed* ■ www.cluboasisps.com

Cafes

Palm Springs Koffi [★WI,GO] 760/416-2244 ■ 515 N Palm Canyon Dr (at Alejo) ■ *5:30am-7pm* ■ www.kofficoffee.com

Restaurants

Amici 760/341-0738 ■ 71380 Hwy 111, Rancho Mirage ■ *lunch & dinner, Sun brunch, Italian, patio, also full bar* ■ www.dineamici.com

Azul 760/325-5533 ■ 369 N Palm Canyon Dr ■ *11am-3pm & 4pm-2am, tapas lounge, full bar upstairs* ■ www.azultapaslounge.com

Bangkok Five 760/770-9508 ■ 70-026 Hwy 111, Rancho Mirage ■ *dinner nightly, Thai* ■ www.bangkok5.com

Billy Reed's [WC] 760/325-1946 ■ 1800 N Palm Canyon Dr (at Vista Chino) ■ *7am-9pm, some veggie, bakery, full bar*

Blame It on Midnight [M,E,GO] 760/323-1200 ■ 777 E Tahquitz Canyon Wy Stes 101-109 (at the Courtyard) ■ *5pm-11pm, clsd Mon in summer, live music Th-Sun, also full bar, patio* ■ www.blameitonmidnight.com

Blue Coyote Grill 760/327-1196 ■ 445 N Palm Canyon Dr ■ *11am-10pm, till 11pm Fri-Sat, Southwestern* ■ www.bluecoyote-grill.com

Bongo Johnny's 760/866-1905 ■ 214 E Arenas Rd ■ *8am-10pm, till 11pm Fri-Sat, burgers & sandwiches*

Boscoso 760/325-4002 ■ 707 N Palm Canyon Dr (at Merito, in Uptown) ■ *from 5pm, Northern Italian, also lounge* ■ www.myboscoso.com

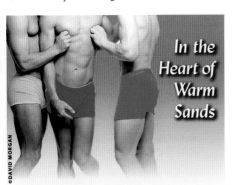

Butterfield's Adobe 760/328-7211 ■ 67-670 Carey Rd (at The Villa resort), Cathedral City ■ *11am-10pm, wknd champagne brunch by pool, full bar* ■ www.thevilla.com/dine.php

The Chop House [R] 760/320-4500 ■ 262 S Palm Canyon Dr ■ *from 5pm, steak* ■ www.palmspringschophouse.com

Copley's 760/327-9555 ■ 621 N Palm Canyon Dr (btwn E Tamarisk Rd & E Granvia Valmonte) ■ *6pm-10pm, Sun brunch, "creative contemporary American cuisine," full bar* ■ www.copleysrestaurant.com

CopyKatz Showroom & Backstage Bistro [GS,TG,E,C,DS,WC] 760/864-9293 ■ 200 S Palm Canyon Dr ■ *lunch & dinner* ■ www.copykatzps.com

The Cove Cafe [WI] 760/321-5557 ■ 68-375 Hwy 111, Cathedral City ■ *lunch & dinner, clsd Sun*

Dale's Lost Highway [MW,E] 760/327-2005 ■ 125 E Tahquitz Canyon ■ *lunch & dinner, full bar, stand-up comedy Th-Sat* ■ www.daleslosthighway.com

Davey's Hideaway [P] 760/320-4480 ■ 292 E Palm Canyon Dr ■ *from 5pm, steak, seafood & pasta, patio, full bar* ■ daveysps@aol.com

El Gallito [BW] 760/328-7794 ■ 68820 Grove St (at Palm Canyon), Cathedral City ■ *10am-9pm, homemade Mexican*

Hamburger Mary's 760/778-6279 ■ 415 N Palm Canyon Dr ■ *11am-close, full bar* ■ www.hamburgermarysps.com

Just Pizza 760/416-2818 ■ 315 E Arenas ■ *11am-10pm, till 2am Fri-Sat, also delivers* ■ www.justpizza.net

Kalaya's Thai Restaurant [R] 760/568-0433 ■ 71-321 Hwy 111, Rancho Mirage ■ *lunch & dinner, clsd Sun*

Las Casuelas 760/325-3213 ■ 368 N Palm Canyon Dr (btwn Amado & Alejo) ■ *11am-10pm, traditional Mexican*

Look 760/778-3520 ■ 139 E Andreas Rd ■ *11am-10pm, patio bar till 2am*

Lotza Mozza 760/325-5571 ■ 119 S Indian Canyon ■ *10am-10pm, till 11pm Fri-Sat, pizza & pasta* ■ www.lotzamozza.com

Matchbox 760/778-6000 ■ 155 S Palm Canyon Dr (in Mercado Plaza, 2nd level) ■ *4pm-1am, pizza* ■ www.matchboxpalmsprings.com

Ming's Chinese Cuisine 760/770-3663 ■ 35300 Date Palm Dr, Cathedral City ■ *11:30am-9pm, clsd Sun*

More Than a Mouthful Cafe 760/322-3776 ■ 134 E Tahquitz Canyon Wy ■ *7:30am-2pm, clsd Tue*

Patrick's Roadhouse 760/325-1551 ■ 611 S Palm Canyon Dr (in the Sun Center) ■ *9am-8pm, till 9pm Fri-Sat, till 3pm Sun, clsd Mon, American* ■ www.patricksroadhouse.com

Philippe's Cafe 760/323-0772 ■ 245 S Palm Canyon Dr ■ *10am-10pm, from 8am wknds, clsd Mon, French*

Picanha 760/674-3434 ■ 73399 El Paseo, Palm Desert ■ *lunch & dinner, Sun brunch, Brazilian churrascaria* ■ www.picanharestaurant.com

Plum [★MW] 760/322-0200 ■ 241 E Tahquitz Canyon Wy ■ *lunch & dinner, champagne brunch wknds, clsd Mon, patio, also martini bar*

Pomme Frite 760/778-3727 ■ 256 S Palm Canyon Dr ■ *5pm-11pm Wed-Mon & noon-3pm wknds, clsd Tue, Belgian beer & French food* ■ www.pomme-frite.com

Rainbow [P] 760/325-3868 ■ 212 S Indian Canyon (at Arenas) ■ *lunch & dinner, Sun brunch, Californian, piano bar* ■ www.psrainbow.com

Red Tomato & House of Lamb [BW,WC] 760/328-7518 ■ 68-784 E Palm Canyon (btwn Date Palm & Cathedral Canyon), Cathedral City ■ *4pm-10pm, Italian*

Rick's Restaurant 760/416-0090 ■ 1973 N Palm Canyon Dr ■ *6am-3pm, Cuban/American*

Rock Garden Cafe 760/327-8840 ■ 777 S Palm Canyon Dr ■ *7am-10pm, Greek, patio*

Shame on the Moon [R,WC] 760/324-5515 ■ 69-950 Frank Sinatra Dr (at Hwy 111), Rancho Mirage ■ *5pm-10:30pm, cont'l, some veggie, patio, full bar* ■ www.shame-onthemoon.com

Sherman's Deli & Bakery 760/325-1199 ■ 401 E Tahquitz Canyon Wy ■ *7am-9pm, till 2pm Th, kosher-style deli*

Simba's [E] 760/778-7630 ■ 190 N Sunrise Wy ■ *lunch & dinner, ribs, clsd summers*

Spencer's Restaurant [R] 760/327-3446 ■ 701 W Baristo Rd ■ *9am-2:30pm & 5pm-10pm, Sun brunch, upscale contemporary* ■ www.spencersrestaurant.com

Thai Palms 760/322-3992 ■ 1418 N Palm Canyon ■ *11am-9pm, clsd Th*

Thai Smile 760/320-5503 ■ 651 N Palm Canyon Dr ■ *11:30am-10pm* ■ www.thaismilerestaurants.com

Tootie's Texas Barbeque 760/202-6963 ■ 68-703 Perez Rd, Cathedral City ■ *11am-8pm, clsd Sun-Mon, the name says it all*

Towne Center Cafe 760/346-2131 ■ 44491 Town Center Wy, Palm Desert ■ *Greek diner* ■ www.townecentercafe.com

The Uptown Grill of Palm Springs [P,NS] 760/320-6116 ■ 150 E Vista Chino (at Indian Canyon) ■ *lunch & dinner, cont'l, full bar* ■ www.uptowngrillofpalmsprings.com

Wang's in the Desert 760/325-9264 ■ 424 S Indian Canyon Dr ■ *from 5:30pm, Chinese* ■ wangsinthedesert.com

Zin American Bistro 760/322-6300 ■ 198 S Palm Canyon (at Arenas) ■ *5pm-10pm, till 11pm Fri-Sat* ■ www.zinamericanbistro.com

ENTERTAINMENT & RECREATION

Desert Dyners 760/202-6645 ■ PO Box 5072, 92263-5072 ■ *lesbian social group, membership required, hosts mixers, dances, dinners & golf, singles & couples welcome* ■ www.desertdyners.com

The Living Desert Zoo & Gardens [$] 760/346-5694 ■ 47-900 Portola Ave, Palm Desert ■ *9am-5pm (8am-1pm June-Aug), "zoo & endangered species conservation center, botanical gardens, natural history museum, wilderness park, nature preserve, education center"* ■ www.livingdesert.org

Palm Springs Art Museum 760/325-7186 ■ 101 Museum Dr ■ *10am-5pm, noon-8pm Th, clsd Mon, some LGBT events* ■ www.psmuseum.org

Palm Springs Caballeros 760/322-3112 ■ PO Box 8057, 92263-8057 ■ *gay men's chorus* ■ www.pscaballeros.org

Ruddy's 1930s General Store Museum 760/327-2156 ■ 221 S Palm Canyon Dr ■ *10am-4pm Th-Sun, clsd summers, "the most you can spend is 95¢"*

BOOKSTORES

Peppertree Bookstore & Cafe [★] 760/325-4821 ■ 155 S Palm Canyon Dr ■ *10am-8pm, till 10pm Th-Sat, independent, some LGBT titles, readings* ■ www.peppertreebookstore.com

54 **Q Trading Company** 760/416-7150, 800/756-2290 ■ 606 E Sunny Dunes Rd (at Indian Canyon) ■ *10am-6pm, LGBT, also cards, gifts, videos* ■ www.qtrading.com

RETAIL SHOPS

Bear Wear Etc 760/323-8940 ■ 319 E Arenas Rd ■ *10am 6pm, till 10pm Th-Sat, noon-5pm Sun, men's clothing, leatherwear, resortwear (shorts, swimwear, tanks & T-shirts)* ■ bearzwear@aol.com

The Drag Bag 760/322-9500 ■ 650 E Sunny Dunes #3 ■ *noon-5pm, clsd Sun-Mon, everything a drag queen needs* ■ www.thedragbag.com

GayMartUSA 760/416-6436 ■ 305 E Arenas Rd (at Indian Canyon) ■ *10am-midnight*

Mischief 760/322-8555 ■ 210 E Arenas Rd (at Indian Canyon) ■ *11am-7pm, 10am-10pm Th, 10am-11pm Fri-Sat, cards, novelties, gifts, toys & DVDs*

Tuff Stuff 760/864-8539 ■ 407 Industrial Pl ■ *custom leather, some bear & pride items* ■ www.tuffstuffleather.com

PUBLICATIONS

The Bottom Line 760/323-0552 ■ *the desert's LGBT guide & classifieds* ■ www.psbottomline.com

Buzz 760/323-0552 ■ *bi-weekly, news, entertainment & listings, covers San Diego & Palm Springs* ■ www.buzzpublication.com

Desert Daily Guide 760/320-3237 ■ *LGBT weekly, travel, activity & lodging info for Palm Springs* ■ www.desertdailyguide.com

Palm Springs Gay Yellow Pages 760/324-8299 ■ www.psgyp.com

GYMS & HEALTH CLUBS

Basic Gym 760/320-1009 ■ 1584 S Palm Canyon Dr (at E Olancha) ■ *7am-8pm, 8am-6pm Sat, 11am-3pm Sun* ■ www.thebasicgym.com

Gold's Gym [GF] 760/322-4653 ■ 4070 Airport Center Dr (at Ramon) ■ *24hrs* ■ www.goldsgym.com/palmspringsca

Urban Yoga Center 760/320-7702 ■ 750 N Palm Canyon Dr (at Healing Arts Community) ■ www.urbanyoga.org

World Gym Palm Springs [M,MR,WC,GO] 760/327-7100 ■ 1751 N Sunrise Way (at Vista Chino) ■ *5am-10pm, from 6am wknds, day passes available, steam & sauna, club-quality sound system* ■ www.worldgympalmsprings.com

EROTICA

Hidden Joy Book Shop 760/328-1694 ■ 68-424 Commercial (at Cathedral Canyon), Cathedral City ■ *clsd 3am-5am, also arcade*

World Wide Book Store 760/321-1313 ■ 68-300 Ramon Rd (at Cathedral Canyon), Cathedral City ■ *also arcade*

Russian River

ACCOMMODATIONS

1 **Applewood Inn** [GF,F,SW,NS,WI,WC,GO] 707/869-9093, 800/555-8509 ■ 13555 Hwy 116 (at Mays Canyon), Guerneville ■ *full brkfst* ■ www.applewoodinn.com

2 **Dawn Ranch Lodge** [GF,F,SW,NS,WI,WC,GO] 707/869-0656, 800/734-3371 ■ 16467 River Rd (at Brookside Ln), Guerneville ■ *55 cottages & cabins, also 2 full bars & restaurant* ■ www.dawnranch.com

3 **Eagle's Peak** [M,GO] 707/480-3328, 877/891-6466 ■ 11644 Our Peak Rd (at McPeak Rd), Forestville ■ *vacation house w/ deck & spa on 26 acres* ■ www.eaglespeak.net

Far Reaches [GF,GO] 415/864-4554 ■ Highland Terrace (at Huckleberry St), Monte Rio ■ *cottage, kids/ pets ok, large deck* ■ www.russianrivercottage.com

RUSSIAN RIVER

Local Food:

There are nearly 200 wineries in surrounding Sonoma County, many of which offer free tours. Take advantage of the plentiful produce stands and farmers markets scattered around the county, or make reservations at one of the many top-notch restaurants in the area. Talented, creative chefs use fresh local ingredients to create an unforgettable dining experience.

Tourist Info

AIRPORT DIRECTIONS

The closest airport is the Sonoma County Airport in Santa Rosa, or San Francisco International, 2 hours to the south.

PUBLIC TRANSIT & TAXIS

Bill's Taxi Service 707/869-2177.
As far as public transit goes, this area is easiest to reach by car.

TOURIST SPOTS & INFO

Armstrong Redwood State Park.
Bodega Bay, web: www.bodegabay.com.
Jenner.
Healdsburg.
Mudbaths of Calistoga.
Wineries of Napa and Sonoma Counties, web: www.napavalley.com & www.sonomacounty.com.
Visitor's Center: Russian River Chamber of Commerce & Visitors Center 877/644-9001, web: www.russianriver.com.

Weather

Summer days are sunny and warm (80°s-90°s) but usually begin with a dense fog. Winter days have the same pattern but are a lot cooler and wetter. Winter nights can be very damp and chilly (low 40°s).

Best Views

Anywhere in Armstrong Woods, the Napa Wine Country, and on the ride along the picture-postcard-perfect coast on Highway 1.

City Calendar

ANNUAL EVENTS

May - Women's Weekend 877/644-9001 (chamber of commerce #), web: www.rrwomensweekend.com.
June - Blues Festival, web: rrfestivals.com/blues.
August - Lazy Bear Weekend, thousands of bears take over the River, web: www.lazybearweekend.com.
September - Jazz Festival, web: www.jazzon-theriver.com.

Queer Resources

COMMUNITY INFO

Gay Russian River, web: www.gayrussianriver.com.
Santa Rosa AA 707/544-1300.
Face To Face 707/869-7390.

---

4   **Fern Grove Cottages** [GF,SW,NS,WI] 707/869-8105 ■ 16650 River Rd, Guerneville ■ *restored 1920s cottages, kids/ pets ok* ■ www.ferngrove.com

5   Grandma's House [MW,WC,GO] 707/865-1865, 800/433-6673 ■ 20280 River Blvd, Monte Rio ■ *B&B on river, private beach, lesbian-owned* ■ www.rrgetaways.com/grandmas_1.htm
HearthSide Cabin [GS,WI,GO] 415/255-1099 ■ 2320 Cazadero Hwy, Cazadero ■ *2-bdrm cabin (sleeps 6), hot tub* ■ hearthsidecabin.com

6   **Highland Dell Resort** [GF,WI] 707/865-2300 ■ 21050 River Blvd (at Bohemian Hwy), Monte Rio ■ *riverside hotel w/ full bar & restaurant* ■ www.highlanddell.com

7   **Highlands Resort** [MW,SW,N] 707/869-0333 ■ 14000 Woodland Dr, Guerneville ■ *country retreat on 4 wooded acres, hot tub* ■ www.HighlandsResort.com

8   Huckleberry Springs Country Inn & Spa [GS,V,SW,NS] 707/865-2683, 800/822-2683 ■ 8105 Old Beedle, Monte Rio ■ *full brkfst, private cottages, Japanese spa, massage therapy, no smoking anywhere on property* ■ www.huckleberrysprings.com

9   **Inn at Occidental** [GF,NS,WC] 707/874-1047, 800/522-6324 ■ 3657 Church St, Occidental ■ *luxury Sonoma Wine Country inn, full brkfst* ■ www.innatoccidental.com

10   **Inn at the Willows** [MW,NS,GO] 707/869-2824 (8am-8pm PST), 800/291-1905 ■ 15905 River Rd (at Hwy 116), Guerneville ■ *old-fashioned country lodge & campground, hot tub* ■ www.innatthewillows.com

11   **New Dynamic Inn** [GF,NS,WI,WC] 707/869-5082 ■ 14030 Mill St (at Main St), Guerneville ■ *kids/ pets ok* ■ www.newdynamicinn.com

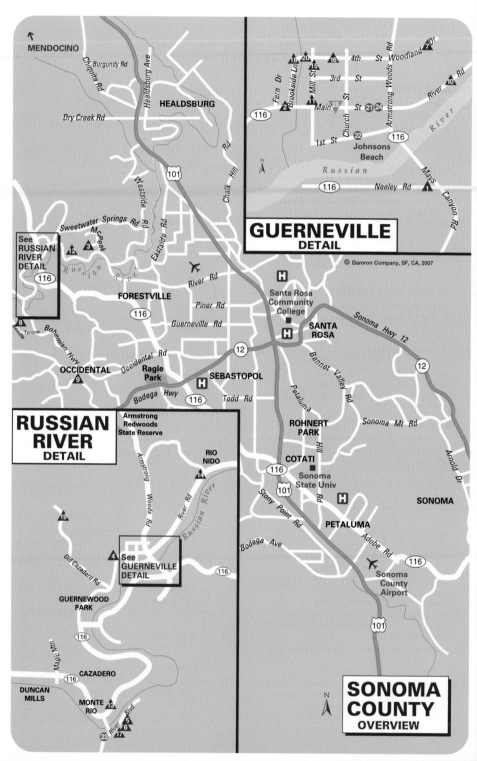

Pacha Mama Home [MW,NS,WI,GO] 415/648-9333 ■
*2-bdrm home on wooded hillside, hot tub, wood stove, dog-
friendly, near river, lesbian-owned* ■ www.pachamama-
home.info

12 Ridenhour Ranch House Inn & Cottages [GF,NS,WI]
707/887-1033, 888/877-4466 ■ 12850 River Rd,
Guerneville ■ *1906 B&B, hot tub* ■ www.ridenhourranch-
houseinn.com

13 Rio Villa Beach Resort [GF,NS,WI,GO] 707/865-1143,
877/746-8455 ■ 20292 Hwy 116 (at Bohemian Hwy),
Monte Rio ■ *cabins on the river* ■ www.riovilla.com

13 River Gem Resort [GS,NS] 707/865-1467, 800/865-1467
■ 20284 Hwy 116 (at F St), Monte Rio ■ *historic riverfront
cottages* ■ www.rivergemresort.com

14 River Village Resort & Spa [GS,SW,NS,WI,WC]
707/869-8139 ■ 14880 River Rd, Guerneville ■ *cottages,
hot tub, full-service spa* ■ www.rivervillageresort.com

15 Russian River Getaways [MW,SW,NS,WI,GO]
707/869-4560, 800/433-6673 ■ 14070 Mill St (at 4th St),
Guerneville ■ *vacation rental service, lesbian-owned* ■
www.rrgetaways.com

16 Russian River Resort/ Triple R Resort
[MW,E,P,V,SW,N,WC,GO] 707/869-0691, 800/417-3767
■ 16390 4th St (at Mill), Guerneville ■ *hot tub, also bar &
restaurant, some veggie* ■ www.RussianRiverResort.com

Russian River View Retreat [GF,NS] 707/869-3040
(8am-8pm PST) ■ *vacation home w/ deck, hot tub, private
dock & boat* ■ RussianRiverView.com

Tim & Tony's Treehouse [GS,SW,N,NS,GO] 707/887-9531,
888/887-9531 ■ *studio cottage, hot tub, sauna* ■
www.timntony.com

17 Village Inn & Restaurant [GS,NS,WC,WI,GO]
707/865-2304, 800/303-2303 ■ 20822 River Blvd, Monte
Rio ■ *historic inn w/ restaurant & full bar* ■
www.villageinn-ca.com

18 West Sonoma Inn [GS,SW,NS,WI,WC] 707/869-2470,
800/551-1881 ■ 14100 Brookside Ln (at Main St),
Guerneville ■ *6-acre resort a short walk from Johnson's
Beach, spa, some jacuzzis* ■ www.westsonomainn.com

19 Wildwood Retreat [GS,SW,WC] 707/632-5321 ■ Old
Cazadero Rd (off River Rd), Guerneville ■ *facilities are for
groups of 20 or more* ■ www.wildwoodretreat.com

20►The Woods Resort [MW,SW,N,NS,WC,GO] 707/869-0600,
877/887-9218 ■ 16484 4th St (at Mill St), Guerneville
■ *centrally located in downtown area, cottages, guest cabins
& suites* ■ rrwoods.com

BARS

21 Liquid Sky [M,NH,D,K,WC] 707/869-9910 ■ 16225 Main St
(at Armstrong Woods Rd), Guerneville ■ *5pm-2am, from 1pm
wknds, DJ Th-Sun*

22 Mc T's Bullpen [GS,NH,WC] 707/869-3377 ■ 16246 1st St
(at Church), Guerneville ■ *8am-2am, sports bar, patio*

23 The Pink Elephant [GF,NH] 707/865-0500 ■ 9895 Main
St, Monte Rio ■ *10am-2am*

24 Rainbow Cattle Co [GS,NH] 707/869-0206 ■ 16220 Main
St (at Armstrong Woods Rd), Guerneville ■ *6am-2am* ■
DJ Bruce Sat night ■ www.queersteer.com

CAFES

Coffee Bazaar [WI] 707/869-9706 ■ 14045 Armstrong
Woods Rd (at River Rd), Guerneville ■ *6am-8pm, soups,
salads & sandwiches*

Coffee Catz [E,WI,WC] 707/829-6600 ■ 6761 Sebastopol
Ave (at Hwy 116), Sebastopol ■ *7am-6pm, till 8pm Th, till
10pm Wed & Fri-Sat*

RESTAURANTS

Applewood [★R,WC] 707/869-9093, 800/555-8509
■ 13555 Hwy 116 (at Applewood Inn), Guerneville ■ *dinner,
clsd Sun-Mon, gourmet meals in the heart of the redwoods* ■
www.applewoodinn.com/dine/

Bob N' Boy [BW] 707/869-0780 ■ 16248 Main St (at Hwy
116), Guerneville ■ *11:30am-5:30pm, clsd Mon-Tue, burgers*
■ www.bobnboy.com

Cape Fear Cafe 707/865-9246 ■ 25191 Main St, Duncans
Mills ■ *9am-3pm & 5pm-9pm*

Charizma Wine Lounge & Deli [BW,WC] 707/869-0909
■ 16337 Main St (at Church St), Guerneville ■ *10am-9pm, till
4pm Wed (clsd Nov-March), 8am-9pm wknds* ■
www.charizmawinelounge.com

Farmhouse Inn Restaurant [BW] 707/887-3300 ■ 7871
River Rd, Forestville ■ *dinner, clsd Tue-Wed* ■ www.farm-
houseinn.com/restaurant.htm

Guerneville Grill [MW,WC] 707/869-0691 ■ 16390 4th St
(at Triple R Resort), Guerneville ■ *dinner, Sun brunch, clsd
Tue-Wed, American, some BBQ, some veggie, full bar, patio* ■
www.RussianRiverResort.com

Main Street Station [C,BW] 707/869-0501 ■ 16280 Main
St, Guerneville ■ *11am-8:30pm, from 4pm Wed, Italian
restaurant & pizzeria, cabaret dinner shows nightly* ■
www.mainststation.com

Mom's Apple Pie [★] 707/823-8330 ■ 4550 Gravenstein
Hwy N, Sebastopol ■ *10am-6pm, pie worth stopping for on
your way to and from Russian River!* ■ www.momsap-
plepieusa.com

Mosaic [TG,WC] 707/887-7503 ■ 6675 Front St (Hwy 116),
Forestville ■ *dinner, Sun brunch, clsd Mon, also wine lounge*
■ www.mosaiceats.com

River Inn Grill [★WC] 707/869-0481 ■ 16141 Main St,
Guerneville ■ *8am-2pm, till 8pm Fri-Sat, local favorite* ■
www.riverinngrill.com

Underwood Bar & Bistro 707/823-7023 ■ 9113 Graton
Rd, Graton ■ *lunch & dinner, clsd Mon* ■ www.underwood-
graton.com

Willow Wood Market Cafe [★] 707/823-0233 ■ 9020
Graton Rd, Graton ■ *8am-9pm, from 9am Sat, brunch 9am-
3pm Sun* ■ www.willowwoodgraton.com

ENTERTAINMENT & RECREATION

Pegasus Theater [WC] 707/522-9043 ▪ 20347 Hwy 116 (at Bohemian Hwy), Monte Rio ▪ *classic to contemporary plays* ▪ www.pegasustheater.com

River's Edge Kayak & Canoe Company [GO] 707/433-7247, 800/345-0869 ▪ 13840 Healdsburg Ave (at Hwy 101), Healdsburg ▪ *river excursions* ▪ riversedgekayakandcanoe.com

BOOKSTORES

25 **River Reader** [WC] 707/869-2240 ▪ 16355 Main St (at Mill), Guerneville ▪ *10am-6pm, till 5pm Sun, extended summer hours*

RETAIL SHOPS

Guerneville 5 &10 [GO] 707/869-3404 ▪ 16252 Main St, Guerneville ▪ *10am-6pm, old-fashioned five & dime, lesbian-owned* ▪ www.guerneville5and10.com

Touch of Greene [GO] 707/869-3180 ▪ 16377 B Main St, Guerneville ▪ *11am-5pm, clsd Mon-Tue, bath & body shop, massage, lesbian-owned* ▪ www.touchofgreene.com

Up the River 707/869-3167 ▪ 16212 Main St (at Armstrong Woods Rd), Guerneville ▪ *cards, gifts, T-shirts & more*

Vine Life 707/869-1234 ▪ 16359 Main St (at Mill St), Guerneville ▪ *11am-5pm, wine, cards & gifts* ▪ www.vinelifegifts.com

San Diego

ACCOMMODATIONS

1 **Balboa Park Inn** [GF,NS] 619/298-0823, 800/938-8181 ▪ 3402 Park Blvd (at Upas) ▪ *charming guesthouse in the heart of San Diego, theme rooms* ▪ www.balboaparkinn.com

2 **Beach Area B&B/ Elsbree House** [GF,NS] 619/226-4133, 800/607-4133 ▪ 5054 Narragansett Ave (at Sunset Cliffs Blvd) ▪ *B&B & 3-bdrm condo* ▪ www.bbinob.com

3 **The Beach Place** [M,N,W,GO] 619/225-0746 ▪ 2158 Sunset Cliffs Blvd (at Muir) ▪ *apts, hot tub, near beach* ▪ www.beachplace.us

4 **Best Western Blue Sea Lodge** [GF,SW,WC] 858/488-4700, 800/258-3732 ▪ 707 Pacific Beach Dr ▪ *beachfront hotel, hot tub, kids ok* ▪ www.bestwestern-bluesea.com

5 **The Bristol Hotel** [GS,WI,WC] 619/232-6141, 800/662-4477 ▪ 1055 First St ▪ *restaurant, great collection of pop art* ▪ www.thebristolsandiego.com

36 **Carole's B&B Inn** [GF,SW,WI,NS] 619/280-5258, 800/975-5521 ▪ 3227 Grim Ave ▪ *comfy early California bungalow, full brkfst* ▪ www.carolesbnb.com

6 **Casa Granada** [GS,NS,WI,GO] 619/501-5911, 866/524-2312 ▪ 1720 Granada Ave (at Dante St) ▪ *near beach* ▪ www.casa-granada.com

Crown City Inn [GF,SW,WI,WC] 619/435-3116, 800/422-1173 ▪ 520 Orange Ave, Coronado Island ▪ *near beach, also restaurant* ▪ www.crowncityinn.com

7 **da Vinci's** [MW,NS,WI,GO] 619/338-9966 ▪ 642 W Hawthorn (btwn Columbia & State) ▪ *also T's bar* ▪ www.myspace.com/hoteldavinci

8 **Handlery Hotel & Resort** [GF,SW,NS,WI,WC] 619/298-0511, 800/676-6567 ▪ 950 Hotel Circle N ▪ *centrally located in Mission Valley* ▪ www.handlery.com

9 **Hillcrest Inn Hotel** [MW,WI,WC] 619/293-7078, 800/258-2280 ▪ 3754 5th Ave (btwn Robinson & Pennsylvania) ▪ *int'l hotel in the heart of Hillcrest, hot tub* ▪ www.hillcrestinn.net

10 **Keating House** [GF,NS,WI,GO] 619/239-8585, 800/995-8644 ▪ 2331 2nd Ave (at Juniper) ▪ *150-yr-old Victorian on Bankers Hill, full brkfst* ▪ www.keatinghouse.com

11 **Mike's Place** [M,GO] 619/992-7466 ▪ 1252 Lincoln Ave (at Washington St) ▪ *private guest cottage* ▪ www.MikesPlace1252.com

12 **Park Manor Suites** [GF,WI] 619/291-0999, 800/874-2649 ▪ 525 Spruce St (btwn 5th & 6th) ▪ *1926 hotel, bar [P] & 2 restaurants, popular Fri happy hour* ▪ www.parkmanorsuites.com

13 **Sunburst Court Inn** [GS,NS,GO] 619/294-9665 ▪ 4086 Alabama St (at Polk) ▪ *all-suite inn* ▪ www.sunburstcourtinn.com

14 **W San Diego** [GF,SW,NS,WI,WC] 619/398-3100, 877/WHOTELS (reservations only) ▪ 421 W B St ▪ *rooftop bar, also restaurant* ▪ www.whotels.com/sandiego

BARS

15 **Airport Lounge** [GF,D,F,YC] 619/685-3881 ▪ 2400 India St (in Little Italy) ▪ *8pm-2am Th-Sat, futuristic airplane-themed restaurant to match the planes booming by overhead* ▪ www.airportloungesd.com

16 **Bourbon Street** [★M,E,V] 619/291-4043 ▪ 4612 Park Blvd (at Adams) ▪ *4pm-2am, front bar [E] & lounge [DJ], patio, [K] Tue, go-go boys Sat* ▪ www.bourbonstreetsd.com

17 **The Brass Rail** [MW,D,WC] 619/298-2233 ▪ 3796 5th Ave (at Robinson) ▪ *2pm-2am, clsd Wed, theme nights, Latin night Sat* ▪ www.brassrailsd.com

18 **The Caliph** [M,E,K,P,OC,WC] 619/298-9495 ▪ 3100 5th Ave (at Redwood) ▪ *11am-2am, piano bar*

19 **Chee Chee Club** [M,NH,TG] 619/234-4404 ▪ 929 Broadway (at 9th Ave) ▪ *6am-2am*

20 **Cheers** [M,NH,F] 619/298-3269 ▪ 1839 Adams Ave (at Park) ▪ *11am-2am, patio*

21 **The Flame** [★MW,D] 619/295-4163 ▪ 3780 Park Blvd (at University) ▪ *Boys Night Out Fri, Girls Night Out Sat, Sabbat (goth night) 2nd Sat, patio* ▪ www.flamesd.com

22 **Flicks** [★M,V,YC] 619/297-2056 ▪ 1017 University Ave (at 10th Ave) ▪ *2pm-2am, Latin night Fri w/ go-go dancers, wet underwear contest Sat* ▪ www.sdflicks.com

23 **The Hole** [M,NH,L] 619/226-9019 ▪ 2820 Lytton St (at Rosecrans) ▪ *4pm-close, from 6pm Tue-Wed, from 1pm Fri & Sun, from 5pm Sat, Wet & Wild Mon (wet underwear contest)* ▪ www.thehole.com

24 **Kickers** [★M,D,K,WC] 619/491-0400 ▪ 308 University Ave (at 3rd Ave) ▪ *9pm-2am, theme nights, Latin Mon, hip hop Fri, CW Tue & Sat, brunch Sun and T-dance from 5pm, patio* ▪ www.urbanmos.com

25 **The Loft** [M,NH,WC] 619/296-6407 ▪ 3610 5th Ave (at Brookes) ▪ *11am-2am*

26 **No 1 Fifth Ave (no sign)** [M,NH,V] 619/299-1911 ▪ 3845 5th Ave (at University) ▪ *noon-2am, patio*

27 **Numbers** [★MW,D,S,V,WC] 619/294-7583 ▪ 3811 Park Blvd (at University) ▪ *Bad Kitties [W] Fri, Recharge [M] Sat, patio* ▪ www.numberssd.com

28 **Pecs** [M,NH,B,L,WC] 619/296-0889 ▪ 2046 University Ave (at Alabama) ▪ *noon-2am, from 10am Sun, patio, cruisy* ▪ www.pecsbar.com

29 **Redwing Bar & Grill** [M,NH] 619/281-8700 ▪ 4012 30th St (at Lincoln, North Park) ▪ *10am-2am, patio* ▪ www.redwingbar.com

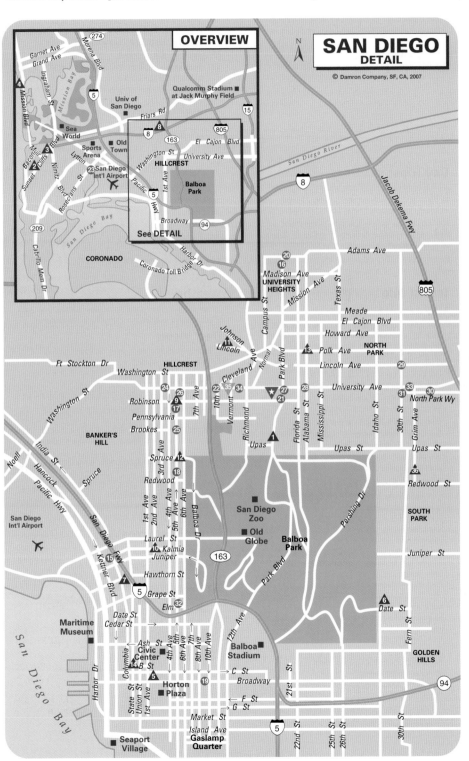

OVERVIEW

274

Garnet Ave
Grand Ave
Morena Blvd
Ingraham St
Mission Blvd
4
Sea World
Univ of San Diego
Qualcomm Stadium at Jack Murphy Field
5
15
Friars Rd
8
8
163
805
3
Old Town
El Cajon Blvd
Sports Arena
Washington St
University Ave
HILLCREST
2
Lytton
San Diego Int'l Airport
23
Barnett
Sunset
Nimitz Blvd
Rosecrans St
Pacific Hwy
1st Ave
5
Balboa Park
209
San Diego Bay
Cabrillo Mem Dr
Harbor Dr
Broadway
94
See DETAIL

CORONADO
Coronado Toll Bridge

San Diego River
8
Jacob Dekema Fwy

SAN DIEGO
DETAIL
© Damron Company, SF, CA, 2007

N

20
16
Adams Ave
Madison Ave
UNIVERSITY
HEIGHTS
Campus St
Mission Ave
Texas St
805

Meade
El Cajon Blvd
Howard Ave
13
Polk Ave
NORTH PARK
Ft Stockton Dr
HILLCREST
Washington St
Johnson
Lincoln
11
Cleveland Ave
Normal
Park Blvd
Lincoln Ave
29
24 26
22 35 34
27
28
University Ave
33
30
Robinson
9
7th Ave
10th
Vermont
21
31
North Park Wy
17
Pennsylvania
Richmond
Florida St
Alabama St
Mississippi St
Idaho St
30th St
Grim Ave
Brookes
25
BANKER'S
HILL
Upas
Upas St
Upas St
Spruce
3rd Ave
12
Spruce
18
36
Redwood
Redwood St
India St
Noell
Hancock
Pacific Hwy
1st Ave
2nd Ave
4th Ave
5th Ave
6th Ave
Balboa Dr
San Diego Zoo
SOUTH PARK
San Diego Int'l Airport
Laurel St
Old Globe
Balboa Park
Kalmia
10
Juniper
163
Pershing Dr
Juniper St
15
Hawthorn St
Kettner Blvd
5
Grape St
Elm
32
6
Date St
Fern St
GOLDEN HILLS
Maritime Museum
Date St
Cedar St
Ash St
12th Ave
Balboa Stadium
Civic Center
14
Columbia
B St
4th Ave
5th
6th Ave
7th
8th Ave
10th Ave
C St
Broadway
21st St
94
5
Horton Plaza
19
F St
G St
State St
Union St
1st Ave
Market St
Island Ave
Gaslamp Quarter
22nd St
25th St
26th St
30th St
Seaport Village
San Diego Bay

30 **San Diego Eagle** [M,NH,L,WC] **619/295-8072** ■ 3040 North Park Wy (at 30th) ■ *4pm-2am, from 2pm Fri-Sun, leather & fetish dress encouraged*

31 **Shooterz/ Club Odyssey** [GS,NH,D,V] **619/574-0744** ■ 3815 30th St (at University) ■ *3pm-2am, till 4am Fri, noon-4am Sat, noon-2am Sun, sports bar & dance club (from 9:30pm)*

32 **SRO Lounge** [M,NH,OC] **619/232-1886** ■ 1807 5th Ave (btwn Elm & Fir) ■ *10am-2am, cocktail lounge, Ladies Night Out 1st & 3rd Sat [W,TG]* ■ www.srolounge.com

NIGHTCLUBS

33 **Bacchus House** [★M,D,MR,TG,E,DS,S,V,YC,WC,GO] **619/299-2032** ■ 3054 University Ave (at 30th St) ■ *4pm-2am, clsd Mon, theme nights, Latin night Wed & Sun, wet underwear contest Th, strippers & go-go boys Th-Sun* ■ www.bacchushouse.com

SAN DIEGO

Day Trips: Tijuana/ Rosarito Beach

You can't go to San Diego without a trip south of the border! While Tijuana might be best-known to some of us as the place to party before turning 21 (you know who you are!), you may not know that there are also several museums and galleries here. Take note especially of CECUT-Centro Cultural de Tijuana (www.cecut.gob.mx), which contains several gallery spaces, a planetarium, a theater and a bookstore. Tijuana is also a great place to buy beautiful and inexpensive native arts and crafts, furniture, cigars, and, of course, tequila.

Just a stone's throw from Tijuana, about 18 miles south of the US/Mexico border is the laid-back town of Rosarito Beach. Beautiful beaches, great shopping, golf, and restaurants—what more do you need for a great day out?

Tourist Info

AIRPORT DIRECTIONS

San Diego International – Take Harbor Dr east, then left on Laurel. For the women's bars, go left toward India. To get to Hillcrest area, take a left on 5th up to University.

PUBLIC TRANSIT & TAXIS

Yellow Cab 619/234-6161.
San Diego Cab 619/226-8294.
Silver Cab/Co-op 619/280-5555.
Cloud Nine Shuttle 800/974-8885.
San Diego Transit System 619/233-3004, 800/266-6883 (Northern San Diego County), web: www.sdcommute.com. San Diego Trolley (through downtown or to Tijuana).

TOURIST SPOTS & INFO

Coronado Island (& Hotel Del Coronado), web: www.coronado.ca.us.
Fleet Space Center 619/238-1233, web: www.rhfleet.org.
Hillcrest, web: www.hillquest.com.
Gaslamp Quarter, web: www.gaslamp.org.
Mingei Int'l Museum 619/239-0003, web: www.mingei.org.
La Jolla, web: www.lajollabythesea.com.
The Old Globe Theatre 619/234-5623 (box office), web: www.oldglobe.org.
San Diego Museum of Art 619/232-7931, web: www.sdmart.org.
San Diego Wild Animal Park 760/747-8702, web: www.sandiegozoo.org/wap.
San Diego Zoo 619/231-1515, web: www.sandiegozoo.org.
Sea World 800/257-4268, web: www.seaworld.com.
Visitor's Center: San Diego Convention & Visitors Bureau, web: www.sandiego.org.
SanDiego.com, web: www.sandiego.com.

Weather

San Diego is sunny and warm (upper 60°s-70°s) year-round, with higher humidity in the summer.

Best Views

Cabrillo National Monument on Point Loma or from a harbor cruise.

City Calendar

LGBT PRIDE

July. 619/297-7683, web: www.sdpride.org.

ANNUAL EVENTS

February - Hillcrest Mardi Gras, web: www.hillcrestmardigras.org.
April - FilmOut San Diego, web: www.filmoutsandiego.com.
August - Hillcrest CityFest Street Fair, web: www.hillcrestassociation.com.
August - Street Scene, web: www.streetscene.com. California's largest music festival.

Queer Resources

COMMUNITY INFO

San Diego LGBT Community Center 619/692-2077. 3909 Centre St, 9am-10pm, till 7pm Sat, clsd Sun, web: www.thecentersd.org.
Live & Let Live Alano Club 619/298-8008, web: www.lllac.org. 1730 Monroe Ave, 10:30am-10pm, from 8:30am wknds.
Being Alive 619/291-1400, web: www.beingalive.org. 4070 Centre St.

34 **Rich's** [★M,D,V,S,YC] 619/295-2195 ■ 1051 University Ave (at Vermont) ■ open Th-Sun, theme nights, go-go boys Fri, L.L. Bear [B,L] Sat ■ www.richssandiego.com

CAFES

The Big Kitchen [WC] 619/234-5789 ■ 3003 Grape St (at 30th) ■ 7am-2pm, 7:30am-3pm wknds, some veggie

Claire de Lune 619/688-9845 ■ 2906 University Ave ■ 5am-midnight, till 1am Fri-Sat ■ www.clairedelune.com

Cream Coffee Bar [WI] 619/260-1917 ■ 4496 Park Blvd (University Heights) ■ 7am-11pm

David's Coffeehouse [MW,E] 619/296-4173 ■ 3766 5th Ave (at Robinson) ■ 7am-11pm, till midnight wknds, coffeehouse for positive people & their friends, patio

Espresso Roma 858/450-2141 ■ UCSD Price Center #76 (at Voight), La Jolla ■ 7am-10pm, hours vary wknds

Extraordinary Desserts 619/294-2132 ■ 2929 5th Ave ■ 8:30am-11pm, till midnight Fri, 10am-midnight Sat, 10am-11pm Sun, the name says it all ■ www.extraordinary-desserts.com

Gelato Vero Caffee [WI] 619/295-9269 ■ 3753 India St ■ 6am-midnight, till 1am Fri, 7am-1am Sat, 7am-midnight Sun, great desserts (yes, the gelato is truly delicious) as well as coffee ■ www.gelatovero.net

Twiggs [E] 619/296-0616 ■ 4590 Park Blvd (at Madison Ave, University Heights) ■ 7am-11pm, till midnight Fri-Sat, live music ■ www.twiggs.org

Urban Grind [★GO] 619/299-4763 ■ 3797 Park Blvd (at University) ■ 7am-11pm

RESTAURANTS

Adams Avenue Grill [BW,WC,GO] 619/298-8440 ■ 2201 Adams Ave (at Mississippi) ■ lunch, dinner, brunch wknds, bistro

Apertivo 619/297-7799 ■ 3926 30th St ■ dinner Tue-Sun, clsd Mon, Italian tapas & wine bar ■ www.apertivo.com

Aqua Blu [WC] 619/544-6456 ■ 734 5th Ave (near G St) ■ 11:30am-11pm, till midnight Fri-Sat, "fusion seafood," upscale ■ www.aquabluseafood.com

Arriverderci 619/299-6282 ■ 3845 4th Ave ■ lunch & dinner, Italian ■ www.arriverderristorante.com

Asian Bistro 619/296-4119 ■ 414 University Ave ■ 3pm-3am, Asian fusion

Bai Yook Thai 619/296-2700 ■ 1260 University Ave ■ lunch & dinner, dinner only Sun ■ www.baiyookthaicuisine.com

Baja Betty's [MW,WC] 619/269-8510 ■ 1421 University Ave (at Normal St) ■ 11am-midnight, till 1am Fri-Sat, Mexican, also tequila bar, patio ■ www.bajabettyssd.com

Brazil by the Hill 619/692-1919 ■ 142 University Ave ■ 11am-10pm, noon-11pm wknds, Brazilian

Brian's American Eatery [BW] 619/296-8268 ■ 1451 Washington St ■ 6:30am-10pm, 24hrs Fri-Sat

Cafe Eleven [WC] 619/260-8023 ■ 1440 University Ave (at Normal) ■ 5pm-close, Sun brunch from 10am, clsd Mon, country French, some veggie, patio

California Cuisine [WC] 619/543-0790 ■ 1027 University Ave (at 10th Ave) ■ 5pm-10pm, some veggie, also bar ■ www.californiacuisine.cc

Celadon 619/297-8424 ■ 540 University Ave (at 6th) ■ lunch & dinner, upscale Thai ■ www.celadonrestaurant.com

City Deli 619/295-2747 ■ 535 University Ave (at 6th Ave) ■ 7am-midnight, till 2am wknds, NY deli, plenty veggie, full bar ■ citydeli.com

Cody's La Jolla [R,E] 858/459-0040 ■ 8030 Girard Ave (at Coast Blvd S), La Jolla ■ brkfst & lunch daily, dinner Wed-Sun, contemporary California cuisine, live music ■ www.codyslajolla.com

The Cottage 858/454-8409 ■ 7702 Fay (at Klein), La Jolla ■ 7:30am-3pm, fresh-baked items ■ www.cottagelajolla.com

Crest Cafe [WC] 619/295-2510 ■ 425 Robinson (btwn 4th & 5th) ■ 7am-midnight, some veggie ■ www.crestcafe.net

Green Tomato 619/283-7546 ■ 4090 Adams Ave ■ lunch Mon-Fri, dinner nightly, Sun brunch, gourmet meats, seafood & pastas, also full bar ■ www.greentomato.net

Gulf Coast Grill 619/295-2244 ■ 4130 Park Blvd ■ lunch & dinner, also Sun brunch, New Orleans-inspired menu ■ www.gulfcoastgrill.net

Hash House A Go Go 619/298-4646 ■ 3628 5th Ave ■ brkfst, lunch & dinner, great brkfst ■ www.hashhouseagogo.com

Hawthorn's 619/544-0940, 619/295-1688 ■ 2895 University Ave ■ dinner nightly, Sun brunch, seasonal food & wine, American ■ www.hawthornssandiego.com

Inn at the Park [★M] 619/296-0057 ■ 525 Spruce St (btwn 5th & 6th, at Park Manor Suites) ■ dinner nightly, also bar [P] ■ www.parkmanorsuites.com/restaurants.html

Jimmy Carter's Mexican Cafe 619/296-6952 ■ 807 W Washington St (Mission Hills) ■ 11am-9pm, from 9am wknds

Kemo Sabe [R] 619/220-6802 ■ 3958 5th Ave ■ 5:30pm-close, int'l, lesbian celeb chef Deborah Scott ■ www.cohnrestaurants.com

Kous Kous 619/295-5560 ■ 3940 4th Ave, Suite 110 (beneath Martinis on Fourth) ■ 5pm-midnight, Moroccan

Lips [DS] 619/295-7900 ■ 3036 El Cajon Blvd ■ 5pm-close, Sun gospel brunch, clsd Mon, "the ultimate in drag dining," Bitchy Bingo Wed, celeb impersonation Th, DJ wknds ■ www.lipsshow.biz

The Lumberjack Grille [BW] 619/294-3804 ■ 3949 Ohio St (North Park) ■ 7am-9pm, till midnight Fri-Sat, hearty food for your inner lumberjack

Magnolias [E] 619/262-6005 ■ 342 Euclid Ave Suite 403 ■ Southern, live jazz ■ www.magnoliasdining.com

Martinis Above Fourth [MW,C,P,GO] 619/400-4500 ■ 3940 4th Ave, Ste 200 (btwn Washington & University) ■ 3pm-11pm, till midnight Fri-Sat, 11am-11pm Sun (brunch), clsd Mon, also cabaret lounge, indoor & outdoor bar ■ www.martinisabovefourth.com

Medgrill [E] 619/683-2233 ■ 1263 University Ave ■ Middle Eastern, belly dancing Th-Sat ■ www.medgrill-cafe.com

The Mission [MW] 858/488-9060 ■ 3795 Mission Blvd (at San Jose), Mission Beach ■ 7am-3pm; also 2801 University Ave in North Park, 619/220-8992

Modus Supper Club [WC] 619/236-8516 ■ 2202 4th Ave (at Ivy) ■ 5pm-2am, full bar, patio ■ www.modusbar-lounge.com

Ono Sushi 619/298-0616 ■ 1236 University Ave ■ lunch Fri-Sun, dinner nightly ■ www.onosushi.com

The Prado 619/557-9441 ■ 1549 El Prado (in Balboa Park) ■ lunch Mon-Sat, dinner Tue-Sun, Latin/ Italian fusion ■ www.cohnrestaurants.com

Roberto's 858/488-1610 ■ 3202 Mission Blvd ■ the best rolled tacos & guacamole, multiple locations—imitators, even drive-thru versions—throughout San Diego

Rudford's 619/282-8423 ■ 2900 El Cajon Blvd (at Kansas St) ■ *24hrs, popular homestyle cooking since 1949* ■ www.rudfords.com

Saigon on Fifth 619/220-8828 ■ 3900 5th Ave, Suite 120 ■ *11am-midnight, Vietnamese*

South Park Bar & Grill [E] 619/696-0096 ■ 1946 Fern St (at Grape St) ■ *5pm-9pm, till midnight Wed-Sat, bar till 2am, "California comfort food"* ■ www.southparkbarandgrill.com

Taste of Szechuan 619/298-1638 ■ 670 University Ave ■ *11:30am-11pm, noon-10pm Sun, Chinese*

Terra 619/293-7088 ■ 3900 block of Vermont St (at 10th Ave) ■ *lunch & dinner, Sun brunch, American* ■ www.terrasd.com

Tioli's Crazy Burger 619/282-6044 ■ 4201 30th St ■ *11am-9pm, till 10pm Fri-Sat, handcrafted burgers & brats* ■ www.tioliscrazyburger.com

Top of the Park [★M] 619/296-0057 ■ 525 Spruce St (btwn 5th & 6th, at Park Manor Suites) ■ *lunch only 11:30am-2pm, penthouse restaurant w/ panoramic views, popular Fri happy hour* ■ www.parkmanorsuites.com/restaurants.html

Urban Mo's [MW,WC] 619/491-0400 ■ 308 University Ave (at 3rd) ■ *9am-2am, 10am-midnight Sun, some veggie, full bar, patio* ■ www.urbanmos.com

Veg N Out 619/546-8411 ■ 3442 30th St (North Park) ■ *11am-3pm & 4pm-9pm, 11am-9pm Sat, 11am-4pm only Sun, veggie burgers, dogs, sandwiches & more* ■ www.vegnout.net

Waffle Spot 619/297-2231 ■ 1333 Hotel Circle S (at King's Inn) ■ *7am-2pm* ■ www.wafflespot.com

ENTERTAINMENT & RECREATION

Diversionary Theatre 619/220-0097 (box office #), 619/220-6830 ■ 4545 Park Blvd #101 (at Madison) ■ *LGBT theater* ■ www.diversionary.org

Womenmoto PO Box 3390, 92163 ■ *women's motorcycling organization* ■ www.womenmoto.com

BOOKSTORES

Groundwork Books Collective [WC] 858/452-9625 ■ UCSD Student Center 0323 (at Gilman Dr), La Jolla ■ *10am-6pm, till 5pm Fri, clsd wknds, alternative, LGBT section* ■ www.groundwork.ucsd.edu

35 **Obelisk the Bookstore** [WC] 619/297-4171 ■ 1029 University Ave (at 10th) ■ *10am-10pm, LGBT*

Traveler's Depot 858/483-1421 ■ 1655 Garnet Ave (in Pacific Beach) ■ *10am-6pm, till 5pm Sat, noon-5pm Sun, travel guides, maps, luggage & more* ■ www.travelersdepot.com

RETAIL SHOPS

Auntie Helen's [WC] 619/584-8438 ■ 4028 30th St (at Lincoln) ■ *10am-4:30pm, clsd Sun-Mon, thrift shop benefits PWAs* ■ www.auntiehelens.org

Babette Schwartz [GO] 619/220-7048 ■ 421 University Ave (at 5th Ave) ■ *11am-9pm, till 5pm Sun, campy novelties & gifts* ■ www.babette.com

Firefly Factory [GO] 619/291-3774 ■ 3774 Park Blvd (2 blks S of University Ave) ■ *10am-8am, home decor, cards & gifts* ■ www.fireflyfactory.com

Flesh Skin Grafix 619/424-8983 ■ 1155 Palm Ave, Imperial Beach ■ *tattoos & piercing* ■ www.fleshskingrafix.com

MacLeo Sexy Leather 619/688-0504 ■ 3750 30th St (in North Park) ■ *noon-8pm, by appt only Sun, clsd Mon, custom-made leather fashions* ■ www.sexyleather.com

Mastodon 858/272-1188 ■ 4638 Mission Blvd (at Emerald), Pacific Beach ■ *body piercing*

PUBLICATIONS

Buzz 619/291-6690 ■ 3314 4th Ave ■ *bi-weekly, news, entertainment & listings, covers San Diego & Palm Springs* ■ www.sdbuzz.com

Gay/ Lesbian Times 619/299-6397, 800/438-8786 ■ 1730 Monroe Ave, Ste A ■ *LGBT newsmagazine* ■ www.gaylesbiantimes.com

The Lavender Lens 619/291-8223 ■ *California's monthly lesbian magazine* ■ www.thelavenderlens.com

Rocket Magazine 619/299-6397, 800/438-8786 ■ 1730 Monroe Ave, Ste A ■ *all the dirt on San Diego's nightlife for the boys* ■ www.rocketsandiego.com

GYMS & HEALTH CLUBS

Frog's Athletic Club 619/291-3500 ■ 901 Hotel Circle S (at Washington), Mission Valley ■ www.frogsfit.com

PowerHouse Gym 619/296-7878 ■ 734 University Ave #D (at 7th Ave) ■ *5am-11pm, till 10pm Fri, 8am-8pm wknds* ■ www.powerhousegym.com

Urbanbody Gym 619/795-9712 ■ 3148 University Ave (at Iowa St, North Park) ■ *5am-10pm, till 9pm Fri, 7am-7pm wknds, gym & classes* ■ www.urbanbodygym.com

MEN'S CLUBS

Club San Diego [PC] 619/295-0850 ■ 3955 4th Ave (btwn Washington & University) ■ *24hrs*

➤**Vulcan Steam & Sauna** [PC] 619/238-1980 ■ 805 W Cedar St (at Pacific Hwy) ■ *24hrs*

EROTICA

Adult Emporium [GO] 619/239-1878 ■ 3576 Main St (at 32nd St) ■ *24hrs*

Barnett Ave Adult Superstore 619/224-0187 ■ 3610 Barnett Ave (near intersection of Barnett & Jessop Ln) ■ *24hrs*

The Crypt 619/692-9499 ■ 3847 Park Blvd (at University)

F St Bookstore 619/298-2644 ■ 2004 University Ave (at Florida)

F St Bookstore 619/236-0841 ■ 751 4th Ave (at F St)

Gemini Adult Books [WC] 619/287-1402 ■ 5265 University Ave (at 52nd)

Romantix Adult Superstore 619/299-7186 ■ 1407 University Ave (at Richmond) ■ *also Hillcrest location* ■ www.romantixonline.com

Romantix Adult Superstore 619/237-9056 ■ 836 5th Ave (btwn E & F Sts) ■ www.romantixonline.com

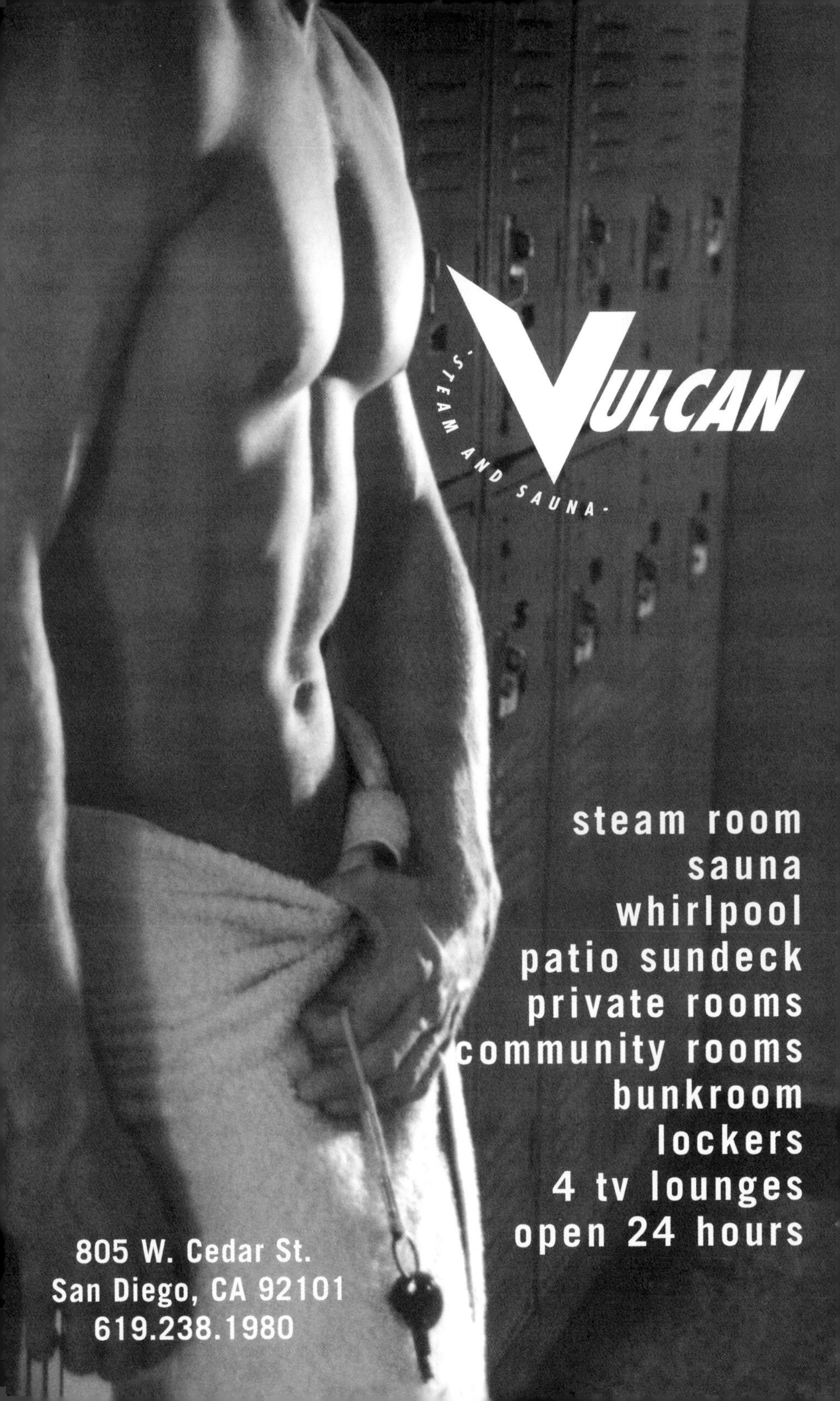

VULCAN
· STEAM AND SAUNA ·

steam room
sauna
whirlpool
patio sundeck
private rooms
community rooms
bunkroom
lockers
4 tv lounges
open 24 hours

805 W. Cedar St.
San Diego, CA 92101
619.238.1980

San Francisco

San Francisco is divided into 7 geographical areas:
- SF—Overview
- SF—Castro & Noe Valley
- SF—South of Market
- SF—Polk Street Area
- SF—Downtown & North Beach
- SF—Mission District
- SF—Haight, Fillmore, Hayes Valley

SF—Overview

ENTERTAINMENT & RECREATION

Bay Area Derby Girls ■ *SF Bay Area's female roller derby league, check web for upcoming events* ■ bayareaderbygirls.com

Beach Blanket Babylon [★GF] 415/421-4222 ■ 678 Green St (at Powell, in Club Fugazi) ■ *8pm Wed, 7pm & 10pm Fri-Sat, 2pm & 5pm Sun, the USA's longest running musical revue & wigs that must be seen to be believed; also restaurant, full bar* ■ www.beachblanketbabylon.com

Betty's List ■ *LGBT directory & community calendar* ■ www.bettyslist.com

Black Sand Beach first exit past Golden Gate Bridge (Alexander) (go left under fwy, right on Outlook Rd, look for dirt parking lot), Golden Gate Nat'l Rec Area ■ *popular nude beach, look for trail*

Brava! [WC] 415/641-7657, 415/647-2822 (box office) ■ 2781 24th St (btwn York & Hampshire) ■ *culturally diverse performances by women* ■ www.brava.org

Castro Theatre 415/621-6120 ■ 429 Castro (at Market) ■ *art house cinema, many LGBT & cult classics, live organ evenings (see Castro detail)* ■ www.thecastrotheatre.com

Cruisin' the Castro Tours 415/255-1821 ■ tour meets at the rainbow flag at Harvey Milk Plaza (corner of Castro & Market) ■ *"The 'original' historical walking tour of the Castro, the world's largest gay mecca. Fun & easy!"* ■ www.cruisinthecastro.com

Femina Potens 415/217-9340 ■ 465 S Van Ness (at 16th) ■ *nonprofit art gallery & performance space promoting women & transfolk in the arts* ■ www.feminapotens.com

Frameline 415/703-8650 ■ *LGBT media arts foundation that sponsors annual SF Int'l LGBT Film Festival in June* ■ www.frameline.org

The Intersection for the Arts [GF] 415/626-2787, 415/626-3311 (box office) ■ 446 Valencia St (btwn 16th & 15th Sts) ■ www.theintersection.org

Jon Sims Center for the Arts 415/554-0402 ■ 1519 Mission St (at 11th) ■ *LGBT performing arts organization; check web for events (see South of Market detail)* ■ www.jonsimsctr.org

K'vetsh [★21+] 415/551-7988 ■ 491 Potrero (at Mariposa, at Sadie's Flying Elephant) ■ *8pm 1st Sun (7:30pm sign-up), San Francisco's coolest queer open mic* ■ www.flyingelephant.com

Local Tastes of the City Tours [GO] 415/665-0480, 888/358-8687 ■ *3-hour walking tours of culture & cuisine of San Francisco's most colorful neighborhoods, including North Beach, Chinatown & Haight-Ashbury; ends w/ optional dinner; "We eat our way through San Francisco"* ■ www.localtastesofthecitytours.com

The Marsh 415/641-0235, 800/838-3006 (box office) ■ 1062 Valencia (at 22nd St) ■ *queer-positive theater* ■ www.themarsh.org

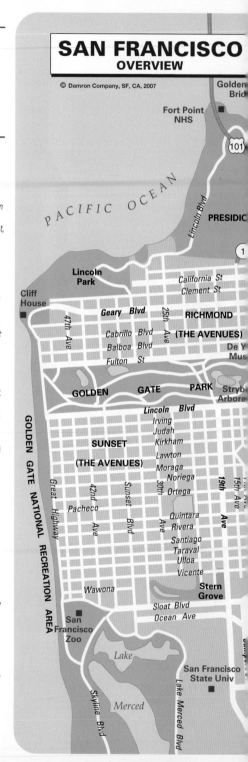

SAN FRANCISCO
OVERVIEW

© Damron Company, SF, CA, 2007

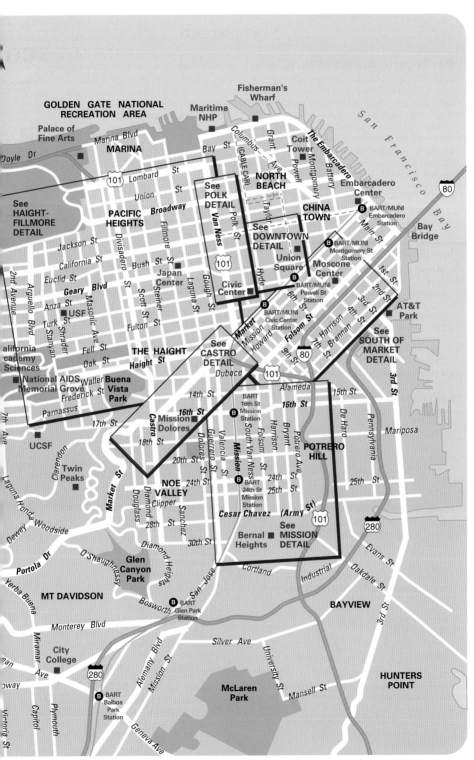

SAN FRANCISCO

Day Trips: Cruise across the Golden Gate Bridge to visit Muir Woods, a majestic grove of redwood trees in Mill Valley. Afterward, wind your way into Tiburon, where you'll enjoy quaint shopping and a new perspective on San Francisco. Grab an outdoor table at Guaymas restaurant (5 Main St, 415/435-6300) and soak up the view of Angel Island and the Bay. Those without a car can experience this up close and personal by taking a ferry from Fisherman's Wharf. Angel Island is also accessible by ferry, and offers trails for hiking and biking, plus guided tours.

Napa Valley wineries and the spas of Calistoga are a short drive northeast of the city. To maximize your bridge views, exit the city via the Golden Gate Bridge, and return through the East Bay. On the way back, you'll cross the erector-set-inspired Carquinez Bridge, and you'll be on the upper deck of the Bay Bridge when you come back into San Francisco. Get your camera ready, because a picture here (including Coit Tower, the Trans-America Building, the Port of San Francisco, and Twin Peaks) is truly worth a thousand words.

Local Food:

Locals fill up on hearty burritos from the taquerias in the Mission, and a visit to the City by the Bay would not be complete without some dim sum. Award-winning Yank Sing, inside the Rincon Center, is one of our faves.

Tourist Info

AIRPORT DIRECTIONS

San Francisco International. To get to the Castro District take 101 North. Follow signs to Golden Gate Bridge. Take Mission/Van Ness exit. Continue up Duboce St (13th St) for 3 blocks to Market St. Take a left, go 5 blocks, and begin to pray to "Asphalta," the goddess of parking. (Or, better yet, hitch a ride on BART—the public transit system that connects SF and the East Bay and leaves directly from SFO—or one of the reasonably priced shuttles.)

PUBLIC TRANSIT & TAXIS

Yellow Cab 415/626-2345.
Luxor Cab 415/282-4141.
Quake City Shuttle 415/255-4899.
511, web: 511.org. Covers all Bay Area transit (also traffic).
Muni 415/673-6864, web: www.sfmuni.org.
Bay Area Rapid Transit (BART) 415/989-2278, subway, web: www.bart.gov.

TOURIST SPOTS & INFO

Alcatraz 415/981-7625, web: www.nps.gov/alcatraz.
Asian Art Museum 415/ 581-3500, www.asianart.org.
Cablecars.
Chinatown.
Coit Tower.
Exploratorium 415/561-0360, web: www.exploratorium.edu.
Fisherman's Wharf & Pier 39 (take the F car down Market St & along the Embarcadero).
Golden Gate Park.
Haight & Ashbury Sts.
Japantown.
North Beach.
Mission San Francisco de Assisi.
SF Museum of Modern Art 415/357-4000, web: www.sfmoma.org.
Twin Peaks.
Visitor's Center: San Francisco Convention & Visitors Bureau 415/391-2000, web: www.sfvisitor.org.

Weather

A beautiful summer comes at the end of September and lasts through October. Much of the city is cold and fogged-in June through September, though the Castro and Mission are usually sunny. The cold in winter is damp, so bring lots of layers. When there isn't a drought, it also rains in the winter months of November through February.

City Calendar

LGBT PRIDE

June. 415/864-3733, web: www.sfpride.org.

ENTERTAINMENT

Theatre Rhinoceros 415/861-5079, 2926 16th St.

ANNUAL EVENTS

June - San Francisco Int'l Lesbian/Gay Film Festival 415/703-8650, web: www.frameline.org.
July - Up Your Alley Fair 415/861-3247, web: folsomstreetevents.org. Local SM/leather street fair held in Dore Alley, South-of-Market.
September - Folsom Street Fair 415/861-3247, web: folsomstreetevents.org. Huge SM/leather street fair, topping a week of kinky events.
September - MadCat Women's Int'l Film Festival 415/436-9523, web: www.madcatfilmfestival.org.
October - Castro Street Fair 415/841-1824, web: www.castrostreetfair.org. Arts and community groups street fair.

Queer Resources

COMMUNITY INFO

The San Francisco LGBT Community Center 415/865-5555, web: www.sfcenter.org. 1800 Market St (at Octavia), noon-10pm, from 9am Sat, clsd Sun.
Pacific Center for Human Growth 510/548-8283, web: www.pacificcenter.org. 2712 Telegraph Ave, Berkeley. 4pm-10pm Mon-Fri.
AA Gay/Lesbian 415/674-1821, web: www.aasf.org.
CA AIDS, STD & Hepatitis Hotline 415/863-2437.

National AIDS Memorial Grove [WC] 415/750-8340, 888/294-7683 ■ Golden Gate Park (on corner of Middle Drive East & Bowling Green Dr) ■ guided tours available 9am-noon every 3rd Sat ■ www.aidsmemorial.org

The New Conservatory Theatre Center 415/861-8972 ■ 25 Van Ness Ave, Lower Lobby (at Market) ■ gay theater in historic Masonic Bldg ■ www.nctcsf.org

QComedy Gay Comedy Showcase [★MW,$] 415/541-5610 ■ 1519 Mission St (at Van Ness, at Jon Sims Center) ■ 8pm 2nd & 4th Sun, see www.qcomedy.com for location ■ www.qcomedy.com

Queer Things to Do in the San Francisco Bay Area ■ your one-stop spot to find out all things queer & fabulous & fun to do in the Bay Area; a must visit! ■ www.sfqueer.com

Radar [★] 415/557-4400 (library #) ■ 100 Larkin St (at Grove, in Latino/ Hispanic Rm of SF Public Library) ■ 6pm-7:30pm, San Francisco literary superstar Michelle Tea hosts monthly reading series, very cool & very queer-friendly, all genres welcome, followed by Q&A & Tea's own home-baked cookies

San Francisco City Hikes [GF,WC,GO] 510/758-9313 ■ 3-hour hiking tours of San Francisco for groups of 10+, $15-20/ person, lesbian-owned, "the best way to see the city" ■ www.cityhikes.com

Theatre Rhinoceros 415/861-5079 (box office), 415/552-4100 ■ 2926 16th St (at S Van Ness) ■ LGBT theater (see Mission detail map) ■ www.therhino.org

Victorian Home Walks [GO] 415/252-9485 ■ custom-tailored walking tours w/ San Francisco resident ■ www.victorianwalk.com

Yerba Buena Center for the Arts [GF] 415/978-2787 (box office), 415/978-2700 (administrative) ■ 701 Mission St (at 3rd St) ■ www.ybca.org/b_ybca.html

PUBLICATIONS

BAR (Bay Area Reporter) 415/861-5019 ■ the weekly LGBT newspaper ■ www.ebar.com

Bay Times 415/626-0260 ■ bi-weekly, good Bay Area resource listings ■ www.sfbaytimes.com

Gloss Magazine 510/451-2090 ■ CA arts/ entertainment magazine, bi-weekly ■ www.sfgloss.com

Odyssey Magazine 415/621-6514 ■ all the dish on SF's club scene ■ www.odysseymagazine.net

Outword Magazine 415/437-2886 ■ www.outword-magazine.com

Pink Pages 415/552-5697, 877/769-7465 ■ LGBT business directory & lifestyle magazine ■ lesgaypinkpages.com

SF—Castro & Noe Valley

ACCOMMODATIONS

1   24 Henry & Village House [M,NS,WI,GO] 415/864-5686, 800/900-5686 ■ 24 Henry St & 4080 18th St (btwn Sanchez & Noe) ■ B&B, some shared baths, 1-bdrm apt also available ■ www.24Henry.com

2   Albion House Inn [GF,NS] 415/621-0896, 800/400-8295 ■ 135 Gough St (at Fell) ■ full brkfst ■ www.AlbionHouseInn.com

3   Beck's Motor Lodge [GF,WC] 415/621-8212, 800/955-2325 ■ 2222 Market St (at Sanchez) ■ in the heart of the Castro (ie, cruisy) ■ becksSF@aol.com

▶Belvedere House [★MW,NS,WI,GO] 415/731-6654, 877/226-3273 ■ 598 Belvedere St (at 17th St) ■ wall-to-wall books, art & style, German spoken ■ www.GayBedAndBreakfast.net

Casa Buena Vista [GF,NS,WI] 916/974-7409, 916/813-3119 (cell) ■ near Market & Castro ■ rental apts ■ www.vacationhomes.com/14017

4   Castillo Inn 415/864-5111, 800/865-5112 ■ 48 Henry St ■ castilloinn@yahoo.com

5   Castro Suites [GS,NS,WI,GO] 415/437-1783 ■ 927 14th St (at Noe) ■ furnished apts, kitchen ■ www.castrosuites.com

Collingwood Cottage in Castro [GS,NS,WI,GO] 415/425-8157 ■ collingwoodcottageincastro@yahoo.com

6   Dolores Park Inn [GF,NS] 415/621-0482 ■ 3641 17th St (btwn Church & Dolores) ■ 1874 Italianate Victorian mansion, subtropical garden, hot tub, kitchens, fireplaces ■ www.doloresparkinn.net

7   Edwardian San Francisco [GF,NS] 415/864-1271, 888/864-8070 ■ 1668 Market St (btwn Franklin & Gough) ■ some shared baths, hot tub, jacuzzi ■ www.edwardiansfhotel.com

BELVEDERE HOUSE
Bed and Breakfast
San Francisco's #1 Gay B&B

www.GayBedAndBreakfast.net
toll free   1.877 B and B SF
fax   415.681.0719
email   Info@GayBedAndBreakfast.net

598 Belvedere Street (at 17th Street)

– We're right above the Castro
– You can walk to the restaurants,
bars, shops, and all the fun
– Great views of Golden Gate Bridge
and the Pacific Ocean *

– Breakfast until noon
– Complimentary refreshments
– FREE wi-fi and computer access
– Laundry service available

Rooms from $115.00

10% DISCOUNT
for reservations made
four weeks in advance

(*some restrictions apply)

8   **Inn on Castro** [MW,NS,WI,GO] 415/861-0321 ■ 321 Castro St (btwn 16th & 17th) ■ *full brkfst* ■ www.innoncastro.com

9   **Just Off Castro** [M,GO] 415/621-2915 ■ 4408 18th St ■ *Victorian, some shared baths, 1 single bed for 1 person* ■ home.pacbell/psgreene

10   **Le Grenier** [MW] 415/864-4748 ■ 347 Noe St (at 16th St) ■ *suite* ■ annfisher347@sbcglobal.net

     Nancy's Bed [WO,NS,GO] 415/239-5692 ■ *kitchen* ■ nancysbed@aol.com

     Noe's Nest B&B [GF,NS] 415/821-0751 ■ 1257 Guerrero St (btwn 24th & 25th Sts) ■ *full brkfst, kitchens, fireplace* ■ www.noesnest.com

     Olive's Gate Guesthouse [GS,NS,WI,GO] 415/821-6039 ■ 3796 23rd St (at Church) ■ *studio apt in Noe Valley, lesbian-owned* ■ www.olivesgate.com

11 ► **The Parker Guest House** [★M,NS,WI,GO] 415/621-3222, 888/520-7275 ■ 520 Church St (at 17th) ■ *guesthouse complex w/ gardens, steam spa* ■ www.parkerguesthouse.com

     SF Noe Valley Tourist Apartment [GF,NS,GO] 415/695-9782, 415/312-0138 (cell) ■ 225 28th St (at Church) ■ *cozy upstairs apt, kids ok* ■ hometown.aol.com/bewessie/myhomepage/index.html

     Terrace Place [M,WI,GO] 415/241-0425 ■ *guest suite* ■ www.terraceplace.com

12   **Tom's Place** [M,L,WI,GO] 415/861-0516 ■ 4510 18th St (at Douglass) ■ *slinged play area* ■ Tomfister@aol.com

13   **Travelodge Central** [GF] 415/621-6775, 800/578-7878 (reservations) ■ 1707 Market St (at Valencia) ■ *nonsmoking rooms available, close to LGBT center* ■ www.sanfrancisco-centralhotel.com

14   **The Willows Inn** [MW,NS,WI,GO] 415/431-4770, 800/431-0277 ■ 710 14th St (at Church) ■ *"amenities, comfort, great location"* ■ www.WillowsSF.com

BARS

15   **18th Street Bar** [M,NH] 4146 18th St

16   **440 Castro** [★M,NH,B,L] 415/621-8732 ■ 440 Castro St ■ *noon-2am, from 11am wknds, very cruisy, rock 'n' roll beer bust Sun* ■ daddysbar.com

17   **Amber** [GS] 415/626-7827 ■ 718 14th St (at Market) ■ *6pm-2am, from 7pm wknds, smoking bar*

18   **The Bar on Castro** [★M,NH,D,WC] 456 Castro St ■ *4pm-2am, from 1pm wknds* ■ www.thebarsf.com

19   **The Cafe** [★MW,D,YC] 415/861-3846 ■ 2369 Market St (at Castro) ■ *4pm-2am, from 3pm Sat, from 2pm Sun, deck overlooking Castro & Market* ■ www.cafesf.com

20   **Cafe du Nord** [GF,A,F,E] 415/861-5016 ■ 2170 Market St (at Sanchez) ■ *live music, various theme nights* ■ www.cafedunord.com

21   **CAV Winebar** [GS] 415/437-1770 ■ 1666 Market St (at Gough) ■ *5:30pm-close, clsd Sun, also restaurant* ■ www.cavwinebar.com

19   **Delicious** [W,D,S,$] 408/792-3466 (info line) ■ 2369 Market St (at the Cafe) ■ *3:30pm-9pm 3rd Sat only, smoking patio* ■ www.creamsf.com

22   **The Edge** [★M,NH,L] 415/863-4027 ■ 4149 18th St ■ *noon-2am, classic cruise bar* ■ www.edgesf.com

23   **Expansion Bar** [GS,NH] 415/863-4041 ■ 2124 Market St ■ *noon-2am, all beer $2 Tue*

24   **Harvey's** [★MW,NH,E,DS,WC] 415/431-4278 ■ 500 Castro St ■ *11am-midnight, 10am-2am wknds, also restaurant*

25 **The Jet** [M,D] 2348 Market St (at Castro) ■ *8pm-close* ■ www.jetsf.com

26 **Ladies Night at Mecca** [★E,F,WC] 415/621-7000 ■ 2029 Market St (at 14th) ■ *Th only, also swanky restaurant* ■ www.sfmecca.com

27 **Martuni's** [GS,NH,P] 415/241-0205 ■ 4 Valencia St (at Market) ■ *4pm-2am, lounge, great martinis*

28 **Men's Room** [M,NH] 415/861-1310 ■ 3988 18th St ■ *noon-2am*

29 **The Metro** [M,F] 415/703-9751 ■ 3600 16th St (at Noe & Market) ■ *11am-2am, overlooks Market St, also The Grill restaurant*

30 **Midnight Sun** [★M,V] 415/861-4186 ■ 4067 18th St (at Castro) ■ *2pm-2am, from 1pm Sat-Sun* ■ www.midnight-sunsf.com

31 **The Mint** [MW,K] 415/626-4726 ■ 1942 Market St (at Buchanan) ■ *noon-2am, popular karaoke bar nights, also sushi restaurant* ■ www.themint.net

32 **The Mix** [M,NH] 415/431-8616 ■ 4086 18th St ■ *3pm-2am, from 8am wknds, heated patio, wknd BBQ*

33 **Moby Dick's** [M,NH,V] 4049 18th St (at Hartford) ■ *2pm-2am, from noon wknds* ■ www.mobydicksf.com

19 **Pan Dulce** [MW,D,MR-L] 415/861-3846 ■ 2369 Market St (at The Cafe) ■ *9pm-2am Th only, "The Castro's Biggest Latino Party!"*

34 **Pilsner Inn** [★M,NH,YC] 415/621-7058 ■ 225 Church St (at Market) ■ *10am-2am, great patio* ■ www.pilsnerinn.com

35 **SF Badlands** [★M,NH,D,V,WC] 415/626-9320 ■ 4121 18th St (at Castro) ■ *2pm-2am, Sun beer busts* ■ www.sfbad-lands.com

36 **The Transfer** [M,NH] 415/861-7499 ■ 198 Church St (at Market) ■ *5pm-2am, more women 3rd Fri for Cockblock*

37 **Twin Peaks** [M,OC,WC] 415/864-9470 ■ 401 Castro St ■ *noon-2am, from 8am Th-Sun* ■ twinpeakstavern@aol.com

CAFES

Cafe Flore [★MW] 415/621-8579 ■ 2298 Market St (at Noe) ■ *7am-midnight, some veggie, full bar, great patio to see & be seen, come early for a seat* ■ cafeflore.com

Caffe Trieste [★E] 415/551-1000 ■ 1667 Market St (at Gough) ■ *6:30am-10pm, till 11pm Fri-Sat, great coffee, live music* ■ www.caffetrieste.com

Duboce Park Cafe [F] 415/621-1108 ■ 2 Sanchez St (at Duboce) ■ *7am-8pm, overlooks Duboce Park, outdoor seating* ■ www.duboceparkcafe.com

Jumpin' Java [WI] 415/431-5282 ■ 139 Noe St (at 14th St) ■ *6:30am-7:30pm, 7am-8pm wknds*

Just Desserts [MW] 415/602-9245 ■ 248 Church St ■ *10am-7pm, from noon Sat, noon-6pm Sun, delicious cakes* ■ www.justdesserts.com

Lovejoy's Tea Room [★] 415/648-5895 ■ 1351 Church St (at Clipper) ■ *11am-6pm, clsd Mon-Tue, for a tea party fit for a queen, reservations highly recommended* ■ www.lovejoys-tearoom.com

Orbit Room Cafe 415/252-9525 ■ 1900 Market St (at Laguna) ■ *8am-2am, till midnight Sun, great view of Market St, also bar*

Peet's Coffee & Tea Inc [★M] 415/626-6416 ■ 2257 Market St (at 16th St) ■ *6am-8pm, till 9pm Fri-Sat, small cafe but always cute crowd inside & out*

Red Door Cafe [GO] 415/447-4102 ■ 1494 California St ■ *9:30am-2pm, till 3pm wknds*

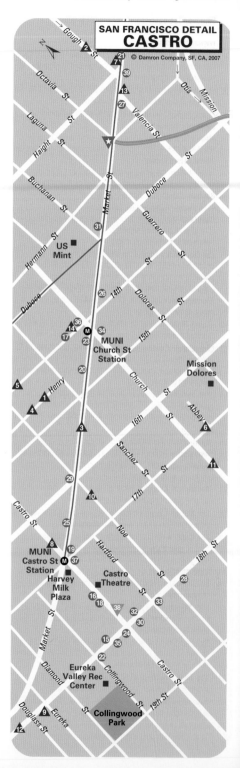

Samovar Tea Lounge 415/626-4700 ■ 498 Sanchez St (at 18th St) ■ 10am-10pm, tea culture from around the world ■ www.samovartea.com

Starbucks [B] 415/626-6263 ■ 4094 18th St (at Castro) ■ 5am-10:30pm, till 10:30pm Fri-Sat, always a bear jamboree

Sweet Inspiration [F] 415/621-8664 ■ 2239 Market St ■ 7am-11:30pm, 8am-12:30am Fri-Sat, popular wknd nights, fabulous desserts

RESTAURANTS

2223 Market [★WC] 415/431-0692 ■ 2223 Market St ■ dinner, Sun brunch, contemporary American, full bar ■ www.2223restaurant.com

Anchor Oyster Bar [MW,BW] 415/431-3990 ■ 579 Castro St (at 19th) ■ 11:30am-10pm, from 4pm Sun, seafood, some veggie

Bagdad Cafe [MW] 415/621-4434 ■ 2295 Market St ■ 24hrs, diner, some veggie, great for people watching

Blue [★BW] 415/863-2583 ■ 2337 Market St (btwn Castro & Noe) ■ 11:30am-11pm, wknd brunch from 10:30am, homecooking served w/ style

Catch [E] 415/431-5000 ■ 2362 Market St ■ lunch & dinner [R], brunch Sat-Sun, seafood ■ www.catchsf.com

Chloe's [★] 415/648-4116 ■ 1399 Church St (at 26th St) ■ 8am-3pm, till 3:30pm wknds, come early for the excellent wknd brunch

Chow [★] 415/552-2469 ■ 215 Church St (at Market) ■ 11am-11pm, 10am-midnight wknds, wknd brunch, eclectic & affordable, patio

Cove Cafe [MW,WC] 415/626-0462 ■ 434 Castro St ■ 7:30am-9pm, till 10pm Fri-Sat, some veggie

39►**DeLessio Market & Bakery** 415/552-5559 ■ 1695 Market St (at Gough) ■ 7am-7:30pm, 9am-5:30pm wknds, great chocolate & cake ■ www.delessiomarket.com

Eric's Chinese Restaurant [★] 415/282-0919 ■ 1500 Church St (at 27th St) ■ 11am-9pm

Firewood Cafe 415/252-0999 ■ 4248 18th St (at Diamond St) ■ 11am-11pm, rotisserie chicken, pastas, oven-fired pizzas, salads ■ firewoodcafe.com

Home [★] 415/503-0333 ■ 2100 Market St (at Church) ■ 5pm-10pm, till 11pm Fri-Sat, wknd brunch 10am-2pm, American ■ www.home-sf.com

It's Tops 415/431-6395 ■ 1801 Market St (at Octavia) ■ 8am-3pm & 8pm-3am, classic diner, great hotcakes

La Mediterranée [BW] 415/431-7210 ■ 288 Noe (at Market) ■ 11am-10pm, till 11pm Sat-Sun, Mediterranean/ Middle Eastern ■ www.lamediterranee.net

Lime [★] 415/621-5256 ■ 2247 Market St ■ 5pm-midnight, wknd brunch, Mediterranean, full bar

Luna [★MW] 415/621-2566 ■ 558 Castro St (btwn 18th & 19th) ■ 9am-9pm, till 10pm Fri-Sat, patio

M&L Market (May's) 415/431-7044 ■ 691 14th St (at Market) ■ 11:30am-4pm, clsd wknds, great huge sandwiches

Mecca [★E,WC] 415/621-7000 ■ 2029 Market St (at Dolores) ■ 5pm-11pm, till midnight Fri-Sat, from 4pm Sun, American, also swanky bar, DJ nightly, ladies night Th, Men's Night Out 4pm Sun, valet parking ■ www.sfmecca.com

Nirvana Restaurant & Bar [MW] 415/861-2226 ■ 544 Castro St (btwn 18th & 19th) ■ 11:30am-10pm, from noon Sun, from 4:30pm Tue & Th, Southeast Asian, patio ■ www.nirvanarestaurant.net

Octavia Lounge [E,GO] 415/863-3516 ■ 1772 Market St (near Gough) ■ 5pm-11pm, till 1am Fri-Sat, 11am-10pm Sun ■ octavialounge.com

Orphan Andy's [GO] 415/864-9795 ■ 3991 17th St ■ 24hrs, diner

Pasta Pomodoro [MW] 415/558-8123 ■ 2304 Market St ■ 11am-11pm, Italian, outdoor seating; also 24th & Noe location, 415/920-9904 ■ www.pastapomodoro.com

Red Jade 415/621-3020 ■ 245 Church St ■ from 11am, Chinese, plenty veggie

The Sausage Factory [MW,BW] 415/626-1250 ■ 517 Castro St ■ 11:30am-midnight, pizza & pasta, some veggie ■ www.castrosausagefactory.com

Sparky's 415/626-8666 ■ 242 Church St (at Market) ■ 24hrs, diner, some veggie, popular after-hours

Squat & Gobble 415/552-2125 ■ 3600 16th St (beneath the Metro) ■ 8am-10pm, popular wknds for brkfst, outdoor seating ■ www.squatandgobble.com

Sumi [MW] 415/626-7864 ■ 4243 18th St (at Diamond) ■ 5:30pm-10:30pm, cont'l/ Japanese ■ www.suminthecastro.com

Thailand Restaurant 415/863-6868 ■ 438-A Castro St ■ 11am-10pm, plenty veggie

Welcome Home [★MW,BW] 415/626-3600 ■ 464 Castro St ■ 8am-10pm, homestyle, some veggie

Yokoso Nippon Sushi (aka No Name Sushi) [★] 314 Church St ■ noon-10pm, some veggie, always a line & always worth the wait

Zuni Cafe [★] 415/552-2522 ■ 1658 Market St (at Franklin) ■ lunch & dinner, clsd Mon, upscale cont'l/ Mediterranean, full bar

ENTERTAINMENT & RECREATION

36 **Castro Country Club** [MW] 415/552-6102 ■ 4058 18th St (at Hartford) ■ 11am-11pm, till 1am Fri-Sat, open holidays, alcohol- & drug-free space ■ www.castrocountryclub.org

Pink Triangle Park near Market & Castro ■ "in remembrance of LGBT victims of the Nazi regime" ■ www.pinktrianglepark.net

Three Dollar Bill Cafe [WI] 415/503-1532 ■ 1800 Market St (in the SF LGBT Center) ■ 7am-10pm, 9am-8pm Sat, clsd Sun, cafe & so much more: hosts open mic, micro-cinema (film) night, games night ■ www.threedollarbill.com

BOOKSTORES

38   **A Different Light** 415/431-0891 ■ 489 Castro St ■ *10am-10pm, till 11pm Fri-Sat, LGBT, readings* ■ www.adlbooks.com

Aardvark Books 415/552-6733 ■ 227 Church St ■ *10:30am-10:30pm, used, good LGBT section*

Books, Inc [WC] 415/864-6777 ■ 2275 Market St ■ *9:30am-11pm, till 10pm Sun, LGBT section, readings* ■ www.booksinc.net

Cover to Cover Booksellers 415/282-8080 ■ 1307 Castro St ■ *10am-9pm, till 6pm Sun, independent*

Get Lost [★] 415/437-0529 ■ 1825 Market St (at Guerrero) ■ *10am-7pm, till 6pm Sat, 11am-5pm Sun, travel books, LGBT section* ■ www.getlostbooks.com

Phoenix Books 415/821-3477 ■ 3850 24th St (at Vicksburg) ■ *9am-9pm, till 8pm Sun, new & used, also new & used music* ■ www.dogearedbooks.com

RETAIL SHOPS

All American Boy 415/861-0444 ■ 463 Castro St ■ *10am-9pm, men's clothing*

Best in Show 415/863-7387, 877/863-7387 ■ 300 Sanchez St (at 16th St) ■ *11am-7:30pm, 10am-6pm Sat, 11am-6pm Sun, pet supply boutique* ■ www.bestinshowsf.com

Cold Steel America 415/621-7233 ■ 2377 Market St (at 17th St, 2nd floor) ■ *noon-8pm, piercing & tattoo studio; also 1783 Haight St, 415/933-7233*

De La Sole Footwear 415/255-3140 ■ 4126 18th St ■ *11am-7pm, till 8pm Sat* ■ www.delasole.com

Does Your Mother Know? 415/864-3160 ■ 4141 18th St (at Castro) ■ *9:30am-10pm, till 11pm Fri-Sat, 10am-9pm Sun, cards & T-shirts*

Dragonfly Ink 415/550-1445 ■ 3409 23rd St ■ *woman-owned/ run tattoo studio* ■ www.dragonflyink.com

Gotham Body Piercing 415/701-1970 ■ 3991 17th St ■ *noon-8pm*

Image Leather 415/621-7551 ■ 2199 Market St (at Sanchez) ■ *9am-10pm, 11am-7pm Sun, custom leather clothing, accessories & toys*

Just for Fun [WC] 415/285-4068 ■ 3982 24th St (btwn Noe & Sanchez) ■ *9am-8pm, till 7pm Sat, 10am-6pm Sun, gift shop* ■ justforfun.invitations.com

La Sirena Botanica 415/285-0612 ■ 1509 Church St (at 27th St) ■ *noon-7pm, Afro-Caribbean religious articles*

Rolo 415/431-4545 ■ 2351 Market St ■ *11am-8pm, till 7pm Sun, designer labels*

See Jane Run Sports 415/401-8338 ■ 3910 24th St (at Noe) ■ *11am-7pm, 10am-6pm Sat, till 5pm Sun, women's athletic apparel* ■ www.seejanerunsports.com

Under One Roof [WC] 415/503-2300, 800/525-2125 ■ 549 Castro ■ *10am-8pm, 11am-7pm Sun, 100% donated to AIDS relief* ■ www.underoneroof.org

GYMS & HEALTH CLUBS

Gold's Gym Castro [★MW] 415/626-4488 ■ 2301 Market St ■ *day passes available* ■ www.goldsgym.com/sanfranciscocastroca

The Gym SF [MO,GO] 415/863-4700 ■ 2275 Market St ■ *day passes available* ■ www.thegymsf.com

MEN'S CLUBS

Eros [PC] 415/864-3767 ■ 2051 Market St (btwn Church & Dolores) ■ *4pm-midnight, till 4am Fri, 2pm-4am Sat, 2pm-midnight Sun, safer-sex club, theme nights, massage available, day passes* ■ www.erossf.com

EROTICA

Auto-Erotica 415/861-5787 ■ 4077-A 18th St, 2nd flr ■ *"purveyor of vintage porn & fine dildos"*

➤ **Castro Gulch** 415/934-8524 ■ 2353 Market St (at Castro) ■ *10am-midnight, till 2am Fri-Sat, toys, videos, DVDs, magazines, men's sexy clothing, fetish items* ■ www.sfgulch.com

Chaps 415/863-1699 ■ 4057 18th St (btwn Castro & Hartford) ■ *10am-11pm, till midnight Fri-Sat* ■ www.chapssf.com

Rock Hard 415/437-2430 ■ 518 Castro St (at 18th St) ■ *9:30am-11pm, till midnight Fri-Sat, toys, DVDs, lube, leather, cockrings & more* ■ sfrockhard@aol.com

Romantasy Exquisite Corsetry 415/585-0760 ■ *call for appt, corsets & fetish clothing* ■ www.romantasy.com

SAN FRANCISCO DETAIL
SOUTH OF MARKET

© Damron Company, SF, CA, 2007

SF — South of Market

ACCOMMODATIONS

1 **Argent Hotel** [GF,NS] 415/974-6400, 877/222-6699 ■ 50 3rd St ■ *sauna, kids ok* ■ www.argenthotel.com

Hotel Vitale [GF,NS,WI,WC] 415/278-3700, 888/890-8688 ■ 8 Mission St ■ www.hotelvitale.com

2 **Howard Johnson Express Inn** [GS,WI,WC] 415/431-5131, 800/446-4656 ■ 385 9th St (at Harrison) ■ *motel, close to SOMA bars* ■ www.hojo.com

3 **The Mosser Hotel** [GS,NS] 415/986-4400, 800/227-3804 ■ 54 4th St (btwn Market & Mission) ■ *1913 landmark, also restaurant & full bar, kids ok* ■ www.themosser.com

4 **National Hotel** [GF] 415/864-9343 ■ 1139 Market St ■ *hostel* ■ nationalhotelsf@yahoo.com

5 **Ramada Market St** [GF,WI,WC] 415/626-8000, 800/227-4747 ■ 1231 Market St (btwn 8th & 9th) ■ *also restaurant & Starbucks on-site* ■ www.ramadaplazasf.com

6 **Renoir Hotel** [GS,NS,WC] 415/626-5200, 800/576-3388 ■ 45 McAllister (at Market St) ■ *boutique-style, bar & Brazilian restaurant* ■ www.renoirhotel.com

7 **W San Francisco** [GF,SW,WI,WC] 415/777-5300, 877/WHOTELS (reservations only) ■ 181 Third St ■ *also XYZ Bar* ■ www.whotels.com/sanfrancisco

BARS

8 **111 Minna Gallery** [GS,D,E] 415/974-1719 ■ 111 Minna St (at 2nd St) ■ *also art gallery, [D] Wed for Qool, call for events* ■ www.111minnagallery.com

9 **Dada SF Studio** [GS,GO] 415/357-1367 ■ 86 2nd St (btwn Market & Mission) ■ *4pm-midnight, till 2am Fri-Sat, from 7pm Sat, clsd Sun, art gallery* ■ www.thegallerylounge.com

10 **The Eagle Tavern** [★M,L,E] 415/626-0880 ■ 398 12th St (at Harrison) ■ *noon-2am, great beer bust Sun, patio* ■ www.sfeagle.com

11 **Gallery Lounge** [GS] 415/227-0449 ■ 510 Brannan St ■ *4pm-midnight, till 2am Th-Fri, 7pm-2am Sat, clsd Sun, also (unsurprisingly) an art gallery* ■ www.thegallerylounge.com

12 **Hole in the Wall Saloon** [★M,NH,L] 415/431-4695 ■ 1369 Folsom (at 10th) ■ *noon-2am, "a nasty little biker bar"* ■ www.holeinthewallsaloon.com

13 **Lone Star Saloon** [★M,B,L] 415/863-9999 ■ 1354 Harrison St (btwn 9th & 10th) ■ *noon-2am, from 9am wknds, patio, bear bar, beer bust wknds* ■ www.lonestarsaloon.com

14 **My Place** [M] 415/863-1290 ■ 1225 Folsom St (at 8th) ■ *7pm-close, from noon wknds, "A rock n roll dude bar"*

15 **Powerhouse** [M,NH,L] 415/552-8689 ■ 1347 Folsom St (at Dore Alley) ■ *4pm-2am, theme nights, popular wknds w/ DJ, patio, cruisy* ■ www.powerhouse-sf.com

16 **VinoVenue** [GF] 415/341-1930 ■ 686 Mission St (at 3rd) ■ *2pm-9pm, till 10pm Fri-Sat, till 6pm Sun, women's night Wed* ■ www.vinovenue.net

NIGHTCLUBS

17 **1015 Folsom** [★GS,D,$] 415/431-1200 ■ 1015 Folsom St (at 6th) ■ *10pm-close Fri-Sat, call for events* ■ www.1015.com

18 **Asia SF** [★GS,D,MR-A,$] 415/255-2742 ■ 201 9th St (at Howard) ■ *10pm-close Wed-Sat, theme nights, go-go boys, also Cal-Asian restaurant w/ en-drag service rom 6:30pm, from 6pm Th & Sun, from 5pm Sat* ■ asiasf.com

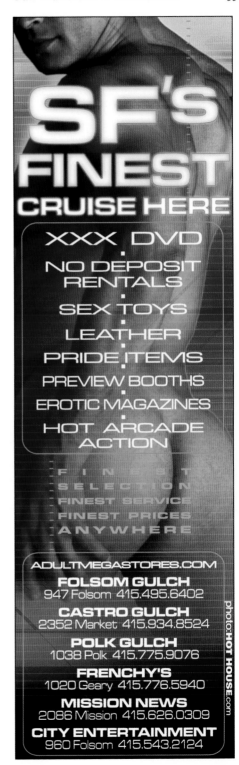

19 **Bootie** [★GF,D,A,E,$] 415/626-1409 (DNA info line) ■ 375 11th St (at Harrison, at DNA Lounge) ■ *9pm-close 2nd Sat, mashups, bootlegs, bastard pop* ■ www.bootiesf.com

20 **Club Dragon** [★M,D,MR-A,S,$] 415/431-1151 ■ 1151 Folsom St (at Eight) ■ *9pm-3am Fri, go-go boys* ■ www.eightsf.com

21 **The Crib SF** [MW,D,V,18+,$] 715 Harrison St (at 3rd) ■ *9:30pm-2am Th only, "all-video pop club"* ■ www.thecribsf.com

22 **Dirty** [M,D,A,YC] 415/252-7666 ■ 1190 Folsom (at 8th, in Cat Club) ■ *4th Sat* ■ www.clubdirtysf.com

20 **Eight** [★GS,D,$] 415/431-1151 ■ 1151 Folsom St (btwn 7th & 8th St) ■ *9pm-3am, clsd Mon-Wed, 2 flrs, theme nights, smoking patio* ■ www.eightsf.com

23 **Endup** [M,D,MR] 415/646-0999 (info line), 415/357-0827 ■ 401 6th St (at Harrison) ■ *clsd Tue-Wed, theme nights, popular Sun mornings* ■ www.theendup.com

23 **Fag Fridays** [★M,D,YC,$] 415/263-4850 ■ 401 6th St (at The Endup) ■ *10pm-5:30am Fri* ■ www.fagfridays.com

GusPresents.com ■ *The host with the most—Gus always throws one hell of a party for the boys!* ■ www.guspresents.com

22 **Hot Pants** [W,D] 415/703-8965 (club #) ■ 1190 Folsom St (at Cat Club) ■ *10pm-3am 2nd & 4th Fri, '80s electro, indie, hip-hop, punk* ■ www.catclubsf.com

24 **Mezzanine** [GS,D,MR,TG,E,WC,$] 415/625-8880 ■ 444 Jessie (at Mint) ■ *9pm-close, live music, call for events* ■ www.mezzaninesf.com

19 **Pop Roxx** [★GF,D,A,E,$] 415/626-1409 (DNA info line) ■ 375 11th St (at Harrison, at DNA Lounge) ■ *9pm-close last Sat; DJs spin electro, indie, rock, new wave, goth & mod; upstairs Mini-Bootie mashup* ■ www.poproxxsf.com

25 **The Stud** [★MW,D,YC] 415/863-6623 ■ 399 9th St (at Harrison) ■ *5pm-2am, theme nights, Trannyshack Tue* ■ www.studsf.com

20 **Thick** [★M,D,$] 415/431-1151 ■ 1151 Folsom St (at Eight) ■ *11pm-3am 1st & 3rd Sun, after-hours party* ■ www.eightsf.com

25 **Trannyshack** [★M,D,TG,E,GO] 415/863-6623 ■ 399 9th St (at The Stud) ■ *10pm-3am Tue, weekly party for trannies & their friends & admirers* ■ www.trannyshack.com

CAFES

Brain Wash [★E,BW] 415/861-3663, 415/431-9274 ■ 1122 Folsom St (at 7th St) ■ *7am-11pm, till midnight Fri-Sat, 8am-11pm Sun, laundromat & cafe* ■ www.brainwash.com

Pick Me Up [WI] 415/864-7425 ■ 298 9th St (at Folsom) ■ *6am-7pm, 8am-5pm wknds*

RESTAURANTS

Ame [R] 415/284-4040 ■ 689 Mission St (at 3rd St, in St Regis Hotel) ■ *lunch & dinner, seasonal New American cuisine, full bar* ■ www.amerestaurant.com

Ananda Fuara 415/621-1994 ■ 1298 Market St (at 9th) ■ *8am-8pm, till 3pm Wed, clsd Sun, vegetarian* ■ anandafuara.com

Bacar Restaurant & Wine Salon [★E,R,WC] 415/904-4100 ■ 448 Brannan St (btwn 3rd & 4th) ■ *lunch Fri, dinner nightly* ■ www.bacarsf.com

Bong Su [R] 415/536-5800 ■ 311 3rd St (at Folsom) ■ *lunch Mon-Fri, dinner nightly, Vietnamese* ■ www.bongsu.com

Boulevard [★] 415/543-6084 ■ 1 Mission St (at Steuart) ■ *lunch Mon-Fri & dinner nightly, one of SF's finest* ■ www.boulevardrestaurant.com

Butter 415/863-5964 ■ 354 11th St (btwn Folsom & Harrison) ■ *6pm-2am, clsd Mon, "white trash bistro," full bar, theme nights* ■ www.smoothasbutter.com

Dogzilla Cafe [BW,GO] 415/442-1889 ■ 215 Fremont #2A (enter on Howard) ■ *11am-7pm, clsd Sat-Sun, hot dog & sausage creations, lesbian-owned* ■ www.dogzillacafe.com

Don Ramon's Mexican Restaurant 415/864-2700 ■ 225 11th St (btwn Howard & Folsom)

Fringale [WC] 415/543-0573 ■ 570 4th St (btwn Bryant & Brannan) ■ *lunch Tue-Fri & dinner nightly, French bistro*

Hawthorne Lane 415/777-9779 ■ 22 Hawthorne St (btwn 2nd & 3rd, off Howard) ■ *dinner nightly, lunch Mon-Fri* ■ www.hawthornelane.com

Le Charm 415/546-6128 ■ 315 5th St (at Folsom) ■ *lunch Mon-Fri & dinner Tue-Sun, French bistro* ■ www.lecharm.com

Levende Lounge [E] 415/864-5585 ■ 1710 Mission St (at Duboce) ■ *dinner Tue-Sat, Boogie Brunch Sun, clsd Mon, full bar, live DJs nightly* ■ www.levendesf.com

Manora's Thai Cuisine 415/861-6224 ■ 1600 Folsom (at 12th) ■ *lunch Mon-Fri, dinner nightly*

Restaurant LuLu [★WC] 415/495-5775 ■ 816 Folsom St (at 4th St) ■ *lunch & dinner, upscale Mediterranean, some veggie, full bar* ■ restaurantlulu.com

Rocco's Cafe [★] 415/554-0522 ■ 1131 Folsom St (at 7th) ■ *brkfst & lunch daily, dinner Wed-Sat only* ■ www.roccoscafe.com

The Slanted Door [★R] 415/861-8032 ■ 1 Ferry Building #3 ■ *lunch & dinner, Vietnamese, full bar* ■ www.slanteddoor.com

Supperclub [E] 415/348-0900 ■ 657 Harrison St (btwn 2nd & 3rd) ■ *6:30pm-close, live performance art & acrobatics, also full bar & nightclub* ■ www.supperclub.com

Tu Lan 415/626-0927 ■ 8 6th St (at Market) ■ *lunch & dinner, dingy Sun, Vietnamese, some veggie, dicey neighborhood but delicious (& cheap) food*

Woodward's Garden [WC] 415/621-7122 ■ 1700 Mission St (at Duboce) ■ *dinner from 6pm, clsd Sun-Mon*

Yank Sing [★] 415/957-9300 ■ 101 Spear St (One Rincon Center, at Mission) ■ *11am-3pm Mon-Fri, 10am-4pm wknds, dim-sum heaven!* ■ www.yanksing.com

RETAIL SHOPS

A Taste of Leather 415/252-9166 ■ 1285 Folsom (btwn 9th & 10th) ■ *noon-8pm, till 10pm Th-Sat* ■ www.atasteofleather.com

Dandelion [GO] 415/436-9500, 888/548-1968 ■ 55 Potrero Ave (at Alameda St) ■ *10am-7pm, till 6pm Fri-Sat, noon-5pm Sun, gifts, books, erotica & more* ■ www.tampopo.com

Leather Etc 415/864-7558 ■ 1201 Folsom St (at 8th St) ■ *10:30am-7pm, 11am-6pm Sat, noon-5pm Sun* ■ www.leatheretc.com

Madame S 415/863-9447 ■ 385 8th St (at Harrison) ■ *women's bondage & fetish fashion & equipment* ■ www.madame-s.com

Mr S Leather & Fetters USA San Francisco 415/863-7764, 800/746-7677 (orders) ■ 385 8th St (at Harrison) ■ *11am-7pm, erotic goods, custom leather & latex* ■ www.mr-s-leather.com

Stompers 415/255-6422, 888/BOOTMAN ■ 323 10th St (at Folsom) ■ *11am-6pm, noon-4pm Sun, clsd Mon, boots, cigars & gloves* ■ stompersboots.com

Stormy Leather 415/626-1672, 800/486-9650 ■ 1158 Howard St (btwn 7th & 8th) ■ *noon-7pm, leather, latex, toys & magazines* ■ www.stormyleather.com

GYMS & HEALTH CLUBS

Gold's Gym San Francisco [★] 415/552-4653 ■ 1001 Brannan St (at 9th) ■ *day passes available* ■ www.goldsgym.com/sanfranciscosomaca

MEN'S CLUBS

Blow Buddies [★MO,LV,PC,GO] 415/777-4323 ■ 933 Harrison (btwn 5th & 6th) ■ *open late Wed-Sun, clsd Mon-Tue* ■ www.blowbuddies.com

Mack Folsom Prison [MO,L,PC] 415/252-7127 (club line) ■ 1285 Folsom (at 9th) ■ *6pm-5am, 24hrs wknds, fetish parties* ■ www.mackfolsomprison.com

Men's Spanking Party [18+] 415/864-2766 ■ 74 Otis St (at The Power Exchange, btwn Gough St & South Van Ness) ■ *1pm-7pm 2nd Sun only* ■ sanfranparty@yahoo.com

Power Exchange Mainstation [TG,18+,$] 415/487-9944 ■ 74 Otis St (btwn S Van Ness & Gough) ■ *9pm-6am Th-Sat, cover charge for men, free for women and transgender people* ■ www.powerexchange.com

SEX CLUBS

Power Exchange Level 3 415/487-9944 ■ 86 Otis St (btwn S Van Ness & Gough) ■ *10pm-5am Fri-Sat, couples & single women only* ■ www.powerexchange.com

EROTICA

► **City Entertainment** 415/543-2124 ■ 960 Folsom St (btwn 5th & 6th) ■ *10am-2am, 24hrs wknds, the best in adult entertainment* ■ www.adultmegastores.com

► **Folsom Gulch** 415/495-6402 ■ 947 Folsom (btwn 5th & 6th) ■ *10am-2am, 24hrs Fri-Sat, hot arcade action, serving the gay community for over 25 years!* ■ www.sfgulch.com

Secrets 415/863-7115 ■ 1036 Market St (at 7th) ■ *24hrs, huge selection of DVDs, magazines & lots of arcade action* ■ www.adultmegastores.com

SF—Polk Street Area

ACCOMMODATIONS

1 **Broadway Manor Inn** [WI,WC] 415/776-7900, 800/727-6239 ■ 2201 Van Ness Ave (at Broadway) ■ *motel close to Fisherman's Wharf, free parking, kids ok* ■ www.broadwaymanor.com

2 **Hostelling International–San Francisco City Center** [GF,NS,WI] 415/474-5721, 888/464-4872 ■ 685 Ellis St (at Larkin) ■ *hostel, shared & private rooms available, free brkfst, kids ok* ■ www.sfhostels.com

3 **The Monarch Hotel** [GF] 415/673-5232, 800/777-3210 ■ 1015 Geary St (at Polk) ■ *Edwardian boutique-style hotel* ■ www.themonarchhotel.com

4 **Nob Hill Motor Inn** [GF,NS,WI,WC] 415/775-8160, 800/343-6900 ■ 1630 Pacific Ave (at Van Ness Ave) ■ *hotel* ■ www.staysf.com/nobhill

5 **The Phoenix Hotel** [★GF,SW,WI] 415/776-1380, 800/248-9466 ■ 601 Eddy St (at Larkin) ■ *1950s-style motor lodge, fave of celebrity rockers, also Bambuddha lounge & restaurant* ■ www.thephoenixhotel.com

BARS

6 **The Cinch** [M,NH,WI,WC] 415/776-4162 ■ 1723 Polk St (at Clay) ■ *6am-2am, patio, lots of pool tables & no attitude, [D] Th-Sat, [DS] Fri* ■ www.thecinch.com

7 **Deco Lounge** [M,NH,P] 415/346-2025 ■ 510 Larkin (at Turk) ■ *10am-2am, happy hour noon-8pm, monthly drag shows*

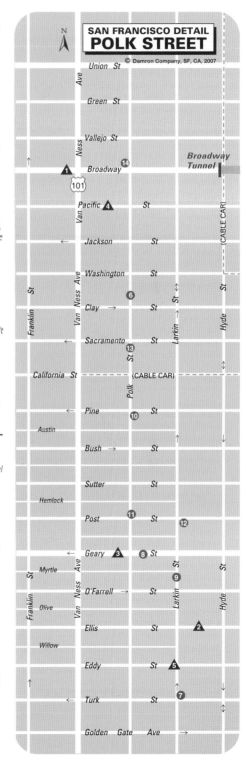

8   **Edinburgh Castle** [GF,NH,E] 415/885-4074 ■ 950 Geary St (at Polk) ■ *5pm-2am, mostly straight but rockin' Scottish pub w/ single malts, beer, darts & authentic fish & chips, live bands* ■ www.castlenews.com

9   **Gangway** [M,NH] 415/776-6828 ■ 841 Larkin St (btwn Geary & O'Farrell) ■ *8am-2am*

10   **Kimo's** [M,NH,GO] 415/885-4535 ■ 1351 Polk St (at Pine) ■ *8am-2am, live bands upstairs [GS,A,YC]*

11   **Lush Lounge** [★GS,NH,E,P,WC] 415/771-2022 ■ 1092 Post (at Polk) ■ *4pm-2am, martini bar & piano lounge* ■ www.thelushlounge.com

NIGHTCLUBS

7   **Bearracuda** [M,D,B] 415/346-2025 ■ 510 Larkin (at Deco Lounge) ■ www.bearracuda.com

12   **Divas** [M,NH,D,TG,DS] 415/474-3482 ■ 1081 Post St (at Larkin) ■ *6am-2am, TS/TVs & their admirers* ■ www.divassf.com

13   **N' Touch** [M,NH,D,MR-A,S] 415/441-8413 ■ 1548 Polk St (at Sacramento) ■ *3pm-2am, [K] Mon-Tue, Club T Th w/ strippers, go-go boys Fri-Sat* ■ www.ntouchsf.com

14   **Respect** [W,D,MR,OC,WC,$] 415/647-8258 ■ Broadway & Polk (at Harry Denton's Rouge) ■ *4pm-9pm 2nd Sun only, "a monthly tea dance for women"* ■ respectforwomen@aol.com

CAFES

La Boulange de Polk 415/345-1107 ■ 2310 Polk St (at Green St) ■ *7am-6:30pm, till 6pm Sun, clsd Mon, French bakery & cafe, outdoor seating, Parisian down to the attitude*

Quetzal Internet Cafe [★E,V,BW,WI] 415/673-4181, 888/673-4181 ■ 1234 Polk St (at Sutter) ■ *6:30am-10pm, roasts own coffee* ■ www.quetzal.org

Royal Ground [WI] 415/474-5957 ■ 2216 Polk St (at Vallejo) ■ *6:30am-11pm, from 7am wknds*

RESTAURANTS

Antica Trattoria 415/928-5797 ■ 2400 Polk St (at Union) ■ *dinner, clsd Mon, Italian, wine served*

California Culinary Academy [★] 415/771-3500, 415/216-4329 (reservations) ■ 625 Polk St (at Turk) ■ *lunch & dinner Tue-Fri, cooking school where future top chefs serve up what they've learned* ■ www.baychef.com/about_restaurants_catering.asp

El Super Burrito 415/771-9700 ■ 1200 Polk St (at Sutter) ■ *9am-11pm*

Grubstake II [MW,BW] 415/673-8268 ■ 1525 Pine St (at Polk) ■ *5pm-4am, from 10am wknds, diner*

Lemongrass 415/929-1183, 415/346-1818 ■ 2348 Polk St (at Union) ■ *11am-10pm, till 10:30pm Fri-Sat, Thai, beer served* ■ www.lemongrasssf.com

Le Petit Robert 415/922-8100 ■ 2300 Polk St (at Green St) ■ *lunch & dinner, also wknd brunch, French, outdoor seating* ■ www.lepetitrobert.com

Rex Cafe 415/441-2244, 415/441-9244 ■ 2323 Polk St ■ *from 5pm, dinner, also brunch 10am-3pm Sat-Sun, clsd Mon, American, full bar*

Street 415/775-1055 ■ 2141 Polk St (btwn Broadway & Vallejo) ■ *dinner, clsd Mon, New American, incredible hamburgers along w/ fancier fare, full bar* ■ www.streeton-polk.com

Tai Chi [★] 415/441-6758 ■ 2031 Polk St (at Pacific) ■ *lunch Mon-Fri, dinner nightly, Chinese*

EROTICA

➤ **Frenchy's** 415/776-5940 ■ 1020 Polk St (at Polk) ■ *10am-2am Mon-Th, 24hrs wknds, hot adult entertainment* ■ www.adultmegastores.com

➤ **Good Vibrations** [★W] 415/345-0400 ■ 1620 Polk St (btwn Sacramento & Clay) ■ *11am-7pm, till 8pm Th, till 9pm Fri-Sat, clean, well-lighted sex toy store, also mail order* ■ www.goodvibes.com

➤ **The Polk Gulch** 415/775-9076 ■ 1038 Polk St (at Post) ■ *City's newst Gulch, hot arcade action* ■ www.sfgulch.com

SF—Downtown & North Beach

ACCOMMODATIONS

1   **Andrews Hotel** [GF,NS,WI] 415/563-6877, 800/926-3739 ■ 624 Post St (at Taylor) ■ *Victorian hotel, also Italian restaurant* ■ www.andrewshotel.com

2   **Cartwright Hotel on Union Square** [GF,WI] 415/421-2865, 800/919-9779 ■ 524 Sutter St (at Powell) ■ *B&B-inn on Union Square, afternoon tea, wine hour* ■ www.cartwrighthotel.com

3   **Dakota Hotel** [GF,WI] 415/931-7475 ■ 606 Post St (at Taylor) ■ *near Union Square* ■ www.hotelsanfrancisco.com

4   **Executive Hotel Vintage Court** [GF,NS,WC] 415/392-4666, 800/654-1100 ■ 650 Bush St (at Powell) ■ *also world-famous 5-star Masa's restaurant, French* ■ www.vintagecourt.com

5   **Galleria Park Hotel** [GS,WI,WC] 415/781-3060, 800/792-9639 ■ 191 Sutter St (at Kearny) ■ *boutique hotel, kids ok* ■ www.galleriapark.com

6   **Grand Hyatt San Francisco** [GF] 415/398-1234, 800/233-1234 ■ 345 Stockton St (at Sutter) ■ *restaurant & lounge, gym* ■ grandsanfrancisco.hyatt.com

7   **Halcyon Hotel** [GF] 415/929-8033, 800/627-2396 ■ 649 Jones St (at Post) ■ www.halcyonsf.com

8   **Handlery Union Square Hotel** [GF,SW,WC] 415/781-7800, 800/995-4874 ■ 351 Geary St ■ *steps from Union Square* ■ www.handlery.com/sf/home.html

     Harbor Court Hotel [GF,SW,WI,WC] 415/882-1300, 866/792-6283 ■ 165 Steuart St (btwn Howard & Mission) ■ *in Financial District, gym* ■ www.harborcourthotel.com

9   **Hostelling International—San Francisco Downtown** [GS,WC] 415/788-5604, 800/909-4776 ■ 312 Mason St (at O'Farrell) ■ www.norcalhostels.org

10   **Hotel Bijou** [GS,NS,WI,WC] 415/771-1200, 800/771-1022 ■ 111 Mason St (at Eddy) ■ www.hotelbijou.com

11   **Hotel Carlton** [GF] 415/673-0242, 800/922-7586 ■ 1075 Sutter St (at Larkin) ■ *also Saha restaurant, Arabic-fusion* ■ www.carltonhotel.com

12 ➤ **Hotel Diva** [GF,NS,WI] 415/885-0200, 800/553-1900 ■ 440 Geary (at Mason) ■ *hip hotel, gym* ■ www.hoteldiva.com

13   **Hotel Fusion** [GS,NS,WI,WC] 415/568-2525, 877/812-0157 ■ 140 Ellis St (at Powell St) ■ www.hotel-fusionsf.com

➤ **Hotel Griffon** [GS,WI,WC] 415/495-2100, 800/321-2201 ■ 155 Steuart St (at Mission) ■ *also restaurant, bistro/ cont'l* ■ www.hotelgriffon.com

14   **Hotel Mark Twain** [GF,WI,WC] 415/673-2332 ■ 345 Taylor St (at Ellis) ■ *also Indian restaurant (serves American brkfst)* ■ www.hotelmarktwainsanfrancisco.com

15 ➤ **Hotel Metropolis** [GF,WI] 800/553-1900 ■ 25 Mason St ■ *near Union Square shopping* ■ www.hotelmetropolis.com

16   **Hotel Monaco** [GF] 415/292-0100, 866/622-5284 ■ 501 Geary St (at Taylor) ■ *non-smoking rooms available, pets ok, also Grand Cafe restaurant, French* ■ www.monaco-sf.com

17   **Hotel Nikko San Francisco** [GF,SW,NS,WC] 415/394-1111, 800/248-3308 ■ 222 Mason St ■ *health club & spa, also ANZU restaurant* ■ www.hotelnikkosf.com

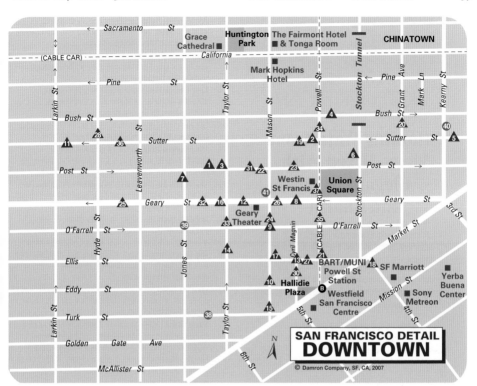

SAN FRANCISCO DETAIL
DOWNTOWN
© Damron Company, SF, CA, 2007

18 **Hotel Palomar** [GS,WI] 415/348-1111, 866/373-4941 ■ 12 4th St (at Market) ■ *boutique hotel* ■ www.hotelpalomar.com

19 **The Hotel Rex** [GF,WC] 415/433-4434, 800/433-4434 ■ 562 Sutter St (at Powell) ■ *also full bar* ■ www.thehotelrex.com

20 **Hotel Triton** [GF,WI,WC] 415/394-0500, 800/433-6611 ■ 342 Grant Ave (at Bush) ■ *designer theme rooms* ■ www.hoteltriton.com

21▶ **Hotel Union Square** [GF,WI] 800/553-1900 ■ 114 Powell St ■ *1930s art deco lobby, original art by Gladys Perint Palmer in rms* ■ www.hotelunionsquare.com

Hyatt Regency San Francisco [GF,NS,WI] 415/788-1234, 800/233-1234 ■ 5 Embarcadero Center (at California) ■ *luxury waterfront hotel* ■ sanfranciscoregency.hyatt.com

The Inn at Union Square [GF,NS,WI] 415/397-3510, 800/288-4346 ■ 440 Post St ■ *steps from Union Square* ■ www.unionsquare.com

22 **JW Marriott Hotel San Francisco** [GF,NS,WI,WC] 415/771-8600, 800/605-6568 ■ 500 Post St (at Mason) ■ www.jwmarriottunionsquare.com

23► **Kensington Park Hotel** [GF,NS,WI] 800/553-1900 ■ 450 Post St ■ *on Union Square, also Farallon Restaurant* ■ www.kensingtonparkhotel.com

24 **King George Hotel** [GS,F,WI,WC] 415/781-5050, 800/288-6005 ■ 334 Mason St (at Geary) ■ *also The Windsor Tearoom* ■ www.kinggeorge.com

25 **Luz Hotel** [M,N,GO] 415/928-1917 ■ 725 Geary Blvd (at Leavenworth) ■ *clothing-optional jacuzzi* ■

26 **The Maxwell Hotel** [GS,WC] 415/986-2000, 888/734-6299 ■ 386 Geary St (at Mason) ■ *1908 art deco masterpiece, full brkfst* ■ www.maxwellhotel.com

27 **Monticello Inn** [GF,WI] 415/392-8800, 866/778-6169 ■ 127 Ellis St (at Powell) ■ *boutique hotel, restaurant & bar* ■ www.monticelloinn.com

28 **Nob Hill Hotel** [GS,NS,WC] 415/885-2987, 877/662-4455 ■ 835 Hyde St (btwn Bush & Sutter) ■ *European-style hotel, jacuzzi* ■ www.nobhillhotel.com

30 **The Powell Hotel** [GS,WI] 415/398-3200, 800/368-0700 ■ 28 Cyril Magnin St ■ *at Powell St cable-car turnaround* ■ www.thepowellhotel.com

31 **Prescott Hotel** [GF,NS,WI] 415/563-0303, 866/271-3632 ■ 545 Post St (btwn Taylor & Mason) ■ *small luxury hotel* ■ www.prescotthotel.com

32 **Savoy Hotel** [GF,NS] 415/441-2700, 800/227-4223 ■ 580 Geary St (at Jones) ■ *also popular Millennium gourmet vegetarian restaurant & bar* ■ www.thesavoyhotel.com

33 **Serrano Hotel** [GF,WI,WC] 415/885-2500, 866/289-6561 ■ 405 Taylor St (at O'Farrell) ■ *in heart of Theater District* ■ www.serranohotel.com

34► **Sir Francis Drake Hotel** [GF,WI] 415/392-7755, 800/795-7129 ■ 450 Powell St (at Sutter) ■ *1928 landmark, also restaurant & Starlight Room* ■ www.sirfrancisdrake.com

The Stratford Hotel [GS,WI,WC] 415/397-7080, 877/922-5928 ■ 242 Powell St (at Geary) ■ *near Union Square* ■ www.hotelstratford.com

The Touchstone Hotel [GF,WC] 415/771-1600, 800/620-5889 ■ 480 Geary St (btwn Mason & Taylor) ■ *in Theater District, full brkfst* ■ www.TheTouchstone.com

Tuscan Inn [GF,WC] 415/561-1100, 888/648-4626 ■ 425 N Point St (at Mason) ■ *boutique inn* ■ www.tuscaninn.com

35 **Union Square Plaza Hotel** [GF] 415/776-7585, 800/841-3135 ■ 432 Geary St ■ *1 block from Union Square* ■ www.unionsqplzahotl.citysearch.com

36 **Vertigo** [GS,NS,WI,WC] 415/885-6800, 800/808-9675 ■ 940 Sutter St (at Leavenworth) ■ *boutique hotel, also Plush Room cabaret* ■ www.yorkhotel.com

37 **Villa Florence Hotel** [GF,WI] 415/397-7700, 866/823-4669 ■ 225 Powell St (at Geary) ■ *Union Square boutique hotel, also Kuleto's restaurant, Italian* ■ www.villaflorence.com

Bars

38 **Aunt Charlie's Lounge** [M,NH,DS] 415/441-2922 ■ 133 Turk St (at Taylor) ■ *noon-2am, till midnight Mon & Wed, from 10am wknds, drag shows wknds* ■ www.auntcharlieslounge.com

39 **Bourbon & Branch** [GS,R] 501 Jones St (at O'Farrell) ■ *in Prohibition-era speakeasy, drinks are worth the price* ■ www.bourbonandbranch.com

36 **Empire Plush Room** [★GS,C,WC] 415/885-2800, 866/468-3399 ■ 940 Sutter St (at York Hotel) ■ *cabaret w/ world-class performers* ■ www.empireplushroom.com

40 **Ginger's Trois** [M,NH,P] 415/989-0282 ■ 246 Kearny St (at Sutter) ■ *10am-10pm, professional crowd*

NIGHTCLUBS

41 **Fresh @ Ruby Skye** [★M,D,$] 415/693-0777 ■ 420 Mason (at Geary) ■ *6pm-midnight Sun, T-dance, check local listings for dates* ■ www.freshsf.com

CAFES

Caffe Trieste [★] 415/392-6739 ■ 601 Vallejo St ■ *6:30am-11pm, till midnight Fri-Sat, get a taste of the real North Beach (past & present) & a great cappuccino* ■ www.caffetrieste.com

RESTAURANTS

Ar Roi 415/771-5146 ■ 643 Post St (at Jones) ■ *lunch Mon-Sat, dinner nightly, Thai*

The Buena Vista 415/474-5044 ■ *9am-2am, from 8am wknds, the restaurant that introduced Irish coffee to America* ■ www.thebuenavista.com

Cafe Claude [E,BW] 415/392-3515 ■ 7 Claude Ln (near Bush & Kearny) ■ *11:30am-10:30pm, from 5:30 pm Sun, live music Th-Sat, as close to Paris as you can get in SF* ■ www.cafeclaude.com

Le Colonial 415/931-3600 ■ 20 Cosmo Pl (btwn Taylor & Jones) ■ *5:30pm-10pm, till 11pm Th-Sat, Vietnamese, full bar* ■ www.lecolonialsf.com

Dottie's True Blue Cafe [GO] 415/885-2767 ■ 522 Jones St (at Geary) ■ *7:30am-3pm, clsd Tue, plenty veggie, great brkfst*

Golden Era [★] 415/673-3136 ■ 572 O'Farrell St ■ *11am-9pm, clsd Tue, vegetarian/ vegan* ■ www.goldeneravegetarian.com

Mario's Bohemian Cigar Store Cafe [BW,WI] 415/362-0536 ■ 566 Columbus Ave (at Union) ■ *10am-close, great foccacia sandwiches, some veggie* ■ www.mariosbohemiancigarstore.com

Masa's [★WC] 415/989-7154 ■ 648 Bush St (at Hotel Vintage Court) ■ *dinner Tue-Sat, world-famous 5-star French restaurant* ■ www.masasrestaurant.com

Max's on the Square [★] 415/646-8600 ■ 398 Geary St (at Mason) ■ *7am-10pm, till 11pm Fri-Sat, full bar* ■ www.maxsworld.com

Millennium 415/345-3900 ■ 580 Geary St (at Jones, at the Savoy Hotel) ■ *dinner only, Euro-Mediterranean, upscale vegetarian* ■ www.millenniumrestaurant.com

Moose's [★] 415/989-7800, 800/286-6673 ■ 1652 Stockton (btwn Filbert & Union) ■ *lunch Wed-Fri, dinner nightly, wknd brunch, upscale bistro menu* ■ www.mooses.com

Original Joe's 415/775-4877 ■ 144 Taylor (btwn Turk & Eddy) ■ *lunch & dinner, Italian, since 1937, also art deco cocktail lounge*

BOOKSTORES

Book Passage 415/835-1020 ■ 1 Ferr Bldg #42 ■ *10am-8pm, from 8am Sat, 10am-7pm Sun-Mon, independent* ■ www.bookpassage.com

City Lights Bookstore 415/362-8193 ■ 261 Columbus Ave (at Pacific) ■ *10am-midnight, historic beatnik bookstore, many progressive titles, LGBT section, whole floor dedicated to poetry* ■ www.citylights.com

Stacey's Bookstore 415/421-4687, 800/926-6511 ■ 581 Market St ■ *9:30am-7pm, 11am-6pm Sat, clsd Sun, independent, LGBT section* ■ www.staceys.com

EROTICA

Nob Hill Adult Theater [MO,$] 415/781-9468 (info line), 415/989-8552 ■ 729 Bush St (at Powell) ■ *9am-2:30am, male dancers, over 25 shows daily* ■ www.nobhilltheatre.com

The Tearoom Theater 415/885-9887 ■ 145 Eddy St (btwn Mason & Taylor) ■ *9am-2am, till 4am Fri-Sat, all-male porn theater w/ live J/O shows several times daily*

SF—Mission District

includes Bernal Heights

ACCOMMODATIONS

Bernal Heights Duplex, Carriage House [GS,NS,WI] 415/601-6460 ■ 3 Porter St (at Crescent) ■ *1-bdrm & studio apt vacation rentals* ■ www.sfholidayrentals.com

1 **Elements** [★GS,F,WI] 415/647-4100, 866/327-8407 ■ 2516 Mission St (at 21st St) ■ *hostel w/ private or shared rooms* ■ www.elementssf.com

2 **The Inn San Francisco** [GF,NS,WI] 415/641-0188, 800/359-0913 ■ 943 S Van Ness Ave (btwn 20th & 21st) ■ *Victorian mansion, hot tub* ■ www.innsf.com

BARS

3 **Argus Lounge** [GS] 415/824-1447 ■ 3187 Mission St, Bernal Heights (at Valencia) ■ *4pm-2am, from 5pm Sun, pool table* ■ www.arguslounge.com

4 **El Rio** [★GS,NH,MR,E] 415/282-3325 ■ 3158 Mission St (at Cesar Chavez) ■ *5pm-close Mon-Th, from 3pm wknds, patio, frequent women's events, free oysters Fri* ■ www.elriosf.com

5 **Lexington Club** [★NH,GO] 415/863-2052 ■ 3464 19th St (btwn Mission & Valencia) ■ *5pm-2am, from 3pm Fri-Sun, hip younger crowd* ■ www.lexingtonclub.com

6 **Lone Palm** [GS] 415/648-0109 ■ 3394 22nd St (at Guerrero) ■ *4pm-2am, a bar for grown ups (we know you're out there)* ■ www.lonepalmbar.com

Nihon [GS,D,F] 415/552-4400 ■ 1779 Folsom St (at 14th St) ■ *6pm-close, clsd Sun, whiskey lounge, also Japanese restaurant* ■ www.nihon-sf.com

7 **Phone Booth** [MW,NH] 415/648-4683 ■ 1398 S Van Ness Ave (at 25th) ■ *noon-2am, from 1pm wknds*

8 **Sadie's Flying Elephant** [★GS,NH,E] 415/551-7988 ■ 491 Potrero (at Mariposa) ■ *4pm-2am, K'vetsh queer open mic 8pm 1st Sun*

9 **Stray Bar** [GS,NH,GO] 415/821-9263 ■ 309 Cortland Ave, Bernal Heights (at Bocana) ■ *4pm-2am, from 1pm wknds, women's night Wed, lesbian-owned* ■ www.straybarsf.com

Truck Bar [MW,NH,F,GO] 415/252-0306 ■ 1900 Folsom St (at 15th) ■ *4pm-2am, from 2pm wknds* ■ www.trucksf.com

10 **Wild Side West** [GS,WC] 415/647-3099 ■ 424 Cortland, Bernal Heights (at Bennington) ■ *1pm-2am, patio, magic garden*

Zeitgeist [★GS,F] 415/255-7505 ■ 199 Valencia St (at Duboce) ■ *9am-2am, divey biker bar & beer garden*

NIGHTCLUBS

11 **Booty** [MW,D,MR] 415/550-8286 ■ 550 Barneveld (at space550, 2 blocks E of Bayshore Blvd) ■ *9:30pm-2am Fri only, "gay & lesbian hip-hop"* ■ www.thecribsf.com/booty

11 **Club Papi SF** [M,D,MR-L] 415/675-9763 ■ 550 Barneveld (at space550, 2 blocks off Bayview) ■ *monthly party from 10pm-4am, call for dates* ■ www.clubpapi.com

12 **Esta Noche** [M,D,MR-L,TG,S] 415/861-5757 ■ 3079 16th St (at Mission) ■ *1pm-2am, salsa & disco in a classic Tijuana dive*

4 **Heavy Rotation** [MW,D] 415/282-3325 ■ 3158 Mission St (at El Rio) ■ *10pm 3rd Fri, "queer flavored, fat dance club"* ■ www.elriosf.com

13 **In Bed With Fairy Butch** [W,D,MR,TG,C,S] 415/339-8000 ■ 2565 Mission (at 22nd, at 12 Galaxies) ■ *occasional parties, strippers, cabaret, "for gals & trannies of all colors & pals"* ■ www.fairybutch.com

4 **Mango** [WO,D,MR,F,$] 415/339-8310 ■ 3158 Mission (at El Rio) ■ *3pm-8:30pm 4th Sat April-Nov* ■ backstreetssf@hotmail.com

14 **Pink** [GS,D,$] 415/431-8889 ■ 2925 16th St (btwn Mission & S Van Ness) ■ *9pm-2am, theme nights, more gay Tue for Taboo* ■ www.pinksf.com

11 **Sundance Saloon** [★M,D,CW,GO,$] 415/820-1403 ■ 550 Barneveld Ave (at space550, 2 blocks off Bayshore Blvd) ■ *5pm-10:30pm Sun (lessons at 5:30) & 6:30pm-10:30pm Th (lessons at 7pm), women welcome!* ■ www.sundancesaloon.org

CAFES

Dolores Park Cafe [★F,E] 415/621-2936 ■ 501 Dolores St (at 18th St) ■ *7am-8pm, outdoor seating overlooking Dolores Park, live music Fri till 10pm* ■ www.doloresparkcafe.org

Farleys [E] 415/648-1545 ■ 1315 18th St (at Texas St, Potrero Hill) ■ *6:30am-10pm, from 7:30am Sat & 8am Sun* ■ www.farleyscoffee.com

Ritual [★WI] 415/641-1024 ■ 1026 Valencia St (at 21st St, next to Lost Weekend Video) ■ *6am-11pm, from 7am Sat, 7am-9pm Sun, primo coffee, pastries* ■ www.ritualroasters.com

Tartine Bakery [★] 415/487-2600 ■ 600 Guerrero St (at 18th St) ■ *8am-7pm, from 9am Sun, French bakery w/ a line out the door every day all day, wine & espresso bar, outside tables* ■ www.tartinebakery.com

RESTAURANTS

Aslam's Rasoi 415/695-0599 ■ 1037 Valencia St (at 21st) ■ *5pm-11pm, Indian & Pakistani* ■ www.aslamsrasoi.com

Boogaloos [★] 415/824-4088 ■ 3296 22nd St (at Valencia) ■ *8am-3pm, worth the wait*

Charanga [★BW,WC] 415/282-1813 ■ 2351 Mission St (at 20th St) ■ *5:30pm-close, clsd Sun-Mon, Cuban-Caribbean tapas* ■ www.charangasf.com

Circolo 415/553-8560 ■ 500 Florida St (at Mariposa) ■ *5pm-close, clsd Mon, Latin-Asian fusion, full bar* ■ www.circolosf.com

Delfina [★R] 415/552-4055 ■ 3621 18th St (at Dolores) ■ *5:30pm-10pm, excellent Tuscan cuisine, full bar, patio (summers)* ■ delfinasf.com

El Farolito [★] 415/824-7877 ■ 2779 Mission St (at 24th) ■ *11am-8pm, till 3am Fri-Sat, delicious, cheap burritos*

Firecracker [★] 415/642-3470 ■ 1007 Valencia St (at 21st) ■ *5:30pm-11pm, clsd Sun, Chinese*

Herbivore [BW] 415/826-5657 ■ 983 Valencia St (at 21st) ■ *9am-10pm, till 11pm Fri-Sat, moderately priced vegan food in upscale setting*

Mabel's Just For You [★MW] 415/647-3033 ■ 722 22nd St (at 3rd St) ■ *7:30am-3pm, from 8am wknds, Southern brkfst, some veggie* ■ justforyoucafe.com

Maverick 415/863-3061 ■ 3316 17th St (btwn Mission & Valencia) ■ *5:30pm-11pm Mon-Sat, also wknd brunch, upscale American, great wine selection* ■ www.sfmaverick.com

Medjool [★WC] 415/550-9055 ■ 2522 Mission St (at 21st St) ■ *5pm-10pm, till 11pm Fri-Sat, clsd Sun, tapas, also cafe, lounge & rooftop bar* ■ www.medjoolsf.com

Pancho Villa [★BW,WC] 415/864-8840 ■ 3071 16th St (btwn Mission & Valencia) ■ *11am-midnight, some veggie; also El Toro at 18th & Valencia*

Pauline's Pizza Pie [★MW,BW] 415/552-2050 ■ 260 Valencia St (btwn 14th & Duboce) ■ *5pm-10pm, clsd Sun-Mon, gourmet pizza* ■ www.paulinespizza.com

Picaro [BW,WC] 415/431-4089 ■ 3120 16th St (at Valencia) ■ *5pm-10pm, till 11pm Fri, 1pm-11pm Sat, 1pm-10pm Sun, Spanish tapas bar*

Pizzeria Delfina [WC] 415/437-6800 ■ 3611 18th St (at Guerrero) ■ *lunch Tue-Sun, dinner nightly, outdoor seating* ■ www.pizzeriadelfina.com

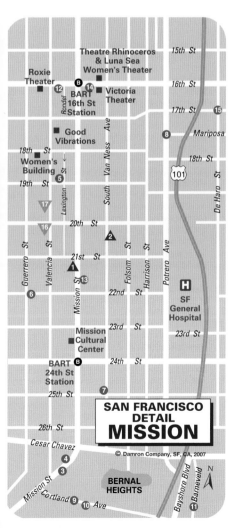

SAN FRANCISCO
DETAIL
MISSION

© Damron Company, SF, CA, 2007

BERNAL
HEIGHTS

Pork Store Cafe [★BW] 415/626-5523 ■ 3122 16th St (at Valencia) ■ 8am-4pm daily & 7pm-3am Th-Sat, cool American/ diner food, great brkfsts; also 1451 Haight St, 415/864-6981

Range [★] 415/282-8283 ■ 842 Valencia St (btwn 19th & 20th Sts) ■ dinner nightly, California contemporary, full bar ■ www.rangesf.com

Slow Club [WC] 415/241-9390 ■ 2501 Mariposa (at Hampshire) ■ lunch Mon-Fri, dinner Mon-Sat, wknd brunch, full bar ■ www.slowclub.com

Ti-Couz [BW,WC] 415/252-7373 ■ 3108 16th St (at Valencia) ■ 5pm-11pm, from 11am Mon & Fri, from 10am wknds, dinner & dessert crepes, plenty veggie, outdoor seating

Yamo Thai Kitchen 415/553-8911 ■ 3406 18th St (at Mission) ■ 10:30am-9:30pm, clsd Sun, small, no frills outfit w/ great cheap food

Yum Yum House [★] 415/861-8698 ■ 581 Valencia St ■ 11am-10pm, great Chinese

ENTERTAINMENT & RECREATION

Brendita's Latin Tour 415/921-0625 ■ walking tours of the Mission District, call between 8am-10pm ■ www.imageoz.com/brendita

15 **Metronome Ballroom** [GS,$] 415/252-9000 ■ 1830 17th St (at De Haro) ■ dance lessons, salsa to swing, dance parties wknds, call for events ■ www.metronomedancecenter.com

Women's Building 415/431-1180 ■ 3543 18th St (btwn Valencia & Guerrero) ■ check out some of the most beautiful murals in the Mission District ■ www.womensbuilding.org

BOOKSTORES

Borderlands Books [★] 415/824-8203, 888/893-4008 ■ 866 Valencia St (at 19th) ■ noon-8pm, new & used, "San Francisco's home for science fiction, fantasy & horror books" ■ www.borderlands-books.com

16 **Dog Eared Books** 415/282-1901 ■ 900 Valencia St (at 20th) ■ 10am-10pm, till 8pm Sun, new & used, good LGBT section ■ www.dogearedbooks.com

17 **Modern Times Bookstore** [WC] 415/282-9246 ■ 888 Valencia St ■ 10am-9pm, 11am-6pm Sun, progressive, LGBT section, readings ■ www.mtbs.com

RETAIL SHOPS

Black & Blue Tattoo [★W] 415/626-0770 ■ 381 Guerrero (at 16th St) ■ noon-7pm, women-owned/ run ■ www.blackandbluetattoo.com

Body Manipulations 415/621-0408 ■ 3234 16th St (btwn Guerrero & Dolores) ■ noon-7pm, from 2pm Mon-Th, piercing (walk-in basis), jewelry ■ www.bodym.com

The Scarlet Sage 415/821-0997 ■ 1173 Valencia St (near 23rd St) ■ 11:30am-6pm, medicinal herbs, books, gifts, cards ■ www.scarletsageherb.com

GYMS & HEALTH CLUBS

Osento [WO] 415/282-6333 ■ 955 Valencia St (at 20th) ■ noon-midnight, baths, hot tub, massage ■ www.osento.com

EROTICA

➤ **Good Vibrations** [★W,WC] 415/522-5460, 800/289-8423 ■ 603 Valencia St (at 17th St) ■ 11am-7pm, till 8pm Th, till 9pm Fri-Sat, clean, well-lighted sex toy store, also mail order ■ www.goodvibes.com

➤ **Mission St News** 415/626-0309 ■ 2086 Mission St (at 17th) ■ 24hrs, DVDs, magazines & much more! ■ www.adultmegastores.com

SF—Haight, Fillmore, Hayes Valley

ACCOMMODATIONS

1 **555 Haight Guesthouse** [GS,NS] 415/551-2555, 800/785-5504 ■ 555 Haight St ■ hostel

2 **The Archbishop's Mansion** [GF,NS,GO] 415/563-7872, 800/543-5820 ■ 1000 Fulton St (at Steiner) ■ one of San Francisco's grandest homes ■ www.thearchbishopsmansion.com

3 **The Chateau Tivoli** [GF,NS,WI] 415/776-5462, 800/228-1647 ■ 1057 Steiner St (at Golden Gate) ■ historic SF B&B ■ www.chateautivoli.com

4 **Edward II Inn & Suites** [GF,WI] 415/922-3000, 800/473-2846 ■ 3155 Scott St ■ European-style B&B w/ own pub & gym ■ www.edwardii.com

5 **Francisco Bay Inn** [GF,NS,WI] 415/474-3030, 800/410-7007 ■ 1501 Lombard St (at Franklin) ■ motel, free parking ■ www.staysf.com/franciscobay

6 **Hayes Valley Inn** [GS,NS,WI] 415/431-9131, 800/930-7999 ■ 417 Gough St (at Hayes) ■ European-style pension, shared baths ■ www.hayesvalleyinn.com

7 **Heritage Marina Hotel** [GF,SW] 415/776-7500, 866/714-6835 ■ 2550 Van Ness Ave ■ vintage '50s hotel in the Marina District ■ www.heritagemarinahotel.com

Hostelling International—Fisherman's Wharf [GS,F,WI,WC] 415/771-7277, 800/909-4776 ■ Fort Mason, Bldg 240 (at Franklin) ■ hostel, close to Golden Gate Nat'l Recreation Area, shared baths, cafe & open kitchen ■ www.norcalhostels.org

8 **Hotel Del Sol** [★GS,NS,SW,WI,WC] 415/921-5520, 877/433-5765 ■ 3100 Webster St (at Greenwich) ■ bright & fun California decor ■ www.thehoteldelsol.com

15 **Hotel Kabuki** [GF,WC] 415/922-3200, 800/333-3333 ■ 1625 Post St (at Laguna) ■ in the heart of Japantown ■ www.miyakohotel.com

9 **Hotel Majestic** [GF,NS,WI,WC] 415/441-1100, 800/869-8966 ■ 1500 Sutter St (at Gough) ■ one of SF's earliest grand hotels, also restaurant, some veggie, full bar ■ www.thehotelmajestic.com

10 **Inn 1890** [GS,NS,GO] 415/386-0486, 888/INN-1890 ■ 1890 Page St (near Stanyan) ■ kitchens, fireplaces, apt available ■ www.inn1890.com

11 **Inn at the Opera** [GF,NS,WC] 415/863-8400, 800/590-0157 ■ 333 Fulton St (at Franklin) ■ www.innattheopera.com

12 **Jackson Court** [GF,NS,WI] 415/929-7670 ■ 2198 Jackson St (at Buchanan) ■ 19th-c brownstone mansion ■ www.jacksoncourt.com

13 **Metro Hotel** [GF,F,WI] 415/861-5364 ■ 319 Divisadero St (at Haight) ■ European-style pension ■ www.metrohotelsf.com

14 **Queen Anne Hotel** [★GF,NS,WI,GO] 415/441-2828, 800/227-3970 ■ 1590 Sutter St (at Octavia) ■ beautifully restored 1890 landmark, fireplaces ■ www.queenanne.com

16 **Shannon-Kavanaugh Guest House** [GF,NS,GO] 415/563-2727 ■ 722 Steiner St (at Hayes) ■ 1-bdrm garden apt w/ house on SF's famous "Postcard Row" ■ www.shannon-kavanaugh.com/rental.html

17 **Stanyan Park Hotel** [GF,NS,WC] 415/751-1000 ■ 750 Stanyan St (at Waller) ■ historic Victorian hotel, evening snacks ■ www.stanyanpark.com

BARS

18 **Drunk & Horny** [M,NH] 424 Haight St (at Underground SF) ■ 9pm Sat, "gay boozin & cruizin" ■ www.drunkandhorny.net

19 **Jade Bar** [GF] 415/869-1900 ■ 650 Gough St (at McAllister) ■ 5pm-2am, from 8pm Sun, upscale cocktails & Asian-inspired "nibbles," indoor waterfall ■ www.jadebar.com

20 **Marlena's** [M,NH,DS,P,WC] 415/864-6672 ■ 488 Hayes St (at Octavia) ■ noon-2am, drag shows Sat, piano bar, Cheers for drag queens (a friendly oasis in hip & het Hayes Valley)

21 **Noc Noc** [GF,BW] 415/861-5811 ■ 557 Haight St (at Fillmore) ■ 5pm-2am

22 **Rickshaw Stop** [★GF,F,E] 415/861-2011 ■ 155 Fell St (btwn Van Ness & Franklin) ■ Wed-Sat only, hipster bar, nightclub (live bands) & restaurant ■ www.rickshawstop.com

18 **Sexy** [M,NH,D,S,$] 866/861-6680 ■ 424 Haight St (at Underground SF) ■ 9pm 1st Sat, "a boy bar," go-go dancers ■ sexy_boybar@onebox.com

18 **Traxx** [M,NH] 415/864-4213 ■ 1437 Haight St (at Masonic) ■ noon-2am ■ www.traxsf.com

NIGHTCLUBS

23 **The Underground** [GS,D,A] 415/864-7386 ■ 424 Haight St (at Webster) ■ 5:30pm-2am, clsd Mon, theme nights, call for events, more gay Sat ■ undergroundsf.com

CAFES

Blue Bottle Coffee Company [★] 415/252-7535 ■ 315 Linden St (at Gough St) ■ 7am-5pm, from 8am wknds, organic coffee & treats from kiosk in front of artists' workshop ■ www.bluebottlecoffee.net

Fillmore Grind 415/775-5680 ■ 711 Fillmore (at Hayes) ■ 7am-7pm

Java Beach Cafe [WI] 415/665-5282 ■ 1396 La Playa St ■ 5:30am-11pm, from 6am wknds, at the end of the N Judah line, right at Ocean Beach–great location ■ www.javabeachcafe.com

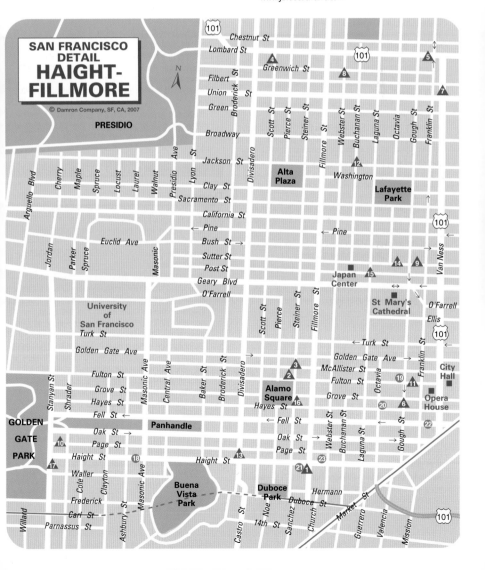

SAN FRANCISCO DETAIL **HAIGHT-FILLMORE**
© Damron Company, SF, CA, 2007

Restaurants

Alamo Square Seafood Grill 415/440–2828 ■ 803 Fillmore (at Grove) ■ *dinner only*

Blue Muse [WC] 415/626–7505 ■ 409 Gough St (at Fell) ■ *7am-9:30pm, Sun brunch, cont'l, some veggie, full bar (open later)*

Burma Superstar [★] 415/387–2147 ■ 309 Clement St ■ *lunch & dinner, Burmese food that will rock your world* ■ www.burmasuperstar.com

Caffe Delle Stelle [★BW] 415/252–1110 ■ 395 Hayes (at Gough) ■ *lunch Mon-Sat, dinner nightly, Italian*

Cha Cha Cha 415/386–7670 ■ 1801 Haight St (at Shrader) ■ *lunch & dinner, Cuban/ Cajun, excellent sangria, worth the wait!* ■ www.cha3.com

Cheese Steak Shop 415/346–3712 ■ 1716 Divisadero St (btwn Bush & Sutter) ■ *9am-9pm, from 11am Sun, from 10am Mon, best cheese steak outside Philly, also veggie versions* ■ www.cheesesteakshop.com

Citizen Cake [★] 415/861–2228 ■ 399 Grove St (at Gough) ■ *8am-10pm Tue-Fri, from 10am Sat, 10am-5pm Sun, clsd Mon* ■ www.citizencake.com

Eliza's [★] 415/621–4819 ■ 2877 California (at Broderick) ■ *lunch Mon-Wed, dinner nightly, excellent Chinese food & stylish decor*

Ella's 415/441–5669 ■ 500 Presidio Ave (at California) ■ *brkfst & lunch Mon-Fri, dinner Wed-Sun, popular wknd brunch* ■ www.ellassanfrancisco.com

Garibaldi's [WC,GO] 415/563–8841 ■ 347 Presidio Ave (at Sacramento) ■ *open for lunch wkdays & dinner nightly, Mediterranean, full bar* ■ garibaldisrestaurant.com

Greens [★] 415/771–6222 ■ Fort Mason, Bldg A (near Van Ness & Bay) ■ *lunch Tue-Sat, dinner Mon-Sat, Sun brunch, gourmet vegetarian, spectacular view of the Golden Gate Bridge* ■ greensrestaurant.com

Herbivore [BW] 415/885–7133 ■ 531 Divisadero St (at Fell St) ■ *9am-10pm, till 11pm Fri-Sat, moderately priced vegan food in upscale setting*

Indian Oven [★BW] 415/626–1628 ■ 233 Fillmore St (at Haight) ■ *5pm-11pm* ■ indianovensf.com

Jardinière [★] 415/861–5555 ■ 300 Grove St (at Franklin) ■ *5pm-midnight, till 10:30pm Sun-Mon, oh-so-chic Californian-French cuisine, full bar* ■ www.jardiniere.com

Kan Zaman [★BW] 415/751–9656 ■ 1793 Haight (at Shrader) ■ *5pm-midnight, from noon wknds, Mediterranean, hookahs & tobacco available*

Kate's Kitchen 415/626–3984 ■ 471 Haight St (at Fillmore St) ■ *8am-2:45pm, long lines wknds*

Little Star Pizza [★BW] 415/441–1118 ■ 846 Divisadero St (btwn Fulton & McAllister Sts) ■ *5pm-10pm, till 11pm Fri-Sat, clsd Mon, Chicago-style deep dish pizza* ■ www.littlestarpizza.com

Park Chow [★] 415/665–9912 ■ 1238 9th Ave (btwn Irving & Lincoln) ■ *11am-10pm, brunch from 10am wknds, eclectic & affordable*

Patxi's Chicago Pizza 415/558–9991 ■ 511 Hayes St (at Octavia St) ■ *11am-10pm, clsd Mon, Chicago-style deep dish pizza, also thin crust* ■ www.patxispizza.com

Pluto's Fresh Food for a Hungry Planet 415/753–8867 ■ 627 Irving St (btwn 7th & 8th Aves) ■ *11am-10pm, design your own sandwiches, salads, plenty veggie*

Sheba Piano Lounge [P] 415/440–7414 ■ 1419 Fillmore St ■ *5pm-midnight, till 2am Fri-Sat, wknd brunch from 10am, Ethiopian, full bar* ■ www.shebalounge.com

Solstice Restaurant & Lounge 415/359–1222 ■ 2801 California St (at Divisadero) ■ *5pm-midnight, comfort food, full bar* ■ www.solsticelounge.com

Suppenküche [BW,GO] 415/252–9289 ■ 601 Hayes (at Laguna) ■ *dinner, Sun brunch, German cuisine served at communal tables* ■ www.suppenkuche.com

Thep-Phanom [★BW] 415/431–2526 ■ 400 Waller St (at Fillmore) ■ *5:30pm-10:30pm, excellent Thai food, worth the wait!* ■ www.thepphanom.com

Entertainment & Recreation

Kabuki Springs & Spa 415/922–6000 ■ 1750 Geary Blvd (at Fillmore) ■ *10am-9:45pm, traditional Japanese bath w/ extensive menu of spa sevices* ■ www.kabukisprings.com

Bookstores

Bibliohead Bookstore 415/621–6772 ■ 334 Gough St (at Hayes) ■ *eclectic used books, queer section*

The Booksmith 415/863–8688, 800/493–7323 (in US) ■ 1644 Haight St ■ *cool independent, big-name author readings* ■ www.booksmith.com

Green Apple Book & Music [★] 415/387–2272 ■ 506 Clement St ■ *10am-10:30pm, till 11:30pm Fri-Sat, new & used books & CDs* ■ www.greenapplebooks.com

Retail Shops

Flight 001 415/487–1001, 877/354–4481 ■ 525 Hayes St (btwn Octavia & Laguna) ■ *11am-7pm, till 6pm Sun, way cool travel gear* ■ www.flight001.com

COLORADO

Denver

Accommodations

1 **Adam's Mark Hotel Denver** [GF,SW] 303/893–3333, 800/444–2326 ■ 1550 Court Pl ■ *near convention center, 4 restaurants, 3 lounges, 1 nightclub, gym* ■ www.adams-mark.com/denver

2 **Capitol Hill Mansion B&B** [GF,NS,WI] 303/839–5221, 800/839–9329 ■ 1207 Pennsylvania (at 12th) ■ *full brkfst, hot tub* ■ www.capitolhillmansion.com

   Courtyard Denver South [GF,NS] 720/895–0300, 800/321–2211 ■ 8320 S Valley Hwy, Englewood ■ www.courtyard.com/deniv

3 **Elyria's Western Guest House** [M,NS,GO] 303/291–0915 ■ 1655 E 47th Ave (near I-70 & Brighton, check in here) ■ www.Bedandbreakfast.com/colorado/elyrias-western-guest-house.html

4 **The Gregory Inn, LoDo** [GF,NS] 303/295–6570, 800/925–6570 ■ 2500 Arapahoe St (at 25th St) ■ *full brkfst, jacuzzis* ■ www.gregoryinn.com

5 **Hotel Monaco** [GF,NS,WI] 303/296–1717, 800/990–1303 ■ 1717 Champa St (at 17th) ■ *gym, spa, also Italian restaurant* ■ www.monaco-denver.com

6 **Hotel Teatro** [GF] 303/228–1100, 888/727–1200 ■ 1100 14th St ■ *luxury boutique hotel, 2 restaurants* ■ www.hotelteatro.com

DENVER

Day Trips: Summit County

A little over an hour west of Denver, the towns of Summit County have plenty to offer visitors year-round. In the old gold-mining town of Breckenridge, not only will you enjoy great skiing, but you will also find great shopping and eats. In late January, the town hosts the not-to-be-missed International Snow Sculpture Fesitval. Keystone, a more modern, upscale resort town, also has great restaurants and great skiing, and boasts a gondola that runs even in the warmer months, offering breathtaking views of the mountains.

Other Summit County towns that you may want to kick around around are Frisco and Copper Mountain.

Local Food:

"Rocky Mountain Oysters" contain no oysters. Let's get that right out in the open. But if bull testicles sound good to you, you will find no shortage of places that serve 'em up, as well as other Wild West treats like rattlesnake and buffalo. You may be in more of a mood to sample these dishes after a couple beers from one of the many micro-breweries in town.

Tourist Info

AIRPORT DIRECTIONS

Denver International. Take Pena Blvd to I-70 W. Follow I-70 W till you come to I-25. Then take I-25 S and exit on Speer Blvd. Once on Speer Blvd, follow it until you reach Colfax Ave and the heart of Denver.

PUBLIC TRANSIT & TAXIS

Yellow Cab 303/777-7777.
Metro Taxi 303/333-3333.
Super Shuttle 303/370-1300 or 800/525-3177, web: www.supershuttledenver.com.
RTD 303/628-9000 or 303/299-6000 & 800/366-7433 (infoline), web: www.rtd-denver.com.

TOURIST SPOTS & INFO

16th Street Mall (pedestrian mall in Lower Downtown or LoDo).
Black American West Museum 303/292-2566, web: www.blackamericanwest.org.
Cherry Creek Shopping Center 303/388-3900, web: www.shopcherrycreek.com.
Denver Art Museum 720/865-5000, web: denverartmuseum.org.
Denver Botanic Gardens 720/865-3500, web: www.botanicgardens.org.
Denver Center for the Performing Arts 303/893-4100, web: www.denvercenter.org.
Denver Zoo 303/376-4800, web: www.denver-zoo.org.
Downtown Aquarium 303/561-4450.
Six Flags Elitch Gardens 303/595-4386, web: www.sixflags.com.
LoDo (Lower Downtown).
Molly Brown House 303/832-4092, web: www.mollybrown.org.
Visitor's Center: 800/233-6837, web: www.denver.org.

Weather

Summer temperatures average in the 90°s and winter ones in the 40°s. The sun shines an average of 300 days a year with humidity in the single digits.

Best Views

Lookout Mountain (at night especially) or from the top of the Capitol rotunda.

City Calendar

LGBT PRIDE

June. 303/733-7743, web: www.denverpridefest.org.

ENTERTAINMENT

Denver Women's Chorus 303/274-4177.

ANNUAL EVENTS

July- 2nd weekend, Rocky Mountain Regional Rodeo (gay rodeo), web: cgra.net.
August- Cinema Q - Denver International LGBT film festival, web: www.cinemaq.org.
August/September - AIDS Walk, web: coloradoaidsproject.org
September/October- Great American Beer Festival, web: www.gabf.org.

Queer Resources

COMMUNITY INFO

The GLBT Center of Colorado 303/733-7743. 1050 Broadway, 10am-6pm Mon-Fri, web: www.coloradoglbt.org.
Lesbian/ Gay AA 303/322-4440, web: www.daccaa.org.
Crystal Meth Anonymous 303/733-7743 (at The Center).
Colorado AIDS Project 303/837-0166, web: www.coloradoAIDSproject.org.

7   **Lumber Baron Inn** [GF,WI] 303/477-8205 ■ 2555 W 37th Ave (at Bryant) ■ *Victorian mansion, full brkfst, hot tub* ■ www.lumberbaron.com

8   **The Oxford Hotel** [GF,F,WI] 303/628-5400, 800/228-5838 ■ 1600 17th St ■ *health club & spa, also restaurant & art deco lounge* ■ www.theoxfordhotel.com

9   **Radisson Hotel Denver Stapleton Plaza** [GF,SW,WI,WC] 303/321-3500, 800/333-3333 ■ 3333 Quebec St (at 35th) ■ *gym, restaurant* ■ www.radisson.com

10   **Ramada Inn Denver Downtown** [GS,SW,WI,WC] 303/831-7700, 800/272-6232 ■ 1150 E Colfax Ave (at Downing) ■ *hotel in the heart of Capitol Hill, hot tub, full brkfst* ■ www.ramadadenverdowntown.com

5   **Residence Inn Denver City Center** [GF,NS] 303/296-3444, 800/331-3131 ■ 1725 Champa St ■ *all-suite hotel, 8th-flr patio w/ hot tub* ■ www.marriott.com/denrd

Bars

11   **The Atrium Bar** [GS,D,S] 303/744-1923 ■ 554 S Broadway ■ *7am-2am, strippers Wed, Fri & Sat*

12   **Barker Lounge** [M,NH] 303/778-0545 ■ 255 S Broadway (at Byers) ■ *noon-2am, also patio w/ bar*

13   **Bender's Tavern** [GF,F,E,K] 303/861-7070 ■ 314 E 13th Ave (at Grant) ■ *noon-2am, live bands, [K] Tue & Th* ■ www.benderstavern.com

14   **BJ's Carousel** [★,MW,NH,TG,F,K,DS,S,WC,GO] 303/777-9880 ■ 1380 S Broadway (at Arkansas) ■ *4pm-2am, from 10am Sat-Mon, male strippers Tue, [K] Wed, [C,DS] Fri-Sat, also restaurant for dinner (clsd Mon) & Sun brunch* ■ www.bjsdenver.com

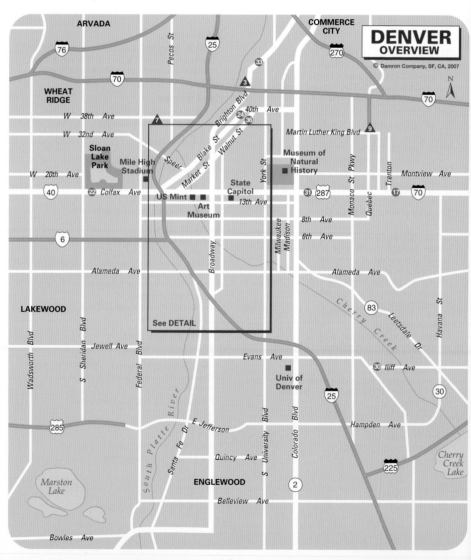

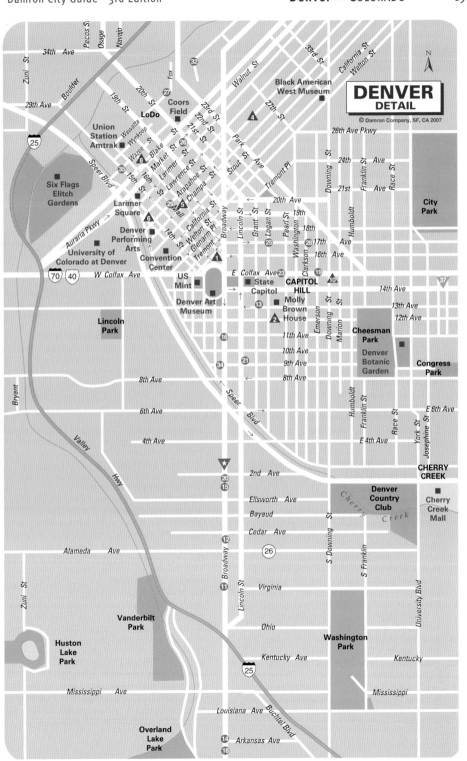

15 **Boyztown** [M,NH,S,WI] 303/722-7373, 303/777-9378 ■ 117 Broadway (btwn 1st & 2nd Aves) ■ *3pm-2am, from noon Fri-Sun, male dancers Tue-Sun* ■ www.boyztowndenver.com

16 **Broadways** [M,NH,WI] 303/623-0700 ■ 1027 Broadway (at 11th Ave) ■ *2pm-2am, from noon Sat-Sun, [K] Th* ■ www.Broadways.biz

17 **C's** [W,D,CW] 303/322-4436 ■ 7900 E Colfax Ave (at Trenton) ■ *5pm-midnight, till 2am Fri-Sat*

18 **Cafe Cero** [GS,NH,F,E] 303/282-1446 ■ 1446 S Broadway (btwn Arkansas & Florida) ■ *3pm-2am, gourmet bar food served 4pm-midnight, 2 patios* ■ www.cafecero.net

19 **Charlie's** [★M,D,CW,WC] 303/839-8890 ■ 900 E Colfax Ave (at Emerson) ■ *11am-2am, 2 clubs, also restaurant* ■ www.charliesonline.com

20 **The Compound** [★M,NH,D,A] 303/722-7977 ■ 145 Broadway (at 2nd Ave) ■ *7am-2am, [D] Fri-Sat* ■ www.compounddenver.com

21 **Dazzle** [GF,F,E] 303/839-5100 ■ 930 Lincoln St (btwn 9th & 10th Aves) ■ *from 4pm, from 5pm Sat-Sun, also Sun brunch (9:30am-1pm), jazz club & restaurant* ■ www.dazzlejazz.com

22 **The Den** [MW,NH,F,K,WC] 303/623-7998 ■ 5110 W Colfax Ave (at Sheridan) ■ *1pm-2am, from 10am Sun, also restaurant: dinner 5pm-10pm Wed-Sat & Sun brunch 10am-3pm*

23 **Denver Detour** [★W,NH,E,WC] 303/861-1497 ■ 551 E Colfax Ave (at Pearl, use back entrance) ■ *11am-2am, lunch & dinner daily, [K] 2nd & 4th Fri*

24 **Denver Eagle** [M,NH,B,L,WC,GO] 303/291-0250 ■ 1475 36th St (at Blake) ■ *levi/ leather/ cruise bar* ■ www.denvereagle.com

25 **The Denver Wrangler** [M,B,WC] 303/837-1075 ■ 1700 Logan Ave (at 17th Ave) ■ *11am-2am, levi/ bear bar, popular Sun beer bust* ■ www.denverwrangler.com

26 **El Chapultepec** [★GF,F,E,$] 303/295-9126 ■ 1962 Market St (at 20th) ■ *9am-2am, live jazz & blues, 2-drink minimum per set*

27 **Fox Hole** [MW] 303/298-7391 ■ 2936 Fox St (at 20th St) ■ *6pm-2am, from 3pm wknds, bi-level patio, outdoor dance Sun*

28 **JR's Bar** [★M,NH,K,DS,V,GO] 303/831-0459 ■ 777 E 17th Ave (at Clarkson) ■ *3pm-2am* ■ www.myjrs.com

29 **Lannie's Clocktower Cabaret** [GF,F,E,C] 303/293-0075 ■ 16th St Mall at Arapahoe (in historic D&F Tower) ■ *upscale cabaret w/ variety of acts weekly including drag (Tue) & burlesque (Th)* ■ www.lannies.com

30 **Metroroom** [MW,NH,D,TG,K] 303/695-5134 ■ 7449 E Iliff Ave ■ *4pm-11pm, till 2am Fri-Sat, 11am-11pm Sun, [K] Wed, [D] Fri-Sat*

31 **R&R Denver** [MW,NH] 303/320-9337 ■ 4958 E Colfax Ave (at Elm) ■ *3pm-2am, from 1pm Fri, from 11am wknds* ■ www.rrlounge.com

32 **Safari Bar** [MW,D,DS] 303/298-7959 ■ 500 Denargo St (at 31st) ■ *1pm-2am, clsd Mon, [D] Fri-Sun, [DS] Sun*

33 **Tequila Rosa's** [M,NH,MR-L] 303/295-2819 ■ 5190 Brighton Blvd ■ *noon-2am*

NIGHTCLUBS

34 **La Rumba** [GF,D,E,$] 303/572-8006 ■ 99 W 9th Ave (at Broadway) ■ *salsa dancing & lessons Th & Sat, more gay Fri for Lipgloss (Brit-pop & indie music)*

35 **Rock Island** [GF,D,A,YC,WC] 303/572-7625 ■ 1614 15th St (at Wazee) ■ *9pm-2am, clsd Mon-Wed, more gay Tue, Sat is all ages w/ no alcohol, call for events (closed for remodelling & will reopen fall 2007)* ■ www.rockislandclub.com

36 **Tracks** [GS,D,MR] 303/863-7326 ■ 3500 Walnut St (at 35th) ■ *9pm-2am, clsd Sun-Wed, 2 rooms, theme nights* ■ www.tracksdenver.com

CAFES

Bump & Grind Cafe 303/861-4841 ■ 439 E 17th Ave (at Pennsylvania) ■ *brkfst & lunch 7am-3:30pm, popular Petticoat Bruncheon w/ drag servers 10am-2pm Sat-Sun, clsd Mon-Tue*

Common Grounds [WI] 303/458-5248 ■ 3484 W 32nd Ave ■ *6:30am-10pm, till 11pm Fri-Sat; also 1601 17th St, 303/296-9248 [WI]*

Diedrich Coffee [★GS,WI] 303/837-1275 ■ 1201 E 9th Ave (at Downing) ■ *6am-10pm, from 7am Sun, outdoor seating, heated patio*

Java Creek [WI,WC] 303/377-8902 ■ 287 Columbine St (at 3rd Ave) ■ *7am-6pm, 8:30am-3pm Sun, patio*

Paris on the Platte [F,WI] 303/455-2451 ■ 1553 Platte St (at 15th) ■ *7am-1am, till 3am Fri-Sat, from 8am wknds, soups, salads, sandwiches, popular after-hours* ■ www.parisontheplatte.com

Simple Foods Market 303/561-4740 ■ 3901 Tennyson ■ *7am-8pm, 10am-5pm Sun, all-organic grocery w/ full-serivce deli & java/ juice bar* ■ www.simplefoodsmarket.com/denver/denver.html

tHERe Coffee Bar & Lounge [W,WI,GO] 303/830-8437 ■ 1526 E Colfax (btwn Humboldt & Franklin) ■ *9am-11pm, 10am-8pm Sun* ■ www.theredenver.com

Wired Coffee & Art [WI] 303/733-3977 ■ 19 E Bayaud ■ *8am-5:30pm, 9am-2pm Sun, clsd Mon* ■ www.wiredcoffeeandart.com

RESTAURANTS

Annie's Cafe [★] 303/355-8197 ■ 4012 E 8th Ave ■ *7am-9pm, from 8am Sat, till 3pm Sun, diner popular for comfort food & all-day brkfsts*

The Avenue Grill 303/861-2820 ■ 630 E 17th Ave (at Washington) ■ *11:30am-11pm, till midnight Fri-Sat, 5pm-10pm Sun* ■ www.avenuegrill.com

Benny's Restaurante y Tequila Bar [NS] 303/894-0788 ■ 301 E 7th Ave (at Grant St) ■ *11am-1pm, from 9am Sat, till 10pm Sun, Mexican, patio* ■ www.bennysrestaurant.com

Brio [E] 303/893-2746 ■ 1320 15th St (at Larimer, LoDo) ■ *contemporary northern Italian* ■ www.briodenver.com

Dixon's Downtown Grill [WC] 303/573-6100 ■ 1610 16th St (at Wazee) ■ *7am-close, from 8am wknds, American* ■ www.dixonsrestaurant.com

Duo 303/477-4141 ■ 2413 W 32nd Ave (at Zuni) ■ *dinner nightly, wknd brunch, hip, organic, creative American, full bar* ■ www.duodenver.com

The Earl of Sandwich [GO] 303/832-7411 ■ 1431 Ogden St (btwn 14th Ave & Ogden Theatre) ■ *10am-8pm, till 6pm Sat, till 4pm Sun, sandwiches & salads*

Goodfriends Restaurant 303/399-1751 ■ 3100 E Colfax Ave (at St Paul) ■ *lunch, dinner, wknd brunch* ■ www.goodfriendsrestaurant.com

Hamburger Mary's [★GS] 303/832-1333 ■ 700 E 17th Ave (across from JR's bar) ■ *11am-2am, from 10am Sun, also full bar* ■ www.hamburgermarysdenver.com

Joseph's Southern Food, Carry Out & Drive In [GO] 303/333-5332 ■ 2868 Fairfax St (at 29th) ■ 11am-8pm, noon-6pm Sun, clsd Mon, traditional Southern, carry out & drive thru, also bakery, ice cream parlor, candy ■ www.josephssouthernfood.com

Kiva 303/832-5482 ■ 3090 Downing St (at 31st Ave) ■ 11am-close, Mexican/ Southwestern, full bar ■ www.kivadenver.com

Las Margaritas Uptown [★GO] 303/830-2199 ■ 1035 E 17th Ave (at Downing) ■ 11am-1am, Mexican, some veggie, also bar ■ www.lasmargs.com

Le Central [BW] 303/863-8094 ■ 112 E 8th Ave (at Lincoln St) ■ lunch & dinner, brunch Sat-Sun, "affordable French" ■ www.lecentral.com

Manny's Underground [BW] 303/308-0110 ■ 1836 Blake ■ 7am-3pm, clsd wknds, deli/ coffeehouse

Pete's Kitchen [★] 303/321-3139 ■ 1962 E Colfax Ave ■ 24hrs, diner, popular after bars close ■ www.petesrestaurantstoo.com/petesKitchen.html

Racine's 303/595-0418 ■ 650 Sherman St (at 6th Ave) ■ brkfst, lunch, dinner, late night & Sun brunch, full bar ■ www.racinesrestaurant.com

Ristorante Amore 303/321-2066 ■ 2355 E 3rd Ave ■ lunch Mon-Fri, dinner nightly, Sun brunch, northern Italian, full bar ■ www.amoredenver.com

Sparrow 303/831-1003 ■ 410 E 7th Ave ■ lunch (Tue-Fri) & dinner, clsd Mon, upscale American bistro, patio, full bar ■ www.sparrowdenver.com

Steuben's 303/830-1001 ■ 523 E 17th Ave ■ 11am-11pm, till midnight Fri, 10am-midnight Sat, till 11pm Sun, American comfort food served up hip, patio, full bar ■ www.steubens.com

Tom's Home Cookin' [GO] 303/388-8035 ■ 800 E 26th Ave ■ 11am-3pm, clsd Sat-Sun, Southern comfort food

Vesta Dipping Grill 303/296-1970 ■ 1822 Blake St (near 18th St) ■ 5pm-10pm Sun-Th, till 11pm Fri-Sat, upscale ■ www.vestagrill.com

Wazee Supper Club 303/623-9518 ■ 1600 15th St (at Wazee) ■ 11am-2am, noon-midnight Sun, classic comfort food, full bar ■ www.wazeesupperclub.com

Zaidy's Deli 303/333-5336 ■ 121 Adams (at First) ■ 6:30am-5pm, till 8pm Th-Sat, 7:30am-5pm Sun; also 15th at Lawrence, 303/893-3600 ■ www.zaidysdeli.com

ENTERTAINMENT & RECREATION

Colorado OUT Spoken 303/861-0829 ■ PBS KBDI, channel 12 ■ 10pm Sun, LGBT news & entertainment TV program ■ www.coloradooutspoken.org

Denver Gay Men's Chorus 303/832-3462 ■ www.dgmc.org

Denver Women's Chorus 303/274-4177 ■ www.denverwomenschorus.org

Mercury Cafe [F,E,NS] 303/294-9281 ■ 2199 California St ■ 5:30pm-close, swing, tango, salsa dancing, live shows, also restaurant, dinner only Tue-Sun, wknd brunch ■ www.mercurycafe.com

Rocky Mountain Rainbeaus 303/863-7739 ■ all-inclusive, all-levels, high-energy square dance club ■ www.rainbeaus.org/cms/

Rocky Mountain Rollergirls 720/984-3132 ■ Denver's female roller derby league, check web for upcoming events ■ www.rockymountainrollergirls.com

BOOKSTORES

Isis Books & Gifts [WC] 303/321-0867, 800/808-0867 (orders) ■ 5701 E Colfax Ave (at Ivanhoe) ■ 10am-7pm, till 6pm Fri-Sat, noon-5pm Sun, New Age, metaphysical ■ www.isisbooks.com

37 **Tattered Cover Book Store** [WC] 303/322-7727, 800/833-9327 ■ 2526 Colfax Ave (at Elizabeth) ■ 9am-11pm, 10am-6pm Sun, local independent, coffee shop; also 1628 16th St, 303/ 436-1070 ■ www.tatteredcover.com

RETAIL SHOPS

Arco Iris Design 303/765-5116 ■ 82 S Broadway ■ pride jewelry & design ■ www.a-iris.net

Bound By Design 303/830-7272, 303/832-TAT2 ■ 1332 E Colfax (at Humboldt) ■ 11am-11pm, noon-10pm Sun, piercing & tattoos ■ www.bodyartusa.com

Heaven Sent Me [WC] 303/733-9000 ■ 116 S Broadway (btwn Alameda & Virginia) ■ 11am-9pm, 10am-8pm Sat, 11am-6pm Sun, pride items, clothing, gifts ■ www.heavensentme.com

Hysteria [GF] 303/733-3373 ■ 114 S Broadway (at Bayaud Ave) ■ 11am-7pm, from noon Sat, till 5pm Sun, clsd Tue ■ hysteriashop.com

Needz [GO] 303/722-0969 ■ 135 Broadway (at 1st Ave) ■ 10am-10pm, cards, gifts, sexy menswear & toys for adults ■ denverneedz@yahoo.com

PUBLICATIONS

Out Front Colorado 303/778-7900 ■ statewide bi-weekly LGBT newspaper, since 1976 ■ www.outfrontcolorado.com

Pink Pages 303/316-4688, 877/769-7465 ■ LGBT business directory & lifestyle magazine ■ lesgaypinkpages.com

MEN'S CLUBS

CCC (Community Country Club) [V,PC] 303/297-2601 ■ 2151 Lawrence St (at 21st) ■ 24hrs, outdoor patio

Denver Swim Club [★MO,V,YC,SW,PC] 303/321-9399 ■ 6923 E Colfax Ave (at Olive) ■ 24hrs ■ www.denverswimclub.com

Midtowne Spa–Denver [PC] 303/458-8902 ■ 2935 Zuni St (at 29th) ■ 24hrs, sundeck, whirlpool, private rooms, basement play area ■ www.midtowne.com

EROTICA

Circus Cinema 303/455-3144 ■ 5580 N Federal Blvd ■ 24hrs

The Crypt 303/733-3112 ■ 8 Broadway (at Ellsworth) ■ 11am-11pm, till 8pm Sun, leather & more ■

Crypt Adult Entertainment 303/778-6584 ■ 139 Broadway (btwn 1st & 2nd) ■ 10am-2am, till 4am Fri-Sat, all-male theaters & arcades

Dove Theater 303/893-0037 ■ 3480 W Colfax ■ 24hrs wknds

Pleasure Entertainment Center 303/722-5852 ■ 127 S Broadway (at Bayaud) ■ open 23hrs; also 3250 W Alameda, 303/934-2373 & 3490 W Colfax, 303/825-6505 ■ www.pleasuresxxx.com

Romantix Adult Superstore 303/831-8319 ■ 633 E Colfax Ave (at Washington) ■ 24hrs ■ www.romantixonline.com

CONNECTICUT

Hartford

ACCOMMODATIONS
1 **Butternut Farm** [GS,NS] 860/633-7197 ■ 1654 Main St, Glastonbury ■ *18th-c house furnished w/ antiques, full brkfst* ■ www.butternutfarmbandb.com
2 **The Mansion Inn** [GF] 860/646-0453 ■ 139 Hartford Rd (at Main St), Manchester ■ *B&B, full brkfst, in-room fireplaces* ■ www.themansioninnct.com

BARS
3 **Chez Est** [★MW,D,F,K,DS] 860/525-3243 ■ 458 Wethersfield Ave (at Main St) ■ *3pm-1am, till 2am Fri-Sat, women's night 2nd Sat, Latin night 3rd Sat* ■ www.chezest.com
4 **The Polo Club** [MW,D,E,K,DS,S] 860/278-3333 ■ 678 Maple Ave (btwn Preston & Mapleton) ■ *8pm-1am, till 2am Fri-Sat, clsd Sun-Wed* ■ www.hartfordpoloclub.com
5 **Women After Hours** [WO,D,$] 860/930-8844 ■ 30 Roberts St (at East Hartford Holiday Inn), East Hartford ■ *monthly dance/ social, please call for schedule* ■ www.wahdance.com

NIGHTCLUBS
3 Club Lucy [W,D] 860/525-3243 ■ 458 Wethersfield Ave (at Chez Est) ■ *2nd Sat only, monthly women's party* ■ www.clublucy.com

CAFES
Tisane Tea & Coffee Bar 860/523-5417 ■ 537 Farmington Ave ■ *7am-1am, 8am-1:30am wknds*

RESTAURANTS
Arugula [R,WC] 860/561-4888 ■ 953 Farmington Ave, West Hartford ■ *lunch & dinner, clsd Sun-Mon, Mediterranean*
Dishes Restaurant & Comet Lounge [MW] 860/525-3474 ■ 267 Farmington Ave ■ *brkfst, lunch & dinner, full bar* ■ www.dishesrestaurant.com
Peppercorns Grill 860/547-1714 ■ 357 Main St ■ *lunch Mon-Fri, dinner only Sat, Northern Italian* ■ www.peppercornsgrill.com
Pond House Cafe [BYOB,WC] 860/231-8823 ■ 155 Asylum Ave ■ *lunch & dinner Tue-Sat, Sun brunch, patio* ■ www.pondhousecafe.com
Trumbull Kitchen 860/493-7417 ■ 150 Trumbull St (at Pearl St) ■ *lunch Mon-Fri, dinner nightly, global cuisine/ tapas* ■ www.trumbullkitchen.com

HARTFORD

Day Trips: Get out and enjoy those glorious New England fall colors! For a nearby country-mouse excursion, tour the Farmington Valley just west of Greater Hartford.
   In warm weather, you may enjoy a jaunt to the shore. Try Hammonasset Beach, in Madison, the state's largest public beach. Two miles of white-sand beach!

Tourist Info
AIRPORT DIRECTIONS
Hartford Bradley Airport. To get to State Capitol, take 91 North toward Hartford and exit on Capitol Ave. Head west on Capitol Ave.
PUBLIC TRANSIT & TAXIS
Yellow Cab 860/666-6666.
Kne Transportation 860/522-8101.
Connecticut Transit 860/522-8101, web: www.cttransit.com.
TOURIST SPOTS & INFO
Bushnell Park Carousel & Museum 860/585-5411, web: www.bushnellpark.org.
Harriet Beecher Stowe Center 860/522-9258, web: www.harrietbeecherstowecenter.org.
Mark Twain House 860/247-0998, web: www.marktwainhouse.org.
Real Art Ways 860/232-1006, web: www.realartways.org.
Wadsworth Atheneum Museum of Art 860/278-2670, web: www.wadsworthatheneum.org.
Visitor's Center: Greater Hartford Tourism District 800/446-7811, web: www.enjoyhartford.com.

Weather
Summer highs are in the low 80°s. But that 50%+ humidity will make it feel like more. Humidity all year round. Winter drops into the low 20°s. January is the coldest and snowiest month. The full four seasons are in effect.

City Calendar
LGBT PRIDE
September, web: www.connecticutpride.com.
ANNUAL EVENTS
June - Conneticut Gay & Lesbian Film Festival, web: ctglff.org

Queer Resources
COMMUNITY INFO
Connecticut Pride Center 860/724-5542. 1841 Broad St, 10am-6pm, wknd hours vary, web: www.ctpridecenter.org.
AA at Community Center 860/724-5542.
Hartford Gay & Lesbian Health Collective 860/278-4163, web: www.hglhc.org.

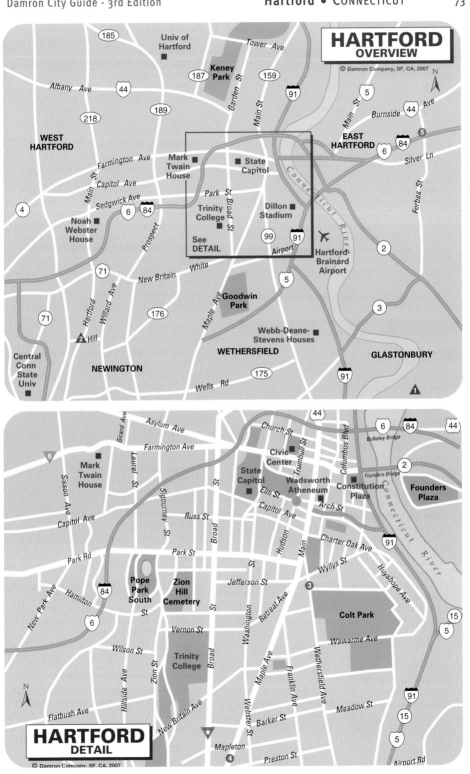

HARTFORD OVERVIEW
© Damron Company, SF, CA, 2007

Univ of Hartford
Tower Ave
Keney Park
WEST HARTFORD
Albany Ave
Garden St
Main St
EAST HARTFORD
Burnside
Ave
Silver Ln
Main St
Connecticut River
Mark Twain House
State Capitol
Farmington Ave
Capitol Ave
Sedgwick Ave
Noah Webster House
Prospect
Park St
Broad St
Trinity College
Dillon Stadium
Airport
Hartford-Brainard Airport
See DETAIL
White
New Britain
Forbes St
Maple Ave
Hill
Goodwin Park
Central Conn State Univ
NEWINGTON
Webb-Deane-Stevens Houses
WETHERSFIELD
GLASTONBURY
Wells Rd

HARTFORD DETAIL
© Damron Company, SF, CA, 2007

Asylum Ave
Girard Ave
Farmington Ave
Church St
Trumbull St
Columbus Blvd
Bulkeley Bridge
Mark Twain House
Sisson Ave
Laurel St
Sigourney St
Civic Center
State Capitol
Wadsworth Atheneum
Elm St
Arch St
Constitution Plaza
Founders Bridge
Founders Plaza
Capitol Ave
Capitol Ave
Russ St
Broad St
Hudson St
Main St
Charter Oak Ave
Connecticut River
Park Rd
Park St
Pope Park South
Zion Hill Cemetery
Jefferson St
Wyllys St
Huyshope Ave
New Park Ave
Hamilton
Wilson St
Zion St
Vernon St
Washington St
Retreat Ave
Colt Park
Wawarme Ave
Broad St
Hillside Ave
Trinity College
Maple Ave
Wetherfield Ave
Franklin Ave
Meadow St
Flatbush Ave
New Britain Ave
Webster St
Barker St
Mapleton
Preston St
Airport Rd

ENTERTAINMENT & RECREATION

Connecticut Sun 877/786-8499 ■ 1 Mohegan Sun Blvd (Mohegan Sun Area), Uncasville ■ *check out the Women's National Basketball Association while you're in Hartford* ■ www.wnba.com/sun

UConn Huskies 877/288-2666 ■ 1266 Storrs Rd (at Gampel Pavilion), Storrs ■ *basketball, also plays at Hartford Civic Center, 860/ 727-8010* ■ uconnhuskies.com

RETAIL SHOPS

6 **MetroStore** 860/231-8845 ■ 493 Farmington Ave (at Sisson Ave) ■ *8:30am-8pm, till 5:30pm Tue, Wed & Sat, clsd Sun, magazines, travel guides, leather, DVD rentals & more* ■ metrostore@metroline-online.com

PUBLICATIONS

Metroline 860/233-8334 ■ *regional newspaper & entertainment guide, covers CT, RI & MA* ■ www.metroline-online.com

EROTICA

Aircraft Book & News 860/569-2324 ■ 349 Main St (at Pratt), East Hartford ■ *adult videos & DVDs, toys* ■ www.bookends2.com

Erotic Zone [AYOR] 860/549-1896 ■ 35 W Service Rd (at Hwy 91 N) ■ *hustlers*

Very Intimate Pleasures 860/246-1875 ■ 100 Brainard Rd (exit 27, off I-91)

DELAWARE

Rehoboth Beach

ACCOMMODATIONS

An Inn by the Bay [GS,NS,GO] 302/644-8878, 866/833-2565 ■ 205 Savannah Rd, Lewes ■ *hot tub* ■ www.aninnbythebay.com

1 **At Melissa's B&B** [GS,NS] 302/227-7504, 800/396-8090 ■ 36 Delaware Ave (btwn 1st & 2nd) ■ *women-owned/ run, 1 block from beach* ■ www.atmelissas.com

2 **Bellmoor Inn** [GF,SW,WI] 302/227-5800, 800/425-2355 ■ 6 Christian St ■ *upscale inn & spa* ■ www.thebellmoor.com

3 **Breakers Hotel & Suites** [GF,WC] 302/227-6688, 800/441-8009 ■ 105 Second St ■ *hotel adjacent to Lake Gerar* ■ www.thebreakershotel.com

4 **Cabana Gardens B&B** [GS,SW,NS,GO] 302/227-5429 ■ 20 Lake Ave (at 3rd St) ■ *ocean views, rooftop deck* ■ www.cabanagardens.com

5 **Canalside Inn** [GS,SW,NS,WI,WC,GO] 302/226-2006, 866/412-2625 ■ Canal at 6th ■ *inn w/in walking distance of beach* ■ www.canalside-inn-rehoboth.com

6 **Delaware Inn B&B** [GF,SW,GO] 302/227-6031, 800/246-5244 ■ 55 Delaware Ave ■ *country inn atmosphere, near beach* ■ www.delawareinn.com

The Homestead at Rehoboth B&B [GF,SW,NS,WC,GO] 302/226-7625 ■ 35060 Warrington Rd ■ *small dogs ok, lesbian-owned* ■ www.homesteadatrehoboth.com

Lazy L at Willow Creek [GS,SW,WI,GO] 302/644-7220 ■ 16061 Willow Creek Rd (at Hwy 1), Lewes ■ *full brkfst, hot tub, very pet-friendly, lesbian-owned* ■ www.lazyl.net

7 **The Lighthouse Inn B&B** [GS,NS,WI,GO] 302/226-0407 ■ 20 Delaware Ave ■ *seasonal, B&B, also apt (weekly rental), 1 block from beach, kids/ pets ok* ■ www.lighthouseinn.net

8 **Pine-n-Brine 101** [GF,NS,WC,GO] 410/757-6951 ■ 29 Maryland Ave, #101 ■ *2-bdrm condo* ■ www.rehobothcondo.com

The Ram's Head [MO,SW,N,GO] 302/226-9171 ■ 35006 Warrington Rd ■ *hot tub & sauna, gym* ■ www.theramshead.com

9 **Rehoboth Guest House** [MW,NS,WI,GO] 302/227-4117, 800/564-0493 ■ 40 Maryland Ave (btwn 1st & 2nd Sts) ■ *Victorian beach house, near boardwalk & beach* ■ www.rehobothguesthouse.com

10 **The Royal Rose Inn** [GS,GO] 302/226-2535 ■ 41 Baltimore Ave ■ *sundeck* ■ royalroseinn.com

11 **Sea Witch Manor Inn & Spa** [GS,NS,WC,GO] 302/226-9482, 866/732-9482 ■ 71 Lake Ave (at Rehoboth Ave) ■ *3-house B&B (2 Hollywood-themed: Bewitched & BEDazzled), full brkfst, hot tub* ■ www.seawitchmanor.com

12 **Shore Inn at Rehoboth** [MO,SW,WI,N,GO] 302/227-8487, 800/597-8899 ■ 703 Rehoboth Ave (across from Double L Bar) ■ *hot tub, sundeck, across from Double L bar* ■ www.shoreinn.com

13 **Silver Lake Guest House** [MW,NS,WI,GO] 302/226-2115, 800/842-2115 ■ 133 Silver Lake Dr ■ *near Poodle Beach* ■ www.silverlakeguesthouse.com

14 **Summer Place Hotel** [GS] 302/226-0766, 800/815-3925 ■ 30 Olive Ave (at 1st) ■ *also apts, near beach* ■ www.rehobothsummerplace.com

BARS

15 **The Blue Moon** [★MW] 302/227-6515 ■ 35 Baltimore Ave (btwn 1st & 2nd) ■ *6pm-2am, clsd Jan, popular happy hour, [E,DS] Th (summers), also top-rated restaurant, dinner, Sun brunch* ■ www.bluemoonrehoboth.com

16 **Dogfish Head Brewings & Eats** [GF,F,E] 302/226-2739 ■ 320 Rehoboth Ave ■ *micro-brewery, wood-grilled food* ■ www.dogfish.com

17 **Double L Bar** [M,L,B] 302/227-0818 ■ 622 Rehoboth Ave ■ *3pm-2am, patio* ■ www.doublelbar.com

18 **Finbar** [GF,F,E] 302/227-1873 ■ 316-318 Rehoboth Ave ■ *from 3pm, from noon Sat-Sun, clsd Mon-Tue, traditional pub, popular happy hour, also restaurant*

19 **Frogg Pond** [GF,NH,F,E,K] 302/227-2234 ■ 3 S 1st St (near Rehoboth Ave) ■ *11am-1am, from 10am Sun, popular happy hour, popular w/ women in summer, women's T-dance Sun* ■ www.thefroggpond.com

20 **Partners Bistro & Piano Bar** [GS,F,P,GO] 302/226-0207 ■ 404 Rehoboth Ave (at State St) ■ *noon-1am, from 11am Sun, also restaurant* ■ www.partners-bistro.com

NIGHTCLUBS

Ladies 2000 856/869-0193 ■ *seasonal parties, call hotline or check website for details* ■ www.ladies2000.com

21 **Rouge** [★M,D,$] 302/226-5900 ■ 59 Lake Ave (at 59 Lake), Dewey Beach ■ *10pm-2am Sat, [D] from 11pm* ■ www.myspace.com/rougerehoboth

22 **Sky Bar** [★MW,D,WC] 302/226-1999 ■ 234 Rehoboth Ave (at Cloud 9) ■ *nightly, men's dance 10pm Fri-Sat, Ladies Tea 5pm Fri-Sat, [K] Mon & Th*

CAFES

The Coffee Mill [WI,GO] 302/227-7530, 888/227-7530 ■ 127B Rehoboth Mews ■ *7:30am-11pm, till 5pm (off-season), lesbian-owned* ■ www.coffees2u.com

Lori's Cafe [GO] 302/226-3066 ■ 39 Baltimore Ave (at 1st) ■ *seasonal, also sandwiches, courtyard* ■ www.lorisoyvey-cafe.com

RESTAURANTS

59 Lake [E,C] 302/226-5900 ▪ 59 Lake Ave ▪ *from 6pm Wed-Sun, upscale contemporary, also martini lounge from 4pm [E,C], also Rouge [M,D] 10pm Sat* ▪ www.59lake.com

Abstractions Sushi Bar & Restaurant 302/226-0877 ▪ 203 Rehoboth Ave ▪ *5pm daily (March-Jan)* ▪ www.rehoboth.com/abstractions/

Aqua Grill [E,P] 302/226-9001 ▪ 57 Baltimore Ave ▪ *seasonal, deck, full bar* ▪ www.aquagrillrehoboth.com

Back Porch Cafe [WC] 302/227-3674 ▪ 59 Rehoboth Ave ▪ *lunch & dinner, Sun brunch, seasonal* ▪ www.backporch-cafe.com

Blue Plate Diner 302/644-8400 ▪ 329 Savannah Rd, Lewes ▪ *Fri-Mon (seasonal)*

Buttery 302/645-7755 ▪ 102 2nd St, Lewes ▪ *lunch, dinner, Sun brunch, fine dining in elegant Victorian, reservations suggested* ▪ butteryrestaurant.com

Cafe Sole 302/227-7107 ▪ 44 Baltimore Ave ▪ *lunch daily, dinner Wed-Sun, casual, patio, also full bar* ▪ www.rehoboth.com/cafesole

Cafe Zeus [★GO] 302/226-0400 ▪ 37 Wilmington Ave ▪ *dinner only, Mediterranean, patio, also bar, Sun T-dance* ▪ www.cafezeus.com

Celsius [WC] 302/227-5767 ▪ 50-C Wilmington Ave ▪ *dinner (clsd Th), Sun brunch, French-Mediterranean*

Cloud 9 [★D,WC] 302/226-1999 ▪ 234 Rehoboth Ave (at 2nd) ▪ *4pm-2am, Sun brunch from 11am, fusion bistro, also Sky Bar nightly, men's dance 10pm Fri-Sat, Ladies Tea 5pm Fri-Sat, [K] Mon & Th*

The Cultured Pearl 302/227-8493 ▪ 301 Rehoboth Ave (2nd flr) ▪ *dinner, lunch Th-Mon, clsd Mon-Wed off-season, pan-Asian, cocktail lounge* ▪ culturedpearl.us

Dish 302/226-2112 ▪ 26 Baltimore Ave ▪ *dinner Th-Sun, "a retro dining gallery," also Lava Lounge* ▪ www.dishrehoboth.com

Dos Locos [★] 302/227-3353 ▪ 10 Wilmington Ave (btwn Baltimore & Rehoboth) ▪ *5pm-10pm, till 11pm wknds, full bar till 1am, clsd Mon-Wed, Mexican* ▪ www.rehoboth.com/doslocos

Eden [★WC] 302/227-3330 ▪ 23 Baltimore Ave ▪ *dinner Wed-Sat, seasonal, "bold" American, wine list & martini bar* ▪ www.edenrestaurant.com

Espuma 302/227-4199 ▪ 28 Wilmington Ave ▪ *6pm-10pm, clsd Mon, modern Mediterranean, full bar from 5pm* ▪ www.espumarestaurant.com

Go Fish! 302/226-1044 ▪ 24 Rehoboth Ave ▪ *11:30am-9:30pm (in-season), seafood & authentic British fish & chips* ▪ www.gofishdelaware.com

Iguana Grill 302/227-0948 ▪ 52 Baltimore Ave ▪ *lunch & dinner (summers), Southwestern, full bar, patio* ▪ www.iguanagrill.com

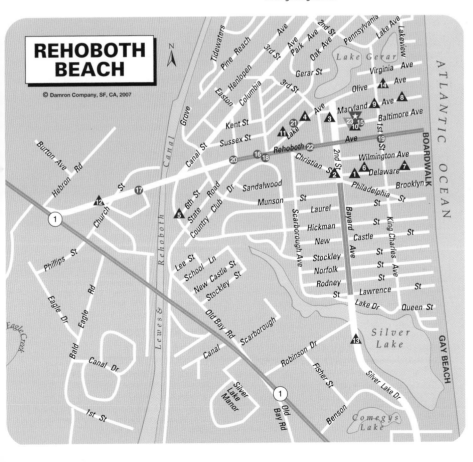

REHOBOTH BEACH

© Damron Company, SF, CA, 2007

Jerry's Seafood 302/645-6611 ■ 108 2nd St, Lewes ■ *lunch & dinner daily, "home of the crab bomb"* ■ www.jerrys-seafood.com

Just in Thyme 302/227-3100 ■ 31 Robinson St ■ *seafood & steak by candlelight, also Sun brunch, local favorite*

La La Land 302/227-3887 ■ 22 Wilmington Ave ■ *6pm-1am (seasonal), seafood & more, full bar, patio* ■ www.lalalandrestaurant.com

Mariachi [NS,WC] 302/227-0226 ■ 14 Wilmington Ave ■ *11am-10pm, till 11pm Fri-Sat, Mexican-Latin American, 2 bars* ■ www.mariachirehobothde.com

Planet X Cafe 302/226-1928 ■ 35 Wilmington Ave ■ *seasonal, lunch, dinner, Sun brunch, organic global cuisine, some veggie, friendly service, kitschy decor housed in converted Victorian*

Purple Parrot Grill [K,DS,WC] 302/226-1139 ■ 134 Rehoboth Ave ■ *lunch & dinner daily, brunch Sun, karaoke & drag shows wknds* ■ ppgrill@aol.com

Queenz Quizine 302/227-0447 ■ 20200 Coastal Hwy ■ *11am-4pm, clsd Sat-Sun, carryout & catering, homemade soups, sandwiches & salads*

Retro Cafe 302/227-9752 ■ 12 Wilmington Ave ■ *8am-3pm Fri-Mon, brkfst & lunch, Beignet Day Fri w/ chicory coffee*

S.O.B.'s Deli 302/226-2226 ■ 56 Baltimore Ave ■ *from 10am (in-season)* ■ rehobothdirectory.com/sobsdeli.html

Seaside Thai 302/227-9525 ■ 19 Rehoboth Ave ■ *1 block from beach*

Tijuana Taxi [WC] 302/227-1986 ■ 207 Rehoboth Ave (at 2nd St) ■ *dinner Wed-Sun, lunch Fri-Sun, full bar*

REHOBOTH BEACH

A popular seaside resort, Rehoboth Beach attracts vacationers from Washington, DC, and the surrounding areas each summer. The charming mixture of eateries, shops (no sales tax!), and beaches makes for a relaxing atmosphere.

Tourist Info

AIRPORT DIRECTIONS

Rehoboth Beach is within 1 1/2 hours of several airports: Baltimore-Washington International, Greater Wilmington, Ronald Reagan Washington National, Philadelphia International.

PUBLIC TRANSIT & TAXIS

Seaport Taxi 302/645-6800.

Jolly Trolley 302/227-1197 (seasonal tour & shuttle), web: www.jollytrolley.com.

Cape May-Lewes Ferry (80-minute ferry ride between N Cape May, NJ & Lewes, DE), 800/643-3779, web: www.capemaylewesferry.com.

TOURIST SPOTS & INFO

Anna Hazzard Museum, 302/226-1119. Photos & memorabilia from when Rehoboth was a Christian resort.

DiscoverSea Shipwreck Museum, Fenwick Island, 302/539-9366, web: discoversea.com.

Dolphin- & whale-watching July-Oct. Boat tours leave from Fisherman's Wharf in Lewes, DE. 302/645-8862, web: www.fishlewes.com/sightseeing.html.

Main Street 302/227-2772, web: www.rehomain.com.

Rehoboth Beach Boardwalk with 2 amusement parks (Funland, web: www.funlandRehoboth.com, & Playland).

Tanger Outlets, 302/226-9223, web: www.tanger-outlet.com. 130 designer stores with no sales tax.

Visitor's Center: Rehoboth Beach-Dewey Beach Chamber of Commerce 302/227-2233 & 800/441-1329, web: www.beach-fun.com.

Weather

You're not far from DC, but you're on the coast. So, yes, it does get hot and muggy in the summers (90s for temps and humidity), but you can take a dip in the ocean. In the winter, a lot of businesses close as the temperatures drop along with the occasional snow flurries.

Best Views

Watching the sun rise over the bay at Dewey Beach or eating a swanky sunset dinner at Victoria's (www.boardwalkplaza.com/restaurant.htm) on the Boardwalk.

City Calendar

LGBT PRIDE

Every day, but Wilmington has their pride here in September.

ANNUAL EVENTS

April/ May - Cabaret Fest.

July - Fireworks 302/227-2772, web: www.rehomain.com/fireworks.html.

October - Rehoboth Beach Autumn Jazz Festival, web: www.rehobothjazz.com.

October - Sea Witch Halloween Festival.

November - Rehoboth Beach Independent Film Festival 302/645-9095, web: www.rehobothfilm.com.

Queer Resources

COMMUNITY INFO

Camp Rehoboth 302/227-5620. 37 Baltimore Ave, web: www.camprehoboth.com. Drop-in community center, 9am-5:30pm Mon-Fri, 10am-4pm wknds (April-Dec).

Lesbian/ Gay AA 302/856-6452, web: www.sussexaa.org. Narcotics Anonymous 302/227-5620 (Camp Rehoboth #).

Venus on the Halfshell [★] 302/227-9292 ■ 136 Dagsworth St, Dewey Beach ■ *seasonal, waterside Asian-inspired restaurant w/ fun Morocco-Meets-the-Far-East setting*

ENTERTAINMENT & RECREATION

Cape Henlopen State Park Beach 302/645-8983 ■ 42 Cape Henlopen Dr, Lewes ■ *8am-sunset* ■ www.destateparks.com/chsp/chsp.htm

North Shores S end of Cape Henlopen State Park (at jetty S of watch tower) ■ *popular women's beach, 20-minute walk from boardwalk*

Poodle Beach S of boardwalk at Queen St ■ *popular gay beach*

BOOKSTORES

23 Lambda Rising [WC] 302/227-6969 ■ 39 Baltimore Ave (btwn 1st & 2nd) ■ *11am-8pm, till 10pm Fri-Sat, 10am-midnight summers, LGBT* ■ www.lambdarising.com

RETAIL SHOPS

Leather Central 302/227-0700 ■ 4284A Hwy 1 (on the service road) ■ *10am-6pm, till 5pm Sun, clsd Tue-Wed, leather uniforms, toys, accessories* ■ www.leathercentral.net

The Pelican Loft Home & Garden Gift Shop [GO] 302/226-5080 ■ 49 Baltimore Ave ■ *lesbian-owned* ■ www.pelicanloft.com

PUBLICATIONS

EXP Magazine 302/227-5787, 877/397-6244 ■ *bi-weekly gay magazine for Mid-Atlantic* ■ www.expmagazine.com

Letters from Camp Rehoboth 302/227-5620 ■ *newsmagazine w/ events & entertainment listings* ■ www.camprehoboth.com

GYMS & HEALTH CLUBS

Body Shop 302/226-0920 ■ 401 N Boardwalk (at Virginia) ■ *8am-7pm, till 6pm Sun, on the beach, $12 day pass* ■ www.rehoboth.com/bodyshop

The Firm Fitness Center 302/227-8363 ■ 6 Camelot Shopping Center/ Rte 1 ■ *$10 day pass*

Gold's Gym 302/226-4653 ■ 3712 Hwy 1, #11 ■ *6am-10pm, 7am-8pm Sat, 8am-5pm Sun* ■ www.goldsgym.com/rehobothbeachde

Midway Fitness 302/645-0407 ■ Midway Shopping Center #28B (on Rte 1, NW of John J Williams Hwy) ■ *$12 day pass, racquetball* ■ www.midwayfitness.com

Washington

ACCOMMODATIONS

1 ➤The Bed & Breakfast at the William Lewis House [★M,GO] 202/462-7574, 800/465-7574 ■ 1309 R St NW (at 13th) ■ *2 turn-of-the-century buildings, full brkfst wknds, hot tub* ■ www.wlewishous.com

2 Bloomingdale Inn [GF] 202/319-0801 ■ 2417 1st St NW (at Bryant) ■ *Victorian town house* ■ www.BloomingdaleInn.com

11 The Braxton Hotel [GS,WI] 202/232-7800 ■ 1440 Rhode Island Ave NW (btwn 14th & 15th) ■ *conveniently located in Dupont/ Logon Circle Historic District* ■ www.braxtonhotel.com

3 The Carlyle Suites Hotel [GS,F,WC] 202/234-3200, 866/468-3532 ■ 1731 New Hampshire Ave NW (btwn R & S Sts) ■ *art deco hotel, gym, also restaurant & bar, popular gay Sun brunch* ■ www.carlylesuites.com

Chez Aimee [GF,NS,WI] 202/669-7708, 202/669-7708 (cell) ■ *flat in 1910-era rowhouse in Adams Morgan district* ■ www.staychezaimee.com

4 Comfort Inn Downtown DC—Convention Center [GS,WC] 202/682-5300, 877/424-6423 ■ 1201 13th St NW ■ www.choicehotels.com/hotel/DC601

5 DC GuestHouse [GS,WI,GO] 202/332-2502 ■ 1337 10th St NW ■ *full brkfst* ■ www.dcguesthouse.com

6 Doubletree Hotel–Washington [GF] 202/232-7000 ■ 1515 Rhode Island Ave NW ■ www.doubletreewashington.com

7 Dupont at The Circle [GS,NS,WI] 202/332-5251, 888/412-0100 ■ 1604 19th St NW (at Q St) ■ *Victorian at Dupont Circle* ■ www.dupontatthecircle.com

8 The Embassy Inn [GF,WI] 202/234-7800, 800/423-9111 ■ 1627 16th St NW ■ *small hotel w/ B&B atmosphere*

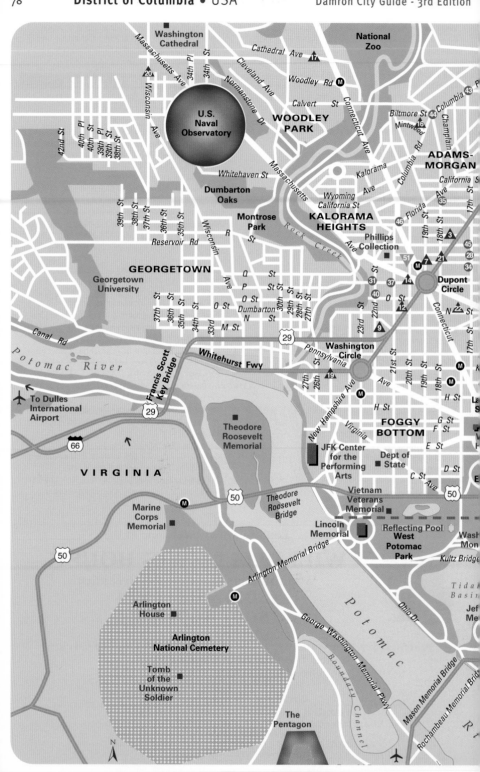

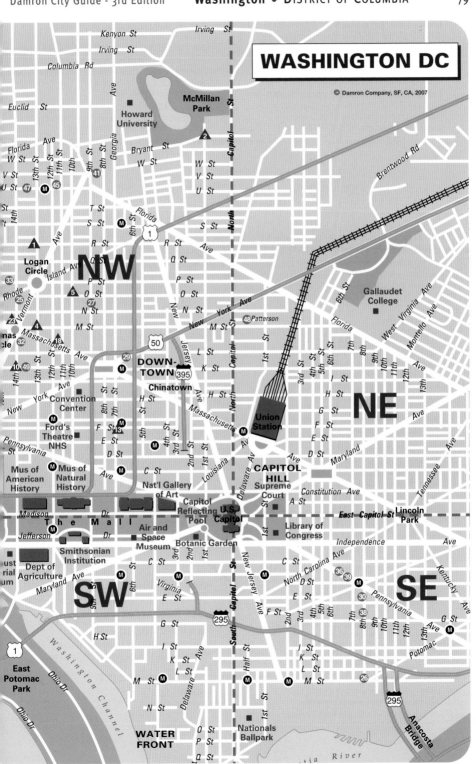

WASHINGTON DC

© Damron Company, SF, CA, 2007

Embassy Suites Alexandria [GS,SW] 703/684-5900, 800/362-2779 ■ 1900 Diagonal Rd, Alexandria, VA ■ *full brkfst* ■ www.embassysuites.com/en/es

Embassy Suites Hotel at the Chevy Chase Pavilion [GF,SW,WC] 202/362-9300, 800/362-2779 ■ 4300 Military Rd NW ■ www.embassysuitesdcmetro.com

Embassy Suites Tysons Corner [GF,SW,WC] 703/883-0707, 800/362-2779 ■ 8517 Leesburg Pike, Vienna, VA ■ *upscale hotel in heart of Tysons Corner, full brkfst, kids ok* ■ www.embassysuites.com

9   **Embassy Suites Washington, DC** [GF,SW,WI] 202/857-3388, 800/362-2779 ■ 1250 22nd St NW ■ *luxury hotel between Dupont Circle & Georgetown, full brkfst* ■ www.embassysuites.com

10   **Hamilton Crowne Plaza Hotel** [GF,NS,WC] 800/263-9802 ■ 14th & K St, NW ■ *full brkfst* ■ www.hamiltonhoteldc.com

11   **Hotel Helix** [GF,WC,WI] 202/462-9001, 800/706-1202 ■ 1430 Rhode Island Ave NW ■ *full-service boutique hotel, also Helix Lounge* ■ www.hotelhelix.com

12   **Hotel Madera** [GF,WI,WC] 202/296-7600, 800/430-1202 ■ 1310 New Hampshire Ave NW (at N) ■ *boutique hotel, Firefly bistro adjacent* ■ www.hotelmadera.com

WASHINGTON DC

Day Trips: New Market, MD (approximately 50 miles)

This small historic town is an antique-collector's paradise. Though fairly quiet during the week (look for flags flying signifying an open shop), the town can get pretty busy with tourists on weekends. Stroll Main Street for all kinds of shops full of china, clocks, porcelain, jewelry, furniture, and much more. Stop in at the Village Tea Room or Mealey's to recharge over a leisurely meal, and then get back out there and shop till the sun drops!

Tourist Info

AIRPORT DIRECTIONS

Washington Dulles International. To get downtown, take Dulles Airport Access and Toll Rd to I-66 and head east into Washington. Baltimore/Washington International. To get downtown, follow 46 out of airport to the Baltimore/Washington Expressway. Take a left on the Expressway and head south to Washington.

PUBLIC TRANSIT & TAXIS

Yellow Cab 202/544-1212.
Washington Flier 703/661-6655 (from Dulles or Ronald Reagan National).
Super Shuttle 800/258-3826.
Metro Transit Authority 202/637-7000, web: www.wmata.com.

TOURIST SPOTS & INFO

Ford's Theatre 202/347-4833, web: www.fordstheatre.org.
Jefferson Memorial.
JFK Center for the Performing Arts 800/444-1324, web: www.kennedy-center.org.
Lincoln Memorial.
National Gallery 202/737-4215, web: www.nga.gov.
National Museum of Women in the Arts 202/783-5000, web: www.nmwa.org.
National Zoo 202/633-4800, web: natzoo.si.edu.
Smithsonian 202/357-2425, web: www.smithsonianeducation.org.
Vietnam Veteran's Memorial.
United States Holocaust Memorial Museum 202/488-0400, web: www.ushmm.org.
Visitor's Center: DC Convention & Tourism Corporation. 800/422-8644, web: www.washington.org.

Weather

Summers are hot (90°s) and MUGGY (the city was built on marshes). In the winter, temperatures drop to the 30°s and 40°s with rain and sometimes snow. Spring is the time of cherry blossoms.

Best Views

From the top of the Washington Monument.

City Calendar

LGBT PRIDE

May. Black Lesbian/ Gay Pride 202/737-5767, web: www.dcblackpride.org.
June. 202/797-3510, web: www.capitalpride.org.

ENTERTAINMENT

Gay Men's Chorus of Washington 202/338-7464, web: www.gmcw.org.

ANNUAL EVENTS

March - Women's History Month at various Smithsonian Museums 202/357-2425, web: www.smithsonianeducation.org.
October - Reel Affirmations Film Festival 202/986-1119, web: www.reelaffirmations.org.

Queer Resources

COMMUNITY INFO

Metro Weekly, web: www.metroweekly.com.
Washington Blade, web: www.washblade.com.
AA 202/966-9115.
Whitman-Walker Clinic 202/797-3500, web: www.wwc.org.

13 **Hotel Monaco Washington DC** [GF,WC,WI] 202/628-7177, 800/649-1202 ■ 700 F St NW (at 7th) ■ *boutique hotel* ■ www.monaco-dc.com

14 **Hotel Palomar** [GF,F,SW,WC] 202/448-1800, 800/546-7866 ■ 2121 P St NW (at 21st St) ■ *in Dupont Circle* ■ www.hotelpalomar-dc.com

15 **Hotel Rouge** [GF,WI,WC] 202/232-8000, 800/368-5689 ■ 1315 16th St NW (at Rhode Island) ■ *ultra-hip, high-tech luxury hotel, also restaurant & bar* ■ www.rougehotel.com

16 **Kalorama Guest House at Kalorama Park** [GS,NS,WI] 202/667-6369 ■ 1854 Mintwood Pl NW (at Columbia Rd) ■ *Victorian town house near Dupont Circle, restaurants* ■ www.kaloramaguesthouse.com

17 **Kalorama Guest House at Woodley Park** [GS,NS,WI] 202/328-0860 ■ 2700 Cathedral Ave NW (off Connecticut Ave) ■ *near National Zoo & Washington Cathedral* ■ www.kaloramaguesthouse.com

18 **Morrison-Clark Historic Inn & Restaurant** [GF,WI] 202/898-1200, 800/322-7898 ■ 1015 L St NW (at Massachusetts Ave NW) ■ *hotel in 2 Victorian town houses w/ very popular restaurant* ■ www.morrisonclark.com

Otis Place B&B [GS,GO] 202/483-0241, 877/893-3233 ■ 1003 Otis Place NW ■ *Victorian townhouse* ■ ww.bedandbreakfastdc.com

19 **The River Inn** [GF,WI,WC] 202/337-7600, 888/874-0100 ■ 924 25th St NW (at K St) ■ *suites w/ kitchen, gym, also Dish restaurant* ■ www.theriverinn.com

20 **Savoy Suites Hotel** [GF,WI,WC] 202/337-9700, 800/944-5377 ■ 2505 Wisconsin Ave NW (at Calvert, in Georgetown) ■ *also Italian restaurant* ■ www.savoysuites.com

21 **Swann House Historic B&B** [GS,SW,WI] 202/265-4414 ■ 1808 New Hampshire Ave NW (at Swann St) ■ *1883 Victorian mansion in Dupont Circle, roof deck, fireplaces* ■ www.swannhouse.com

22 **Topaz Hotel** [GF,WI,WC] 202/393-3000, 800/424-2950 ■ 1733 N St NW ■ *boutique hotel, also restaurant & bar* ■ www.topazhotel.com

23 **Washington Plaza** [GF,SW] 202/842-1300, 800/424-1140 ■ 10 Thomas Cir NW (at 14th & Massachusetts) ■ *full-service hotel, also restaurant* ■ www.washingtonplazahotel.com

24 **The Windsor Inn** [GF,WI] 202/667-0300, 800/423-9111 ■ 1842 16th St NW ■ *small hotel w/ B&B atmosphere*

Bars

25 **1409 Playbill Cafe** [MW,F] 202/265-3055 ■ 1409 14th St NW ■ *4pm-2am, till 3am Fri-Sat, 11am-2am Sun, also theater*

26 **Back Door Pub** [M,D,MR-AF,F,S,WC] 202/546-5979 ■ 1104 8th St SE, 2nd flr (at L St) ■ *5pm-2am, till 3am Fri-Sat*

27 **Be Bar** [MW,D] 202/232-7450 ■ 1318 9th St NW ■ *5pm-2am, till 3am Fri-Sat, Ladies Night Wed* ■ www.bebardc.com

28 **Club Chaos** [MW,D,MR,TG,F,WC] 202/232-4141 ■ 1603 17th St NW (at Q St) ■ *6pm-2am, till 3am Fri-Sat, women's night Wed, also restaurant* ■ www.chaosdc.com

29 **DC Eagle** [★M,L,WC] 202/347-6025 ■ 639 New York Ave NW (btwn 6th & 7th) ■ *4pm-2am, noon-3am Fri-Sat, noon-2am Sun* ■ www.dceagle.com

29 **DC Eagle Dyke Night** [★W,L,WC] 639 New York Ave NW (btwn 6th & 7th) ■ *women's night 4th Wed only* ■ groups.yahoo.com/group/dceagleladykenight/

28 **DIK Bar/ Windows** [M,D,K,OC] 202/328-0100, 202/234-5747 ■ 1637 17th St NW (near 16th St NW, upstairs) ■ *4pm-2am, till 3am Fri-Sat, 3pm-2am Sun* ■ dupontitaliankitchen.com/D_I_K__Bar/d_i_k__bar.html

30 **Ellington's on 8th** [MW,F,E] 202/546-8308 ■ 424-A 8th St SE ■ *dinner, brunch wknds, clsd Mon-Tue, live jazz* ■ www.ellon8thjazz.tk

31 **The Fireplace** [M,NH,MR,V,WC] 202/293-1293 ■ 2161 P St NW (at 22nd St) ■ *1pm-2am, till 3am Fri-Sat*

32 **Green Lantern** [M,NH,K,V] 202/347-4533 ■ 1335 Green Court NW (in alley, L St btwn 13th & 14th) ■ *1:30pm-2am, till 3am Fri, 4pm-3am Sat, 1pm-2am Sun* ■ greenlanterndc.com

33 **Halo** [MW,NH] 202/797-9730 ■ 1435 P St NW ■ *5pm-close* ■ www.theartoflounge.com

34 **JR's** [★M,NH,F,V,YC] 202/328-0090 ■ 1519 17th St NW (at Church) ■ *2pm-2am, till 3am Fri, 1pm-3am Sat, 1pm-2am Sun, cruisy, hot cocktail hour* ■ www.jrswdc.com

35 **Larry's Lounge** [MW,NH,F,WC] 202/483-1483 ■ 1840 18th St NW (at T St) ■ *4pm-1am, till 3am Fri-Sat, also Malaysian restaurant* ■ www.straitsofmalaya.com

36 **Mr Henry's Capitol Hill** [★GF,MR,E,NS] 202/546-8412 ■ 601 Pennsylvania Ave SE (at 6th St) ■ *11:30am-11:30pm, live jazz Fri, also restaurant*

37 **Omega** [★M,MR,K,DS,S,V] 202/223-4917 ■ 2122 P St NW (enter rear) ■ *4pm-2am, till 3am Fri, 8pm-3am Sat, 7pm-2am Sun* ■ www.omegadc.com

38 **Phase One** [W,NH,D,MR,WC] 202/544-6831 ■ 525 8th St SE (btwn E & G Sts) ■ *7pm-2am, till 3am Fri-Sat (clsd Mon-Wed winter)* ■ www.phase1dc.com

39 **Remington's** [★M,D,CW,K,DS,V] 202/543-3113 ■ 639 Pennsylvania Ave SE (btwn 6th & 7th) ■ *4pm-2am, till 3am Fri-Sat, 2 flrs, CW dance lessons Sun-Mon & Wed, T-dance Sun* ■ www.remingtonswdc.com

25 **Titan** [MW,D,F,V] 202/232-7010 ■ 1337 14th St NW (above Dakota Cowgirl) ■ *5pm-midnight, till 2am Fri-Sat, more women Fri* ■ www.dakotacowgirldc.com

32 **Tool Shed** [M,D,L] 202/347-4533 ■ upstairs at Green Lantern ■ *from 9pm Wed-Sat, from 6pm Sun*

Nightclubs

40 **Apex** [MW,D,K,V,YC,WC,$] 202/296-0505 ■ 1415 22nd St NW (btwn O & P Sts) ■ *9pm-2am, till 3am Fri-Sat, clsd Sun-Wed* ■ www.apex-dc.com

40 **Aqua** [M,D,MR-A,18+,$] 202/296-0505 ■ 1415 22nd St NW (at Apex) ■ *video bar at midnight, first Fri, unofficial Asian night* ■ www.aquadc.org

26 **Bachelors Mill** [★M,D,MR-AF,S,WC] 202/544-1931 ■ 1104 8th St SE (downstairs at Back Door Pub) ■ *10:30pm-close, 2 flrs*

41 **Blowoff** [★GS,D,$] 815 V St NW (at 9:30 Club) ■ *10:30pm-3am monthly, varying Sat* ■ www.blowoff.us

Blush [WO,D,MR-AF] 301/669-7148 ■ *8pm-2am last Fri only, call for location* ■ www.blushdc.com

42 **Cada Vez** [GS] 202/667-0785 ■ 1438 U St NW (at 15th) ■ *check local listings for gay events*

Calor [M,D] 888/269-3349 ■ *occasional parties, call for date & location* ■ www.experiencecalor.com

43 **Chief Ike's Mambo Room** [GF,D,E,WC] 202/332-2211 ■ 1725 Columbia Rd NW (btwn 17th & 18th) ■ *4pm-2am, till 3am Fri, 6pm-3am Sat, clsd Sun, also restaurant, American* ■ www.chiefikes.com

44 **Chloe** [GS,D] 202/265-6592 ■ 2473 18th St NW (at Chloe) ■ *5:30pm-11:30pm, till 2am Fri-Sat, till 2am Sun, clsd Mon, more gay Sun* ■ www.chloedc.com

42 **Club Fuego** [MW,D,MR-L] 1438 U St NW (at Cada Vez) ■ *10pm-close Sat only, salsa, merengue, Latin pop* ■ www.clubfuegodc.com

45 Cobalt/ 30 Degrees Lounge [M,D,E,DS] 202/462-6569 ■ 1639 R St NW (at 17th) ■ *5pm-2am, till 3am Fri-Sat* ■ www.cobaltdc.com

Delta Elite [MW,D,MR-AF] 202/529-0626 ■ 3734 10th St NE (at Perry St NE, in Brookland) ■ *ladies night Fri w/ female strippers, men's night Sat* ■ www.thedeltaelite.com

A Different Kind of Ladies' Night ■ *see web for events* ■ www.adifferentkindofladiesnight.com

46 Fab Lounge 202/797-1122 ■ 1805 Connecticut Ave NW, 2nd flr ■ *5pm-close* ■ www.thefablounge.com

47 First Friday Melt Down [W,D,MR-AF] 202/232-2710 ■ 1355 U St NW (at Republic Gardens) ■ *6pm-close 1st Fri* ■ www.jamorr.com

48 Fusion [W,D,MR-AF,$] 202/277-1583 ■ 33 Patterson St NE (at N Capitol St NE, in Fur Nightclub) ■ *9pm-3am 2nd Fri* ■ www.inhertwined.com

49 Merge Happy Hour [WO,D,MR] 202/277-1583, 800/878-3899 ■ 1301 K St NW (at K Street Lounge) ■ *5pm-10pm 2nd Fri only, dress code* ■ www.inhertwined.com

CAFES

Cosi [★] 202/332-6364 ■ 1647 20th St NW ■ *7am-midnight, till 1am Fri, 7:30am-1am Sat, 7:30am-midnight Sun, full bar from 4pm, make your own s'mores* ■ www.getcosi.com

Jolt 'n' Bolt [★] 202/232-0077 ■ 1918 18th St NW (at Florida) ■ *7am-11pm, 8am-midnight Fri-Sat, patio*

Soho Tea & Coffee [F,WC] 202/463-7646 ■ 2150 P St NW (at 22nd St) ■ *open 7:30am till late, cybercafe & more, patio*

RESTAURANTS

18th & U Duplex Diner [GS] 202/265-7828 ■ 2004 18th St NW (at Ave U) ■ *6pm-11pm, till 12:30am Tue-Th, till 1:30am Fri-Sat, American comfort food, full bar* ■ www.duplexdiner.com

2 Amys Pizza 202/885-5700 ■ 3715 Macomb St NW ■ *11am-11pm, noon-10pm Sun* ■ www.2amyspizza.com

Acadiana [R] 202/408-8848 ■ 901 New York Ave NW ■ *lunch Mon-Fri, dinner Mon-Sat, clsd Sun, Cajun, great bourbon selection* ■ www.acadianarestaurant.com

Annie's Paramount Steak House [★] 202/232-0395 ■ 1609 17th St NW (at Corcoran) ■ *10am-11:30pm, till 1am Th & Sun, 24hrs Fri-Sat, full bar*

Armand's Chicago Pizza 202/363-5500 ■ 4231 Wisconsin Ave NW (at Veazey) ■ *11am-10pm, till 11pm Fri-Sat, noon-10pm Sun, full bar; also 226 Massachusetts Ave NE, Capitol Hill, 202/547-6600* ■ www.armandspizza.com

Asylum 202/319-9353 ■ 2471 18th St NW ■ *5pm-2am, till 3am Fri, 10am-3am Sat, 10am-2am Sun, plenty veggie, also bar* ■ www.asylumdc.com

Banana Cafe & Piano Bar [E,P,GO] 202/543-5906 ■ 500 8th St SE (at E St) ■ *11am-10:30pm, till 11pm Fri-Sat, till 10pm Sun, Puerto Rican/ Cuban, some veggie, famous margaritas* ■ www.bananacafedc.com

Beacon Bar & Grill [★] 202/872-1126 ■ 1516 Rhode Island Ave NW (at 17th, at Beacon Hotel) ■ *brkfst, lunch & dinner, popular Sun brunch, patio* ■ www.beaconbarandgrill.com

Busboys & Poets [E,WI] 202/387-7638 ■ 2021 14th St NW ■ *8am-midnight, till 2am Fri, 10am-2am Sat, 10am-midnight Sun, also bookstore, live jazz & poetry* ■ www.busboysandpoets.com

Cafe Berlin [WC] 202/543-7656 ■ 322 Massachusetts Ave NE (btwn 3rd & 4th) ■ *lunch & dinner, dinner only Sun, German, patio* ■ www.cafeberlindc.com

Cafe Japoné [★MR-A,K] 202/223-1573 ■ 2032 P St NW (at 21st) ■ *6pm-midnight, till 1am Fri-Sat, Japanese, full bar, live jazz Wed*

Cafe Luna [★MW] 202/387-4005 ■ 1633 P St NW (at 17th) ■ *8am-midnight, 10am-11:30pm wknds, plenty veggie* ■ skewers-cafeluna.com

Chartwell Grill [WC] 202/797-2000 ■ 1914 Connecticut Ave (in The Churchill Hotel) ■ *6:30am-10:30pm, also lounge till 12:30am, till 11pm Sun, cont'l* ■ www.thechurchillhotel.com

Dupont Italian Kitchen & Bar 202/328-3222, 202/328-0100 ■ 1637 17th St NW (at R St) ■ *11:30am-11pm, from 10:30am Sun, bar 4pm-2am, some veggie* ■ dupontitaliankitchen.com

Floriana's [GO] 202/667-5937 ■ 1602 17th St NW (at Q St NW) ■ *dinner nightly, Italian, full bar, patio*

Food For Thought [NS] 202/667-7960 ■ 1811 14th St NW (at the Black Cat) ■ *8pm-1am, 7pm-2am Fri-Sat, mostly vegan/ veggie, indie/ punk music shows, readings* ■ www.blackcatdc.com/food.html

Guapo's [WC] 202/686-3588 ■ 4515 Wisconsin Ave NW (at Albemarle) ■ *lunch & dinner, Mexican, full bar* ■ guaposrestaurant.com

The Islander [E] 202/234-4955 ■ 1201 U St NW (at 12th) ■ *lunch & dinner, Caribbean, full bar* ■ u_streetjazz@hotmail.com

Jaleo [WC,E] 202/628-7949 ■ 480 7th St NW (at E St) ■ *lunch & dinner, tapas, full bar, Sevillanas dancers Wed* ■ www.jaleo.com

La Frontera Cantina 202/232-0437 ■ 1633 17th St NW (btwn R & Q Sts) ■ *11am-11pm, till 1am Fri-Sat, Tex-Mex*

Lauriol Plaza 202/387-0035 ■ 1835 18th St NW (at S St) ■ *11:30am-11pm, till midnight Fri-Sat, Latin American* ■ www.lauriolplaza.com

Lillies' [GS,WC] 202/234-3200 ■ 1731 New Hampshire (at 18th & R Sts, in the Carlyle Suites) ■ *lunch & dinner, also art deco bar, internet access* ■ www.carlylesuites.com

Logan Tavern [GO] 202/332-3710 ■ 1423 P St NW ■ *lunch & dinner, wknd brunch, American comfort food, also neighborhood bar* [GF] ■ www.logantavern.com

Mimi's American Bistro 202/464-6464 ■ 2120 P St NW ■ *11:30am-11pm, till midnight Fri-Sun, brunch wknds, waiters spontaneously break into song* ■ www.mimisdc.com

Occidental Grill 202/783-1475 ■ 1475 Pennsylvania Ave NW (btwn 14th & 15th) ■ *lunch Mon-Sat, dinner nightly, clsd Sun, upscale, political player hangout* ■ www.occidentaldc.com

Perry's 202/234-6218 ■ 1811 Columbia Rd NW (at 18th) ■ *5:30pm-10:30pm, till 11:30pm wknds, contemporary American & sushi, popular drag Sun brunch, full bar, roof deck* ■ www.perrysadamsmorgan.com

Rasika 202/637-1222 ■ 633 D St NW ■ *lunch Mon-Fri, dinner Mon-Sat, clsd Sun, Indian* ■ www.rasikarestaurant.com

Rocklands 202/333-2558 ■ 2418 Wisconsin Ave NW (at Calvert) ■ *11am-10pm, till 9pm Sun, BBQ & take-out* ■ www.rocklands.com

Sala Thai 202/872-1144 ■ 2016 P St NW (at 21st) ■ *lunch & dinner, some veggie* ■ salathaidc.com

Skewers [★E] 202/387-7400 ■ 1633 P St NW (at 17th) ■ *11am-11pm, noon-midnight wknds, Middle Eastern, belly dancing Sat, full bar* ■ skewers-cafeluna.com

Soul Vegetarian 202/328-7685 ■ 2606 Georgia Ave NW ■ *11am-9pm, till 3pm Sun (brunch), all-vegan menu*

Tapatinis 202/546-8272 ■ 711 8th St SE ■ *5pm-midnight, till 2am Fri-Sat, from 7pm Sat, clsd Sun-Mon, tapas & martinis* ■ www.Tapatinis.com

Trio 202/232-6305 ■ 1537 17th St NW (at Q St NW) ■ *8am-midnight, American, full bar, sidewalk cafe*

Two Quail [★GO] 202/543-8030 ■ 320 Massachusetts Ave NE ■ *lunch Mon-Fri, dinner nightly, full bar* ■ www.TwoQuail.com

ENTERTAINMENT & RECREATION

Anecdotal History Tours [GF] 301/294-9514 ■ *variety of guided tours* ■ www.dcsightseeing.com

Bike the Sites [GF] 202/842-2453 ■ 1100 Pennsylvania Ave NW (off 12th St) ■ *9am-6pm, tour the nation's capital on bike!* ■ www.bikethesites.com

Gay Men's Chorus of Washington 202/293-1548 ■ www.gmcw.org

Hillwood Museum & Gardens [R] 202/686-5807, 877/445-5966 ■ 4155 Linnean Ave NW (at Tilden St NW) ■ *10am-5pm Tue-Sat, Fabergé, porcelain, furniture & more* ■ www.hillwoodmuseum.org

Lesbian & Gay Chorus of Washington, DC 202/546-1549 ■ www.lgcw.org

Phillips Collection 202/387-2151 ■ 1600 21st St NW (at Q St) ■ *clsd Mon, America's first museum of modern art, near Dupont Circle* ■ www.phillipscollection.org

Rainbow History Project 202/907-9007 ■ *self-guided walking tours of gay DC; visit web to download free PDF* ■ www.rainbowhistory.org

Washington Mystics 202/266-2277 ■ *check out the Women's National Basketball Association while you're in DC* ■ www.wnba.com/mystics

BOOKSTORES

ADC Map & Travel Center 202/628-2608, 800/544-2659 ■ 1636 I St NW (at 17th St) ■ *9am-6:30pm, till 5:30pm Fri, 11am-5pm Sat, clsd Sun, extensive maps & travel guides* ■ www.adcmap.com

50 **G Books** [GO] 202/986-9697 ■ 1520 U St NW, BSMT (btwn 15th St & U St) ■ *noon-10pm, till 11pm Fri-Sat, new & used LGBT books, magazines, pride items, etc* ■ BrandonChan99@msn.com

Kramerbooks & Afterwords Cafe & Grill [E,F,WC] 202/387-1400 ■ 1517 Connecticut Ave NW (at Q St) ■ *7:30am-1am, 24hrs wknds, also cafe* ■ www.kramers.com

51 **Lambda Rising** [WC] 202/462-6969 ■ 1625 Connecticut Ave NW (btwn Q & R Sts) ■ *10am-10pm, till midnight Fri-Sat, LGBT* ■ www.lambdarising.com

RETAIL SHOPS

Leather Rack 202/797-7401 ■ 1723 Connecticut Ave NW (btwn R & S Sts) ■ www.leatherrack.com

Pleasure Place [WC] 800/386-2386 ■ 1063 Wisconsin Ave NW, Georgetown (btwn M & K Sts) ■ *10am-10pm, till midnight Wed-Sat, noon-7pm Sun, erotica, clubwear, leather, adult toys, DVDs, clothing & more* ■ pleasureplace.com

Pleasure Place 202/483-3297 ■ 1710 Connecticut Ave NW (btwn Florida Ave & R St) ■ *10am-10pm, till midnight Wed-Sat, noon-7pm Sun, erotica, clubwear, leather, adult toys, DVDs, clothing & more* ■ pleasureplace.com

Pulp 202/462-7857 ■ 1803 14th St NW ■ *10am-8pm, till 6pm Sun, cards, gifts, music* ■ pulpdc.com

Universal Gear 202/319-0136 ■ 1601 17th St NW (at Q St) ■ *11am-10pm Sun-Th, till midnight Fri-Sat, casual, club, athletic & designer clothing* ■ www.universalgear.com

PUBLICATIONS

EXP Magazine 302/227-5787, 877/397-6244 ■ *bi-weekly gay magazine for Mid-Atlantic* ■ www.expmagazine.com

Metro Weekly 202/638-6830 ■ *lesbian/gay news-magazine, extensive club listings* ■ www.metroweekly.com

Washington Blade 202/797-7000 ■ *huge LGBT newspaper w/ extensive resource listings* ■ www.wash-blade.com

GYMS & HEALTH CLUBS

Results—The Gym [GF] 202/518-0001 ■ 1612 U St NW (at 17th St) ■ *also women-only fitness area, also cafe* ■ www.resultsthegym.com

Washington Sports Club 202/332-0100 ■ 1835 Connecticut Ave NW (at Columbia & Florida) ■ www.washingtonsports.com

MEN'S CLUBS

Crew Club 202/319-1333 ■ 1321 14th St NW (at Rhode Island) ■ *24hrs* ■ www.crewclub.net

EROTICA

K&B Newsstand Video Arcade [AYOR] 202/628-8306 ■ 1004 F St (at 10th)

Pleasure Place [WC] 800/386-2386 ■ 1063 Wisconsin Ave NW, Georgetown (btwn M & K Sts) ■ *10am-10pm, till midnight Wed-Sat, noon-7pm Sun, erotica, clubwear, leather, adult toys, DVDs, clothing & more* ■ pleasureplace.com

Pleasure Place 202/483-3297 ■ 1710 Connecticut Ave NW (btwn Florida Ave & R St) ■ *10am-10pm, till midnight Wed-Sat, noon-7pm Sun, erotica, clubwear, leather, adult toys, DVDs, clothing & more* ■ pleasureplace.com

FLORIDA

Fort Lauderdale

ACCOMMODATIONS

1 **Alcazar Resort** [MO,SW,N,NS,WI,GO] 954/567-2525, 888/830-9931 ■ 555 N Birch Rd (at Terramar) ■ *at the beach* ■ www.alcazarresort.com

2 **Alhambra Beach Resort** [GS,SW,NS,WI,GO] 954/525-7601, 877/309-4014 ■ 3021 Alhambra St ■ *motel, close to gay beach* ■ www.alhambrabeachresort.com

3 **Bamboo Resort** [MO,SW,N,NS,WI,GO] 954/565-7775, 800/479-1767 ■ 2733 Middle River Dr (near 26th St NE) ■ www.thebambooresort.com

4 **The Blue Dolphin** [★MO,V,SW,WI,WC,GO] 954/565-8437, 800/893-2583 ■ 725 N Birch Rd (at Vistamar) ■ *near beach* ■ www.bluedolphinhotel.com

5 **The Cabanas** [M,SW,NS,WI,GO] 954/564-7764, 866/564-7764 ■ 2209 NE 26th St ■ *riverfront, kayaks available, clothing-optional jacuzzi, spa* ■ www.TheCabanasGuesthouse.com

1 **Cheston House** [MO,SW,N,NS,WI,GO] 954/566-7950, 866/566-7950 ■ 520 N Birch Rd (at Viramar) ■ *on beach* ■ www.chestonhouse.com

6   **Coconut Cove Guesthouse** [MO,SW,NS,WI,GO] 954/523-3226, 888/414-3226 ■ 3012 Granada St (at Birch St & A1A) ■ *courtyard gardens* ■ www.coconutcove-guesthouse.com

7   **Comfort Suites Airport & Cruise Port** [GS,SW,WI] 954/767-8700, 800/760-0000 ■ 1800 S Federal Hwy (at 17th St) ■ www.comfortsuitesftlauderdale.com

8   **Coral Reef Guesthouse** [MO,SW,N,WI,WC,GO] 954/568-0292, 888/365-6948 ■ 2609 NE 13th Ct (off Sunrise Blvd) ■ *12-man jacuzzi, very secluded* ■ www.coralreefguesthouse.com

9   **Deauville Inn** [MO,SW,WI,GO] 954/568-5000 ■ 2916 N Ocean Blvd (Oakland Park Blvd & A1A) ■ *in the heart of Fort Lauderdale Beach* ■ www.thedeauvilleinn.com

10 **Doubletree Guest Suites Fort Lauderdale Galleria** [GF,SW,WI,WC] 954/565-3800 ■ 2670 E Sunrise Blvd ■ *bar & grill, patio* ■ www.doubletreegalleria.com

11 **The Dunes Guest House** [MO,SW,NS,WI,GO] 954/568-6161, 800/425-8105 ■ 2835 Terramar St (at Orton) ■ *charming Bahamian-style villa, clothing-optional pool, hot tub* ■ www.dunesguesthouse.com

12 **Elysium Resort** [MO,SW,NS,WI,GO] 954/564-9601, 800/533-4744 ■ 552 N Birch Rd (at Terramar) ■ *sundeck, near beach* ■ www.elysiumresort.net

13 **Embassy Suites Hotel** [GF,SW,WI,WC] 954/527-2700, 800/362-2779 ■ 1100 SE 17th St ■ *full brkfst, hot tub, tropical outdoor pool* ■ www.embassysuitesftl.com

14 **The Flamingo—Inn Amongst the Flowers** [MO,SW,NS,WI,GO] 954/561-4658, 800/283-4786 ■ 2727 Terramar St (near Birch) ■ *luxury hotel* ■ www.theflamingoresort.com

15 **Fort Lauderdale Oceanfront Hotel** [GF,SW] 954/524-8733, 866/273-9593 ■ 440 Seabreeze Blvd ■ *sundeck bar, beach across street* ■ www.ftlauderdaleoceanfront.com

1   **The Grand Resort & Spa** [MO,SW,N,NS,WI,WC,GO] 954/630-3000, 800/818-1211 ■ 539 N Birch Rd (at Windamar) ■ *sundeck, spa, gym, clothing-optional courtyard* ■ www.grandresort.net

16 **Inn Leather Guesthouse** [★MO,L,SW,N,WI,GO] 954/467-1444, 877/532-7729 ■ 610 SE 19th St (at SW 1st Ave) ■ *sling in each room, dungeon, hot tub* ■ www.innleather.com

FORT LAUDERDALE

Snowbirds from points north come to Fort Lauderdale every winter to soak up the sun on the city's beautiful beaches. The "Venice of America"—so called for its canals—has recently benefited from developers who've spruced up the city, making it a world-class vacation spot. The tropical surroundings are also home to a spectacular range of flora and fauna, from Butterfly World (954/977-4400) to Flamingo Gardens (954/473-2955).

Tourist Info

AIRPORT DIRECTIONS
Fort Lauderdale/Hollywood International Airport. Take Federal Hwy 1 north. This crosses Las Olas Blvd, Broward Blvd, and Sunrise Blvd, three of Fort Lauderdale's major avenues.

PUBLIC TRANSIT & TAXIS
Yellow Cab 954/565-5400.
Super Shuttle 954/764-1700.
Broward County Transit 954/357-8400, web: www.broward.org/bct.

TOURIST SPOTS & INFO
Broward Center for the Performing Arts 954/462-0022, web: www.browardcenter.org.
Butterfly World 954/977-4400, web: www.butterflyworld.com.
Everglades.
Flamingo Gardens 954/473-2955, web: www.flamingogardens.org.
Museum of Art 954/525-5500, web: www.moafl.org.
Museum of Discovery & Science 954/467-6637, web: www.mods.org.
Sawgrass Mills, world's largest outlet mall 954/846-2300, web: www.sawgrassmillsmall.com.
Visitor's Center: Greater Fort Lauderdale Convention & Visitors Bureau 954/765-4466 or 800/227-8669 (code 187), web: www.sunny.org.

Weather
The average year-round temperature in this sub-tropical climate is 75-90°.

City Calendar
LGBT PRIDE
March. 954/745-7070, web: www.pridesouthflorida.org.

ANNUAL EVENTS
April - AIDS Walk, web: www.aidswalk.net/ftlauderdale.
October-November - Int'l Film Fest 954/760-9898, web: www.fliff.com.

Queer Resources
COMMUNITY INFO
Gay/Lesbian Community Center 954/463-9005. 1717 N Andrews Ave, 10am-10pm, noon-5pm wknds, web: www.glccsf.org.
Gay Ft Lauderdale, web: www.gayftlauderdale.com.
South Florida Fun, web: www.southfloridafun.com.
Lambda South 954/761-9072, web: www.lambdasouth.com.
Broward House 954/522-4749, web: www.browardhouse.org.

Liberty Apartment & Garden Suites [MW,SW,WI,WC,GO] 954/927-0090, 877/927-0090 ■ 1501 SW 2nd Ave (at Sheridan), Dania Beach ■ *furnished apts, near beach, weekly rates* ■ www.LibertySuites.com

17 The Mangrove Villas [MO,SW,N,NS,WC,GO] 954/527-5250, 800/238-3538 ■ 1100 N Victoria Park Rd (at 11th St) ■ *self-contained houses, sundeck* ■ www.mangrovevillas.com

18 Manor Inn [MO,SW,N,NS,WI,GO] 954/566-8223, 866/682-7456 ■ 2408 NE 6th Ave (at NE 24th St), Wilton Manors ■ *B&B, hot tub* ■ www.wiltonmanorsinn.com

19 Mary's Resort [M,SW,NS,WI,GO] 954/523-3500, 866/805-6570 ■ 1115 Tequesta/ SW 4th St (at 11th Ave) ■ *4 unique Key West-style structures separated by tropical gardens, hot tub, clothing-optional pool area* ■ www.marysresort.com

20 The New Zealand House B&B [M,SW,N,WI,WC,GO] 954/523-7829, 888/234-5494 ■ 908 NE 15th Ave (at Sunrise) ■ *Key West-style guesthouse* ■ www.newzealand-house.com

21 Orton Terrace [MO,SW,N,WI,GO] 954/566-5068, 800/323-1142 ■ 606 Orton Ave (at Terramar) ■ *1- & 2-bdrm apts* ■ www.ortonterrace.com

22 Palm Plaza Resort [★MO,L,SW,N,WI,WC,GO] 954/260-6568 ■ 2801 Riomar St (at Birch) ■ *tropical garden, steps to beach* ■ www.palmplazaresort.com

23 Pineapple Point Guest House [MO,SW,N,NS,WI,GO] 954/527-0094, 888/844-7295 ■ 315 NE 16th Terr (at NE 3rd Ct) ■ *luxury guesthouse* ■ www.pineapplepoint.com

12▶ The Royal Palms Resort [★M,SW,NS,WI,GO] 954/564-6444, 800/237-7256 ■ 2901 Terramar St (at Birch) ■ *sundeck, jacuzzi, rated one of the very best gay accommodations in North America by PlanetOut* ■ www.royalpalms.com

24 Sandra Lee Inn [GS,SW,NS,GO] 954/249-0565 ■ 2307 NE 33rd Ave ■ *apts in 1960s hotel, full kitchen* ■ www.sandraleeinn.com

25 The Schubert Resort [★MO,SW,NS,WI,WC,GO] 954/763-7434, 866/763-7435 ■ 855 NE 20th Ave ■ *full-service resort* ■ www.schubertresort.com

26 Sea Grape House Inn [M,SW,N,NS,WI,GO] 954/525-6586, 800/377-8802 ■ 1109 NE 16th Pl (at Dixie Hwy) ■ *2 clothing-optional pools, 7-man spa* ■ www.seagrape.com

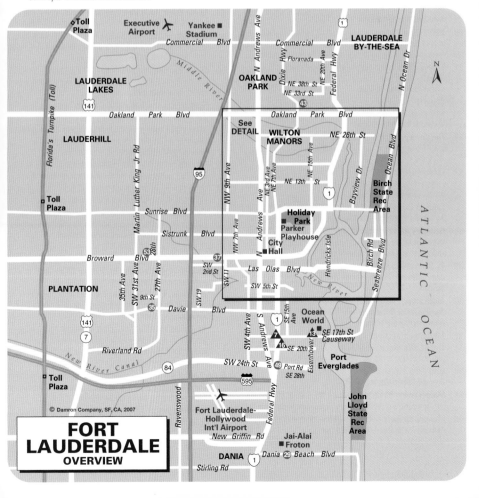

27 **Sheraton Yankee Trader Beach Hotel** [GF,SW,WC] 954/467-1111, 888/627-7109 ■ 321 N Fort Lauderdale Beach Blvd (A1A) ■ *beachfront hotel w/ sports deck, gym, 2 pools, tennis court* ■ www.starwood.com

6   **Soberano Resort La Casa Del Mar** [MW,SW,NS,WI,WC,GO] 954/467-2037, 866/467-2037 ■ 3003 Granada St ■ *Mediterranean villa* ■ www.lacasadelmar.com

21 **Villa Venice Resort** [MO,SW,NS,WI,WC,GO] 954/564-7855, 877/284-5522 ■ 2900 Terramar St (at Orton) ■ *2 blocks to beach* ■ www.villavenice.com

    The Westin Fort Lauderdale [GF,SW,NS] 954/772-1331, 800/937-8461 ■ 400 Corporate Dr (at Cypres Creek Rd) ■ *full brkfst, use of health club, hot tub* ■ www.westin.com/fortlauderdale

28 **Windamar Beach Resort** [M,SW,N,WI,GO] 954/561-0039, 866/554-6816 ■ 543 Breakers Ave (near Bayshore) ■ *just steps to the ocean* ■ www.windamar.com

1   **The Worthington Guest House** [MO,SW,NS,GO] 954/563-6819, 800/445-7036 ■ 543 N Birch Rd (at Terramar) ■ *resort, clothing-optional hot tub* ■ www.theworthington.com

Bars

29 **Beach Betty's** [W,NH,D,E,K,GO] 954/921-9893 ■ 625 Dania Beach Blvd (at Fronton Blvd), Dania ■ *noon-3am* ■ www.beachbettysbar.com

30 **Bill's Filling Station** [★M,NH,F,K,DS,WC] 954/525-9403 ■ 1243 NE 11th Ave (at 13th St) ■ *2pm-2am, till 3am Fri-Sat, from noon Sat-Sun, patio* ■ www.billsfillingstation.com

31 **Boardwalk** [★M,NH,S,18+] 954/463-6969 ■ 1721 N Andrews Ave ■ *3pm-2am, till 3am Fri-Sat, strippers from 5pm* ■ www.boardwalkbar.com

    Cloud 9 Lounge [★W,D,E,DS] 954/499-3525 ■ 7126 Stirling Rd, Davie ■ *noon-4am* ■ www.thecloud9online.com

32 **The Corner Pub, Bar & Cafe** [GS,NH,GO] 954/564-7335 ■ 1915 N Andrews ■ *11am-2am, till 3am Fri-Sat, from 9am Fri-Sun*

33 **Cubby Hole** [M,NH,B,L,F,WC] 954/728-9001 ■ 823 N Federal Hwy (at 8th St) ■ *11am-2am, till 3am Fri-Sat, internet access* ■ www.thecubbyhole.com

    Eagle in Exile [M,D,L,N,PC,$] 954/590-4046 ■ 523 E Sample Rd, Pompano Beach ■ www.ftlauderdaleeagle.com

34 **Georgie's Alibi** [★MW,F,V,NS,WC] 954/565-2526 ■ 2266 Wilton Dr (at NE 4th Ave) ■ *11am-2am, till 3am Fri-Sat, sports bar* ■ www.georgiesalibi.com

35 **J's Bar** [W,NH,D] 954/581-8400 ■ 2780 Davie Blvd ■ *9am-2am, till 3am Fri-Sat, from noon Sun* ■ www.jsbartheoriginal.com

36 **Jackhammer** [M,D,B,L,WC] 954/522-9985 ■ 1951 NW 9th Ave (Powerline Rd) ■ *3pm-3am, theme nights, cruisy* ■ www.jackhammerbar.com

37 **Johnny's** [M,NH,F,S,WC] 954/522-5931 ■ 1116 W Broward Blvd (at 11th Ave) ■ *10am-2am, till 3am Fri-Sat, from noon Sun, male dancers nightly* ■ info@johnnysboys.com

38 **Lush** [MW] 954/568-6950 ■ 3074 NE 33rd Ave ■ *5pm-2am, till 3am Fri-Sat, lounge*

39 **Mona's** [M,NH] 954/525-6662 ■ 502 E Sunrise Blvd (at 6th Ave) ■ *noon-2am, till 3am wknds* ■ www.monasbar.com

40 **Monkey Business** [M,C,DS] 954/565-3550 ■ 2740 N Andrews Ave ■ *9am-2am, till 3am wknds*

41 **New Moon** [W,NH,D,E,K] 954/563-7660 ■ 2440 Wilton Dr, Wilton Manors ■ *2pm-2am, from noon Tue & Sat-Sun, from 4pm Mon, karaoke Th, DJ Fri, live music Sat* ■ www.newmoonbar.com

42 **Ramrod** [★M,B,L] 954/763-8219 ■ 1508 NE 4th Ave (at 16th St) ■ *3pm-2am, till 3am wknds, cruisy, patio, also LeatherWerks leather store* ■ www.ramrodbar.com

43 **Roxanne's** [GS,GO] 954/567-9552 ■ 3148 NE 12th Ave (NE corner Oakland & Dixie, Oakland Park) ■ *2pm-2am, till 3am Fri-Sat, more gay Tue, theme nights*

44 **Scandals** [M,NH,CW] 954/567-2432 ■ 3073 NE 6th Ave, Wilton Manors ■ *noon-2am, till 3am wknds* ■ www.scandalsfla.com

45 **Sidelines Sports Bar** [MW] 954/563-8001 ■ 2031 Wilton Dr, Wilton Manors ■ *2pm-2am, from noon wknds* ■ www.sidelinessports.com

46 **Smarty Pants** [★M,NH,E,K,DS,WC] 954/561-1724 ■ 3038 N Federal Hwy (at Oakland Park Blvd) ■ *9am-2am, till 3am Sat, noon-2am Sun* ■ smartypantsbar.com

Nightclubs

47 **Boom** [★M,D,E,K,DS,V,GO] 954/630-3556 ■ 2232 Wilton Dr, Wilton Manors ■ *noon-2am, till 3am wknds, T-dance Sun* ■ www.clubboom.com

48 **China White** [GS,D] 954/759-7047 ■ 109 SW 2nd Ave ■ *10pm-4am, more men Wed & Fri, more women Sat-Sun*

49 **Coliseum** [M,D,E,S,18+] 954/832-0100 ■ 2520 S Miami Rd (at US1 & State Rd 84) ■ *11:30pm-4am Th, 9pm-5am Fri-Sat, [18+] Fri* ■ www.coliseumnightclub.com

50 **Dudes Bar** [MO,E,P,S,V] 954/568-7777 ■ 3270 NE 33rd St ■ *4pm-2am, till 3am Fri-Sat, live music 6pm, male dancers nightly* ■ www.dudesbar.com

48 **Snatch** [W,D] 954/288-8691 ■ 109 SW 2nd Ave ■ *9pm Sat* ■ www.pandoraultra.com

36 **Steel Video Lounge** [★M,D,V,WC] 561/347-8044 ■ 1951 Powerline Rd (at NW 29th St) ■ *4pm-3am, [CW] Th* ■ www.warehouse250.com

53 **Torpedo** [M,D,S] 954/587-2500 ■ 2829 W Broward Blvd (at 28th Ave) ■ *10pm-4am nightly* ■ www.torpedobar.com

54 **Ultra Saturdays** [W,D] 954/288-8691 ■ 3073 NE 6th (at Elements) ■ *Sat only* ■ www.ultra-events.com

48 **The Voodoo Lounge** [M,D,DS] 954/522-0733 ■ 111 SW 2nd Ave (at Moffat St) ■ *gay Sun only for afternoon Babylon T-dance & drag show* ■ www.garysantis.com

Cafes

    Fantasia's of Boston 954/522-4886 ■ 1826 E Sunrise Blvd (next to Gateway Theater) ■ *noon-9:30pm* ■ www.fantasiasofboston.com

    Java Boys [★] 954/564-8828 ■ 2230 Wilton Dr, Wilton Manors ■ *8am-midnight, coffee, tea & desserts* ■ www.javaboys.net

    The Storks [WC] 954/567-3220 ■ 2505 NE 15th Ave (at NE 26th St, Wilton Manors) ■ *6:30am-midnight, from 7am wknds, patio; also at 1109 E Las Olas Blvd, 954/522-4670* ■ www.storkscafe.com

Restaurants

    Canyon 954/765-1950 ■ 1818 E Sunrise Blvd ■ *dinner, Southwestern, full bar* ■ canyonfl.com

    Chardee's [MW,D,E,K,P,WC] 954/563-1800 ■ 2209 Wilton Dr (at NE 6th Ave) ■ *dinner from 6pm, also bar from 4:30pm-2am*

The Floridian 954/463–4041 ■ 1410 E Las Olas Blvd
■ *24hr diner*

Food Amongst the Flowers [E] 954/563–7752 ■ 2345
Wilton Dr, Wilton Manors ■ *5:30pm-11pm, full bar* ■
www.flowers2345.com

Galanga 954/202–0000 ■ 2389 Wilton Dr, Wilton Manors
■ *dinner nightly, lunch weekdays, Thai, also sushi*

Grandma's French Cafe 954/564–3671 ■ 3354 N Ocean
Blvd (N of Oakland Park Blvd) ■ *11:30pm-10pm, clsd Mon,
also ice cream parlor*

Herban Kitchen [BW] 954/566–1110 ■ 2823 E Oakland
Park Blvd ■ *5pm-10pm nightly, Italian/ Mediterranean, some
veggie* ■ www.herban-kitchen.com

Hi-Life Cafe [R] 954/563–1395 ■ 3000 N Federal Hwy
#12 (at Oakland Park Blvd, in the Plaza 3000) ■ *dinner, clsd
Mon, bistro, some veggie* ■ www.hilifecafe.com

Kitchenetta 954/567–3333 ■ 2850 N Federal Hwy
■ *dinner nightly, clsd Mon* ■ kitchenetta.com

Lester's Diner [★] 954/525–5641 ■ 250 State Rd 84
■ *24hrs, more gay late nights*

Mykonos Souvlaki 954/563–8094 ■ 2909 NE 6th Ave,
Wilton Manors

Peter Pan Diner 954/565–7177 ■ 1216 E Oakland Park
Blvd ■ *24hrs*

Rosie's Bar & Grill [★] 954/567–1320 ■ 2449 Wilton Dr,
Wilton Manors ■ *11am-midnight, till 1am Fri-Sat, full bar* ■
www.rosiesbarandgrill.com

Simply Delish Cafe [R] 954/565–8646 ■ 2287 Wilton Dr,
Wilton Manors ■ *8am-3pm, clsd Mon*

Sublime 954/615–1431 ■ 1431 N Federal Hwy ■ *5:30pm-
10pm, clsd Mon, vegan/ vegetarian* ■ www.sublimeveg.com

Tasty Thai 954/396–3177 ■ 2254 Wilton Dr, Wilton
Manors ■ *lunch & dinner*

Tequila Sunrise Mexican Cafe 954/938–4473 ■ 4711 N
Dixie Hwy ■ www.tequilasunrise.us

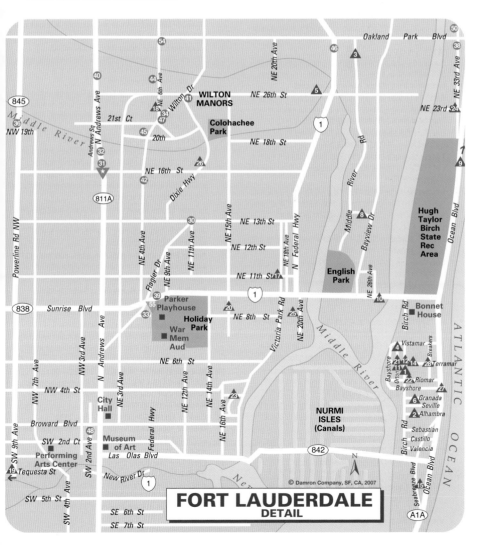

Tropics Cabaret & Restaurant [MW,P,WC] 954/537-6000 ■ 2000 Wilton Dr (at 20th) ■ *lunch & dinner, Sun brunch, new American, also piano bar, till 3am Sat*

The Wine Cellar [GO] 954/565-9021 ■ 199 E Oakland Park Blvd ■ *dinner, clsd Mon, Eastern European*

ENTERTAINMENT & RECREATION

Gallery at Beach Place [GF,F,E] 954/764-3460 ■ 17 S Ft Lauderdale Beach Blvd ■ *10am-10pm, till midnight Fri-Sat* ■ www.galleryatbeachplace.com

Gay Tea Cruise [M,D,F,DS] 888/211-3266 ■ *1st Sun, also women's cruise quarterly* ■ www.gayteacruise.com

Gold Coast Roller Rink 954/523-6783 ■ 2604 S Federal Hwy ■ *8pm-midnight Tue, gay skate*

Laffing Matterz [GF,WC] 954/763-5236 ■ 219 S Andrews Ave (NW corner at Las Olas) ■ *7:15pm Wed-Fri, 6:45pm Sat, 4:30pm Sun, unique & surprising dinner fare followed by cutting-edge musical satire* ■ www.laffingmatterz.com

BOOKSTORES

55 **Pride Factory & CyberCafe** 954/463-6600 ■ 845 N Federal Hwy (at E Sunrise Blvd) ■ *10am-11pm, 11am-9pm Sun, books, clothing, gifts, coffee & cybercafe* ■ www.pridefactory.com

RETAIL SHOPS

Audace 954/522-7503, 888/522-7502 ■ 813 E Las Olas Blvd (at 8th St) ■ *10am-10pm, till midnight Fri-Sat, men's underwear & sportswear* ■ www.audace.com

Bottoms & Tops [GO] 954/561-6670 ■ 2258 Wilton Dr (in Shoppes of Wilton Manors), Wilton Manors ■ *designer men's apparel* ■ www.bottomsandtops.net

GayMartUSA 954/630-0360 ■ 2240 Wilton Dr (at NE 6th Ave) ■ *10am-midnight, clothes & gifts*

J Miles 954/463-3988 ■ 721 E Broward Blvd (off Las Olas, E of US1, enter rear) ■ *10am-6pm, noon-5pm Sun, swimwear, underwear & more*

LeatherWerks 954/761-1236 ■ 1226 NE 4th Ave ■ *noon-8pm, till 6pm Sun, leatherwear & gear, adult toys; also inside the Ramrod (8pm-close)* ■ www.leatherwerks.com

PUBLICATIONS

The 411 Magazine 954/568-1880 ■ *weekly entertainment guide* ■ www.the411mag.com

Buzz Magazine 954/630-3304, 877/429-2899 ■ *LGBT lifestyle magazine for South FL* ■ www.buzzpublications.com

Express South Florida 954/568-1880 ■ www.express-gaynews.com

HOTSPOTS! Magazine 954/928-1862 ■ *Florida's weekly bar guide* ■ www.HotSpotsMagazine.com

The Independent Gay News 954/563-0470 ■ *LGBT newspaper for South FL* ■ www.ourindependent.com

The Rimmer 954/767-9384 ■ *monthly "fun & sleaze magazine" for gay men* ■ www.therimmer.com

GYMS & HEALTH CLUBS

Better Bodies [★GO] 954/561-7977 ■ 1164 Oakland Blvd (at Dixie Hwy), Wilton Manors ■ *also cafe & juice bar* ■ www.bbgftl.com

Main Street Gym [★] 954/563-2655 ■ 2270 Wilton Dr, Wilton Manors ■ *5am-11pm, 8am-10pm wknds, also variety of classes* ■ www.mainstreetgymflorida.com

MEN'S CLUBS

Club Fort Lauderdale [★SW,18+,PC] 954/525-3344 ■ 110 NW 5th Ave (at Broward) ■ *24hrs, multi-level sundeck, outdoor whirlpool, steam cavern, sauna* ■ www.theclubs.com

Clubhouse II [V,PC] 954/566-6750 ■ 2650 E Oakland Park Blvd ■ *24hrs, gym, [L] Tue* ■ clubhouse2.com

EROTICA

Fetish Factory 954/563-5777 ■ 855 E Oakland Park Blvd ■ *11am-9pm, noon-6pm Sun, fetishwear, toys, books, magazine, videos* ■ www.fetishfactory.com

Secrets 954/748-5855 ■ 4509 N Pine Island Rd (btwn Oakland Park & Commercial), Sunrise

Strut Shoes 954/561-1001 ■ 859 E Oakland Park Blvd ■ *11am-9pm, noon-6pm Sun, fetishwear, toys, books, magazine, videos* ■ www.strutshoes.com

Tropixxx Video 954/522-5988 ■ 1514 NE 4th Ave (at 16th St), Wilton Manors ■ tvxusa.com

Key West

ACCOMMODATIONS

1 **Abaco Inn** [GS,NS,GO] 305/292-4040, 866/518-4040 ■ 415 Julia St ■ *private garden* ■ www.abaco-inn.com

2 **Alexander Palms Court** [GF,SW,WC,GO] 305/296-6413, 800/858-1943 ■ 715 South St (at Vernon) ■ www.alexanderpalms.com

3 **Alexander's Guest House** [MW,SW,N,WI,WC,GO] 305/294-9919, 800/654-9919 ■ 1118 Fleming St (at Frances) ■ *sundecks, whirlpool, private patios* ■ www.alexanderskeywest.com

4 **Ambrosia House Tropical Lodging** [GF,SW,WI,WC] 305/296-9838 ■ 615 & 618-622 Fleming St (at Simonton) ■ *sea captain's house, lagoon pool; also Ambrosia Two* ■ www.ambrosiakeywest.com

5 **Andrews Inn** [GF,SW,NS,WI] 305/294-7730, 888/263-7393 ■ Zero Whalton Ln (at Duval) ■ *steps from Duval St, tropical courtyard* ■ www.andrewsinn.com

6 **The Artist House** [GS,NS] 305/296-3977, 800/582-7882 ■ 534 Eaton St (at Duval) ■ *Victorian guesthouse, jacuzzi* ■ www.artisthousekeywest.com

7 **Atlantic Shores Resort** [★MW,F,SW,N,WC] 305/296-2492, 800/526-3559 ■ 510 South St (at Duval) ■ *complete resort w/ pool, pier, bars, restaurant, rooms & T-dance Sun* ■ www.atlanticshoresresort.com

8 **Avalon B&B** [GF,SW,WI] 305/294-8233, 800/848-1317 ■ 1317 Duval St (at United) ■ *restored Victorian, close to beach, sundeck* ■ www.avalonbnb.com

Beach Bungalow & Beach Guest Suite [GS,NS,WI] 305/293-9611, 800/407-8417 ■ *vacation rental, 3-day minimum stay* ■ www.vacationdepot.com

9 **Big Ruby's Guesthouse** [M,SW,N,WI,NS,WC,GO] 305/296-2323, 800/477-7829 ■ 409 Appelrouth Ln (at Duval & Whitehead) ■ *full brkfst, hot tub, evening wine, sundeck* ■ www.bigrubys.com

10 **Blue Parrot Inn** [GF,SW,N,WC,GO] 305/296-0033, 800/231-2473 ■ 916 Elizabeth St (at Olivia) ■ *historic Bahamian home, sundeck, 2 cats on premises* ■ www.blueparrotinn.com

11 **Casa de Luces** [GF,NS,WI,WC] 305/296-3993, 800/432-4849 ■ 422 Amelia St (at Whitehead) ■ *early 1900s Conch house & condos, jacuzzi* ■ www.casadeluces.com

12 **Coral Tree Inn/ Oasis/ Coconut Grove Guest House** [★MO,SW,N,NS,WI,WC,GO] 305/296-2131, 800/362-7477 ■ 817 & 822 & 823 Fleming St (at Margaret) ■ *3 historic homes w/ roof decks w/ 50-mile vistas of the Gulf of Mexico, 3 hot tubs, gym* ■ www.keywest-allmale.com

13 **Cuban Club Suites** [GF] 305/296-0465, 800/432-4849 ■ 1102-1108 Duval St (at Virginia) ■ *award-winning historic hotel, suites w/ kitchens* ■ www.keywestcubanclub.com

14 **Curry House** [GS,SW,NS] 305/294-6777, 800/633-7439 ■ 806 Fleming St (at William) ■ *full brkfst, patio* ■ www.curryhousekeywest.com

15 **Cypress House & Guest Studios** [GF,SW,WI,WC] 305/294-6969, 800/525-2488 ■ 601 Caroline (at Simonton) ■ *1888 Grand Conch mansion, sundeck* ■ www.cypresshousekw.com

16 **Duval House** [GF,SW,NS] 305/292-9491, 800/223-8825 ■ 815 Duval St (at Petronia) ■ *Victorians w/ gardens, sundeck* ■ www.duvalhousekeywest.com

17 **Equator Guest House** [MO,SW,N,NS,WI,WC,GO] 305/294-7775, 800/278-4552 ■ 818 Fleming St (at William) ■ www.equatorresort.com

18 **The Grand Guest House** [MW,NS,GO] 305/294-0590, 888/947-2630 ■ 1116 Grinnell St ■ *in converted rooming house built in 1880s for cigar workers* ■ www.grandguesthouse.com

19 **Heartbreak Hotel** [MW,GO] 305/296-5558 ■ 716 Duval St (near Petronia) ■ *kitchens* ■ www.heartbreakhotel.org

20 **Heron House** [GF,SW,WI,WC] 305/294-9227, 888/861-9066 ■ 512 Simonton St (at Fleming) ■ *evening wine* ■ www.heronhouse.com

21 **Island House** [MO,F,SW,N,NS,WI,WC,GO] 305/294-6284, 800/890-6284 ■ 1129 Fleming St (at White) ■ *some shared baths, hot tub, sauna, steam, gym, very cruisy* ■ www.islandhousekeywest.com

22 **Key Lodge Motel** [GF,SW,WI] 305/296-9915, 800/845-8384 ■ 1004 Duval St (at Truman) ■ www.keylodge.com

23 **Key West Harbor Inn B&B** [GS,SW,NS,WI] 305/296-2978, 800/608-6569 ■ 219 Elizabeth St (at Greene) ■ *hot tub* ■ www.keywestharborinn.com

24 **Knowles House B&B** [GS,SW,N,NS,GO] 305/296-8132, 800/352-4414 ■ 1004 Eaton St (at Grinnell) ■ *restored 1880s Conch house, sundeck* ■ www.knowleshouse.com

25 **La Te Da** [★MW,S,21+,SW,WI,WC,GO] 305/296-6706, 877/528-3320 ■ 1125 Duval St (at Catherine) ■ *full brkfst, tropical setting, also restaurant & 3 bars* ■ www.lateda.com

26 **Marquesa Hotel** [GF,SW,NS,WI,WC] 305/292-1919, 800/869-4631 ■ 600 Fleming St (at Simonton) ■ *also Cafe Marquesa 6pm-10:30pm, full bar* ■ www.marquesa.com

27 **Marrero's Guest Mansion** [GF,SW,NS,WI] 305/294-6977, 800/459-6212 ■ 410 Fleming St (btwn Duval & Whitehead) ■ *1890 Victorian mansion, wknd sunset cocktails* ■ www.marreros.com

28 **The Mermaid & the Alligator** [GS,SW,NS,WI,GO] 305/294-1894, 800/773-1894 ■ 729 Truman Ave (at Windsor Ln) ■ *full brkfst* ■ www.kwmermaid.com

29 **Nassau House** [GF,SW,NS,WI,WC] 305/296-8513, 800/296-8513 ■ 1016 Fleming St (at Grinnell) ■ *sundeck, hot tub* ■ www.nassauhouse.com

30 **The New Orleans House Guesthouse** [M,SW,GO] 305/293-9800, 888/293-9893 ■ 724 Duval St, upstairs (at Angela) ■ www.neworleanshousekw.com

31 **Old Town Manor** [GF,NS,WI] 305/292-2170, 800/294-2170 ■ 511 Eaton St (at Duval) ■ *1886 Victorian mansion w/ gardens* ■ www.eatonlodge.com

32 **Pearl's Rainbow** [★WO,SW,N,NS,WI,WC,GO] 305/292-1450, 800/749-6696 ■ 525 United St (at Duval) ■ *sundeck, hot tub, also bar & restaurant, lesbian-owned* ■ www.pearlsrainbow.com

33 **Pier House Resort & Caribbean Spa** [GF,SW,NS,WI,WC] 305/296-4600, 800/327-8340 ■ 1 Duval St (at Front) ■ *private beach, hot tub, restaurants, bars, spa* ■ www.pierhouse.com

34 **Pilot House Guest House** [GS,SW,N,NS,WI,WC] 305/293-6600, 800/648-3780 ■ 414 Simonton St (at Eaton) ■ *Victorian mansion in Old Town, hot tub available* ■ www.PilotHouseKeyWest.com

35 **Seascape Tropical Inn** [GF,SW,NS] 305/296-7776, 800/765-6438 ■ 420 Olivia St (at Duval) ■ *also cottages, hot tub, sundeck* ■ www.seascapetropicalinn.com

36 **Sheraton Suites Key West** [GF,SW,NS,WI,WC] 305/292-9800, 800/452-3224 ■ 2001 S Roosevelt Blvd ■ *also restaurant*

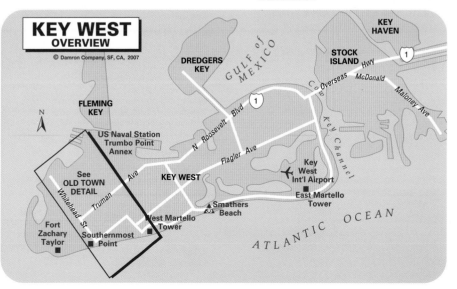

37 **Simonton Court Historic Inn & Cottages** [GF,SW,NS,WI] 305/294-6386, 800/944-2687 ■ 320 Simonton St (at Caroline) ■ built in 1880s, sundeck ■ www.simontoncourt.com

38 **Travelers Palm** [GF,SW] 305/294-9560, 800/294-9560 ■ 915 Center St ■ in Old Town Key West, shared jacuzzi ■ www.travelerspalm.com

39 **Tropical Inn** [GF,SW] 305/294-9977, 888/611-6510 ■ 812 Duval St (at Petronia) ■ old Conch house, also cottages, hot tub, sundeck ■ www.tropicalinn.com

BARS

40 **The 801 Bourbon Bar** [★MW,NH,D,C,DS,P,S] 305/296-1992 ■ 801 Duval St (at Petronia) ■ 11am-4am, Sun bingo, also One Saloon [M,L] ■ www.801bourbon.com

41 **Bobby's Monkey Bar** [M,NH,E,K,WC] 305/294-2655 ■ 900 Simonton St (at Olivia) ■ noon-4am

30 **Bootleggers** [M,CW] 305/296-1992 ■ 411 Petronia (part of Bourbon St Pub Complex) ■ 5pm-midnight ■ www.bootleggerskeywest.com

30 **Bourbon Street Pub** [★M,S,V,SW,WC] 305/296-1992 ■ 724 Duval St (at Angela) ■ 11am-4am, from noon Sun, popular daytime bar, includes garden bar w/ pool & hot tub, start your "Duval Crawl" here ■ www.bourbonstreetpub.com

42 **Kwest Men** [★M,S] 305/292-8500 ■ 705 Duval St ■ noon-4am, strippers ■ www.kwestmen.com

25 **La Te Da** [★MW,C,P,WC,GO] 305/296-6706 ■ 1125 Duval St (at Catherine) ■ 3 bars & restaurant ■ www.lateda.com

32 **Pearl's Patio** [WO,F,K] 305/292-1450, 800/749-6696 ■ 525 United St (at Duval & Simonton, at Pearl's Rainbow) ■ noon-10pm, later on wknds, special events ■ www.pearlspatio.com

43 **Virgilio's** [GS,D,F,E] 305/296-8118 ■ 524 Duval St (at Fleming in La Trattoria) ■ 7pm-4am, martini bar, garden ■ www.virgilioskeywest.com

NIGHTCLUBS

42 **Aqua** [MW,D,E,K,DS,V] 305/294-0555 ■ 711 Duval St ■ 3pm-2am, till 4am Th-Sat, also Wet Bar, from 9pm Fri-Sat, garden w/ waterfall ■ www.aquakeywest.com

CAFES

Croissants de France [BW] 305/294-2624 ■ 223 Petronia ■ 7:30am-6pm, restaurant open till 3pm, clsd Wed, French pastries, patio

RESTAURANTS

Antonia's [★] 305/294-6565 ■ 615 Duval St (at Southard) ■ 6pm-11pm, Italian, full bar ■ www.antoniaskeywest.com

Bo's Fish Wagon [★] 305/294-9272 ■ 801 Caroline (at Williams) ■ lunch, dinner, "seafood & eat it"

KEY WEST

Local Food:
Tiny, yellow Key limes surrender their tart juice for the famous Key Lime pie. Don't leave town without trying a slice; it's the official dessert of Key West.

Tourist Info
AIRPORT DIRECTIONS
Key West International Airport. To get to Duval St, turn left on S Roosevelt. After traffic signal, S Roosevelt becomes N Roosevelt. Follow Truman Ave to Duval St.

PUBLIC TRANSIT & TAXIS
Friendly Cab 305/292-0000.
Key West Express 888/539-2628
Key West Transit Authority 305/292-8160.

TOURIST SPOTS & INFO
Audubon House and Gardens 305/294-2116, web: www.audubonhouse.com.
Dolphin Research Center 305/289-1121, web: www.dolphins.org.
Glass-bottom boats 305/293-0099, web: www.discoveryunderseatours.com.
Hemingway House, web: www.hemingwayhome.com.
Sunset Celebration at Mallory Square.
Red Barn Theatre 305/296-9911, web: www.redbarntheatre.com.
Southernmost Point USA.

Weather
The average temperature year-round is 78°, and the sun shines nearly every day. Any time is the right time for a visit.

Best Views
Old Town Trolley Tour (1/2 hour) 305/296-6688, web: www.historictours.com/keywest.

City Calendar
LGBT PRIDE
June. 305/292-3223, web: www.pridefestkeywest.com.

ANNUAL EVENTS
February - Kelly McGillis Classic Women's & Girls' Flag Football Tournament 888/464-9332, web: www.iwffa.com.
September - WomenFest, web: www.womenfest.com.
October - Fantasy Fest 305/296-1817, web: www.fantasyfest.net. Weeklong Halloween celebration with parties, masquerade balls & parades.

Queer Resources
COMMUNITY INFO
Gay/Lesbian Community Center 305/292-3223.
513 Truman Ave, web: www.glcckeywest.org.
Key West Business Guild 305/294-4603, 800/535-7797, web: www.gaykeywestfl.com.
AA 305/296-8654.
KISS (Keep It Simple, Sweetie), 305/294-8912, 1215 Petronia St (at the MCC).
AIDS Help 305/296-6196.

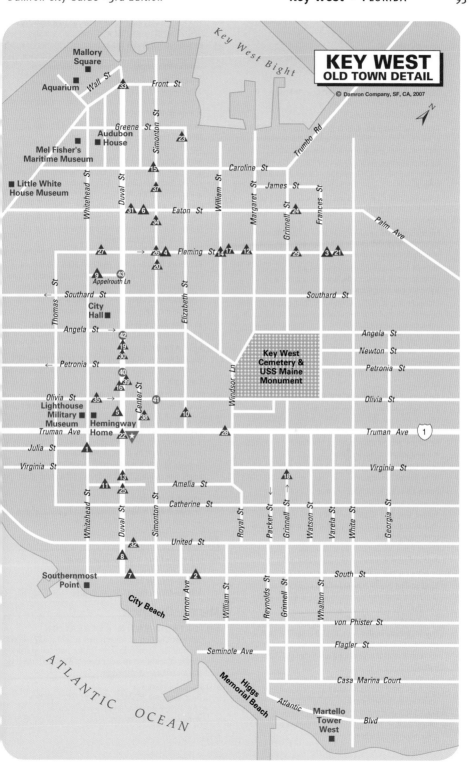

KEY WEST
OLD TOWN DETAIL

© Damron Company, SF, CA, 2007

Cafe Sole 305/294-0230 ■ 1029 Southard St (at Frances) ■ *dinner nightly, Sun brunch, romantic, candlelit backyard* ■ www.cafesole.com

Camille's 305/296-4811 ■ 1202 Simonton (at Catherine) ■ *brkfst, lunch & dinner, bistro, hearty brkfst* ■ www.camilleskeywest.com

Half Shell Raw Bar 305/294-7496 ■ 231 Margaret St ■ *11am-10pm, waterfront, full bar* ■ www.halfshellrawbar.com

Kelly's Caribbean Bar Grill & Brewery 305/293-8484 ■ 301 Whitehead St (at Caroline) ■ *lunch & dinner, owned by actress Kelly McGillis* ■ www.kellyskeywest.com

La Trattoria Venezia 305/296-1075 ■ 524 Duval St (at Fleming) ■ *5:30pm-10:30pm, Italian, full bar* ■ www.latrattoria.us

Lobos [BW] 305/296-5303 ■ 613 Duval St, #5 Key Lime Square (south of Southard St) ■ *11am-6pm, sandwiches, plenty veggie*

Louie's Backyard [★] 305/294-1061 ■ 700 Waddell Ave (at Vernon) ■ *lunch & dinner, fine dining, bar till 2am, deck* ■ www.louiesbackyard.com

Mangia Mangia [BW] 305/294-2469 ■ 900 Southard St (at Margaret St) ■ *dinner only, fresh pasta, patio* ■ www.mangia-mangia.com

Mangoes [WC] 305/292-4606 ■ 700 Duval St (at Angela) ■ *lunch & dinner, bar till 1am, "Floribbean" cuisine, full bar* ■ www.mangoeskeywest.com

New York Pizza Cafe 305/292-1991 ■ 1075 Duval St (Duval Square) ■ *11am-midnight, very reasonable prices*

Pisces 305/294-7100 ■ 1007 Simonton St (at Truman) ■ *6pm-11pm, tropical French, full bar* ■ www.pisceskeywest.com

Restaurant at La Te Da [★P] 305/296-6706, 877/528-3320 ■ 1125 Duval St (at La Te Da accommodations) ■ *brkfst, lunch & dinner, fusion* ■ www.lateda.com

Rooftop Cafe 305/294-2042 ■ 308 Front St (at Fitzpatrick) ■ *bkfst, lunch & dinner, best Key Lime pie, full bar* ■ www.rooftopcafekeywest.com

Salsa Loca 305/292-1865 ■ 918 Duval St ■ *clsd Mon, tasty, inexpensive Mexican*

Seven Fish [★] 305/296-2777 ■ 632 Olivia St (at Elizabeth) ■ *6pm-10pm, clsd Tue* ■ www.7fish.com

Square One [WC] 305/296-4300 ■ 1075 Duval St (at Truman) ■ *6pm-10pm, American, full bar* ■ www.squareonerestaurant.com

Upper Crust 305/293-8890 ■ 611 Duval St ■ *noon-11pm, excellent pizza* ■ www.uppercrustkeywest.com

ENTERTAINMENT & RECREATION

BluQ Sailing [M,GO] 305/923-7245 ■ 201 William St (at Caroline) ■ *all-gay sails, meals included* ■ www.captainstevekw.com

Fort Zachary Taylor Beach ■ *more gay to the right*

Gay & Lesbian Trolley Tour 305/294-4603 ■ *11am Sat, check out all of the gay hotspots & historical points, look for rainbow-decorated trolley* ■ www.gaykeywestfl.com/trolleytour

The Key West Butterfly & Nature Conservatory [GO] 305/296-2988, 800/839-4647 ■ 1316 Duval Street ■ www.keywestbutterfly.com

Moped Hospital 866/296-1625 ■ 601 Truman ■ *forget the car—mopeds are a must for touring the island* ■ www.mopedhospital.com

The Rude Awakening Radio Extravaganza Ministry [W] 305/296-7511 ■ 92.7 FM WEOW ■ *6am-10am Mon-Fri, morning zoo show w/ a lesbian twist; music, comedy, contests, news* ■ www.weow97.com/pages/rudegirl&mollyblue.html

Sebago Gay Cruises [W,BW,$] 305/292-4768, 305/294-5687 ■ 201 William St (at historic Key West Seaport) ■ *women's sunset cruises Th, call for additional info* ■ www.keywestsebago.com

Skinny Dipper Cruises 305/240-0517 ■ Garrison Bight Marina ■ *clothing-optional chartered cruises* ■ www.skinnydippercruises.com

Venus Charters [GO] 305/304-1181, 305/292-9403 ■ Garrison Bight Marina slip #10 ■ *snorkeling, light-tackle fishing, dolphin-watching, lesbian-owned* ■ www.venuscharters.com

BOOKSTORES

Key West Island Books 305/294-2904 ■ 513 Fleming St (at Duval) ■ *10am-9pm, new & used rare books, also LGBT section* ■ kwbook@aol.com

RETAIL SHOPS

Fast Buck Freddie's [WC] 305/294-2007 ■ 500 Duval St (at Fleming) ■ *10am-6pm, till 8pm Th-Fri, till 10pm Sat, from 11am Sun, clothing, gifts* ■ www.fastbuckfreddies.com

Fausto's Food Palace 305/296-5663 ■ 522 Fleming St (at Duval) ■ *8am-8pm, till 7pm Sun, cruisy grocery store*

In Touch 305/292-7293 ■ 715 Duval St (at Angela) ■ *9am-11pm, gay gifts*

PUBLICATIONS

Buzz Magazine 305/394-9722, 877/429-2899 ■ *LGBT lifestyle magazine for Southern Florida* ■ www.buzzpublications.com

GYMS & HEALTH CLUBS

Bodies on South 305/292-2930 ■ 2740 N Roosevelt Blvd

EROTICA

Fairvilla Megastore 305/292-0448 ■ 520 Front St ■ *9am-midnight, clean, well-lighted adult store w/ emphasis on couples: "store for lovers"* ■ www.fairvilla.com

Leather Master 305/292-5051, 800/565-9447 ■ 418 Appelrouth Ln (btwn Duval & Whitehead) ■ *11am-10pm, noon-8pm Sun, custom leather, toys & more* ■ www.leathermaster.com

Truman Books & Video 305/295-0120 ■ 922 Truman Ave ■ *arcade*

Miami

Miami is divided into 3 geographical areas:
Miami—Overview
Miami—Greater Miami
Miami—Miami Beach/ South Beach

Miami—Overview

ENTERTAINMENT & RECREATION

Sailboat Charters of Miami [MW] 305/772-4221 ■ 3400 Pan American Dr (at S Bayshore Dr) ■ *private sailing charters aboard all-teakwood 46-foot clipper to Bahamas & the Keys* ■ www.sailboat-charters.com

PUBLICATIONS

Buzz Magazine 305/420-5120, 877/429-2899 ■ *LGBT lifestyle magazine for Southern Florida* ■ www.buzzpublications.com

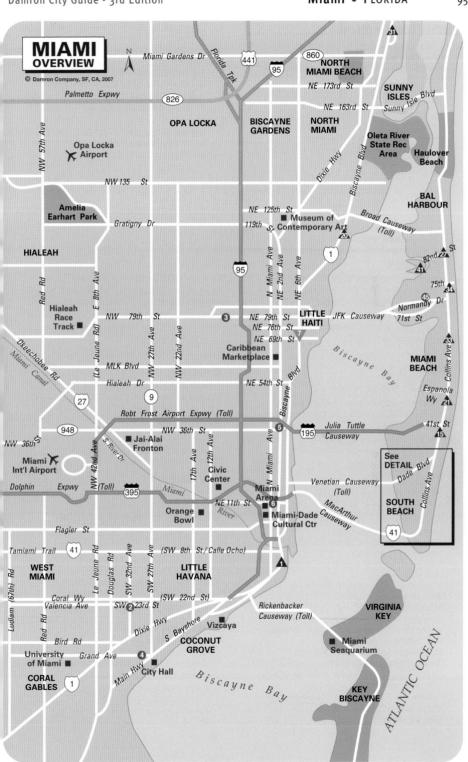

Miami—Greater Miami

ACCOMMODATIONS

1   **Miami River Inn** [GF,SW,WI,WC] 305/325-0045, 800/468-3589 ■ 118 SW S River Dr ■ B&B located in Miami's Little Havana district, jacuzzi ■ www.miamiriverinn.com

NIGHTCLUBS

2   **Azucar** [MW,D,MR-L,DS] 305/441-6974 ■ 2301 SW 32nd Ave (at Coral Wy) ■ 10:30pm-5am Th-Sat, 8pm-3am Sun, clsd Mon-Wed ■ www.clubazucar.com

3   **Club Boi** [M,D,MR-AF] 305/836-8995 ■ 726 NW 79th St (1 block W of I-95) ■ 11pm-close Tue & Fri-Sat ■ www.clubboi.com

4   **Oxygen Lounge** [GS,D,F] 305/476-0202 ■ 2911 Grand Ave, Subterranean level, Coconut Grove ■ 10pm-5am, chic lounge w/ lesbian following, also sushi restaurant ■ www.oxygen-lounge.biz

5   **Pink** [W,D,S] 305/576-1988 ■ 175 NE 36th St (at SOHO Lounge) ■ 10pm-close Fri ■ www.ultra-events.com

6   **Twilo** [M,D,$] 305/350-1851 ■ 30 NE 11th St ■ 11pm-close Fri-Sat only ■ www.twilomiami.com

CAFES

Gourmet Station 305/762-7229 ■ 7601 Biscayne Blvd (at NE 71st St) ■ 9am-9pm, till 8pm Fri, till 4pm Sat, clsd Sun, also catering ■ Rickmia@bellsouth.net

MIAMI

Local Food:

Known by many as the "Capital of Latin America," sizzling Miami serves up some enticing eats. Local "Floribbean" fusion cuisine is a melding of Caribbean, Continental, and South American influences. Thrill-seekers should sample the spicy Cuban fare in Little Havana. South Beach is a see-and-be-seen kind of scene, so grab a table at one of the outdoor restaurants along Lincoln Road or Ocean Drive, and settle in for some world-class people-watching. A warning: many SoBe restaurants automatically include the gratuity in your bill, so double-check before handing over your credit card.

Tourist Info

AIRPORT DIRECTIONS

Miami International. To South Beach, take 953 South to 836 East, to 395 East. 395 becomes 5th St in Miami Beach.

PUBLIC TRANSIT & TAXIS

Yellow Cab 305/266-7799.
Metro Taxi 305/888-8888.
A Plus 305/219-8219.
Metro Bus 305/770-3131.

TOURIST SPOTS & INFO

Bayside Marketplace 305/577-3344, web: www.baysidemarketplace.com.
Miami Beach Botanical Garden 305/673-7256, web: www.mbgarden.org.
Miami Design Preservation League 305/672-2014. web: mdpl.org.
Miami Museum of Science & Planetarium 305/646-4200, web: www.miamisci.org.
Monkey Jungle 305/235-1611, web: www.monkeyjungle.com.
Museum of Contempory Art, N Miami 305/893-6211, web: www.mocanomi.org.
Parrot Jungle Island 305/258-6453, web: www.parrotjungle.com.
Sanford L Ziff Jewish Museum of Florida 305/672-5044, web: www.jewishmuseum.com.

Visitor's Center: Greater Miami Convention & Visitors Bureau 305/539-3000. 701 Brickell Ave, web: www.miamiandbeaches.com.

Weather

Warm all year. Temperatures stay in the 90°s during the summer and drop into the mid-60°s in the winter. Be prepared for sunshine!

Best Views

If you've got money to burn, a helicopter flight over Miami Beach is a great way to see the city. Otherwise, hit the beach.

City Calendar

ANNUAL EVENTS

Feb/March - Winter Party 202/393-5177, web: www.winterparty.com. Beach dance party benefiting the National Gay & Lesbian Task Force.
April/May - Gay & Lesbian Film Festival 305/534-9924, web: www.mglff.com.
May - Aqua Girl 305/532-1997, web: www.aqaugirl.org. A women's weekend.
November - White Party Vizcaya 305/576-1234, web: www.whiteparty.net. AIDS benefit.

Queer Resources

COMMUNITY INFO

Switchboard of Miami 305/358-4357.
Miami-Dade Gay & Lesbian Chamber of Commerce 305/573-4000 web: www.gogaymi-ami.com.
Lambda Dade AA 305/573-9608. web: www.lambdadadeclubhouse.org. 212 NE 24th St.
SoBe AIDS Project 305/532-1033. web: www.sobeaids.org.

RESTAURANTS

The Bal Harbour Bistro [WC,GO] 305/861-4544 ■ 9700 Collins Ave (in the Bal Harbour Shops), Bal Harbour ■ *9am-11pm, full bar, patio* ■ www.balharbourbistro.com

Cafe Tu Tu Tango 305/529-2222 ■ 3015 Grand Ave, Coconut Grove ■ *11:30am-midnight, till 1am Th, till 2am Fri-Sat, eclectic small plates* ■ www.cafetututango.com/grove

Delicias de España 305/669-4485, 305/661-9610 ■ 4016 SW 57th Ave (at Bird Rd) ■ *7am-9pm, till 10pm Th-Sat, till 4pm Sun, Spanish* ■ www.deliciasdeespana.com

Magnum Lounge & Restaurant [★GS,NH,E,P,R] 305/757-3368 ■ 709 NE 79th St ■ *6pm-midnight, bar open 5pm-2am, till 3am wknds, clsd Mon, cont'l*

Ortanique on the Mile [★] 305/446-7710 ■ 278 Miracle Mile (at Salzedo), Coral Gables ■ *lunch Mon-Fri, dinner nightly, New World Caribbean, full bar*

Royal Bavarian Schnitzel Haus 305/754-8002 ■ 1085 NE 79th St ■ *5pm-11pm, till midnight Fri-Sat*

BOOKSTORES

7 **Lambda Passages Bookstore** 305/754-6900 ■ 7545 Biscayne Blvd (at 76th) ■ *11am-9pm, noon-6pm Sun, LGBT/feminist* ■ lambdapassages@aol.com

MEN'S CLUBS

Club Body Center Miami [★MO,SW,PC] 305/448-2214 ■ 2991 Coral Wy ■ *24hrs, poolside cookouts, over 30 years popular!* ■ www.cbcresorts.com

EROTICA

Biscayne Books & Video 305/891-3475 ■ 117 Biscayne Blvd ■ *24hrs*

J&R Book & Video 305/262-6570 ■ 7455 Bird Rd (at Palmetto/826)

Miami—Miami Beach/ South Beach

ACCOMMODATIONS

8 **Aqua Hotel & Lounge** [GS,WI] 305/538-4361 ■ 1530 Collins Ave ■ *boutique hotel, jacuzzi* ■ www.aquamiami.com

9 **Beachcomber Hotel** [GF,NS,WI] 305/531-3755, 888/305-4683 ■ 1340 Collins Ave (at 13th St) ■ *intimate art deco hotel, near beach* ■ www.beachcombermiami.com

10 **The Blue Moon Hotel** [GF,SW] 305/673-2262, 800/553-7739 ■ 944 Collins Ave ■ *Mediterranean-style hotel, also bar* ■ www.bluemoonhotel.com

11 **Bresaro Suites at the Mantell** [GS,SW,GO] 305/772-5665 ■ 255 W 24th St ■ *in 1942 art deco bldg, kitchens, no more than 2 people per suite* ■ www.bresaro.com

12 **The Cardozo Hotel** [GF,F,WI,WC] 305/535-6500, 800/782-6500 ■ 1300 Ocean Dr ■ *Gloria Estefan's plush hotel* ■ www.cardozohotel.com

13 **The Century** [GF,F,NS,WI,WC] 305/674-8855, 888/982-3688 ■ 140 Ocean Dr ■ *restored art deco, Joia restaurant, celebrity hangout* ■ www.centurysouthbeach.com

14 **Chesterfield Hotel** [GS] 305/531-5831, 877/762-3477 ■ 855 Collins Ave ■ www.thechesterfieldhotel.com

15 **Circa 39** [GF,SW,NS,WI,WC] 305/538-4900, 877/824-7223 ■ 3900 Collins Ave (at 39th St) ■ *art deco hotel, also wine bar & lounge; evening cocktails (see Miami Overview map)* ■ www.circa39.com

16 **The Colony Hotel** [GF,F,WI,WC] 305/673-0088 ■ 736 Ocean Dr (at 7th St) ■ *newly renovated art deco, oceanfront* ■ colonymiami.com

17 **Crescent Suites** [GF,NS] 305/531-5197, 800/880-9041 ■ 1420 Ocean Dr, Miami Beach ■ *art deco boutique all-suite property in heart of South Beach* ■ www.crescentsuites.com

18 **Delano Hotel** [GF,F,SW,WC] 305/672-2000, 800/697-1791 ■ 1685 Collins Ave ■ *hip hotel designed by Philippe Starck, great bar scene (see & be seen)* ■ www.delanohotelmiamibeach.com

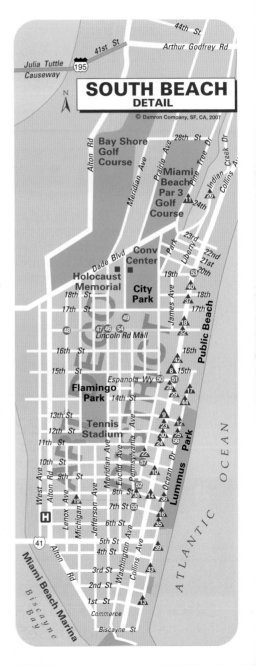

19 **The European Guesthouse** [MW,WI,GO] 305/673-6665 ■ 721 Michigan Ave (btwn 7th & 8th) ■ B&B, full brkfst, hot tub, tropical garden w/ bar ■ www.europeanguesthouse.com

20 **Florida Hotel Network** [★] 800/293-2419 ■ hotel reservations, vacation rentals ■ www.floridahotels.com

21 **Fontainebleau Hilton Resort & Spa** [GF,SW,WC] 305/538-2000, 800/548-8886 ■ 4441 Collins Ave ■ all-suite hotel, (see Miami Overview map) ■ www.fontainebleauresort.com

14 **The Hotel** [GF,F,SW,WI,WC] 305/531-2222, 877/843-4683 ■ 801 Collins Ave ■ interior design by Todd Oldham, Wish restaurant, full bar ■ www.thehotelofsouthbeach.com

22 **Hotel Astor** [★GF,F,WI,WC] 305/531-8081, 800/270-4981 ■ 956 Washington Ave (at 10th St) ■ www.hotelastor.com

23 **Hotel Impala** [GS,F,NS,WI,WC] 305/673-2021, 800/646-7252 ■ 1228 Collins Ave ■ luxury boutique hotel near beach, also Italian restaurant ■ www.hotelimpalamiamibeach.com

14 **Hotel Lily Leon** [GF,F,WC] 305/673-3767, 877/762-3477 ■ 835-841 Collins Ave (at 8th St) ■ stylish decor, popular w/ photo industry ■ www.lilyleonhotel.com

24 **Hotel Nash** [GF,F,SW,NS,WC] 305/674-7800, 800/403-6274 ■ 1120 Collins Ave ■ sleek & modern new boutique hotel, also restaurant & spa, close to gay beach ■ www.hotelnash.com

25 **Hotel Ocean** [★GS,F,WI,WC] 305/672-2579, 800/783-1725 ■ 1230-38 Ocean Dr ■ great location, jacuzzi ■ www.hotelocean.com

14 **Hotel Shelley** [GS,WI] 305/531-3341 ■ 844 Collins Ave ■ 1930s art deco hotel ■ www.hotelshelley.com

26 **The Indian Creek Hotel** [GF,F,SW,WC] 305/531-2727, 800/491-2772 ■ 2727 Indian Creek Dr ■ oasis of serenity w/ art deco flair ■ www.indiancreekhotel.com

27▶**Island House Miami Beach** [GS,N,NS,GO] 305/864-2422, 800/382-2422 ■ 82nd St ■ patio, jacuzzi (see Miami Overview map) ■ www.islandhousesouthbeach.com

28▶**Island House South Beach** [MO,GO] 305/864-2422, 800/382-2422 ■ 1428 Collins Ave ■ SoBe's largest men's guesthouse, full brkfst ■ www.islandhousesouthbeach.com

24 **The Kent** [GS,F,WI,WC] 305/604-5068, 866/826-5368 ■ 1131 Collins Ave (at 11th St) ■ on the beach, garden ■ www.thekenthotel.com

29 **The Loft Hotel** [GS] 305/534-2244 ■ 952 Collins Ave ■ affordable boutique hotel, 1 block to beach ■ www.thelofthotel.com

30 **Marlin Hotel** [GS,WI,WC] 305/604-3595 ■ 1200 Collins Ave ■ fabulous studios w/ full kitchens ■ www.marlinhotel.com

31 **Miami Habitat** [GS,NS] 305/673-3958, 800/385-4644 ■ furnished apts & hotel rooms in Art Deco District (see Miami Overview map) ■ www.miamihabitat.com

28 **The Nassau Suite Hotel** [GS,NS] 305/532-0043, 866/859-4177 ■ 1414 Collins Ave ■ renovated art deco, near beach ■ www.nassausuite.com

32 **The National Hotel** [GS,F,SW,WI,WC] 305/532-2311, 800/327-8370 ■ 1677 Collins Ave ■ on beach ■ www.nationalhotel.com

33 **The New Casablanca on the Ocean** [GS,SW] 305/868-0010, 800/813-6676 ■ 6345 Collins Ave (at 63rd St) ■ studios & town houses ■ www.casablancaontheocean.com

34 **Ocean Surf Hotel** [GF,WC] 305/866-1648, 800/555-0411 ■ 7436 Ocean Terrace (near 75th St & Collins Ave) ■ beautiful restored art deco, in quiet North Beach (see Miami Overview map) ■ www.theoceansurfhotel.com

35 **The Park Central** [GF,F,SW,WI] 305/538-1611 ■ 640 Ocean Dr ■ ocean views ■ www.theparkcentral.com

36 **The Pelican** [★GS,F,WI,WC] 305/673-3373, 800/773-5422 ■ 826 Ocean Dr (btwn 8th & 9th Sts) ■ designer theme rooms, restaurant w/ live DJ ■ www.pelicanhotel.com

37 **The Raleigh, Miami Beach** [GF,SW,WI,WC] 305/534-6300, 800/848-1775 ■ 1775 Collins Ave (at Ocean Front) ■ www.raleighhotel.com

38 **Royal South Beach Condo Hotel** [GS] 305/673-9009, 888/394-6835 ■ 763 Pennsylvania Ave ■ 1930s hotel restored to retro fabulousness by Jordan Mozer ■ www.royalsouthbeach.com

39 **The Savoy Hotel** [GS,SW,NS,WI,WC] 305/532-0200, 800/237-2869 ■ 425 Ocean Dr (at 5th St) ■ art-deco-meets-eclectic-boutique hotel, kids ok ■ www.savoymiami.com

40 **The Shelborne Beach Resort** [GF,F,SW,WC] 305/531-1271, 800/327-8757 ■ 1801 Collins Ave (at 18th) ■ full brkfst, tropical gardens ■ www.shelborne.com

41 **SoBeYou** [GS,SW,NS,WI,GO] 305/534-5247, 877/599-5247 ■ 1018 Jefferson Ave ■ lush, tropical pool area, gourmet brkfst, near beach, lesbian-owned ■ www.sobeyou.us

Something Special, A Lesbian Venture [WO] 305/696-8826 ■ 1-bdrm apt on beach, also backyard camping & dining ■ somethingspecialalv@yahoo.com

37 **South Seas** [GF,F,SW,WI] 305/538-1411, 800/345-2678 ■ 1751 Collins Ave ■ clean & basic, beach access ■ www.southseashotel.com

25 **The Tides** [GS,F,SW,WI] 305/604-5070, 800/439-4095 ■ 1220 Ocean Dr ■ private beach area ■ www.thetideshotel.com

42 **The Tropics Hotel & Hostel** [GS,SW] 305/531-0361 ■ 1550 Collins Ave (btwn 15th & 16th Sts) ■ modern hotel rooms & hostel, near beach & attractions ■ www.tropicshotel.com

28 **Villa Paradiso Guesthouse** [GF] 305/532-0616 ■ 1415 Collins Ave ■ studios w/ full kitchens, courtyard ■ www.villaparadisohotel.com

43 **The Wave Hotel** [GF] 305/673-0401, 800/501-0401 ■ 350 Ocean Dr ■ tropical-style, newly renovated, popular for fashion shoots ■ www.wavehotel.com

44 **The Winterhaven** [GS,WI,WC] 305/531-5571, 800/553-7739 ■ 1400 Ocean Dr ■ ocean views ■ www.winterhavenhotelsobe.com

BARS

45 **Boy Bar** [M,NH] 305/864-2697 ■ 1220 Normandy (at Rue Notre Dame) ■ 5pm-5am, cruisy, backroom (see Miami Overview map)

46 **Buck15 Lounge** [GS] 305/538-3815 ■ 707 Lincoln Ln ■ 10pm-5am, from 8pm Fri-Sat, gallery lounge, more gay Th ■ www.buck15.com

47 **Creme Lounge** [MW,NH,D] 305/535-1163 ■ 925 Lincoln Ln ■ open Tue & Th-Sat, theme nights, more women Sat for Siren ■ www.cremelounge.net

48 **Funkshion** [GS,F,E,DS] 305/673-0554 ■ 1116 Lincoln Rd ■ 6pm-2am, till 5am Fri-Sat, more gay Fri ■ www.funkshionlounge.com

49 Laundry Bar [MW,NH,D,E] 305/531-7700 ■ 721 N Lincoln Ln ■ noon-5am, drag shows, also laundromat ■ www.laundrybarmiami.com

47 Siren [W,D] 305/535-1163 ■ 925 Lincoln Ln (at Creme Lounge) ■ Sat only ■ www.cremelounge.net

NIGHTCLUBS

50 **Back Door Bamby** [GS,D] 305/604-3644 ■ 1437 Washington Ave (at Snatch) ■ Mon only ■ www.backdoor-bamby.com

51 **Blue** [GS,D,DS] 305/534-1009 ■ 222 Espanola Way (at Collins) ■ 10pm-5am, drag show Sun

52 **Indra Lounge** [★GS,D] 305/673-6047 ■ 841 Washington Ave (btwn 8th & 9th) ■ 10:30pm-5am Tue-Wed & Fri-Sat only, more gay Wed for One Night in Bangkok, more lesbian Sat for G-Spot ■ www.indralounge.com

53 **Mynt Ultra Lounge** [GS,D] 786/276-6132 ■ 1921 Collins Ave ■ 11pm-5am, clsd Sun-Tue ■ www.myntlounge.com

Pandora Events [W,D,MR] 305/975-6933 ■ monthly women's parties, locations rotate so check website ■ www.pandoraevents.com

54 **Score** [★MW,D,K,DS,V] 305/535-1111 ■ 727 Lincoln Rd (at Meridian) ■ 4 bars, lounge opens 3pm, dance club 10pm-5am Tue & Th-Sat ■ www.scorebar.net

55 **Seven** [M,D,MR-L] 305/538-0820 ■ 685 Washington Ave (at 7th) ■ 4pm-5am, clsd Mon-Tue

56 **Strawberry Girls** [W,D] 305/531-7234 ■ 1200 Ocean Dr (at Palace) ■ 7pm-close

57 **Twist** [★M,D,DS,S,V,WC] 305/538-9478 ■ 1057 Washington Ave (at 11th) ■ 1pm-5am, 7 bars, go-go boys ■ www.twist-sobe.com

CAFES

News Cafe [★] 305/538-6397 ■ 800 Ocean Dr ■ 24hrs, healthy sandwiches, also bookstore & bar ■ www.newscafe.com

RESTAURANTS

11th Street Diner 305/534-6373 ■ 11th & Washington ■ 24hrs, full bar

A Fish Called Avalon [R,WC] 305/532-1727, 800/933-3306 ■ 700 Ocean Dr (at Avalon Hotel) ■ 6pm-11pm, full bar, seafood ■ www.afishcalledavalon.com

Balans 305/534-9191 ■ 1022 Lincoln Rd (btwn Michigan & Lennox) ■ 8am-midnight, till 1am Fri-Sat, int'l, some veggie ■ www.balans.co.uk/miami.html

Big Pink 305/532-4700 ■ 157 Collins (at 2nd St) ■ 8am-midnight, open late wknds, "real food for real people"

Cafeteria 305/672-3663 ■ 546 Lincoln Rd (at Pennsylvania) ■ 8am-3am, 24hrs Th-Sat ■ www.cafeteriagroup.com

David's Cafe II 305/672-8707 ■ 1654 Meridian Ave ■ 24hrs, Cuban ■ www.davidscafe.com

El Rancho Grande 305/673-0480 ■ 1626 Pennsylvania Ave (S of Lincoln) ■ 11:30am-11pm, Mexican ■ www.elranchograndemexicanrestaurant.com

The Front Porch 305/531-8300 ■ 1418 Ocean Dr (at Penguin Hotel) ■ 7am-6pm, till 7pm Fri-Sun, healthy homecooking, full bar

Joe's Stone Crab 305/673-0365 ■ 11 Washington Ave (near South Point Dr) ■ lunch & dinner, dinner only Sun-Mon, seasonal ■ www.joesstonecrab.com

Larios on the Beach 305/532-9577 ■ 820 Ocean Dr (at 8th) ■ 11:30am-midnight, Cuban

Madame's Restaurant & Cabaret Lounge [GF,NH,TG,E,C,DS,WC] 305/945-2040 ■ 239 Sunny Isles Blvd (at 163rd St & Collins Ave), Sunny Isles Beach ■ 6pm-close, clsd Tue-Wed, Southern comfort food, full bar ■ www.madamesusa.com

Nemo 305/532-4550 ■ 100 Collins Ave (at 1st St) ■ lunch & dinner, Sun brunch, chic decor, Pacific Rim & South American cuisine ■ www.nemorestaurant.com

Nexxt Cafe [★] 305/532-6643 ■ 700 Lincoln Rd (at Euclid Ave) ■ 11:30am-11pm, till midnight Fri-Sat

Pacific Time 305/534-5979 ■ 915 Lincoln Rd (btwn Jefferson & Michigan) ■ lunch Mon-Fri, dinner nightly, pan-Pacific ■ www.pacifictime.biz

Palace [GS,GO] 305/531-7234 ■ 1200 Ocean Dr (at 12th St) ■ noon-midnight, later Th-Sat, also bar

Prime 112 305/532-8112 ■ 112 Ocean Dr ■ lunch Mon-Fri, dinner nightly, steak house ■ www.prime112.com

Something Special [W,GO] 305/696-8826 ■ 6pm-10pm, clsd Mon-Tue, vegetarian ■ somethingspecialalv@yahoo.com

Spiga 305/534-0079 ■ 1228 Collins Ave (at 12th St) ■ dinner only, tasty homemade pastas ■ www.spigarestaurant.com

Sushi Rock Cafe [★] 305/532-2133 ■ 1351 Collins Ave (at 14th) ■ noon-midnight, 2pm-1am wknds, full bar

Tiramesu 305/532-4538 ■ 721 Lincoln Rd ■ lunch & dinner, Italian ■ www.tiramesu.com

Yuca 305/532-9822 ■ 501 Lincoln Rd (at Drexel Ave) ■ noon-11:30pm, New Cuban cuisine, cocktails ■ www.yuca.com

ENTERTAINMENT & RECREATION

Beach Scooter Rentals 305/538-0977 ■ 1435 Collins Ave ■ www.beachscooter.com

Fritz's Skate & Bike 305/532-1954 ■ 730 Lincoln Rd (at Euclid & Meridian) ■ rentals, in pedestrian mall ■ beachinlineskates.com

The Gay Beach 12th St & Ocean ■ where the boys are

Haulover Beach Park A1A S of Sunny Isle Blvd, North Miami Beach ■ popular nude beach

Lincoln Rd Lincoln Rd (btwn Bay Rd & Collins Aves) ■ pedestrian mall that embodies the rebirth of South Beach—fabulous restaurants, stores, galleries, museums, theaters, people at every step

BOOKSTORES

The 9th Chakra 305/538-0671, 866/538-0671 ■ 530 Lincoln Rd (btwn Drexel & Pennsylvania) ■ New Age books, supplies, gifts ■ www.9thchakra.com

Books & Books Inc 305/532-3222 ■ 933 Lincoln Rd ■ 10am-11pm, till midnight Fri-Sat, independent, LGBT section ■ www.booksandbooks.com

RETAIL SHOPS

Whittall & Shon 305/538-2606 ■ 900 Washington Ave (at 9th) ■ 11am-10pm, funky clothes & clubwear for boys ■ www.whittallandshonmen.com

PUBLICATIONS

Wire 305/588-0000 ■ weekly gay tabloid ■ thewire@att.net

GYMS & HEALTH CLUBS

David Barton Gym [GF] 305/674-5757 ■ 1685 Collins Ave (in the Delano Hotel) ■ www.davidbartongym.com

Iron People 305/532-0089 ■ 715 Lincoln Ln (behind Lincoln Rd) ■ ironpeople.com

SoBe Sports Club [★] 305/531-4743 ■ 1676 Alton Rd (btwn 16th & 17th) ■ www.sobesportsclub.net

EROTICA

Pleasure Emporium 305/673-3311 ■ 1019 5th St ■ *24hrs; also at 1671-A Alton Rd, 305/538-6434* ■ www.pleasureemporium.com

Pleasure Place 305/604-8771 ■ 425 Washington Ave (S of 5th), Miami Beach ■ *erotica, clubwear, leather, adult toys, DVDs, clothing & more* ■ www.pleasureplace.com

Sensations Video 305/534-2330 ■ 1317 Washington Ave ■ *24hrs*

X Spot 305/255-2190 ■ 19800 S Dixie Hwy ■ *24hrs; also 8831 SW 40th St, 305/226-8332*

Orlando

ACCOMMODATIONS

Advantage Vacation Homes [GF,SW,NS] 407/396-2262, 800/527-2262 ■ 7799 Styles Blvd (off Hwy 192), Kissimmee ■ *large selection of pool homes & condominiums near Walt Disney World* ■ www.advantagevacationhomes.com

1   Clarion Hotel Universal [GF,SW,WI,WC] 407/351-5009, 800/445-7299 ■ 7299 Universal Blvd ■ *full-service hotel just outside Universal Studios, 2 jacuzzis, sundeck* ■ www.clarionuniversal.com

2   Embassy Suites Orlando Downtown [GF,WC] 407/841-1000, 800/362-2779 ■ 191 E Pine St ■ *all-suite hotel, full brkfst* ■ embassyorlandodowntown.com

3   EO Inn & Urban Spa [GS,F,NS,WI] 407/481-8485, 888/481-8488 ■ 227 N Eola Dr (at Robinson) ■ *boutique hotel, rooftop terrace, sundeck, hot tub, cafe on-site* ■ www.eoinn.com

4   Grand Bohemian Hotel Orlando [GF,SW,NS,WC] 407/313-9000, 866/663-0024 ■ 325 S Orange Ave ■ *luxury hotel in downtown Orlando* ■ www.grandbohemianhotel.com

Holiday Villas [GF,SW,NS,WI] 407/397-0700, 800/344-3959 ■ 2928 Vineland Rd (btwn SR 535 & 192), Kissimmee ■ *2- & 3-bdrm luxury villas just 4 miles from Walt Disney World* ■ www.holidayvillas.com

Mid-Century Modern Rental Home [GF,SW,NS] 407/758-1190 ■ *restored 1950s rental home, near Disney, online keyword: Leedy* ■ www.homeexchange.com

6   ▶Parliament House Resort [★MW,D,MR,F,S,YC,SW,WC,GO] 407/425-7571 ■ 410 N Orange Blossom Tr ■ *also 6 bars (open at 8pm)* ■ www.parliamenthouse.com

The Perri House Inn [GF,SW] 407/876-4830, 800/780-4830 ■ 10417 Vista Oaks Ct ■ *quiet oasis 3 miles from Disney* ■ www.perrihouse.com

Ramada Plaza Gateway [GF,F,WC] 407/396-4400, 800/327-9170 ■ 7470 Hwy 192 W, Kissimmee ■ www.ramadagateway.com

Rick's B&B [M,N,SW,WI,GO] 407/396-7751, 407/414-7751 (cell) ■ PO Box 22318, 32830 ■ *full brkfst, patio, near Walt Disney World* ■ www.ricksbedandbreakfast.com

1   Sheraton Studio City [GF,SW,WI,WC] 407/351-2100, 800/327-1366 ■ 5905 International Dr ■ *world-class amenities combined w/ elegance & sophisticated excitement of 1940s & 1950s Hollywood, also bar & restaurant* ■ www.sheratonstudiocity.com

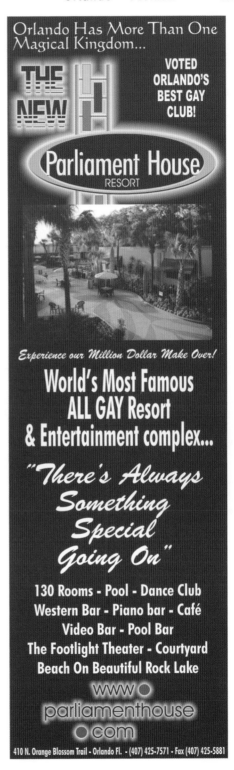

7 **The Veranda B&B** [GF,SW,NS,WC] 407/849-0321, 800/420-6822 ■ 115 N Summerlin Ave ■ *hot tub* ■ www.TheVerandaBandB.com

1 **Westgate Palace Resort** [GF,SW,NS,WI,WC] 407/996-6000, 877/996-6151 ■ 6145 Carrier Dr ■ *hotel, all 2-bdrm suites, kitchens* ■ www.westgateresorts.com

8 **The Winter Park Sweet Lodge** [GS,GO] 407/644-6099 ■ 271 S Orlando Ave (at Fairbanks Ave), Winter Park ■ *motel*

BARS

9 **Beer Bar** [M,NH,F] 407/532-3627 ■ 4453 Edgewater Dr ■ *3pm-2am, from noon Sun, patio* ■ www.ccbeerbar.com

10 **Copper Rocket** [GF,BW,WC] 407/645-0069 ■ 106 Lake Ave (at 17-92), Maitland ■ *2pm-2am, microbrews, full restaurant* ■ www.copperrocketpub.com

11 **Faces Club & Lounge** [★W,NH,D,F,E,K,WC] 407/291-7571 ■ 4910 Edgewater Dr ■ *4pm-midnight, till 2am Fri-Sat*

12 **Full Moon Saloon** [M,CW,B,L,GO] 407/648-8725 ■ 500 N Orange Blossom Tr ■ *4pm-2am, from noon Fri-Sun, popular Sun afternoon, also uniform/ levi, patio* ■ www.fullmoonsaloon.com

13 **Hank's** [M,NH,BW,WC] 407/291-2399 ■ 5026 Edgewater Dr ■ *noon-2am, patio*

New Phoenix [MW,NH,D,E,K] 407/678-9070 ■ 7124 Aloma Ave (at Forsythe), Winter Park ■ www.thenewphoenix.com

15 **Paradise** [M,NH,CW,L,K,WI] 407/898-0090, 407/898-0090 ■ 1300 N Mills Ave (btwn Virginia & Colonial) ■ *4pm-2am, from noon Sun, theme nights*

15 **The Peacock Room** [GF,NH,E] 407/228-0048 ■ 1321 N Mills Ave (at Montana) ■ *4:30pm-2am, from 8pm wknds, trendy lounge, art shows* ■ www.peacockroom.com

16 **Savoy** [M,S] 407/898-6766 ■ 1913 N Orange Ave ■ *5pm-2am, male dancers nightly, buffet Fri* ■ www.SavoyOrlando.com

6 **Western Bar** [M,CW,L,F,P,S] 407/425-7571 ■ 410 N Orange Blossom Tr (at Parliament House) ■ *6pm-2am, from noon wknds, also restaurant* ■ www.parliamenthouse.com

17 **Wylde's** [M,NH] 407/852-0612 ■ 3557 S Orange Ave ■ *5pm-2am* ■ www.wyldesorlando.com

NIGHTCLUBS

18 **The Club at Firestone** [★GS,D,S,V,18+$] 407/872-0066 ■ 578 N Orange Ave ■ *10pm-3am Th-Sun* ■ www.clubatfirestone.com

6 ► **Parliament House Resort** [★MW,D,MR,F,S,V,18+,SW,WC,GO] 407/425-7571 ■ 410 N Orange Blossom Tr ■ *10:30am-3am, 6 bars* ■ www.parliamenthouse.com

19 **Pulse Orlando** [M,K,S,18+] 407/649-3888 ■ 1912 S Orange Ave ■ *9pm-2am, theme nights* ■ www.pulseorlando.com

---

ORLANDO

For most travelers, Orlando is synonymous with Disney World (407/824-4321), but the Magic Kingdom is only one of the many theme parks in Orlando. In addition to Epcot Center and Disney-MGM Studios and the new Animal Kingdom, there's also Universal Studios Florida (407/363-8000), Gatorland (407/855-5496), and Sea World (407/351-3600). Primarily a family vacation area, Orlando will appeal to the kid in all of us.

Tourist Info

AIRPORT DIRECTIONS

Orlando International Airport. To get to Orange Blossom Trail, take 436 North from the airport to the East-West Expressway. Head west on the Expressway and take the Orange Blossom Trail exit.

PUBLIC TRANSIT & TAXIS

Yellow Cab 407/422-2222.
Mears Transportation 407/423-5566.
Lynx 407/841-5969, web: www.golynx.com.

TOURIST SPOTS & INFO

Sea World 800/327-2424, web: www.seaworld.com.
Universal Studios 407/363-8000, web: themeparks.universalstudios.com.
Walt Disney World 407/824-4321, web: www.disneyworld.com.
Wet & Wild Waterpark 407/351-3200, web: www.wetnwildorlando.com.
Gatorland 407/855-5496, web: www.gatorland.com.
Visitor's Center: 407/363-5872. 8723 International Dr, 8am-7pm, web: www.orlandoinfo.com.

Weather

Mild winters, hot summers.

City Calendar

LGBT PRIDE

June.

ANNUAL EVENTS

May-June - Gay Days at Disney World 407/896-8431, web: gaydays.com.

Queer Resources

COMMUNITY INFO

Gay/Lesbian Community Center 407/228-8272. 946 N Mills, noon-9pm, till 6pm Fri-Sat, 1pm-6pm Sun, web: www.glbcc.org.
AA 407/260-5408, web: www.aaorlandointergroup.org.
Hope & Help 407/645-2577, 8am-5pm.

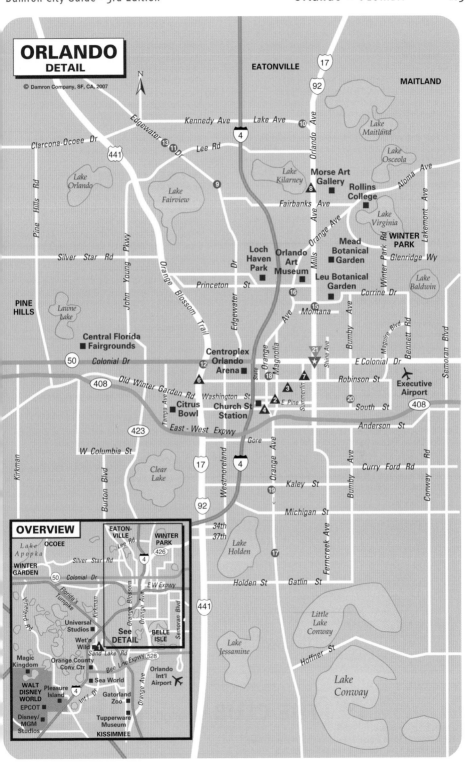

ORLANDO
DETAIL
© Damron Company, SF, CA, 2007

20 **Southern Nights** [★MW,D,MR,DS,S,WC] 407/898-0424 ■ 375 S Bumby Ave ■ 4pm-3am, from 8pm Sat, clsd Sun, theme nights, go-go dancers, patio ■ www.southern-nights.com

CAFES
White Wolf Cafe & Antique Shop [E,BW,WC] 407/895-9911 ■ 1829 N Orange Ave (at Princeton) ■ 11am-10pm, till 9pm Mon, till 11pm Fri-Sat, clsd Sun, salads & sandwiches ■ www.whitewolfcafe.com

RESTAURANTS
Blue Bistro & Grill 407/898-5660 ■ 815 N Mills Ave ■ dinner, clsd Sun, upscale American ■ www.bluebistroand-grill.com

Brian's 407/896-9912 ■ 1409 N Orange Ave (at Virginia) ■ 6am-4pm, popular Sun

Dexter's of Thornton Park [E] 407/648-0620 ■ 808 E Washington St ■ lunch & dinner, brunch Sat-Sun, American, also wine bar; also Winter Park location, 407/629-1150 ■ www.dexwine.com

Friends [BW] 407/895-2444 ■ 1326 N Mills Ave ■ lunch & dinner Tue-Sat, Sun brunch, clsd Mon

Harvey's Bistro 407/246-6560 ■ 390 N Orange Ave (in Bank of America bldg) ■ lunch Mon-Fri, dinner Mon-Sat, clsd Sun, popular cocktail hour ■ www.harveysbistro.com

Hemingway's at the Hyatt [★] 407/239-1234 ■ 1 Grand Cypress Blvd, Lake Buena Vista ■ dinner, seafood ■ www.yattgrandcypress.com

Hue 407/849-1800 ■ 629 E Central Blvd (at N Summerlin Ave) ■ lunch & dinner, wknd brunch, new American, full bar ■ www.huerestaurant.com

Pom Pom's 407/894-0865 ■ 67 N Bumby Ave ■ 11am-8pm, from noon Sat, noon-6pm Sun, tea & sandwiches

▶**The Rainbow Cafe** [MW] 407/425-7571 ■ at Parliament House ■ 7am-11pm, till 3am Fri-Sun ■ www.parliament-house.com

ENTERTAINMENT & RECREATION
The Enzian Theater [BW] 407/629-1088 ■ 1300 S Orlando Ave (at Magnolia), Maitland ■ Central FL's only art house cinema & cafe ■ www.enzian.org

Gay Orlando Talk 407/896-8431 ■ WPRK 91.5 FM ■ noon Fri, LGBT radio ■ www.gayorlando.com

Universal Studios Florida 407/363-8000, 877/801-9720 ■ 1000 Universal Studios Plz ■ www.universalorlando.com

Walt Disney World Resort 407/939-6244 ■ don't even pretend you came to Orlando for any other reason ■ www.disneyworld.com

BOOKSTORES
21 **Mojo** 407/896-0204 ■ 930 N Mills Ave (at E Marks St) ■ 1pm-8pm, till 6pm Sun, LGBT bookstore

Urban Think Bookstore 407/650-8004 ■ 625 E Central Blvd ■ 11am-9pm, till 6pm Sun, clsd Mon, LGBT section, also bar ■ www.urbanthinkorlando.com

RETAIL SHOPS
The Back Room [GO] 407/532-3627 ■ 4453 Edgewater Dr (inside the Beer Bar) ■ 7pm-midnight, till 1am Fri-Sat, DVDs, cards, erotica, sex toys, lube ■ thebackroomguys@aol.com

Harmony Designs [WC,GO] 407/481-9850 ■ 496 N Orange Blossom Tr ■ 6:30pm-1am, pride store

Panache Art & Gifts [GO] 407/830-7890 ■ 155 Cranes Roost Blvd Ste 1110 (at I-4 & 436), Altamonte Springs ■ 10am-8pm, noon-5pm Sun ■ www.panacheartandgifts.com

Urban Body 407/481-7979 ■ 12 N Summerlin (btwn Central & Washington) ■ 11am-7:30pm, till 9pm Th-Sat, noon-5pm Sun, men's clothing ■ www.urbanbody.com

PUBLICATIONS
Buzz Magazine 407/284-1668, 877/429-2899 ■ LGBT lifestyle magazine for Central Florida ■ www.buzzpublica-tions.com

Orlando Gay Yellow Pages 407/788-2008, 877/428-6334 ■ 101 Wymore Rd #215, Altamonte Springs 32174 ■ www.orlandogayyellowpages.com

TLW Magazine 727/522-8888 ■ Southeast's largest entertainment magazine for gay men ■ www.tlwmagazine.com

Watermark 407/481-2243 ■ bi-weekly LGBT newspaper for Central FL ■ www.watermarkonline.com

MEN'S CLUBS
▶**Club Orlando** [SW,PC] 407/425-5005 ■ 450 E Compton St ■ 24hrs ■ www.the-clubs.com

EROTICA

Fairvilla Megastore 407/425-5352 ■ 1740 N Orange Blossom Tr ■ *9am-2am, from 10am Sun, clean, well-lighted adult store w/ emphasis on couples: "store for lovers"* ■ www.fairvilla.com

Midnight News 407/425-7571 ■ *at Parliament House*

Video Express 407/839-8835 ■ 98 N Orange Blossom Trail ■ *11am-midnight, till 1am Fri-Sat*

St Petersburg

ACCOMMODATIONS

1   **Bay Palm Resort** [GF,SW,NS,WI,GO] 727/360-7642 ■ 4237 Gulf Blvd, St Petersburg Beach ■ *mention Damron guide for 10% discount (restrictions apply)* ■ www.baypalmresort.com

2   **Berwin Oak Guesthouse** [MO,NS,GO] 727/321-4272, 727/543-6953 (cell) ■ 5103 28th Ave S (at 51st St S), Gulfport ■ *comprised of 3 apts, courtyard w/ bar, deck & hot tub* ■ www.berwinoak-of-gulfport.com

3   Boca Ciega B&B [WO,SW,GO] 727/381-2755 ■ *B&B in private home* ■ worlddancer@aol.com

4   Changing Tides Cottages [MW,WI] 727/397-7706 ■ 225 Boca Ciega Dr, Madeira Beach ■ *fully furnished rental cottages on harbor* ■ www.changingtidescottages.com

5   **Dicken's House B&B** [GS,WI,GO] 727/822-8622, 800/381-2022 ■ 335 8th Ave NE ■ *newly restored Arts & Crafts home, near museums, full brkfst, jacuzzis* ■ www.dickenshouse.com

6   **Inn at the Bay B&B** [GF,NS,WI,WC] 727/822-1700, 888/873-2122 ■ 126 4th Ave NE (at 1st St) ■ *full brkfst, jacuzzis* ■ www.innatthebay.com

5   **Mansion House** [GF,SW,NS,WI] 727/821-9391, 800/274-7520 ■ 105 Fifth Ave NE ■ *historic B&B inn, full brkfst* ■ www.mansionbandb.com

7   **Pass-A-Grille Beach Motel** [GF,SW] 727/367-4726 ■ 709 Gulf Wy, St Pete Beach ■ PAGBeachMotel@msn.com

8   **Sea Oats by the Gulf** [GF,WC] 727/367-7568, 866/715-9595 ■ 12625 Sunshine Ln, Treasure Island ■ *directly on the Gulf of Mexico* ■ www.flainns.com/seaoats

Suncoast Resort [★MW,SW,NS,WC,GO] ■ *please check website for location* ■ www.suncoastresort.com

BARS

10   **The Back Room Bar @ Surf & Sand Bar** [M,NH,K,WC] 727/391-2680 ■ 14601 Gulf Blvd, Madeira Beach ■ *1pm-2am, beach access, patio*

11   **Chiq Bar** [W,D,E,DS,S] 727/546-7274 ■ 4900 66th St N ■ *4pm-2am, from 1pm Sun, clsd Sat* ■ www.chiqbar.com

12   **Christopher Street Bar** [M,D,DS,S,WI] 727/538-0660, 727/520-4111 ■ 13344 66th St N (at Ulmerton Rd), Largo ■ *2pm-2am* ■ sportspagegirls.com

13   **Grand Central Station** [M,NH,L,K,S,WI,WC] 727/327-8204 ■ 2612 Central Ave (at 26th) ■ *2pm-2am, male dancers, patio* ■ www.grandcentralstationfl.com

14   **Haymarket Pub** [M,NH,WC] 727/577-9621 ■ 8308 4th St N (at 83rd) ■ *5pm-2am, upscale*

14   The Hideaway [W,NH,E,K,WC] 727/570-9025 ■ 8302 4th St N (at 83rd) ■ *2pm-2am* ■ www.thehideawaygirls.com

15   **Oar House** [MW,NH,F,K] 727/327-1691 ■ 4807 22nd Ave S ■ *2pm-2am, from 1pm Sun*

13   **The Platform** [M,NH,B,L,DS] 727/327-8204 ■ 2608 Central Ave ■ *9pm-2am, leather/ levi bar, patio* ■ www.theplatformleatherbar.com

16   **Pro Shop Pub** [★M,NH] 727/447-4259 ■ 840 Cleveland St (at Prospect), Clearwater ■ *11:30am-2am, from 1pm Sun* ■ www.proshoppub.us

17   A Taste for Wine 727/895-1623 ■ 241 Central Ave (at 2nd St N) ■ *1pm-9pm, 2pm-midnight Fri-Sat, clsd Sun-Mon, occasional lesbian events*

ST PETERSBURG

Across the bay from its larger sister city, Tampa, St. Petersburg is best known for its spectacular beaches.

Tourist Info

PUBLIC TRANSIT & TAXIS
Yellow Cab 727/821-7777.

TOURIST SPOTS & INFO
Great Explorations, interactive kids' museum, 727/821-8992, web: www.greatexplorations.org.
Salvador Dalí Museum 727/823-3767, web: www.salvadordalimuseum.org.
Visitor's Center: Chamber of Commerce 727/821-4069, 8am-5pm Mon-Fri, web: www.stpete.com.

Weather
Some say it's the Garden of Eden—winter temperatures occasionally dip into the 40°s, but for the rest of the year temperatures stay in the 70°-80°s.

Best Views
Pass-A-Grille Beach in Tampa.

City Calendar

LGBT PRIDE
June.

ANNUAL EVENTS
May - Tampa Bay Blues Festival 727/502-5000, web: www.tampabaybluesfest.com.

Queer Resources

COMMUNITY INFO
Tampa Bay Business Guild web: www.tbbg.org.
Pinellas County AA 727/530-0415, web: www.aapinellas.org.
Tampa Bay AIDS Network 813/769-5180.

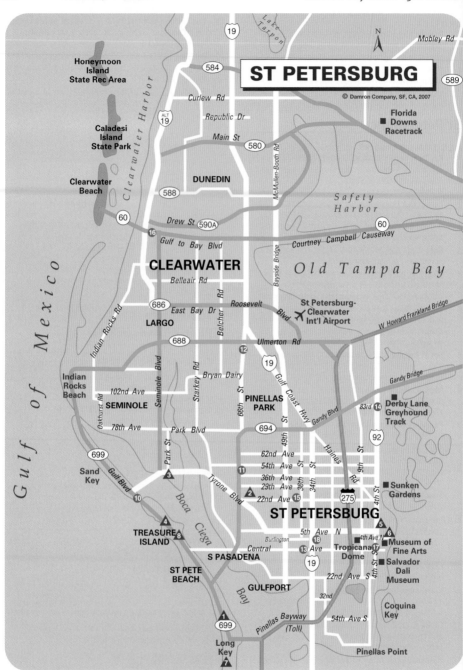

ST PETERSBURG

© Damron Company, SF, CA, 2007

NIGHTCLUBS

18   Georgie's Alibi [MW,NH,D,F,DS,S,V,WC,GO] 727/321-2112 ■ 3100 3rd Ave N (at 31st St N) ■ 11am-2am, 3 bars, patio, wireless internet ■ www.georgiesalibi.com

RESTAURANTS

The Kizmet 727/821-1078 ■ 1101 1st Ave N ■ 11am-2am, steak & lobster, also lounge ■ www.thekizmet.com

Uncle Gizzy's Diner [B,GO] 727/323-4499 ■ 3151 3rd Ave ■ 4pm-close, from 11am Sun, American

RETAIL SHOPS

Tampa Bay Leather Company 727/865-3010 ■ 3400 34th St S (in Suncoast Resort) ■ noon-midnight, till 2am Fri-Sat, leather, fetish ■ www.tampabayleathercompany.com

PUBLICATIONS

Buzz Magazine 727/228-1307, 877/429-2899 ■ LGBT lifestyle magazine for Southern Florida ■ www.buzzpublications.com

The Gazette 727/821-5009 ■ Tampa Bay's gay/ lesbian newsmagazine ■ www.gazettetampabay.com

TLW Magazine 727/522-8888 ■ Southeast's largest entertainment magazine for gay men ■ www.tlwmagazine.com

Watermark 813/655-9890 (Tampa office), 877/926-8118 ■ bi-weekly LGBT newspaper for Central FL ■ www.watermarkonline.com

Tampa

ACCOMMODATIONS

1   Gram's Place Hostel [GS,P,BYOB,N,NS] 813/221-0596 ■ 3109 N Ola Ave ■ hot tub ■ www.Grams-Inn-Tampa.com

Sawmill Camping Resort [★MW,D,E,K,SW,N,GO] 352/583-0664 ■ 21710 US Hwy 98, Dade City ■ www.flsawmill.com

BARS

2   2606 [★M,L,S,WC,GO] 813/875-6993 ■ 2606 Armenia Ave (at St Conrad) ■ 2pm-3am, strippers wknds, also leather shop from 9pm ■ www.2606.com

3   Azalea Lounge [GF,NH,K] 813/228-0139 ■ 1502 N Florida ■ 3pm-3am, till midnight Sun

4   Baxter's [M,NH,K,S,WC] 813/258-8830 ■ 1519 S Dale Mabry (at W Neptune) ■ noon-3am

5   City Side [MW,NH,K] 813/350-0600 ■ 3703 Henderson Blvd (at Dale Mabry) ■ 11am-3am, patio ■ www.clubcityside.com

6   Keith's Bar [M,NH,S,GO] 813/971-3576 ■ 14905 N Nebraska (at Bearss) ■ 1pm-3am, strippers Fri ■ www.keithsbar.com

7   Ki Ki Ki Lounge [M,BW] 813/254-8183 ■ 1908 W Kennedy Blvd (at Melville) ■ 11:30am-3am

TAMPA

West Florida's largest city, Tampa is a relaxing alternative to the more popular Florida destinations. The slower pace of life is ideal for travelers looking for a place to soak up the sun in peace and quiet.

Tourist Info

AIRPORT DIRECTIONS

Tampa International. To get to most gay resorts and bars, follow signs to I-75 North. Take I-275 North and follow it to exits for either Dale Mabry Hwy, Nebraska Ave, or Busch Blvd.

PUBLIC TRANSIT & TAXIS

Yellow Cab 813/253-0121.
Super Shuttle 727/572-1111.
Hartline Transit (bus) 813/254-4278.

TOURIST SPOTS & INFO

Busch Gardens/Adventure Island 813/987-5082, web: www.4adventure.com.
Florida Aquarium 813/273-4000.
Harbour Island.
Museum of Science & Industry 813/987-6300.
Ybor Square.
Visitor's Center: Greater Tampa Chamber of Commerce 813/228-7777, web: www.tampachamber.com.
Tampa/Hillsborough Convention & Visitors Bureau 813/223-1111.
www.visittampa.com.

City Calendar

LGBT PRIDE

June. Central Florida Black Pride 813/236-8809, web: www.floridablackpride.net.
June. St Pete Pride, web: www.stpetepride.com.

ENTERTAINMENT

Tampa Bay Gay Men's Chorus 727/580-5517, web: www.tampabayarts.com.
Crescendo, Tampa Bay Womyn's Chorus 813/679-7585, web: www.crescendochorus.org.

ANNUAL EVENTS

October- Tampa International Gay & Lesbian Film Festival, web: www.pridefilmfest.com.

Queer Resources

COMMUNITY INFO

Gay/ Lesbian Community Center of Tampa 813/875-8116. 3708 W Swann Ave.
The Line 727/586-4297, 24-hour automated info & referral line.

8 **Male Room** [M,NH,K,S] 813/832-9085 ■ 4502 S Dale Mabry Hwy ■ *4pm-3am, male dancers* ■ www.themaleroomtampa.com

9 **Midtown Tavern** [M,NH,GO] 813/915-0819 ■ 9002 N Florida Ave (at Busch) ■ *2:30pm-3am* ■ www.midtowntaverntampa.com

10 **Rainbow Room** [W,BW] 813/871-2265 ■ 421 S MacDill Ave (at Azeele St) ■ *3pm-3am* ■ www.rainbowroompub.com

11 **Wranglers** [M,D,CW,V,GO] 813/247-2950 ■ 1915 E 7th Ave (btwn 19th & 20th Sts), Ybor City ■ *7pm-3am, theme nights, free line dance lessons* ■ www.wranglersbar.com

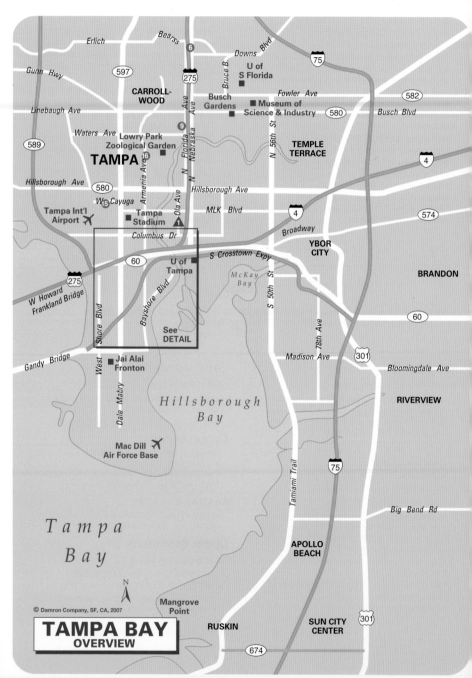

TAMPA BAY
OVERVIEW

© Damron Company, SF, CA, 2007

NIGHTCLUBS

12 **Club Chambers** [MW,D,F,DS,18+] 813/223-1300 ■ 1701 N Franklin St (at E Henderson Ave) ■ 8:30pm-3am Fri-Sat only, 2 flrs, also restaurant ■ www.clubchambers.com

13 <u>Flirt</u> [MW,D,DS,S,18+] 1909 N 15th St (btwn 8th & 9th), Ybor City ■ 10pm-3am Th-Sat, 2 flrs ■ flirtnightclub@aol.com

14 **G. Bar** [M,D,S] 813/247-1016 ■ 1401 E 7th Ave ■ 4pm-3am, theme nights ■ www.gbartampabay.com

15 **Radar** [M,D] 813/870-3081 ■ 4202 W Cayuga St (at Lois), Drew Park ■ www.radartampa.com

16 **Valentines Nightclub** [M,D,K,DS,S] 813/936-1999 ■ 7522 N Armenia Ave (btwn Sligh & Waters) ■ 3pm-3am ■ www.valentinesnightclub.com

CAFES

<u>Sacred Grounds Coffeehouse</u> [MW,E] 813/983-0837 ■ 4819 E Busch Blvd ■ 7pm-1am, till 2am Fri-Sat, open mic Mon, all welcome but popular hangout for lesbians & gay men ■ www.coffeeunchained.com

RESTAURANTS

Ho Ho Chinese [WC,GO] 813/254-9557 ■ 533 S Howard ■ 11am-10pm, dinner only wknds, full bar

Taqueria Quetzalcoatl [BW] 813/259-9982 ■ 402 S Howard Ave (at Azeele St) ■ 11am-11pm, till 1am Fri

ENTERTAINMENT & RECREATION

<u>The Women's Show</u> 813/238-8001 ■ WMNF 88.5 FM ■ 10am-noon Sat ■ www.wmnf.org

PUBLICATIONS

Buzz Magazine 813/425-2087, 877/429-2899 ■ LGBT lifestyle magazine for Southern Florida ■ www.buzzpublications.com

The Gazette 727/821-5009 ■ Tampa Bay's LGBT newsmagazine ■ www.gazettetampabay.com

TLW Magazine 727/522-8888 ■ Southeast's largest entertainment magazine for gay men ■ www.tlwmagazine.com

Watermark 813/655-9890 ■ bi-weekly LGBT newspaper for Central FL ■ www.watermarkonline.com

MEN'S CLUBS

Club Tampa [★PC] 813/223-5181 ■ 215 N 11th St ■ 24hrs ■ www.clubtampaflorida.com

Rainbow Cabaret [AYOR,WI] 813/877-7585 ■ 4421 N Hubert Ave (behind Playhouse Theatre) ■ 24hrs, sauna, jacuzzi ■ www.rainbowcabaret.com

EROTICA

Buddies Video 813/876-8083 ■ 4322 W Crest Ave (at Hillsborough) ■ 24hrs

Playhouse Theatre 813/873-9235 ■ 4421 N Hubert Ave (at Alva) ■ 24hrs

Tres Equis 813/740-8664 ■ 6220 Adamo Dr (behind Goldrush topless bar) ■ 24hrs

XTC Adult Supercenter 813/930-0069 ■ 330 E Fowler Ave ■ 24hrs

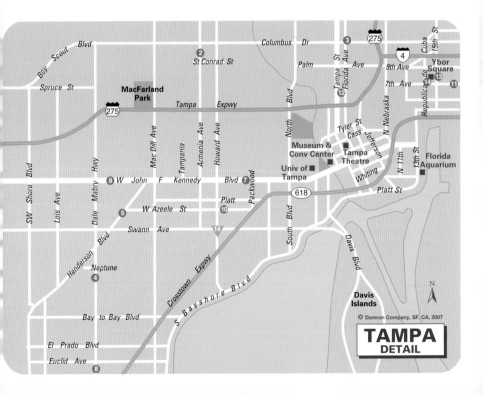

© Damron Company, SF, CA, 2007

TAMPA DETAIL

GEORGIA

Atlanta

ACCOMMODATIONS

2   The Gaslight Inn [GS,NS,WI,GO] 404/875-1001 ■ 1001 St Charles Ave NE ■ *1913 craftsman-style B&B* ■ www.gaslightinn.com

3   The Georgian Terrace Hotel [GF,SW,WI,WC] 404/897-1991, 800/555-8000 ■ 659 Peachtree St ■ *"Atlanta's only historic luxury hotel," hosted Gone with the Wind world-premier reception in 1939, kids ok* ■ www.thegeorgianterrace.com

4   Glenn Hotel [GS] 404/521-2250, 866/404-5366 ■ 110 Marietta St NW ■ www.glennhotel.com

5   Hello B&B [MW,NS,WI,GO] 404/892-8111 ■ 1865 Windemere Dr ■ *hot tub* ■ members.aol.com/hellobnb

6   Hill Street Resort B&B [GS,SW,GO] 404/627-4281 ■ 729 Hill St SE ■ *full brkfst, hot tub* ■ www.hillstreetresort.com

3   Hotel Indigo [WI] 404/874-9200 ■ 683 Peachtree St NE ■ *cozy, stylish no-frills hotel, workout room, also restaurant* ■ www.hotelindigo.com

Microtel Inn & Suites [GF,WI,WC] 404/325-4446 ■ 1840 Corporate Blvd ■ www.microtelinn.com

7   Midtown Carriage House [MW,SW,NS,GO] 404/931-8791 ■ *central location, 2-story house, garden, patio w/ view of Midtown skyline* ■ www.basakamerica.com/1689

8   Midtown Guest House [GS,GO] 404/931-8791 ■ 845 Penn Ave ■ *in the heart of midtown* ■ midtowninn.aol.com

9   Sheraton Atlanta Hotel [GF,F,SW,WC] 404/659-6500, 800/325-3535 ■ 165 Courtland St (at International Blvd) ■ *3 restaurants, full bar, gym* ■ www.sheraton.com

W Atlanta [GF,SW,NS,WI,WC] 770/396-6800, 877/WHOTELS (reservations only) ■ 111 Perimeter Center W ■ *also restaurant* ■ www.whotels.com/atlanta

BARS

10   Amsterdam [★M,D,F,V] 404/892-2227 ■ 502 Amsterdam Ave NE ■ *11:30am-close, video & sports bar* ■ www.amsterdam-atlanta.com

11   Atlanta Eagle [★M,D,B,L,GO] 404/873-2453 ■ 306 Ponce de Leon Ave NE (at Argonne) ■ *8pm-3am, till 4am Fri, clsd Sun, also leather store* ■ www.atlantaeagle.com

12   BJ's [M,NH,K,DS,GO] 404/634-5895 ■ 2345 Cheshire Bridge Rd (at La Vista) ■ *3pm-3am, till midnight Sun* ■ www.bjroosters.com

13   Blake's (on the Park) [★MW,NH,F,P,S,V] 404/892-5786 ■ 227 10th St (at Piedmont) ■ *3pm-3am, till midnight Sun* ■ www.blakesontheparkatlanta.com

14   Bulldogs [★M,NH,D,L,MR-AF,V] 404/872-3025 ■ 893 Peachtree St NE (btwn 7th & 8th) ■ *4pm-3am, clsd Sun, cruise bar* ■ members.aol.com/bulldognco

15   Burkhart's Pub [MW,NH,F,K,S,WC] 404/872-4403 ■ 1492-F Piedmont Ave (at Monroe, in Ansley Square) ■ *4pm-2:30am, from 2pm wknds, till midnight Sun, patio* ■ www.burkharts.com

16   Eastside Lounge [GS,D,MR] 404/521-9666 ■ 485-A Flat Shoals Ave ■ *9pm-2:30am, from midnight Sun* ■ www.eastsidelounge.net

17   Eddie's Attic [GS,E] 404/377-4976 ■ 515-B N McDonough St (at Trinity Place), Decatur ■ *4pm-close, clsd Sun, rooftop deck, live music, comedy 2nd & 4th Tue, restaurant, live music 6 nights/ week, occasional lesbian hangout* ■ www.eddiesattic.com

15   Felix's on the Square [M,F] 404/249-7899 ■ 1510-G Piedmont Ave NE (Ansley Square) ■ *11am-2:30am, 12:30pm-midnight Sun*

18   Friends on Ponce [MW,NH,V] 404/817-3820 ■ 736 Ponce de Leon, NE (at Ponce de Leon Pl) ■ *1pm-2:30am, clsd Sun, rooftop patio*

19   Halo Lounge [GS,F] 404/962-7333 ■ 817 W Peachtree (6th St, btwn W Peachtree & Peachtree) ■ *4pm-3am, from 6pm Sat, clsd Sun* ■ www.halolounge.com

20   Hoedowns [★M,D,CW,E,WC] 404/876-0001 ■ 931 Monroe Dr #B (at Midtown Promenade) ■ *3pm-2am, till 3am Fri-Sat, clsd Sun-Mon, more women Th* ■ www.hoedownsatlanta.com

Le Buzz [MW,NH,D,F,K,DS,S,WC] 770/424-1337 ■ 585 Franklin Rd A-10 (at S Marietta Pkwy, in Longhorn Plaza), Marietta ■ *7pm-3am Sat, clsd Sun, DJ Fri, patio*

21   Mary's [MW,NH,D,K,V] 404/624-4411 ■ 1287B Glenwood Ave (at Flat Shoals) ■ *5pm-3am, clsd Sun-Mon, friendly cocktail bar* ■ www.marysatlanta.com

22   Miss Q's [MW,NH,F] 404/875-6255 ■ 560-B Amsterdam (in Amsterdam Walk) ■ *4pm-close, 3pm-midnight Sun, big-screen TV*

23   Model T [M,NH,F,K,DS,OC,WC] 404/872-2209 ■ 699 Ponce de Leon NE, Ste 11 (at Barnett) ■ *9am-3am, 12:30pm-midnight Sun, [K] Th, [DS] Fri-Sat, cruisy*

15   New Order Lounge [M,NH,E,OC,WC] 404/874-8247 ■ 1544 Piedmont Ave NE (at Monroe, in Ansley Mall) ■ *2pm-2am, till 3am wknds*

25   Opus I [M,NH,WC] 404/634-6478 ■ 1086 Alco St NE (at Cheshire Bridge) ■ *9am-3am, 12:30pm-midnight Sun* ■ www.opus1atlanta.com

15   Oscar's Video Bar [M,V] 404/874-7748 ■ 1510-C Piedmont Ave NE (in Ansley Mall) ■ *3pm-2:30am, clsd Sun*

22   Red Chair [MW,MR-AF,F,V] 404/870-0532 ■ 550-C Amsterdam Ave (at Monroe) ■ *10pm-3am, from 7pm Sat, 6pm-midnight Sun, 8pm-1am Mon, clsd Tue-Wed, more women Th & Sat, also restaurant, wknd brunch, patio* ■ www.redchairatlanta.com

The Stage Door [MW,K,DS,GO] 770/414-9292 ■ 4431 Hugh Howell Rd, Tucker ■ *5pm-4am, 3pm-3am Sat-Sun, [L] 1st & 3rd Th* ■ www.thestagedoor.biz

26   Swinging Richard's [M,S,$] 404/352-0532 ■ 1400 Northside Dr NW (btwn I-75 & Northside Dr) ■ *6:30pm-2:45am, clsd Sun-Mon, gay strip club, gift shop*

27   Tripps [M,NH,F] 404/724-0067 ■ 1931 Piedmont Circle (at Cheshire Bridge) ■ *9am-3am, 12:30pm-midnight Sun*

28   Woofs on Piedmont [★M,NH,F,GO] 404/869-9422 ■ 2425 Piedmont (at Lindbergh) ■ *11:30am-2am, 12:30pm-midnight Sun, sports bar* ■ www.woofsatlanta.com

NIGHTCLUBS

44   Bazzaar [GS,D,MR,F] 404/885-7505 ■ 654 Peachtree St (at Ponce de Leon) ■ *6pm-3am, lounge w/ food served* ■ www.bazzaaratlanta.com

29   Chaparral [M,D,MR-L] 404/634-3737 ■ 2715 Buford Hwy ■ *10pm-4am Wed-Th, Fri & Sun* ■ www.chaparralatlanta.com

Chit Chat Restaurant & Lounge [W,F] 404/243-8182 ■ 2920 Ember Dr, Decatur

30   Club 708 [M,D,E,MR-AF] 404/874-8125 ■ 708 Spring St ■ *10pm-5am, clsd Sun-Mon, go-go dancers* ■ www.legendaryclub708.com

Da Hype [M,D,MR-AF] 404/246-9000 ■ 4830 Fulton Industrial Blvd ■ *midnight-close Sat only* ■ www.wassup-natl.com

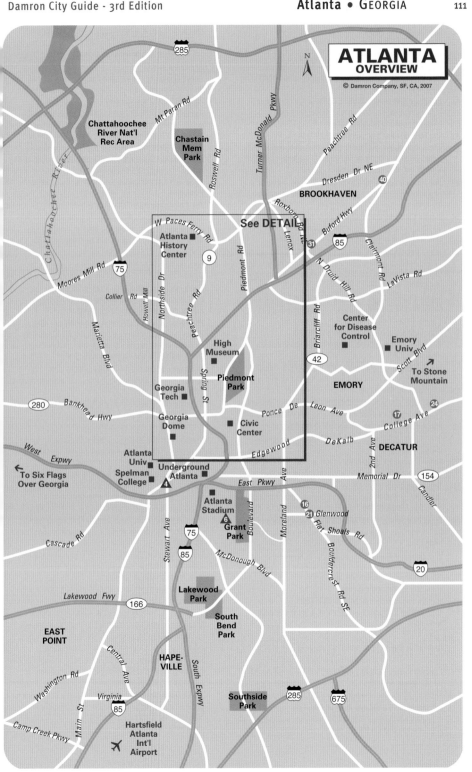

Eye Candy Club [W,D,E,S] 866/503-5903 ■ 4470 Commerce Dr SW ■ 9pm-4am Fri, till 3am Sat, clsd Sun-Th ■ www.icandyclubga.com

31 **Frisky Fridays** [W,D,MR-AF] 404/929-9991 ■ 3011 Buford Hwy (at Club Miami) ■ 10pm-close Fri only ■ www.traxxatlanta.com

45 **Girlology 101** [W,F,E] 404/846-2000 ■ 1197 Peachtree St ■ 6pm-close last Sun only, wet T-shirt contests ■ www.heretoserverestaurants.com

32 **The Heretic** [★M,D,L,F,S,WC] 404/325-3061 ■ 2069 Cheshire Bridge Rd (at Piedmont) ■ 10am-3am, clsd Sun, 3 bars, patio, call for theme nights, also Heretic Leathers toy shop ■ www.hereticatlanta.com

33 **The House** [GS,D] 678/528-7732 ■ 50 Upper Alabama St (in Kenny's Alley) ■ more gay Tue ■ www.thehousenightclub.com

34 **Jungle Club** [★MW,D,DS,$] 404/844-8800 ■ 2115 Faulkner Rd NE ■ 10pm-3am Fri-Sat, also 11pm Mon for Stars of the Century [DS] ■ www.jungleclub.net

35 **Lion's Den** [M,D,MR-AF] 404/315-7676 (club), 770/991-6929 (info line) ■ 2678 Buford Hwy NE (at The Cabin Room) ■ 9pm-3am Sun only ■ www.thelionsdenatlanta.com

36 **Manhunt** [M,D,MR-AF,WC] 404/246-9000 ■ 735 Ralph McGill Blvd NE (at Freedom Pkwy, at Tower II) ■ 10pm Fri only ■ www.wassupnatl.com

37 **Masquerade** [GF,D,F,E,18+,$] 404/577-8178, 404/577-2002 ■ 695 North Ave NE ■ hours vary ■ www.masq.com

31 **My Girl Gotta Girlfriend** [W,D,MR-AF] 404/929-9991 ■ 3011 Buford Hwy (at Club Miami) ■ 10pm-close Sun only ■ www.traxxatlanta.com

Phase One [GS,D,MR-AF,S] 404/291-7171 ■ 4933 Memorial Dr, Decatur ■ 10pm-close Th & Sat only ■ www.phase1.com

38 **Playground South** [M,D,MR-AF] 404/217-3935 ■ 253 Auburn Ave (at the Black Lion Cafe) ■ Sat only ■ www.atl-playground.com

39 **Sutra Lounge** [GF,D] 404/607-1160 ■ 1136 Crescent Ave (at 13th) ■ 9pm-3am Th-Sat ■ www.sutraloungeatl.com

36 **The Tower II** [MW,D,MR,E,YC,WC] 404/523-1535 ■ 735 Ralph McGill Blvd NE (at Freedom Pkwy) ■ 10pm-2am, clsd Sun-Mon, Manhunt [M,D,MR-AF], mostly women Sat & Wed

40 **Traxx** [M,D,MR-AF,E] 678/760-2395 ■ 3595 Clairmont Rd (at Atlanta Live), Decatur ■ Tue & Sat only ■ www.traxxatlanta.com

Wet Dream [S,F] 678/296-0678 ■ 5231 Memorial Dr (at Central Park Club & Bistro), Stone Mountain ■ 10:30pm-close Sun only, male & female revue ■ www.ozonentertainment.com

41 **Wetbar** [★MW,D,V] 404/745-9494 ■ 960 Spring St (at 10th) ■ 8pm-3am, clsd Sun-Tue, patio ■ www.wetbaratlanta.com

Cafes

Australian Bakery Cafe 678/797-6222 ■ 48 S Park Square, Marietta ■ www.australianbakerycafe.com

Caribou Coffee 404/733-5539 ■ 1551 Piedmont Ave NE (at Monroe) ■ 6am-10pm, till 11pm Fri-Sat, 7am-9pm Sun, locations throughout the city ■ www.cariboucoffee.com

Intermezzo [WI] 404/355-0411 ■ 1845 Peachtree Rd NE ■ 10:30am-3am, classy cafe, full bar, great desserts, [WI] till 7pm ■ www.cafeintermezzo.com

Urban Grounds 404/499-2136 ■ 38 N Avondale Rd, Avondale Estates ■ 6:30am-9pm, till 10pm Fri, 7:30am-10pm Sat, 8am-4pm Sun ■ www.urbangrounds.net

Restaurants

Agnes & Muriel's [★BW] 404/885-1000 ■ 1514 Monroe Dr (near Piedmont) ■ 11am-10pm, till 11pm Fri-Sat, 10am-10pm Sun, patio ■ www.mominthekitchen.com

Apres Diem 404/872-3333 ■ 931 Monroe Dr #C-103 ■ 11:30am-midnight, till 1am Fri-Sat, from 11am wknds, brunch Sat-Sun, French bistro, live jazz Wed, full bar ■ www.apresdiem.com

Bacchanalia/ Star Provisions/ Quinones 404/365-0410 ■ 1198 Howell Mill Rd NW ■ lunch Wed-Sat & dinner Mon-Sat, upscale, contemporary American ■ www.starprovisions.com

The Colonnade 404/874-5642 ■ 1879 Cheshire Bridge Rd NE ■ lunch Wed-Sun, dinner nightly, traditional Southern

Cowtippers [TG,WC] 404/874-3469 ■ 1600 Piedmont Ave NE (at Monroe) ■ 11:30am-11pm, till midnight Fri-Sat, steak house

Ecco [R] 404/347-9555 ■ 40 7th St ■ 5:30pm-11pm, till 2am Th-Sat, till 10pm Sun, Italian ■ www.ecco-atlanta.com

Einstein's [★WC] 404/876-7925 ■ 1077 Juniper (at 12th) ■ 11am-midnight, till 1am Fri-Sat, wknd brunch, some veggie, full bar, patio ■ www.einsteinsatlanta.com

The Flying Biscuit Cafe [★BW,WC] 404/687-8888 ■ 1655 McLendon Ave (at Clifton) ■ 7am-10pm, till 10:30pm Fri-Sat, healthy brkfst all day, plenty veggie; also 1001 Piedmont Ave, 404/874-8887 ■ www.flyingbiscuit.com

The Lobby at Twelve [R] 404/961-7370 ■ 361 17th St ■ brkfst, lunch & dinner, upscale American ■ www.lobbyattwelve.com

Majestic Diner [★AYOR] 404/875-0276 ■ 1031 Ponce de Leon (at Highland) ■ 24hrs, diner right from the '50s, cantankerous waitresses included

Murphy's [★WC] 404/872-0904 ■ 997 Virginia Ave NE (at N Highland Ave) ■ 11am-10pm, till midnight Fri-Sat, from 8am wknds, plenty veggie ■ www.murphysvh.com

No Más! Cantina [GO] 404/574-5678 ■ 180 Walker St ■ 11am-11pm, till midnight Fri-Sat, Mexican, also huge furniture & gift store ■ www.nomascantina.com

R Thomas [BW,WC] 404/872-2942 ■ 1812 Peachtree Rd NE (btwn 26th & 27th) ■ 24hrs, healthy Californian/ juice bar, plenty veggie, popular late night ■ www.rthomasdeluxe-grill.com

Repast [R] 404/870-8707 ■ 620 N Glen Iris Dr ■ 5:30pm-10pm, till 10:30pm Fri-Sat, clsd Sun, upscale American ■ www.repastrestaurant.com

Ria's Bluebird Cafe [★BW,TG,WC] 404/521-3737 ■ 421 Memorial Dr ■ 8am-3pm, gourmet brunch in quaint old diner in Grant Park, plenty veggie ■ www.riasbluebird.com

Slice [WI,GO] 404/588-1820 ■ 259 Peters St ■ 11am-midnight, till 3am Fri, noon-3am Sat, noon-midnight Sun, pizza & martinis ■ www.sliceatlanta.com

Swan Coach House 404/261-0636 ■ 3130 Slaton Dr NW ■ 11am-2:30pm, clsd Sun, also gift shop & art gallery ■ www.swancoachhouse.com

Sweet Devil Moon [D,E] 404/347-3600 ■ 980 Piedmont Ave ■ 4pm-midnight, from 3pm Fri-Sun, Ladies Night Tue, Boys Night Out Wed, Peruvian tapas ■ www.sdmatlanta.com

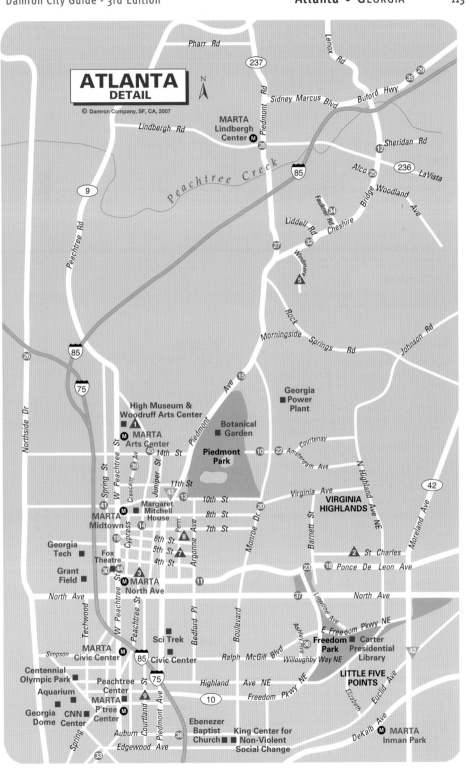

Table 1280 404/897-1280 ■ 1280 Peachtree St NE (at Woodruff Arts Center) ■ *lunch & dinner Tue-Sat, brunch Sun, also lounge 11am-10pm Tue-Sat, till 6pm Sun, clsd Mon, upscale American & tapas* ■ www.table1280.com

TWO. urban licks [E,R] 404/522-4622 ■ 820 Ralph McGill Blvd ■ *dinner nightly, great grill, full bar, live blues* ■ www.twourbanlicks.com

Veni Vidi Vici [WI] 404/875-8424 ■ 41 14th St ■ *lunch Mon-Fri, dinner nightly, upscale Italian, some veggie* ■ www.buckheadrestaurants.com

Wasabi 404/574-5680 ■ 180 Walker St ■ *lunch Tue-Sat, dinner Mon-Sat, clsd Sun, sushi* ■ www.wasabiatl.com

ATLANTA

Day Trips: Savannah & Peach Blossom Trail

You'll have to get up early in the morning to take a day trip to Savannah (about 200 miles southeast of Atlanta), but your troubles will be well rewarded. Perhaps made most famous by the book *Midnight in the Garden of Good and Evil*, Savannah was the state's first settlement, and is now a wonderful example of historic preservation. Check with Savannah Walks, Inc at 912/238-9255 (www.savannahwalks.com) to arrange a walking tour; don't miss the the park-like squares that make up the historic downtown area. Explore the funky shops and eateries on Broughton Street, and visit the childhood home of one of the US's greatest writers, Flannery O'Connor.

Georgia's peach trees blossom in March, so take the Peach Blossom Trail along Hwys 41 and 341 to enjoy these lovely pink-and-white flowers. Visit www.peachblossomtrail.com for more information.

Local Food:

Georgia is just peachy during the summer; this is when peaches are picked around the state. Check locally for an orchard where you can pick your own!

Tourist Info

AIRPORT DIRECTIONS

Hartsfield International. Take 85 North, and get off at 14th to go downtown or to Midtown, or turn left on Piedmont to get to Ansley Square. Or get off of 85 at the Piedmont exit and take a left onto Cheshire Bridge, or go back over the freeway, north, on Piedmont to Buckhead.

PUBLIC TRANSIT & TAXIS

Yellow Cab 404/521-0200.
Superior Shuttle 770/457-4794.
Marta 404/848-5000, web: www.itsmarta.com.

TOURIST SPOTS & INFO

Atlanta Botanical Garden 404/876-5859, web: www.atlantabotanicalgarden.org.
Centennial Olympic Park.
CNN Center 404/827-2300, web: www.cnn.com/StudioTour.
Coca-Cola Museum 404/676-5151, web: www.woccatlanta.com.
Georgia Aquarium (largest aquarium in the US) 404/581-4000, web: www.georgiaaquarium.org.
High Museum of Art 404/733-4444, web: www.high.org.
Margaret Mitchell House 404/249-7015, web: www.gwtw.org.
Martin Luther King Jr. Memorial Center 404/526-8900, web: www.thekingcenter.org.
Piedmont Park.
Stone Mountain Park 770/498-5690, web: www.stonemountainpark.com.
Underground Atlanta 404/523-2311, web: underground-atlanta.com.
Visitor's Center: 404/521-6600 or 800/285-2682, web: www.atlanta.net.

Weather

Summers are warm and humid (upper 80°s to low 90°s) with occasional thunderstorms. Winters are icy with occasional snow. Temperatures can drop into the low 30°s. Spring and fall are temperate – spring brings blossoming dogwoods and magnolias, while fall festoons the trees with awesome fall colors.

Best Views

70th floor of the Peachtree Plaza, in the 3-story revolving Sun Dial restaurant (404/589-7506). Also from the top of Stone Mountain (only 20 feet taller).

City Calendar

LGBT PRIDE

June. 404/929-0071, web: atlantapride.org.

ANNUAL EVENTS

July - National Black Arts Festival 404/730-7315, web: www.nbaf.org.
Labor Day weekend - Femme-nomen-non (lesbian party), web: www.girlsinthenight.com.
November - Out on Film, lesbian/ gay film festival 404/352-4225, web: www.outonfilm.com.

Queer Resources

COMMUNITY INFO

Gay Atlanta, web: gay-atlanta.com.
Galano AA 404/881-9188, web: www.galanoat-lanta.org. 585 Dutch Valley.
AID Atlanta 404/870-7700, web: www.aidatlanta.org.

Watershed 404/378-4900 ▪ 406 W Ponce de Leon Ave, Decatur ▪ 11am-10pm, Sun brunch, wine bar, also gift shop, owned by Emily Saliers of the Indigo Girls ▪ www.watershedrestaurant.com

ENTERTAINMENT & RECREATION

AIDS Memorial Quilt/ NAMES Project 404/688-5500 ▪ 101 Krog St (enter at 725 Lake Ave) ▪ visit The Quilt at the foundation offices ▪ www.aidsquilt.org

Ansley Park Playhouse 404/875-1193 ▪ 1545 Peachtree St ▪ some LGBT-themed productions ▪ www.ansleyparkplayhouse.com

Atlanta Rollergirls ▪ Atlanta's female roller derby league, check web for upcoming events ▪ www.atlantarollergirls.com

Krause Gallery 404/522-6205 ▪ 291 Peters St SW ▪ 1pm-5:30pm, noon-6pm Th-Sat, clsd Sun, contemporary art & photography ▪ www.krausegallery.com

Lambda Radio Report 404/523-8989 ▪ WRFG 89.3 FM ▪ 6pm Tue, LGBT radio program ▪ www.wrfg.org

Little 5 Points, Moreland & Euclid Ave S of Ponce de Leon Ave ▪ hip & funky area w/ too many restaurants & shops to list ▪ www.l5p.com/areamap.html

Martin Luther King, Jr Center for Non-Violent Social Change 404/526-8923 ▪ 449 Auburn Ave NE ▪ 9am-5pm daily, includes King's birth home, the church where he preached in the '60s & his gravesite ▪ www.thekingcenter.org

Sam Romo Gallery [GO] 404/222-9955, 877/615-3183 ▪ 309 Peters St SW ▪ noon-6pm Tue-Sat only, contemporary art & photography ▪ www.romogallery.com

Wertz Contemporary 404/420-4342 ▪ 264 Peters St ▪ art drawn from Africa & the African Diaspora ▪ www.wertzcontemporary.com

BOOKSTORES

15 Brushstrokes/ Capulets [GO] 404/876-6567 ▪ 1510-J Piedmont Ave NE (near Monroe) ▪ 10am-10pm, till 11pm Fri-Sat, LGBT variety store ▪ www.brushstrokesatlanta.com

42 Charis Books & More [WC] 404/524-0304 ▪ 1189 Euclid Ave NE (at Moreland) ▪ 10:30am-6:30pm, till 8pm Wed-Sat, noon-6pm Sun, feminist ▪ www.charisbooksandmore.com

Oakwells 404/373-5190 ▪ 403 W Ponce de Leon Ave, Decatur ▪ 6am-7pm, LGBT section ▪ www.oakwells.com

43 ▶Outwrite Bookstore & Coffeehouse [★F,WC] 404/607-0082 ▪ 991 Piedmont Ave (at 10th) ▪ 10am-11pm, LGBT, music, videos, gifts, cafe ▪ www.outwritebooks.com

RETAIL SHOPS

Atlanta Leather Company 404/320-8989 ▪ 2111 Faulkner Rd NE (at Cheshire Bridge Rd) ▪ 11am-8pm, noon-6pm Sun, leather, fetish ▪ www.atlantaleathercompany.com

The Boy Next Door 404/873-2664 ▪ 1447 Piedmont Ave NE (btwn 14th & Monroe) ▪ 10am-8pm, noon-6pm Sun, clothing

The Junkman's Daughter 404/577-3188 ▪ 464 Moreland Ave (at Euclid) ▪ 11am-7pm, till 8pm Fri, till 9pm Sat, from noon Sun, hip stuff

Piercing Experience 404/378-9100, 800/646-0393 ▪ 1654 McLendon Ave NE (at Clifton) ▪ noon-9pm, till 6pm Sun ▪ www.piercing.org

PUBLICATIONS

David Atlanta 404/876-1819 ▪ gay entertainment magazine w/ extensive nightlife calendar, maps & directory ▪ www.davidatlanta.com

Labrys Atlanta 404/762-6601 ▪ bimonthly lesbian magazine ▪ www.labrysatl.com

Out & Active 404/873-6004 ▪ free gay/ lesbian resource & entertainment guide ▪ www.outandactive.com

Southern Voice 404/876-1819 ▪ weekly LGBT newspaper for AL, FL (panhandle), GA, LA, MS, TN w/ resource listings ▪ www.southernvoice.com

GYMS & HEALTH CLUBS

The Fitness Factory [★GF] 404/815-7900 ▪ 500 N Amsterdam (in Amsterdam Outlets) ▪ full gym ▪ www.ffatl.com

MEN'S CLUBS

Club Eros Atlanta [PC] 2219 Faulkner Rd ▪ 10am-6am, clsd Mon-Wed, "social club exists to support homosexual males who share the ideals of the swinger's lifestyle and the right of private assembly" ▪ www.cluberosatlanta.com

The Den [MO,MR-AF,PC] 404/292-7746 ■ 334 N Clarendon Ave Suite D, Scottsdale ■ www.thedeninc.com

Flex [SW,WI] 404/815-0456 ■ 76 4th St NW (at Spring St) ■ 24hrs ■ www.flexbaths.com

EROTICA

Aphrodite's Toy Box [TG,18+] 404/292-9700 ■ 3040 N Decatur Rd (at Ponce De Leon), Scottdale ■ noon-8pm, till 9pm Fri-Sat, till 6pm Sun, clsd Tue, women-oriented erotic boutique for women & their partners & friends, also classes ■ www.aphroditestoybox.com

Heaven 404/262-9113 ■ 2628 Piedmont (at Sidney Marcus Blvd) ■ www.inserection.com

Inserection 404/888-0878 ■ 505 Peachtree St NE ■ call for other locations ■ www.inserection.com

The Poster Hut/ Scream Boutique 404/633-7491 ■ 2175 Cheshire Bridge Rd ■ noon-7:30pm, till 9pm Fri-Sat, till 6pm Sun, clothing, toys

Southern Nights Videos 404/728-0701 ■ 2205 Cheshire Br Rd (at Woodland Ave NE)

Starship 404/320-9101 ■ 2275 Cheshire Bridge Rd ■ 24hrs, many locations in Atlanta ■ www.shopstarship.com

HAWAII

Honolulu

ACCOMMODATIONS

1 **Aqua Coconut Plaza** [GF,SW,WC] 808/923-8828 ■ 450 Lewers St (at Ala Wai, Waikiki) ■ boutique hotel in the heart of Waikiki, near the Kuhio (gay) District ■ www.aquaresorts.com

2 **Aqua Palms & Spa** [GF,SW,NS,WC] 808/947-7256, 866/406-2782 ■ 1850 Ala Moana Blvd (at Kalia & Ena) ■ boutique hotel w/ retro-Hawaiian style, full spa ■ www.aquaresorts.com

3 **Breakers Hotel** [GF,SW] 808/923-3181, 800/426-0494 ■ 250 Beachwalk ■ also bar & grill ■ www.breakers-hawaii.com

4 **The Cabana at Waikiki** [★M,GO] 808/926-5555, 877/902-2121 ■ 2551 Cartwright Rd (off Kapahulu Ave) ■ 1-bdrm suites w/ kitchens & lanais, 8-man spa, 1 block to gay Queen's Surf beach & 1/2 block to Hula's ■ www.cabana-waikiki.com

5 **Diamond Head View Vacations** [M,SW,WI,WC] 808/258-6636 ■ 134 Kapahulu Ave (in Waikiki Grand Hotel) ■ near beach, view of Diamond Head Crater & "Queen Beach" ■ gayhawaii.com/diamondheadview

5 **Grand Waikiki** 134 Kapahulu Ave (in Waikiki Grand Hotel) ■ private condo located in Waikiki Grand Hotel (same building as Hula's) ■ home.earthlink.net/~loz808/GW/index.html

6 **Ilima Hotel** [GF,WC] 808/923-1877, 800/801-9366 ■ 445 Nohonani St (at Kuhio Ave) ■ offers spacious condo-style studios & suites w/ full kitchens, private lanai ■ www.ilima.com

7 **Kolohe's B No B** [MO,WI,GO] 808/923-2408 ■ 441 Kanekapolei St #102A (at Ala Wai Blvd) ■ "bed w/out brkfst" in private home, DSL internet access ■ www.kolohekea.com

8 **Nui Kai** [MW,R,SW,NS,WI,WC,GO] 719/783-2331 ■ Gold Coast oceanfront condo, huge lanai ■ mike@ranchretreats.com

Outrigger Hotels & Resorts [GF] 808/921-6600, 800/688-7444 ■ many properties in Waikiki ■ www.outrigger.com

5 **Queen's Surf Vacation Rentals** [GS,NS] 808/923-1814, 888/336-4368 ■ 134 Kapahulu (at Lemon Rd, in Waikiki Grand Hotel) ■ deluxe units w/ ocean views, kids ok ■ www.queenssurf.com

ResortQuest Waikiki Circle Hotel [GF,NS] 808/923-1571, 877/997-6667 ■ 2464 Kalakaua Ave (at Uluniu St, Waikiki) ■ overlooking Waikiki Beach ■ www.resortquesthawaii.com

10 **ResortQuest Waikiki Joy Hotel** [GF,F,K,SW,NS,WC] 808/923-2300, 866/774-2924 ■ 320 Lewers St (at Kalakaua Ave, Waikiki) ■ boutique hotel, jacuzzis, near beach ■ www.resortquesthawaii.com

11 **Seashore Vacations Hawaii** [GF,NS] 808/630-0261 ■ 2450 Koa Ave (at Uluniu Ave) ■ rental condo ■ www.seashorevacationshawaii.com

12 **Vivian's 605** [MW,NS,GO] 808/344-3866, 808/780-2070 ■ 1911 Kalakaua Ave #605 (at Ala Moana Blvd) ■ 1-bdrm condo, sleeps up to 4, near beach, in heart of Waikiki ■ tamber401@aol.com

Waikiki GLBT Vacation Rentals [GF,SW,NS,WC] 808/922-1659 ■ reservation service, ask for Walt Flood ■ www.waikiki-vacation-GLBT-rentals.com

5 **Waikiki Grand Hotel** [M,NS] 808/923-1814, 888/336-4368 ■ 134 Kapahulu Ave ■ deluxe hotel that includes rental units as well as Hula's Bar, close to gay beach ■ www.waikikigrand.com

5 **Waikiki Grand Sundeck Suite 1005** 134 Kapahulu Ave (in Waikiki Grand Hotel) ■ private rental in one of largest rooms in hotel, completely renovated, panoramic view, 134 steps to beach, full kitchen ■ www.waikikigrandview.com

BARS

13 **Angles** [MW,NH,D,S,V] 808/926-9766, 808/923-1130 (infoline) ■ 2256 Kuhio Ave, 2nd flr (at Seaside, Waikiki) ■ 10am-2am, DJ Wed-Sun, male dancers Th & Sun, catamaran cruise 1pm Sun ■ www.angleswaikiki.com

14 **In Between** [M,NH,K] 808/926-7060 ■ 2155 Lau'ula St (off Lewers, across from Planet Hollywood, Waikiki) ■ 4pm-2am ■ www.inbetweenonline.com

NIGHTCLUBS

Black Garter Cafe [W,D,WC] 808/737-6446 x2 ■ 9:30pm-2am Fri, venue changes ■ www.blackgartercafe.com

15 **Fusion Waikiki** [★M,D,TG,K,DS,S,V] 808/924-2422 ■ 2260 Kuhio Ave, 2nd flr (at Seaside) ■ 10pm-4am, from 8pm Fri-Sat, [K] Mon-Tue [DS,S] Fri-Sat ■ www.gayhawaii.com/fusion

5 **Hula's Bar & Lei Stand** [★M,D,TG,F,S,V,YC,WI] 808/923-0669 ■ 134 Kapahulu Ave (2nd flr of Waikiki Grand Hotel) ■ 10am-2am, near gay beach, go-go boys Th & Sun, weekly catamaran cruise, lesbian-, transgender-, bear-, & leather-friendly ■ www.hulas.com

16 **Venus Nightclub** [GS,D,MR-A,S,YC] 808/951-8671, 808/955-2640 ■ 1349 Kapiolani Blvd (below China House restaurant, at Piikoi) ■ 8pm-4am, male revue Sat, [18+] 2nd & 4th Sat ■ www.venusnightclub.com

CAFES

Caffe G [WI,GO] 808/979-2299 ■ 1888 Kalakaua Ave, C106 (in Waikiki Landmark Building) ■ 8am-11pm, internet cafe, patio, great coffee, sandwiches & desserts ■ www.caffegiovannini.com

Mocha Java Cafe 808/591-9023 ■ 1200 Ala Moana Blvd (in Ward Center) ■ 8am-9pm, till 10pm Fri-Sat, till 6pm Sun, plenty veggie, outdoor seating

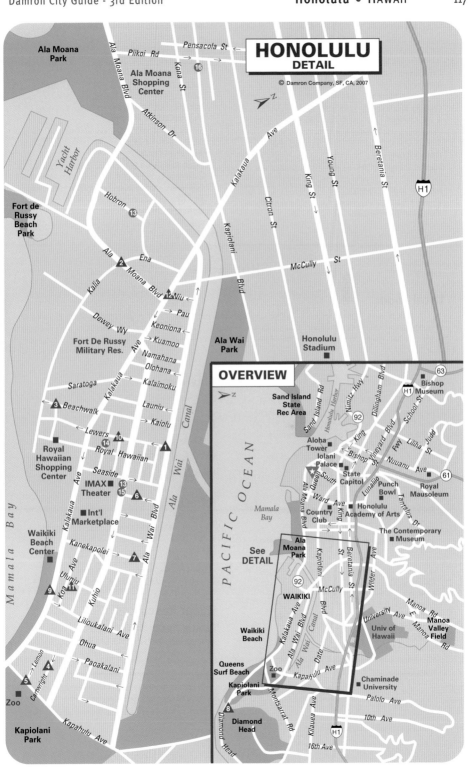

RESTAURANTS

Cafe Che Pasta [MW,D,E] 808/524-0004 ■ 1001 Bishop St, Ste 108 (enter off Alakea St) ■ *lunch & dinner Mon-Fri, clsd wknds, full bar* ■ www.cafechepasta.com

Cafe Sistina [WC] 808/596-0061 ■ 1314 S King St ■ *lunch Mon-Fri, dinner nightly, northern Italian, some veggie, full bar, live music wknds* ■ www.cafesistina.com

Cha Cha Cha 808/923-7797 ■ 342 Seaside Ave ■ *11:30am-11pm, Caribbean Mexican, happy hour, full bar*

Cheeseburger in Paradise 808/923-3731 ■ 2500 Kalakaua Blvd ■ *7am-11pm, full bar* ■ www.cheeseburger-inparadise.com

Eggs 'n' Things 808/949-0820 ■ 1911-B Kalakaua Ave ■ *11pm-2pm, diner, popular after-hours* ■ eggsnthings.com

Indigo [E] 808/521-2900 ■ 1121 Nu'uanu Ave ■ *lunch Tue-Fri, dinner Tue-Sat, bar open later, Eurasian, live music nightly* ■ www.indigo-hawaii.com

Keo's in Waikiki [★R] 808/732-7947 ■ 2028 Kuhio Ave ■ *7am-2pm & 5pm-10:30pm, till 11pm Fri-Sat* ■ www.keosthaicuisine.com

La Cucaracha 808/922-2288 ■ 2310 Kuhio Ave, #102 (at Nahua) ■ *noon-11pm, Mexican, full bar*

Rock Island Cafe 808/923-8033 ■ 131 Kaiulani Ave (off Kalakaua, in King's Village Waikiki) ■ *old-fashioned soda fountain, pizza & shakes, also memorabilia shop* ■ www.rockislandonline.com

Singha Thai [E] 808/941-2898, 800/482-8424 ■ 1910 Ala Moana Blvd ■ *4pm-10pm, Thai dancers 7pm-9pm* ■ www.singhathai.com

Tapa's Restaurant & Lanai Bar [E,GO] 808/921-2288 ■ 407 Seaside, 2nd flr (at Kuhio Ave) ■ *noon-midnight, till 2am wknds, also Sun brunch (summers only 10am-1pm), East-West fusion, some veggie, lanai bar [K], live music Fri* ■ www.tapaswaikiki.com

HONOLULU

Local Food:

Poi, a paste made from taro root, is a staple of the traditional Hawaiian diet. A luau may be the most fun way to sample this local delicacy, enjoyed along with a roasted pig, tropical drinks, and some beautiful hula dancing. Luaus run the gamut from traditional to high kitsch, so check local listings for one that suits your taste.

Tourist Info

AIRPORT DIRECTIONS

Honolulu International Airport. Take Nimitz Hwy South, which becomes Ala Moana South. Go right at Kalakaua into Waikiki. (For a true Hawaiian welcome, contact Leis of Hawaii [www.leisofhawaii.com] and get a fresh lei on arrival.)

PUBLIC TRANSIT & TAXIS

Charley's 808/531-1333.
The Bus 808/848-5555, web: www.thebus.org.

TOURIST SPOTS & INFO

Bishop Museum 808/847-3511, web: www.bishop-museum.org.
Foster Botanical Gardens. 808/522-7066, web: www.hawaiimuseums.org/mc/isoahu_foster.htm.
Hanauma Bay.
Honolulu Academy of Arts 808/532-8700, web: www.honoluluacademy.org.
'Iolani Palace 808/522-0832, web: www.iolani-palace.org.
Polynesian Cultural Center 800/367-7060 or 808/293-3333, web: www.polynesia.com.
USS Arizona Memorial, 808/422-0561, web: www.nps.gov/usar.
Waimea Falls Park.
Visitor's Center: 800/464-2924, web: www.gohawaii.com.
Also City & County of Honolulu, web: www.co.honolulu.hi.us/menu/visitors.

Weather

Usually paradise perfect, but humid. It rarely gets hotter than the upper 80's.

Best Views

Helicopter tour.

City Calendar

LGBT PRIDE

June, web: www.thecenterhawaii.org.

ANNUAL EVENTS

April - Merrie Monarch Festival, hula competition in Hilo, web: www.kalena.com/merriemonarch.
April-May - Golden Week, celebration of Japanese culture.
May - Honolulu Rainbow Film Festival 808/381-1952, web: www.hglcf.org.
September - Aloha Festival, web: alohafestivals.com.

Queer Resources

COMMUNITY INFO

The Center 808/545-2848. 614 South St, 10am-7pm, web: www.thecenterhawaii.org.
Helpful website: www.gayhawaii.com.
Lesbian/ Gay AA 808/946-1438, 277 Ohua (yes, it's Ohua!) (Waikiki Health Ctr), 8pm nightly, web: www.oahucentraloffice.com.
Life Foundation 808/ 521-2437, web: lifefoundation.org.

ENTERTAINMENT & RECREATION

Dolphin Quest 808/739-8918, 800/248-3316 ■ 5000 Kahala Ave (at Kahala Hotel & Resort) ■ *variety of programs for all ages to interact one-on-one with dolphins* ■ www.dolphinquest.org

Girls Who Surf 808/371-8917 ■ PO Box 38095 96837 ■ *surf lessons, beginners welcome* ■ www.girlswhosurf.com

LikeHike 808/455-8193 ■ *gay hiking tours every other Sun, also gay kayaking trips, call for info & locations* ■ www.gayhawaii.com/likehike

Queen's Surf Beach Kapiolani Park (off Kalakaua) ■ *popular gay beach at far end of Kuhio Beach*

Rainbow Sailing Charters [MW,GO] 808/396-5995 ■ *day & overnight sailing adventures, whale-watching, snorkeling, sunset cocktail cruises & commitment ceremonies, lesbian-owned* ■ yachts@hawaii.rr.com

Wahine Divers [GO] 808/358-4137 ■ 94-1052 Ohilau Pl ■ *9am-6pm, freedive, spearfishing & snorkel tours for women, rental equipment & packages, lesbian-owned* ■ www.wahinedivers.com

RETAIL SHOPS

Bethel Street Gallery [GO] 808/524-3552 ■ 1140 Bethel St (at Pauahi St) ■ *10am-6pm, till 3pm Sat, clsd Sun, contemporary art by Hawaiian artists* ■ www.bethelstreetgallery.com

5 **Eighty Percent Straight** 808/923-9996 ■ 134 Kapahulu Ave, Ste B (in Waikiki Grand Hotel) ■ *10am-10pm, till 11pm Fri-Sat, noon-10pm Sun, LGBT clothing, books, videos, cards, toys* ■ www.80percentstraight.com

Over Easy Down Under 808/926-4994 ■ 2301 Kuhio Ave, Ste 220 (Level 2, Waikiki Town Center) ■ *10am-10pm, clsd Sun, men's swimwear & activewear* ■ downunderhi@aol.com

PUBLICATIONS

DaKine Magazine 808/923-7378 ■ *LGBT newsmagazine for Oahu, club & nightlife listings, monthly* ■ www.dakinemagazine.com

Odyssey Magazine Hawaii 808/955-5959 ■ *everything you need to know about gay Hawaii* ■ www.odyssey-hawaii.com

GYMS & HEALTH CLUBS

Gold's Gym 808/533-7111 ■ 768 South St ■ *5am-11pm, till 10pm Fri, 6am-8pm Sat, 7am-7pm Sun* ■ www.goldsgym.com

MEN'S CLUBS

Max's Gym [★V,18+,PC] 808/951-8232 ■ 438 Hobron Ln, 4th flr (at Ala Moana Blvd, in Eaton Square) ■ *24hrs, also Cafe Max*

EROTICA

Backseat Betty's 808/946-7301 ■ 1687 Kapiolani Blvd ■ *10am-2am*

Diamond Head Video 808/943-6066 ■ 1745 Kalakaua Ave (across from Convention Center & Hard Rock Cafe) ■ *24hrs* ■ www.diamondheadvideo.com

Suzie's 808/922-4071 ■ 2162 Kalakaua Ave (at Lewers)

Velvet Video 808/924-0868 ■ 2155 Lau'ula St, 2nd flr (above In Between, Waikiki) ■ *24hrs, videos for sale & rent, preview booths, toys* ■ www.velvet-video.com

---

ILLINOIS

Chicago

Chicago is divided into 5 geographical areas:
    Chicago—Overview
    Chicago—North Side
    Chicago—Boystown/ Lakeview
    Chicago—Near North
    Chicago—South Side

Chicago—Overview

includes some listings for Greater Chicagoland

ACCOMMODATIONS

Chicago Park Hotel [GF,SW] 708/596-1500 ■ 17040 S Halsted St (off I-80), Harvey ■ *kids ok, also restaurant, 30 minutes from Chicago* ■ www.chicagoparkhotel.com

Chicago Sisters' Place [WO,WI,GO] 773/542-9126 ■ 1957 S Spaulding Ave (at S 21st) ■ *furnished rooms in women's residence; please call ahead; lesbian-owned* ■ sophiebella@sbcglobal.net

Days Inn Hotel [GF,SW,WI,WC] 708/474-6300 ■ 17356 Torrence Ave (I-80), Lansing ■ *20 minutes S of Chicago, also restaurant* ■ www.daysinnlansingil.com

BARS

Chesterfield Club [M,D,MR-L] 773/376-9511 ■ 1800 W Pershing Rd ■ *8pm-2am, till 3am Sat, clsd Mon-Th* ■ www.clubchesterfields.com

NIGHTCLUBS

Chix Mix Productions [W,D] ■ *occasional dance parties, see website for info* ■ www.chixmixproductions.com

ENTERTAINMENT & RECREATION

About Face Theatre 773/784-8565 ■ *roving LGBT theater company w/ popular Youth Theatre as well* ■ www.aboutfacetheatre.com

Artemis Singers 773/764-4465 ■ *lesbian feminist chorus* ■ www.artemissingers.org

Bailiwick Arts Center 773/883-1090 (box office #) ■ 1229 W Belmont Ave ■ *many LGBT-themed productions, including the popular Pride Series & Lesbian Theater Initiative* ■ www.bailiwick.org

Cafe Pride 773/281-2655 (church #) ■ 716 W Addison St (at Broadway, at Lake View Presbyterian) ■ *coffeehouse for LGBT youth (17-21) only, 8pm-midnight Fri* ■ www.cafepride.com

Chicago Metropolitan Sports Association (CMSA) ■ *if you want to play a sport, they have a team for it* ■ www.chicagomsa.com

Chicago Neighborhood Tours [GF] 312/742-1190 ■ 77 E Randolph St (at Chicago Cultural Center) ■ *the best way to make the Windy City your kind of town* ■ www.chgocitytours.com

Chicago Sky 877/329-9622 ■ UIC Pavilion ■ *check out the Women's National Basketball Association while you're in Chicago* ■ www.wnba.com/sky

GayCo 312/458-9400, 773/478-6376 ■ 5353 N Magnolia ■ www.gayco.net

The Hancock Observatory 312/751-3681, 888/875-8439 ■ 875 N Michigan Ave (in John Hancock Center) ■ *9am-11pm, renovated 94th-flr observatory w/ outside Skywalk* ■ www.hancockobservatory.com

Chicago

Day Trips: Indiana Dunes

The Indiana Dunes are about 50 miles southeast of the city. Winter or summer, the dunes offer a wide range of things to do on or off the water: swimming, hiking and biking trails, ice-skating, sledding, and golf are just a few things to keep you busy. Exploring the quaint art galleries and local wineries will add some culture to your jaunt.

Local Food:

Chicago is a meat-lover's town. Italian beef, Polish sausage, and "red hots," the Windy City's version of the hot dog, are just some of the local treats to sink your teeth into. And don't forget about the Chicago-style deep-dish pizza.

Curious cooks should take Evelyn's Ethnic Grocery Store Tour, a wonderful way to learn about the ethnic neighborhoods—and foods—that make up Chicago ($70 for 2; 773/ 465-8064; www.ethnic-grocery-tours.com).

Tourist Info

AIRPORT DIRECTIONS

O'Hare International. The Kennedy Expressway heads toward the city. Or take Mannheim Rd to the Eisenhower Expressway. Inquire locally about which is currently the lesser of two evils. Better still, take the train (Blue Line) from the station in O'Hare to the Washington stop downtown. Transfer here to the Red Line and get off at Belmont. Outside the station, hike east along Belmont to Halsted, turn left and for several blocks into the heart of Boystown.

PUBLIC TRANSIT & TAXIS

Yellow Cab 312/ 829-4222.
Continental Airport Express 888/284-3826.
Chicago Transit Authority 312/836-7000, web: www.transitchicago.com.
Metra Rail 312/322-6777, web: www.metrarail.com.

TOURIST SPOTS & INFO

900 North Michigan Shops.
Jane Addams Hull-House Museum 312/413-5353, www.hullhousemuseum.org.
The Art Institute of Chicago 312/443-3600, web: www.artic.edu.
DuSable Museum of African American History 773/947-0600, web: www.dusablemuseum.org.
Historic Water Tower.
LaSalle Bank Theatre (formerly Schubert Theatre).
Museum of Contemporary Art 312/280-2660, web: www.mcachicago.org.
Museum of Science and Industry 773/684-1414, web: www.msichicago.org.
National Museum of Mexican Art 312/738-1503, web: www.nationalmuseumofmexicanart.org.
Peace Museum, 773/638-6450, web: www.peacemuseum.org.
Steppenwolf Theatre Company, 312/335-1650, web: www.steppenwolf.org.
Terra Foundation for American Art, 312/664-3939, web: www.terraamericanart.org.
Wrigley Field, 773/404-CUBS, web: chicago.cubs.mlb.com.
Visitor's Center: Chicago Office of Tourism 877/244-2246, web: www.cityofchicago.org.

Weather

"The Windy City" earned its name. Winter temperatures have been known to be as low as -46°. Summers are humid, normally in the 80°s.

Best Views

Skydeck of the 110-story Sears Tower, web: www.theskydeck.com or the open-air observation deck at the John Hancock Observatory, web: www.hancockobservatory.com.

City Calendar

LGBT PRIDE

June. 773/348-8243, web: www.chicagopridecalendar.org.

ANNUAL EVENTS

May - International Mr. Leather 800/545-6753. Weekend of events and contest on Sunday, web: www.imrl.com.
May - Bear Pride 773/509-5135, web: www.bearpride.org.
May-June- Chicago Blues Festival 312/744-3370, web: www.chicagobluesfestival.org.
August - Northalsted Market Days 773/883-0500, web: www.northalsted.com/daze.htm.
November - Chicago Lesbian & Gay Film Festival 773/293-1447, web: www.reelingfilmfestival.org.

Queer Resources

COMMUNITY INFO

The Center on Halsted 773/472-6469. 3656 N Halsted St, 8am-10pm, web: www.centeronhalsted.org (see Boystown map).
Center on Halsted Infoline, 773/929-4357, 8am-10pm.
Chicago Area Gay/Lesbian Chamber of Commerce, 773/303-0167, web: www.glchamber.org.
Newtown Alano Club (AA), 773/529-0321. 909 W Belmont St, 2nd flr (btwn Clark & Sheffield).
State of Illinois HIV/AIDS/STD Hotline, 800/243-2437 (in IL). 8am-10pm.

CHICAGO
OVERVIEW
© Damron Company, SF, CA, 2007

N

Baha'i House
of Worship ■
EVANSTON

■ Grosse Point
Lighthouse

Northwestern
University ■

DES
PLAINES

Des Plaines River

Rand Rd
Northwest Hwy

294

Waukegan

Harlem Ave

Milwaukee Ave

43

Sheridan Road

Lake Michigan

14

12

21

45

Tollway

Dempster St

41

50

SKOKIE

94

Western Ave

PARK
RIDGE

Horizon
Arena

Forest
Preserve

41

Loyola
University ■

190

Peterson Ave

14

O'Hare
Int'l Airport

90

Chicago River

See
NORTH SIDE
DETAIL

Lincoln
Park

Lake Shore

294

Franklin
Park

Irving Park Rd

Lincoln
Park Zoo

Wrigley
Field

See
BOYSTOWN/
LAKEVIEW
DETAIL

Grand Ave

Mannheim

94

DePaul
Univ

90

Cicero Ave

Milwaukee Ave

Fullerton

North Ave

Harlem Ave

OAK
PARK

Frank Lloyd
Wright Home

Lake St

Dwight D Eisenhower Expwy

Humboldt
Park

Grand Ave

See
WICKER
PARK
DETAIL

■ Chicago
See Hist Soc
NEAR
NORTH   Navy
DETAIL   Pier

Grand Ave

Garfield
Park

Washington Blvd

Art
Institute

290

FOREST
PARK

Roosevelt Rd

■ Mus of Nat History

12

CICERO

Douglas
Park

Cermak Rd

Nat'l Museum
of Mexican
Art

Soldier
Field

20

Brookfield
Zoo ■

43

45

Ogden Ave

Ogden Ave

55

Pershing

Comiskey
Park

Dan Ryan Expwy

Michigan Ave

Lake

Washington
Park

Archer Ave

47th St

Pulaski

Kedzie

Western Ave

Int'l
Ampitheatre

90

DuSable Museum of
African American History

HYDE   Univ of
PARK   Chicago

■ Mus of
Science &
Industry

171

Midway
Airport

55th St

Cicero Ave

Marquette
Park

Ashland

Halsted

Jackson
Park

94

90

Shore Dr

79th St

Ave

Columbus

State St

294

Tri-State Tollway

La Grange Rd

Palos
Forest
Preserve

95th St

OAK
LAWN

50

EVERGREEN
PARK

12   20

Chicago State
■ University

57

94

Heartland Cafe 773/465-8005 ■ 7000 N Glenwood Ave (in Rogers Park) ■ cafe w/ full bar, theater, lots of live music including performers popular on women's music circuit ■ www.heartlandcafe.com

Leather Archives & Museum 773/761-9200 ■ 6418 N Greenview Ave ■ noon-8pm Th-Fri, till 5pm Sat-Sun, or by appointment, membership required (purchase at door) ■ www.leatherarchives.org

The Neo-Futurarium 773/275-5255 ■ 5153 N Ashland Ave ■ alternative theater group ■ www.neofuturists.org

Queer Nerds at Heart ■ hosts monthly social events, check website for details ■ www.nerdsatheart.com

Sears Tower Skydeck 312/875-9696 ■ 233 S Wacker Dr (enter at Jackson Blvd) ■ see the city from the 99th & 103rd floors of North America's tallest building ■ www.theskydeck.com

Second City [GF,E] 312/337-3992, 877/778-4707 ■ 1616 N Wells St (at North) ■ legendary comedy club, call for reservations ■ www.secondcity.com

Windy City Performing Arts 773/404-9242 ■ 3023 N Clark St #329 ■ includes Windy City Gay Chorus, Aria: Windy City Women's Ensemble & Unison: Windy City Lesbian & Gay Singers ■ www.windycitysings.org

Windy City Rollers ■ Chicago's female roller derby league, check web for upcoming events ■ www.windycityrollers.com

PUBLICATIONS

The Alternative Phone Book 773/472-6319 ■ 619 W Stratford Pl ■ directory of local businesses ■ www.apb-chicago.com

boi magazine 773/975-0264 ■ slick glossy w/ bar listings, articles, photos & circuit dish ■ www.boimagazine.com

Chicago Free Press 773/868-0005 ■ LGBT newspaper ■ www.chicagofreepress.com

Gay Chicago 773/327-7271 ■ weekly, extensive resource listings ■ www.gaychicagomag.com

Identity 773/871-7610 ■ monthly news & features for LGBTs of color ■ www.WindyCityTimes.com

Nightspots 773/871-7610 ■ weekly LGBT nightlife magazine ■ www.WindyCityTimes.com

Pink Pages 773/769-6328, 877/769-7465 ■ LGBT business directory & lifestyle magazine ■ lesgaypinkpages.com

Windy City Times 773/871-7610 ■ weekly LGBT newspaper & calendar guide ■ www.WindyCityTimes.com

MEN'S CLUBS

Windy City Bondage Club 312/409-7613 (hotline #) ■ members-only club for bondage & BDSM w/ play parties; guests welcome ■ www.wcbc-chicago.org

Chicago—North Side

ACCOMMODATIONS

1 The Ardmore House [M,WI,GO] 773/728-5414 ■ 1248 W Ardmore Ave (at Magnolia) ■ Victorian B&B, full brkfst wknds, hot tub ■ www.ardmorehousebb.com

2 House 5863 [GS,NS,WI,GO] 773/944-5555 ■ 5863 N Glenwood (at Admore) ■ B&B w/ "hip urban rooms" ■ www.house5863.com

BARS

3 The Anvil [M,NH,V] 773/973-0006 ■ 1137 W Granville (E of Broadway) ■ 9am-2am

4 Big Chicks [MW,NH,D,F,V,WI,WC] 773/728-5511 ■ 5024 N Sheridan (btwn Foster & Argyle) ■ 4pm-2am, from 3pm wknds, patio, Sun BBQ ■ www.bigchicks.com

5 Chicago Eagle [MW,L,WC] 773/728-0050 ■ 5015 N Clark St (at Argyle) ■ 8pm-4am, till 5am Sat, dress code Tue & Fri-Sat ■ www.chicagoeagle.com

6 Crew [MW,F,V] 773/784-2739 ■ 4804 N Broadway St (at Lawrence) ■ 11:30am-2am, from 11am Sat, sports bar & grill, patio ■ www.worldsgreatestbar.com

7 El Gato Negro [GS,D,MR-L,TG,E] 773/472-9353 ■ 1461 W Irving Park (btwn Clark & Ashland) ■ noon-2am, till 3am Sat, live shows Sun ■ www.elgatonegrobar.com

6 Green Mill [★GS,E] 773/878-5552 ■ 4802 N Broadway St (at Lawrence) ■ noon-4am, till 5am Sat, noted jazz venue, hosts the Uptown Poetry Slam ■ www.greenmilljazz.com

8 Jackhammer [★M,NH,D,L,S,V] 773/743-5772 ■ 6406 N Clark St (at Devon) ■ 4pm-4am, till 5am Fri-Sat, from 2pm wknds, 3 bars (dance bar, sports bar & downstairs leather bar), patio ■ www.jackhammer-chicago.com

9 Joie de Vine [W,WI,WC,GO] 773/989-6846 ■ 1744 W Balmoral (at Paulina St) ■ 4pm-2am, till 3am Sat, till midnight Sun, wine bar, patio, lesbian-owned

10 Lost & Found [W,NH] 773/463-7599 ■ 3058 W Irving Park Rd (at Albany) ■ 7pm-2am, clsd Mon (also Tue summers), sports bar

11 Marty's [GF] 773/561-6425 ■ 1511 W Balmoral Ave (at Clark) ■ 5pm-2am, upscale wine & martini bar

12 Scot's [M,NH] 773/528-3253 ■ 1829 W Montrose (at Damen) ■ 3pm-2am, 11am-3am Sat, till 2am Sun

13 Sofo [M,NH,V] 773/784-7636 ■ 4923 N Clark St (at Argyle) ■ 5pm-2am, 3pm-3am Sat, till 2am Sun, video bar, backyard beer garden

14 Star Gaze [W,NH,D,TG,F,K] 773/561-7363 ■ 5419 N Clark St (at Balmoral) ■ 6pm-2am, 5pm-3am Sat, 11:30am-2am Sun, clsd Mon-Tue, sports bar & dance bar, outdoor beer garden, also restaurant ■ www.stargazechicago.com

15 T's [GS,NH,F,WC] 773/784-6000 ■ 5025 N Clark St (at Winnemac) ■ 5pm-2am, 11am-3am, till 2am Sun, also restaurant ■ www.tsbarchicago.com

16 Touché [★M,L] 773/465-7400 ■ 6412 N Clark St (at Devon) ■ 5pm-4am, 3pm-5am Sat, noon-4am, Bear Night 1st Sat ■ www.touchechicago.com

NIGHTCLUBS

17 Atmosphere [MW,D,C,S,GO] 773/784-1100 ■ 5355 N Clark St (at W Balmoral Ave) ■ 5pm-2am, till 3am Sat, 3pm-2am Sun, clsd Mon, [S] Th-Sat ■ www.atmospherebar.com

18 Planet Claire [GS,D,V] 773/348-9600 (Holiday Club #) ■ 4000 N Sheridan Rd (at Irving Park, at the Holiday Club) ■ 10pm-2am Fri only, New Wave ■ www.swingersmecca.com

CAFES

Charmer's Cafe [MW,WI,WC] 773/743-2233 ■ 1500 W Jarvis (at Greenview) ■ 6am-6:30pm, from 7am wknds

Coffee Chicago [F,WI] 773/784-1305 ■ 5256 N Broadway St (btwn Berwyn & Foster) ■ 7am-9pm, till 9:30pm Fri, from 8am Sat, till 9pm Sun, also sandwiches, soups, smoothies, ice cream

KOPI: A Traveler's Cafe [E] 773/989-5674 ■ 5317 N Clark St (at Summerdale) ■ 8am-11pm, till midnight Fri-Sat, from 9am Sat, from 10am Sun, coffee & tea, soup, sandwiches, & pastries; also boutique & gallery w/ travel books & art from around the world

Metropolis Coffee [★WI] 773/764-0400 ■ 1039 W Granville Ave (at Kenmore) ■ 6:30am-8pm, from 7am Sat, from 7:30am Sun ■ metropoliscoffee.com

RESTAURANTS

Andie's [WC] 773/784-8616 ▪ 5253 N Clark (btwn Berwyn & Farragut) ▪ 10:30am-10:30pm, till 11:30pm Fri-Sat, 10am-10pm Sun, eastern Mediterranean, plenty veggie, full bar ▪ www.andiesres.com

Charlie's Ale House [GS] 773/751-0140 ▪ 5308 N Clark St (at Summerdale) ▪ 11:30am-1am, 11am-2am Sat, 11am-midnight Sun, brunch Sun, American food, more lesbian wknds ▪ www.charliesalehouse.com/andersonville.html

Deluxe Diner/ Maria's 773/743-8244 (Deluxe #), 773/743-9900 (Maria's #) ▪ 6349 N Clark St (at Devon) ▪ 24hr diner & pizza/ Italian restaurant till 11pm

Fireside 773/561-7433, 877/878-7433 ▪ 5739 N Ravenswood (at Rosehill) ▪ 11am-4am, till 5am Sat, 10am-4am Sun, Cajun & pizza, patio, full bar ▪ www.firesidechicago.com

Hamburger Mary's [MW,E,K,DS] 773/784-6969 ▪ 5400 N Clark St (at Balmoral) ▪ opens 11am, from 10am Sun, also full bar ▪ www.hamburgermaryschicago.com

Pauline's 773/561-8573 ▪ 1754 W Balmoral (at Ravenswood) ▪ 7am-3pm, hearty brkfsts, home of 5-egg omelette ▪ www.paulinesbreakfast.com

Reza's Restaurant [WC] 773/561-1898 ▪ 5255 N Clark (btwn Berwyn & Farragut) ▪ lunch, dinner & wknd brunch, Mediterranean/ Persian, plenty veggie, full bar ▪ www.rezasrestaurant.com

Svea Restaurant [WC] 773/275-7738 ▪ 5236 N Clark (btwn Berwyn & Farragut) ▪ 7am-3:45pm, Swedish/ American comfort food

Tedino's [★WC] 773/275-8100 ▪ 5335 N Sheridan (at Broadway) ▪ 11am-11pm, till midnight wknds, pizza, full bar

Thai Pastry & Restaurant 773/784-5399 ▪ 4925 N Broadway St, Unit E (at Argyle) ▪ 11am-10pm, till 11pm Fri-Sat ▪ www.thaipastry.com

Tomboy [★WC,GO] 773/907-0636 ▪ 5402 N Clark St (at Balmoral) ▪ 5pm-10pm, till 11pm wknds, clsd Sun, eclectic American, full bar ▪ www.tomboyrestaurant.com

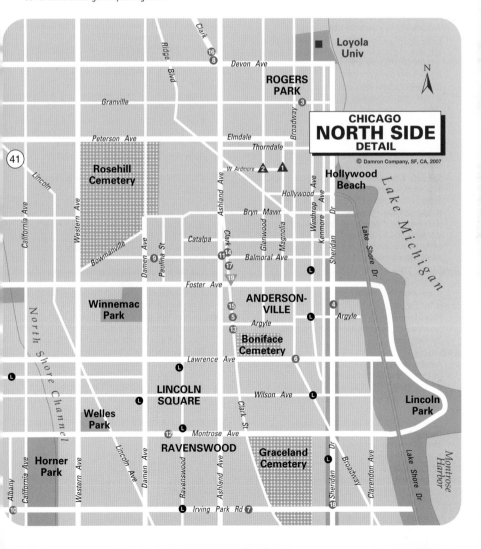

Tweet [WI] 773/728-5576 ■ 5020 N Sheridan Rd (at Argyle) ■ *9am-3pm, clsd Tue, brkfst & brunch, cash only* ■ www.tweet.biz

Unique So Chique Tea & Chocolate Room [GO] 773/561-0324 ■ 4600 N Magnolia, Ste C (entrance on Wilson, next to Starbucks) ■ *lunch 11:30am-3pm, tea service 3pm-5pm, brunch 10am-2:30pm wknds, clsd Mon, also hosts special gay events like Gay-i-Tea* ■ www.uniquesochique.com

ENTERTAINMENT & RECREATION

Hollywood Beach [★] at Hollywood & Sheridan Sts ■ *"the" gay beach*

BOOKSTORES

19 **Women & Children First** [★WC] 773/769-9299, 888/923-7323 ■ 5233 N Clark St (at Foster) ■ *11am-7pm, till 9pm Wed-Fri, 10am-7pm Sat, 11am-6pm Sun, women-owned* ■ www.womenandchildrenfirst.com

RETAIL SHOPS

Bad Boys Chicago [GO] 773/334-9993 ■ 1500 W Balmoral (at Clark) ■ *noon-9pm, from 11am Sat, noon-6pm Sun, men's clothing, accessories; also 335 N Halsted St, 773/549-7701* ■ www.badboyschicago.com

Enjoy, An Urban General Store 773/334-8626 ■ 4727 N Lincoln Ave (Lincoln Square) ■ *from 11am, from 10am Sat-Sun, cards & gifts, pride items* ■ www.urbangeneralstore.com

Gaymart 773/929-4272 ■ 3457 N Halsted St (at Cornelius) ■ *11am-7pm, noon-8pm Fri, till 6pm Sun, lots of kitsch & pride items*

Mephisto Leathers North America [MW,GO] 773/508-0900, 800/910-0666 ■ 6410 N Clark St (at Devon, btwn Jackhammer & Touché) ■ *noon-midnight, till 4am Th, till 5am Fri, till 6am Sat, 4pm-midnight Sun-Mon* ■ www.mephistona.com

Specialty Video Films [GO] 773/878-3434 ■ 5307 N Clark St (at Berwin Ave) ■ *10am-11pm, till midnight Fri-Sat, foreign, cult, art house, LGBT & erotic videos*

Unique So Chique Boutique [GO] 773/561-0324 ■ 4600 N Magnolia, Ste C (entrance on Wilson, next to Starbucks) ■ *11:30am-7:30pm, 10am-6pm Sat, till 5pm Sun, clsd Mon, clothing & accessories; also tea & chocolate room* ■ www.uniquesochique.com

GYMS & HEALTH CLUBS

Cheetah Gym 773/728-7777 ■ 5248 N Clark St (at Foster) ■ www.cheetahgym.com

MEN'S CLUBS

Man's Country [PC,S] 773/878-2069 ■ 5017 N Clark St (at Argyle) ■ *24hrs, nude strippers Fri-Sat* ■ www.manscountrychicago.com

EROTICA

Admiral Theater 773/478-8111 ■ 3940 W Lawrence Ave (at Pulaski) ■ www.admiralx.com

Banana Video 773/561-8322 ■ 4923 N Clark (at Argyle, 2nd flr) ■ *4pm-2am, till 4am Fri, noon-4am Sat, till midnight Sun, arcade*

Early to Bed [GF,TG,18+,GO] 773/271-1219, 866/585-2233 ■ 5232 N Sheridan Rd (at Foster) ■ *clsd Mon, lesbian-owned* ■ www.early2bed.com

Tulip Sex Toy Gallery [W,GO] 773/275-6110, 877/708-8547 ■ 1480 W Berwyn (at Clark) ■ *noon-10pm, till 7pm Sun, lesbian-owned* ■ www.mytulip.com

Chicago—Boystown/ Lakeview

ACCOMMODATIONS

1 **Best Western Hawthorne Terrace** [GF,WI,WC] 773/244-3434, 888/860-3400 ■ 3434 N Broadway St (at Hawthorne Pl) ■ *in heart of Chicago's gay community, gym* ■ www.hawthorneterrace.com

2 **City Suites Hotel** [GF,WI] 773/404-3400, 800/248-9108 ■ 933 W Belmont Ave (btwn Clark & Sheffield) ■ *accommodations w/ touch of European style* ■ www.cityinns.com/citysuites

3 **Inn at Lincoln Park** [GS,WI,GO] 773/348-2810, 866/774-7275 ■ 601 W Diversey Pkwy (at N Clark St) ■ *vintage Victorian inn in Lincoln Park* ■ www.innlp.com

4 **Majestic Hotel** [GF,WI] 773/404-3499, 800/727-5108 ■ 528 W Brompton Ave (at Addison) ■ *romantic 19th-c atmosphere* ■ www.cityinns.com/majestic

5 **Roscoe Rooms** [M,NS,GO] 773/281-4546, 773/392-4546 ■ 1951 W Cornelia (at Damen) ■ *2 rms in Queen Cottage in heart of Roscoe Village*

6 **Villa Toscana B&B** [MW,NS,WI,GO] 773/404-2643, 800/404-2643 ■ 3447 N Halsted St (at Cornelia) ■ *1890s coach house* ■ www.villa-toscana.com

7 **The Willows** [GS,WI] 773/528-8400, 800/787-3108 ■ 555 W Surf St (at Broadway) ■ *hotel w/ 19th-c French flair in Lincoln Park* ■ www.cityinns.com/willows

BARS

8 **3160** [MW,NH,E,WC] 773/327-5969 ■ 3160 N Clark St (at Belmont) ■ *noon-2am, till 3am Sat*

9 **Beat Kitchen** [GF,F,E] 773/281-4444 ■ 2100 W Belmont (btwn Hoyne & Damen) ■ *4pm-2am, from 11:30am Fri-Sun, live bands, also grill* ■ www.beatkitchen.com

10 **Blues** [★GF,E] 773/528-1012, 773/549-9436 ■ 2519 N Halsted St (at Wrightwood) ■ *8pm-2am, till 3am Sat, classic Chicago blues spot* ■ www.chicagobluesbar.com

11 **Bobby Love's** [MW,NH,K,WC] 773/525-1200 ■ 3729 N Halsted St (at Waveland) ■ *3pm-2am, from noon wknds, till 3am Fri-Sat, [K] Fri* ■ bobbyloveschgo@aol.com

12 **Buck's Saloon** [M,NH] 773/525-1125 ■ 3439 N Halsted St (btwn Cornelia & Newport) ■ *noon-2am, till 3am Sat, 11am-2am Sun, beer garden on the street* ■ www.buckssaloonchicago.com

13 **Cell Block** [M,D,B,L,WC] 773/665-8064 ■ 3702 N Halsted St (at Waveland) ■ *4pm-2am, from 2pm wknds, also Holding Cell from 10pm Fri-Sat w/ strict leather/ latex/ uniform code* ■ www.cellblock-chicago.com

14 **Charlie's Chicago** [M,D,CW,DS] 773/871-8887 ■ 3726 N Broadway St (btwn Waveland & Grace) ■ *3pm-4am, till 5am Sat, club music after 1am* ■ www.charlieschicago.com

15 **The Closet** [★MW,NH,V] 773/477-8533 ■ 3325 N Broadway St (at Buckingham) ■ *2pm-4am, noon-5am Sat, till 4am Sun, video bar* ■ www.theclosetbar.com

16 **Cocktail** [MW,NH,D,S,V,WC] 773/477-1420 ■ 3359 N Halsted St (at Roscoe) ■ *4pm-2am, from 2pm wknds, till 3am Sat, go-go dancers Tue & Th*

17 **Gentry on Halsted** [M,E,C,P] 773/348-1053 ■ 3320 N Halsted St (at Aldine) ■ *4pm-2am, till 3am Sat, piano bar* ■ www.gentryofchicago.com

18 **Little Jim's** [★M,NH] 773/871-6116 ■ 3501 N Halsted St (at Cornelia) ■ *noon-4am, till 5am Sat*

19 **The Lucky Horseshoe Lounge** [M,NH,S] 773/404-3169 ■ 3169 N Halsted St (at Briar) ■ *4pm-2am, 2pm-3am Sat, till 2am Sun, dancers nightly, patio*

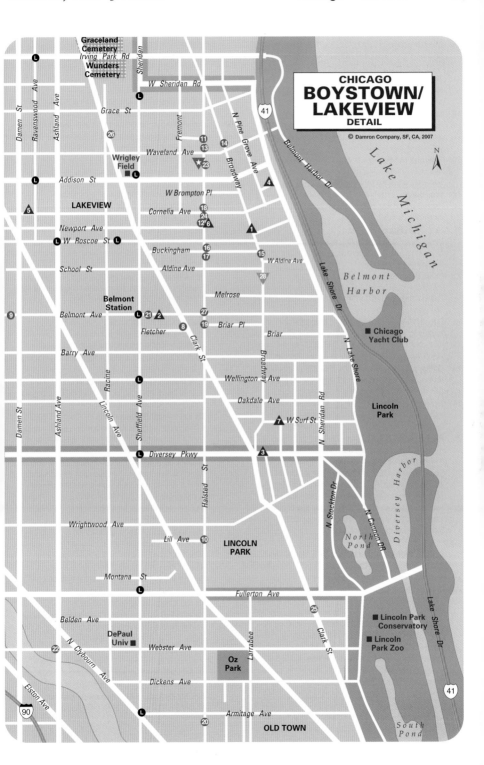

CHICAGO
**BOYSTOWN/
LAKEVIEW**
DETAIL
© Damron Company, SF, CA, 2007

20 **Manhandler Saloon** [★M,NH,V] 773/871-3339 ■ 1948 N Halsted St (at Armitage) ■ noon-4am, till 5am Sat, patio

16 **Minibar** [MW,NS] 773/871-6227 ■ 3341 N Halsted St (at Roscoe) ■ 7pm-2am, 5pm-3am Sat, 5pm-2am Sun, small lounge, specialty martinis ■ www.minibarchicago.com

11 **The North End** [M,NH,WC] 773/477-7999 ■ 3733 N Halsted St (at Grace) ■ 3pm-2am, 11am-3am Sat, till 2am Sun, sports bar ■ northendchgo@yahoo.com

16 **Roscoe's** [★MW,NH,D,F,S,V] 773/281-3355 ■ 3354-56 N Halsted St (at W Roscoe) ■ noon-2am, 11am-3am Sat, till 2am Sun, 6 bars, patio cafe in summer, "Glam 'n Eggs" brunch Sat-Sun ■ www.roscoes.com

16 **Sidetrack** [★MW,NH,V,WC] 773/477-9189 ■ 3349 N Halsted St (at Roscoe) ■ 3pm-2am, till 3am Sat, upscale video bar ■ www.sidetrackchicago.com

16 **Winebar** [MW,F] 773/871-6227 ■ 3341 N Halsted St (at Roscoe) ■ dinner 5pm-11pm, bar till 3am ■ www.mini-barchicago.com/winebar.html

Nightclubs

21 **Berlin** [★MW,D,TG,S,V,WC] 773/348-4975 ■ 954 W Belmont (at Sheffield) ■ 5pm-4am, from 8pm Sun-Mon ■ www.berlinchicago.com

22 **Boom Boom Room** [★GS,D] 773/395-0066, 773/549-0101 (promoter's #) ■ 2200 N Ashland (at Green Dolphin Street bar) ■ 11pm-4am Mon only ■ www.music-101.com

23 **Circuit/ Rehab** [M,D,MR,S] 773/325-2233 ■ 3641 N Halsted St (at Addison) ■ 9pm-4am, till 5am Sat, clsd Mon-Wed, theme nights, Latin nights Th & Sun (T-dance), women's nights 1st-3rd Fri & 1st Sat ■ www.circuitclub.com

23 **Girlbar Chicago** [★W,D,S] 773/325-2233 ■ 3641 N Halsted St (at Addison, at Circuit nightclub) ■ 9pm-4am 1st Sat ■ www.circuitclub.com

24 **Hydrate** [★GS,D,E,DS,S] 773/975-9244 ■ 3458 N Halsted St (at Cornelia) ■ 8pm-4am, till 5am Sat, opens earlier in summer, [DS] Wed, [S] Th ■ www.hydratechicago.com

25 **Planet Earth** [GS,D] 773/528-2622 ■ 2350 N Clark St (at Fullerton Pkwy, at Neo nightclub) ■ 10pm-4am Th, New Wave ■ www.planetearthchicago.com

26 **Smart Bar** [★GF,D,A,E] 773/549-0203 ■ 3730 N Clark St (downstairs at the Metro) ■ 10pm-4am, till 5am Sat, clsd Mon-Tue, theme nights ■ www.smartbarchicago.com

27 **Spin** [MW,D,DS,S,V,YC] 773/327-7711 ■ 800 W Belmont (enter on Halsted) ■ 4pm-2am, till 3am Sat, from 2pm wknds, 3 bars ■ www.spin-nightclub.com

Cafes

Caribou Coffee [WI] 773/477-3695 ■ 3300 N Broadway St (at Aldine) ■ from 5:30am, from 6:30am Sat, from 7am Sun ■ www.cariboucoffee.com

Chicago Room Gallery & Espresso Bar [WI] 773/404-2233 ■ 3318 N Halsted St (at Roscoe) ■ 11am-10pm, till midnight, clsd Tue, coffeehouse & art gallery, patio ■ www.chicagoroomgallerycafe.com

The Coffee & Tea Exchange 773/528-2241 ■ 3311 N Broadway St (at Roscoe) ■ 8am-8pm, till 7pm Fri, 9am-7pm Sat, 10am-6pm Sun, fair-trade coffee & tea by the cup & the pound ■ www.coffeeandtea.com

Starbucks [WI] 773/528-0343 ■ 3358 N Broadway St (at Roscoe) ■ 5:30am-9pm

Restaurants

Angelina Ristorante [WC] 773/935-5933 ■ 3561 N Broadway St (at Addison) ■ 5:30pm-11pm, Sun brunch, Italian, full bar ■ www.angelinaristorante.com

Ann Sather's [★] 773/348-2378 ■ 929 W Belmont Ave (at Sheffield) ■ 7am-3pm, till 4pm Sat-Sun, Swedish diner & Boystown fixture ■ www.annsather.com

Arco de Cuchilleros [MW] 773/296-6046 ■ 3445 N Halsted St (btwn Newport & Cornelia) ■ 5pm-11pm, till midnight Fri-Sat, 4pm-10pm Sun, clsd Mon, tapas, full bar, patio

Buca di Beppo [WC] 773/348-7673 ■ 2941 N Clark (btwn Wellington & Oakdale) ■ 5pm-10pm, 4pm-11pm Fri-Sat, noon-10pm Sun, Italian, full bar ■ www.bucadibeppo.com

Cesar's 773/296-9097 ■ 2924 N Broadway (at Oakdale) ■ "home of the killer margaritas" ■ www.killermargaritas.com

Chicago Diner [BW] 773/935-6696 ■ 3411 N Halsted St (at Roscoe) ■ 11am-10pm, from 10am wknds, till 11pm Fri-Sat, hip & vegetarian ■ www.veggiediner.com

Cornelia's [E,WC] 773/248-8333 ■ 750 W Cornelia Ave (at Halsted) ■ dinner nightly, clsd Mon, late-night menu, upscale Italian, full bar, live music nightly ■ www.ilovecornelias.com

Firefly 773/525-2505 ■ 3335 N Halsted St (at Roscoe) ■ 5:30pm-1:30am, till midnight Sun, clsd Tue, romantic French bistro

HB: A Hearty Boys Spot [★BYOB] 773/244-9866 ■ 3404 N Halsted St (at Roscoe, btwn Addison & Belmont) ■ 5pm-10pm, 9am-2pm & 5pm-10pm Sat-Sun, clsd Mon, upscale American ■ www.heartyboys.com

Horizon Cafe 773/883-1565 ■ 3805 N Broadway (corner w/ Halsted & Grace) ■ 7am-9pm, till 10pm Fri-Sat, diner, brkfst anytime ■ www.horizoncafechgo.com

IHOP 773/296-0048 ■ 3760 N Halsted St (btwn W Grace & W Bradley Pl) ■ 24hrs

Joy's Noodles & Rice 773/327-8330 ■ 3257 N Broadway St (at Melrose) ■ 11am-10pm, till 11pm Fri-Sat, plenty veggie, patio ■ www.joysnoodlesandrice.com

Kit Kat Lounge & Supper Club [C,DS,GO] 773/525-1111 ■ 3700 N Halsted St (at W Waveland Ave) ■ 5:30pm-1am, brunch Sun (seasonal), clsd Mon, great martini menu ■ www.kitkatchicago.com

Kitsch'n On Roscoe 773/248-7372 ■ 2005 W Roscoe (at Damen) ■ 9am-10pm, till 3pm Sun-Mon, brunch wknds, comfort food for hipsters, full bar ■ www.kitschn.com

Las Mananitas [★GS] 773/528-2109 ■ 3523 N Halsted St (at Cornelia) ■ 11am-11pm, till midnight Fri-Sat, Mexican, full bar, strong margaritas

Mon Ami Gabi 773/348-8886 ■ 2300 N Lincoln Park W (at Belden) ■ dinner only, French bistro ■ www.monami-gabi.com

Nancy's Pizza 773/883-1977 ■ 2930 N Broadway (at Oakdale) ■ deep-dish pizza ■ www.nancyspizza.com

Nookie's Tree [★] 773/248-9888 ■ 3334 N Halsted St (at Roscoe) ■ 7am-midnight, 24hrs wknd

Panino's Pizzeria [WC] 773/472-6200 ■ 3702 N Broadway (at Waveland) ■ 11:30am-11pm, from noon Sat, till 10pm Sun, Italian, full bar ■ www.paninospizzeria.com

The Pepper Lounge [MW] 773/665-7377 ■ 3441 N Sheffield (btwn Newport & Clark) ■ 6pm-midnight, till 1am Fri-Sat, 5pm-10pm Sun, supper club, gourmet American, full bar ■ www.pepperlounge.com

Pick Me Up Cafe & All Nite Express Lounge 773/248-6613 ■ 3408 N Clark St (at Roscoe) ■ 11am-3am, 24hrs Fri-Sat, brkfst all day

The Raw Bar & Grill [E,WC] 773/348-7291, 773/348-7961 ■ 3720 N Clark St (at Waveland) ■ *11am-2am, till 3am Sat, seafood, also lounge* ■ www.rawbarand-grill.com

X/O [★MW,C] 773/348-9696 ■ 3441 N Halsted St (btwn Newport & Cornelia) ■ *dinner nightly, clsd Mon (winter), also Sun brunch 11am-3pm, int'l/ fusion, full bar, patio (seasonal)* ■ www.xochicago.com

Yoshi's Cafe [★] 773/248-6160 ■ 3257 N Halsted St (at Melrose) ■ *dinner Tue-Sun, also Sun brunch, Asian-inspired French* ■ www.yoshiscafe.com

BOOKSTORES

28 **Unabridged Books** [★] 773/883-9119 ■ 3251 N Broadway St (at Aldine) ■ *10am-9pm, till 7pm wknds, LGBT section* ■ www.unabridgedbookstore.com

RETAIL SHOPS

Bad Boys Chicago [GO] 773/549-7701 ■ 3352 N Halsted St (at Roscoe) ■ *noon-9pm, from 11am Sat, noon-6pm Sun, men's clothing, accessories* ■ www.badboyschicago.com

Bears Like Us 773/857-7393 ■ 3732 N Broadway St (at Waveland) ■ *noon-8pm, till midnight Fri-Sat, bearwear & more for the "Bear Lifestyle"* ■ www.bearslikeus.com

Ragin' RaeJean's 773/975-5020 ■ 3450 N Halsted St (btwn Newport & Cornelia) ■ *novelties & more*

Specialty Video Films [GO] 773/248-3434 ■ 3221 N Broadway St (at Belmont) ■ *10am-11pm, foreign, cult, art house, LGBT & erotic videos*

Uncle Fun 773/477-8223 ■ 1338 W Belmont (at Racine) ■ *heaven for kitsch lovers* ■ www.unclefunchicago.com

Universal Gear 773/296-1090 ■ 3153 N Broadway St (at Belmont) ■ *10am-9pm, till 10pm Fri-Sat, 11am-8pm Sun, casual, club, athletic & designer clothing* ■ www.universal-gear.com

GYMS & HEALTH CLUBS

Chicago Sweat Shop [GF] 773/871-2789 ■ 3215 N Broadway St (at Belmont) ■ *5am-11pm, till 10pm Fri, 7am-8:30pm, from 8am Sun* ■ www.chicagosweatshop.com

MEN'S CLUBS

Steamworks Men's Gym/ Sauna [★PC] 773/929-6080 ■ 3246 N Halsted St (N of Belmont) ■ *24hrs* ■ www.steam-worksonline.com

EROTICA

Adult Fantasy 773/525-9705 ■ 2928 N Broadway St (at Oakdale) ■ *24hrs*

Batteries Not Included 773/935-9900 ■ 3420 N Halsted St (at Newport) ■ *11am-midnight, till 1am Fri, 10am-2am Sat; also 1439 N Milwaukee Ave, 773/489-2200* ■ www.toysafterdark.com

Cupid's Leather Sport 773/868-0914 ■ 3505 N Halsted St (at Cornelia) ■ *11am-midnight*

Cupid's Treasures 773/348-3884 ■ 3519 N Halsted St (at Cornelia) ■ *11am-midnight*

The Pleasure Chest 773/525-7152 ■ 3436 N Lincoln Ave (btwn Roscoe & Addison) ■ *10am-10pm, till midnight Fri-Sat* ■ www.thepleasurechest.com

The Ram Bookstore 773/525-9528 ■ 3511 N Halsted St (at Cornelia) ■ *24hrs*

Tulip Sex Toy Gallery [W,GO] 773/975-1515, 877/708-8547 ■ 3448 N Halsted St (btwn Newport & Cornelia) ■ *noon-10pm, till 7pm Sun, lesbian-owned* ■ www.mytulip.com

Chicago—Near North

ACCOMMODATIONS

1 **Allegro Chicago** [GF,F,E,WI,WC] 312/236-0123, 866/672-6143 ■ 171 W Randolph St (at LaSalle) ■ *Kimpton hotel, upscale lounge & restaurant* ■ www.allegrochicago.com

2 **Best Western Inn of Chicago** [GF,F,WI,WC] 312/787-3100, 800/780-7234 ■ 162 E Ohio St (at Michigan Ave) ■ *1/2 block E of the Magnificent Mile* ■ www.bestwestern.com/prop_14101

3 **Comfort Inn & Suites Downtown** [GF,WI] 312/894-0900, 888/775-9223 ■ 15 E Ohio St (at State St) ■ *boutique hotel, art deco decor, gym* ■ www.chicagocomfortinn.com

4 **Flemish House of Chicago** [GS,NS,WI,GO] 312/664-9981 ■ 68 E Cedar St (btwn Rush & Lake Shore Dr) ■ *B&B, studios & apts in greystone row house* ■ www.innchicago.com

5 **Gold Coast Guest House B&B** [GF,NS,WI] 312/337-0361 ■ 113 W Elm St (btwn Clark & LaSalle) ■ *1873 town house, long-term rates available* ■ www.bbchicago.com

Hilton Chicago [GF,SW] 312/922-4400 ■ 720 S Michigan Ave (at Balbo Dr) ■ *3 restaurants & 1 lounge, shopping arcade* ■ www.hiltonchicagosales.com/hotels_hiltonchicago.aspx

6 **Holiday Inn Express Magnificent Mile** [GF,F] 312/787-4030 ■ 640 N Wabash Ave (btwn Ontario & Erie) ■ www.casshotel.com

7 **The Hotel Burnham** [GF,WI] 312/782-1111, 877/294-9712 ■ One W Washington St (at State) ■ *Chicago landmark* ■ www.burnhamhotel.com

8 **Hotel Indigo Chicago** [GF,WI,WC] 312/787-4980, 800/972-2494 ■ 1244 N Dearborn Pkwy (btwn Goethe & Division) ■ *designer hotel, gym, restaurant & lounge* ■ www.hotelindigo.com

9 **Hotel Monaco** [GF,WI] 312/960-8500, 866/610-0081 ■ 225 N Wabash (at S Water & Wacker Pl) ■ *4-star luxury hotel, gym, also restaurant* ■ www.monaco-chicago.com

10 **Hyatt Regency Chicago** [GF,WI] 312/565-1234, 800/233-1234 ■ 151 E Wacker Dr (at Michigan Ave) ■ *fitness center, restaurant, cafe & bar* ■ chicagoregency.hyatt.com

11 **Millennium Hotels & Resorts** [GF,F,WC] 312/751-8100, 800/621-8140 ■ 163 E Walton Pl (Michigan Ave) ■ *right off the Magnificent Mile, gym, restaurant & martini bar* ■ www.millenniumhotels.com

12 **Old Town Chicago B&B/ Vacation Rental** [GS,NS,WI] 312/440-9268 ■ *jacuzzi, roof deck, gym, kids ok* ■ www.oldtownchicago.com

13 **Palmer House Hilton** [GF,SW] 312/726-7500 ■ 17 E Monroe St (at State Sts) ■ *fitness center, shopping arcade* ■ www.hiltonchicagosales.com/hotels_palmer.aspx

14 **Parkview Hotel Chicago** [GF,WC] 312/664-3040, 800/329-7466 (reservations) ■ 1816 N Clark St (at Lincoln) ■ *also restaurant & lounge*

15 **W Chicago—City Center** [GF,NS,WI,WC] 312/332-1200, 877/WHOTELS (reservations only) ■ 172 W Adams St (at LaSalle) ■ *in the Loop, also restaurant & bar* ■ www.whotels.com/citycenter

16 **W Chicago—Lakeshore** [GF,SW,NS,WI,WC] 312/943-9200, 877/WHOTELS (reservations only) ■ 644 N Lake Shore Dr (at Ontario) ■ *overlooking Lake Michigan, also restaurant & bar* ■ www.whotels.com/lakeshore

CHICAGO
NEAR NORTH
DETAIL

© Damron Company, SF, CA, 2007

BARS

17   Club Foot [GF,NH,D,A] 773/489-0379 ■ 1824 W Augusta Blvd (in Wicker Park) ■ 8pm-2am, till 3am Sat, kitschy

18   Davenport's [GS,C,P] 773/278-1830 ■ 1383 N Milwaukee (in Wicker Park) ■ 7pm-midnight, till 2am Fri-Sat, till 11pm Sun, clsd Tue ■ www.davenportspianobar.com

19   Gentry on State [★M,E,C,P,V] 312/836-0933 ■ 440 N State (at Illinois) ■ 4pm-2am, till 3am Sat ■ www.gentry-ofchicago.com

20   Second Story Bar [M,NH] 312/923-9536 ■ 157 E Ohio St (at Michigan Ave) ■ noon-2am, till 3am Sat

NIGHTCLUBS

21   Baton Show Lounge [MW,DS,WC] 312/644-5269 ■ 436 N Clark St (btwn Illinois & Hubbard) ■ showtimes at 8:30pm, 10:30pm, 12:30am, clsd Mon-Tue, reservations recommended, since 1969! ■ www.thebatonshowlounge.com

22   Crobar [★GF,D] 312/266-1900 ■ 1543 N Kingsbury (at Sheffield) ■ 10pm-4am, clsd Mon-Th, occasional gay nights Sun ■ www.crobarnightclub.com

23   OTDL (On the Down Low) [M,D,MR] 312/738-9971 ■ 306 S Halsted St (at W Fulton, at Generator) ■ 11pm-4am Sun only ■ www.otdlchicago.com

24   The Rails [★M,D,MR-AF,MR-L,S,$] 773/486-2086 (Prop House #) ■ 1675 N Elston Ave (at North Ave, at Prop House in Wicker Park) ■ 11pm-4am Fri only ■ www.railschi.net

25   Sound Bar/ Y Bar [GS,D] 312/787-4480 ■ 226 W Ontario (btwn Franklin & Wells) ■ 9pm-4am, till 5am Sat, clsd Sun-Wed ■ www.sound-bar.com

CAFES

Earwax Cafe & Film 773/772-4019 ■ 1561 N Milwaukee Ave (in Wicker Park) ■ 9am-11pm, 8am-midnight Fri-Sun, food served (burgers, burritos, salads & vegan soups & stews), also film section w/ 1000 DVDs ■ www.earwaxcafe.com

RESTAURANTS

Blackbird 312/715-0708 ■ 619 W Randolph St (at Des Plaines) ■ lunch Mon-Fri, dinner nightly, clsd Sun ■ www.blackbirdrestaurant.com

Fireplace Inn 312/664-5264 ■ 1448 N Wells St (at North Ave) ■ 4:30pm-midnight, 11:30am-1am Fri-Sat, BBQ, patio, full bar ■ www.thefireplaceinn.com

Hot Chocolate [WC] 773/489-1747 ■ 1747 N Damen Ave (in Wicker Park) ■ lunch, dinner & dessert, wknd brunch, clsd Mon ■ www.hotchocolatechicago.com

Ina's 312/226-8227 ■ 1235 W Randolph St (at Racine) ■ www.breakfastqueen.com

Japonais 312/822-9600 ■ 600 W Chicago Ave (at Larrabee) ■ lunch Mon-Fri, dinner nightly, upscale Japanese, lounge ■ www.japonaischicago.com

Kiki's Bistro 312/335-5454 ■ 900 N Franklin St (at Locust) ■ lunch Mon-Fri, dinner nightly, clsd Sun, French, full bar ■ www.kikisbistro.com

Manny's 312/939-2855 ■ 1141 S Jefferson St (at Roosevelt) ■ 5am-4pm, clsd Sun, killer corned beef ■ www.mannysdeli.com

Nacional 27 312/664-2727 ■ 325 W Huron (at N Orleans) ■ 5:30-9:30pm, till 11pm Fri-Sat, clsd Sun, Nuevo Latino, live music Tue & Fri, salsa dancing 11pm-2am Fri-Sat ■ www.nacional27.net

Park Grill 312/521-7275 ■ 11 N Michigan Ave (in Millennium Park) ■ 10:45am-10pm, classic American, seasonal outdoor dining ■ www.parkgrillchicago.com

Parthenon Restaurant 312/726-2407 ■ 314 S Halsted St (near W Jackson) ■ 11am-midnight, full bar, Greek, "best gyros in Chicago" ■ www.theparthenon.com

Shaw's Crab House [WC] 312/527-2722 ■ 21 E Hubbard St (at State St) ■ lunch & dinner, full bar ■ www.shawscrabhouse.com

Topolobampo/ Frontera Grill 312/661-1434 ■ 445 N Clark St (btwn Illinois & Hubbard) ■ lunch & dinner, Sat brunch (Frontera only), clsd Sun, Mexican ■ fronterakitchens.com/restaurants

Vermillion [★WC] 312/527-4060 ■ 10 W Hubbard St (at State) ■ lunch Mon-Fri, dinner nightly, Latin-Indian fusion, full bar, patio, upscale

BOOKSTORES

After-Words New & Used Books 312/464-1110 ■ 23 E Illinois (at State) ■ 10:30am-10pm, till 11pm Fri-Sat, noon-7pm Sun, internet access, cards, stationery, etc ■ bdvorkin@aol.com

26   Quimby's Bookstore [★WC] 773/342-0910 ■ 1854 W North Ave (at Wolcott, in Wicker Park) ■ noon-10pm, from 11am Sat, noon-6pm Sun, alternative literature & comics ■ www.quimbys.com

RETAIL SHOPS

Flight 001 312/944-1001, 877/354-4481 ■ 1133 N State St (at Division) ■ 11am-7pm, till 6pm Sun, way cool travel gear ■ www.flight001.com

GYMS & HEALTH CLUBS

Cheetah Gym 773/394-5900 ■ 1934 W North Ave (at Damen, in Wicker Park) ■ www.cheetahgym.com

Thousand Waves Spa [WO] 773/549-0700 ■ 1212 W Belmont Ave (at Racine) ■ noon-9pm, 10am-7pm wknds, clsd Mon, health spa for women only, women-owned/ run ■ www.thousandwaves.com/twspa

EROTICA

Bijou Theatre 312/943-5397 ■ 1349 N Wells St (at North Ave) ■ 24hrs ■ www.bijouworld.com

Erotic Warehouse [WC] 312/226-5222 ■ 1246 W Randolph (at Elizabeth) ■ 24hrs ■ www.loversplayground.com

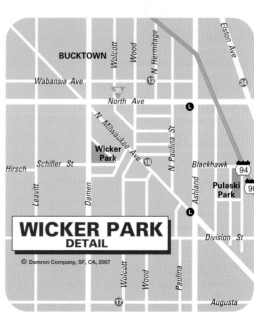

© Damron Company, SF, CA, 2007

BUCKTOWN

Wabansia Ave

North Ave

Wicker Park

Hirsch   Schiller St

WICKER PARK DETAIL

Blackhawk

Pulaski Park

Division St

Augusta

Frenchy's 312/337-9190 ■ 872 N State St (at E Chestnut) ■ 24hrs ■ www.loversplayground.com

Hubbard Books 312/828-0953 ■ 109 W Hubbard (at Clark) ■ 24hrs ■ www.loversplayground.com

Mimi's Adult Bookstore 773/283-0980 ■ 3203 N Cicero (at Belmont) ■ 24hrs

Te' Jay's Adult Books 312/923-9210 ■ 53 W Hubbard (at Dearborn) ■ 24hrs, arcade

Wells Books 312/263-9266 ■ 178 N Wells (at Lake) ■ 7am-10pm, 9am-9pm Sun ■ www.loversplayground.com

Chicago—South Side

BARS

Club Escape [MW,D,MR-AF,F] 773/667-6454 ■ 1530 E 75th St (at Stoney Island) ■ 4pm-2am, till 3am Sat, women's night Th

Inn Exile [M,D,V,WC] 773/582-3510 ■ 5758 W 65th St (at Menard, near Midway Airport; 1 mile W of Midway hotel center at 65th & Cicero) ■ 8pm-2am, till 3am Sat ■ www.innexilchicago.com

Jeffery Pub [★MW,D,MR-AF,DS,WC] 773/363-8555 ■ 7041 S Jeffery (at 71st) ■ 5pm-4am, from 1pm Fri, noon-5am Sat, noon-4am Sun, clsd Mon

BOOKSTORES

57th St Books 773/684-1300 ■ 1301 E 57th St, Hyde Park (at Kimbark St) ■ 10am-9pm, till 8pm Sat-Sun, LGBT section ■ www.semcoop.com

Barbara's Bookstore [★WC] 312/413-2665 ■ 1218 S Halsted St (at W Roosevelt) ■ 9am-10pm, from 10am wknds, till 8pm Sun, women's/ LGBT section; also at Marshall Field's, 111 N State St, 312/781-3033; also 1100 Lake St, Oak Park, 708/848-9140 ■ www.barbarasbookstore.com

INDIANA

Indianapolis

ACCOMMODATIONS

1   Adam's Mark Hotel [GF,SW] 317/248-2481, 800/444-2326 ■ 2544 Executive Dr (off Airport Expy) ■ seasonal pool, WiFi in lobby, restaurant & lounge ■ www.adamsmark.com/indy-airport

East Lake Retreat [NS,GO] 812/376-0784 ■ 335 W Lakeview Dr, Nineveh ■ fully furnished 2-bdrm/ 2-bath rental home 30 minutes from Indianapolis on Prince's Lake, lesbian-owned ■ skbolte@alumni.indiana.edu

The Kendall Inn [GF,NS,WC] 317/638-6000 ■ 5830 N Post Rd ■ luxury inn in historic Fort Harrison in northeast Indianapolis ■ www.thekendallinn.com

Kurt's B&B Inn [MO,SW,N,GO] 317/291-5728 ■ 8 miles from downtown bars & 3 miles from Indy 500

Sycamore Knoll B&B [GS,NS,WI,GO] 317/776-0570 ■ 10777 Riverwood Ave, Noblesville ■ fully-restored 1886 estate near the White River, full brkfst, lesbian-owned ■ www.sycamoreknoll.com

2   Yellow Rose Inn [GS,NS] 317/636-7673 ■ 1441 N Delaware St ■ Victorian B&B, rooftop hot tub ■ www.yellowroseinn.com

BARS

3   501 Eagle [★M,D,B,L] 317/632-2100 ■ 501 N College (at Michigan St) ■ 5:30pm-3am, from 7:30pm Sat, from 4pm Sun ■ www.501eagle.com

Brix [GF,NH,F,E] 317/732-2233 ■ 65 S 1st St (at W Oak St), Zionsville ■ clsd Sun-Mon, wine bar & bistro, full restaurant serving lunch & dinner, patio ■ www.brixzionsville.com

4   Club 2802 [MW,NH,F,DS] 317/955-1840 ■ 2802 Brookside Ave (at Rural) ■ noon-3am, from 11am Sat, noon-12:30am Sun, clsd Mon, lounge, [DS] Fri-Sat, dinner w/ drag show Sun, more [MR-AF] Sat

5   Cosmos [M,NH,E,K,WI,GO] 317/634-9999 ■ 243 N State Ave (at Washington) ■ 5pm-close, clsd Tue, "pianoke" singalongs ■ www.indycosmos.com

6   Downtown Olly's [M,NH,V,WC] 317/636-5597 ■ 822 N Illinois St (at St Clair) ■ 11am-3am, from 10am Sat, till midnight Sun, sports & video bar, brunch Sat-Sun (10am-1pm) ■ www.downtownollys.com

7   Illusions [GS,K,DS] 317/266-0535 ■ 1446 E Washington (at Arsenal) ■ 7am-3am, noon-midnight Sun, drag shows Fri-Sat

8   The Metro Restaurant & Nightclub [★MW,F,K,P,WC] 317/639-6022 ■ 707 Massachusetts Ave (at College) ■ 3pm-3am, 11am-12:30am Sun, patio, also restaurant, giftshop ■ www.metro-indy.com

9   Midwest Wymn, Inc [WO] 317/213-1272 ■ 3508 W 30th St ■ 11pm-3am Fri, membership-only social club for women ■ www.midwestwymninc.com

10 Varsity Lounge [M,NH,F] 317/635-9998 ■ 1517 N Pennsylvania St (S of 16th) ■ 10am-3am, till midnight Sun

NIGHTCLUBS

11 Greg's [★M,D,CW,V,WC] 317/638-8138 ■ 231 E 16th St (at Alabama) ■ 4pm-3am, 6pm-12:30am Sun, [CW] Fri & Sun, DJ Th-Sat, patio ■ www.gregsindiana.com

12 Spin [GF,D,DS] 317/257-0000 ■ 6308 Guilford Ave (at Broad Ripple) ■ 9pm-3am Sun only, drag shows, live bands Th-Sat

13 Talbott Street [★GS,D,DS,GO] 317/931-1343 ■ 2145 N Talbott St (at 22nd St) ■ 9pm-4am, till 1am Sun, clsd Mon-Th, theme nights ■ www.talbottstreet.com

14 The Ten [★MW,D,DS,S,WC] 317/638-5802 ■ 1218 N Pennsylvania St (at 12th, enter rear) ■ 6pm-3am, till 1am Wed, till midnight Sun, clsd Mon-Tue

15 The Unicorn Club [★M,D,S,PC] 317/262-9195 ■ 122 W 13th St (at Illinois) ■ 8pm-3am, till 12:30am Sun, male strippers nightly

CAFES

Ah Barista Cafe [F,WI] 317/638-2233 ■ 201 S Capitol Ave (btwn Maryland & South Sts) ■ 7am-3pm Mon-Fri, brkfst & lunch menu ■ www.ahbarista.com

Cornerstone Coffeehouse [F,WI] 317/726-1360 ■ 651 E 54th St (at N College Ave, Broad Ripple) ■ 6am-9:30pm, 7am-8pm wknds ■ www.moeandjohnnys.com/coffeeshop.htm

Henry's on E Street [★F,WI,GO] 317/951-0335 ■ 627 N East St (next door to Out Word Bound Books) ■ 7am-7pm, t. 11pm Fri, 9am-3pm Sat-Sun

Hubbard & Cravens 317/251-5161 ■ 4930 N Pennsylvania St (in Broad Ripple) ■ 6am-7pm, 7am-3pm Sun also 4 other locations ■ www.hubbardandcravens.com

Lazy Daze Coffee House [WI] 317/353-0777 ■ 10 Johnson Ave (at E Washington St, in Irvington) ■ 6:30am-8pm, till 9pm Fri, 8am-9pm Sat, till 7pm Sun ■ www.lazy-dazecoffeehouse.com

Monon Coffee Company 317/255-0510 ■ 920 E Westfield Blvd (at Guilford) ■ 6:30am-8pm, till 10pm Fri, from 7am Sat, 8am-8pm Sun ■ home.indy.rr.com/mononcoffee

RESTAURANTS

Adobo Grill 317/915-9990 ■ 4939 E 82nd St (W of Allisonville Rd) ■ *lunch Fri-Sun, dinner nightly, Mexican, full bar, also Fiesta Fridays [D] w/ salsa dancing* ■ www.adobo-grill.com

Aesop's Tables [BW,WC] 317/631-0055 ■ 600 N Massachusetts Ave (at East) ■ *lunch & dinner, clsd Sun, authentic Mediterranean*

Agio [NS] 317/488-0359 ■ 635 Massachusetts Ave (at East) ■ *lunch Mon-Fri, dinner nightly, cont'l* ■ www.agiorestaurant.net

Cafe @ Ray 317/636-2233 ■ 946 S Meridian St (at Ray) ■ *10am-2:30pm Mon-Fri, soups & salads, some veggie* ■ www.cafeatray.com

English Ivy's 317/822-5070 ■ 944 S Alabama (at 10th) ■ *lunch & dinner, till 3am Mon-Sat, 11am-midnight Sun, eclectic, also full bar*

India Garden 317/253-6060 ■ 830 Broad Ripple Ave (btwn Carrollton & Guilford) ■ *lunch & dinner, Indian; also 143 N Illinois St, 317/634-6060, lunch & dinner, clsd Sun* ■ www.indiagardenindy.com

Mama Carolla's [★WC] 317/259-9412 ■ 1031 E 54th St (at Winthrop) ■ *5pm-close, clsd Sun-Mon, traditional Italian*

Mikado [★WC] 317/972-4180 ■ 148 S Illinois St (at Georgia) ■ *11:30am-close, Japanese, saketinis*

Naked Tchopstix [★BW] 317/252-5555 ■ 6253 N College Ave (in Broad Ripple) ■ *lunch Mon-Fri, dinner Mon-Sat, Korean, Japanese, Chinese cuisine, also sushi bar* ■ www.tchopstix.com

Oakley's Bistro [★] 317/824-1231 ■ 1464 W 86th St (at Ditch Rd) ■ *lunch & dinner, clsd Sun-Mon, gourmet cont'l, reservations suggested* ■ www.oakleysbistro.com

Pancho's Taqueria [★] 317/202-9015 ■ 7023 Michigan Rd (at Westlane) ■ *10:30am-9:30pm, noon-9pm Sun, authentic Mexican*

Red Eye Cafe [WI] 317/972-1500 ■ 250 S Meridian St (N of Union Station) ■ *24hrs, diner, beer* ■ www.redeyecafe.com

Sawasdee 317/844-9451 ■ 1222 W 86th St (at Ditch Rd) ■ *lunch Mon-Sat, dinner nightly, Thai, some veggie*

Shanghai Lil 317/205-9335 ■ 8505 Keystone Crossing (across from Keystone Mall) ■ *upscale Chinese & Japanese, full bar* ■ www.shanghai-lil.com

Three Sisters Cafe 317/257-5556 ■ 6360 Guilford Ave (at 64th) ■ *lunch & dinner, clsd Mon, plenty veggie & vegan, popular Sun brunch*

Usual Suspects 317/251-3138 ■ 6319 Guilford Ave (at Broad Ripple) ■ *5pm-10pm, till 9pm Sun, clsd Mon, eclectic, full bar, patio*

Yats [★WC] 317/686-6380 ■ 659 Massachusetts Ave (at Walnut) ■ *11am-9pm, till 10pm Fri-Sat, clsd Sun, Cajun; also 5463 N College Ave, 317/ 253-8817* ■ www.yatscajuncre-ole.com

ENTERTAINMENT & RECREATION

Indiana Fever 317/917-2500 ■ 1 Conseco Ct (in Conseco Fieldhouse) ■ *check out the Women's National Basketball Association while you're in Indianapolis* ■ www.wnba.com/fever

Indianapolis Men's Chorus 317/931-9464 ■ PO Box 2919 46206-2919 ■ *various concerts throughout season* ■ www.indychoruses.org

Indianapolis Women's Chorus 317/931-9464 ■ PO Box 2919 46206-2919 ■ *various concerts throughout season* ■ www.indychoruses.org

Indyindie 317/295-9302 ■ 7780 Eagle Valley Pass ■ *monthly women's music concert series, also events at Out Word Bound* ■ www.indyindie.com

Key Cinemas 317/784-7454 ■ 4044 S Keystone Ave (at S Carson Ave) ■ *alternative cinema* ■ www.keycinemas.com

Theatre on the Square 317/685-8687 ■ 627 Massachusetts Ave (at East) ■ *often presents gay-themed productions* ■ www.tots.org

INDIANAPOLIS

Day Trips: Nappanee

This small town, roughly 140 miles north of Indianapolis, is home to one of the largest Amish settlements in the US. Visit Amish Acres, an 80-acre historic farmstead, for tours, demonstrations, theater productions, arts & crafts, tasty homemade goodies, and of course, quilts. If you happen to be visiting in August, you won't want to miss the annual Arts & Crafts Festival, voted the 5th-best traditional craft show in the US. For more info, visit www.-amishacres.com.

Tourist Info

AIRPORT DIRECTIONS

Indianapolis International Airport. To get to downtown, take the Airport Expressway to I-70 East. Take I-70 East and then exit on Washington St or New York St.

PUBLIC TRANSIT & TAXIS

Yellow Cab 317/487-7777.
IndyGo 317/635-3344, web: www.indygo.net.

TOURIST SPOTS & INFO

Benjamin Harrison Home, 317/631-1888, web: www.presidentbenjaminharrison.org.
Eiteljorg Museum of American Indians & Western Art, 317/636-9378, 500 W Washington.
Indianapolis Museum of Art 317/923-1331 & 920-2660, web: www.ima-art.org.
Morris-Butler Home, 317/636-5409, web: www.historiclandmarks.org/what/mbhouse.html.
Speedway 500 317/481-8500, web: www.indi-anapolismotorspeedway.com.
Zoo 317/630-2001, web: www.indyzoo.com.
Visitor's Center: Indianapolis Convention & Visitors Association 317/639-4282, 800/323-INDY, web: www.indy.org.

Weather

The spring weather is moderate (50°s-60°s) with occasional storms. The summers are typically midwestern: hot (mid-90°s) and humid. The autumns are mild and colorful in southeastern Indiana. As for winter, it's the wind chill that'll get to you.

City Calendar

LGBT PRIDE

June, web: www.indyprideinc.com.

ANNUAL EVENTS

April-May - Indianapolis International Film Festival, web: indyfilmfest.org.
May - Broad Ripple Arts Fair, web: www.indplsart-center.org.
Memorial Day Weekend - Indy 500 auto race.
June - Indy Jazz Fest, web: www.indyjazzfest.net.
Aug-Sept - Indianapolis Theatre Fringe Festival, web: www.indyfringe.org.
Nov - Indy LGBT Film Festival, web: indylgbtfilm-fest.com.

Queer Resources

COMMUNITY INFO

GayIndy.Org, virtual LGBT community center, web: www.gayindy.org.
AA Gay/Lesbian 317/632-7864, web: www.indyaa.org.
Damien Center 317/632-0123, web: www.damien.org.

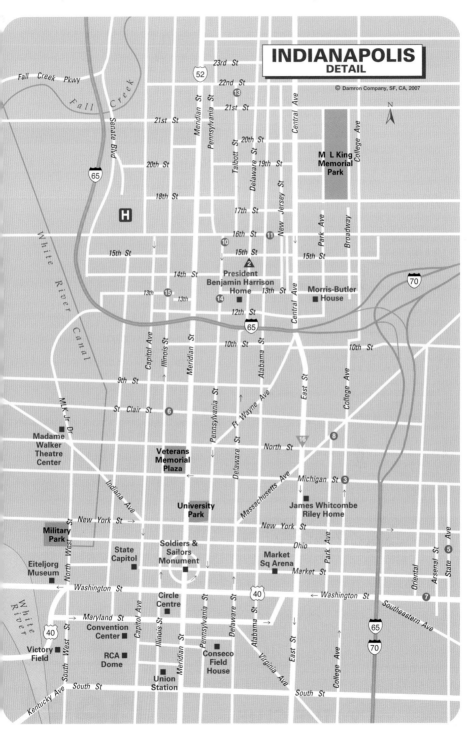

INDIANAPOLIS
DETAIL
© Damron Company, SF, CA, 2007

BOOKSTORES

Big Hat Books 317/202-0203 ■ 922 E Westfield Blvd, Broad Ripple Village (at Guilford) ■ *10am-8pm, till 10pm Fri-Sat, noon-6pm Sun, general independent* ■ www.bighat.booksense.com

Bookmamas 317/375-3715 ■ 9 S Johnson Ave (at E Washington St, in Irvington) ■ *used bookstore, call for hours* ■ www.bookmamas.com

16 Out Word Bound [★GO] 317/951-9100 ■ 625 N East St (at Massachusetts Ave) ■ *from 11am daily, LGBT, special events, lesbian-owned* ■ ww.outwordbound.com

A Shade of Gray Bookstore [MR,GO] 317/423-3316 ■ 1402 N Pennsylvania St (at 14th) ■ *woman-centered store focused on feminism, people of color & the LGBT community, lesbian-owned* ■ www.ashadeofgraybookstore.com

RETAIL SHOPS

All My Relations 317/227-3925 ■ 1008 Main (at 10th) ■ *noon-6pm, till 7pm Wed, 10am-5pm Sat, noon-5pm Sun, New Age/ metaphysical store, also classes* ■ www.allmyrelationsindy.com

Delaware News Company 317/632-9331 ■ 130 N Delaware St (btwn Market & Ohio) ■ *clsd Sun, old-fashioned newsstand, some gay titles*

The Magic Candle 317/357-8801 ■ 204 S Audubon Rd (S of Washington) ■ *10am-7pm, pagan supplies, classes*

Metamorphosis [18+] 317/466-1666 ■ 828 Broad Ripple Ave (at Carrollton) ■ *1pm-9pm, till 5pm Sun, tattoo & piercing parlor* ■ www.myspace.com/metamorphosisinc

Metropolis 317/639-1029 ■ 707 Massachusetts Ave (upstairs at The Metro) ■ *4pm-2am, 1pm-12:30am Sun, also restaurant & nightclub* ■ www.metro-indy.com

PUBLICATIONS

Nuvo 317/254-2400 ■ *Indy's alternative weekly* ■ www.nuvo.net

The Word 317/725-8840 ■ *LGBT newspaper* ■ www.the-word-online.com

MEN'S CLUBS

▶**Club Indianapolis** [18+,SW,PC] 317/635-5796 ■ 620 N Capitol Ave (at North & Walnut) ■ *24hrs, steam, sauna, gym, outdoor patio* ■ www.the-clubs.com

The Works [L,V,PC,GO] 317/547-9210 ■ 4120 N Keystone Ave (at 38th) ■ *24hrs* ■ www.theworks4men.com

EROTICA

Annex Bookstore 317/549-3522 ■ 6767 E 38th St (at Massachusetts) ■ *also arcade*

Fat Dicks Video 822 N Illinois St (behind Downtown Olly's) ■ *noon-7pm, videos & magazines*

Southern Nights Videos 317/329-5505 ■ 3760 Commercial Dr (at 38th St) ■ *10am-midnight, clsd Sun, videos, DVDs, toys, etc* ■ www.southernnights.com

KANSAS

Wichita

ACCOMMODATIONS

1 **Hawthorn Suites** [GF,WC] 316/729-5700 ■ 2405 N Ridge Rd ■ *brkfst buffet* ■ www.wichitahawthorn.com

BARS

2 **The Corner** [W,NH] 316/683-9781 ■ 3210 E Osie (at George Washington) ■ *3pm-2am, mostly women, men welcome*

3 **J's Lounge** [MW,E,K,C,WC] 316/262-1363 ■ 513 E Central (at Emporia) ■ *4pm-2am, till midnight Sun, cabaret, patio, "an upscale dive"* ■ www.Js-Lounge.com

4 **Kirby's Beer Store** [GF,S] 316/685-7013 ■ 3227 E 17th (at Holyoke) ■ *2pm-2am, from 3pm wknds* ■ www.kirbysbeer-store.com

5 **The Other Side** [MW,NH,B] 316/262-7825 ■ 447 N St Francis ■ *2pm-2am*

6 **Side Street** [M,D,CW,L,WC] 316/267-0324 ■ 1106 S Pattie (near Lincoln & Hydraulic) ■ *2pm-2am, patio*

7 **Trends** [MW,D,WC,GO] 316/262-4530 ■ 1507 E Pawnee (at K-15) ■ *2pm-2am*

NIGHTCLUBS

8 **Fantasy Complex** [MW,D,CW,DS,S,18+,WC] 316/682-5494 ■ 3201 S Hillside (at 31st) ■ *3pm-2am, clsd Mon, also South Forty [CW]*

9 **Glacier** [MW,D,E,K,DS,18+] 316/612-9331 ■ 2828 E 31st South (at S Volutsia St) ■ *5pm-2am, from 3pm Sun*

10 **Metro** [M,D,MR,TG,E,DS,S,V,WC,GO] 316/214-1544 ■ 2120 N Woodlawn #450 (at 21st St N) ■ *9pm-2am, till 3am Sat, clsd Mon-Wed* ■ www.clublettuce.com

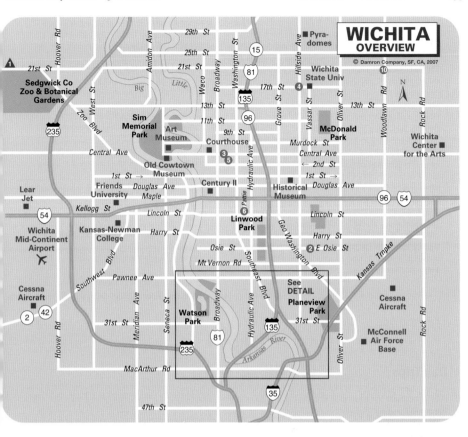

WICHITA OVERVIEW

© Damron Company, SF, CA, 2007

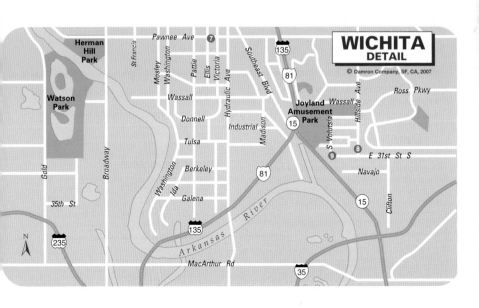

WICHITA DETAIL

© Damron Company, SF, CA, 2007

CAFES

Riverside Perk 316/264-6464 ■ 1144 Bitting Ave (at 11th) ■ *7am-10pm, till midnight Fri-Sat, from 10am Sun, internet access; also Lava Lounge juice bar next door*

The Vagabond [WI] 316/558-5830 ■ 614 W Douglas Ave ■ *theme nights, art gallery*

RESTAURANTS

Moe's Sub Shop 316/524-5511 ■ 2815 S Hydraulic (at Wassall) ■ *11am-8pm, clsd Sun*

Old Mill Tasty Shop 316/264-6500 ■ 604 E Douglas (at St Francis) ■ *11am-3pm, 8am-5pm Sat, clsd Sun, old-fashioned soda fountain, lunch menu*

River City Brewing Company 316/263-2739 ■ 150 N Mosley St ■ *11am-10pm, till 11pm wknds, American, also live music* ■ www.rivercitybrewingco.com

Riverside Cafe 316/262-6703 ■ 739 W 13th (at Bitting) ■ *6am-8pm, till 2pm wknds*

The Upper Crust 316/683-8088 ■ 7038 E Lincoln (at Governor) ■ *lunch only, clsd wknds, homestyle*

Uptown Bistro 316/262-3232 ■ 301 N Mead (at 2nd) ■ *lunch & dinner daily, noon-8pm Sun* ■ www.uptown-bistrowichita.com

ENTERTAINMENT & RECREATION

Cabaret Oldtown Theatre 316/265-4400 ■ 412 1/2 E Douglas (at Topeka) ■ *edgy, kitschy productions* ■ www.cabaretoldtown.com

Mosley Street Melodrama [F,$] 316/263-0222 ■ 234 N Mosley St (btwn 1st & 2nd St) ■ *melodrama, homestyle buffet & full bar!* ■ www.mosleystreet.com

Wichita Arts 316/462-2787 ■ 334 N Mead ■ *promotes visual & performing arts; ArtScene publication has extensive cultural calendar* ■ www.wichitaarts.com

RETAIL SHOPS

Holier Than Thou Body Piercing 316/266-4100 ■ 1115 E Douglas Ave (at Washington) ■ *noon-8pm Tue-Sat*

PUBLICATIONS

The Liberty Press 316/652-7737 ■ www.libertypress.net

SEX CLUBS

Seb's Place [GF,PC] 316/253-3525 ■ *dungeon catering to BDSM & fetish communities, 4,000 square feet, 16 stations, "pansexual & open to all"* ■ www.sebsplace.com

EROTICA

Las Vegas Adult Video 316/722-7808 ■ 8323 W Kellogg ■ *24hrs*

Priscilla's 316/942-1244 ■ 6143 W Kellogg (at Dugan)

Xcitement Video 316/269-9036 ■ 1306 E Harry (at Pattie) ■ *24hrs*

WICHITA

Day Trips: El Dorado State Park/ El Dorado Lake & Kechi

Pack a picnic lunch and head for the hills—the Flint Hills, that is. El Dorado State Park is at the edge of the Flint Hills just outside the town of El Dorado, roughly 30 miles northeast of Wichita. Swim, fish, or just relax and enjoy the scenery.

If antiquing is more your thing, you'll want to head just a bit north of Wichita to the small town of Kechi, the "Antique Capital of Kansas." For more info, visit www.kechiks.com.

Tourist Info

AIRPORT DIRECTIONS

Wichita Mid-Continent Airport. To get to most gay bars, take US 54 East and exit Hillside South.

PUBLIC TRANSIT & TAXIS

American Cab Co. 316/262-7511.

Emu Express 316/734-0100, web: www.emuexpress.com.

Metropolitan Transit Authority 316/265-7221.

TOURIST SPOTS & INFO

Botanica 316/264-0448, web: www.botanica.org.
Kansas African American Museum 316/262-7651, web: www.thekansasafricanamericanmuseum.org.
Mid-America All-Indian Center 316/262-5221, web: www.theindiancenter.org.
Old Cowtown Museum 316/660-1864, web: www.old-cowtown.org.
Oldtown.
Pyradomes.
Wichita Art Museum 316/268-4921, web: www.wichitaartmuseum.org.
Visitor's Center: Kansas Travel & Tourism Dept 800/252-6727, web: www.travelks.com.

City Calendar

LGBT PRIDE

June.

ANNUAL EVENTS

May - River Festival, web: www.wichitariverfestival.org.
October - Tallgrass Film Festival 316/650-2391, web: www.tallgrassfilmfest.com. Gay-friendly independent film festival w/ some LGBT programming.

Queer Resources

One Day At a Time Gay AA 316/522-7411. 8pm Mon, Wed & Th at 156 S Kansas Ave (at MCC, enter on English St).
316/ 262-3611, web: www.hunterhealthclinic.org.

KENTUCKY

Louisville

ACCOMMODATIONS

1   **21c Museum Hotel** [GF] 502/217-6300, 877/217-6400 ■ 700 W Main ■ *boutique hotel w/ museum* ■ www.21cmuseumhotel.com

2   **The Brown Hotel** [GF] 502/583-1234, 888/888-5252 ■ 335 W Broadway (at 4th) ■ www.brownhotel.com

3   **Columbine B&B** [GF,NS,GO] 502/635-5000, 800/635-5010 ■ 1707 S 3rd St (near Lee St) ■ *1896 Greek Revivial mansion, full brkfst* ■ www.thecolumbine.com

4   **Galt House Hotel & Suites** [GF] 502/589-5200, 800/843-4258 ■ 140 N 4th St (at W Main) ■ *waterfront hotel* ■ www.galthotel.com

5   **Holiday Inn Southwest** [GF,F,SW,WC] 502/448-2020 ■ 4110 Dixie Hwy (at I-264) ■ *lounge*

LOUISVILLE

Day Trips: Kentucky is threaded with many Scenic Byways, scenic drives highlighting such things as bluegrass music, the Civil War, the state's breathtaking countryside, and of course, bourbon, the potent local liquor. Check a state map for a trail that interests you. If horses are your thing, Lexington, about 75 miles away, is recognized as the "Horse Capital of the World." Spelunkers and their admirers should check out Mammoth Cave National Park, about 100 miles south.

Local Food:

The Southern staples here won't disappoint: barbecue, country ham, and fried chicken (ever heard of Colonel Sanders?) are all easy to come by in the Bluegrass State. Adventurous meat eaters may want to sample some burgoo, a hearty stew made from pork, veal, chicken, cabbage and potatoes.

Tourist Info

AIRPORT DIRECTIONS

Stadiford Field Airport (located at US 264 and US 65). To get to town, take 65 North.

PUBLIC TRANSIT & TAXIS

Yellow Taxi 502/636-5511.

Louisville Transportation Co 502/637-6511, web: www.loutrans.com.

TARC Bus System 502/585-1234, web: www.ridetarc.org.

Louisville Horse Trams 502/581-0100, web: www.louisvillehorsetrams.com.

TOURIST SPOTS & INFO

Belle of Louisville steamboat 502/574-2992, web: www.belleoflouisville.org.

Churchill Downs 502/636-4400, web: www.churchilldowns.com.

Farmington Historic Home 502/452-9920.

Hadley Pottery 502/584-2171, web: www.hadley-pottery.com.

Kentucky Derby 502/584-6383.

Louisville Slugger Tour 877/775-8443, web: www.sluggermuseum.org.

Locust Grove Historic Farm 502/897-9845, web: www.locustgrove.org.

St. James Court.

Waterfront Park, web: www.louisvillewaterfront.com.

West Main Street Historic District, web: www.mainstreetassociation.com.

Visitor's Center: Louisville Visitor Center 800/626-5646.

Convention & Visitors Bureau, web: www.gotolouisville.com.

Weather

Mild winters and long, hot summers!

Best Views

Aboard the Belle of Louisville steamboat at Waterfront Park.

City Calendar

LGBT PRIDE

June. 502/649-4851, web: www.kentuckianapride-festival.com.

ENTERTAINMENT

Community Chorus 502/327-4099.

ANNUAL EVENTS

May - Kentucky Derby, web: www.kentuckyderby.com.

June-July - Kentucky Shakespeare Festival 502/637-4933, web: www.kyshakes.org.

October - World's Largest Halloween Party, Louisville Zoo, web: www.louisvillezoo.org.

October - St James Court Art Show 502/ 635-1842, web: www.stjamescourtartshow.com.

Queer Resources

AA 502/587-6225. 4:30pm Sun & 6pm Mon at 1432 Highland Ave. 502/574-5490.

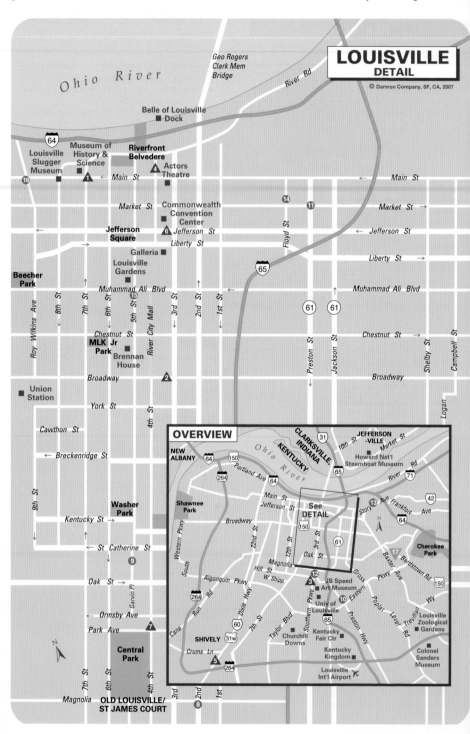

LOUISVILLE
DETAIL
© Damron Company, SF, CA, 2007

Ohio River

Geo Rogers
Clark Mem
Bridge

River Rd

Belle of Louisville
Dock

64 Louisville
Slugger
Museum

Museum of
History &
Science

Riverfront
Belvedere

Actors
Theatre

16   Main St   ← Main St

Market St

Commonwealth
Convention
Center

Jefferson
Square

Jefferson St   ← Jefferson St
Liberty St

14   11

Galleria
Louisville
Gardens

Liberty St →

Beecher
Park

Floyd St

Muhammad Ali Blvd

Muhammad Ali Blvd

Roy Wilkins Ave
8th St
7th St
6th St
5th St
River City Mall
3rd St
2nd St
1st St

61   61

Chestnut St

Chestnut St

MLK Jr
Park

Brennan
House

Preston St
Jackson St
Shelby St
Campbell St

Broadway

Broadway

Union
Station

York St

4th St

Cawthon St

9th St

Breckenridge St

OVERVIEW

CLARKSVILLE
INDIANA
KENTUCKY

JEFFERSON
-VILLE

NEW
ALBANY

64   150

31
10th St
Market St

Howard Nat'l
Steamboat Museum

Ohio River

Washer
Park

264

Portland Ave   64

River Rd   71

Kentucky St

Shawnee
Park

Main St
Jefferson St

See
DETAIL

13   Frankfort
Ave

42

St Catherine St

9

Broadway

22nd St

12th St

150

Story Ave

64

61

Cherokee
Park

Oak St →

Garvin Pl

Magnolia

Hill St
W Shipp

Oak St

17

150

Ormsby Ave

Algonquin Pkwy

3
264   Run Rd

12   JB Speed
Art Museum

Gross

Bardstown Rd

Baxter Ave

Park Ave

7

South

Dixie Hwy

7th St

Univ of
Louisville
65

10   Eastern

Poplar Level

Trevilian

Pkwy

Louisville
Zoological
Gardens

Central
Park

Cane

60
31w

Taylor Blvd
Southern Pkwy

Churchill
Downs

Kentucky
Fair Ctr

Preston Hwy

7th St
6th St
4th St

SHIVELY

Crums Ln

5
264

Kentucky
Kingdom

Colonel
Sanders
Museum

Magnolia   OLD LOUISVILLE/
ST JAMES COURT

3rd St
2nd St
1st St

8

Louisville
Int'l Airport

6   **Hyatt Regency Louisville** [GF,SW,WI,WC] 502/581-1234 ■ 320 W Jefferson St (at 3rd) ■ *tennis* ■ www.hyattregen-cylouisville.com

7   **Inn at the Park** [GF,NS] 502/638-0045 ■ 1332 S 4th St (at Park Ave) ■ *restored mansion, full brkfst* ■ www.innatpark.com

    Mansion at River Walk [GF] 812/941-8100 ■ 704 E Main St (at State St), New Albany, IN ■ www.tcentury.com

BARS

8   **Magnolia Bar** [GF,NH,YC] 502/637-9052 ■ 1398 S 2nd St (at Magnolia) ■ *4pm-4am*

9   **Teddy Bears Bar & Grill** [M,NH,WC] 502/589-2619 ■ 1148 Garvin Pl (at St Catherine) ■ *11am-4am, from 1pm Sun*

10   **Tink's Pub** [MW,NH,K,DS] 502/634-8180 ■ 2235 S Preston St ■ *4pm-close, from noon Sat, from 1pm Sun* ■ www.tinkspub.talkspot.com

11   **Tryangles** [M,K,S,WC] 502/583-6395 ■ 209 S Preston St (at Market) ■ *4pm-4am, from 1pm Sun*

12   **Woody's Tavern** [M] 502/635-9221 ■ 208 E Burnett Ave ■ *4pm-4am*

NIGHTCLUBS

13   **The Alternative** [W,D,CW,E,18+,NS,WC,GO] 502/561-7613 ■ 1032 Story Ave (at Bickel Ave) ■ *6pm-midnight, 7pm-2am Fri-Sat, clsd Sun-Mon* ■ www.louisvillealternative.com

14   **Boots** [★M,L] 502/585-5752 ■ 120 S Floyd St (in Connections Complex) ■ *9pm-2am, till 4am Fri-Sat, clsd Mon-Tue, dress code, fireplace, patio* ■ www.theconnection.net/boots.htm

14   **The Connection Complex** [★MW,D,C,P,V,WC] 502/585-5752 ■ 120 S Floyd St (at Market) ■ *7pm-4am, till 2am Mon-Tue, includes piano bar, video bar, cabaret* ■ www.theconnection.net

15   **Exile** [GS,D,A,E] 514 S 5th St (at E Muhammad Ali Blvd) ■ *from 10pm Fri-Sat only* ■ exileky@yahoo.com

16   **Starbase Q** [M,D,K,V] 921 W Main St (at 9th St) ■ *8pm-close, from 4pm Wed, clsd Mon, industrial video bar* ■ www.starbaseq.com

CAFES

    Days Coffeehouse [GO] 502/456-1170 ■ 1420 Bardstown Rd (at Edenside) ■ *6:30am-10pm, till 11pm wknds*

    Sumshee's Family Room [A,E,DS] 502/589-2018 ■ 204 S Preston ■ *7pm-close, after-hours [D] Fri-Sat* ■ www.sumshee.com

RESTAURANTS

    Cafe Mimosa 502/458-2233 ■ 1216 Bardstown Rd ■ *lunch & dinner, Vietnamese, Chinese & sushi* ■ www.cafemimisatogo.com

    El Mundo [★] 502/899-9930 ■ 2345 Frankfort Ave ■ *11:30am-10pm, full bar till 2am Th-Sat, clsd Sun-Mon, Mexican* ■ www.502elmundo.com

    Lynn's Paradise Cafe [★MW,WI,GO] 502/583-3447 ■ 984 Barret Ave (at Baxter) ■ *7am-10pm, from 8am wknds, also bar, lesbian-owned* ■ www.lynnsparadisecafe.com

    Porcini 502/894-8686 ■ 2370 Frankfort Ave ■ *dinner nightly, clsd Sun, Italian* ■ www.porcinilouisville.com

    Proof on Main 502/217-6360 ■ 702 W Main St (at 7th) ■ *lunch Mon-Fri, dinner nightly, upscale, modern American w/ Tuscan influence* ■ www.proofonmain.com

    Rudyard Kipling [E] 502/636-1311 ■ 422 W Oak St ■ *6:30pm-2am Wed-Sat, full bar* ■ www.therudyard-kipling.com

    Windy City Pizza [GO] 502/636-3708 ■ 2622 S 4th St ■ *11am-10pm, till 11pm Fri-Sat, 4pm-8pm Sun, clsd Mon*

    Zen Garden 502/895-9114 ■ 2240 Frankfort Ave ■ *lunch & dinner, clsd Sun, Asian, vegetarian* ■ www.zengardenrestaurant.org

ENTERTAINMENT & RECREATION

    Pandora Productions PO Box 4185 40204 ■ *LGBT-themed productions* ■ www.pandoraprods.org

    Voices of Kentuckiana 502/583-1013 ■ *LGBT community chorus* ■ www.voicesky.org

BOOKSTORES

    Borders 502/456-6660, 800/844-7323 ■ 3024 Bardstown Rd (in Gardiner Lane Shopping Center) ■ *9am-9pm, 10am-6pm Sun; also 4600 Shelbyville Rd, Shelbyville Plaza, 502/893-2008*

17   **Carmichael's** 502/456-6950 ■ 1295 Bardstown Rd (at Longest Ave) ■ *8am-10pm, till 11pm Fri-Sat, from 10am Sun, large LGBT section*

PUBLICATIONS

    The Letter ■ *LGBT newspaper serving KY & IL, IN, MO, OH & TN* ■ www.theletteronline.com

EROTICA

    Arcade Adult Bookstore 502/637-8388 ■ 2822 7th St (at Arcade)

    Blue Movies 502/585-4627 ■ 140 W Jefferson St (at 2nd) ■ *24hrs*

    Louisville Manor 502/449-1443 ■ 4600 Dixie Hwy ■ *24hrs*

    Metro Station 502/968-2353 ■ 4948 Poplar Level Rd

    Showboat Adult Bookstore 502/361-0007 ■ 3524 S 7th St (at Berry Blvd) ■ *hustlers*

LOUISIANA

New Orleans

ACCOMMODATIONS

1   **1896 O'Malley House B&B** [GS,NS,WI,GO] 504/488-5896, 866/226-1896 ■ 120 S Pierce St (at Canal St) ■ *B&B, jacuzzi, kids ok* ■ www.1896omalleyhouse.com

2   **5 Continents B&B** [GS,WI,GO] 504/324-8594, 800/997-4652 ■ 1731 Esplanade Ave (at Claiborne) ■ *full brkfst* ■ www.fivecontinentsbnb.com

3   **A Creole House** [GS,NS] 504/524-8076, 800/535-7858 ■ 1013 St Ann (btwn Burgundy & N Rampart) ■ *1830s bldg furnished in period style* ■ www.acreolehouse.com

4   **Aaron Ingram Haus** [GS,WI,GO] 504/949-3110 ■ 1012 Elysian Fields Ave (btwn N Rampart & St Claude) ■ *guesthouse, apts, courtyard* ■ www.ingramhaus.com/xgey.htm

5   **Andrew Jackson Hotel** [GF,WI] 504/561-5881, 800/654-0224 ■ 919 Royal St (btwn St Philip & Dumaine) ■ *historic inn, tropical courtyard* ■ www.frenchquarterinns.com

6   **Antebellum Guest House** [GS,N,NS,WI,GO] 504/943-1900 ■ 1333 Esplanade Ave (at Maris St) ■ *B&B in historic 1830s Grand Greek Revival near French Quarter, antique interiors, full brkfst, clothing-optional hot tub & private courtyard* ■ www.antebellumguesthouse.com

7 **Ashton's B&B** [GF,NS,WI] 504/942-7048, 800/725-4131 ■ 2023 Esplanade Ave (at Galvez) ■ 1860s Greek revival mansion, quiet location, close by to French Quarter ■ www.ashtonsbb.com

8 **Auld Sweet Olive B&B** [★GS,NS,WI] 504/947-4332, 877/470-5323 ■ 2460 N Rampart (at Spain) ■ kids 13+ ok ■ www.sweetolive.com

9 **B&W Courtyards B&B** [GF,NS,WI,GO] 504/945-9418, 800/585-5731 ■ 2425 Chartres St (btwn Mandeville & Spain) ■ three 19th-c bldgs connected by courtyards, hot tub ■ www.bandwcourtyards.com

10 **Biscuit Palace Guest House** [GF,WI,WC] 504/525-9949 ■ 730 Dumaine (btwn Royal & Bourbon) ■ 1820s Creole mansion in the French Quarter ■ www.biscuit-palace.com

11 **Block-Keller House** [GS,NS,GO] 504/483-3033, 877/588-3033 ■ 3620 Canal St (at Telemachus) ■ B&B in restored Classical Revival villa; 2 dogs on-site ■ www.block-kellerhouse.com

12 **The Bohemian Armadillo** [GS,NS,WI] 512/297-9883 ■ 735 Touro St (at Dauphine) ■ newly remodeled 1820s Creole cottage, hot tub, kids ok, private courtyard ■ www.bohemianarmadillo.com

13 **Bon Maison Guest House** [★GS,NS,GO] 504/561-8498 ■ 835 Bourbon St (btwn Lafitte's & Bourbon Pub) ■ 1833 town house, patio ■ www.bonmaison.com

14 **Bourbon Orleans Hotel** [★GF,F,SW] 504/523-2222 ■ 717 Orleans (at Bourbon St) ■ also Palliard's restaurant & Napoleon's Itch (popular lounge) ■ www.bourbonorleans.com

13 **Bourgoyne Guest House** [★MW] 504/524-3621, 504/525-3983 ■ 839 Bourbon St (at Dumaine St) ■ 1830s Creole mansion furnished w/ antiques, courtyard ■ www.bourgoynehouse.com

15 **The Burgundy B&B** [GS,NS,WI,GO] 504/942-1463, 800/970-2153 ■ 2513 Burgundy St (at St Roch) ■ 1890s ornate "double shotgun" in Faubourg Marigny, close to French Quarter, hot tub [N] ■ www.theburgundy.com

16 **Bywater B&B** [GF,NS,WI,GO] 985/707-3964 ■ 1026 Clouet St ■ Victorian cottage, fireplace, some shared baths ■ bywaterbnb.com

17 **Chez Palmiers B&B** [GS,SW,NS,GO] 877/233-9449 ■ 1744 N Rampart St ■ near French Quarter, in historic Faubourg Marigny ■ www.chezpalmiers.com

18 **The Chimes B&B** [★GF,NS,WI] 504/899-2621, 504/453-2183 ■ 1146 Constantinople St (in Garden District) ■ 1876 home ■ www.chimesneworleans.com

19 **The Cornstalk Hotel** [GF,WI] 504/523-1515, 800/759-6112 ■ 915 Royal St ■ in historic home ■ www.cornstalkhotel.com

20 **Creole Inn** [GS,NS,WI,GO] 504/948-3230 ■ 2471 Dauphine St (at Spain) ■ B&B in private home, garden ■ www.creoleinn.com

21 **Crescent City Guest House** [GS,N,NS,WI,GO] 504/944-8722, 877/203-2140 ■ 612 Marigny St (at Chartres) ■ near French Quarter, hot tub ■ www.crescentcitygh.com

22 **The Degas House** [GF,WI] 504/821-5009, 800/755-6730 ■ 2306 Esplanade Ave (at Tonti St) ■ French Impressionist Degas' home (1872-1873), full brkfst, jacuzzi ■ www.degashouse.com

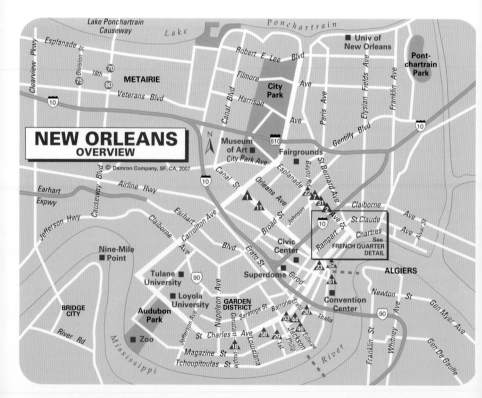

23 **Doubletree Hotel** [GF,F,SW,WI,WC] 504/581-1300, 888/874-9074 ■ 300 Canal St (btwn S Peters & Tchoupitoulas) ■ *gym, restaurants & lounge* ■ www.doubletree.com

24 **Elysian Fields Inn** [GS,NS,WI,WC] 504/948-9420, 866/948-9420 ■ 930 Elysian Fields Ave (at Burgundy) ■ *1860s inn in Faubourg Marigny, full brkfst, jacuzzi* ■ www.elysianfieldsinn.com

25 **Elysian Guest House** [MW,WI,GO] 504/324-4311 ■ 1008 Elysian Fields Ave (at Rampart St) ■ *1880s Victorian "double," large hot tub, kids/ small dogs ok* ■ www.elysianguesthouse.com

26 **Empress Hotel** [GF] 504/529-4100, 888/524-9200 ■ 1317 Ursulines Ave (btwn Treme & Marais) ■ *2 blocks to French Quarter* ■ www.empresshotel.com

French Quarter Guest Apartments 504/451-2495 ■ *unique apts in French Quarter* ■ www.frenchquarterguestapartments.com

French Quarter Reservation Service [MW,GO] 504/565-5344, 866/827-6652 ■ *kids ok, some [SW], some [WC]* ■ www.neworleansreservations.com

27 **French Quarter Suites Hotel** [GF,SW,WI,WC] 504/524-7725, 800/457-2253 ■ 1119 N Rampart (at Ursulines) ■ *all-suite hotel, kitchens* ■ frenchquartersuites.com

28 **The Frenchmen Hotel** [★GS,SW,NS,WI,WC] 504/948-2166, 800/831-1781 ■ 417 Frenchmen St (where Esplanade, Decatur & Frenchmen intersect) ■ *1860s Creole town houses, spa* ■ www.frenchmenhotel.com

29 **Garden District B&B** [GF,WI] 504/895-4302 ■ 2418 Magazine St (at First St) ■ *2 miles from French Quarter* ■ www.gardendistrictbedandbreakfast.com

30 **The Green House Inn** [MW,SW,NS,WI,GO] 504/525-1333, 800/966-1303 ■ 1212 Magazine St (at Erato) ■ *gym, hot tub* ■ www.thegreenhouseinn.com

31 **HH Whitney House on the Historic Esplanade** [GS,SW,NS,WI,GO] 504/948-9448, 877/944-9448 ■ 1923 Esplanade Ave (btwn N Prieur and N Johnson) ■ *1865 B&B, hot tub, some shared baths* ■ www.hhwhitneyhouse.com

Historic Rentals [GS,GO] 800/537-5408 ■ *1- & 2-bdrm apts in French Quarter* ■ www.historicrentals.com

32 **Hotel de la Monnaie** [GF,SW,WI,WC] 504/947-0009 ■ 405 Esplanade Ave (btwn Decatur & N Peters) ■ *all-suite hotel, hot tub, courtyard* ■ www.hoteldelamonnaie.com

33 **Hotel Maison de Ville** [GF,SW,WI] 504/561-5858, 800/634-1600 ■ 727 Rue Toulouse (btwn Bourbon & Royal Sts) ■ *upscale hotel* ■ www.hotelmaisondeville.com

Hotel Monteleone [GF] 504/523-3341, 800/535-9595 ■ 214 Royal St ■ www.hotelmonteleone.com

34 **Hotel Royal** [GS,NS,WC] 504/524-3900, 800/776-3901 ■ 1006 Royal St (at St Philip) ■ *1830s Creole town house* ■ www.melrosegroup.com

35 **Hotel St Pierre** [GF,SW,WI] 504/524-4401, 800/225-4040 ■ 911 Burgundy St ■ *Creole-style hotel, 2 blocks off Bourbon St* ■ www.hotelsaintpierre.com

Inn The Quarter Reservation Service [GF,NS] 888/523-5235 ■ *reservation service w/ over 40 accommodations* ■ www.innthequarter.com

36 **Kerlerec House** [GS,NS,WI,GO] 504/944-8544 ■ 928 Kerlerec St (at Dauphine St) ■ *1 block from the French Quarter, gardens* ■ www.kerlerec.com

37 **La Dauphine, Residence des Artistes** [GS,NS,WI,GO] 504/948-2217 ■ 2316 Dauphine St (btwn Elysian Fields & Marigny) ■ *B&B, no unregistered overnight guests* ■ www.ladauphine.com

38 **La Maison Marigny B&B on Bourbon** [GS,NS,WI,GO] 504/948-3638, 800/570-2014 ■ 1421 Bourbon St (at Esplanade) ■ *on the quiet end of Bourbon St* ■ www.lamaisonmarigny.com

39 **Lafitte Guest House** [★GS,NS,WI] 504/581-2678, 800/331-7971 ■ 1003 Bourbon St (at St Philip) ■ *elegant French manor house* ■ www.lafitteguesthouse.com

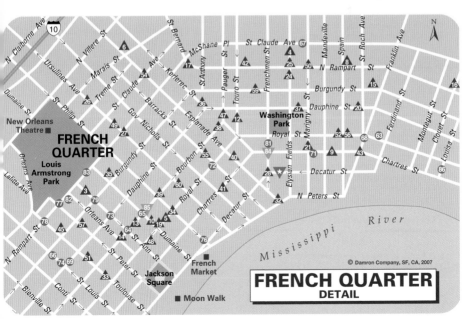

© Damron Company, SF, CA, 2007

FRENCH QUARTER DETAIL

NEW ORLEANS

Day Trips: Creole Nature Trail
   Take some time to discover the natural beauty of this part of the country by driving even a few of the over 180 miles of this scenic byway. The trail winds through the marshlands, farmlands, and coastline of southwestern Louisiana, and starts near the town of Sulpher on Hwy 27. It's a bit of a trip, but nature lovers of all stripes will be in 7th heaven. For more info, visit www.creolenaturetrail.org.

Local Food:
   Creole, Cajun & Soul—all the good stuff is right here, honey. This is also the home of the "po-boy" sandwich, and different restaurants have their own special versions (try Casamento's famous oyster-loaf version, www.casamentosrestaurant.com). Though this town is a meat- and fish-lover's paradise, vegetarians should set a spell at veggie-friendly 13 Monaghan's in the Faubourg Marigny (www.13monaghan.com), or Moon Wok in the Quarter.

Tourist Info

AIRPORT DIRECTIONS
   New Orleans Int'l Airport. Take I-10 southeast.

PUBLIC TRANSIT & TAXIS
   United Cab 504/522-9771.
   New Orleans Regional Transit Authority 504/248-3900, web: www.norta.com.

TOURIST SPOTS & INFO
   Bourbon Street in the French Quarter.
   Cabildo (to see the Louisiana Purchase) 504/568-6968.
   Cafe du Monde for beignets 504/587-0835, web: www.cafedumonde.com.
   Garden District.
   Haunted History Tour 504/861-2727, web: www.hauntedhistorytours.com.
   Moon Walk.
   New Orleans Museum of Art 504/488-2631, web: www.noma.org.
   Pat O'Brien's for a hurricane 504/525-4823, web: www.patobriens.com.
   Preservation Hall 504/522-2841 or 888/946-5299, web: www.preservationhall.com.
   Top of the Market.
   Visitor's Center: 504/566-5011 or 800/672-6124, web: www.neworleanscvb.com.
   Louisiana Office of Tourism 225/342-8100 or 800/677-4082, web: www.louisianatravel.com.

Weather
   Summer temperatures hover in the 90's with subtropical humidity. And on the heels of all that heat and humidity come hurricanes. Hurricane season stretches from June 1 to November 30. Winters can be rainy and chilly. The average temperature in February (Mardi Gras month) is 58°, while the average precipitation is 5.23".

City Calendar

ANNUAL EVENTS
   February - Mardi Gras 504/566-5011, web: www.mardigras.com. North America's rowdiest block party.
   March - Tennesse Williams Festival, web: www.tennesseewilliams.net.
   April - Gulf Coast Womyn's Sister Camp at Camp SisterSpirit (in Ovett, MS) 601/344-1411, web: www.campsisterspirit.com.
   April - Gay Easter Parade 504/522-8049, web: www.gayeasterparade.com.
   April/May - New Orleans Jazz & Heritage Festival, web: www.nojazzfest.com.
   May - Saints & Sinners, LGBT writers' festival 504/581-1144, web: www.sasfest.org.
   Labor Day - Southern Decadence 504/522-8047, web: www.southerndecadence.com. Gay mini-Mardi Gras.
   Labor Day - DecaFest, web: www.decafest.com. Celebration of LGBT culture.

Queer Resources

COMMUNITY INFO
   Lesbian/Gay Community Center 504/945-1103. 2114 Decatur, call for hours, web: www.lgccno.net.
   AA Lambda Center 504/779-1178. 2106 Decatur. 504/821-6050 (hotline #).
   NO/AIDS Task Force 504/821-2601, web: www.noaidstaskforce.org.

40 **Lamothe House Hotel** [★GS,SW,NS,WI,GO] 504/947-1161, 800/367-5858 ■ 621 Esplanade Ave (btwn Royal & Chartres) ■ *antique-furnished Victorian guesthouse w/ wonderful courtyard/ pool area* ■ www.lamothehouse.com

41 **Lanata House** [GS,SW,WI,GO] 504/581-9060, 866/881-9060 ■ 1226 Chartres St (at Gov Nicholls) ■ *furnished residential accommodations* ■ www.lanata-houseapts.com

42 **Le Papillon Guesthouse** [GS,NS,GO] 504/948-4993, 504/884-4008 (cell) ■ 2011 N Rampart St (at Touro St) ■ *restored 1830s guesthouse* ■ www.lepapillongh.com

43 **Lions Inn** [GS,SW,N,NS,WI,GO] 504/945-2339, 800/485-6846 ■ 2517 Chartres St (btwn Spain & Franklin) ■ *handsome 1850s home, patio, hot tub* ■ www.lionsinn.com

44 **Magnolia Mansion** [GS,NS,21+,WI] 504/412-9500, 888/222-9235 ■ 2127 Prytania St (at Jackson) ■ *an enchanting antebellum mansion w/ uniquely themed guestrooms, located in historic Garden District* ■ www.magnoliamansion.com

45 **Maison Dupuy Hotel** [GF,SW] 504/586-8000, 800/535-9177 ■ 1001 Toulouse St ■ *luxury boutique hotel, also Dominique's restaurant* ■ www.maisondupuy.com

40 **Marigny Guest House** [GS,SW,NS] 504/944-9700 (Lamothe House #), 888/696-9575 ■ 621 Esplanade (btwn Royal & Chartres) ■ *quaint Creole cottage that's an affordable annex to Lamothe House, includes visiting privileges to Lamothe House's pool & hot tub* ■ www.lamothehouse.com/marigny_house.html

25 **Marigny Manor House** [GS,NS,WI,GO] 504/943-7826, 877/247-7599 ■ 2125 N Rampart St ■ *in historic 1850s Greek Revival, secret garden* ■ www.marignymanorhouse.com

46 **The McKendrick-Breaux House** [GF,NS,WI] 504/586-1700, 888/570-1700 ■ 1474 Magazine St (at Race St) ■ *1860s restored Greek Revival, hot tub, kids ok* ■ www.mckendrick-breaux.com

47 **Mentone B&B** [GF,NS,WI] 504/943-3019 ■ 1437 Pauger St (at Kerlerec) ■ *suite in Victorian home* ■ www.mentonebandb.com

48 **New Orleans B&B/ French Quarter Accommodations** [GF,SW,NS,WI] 504/561-0447, 888/240-0070 ■ www.neworleansbandb.com

49 **New Orleans Guest House** [GS,NS,WI,GO] 504/566-1177, 800/562-1177 ■ 1118 Ursulines Ave (at N Rampart) ■ *1848 Creole cottage, courtyard* ■ www.neworleans.com/nogh

50 **Olde Town Inn** [GS,WI,WC] 504/949-5815, 800/209-9408 ■ 1001 Marigny St ■ *historic guesthouse, tropical courtyard, walk-ins welcome* ■ www.oldetowninn.com

51 **The Olivier House** [★GF,SW,WI,WC] 504/525-8456, 866/525-9748 ■ 828 Toulouse ■ *upscale hotel in 3 Greek Revival townhouses* ■ www.olivierhouse.com

52 **Pierre Coulon Guest House** [GS,NS,GO] 504/943-6692, 866/328-1497 ■ *quiet apt in Faubourg Marigny, kitchenette, balcony overlooking tropical patio* ■ www.pierrecoulonguesthouse.com

53 **The Pontchartrain Hotel** [GF] 504/524-0581, 800/777-6193 ■ 2031 St Charles Ave (at Josephine St) ■ *landmark hotel in Garden District, also Bayou Bar* ■ www.pontchartrainhotel.com

54 **The Rathbone Mansions** [GS,SW,WC,GO] 504/309-4479, 866/724-8140 ■ 1227 Esplanade Ave (at St Claude) ■ *1850s Greek Revival mansion, hot tub, patio; also at 1244 Esplanade [SW]* ■ www.rathboneinn.com

55 **Royal Barracks Guest House** [GF,NS,WI] 504/529-7269, 888/255-7269 ■ 717 Barracks St (at Bourbon) ■ *jacuzzi, courtyard* ■ www.rbgh.com

56 **Royal Street Courtyard** [GS,WI,GO] 504/943-6818, 888/846-4004 ■ 2438 Royal St (at Spain) ■ *historic 1850s guesthouse, hot tub* ■ www.RoyalStreetCourtyard.com

44 **St Charles Guest House** [GF,SW,NS,WI] 504/523-6556 ■ 1748 Prytania St (at Felicity) ■ *pensione-style guesthouse, some shared baths, special rates for volunteers* ■ www.stcharlesguesthouse.com

57 **St Peter House Hotel** [GS] 504/524-9232, 800/535-7815 ■ 1005 St Peter St (at Burgundy) ■ *antique-furnished early-1800s bldg* ■ www.stpeterhouse.com

58 **Sully Mansion** [GF,NS,WI,GO] 504/891-0457, 800/364-2414 ■ 2631 Prytania St (at Fourth) ■ *1890s mansion in heart of Garden District* ■ www.sullymansion.com

59 **Sun Oak Museum & Guesthouse** [GS,NS,GO] 504/250-6630 ■ 2020 Burgundy St ■ *Greek Revival Creole cottage, circa 1836, w/ gardens* ■ www.sunoaknola.com

60 **Ursuline Guest House** [★GS,WC,GO] 504/525-8509, 800/654-2351 ■ 708 Ursuline St (btwn Royal & Bourbon) ■ *hot tub* ■ www.ursulineguesthouse.com

Vieux Carré Rentals [GF,NS] 504/525-3983 ■ 841 Bourbon St ■ *1 & 2-bdrm apts* ■ www.1822bougainvillea.com

61 **W New Orleans** [GF,SW,WI,WC] 504/525-9444, 877/WHOTELS (reservations only) ■ 333 Poydras St ■ *also bar & restaurant* ■ www.whotels.com/neworleans

62 **W New Orleans—French Quarter** [GF,SW,WI,WC] 504/581-1200, 877/WHOTELS (reservations only) ■ 316 Chartres St ■ *also Bacco restaurant* ■ www.whotels.com/frenchquarter

BARS

63 **Big Daddy's** [MW,NH,WC] 504/948-6288 ■ 2513 Royal St (at Franklin) ■ *24hrs, occasional shows*

64 **Bourbon Pub & Parade** [★MW,D,DS,S,V,18+,YC,WI] 504/529-2107 ■ 801 Bourbon St (at St Ann) ■ *24hrs, theme nights, Sun T-dance* ■ www.bourbonpub.com

65 **Cafe Lafitte in Exile/ The Balcony Bar** [★M,D,S,V] 504/522-8397 ■ 901 Bourbon St (at Dumaine) ■ *24hrs, Balcony Bar upstairs features area's first cyberbar* ■ www.lafittes.com

66 **The Corner Pocket** [★M,NH,DS,S] 504/568-9829 ■ 940 St Louis (at Burgundy) ■ *noon-2am, till 3am Fri-Sat, male dancers nightly, New Meat Contest Fri* ■ www.corner-pocket.net

86 **Country Club** [★GF,F,C,S,SW,N] 504/945-0742 ■ 634 Louisa St (at Royal) ■ *11am-1am, not your father's country club!* ■ www.countryclubneworleans.com

67 **Cowpoke's** [M,NH,D,CW,E,WI] 504/947-0505 ■ 2240 St Claude Ave (at Marigny) ■ *5pm-close, clsd Mon, dance lessons 8pm Tue, lube wrestling last Wed, also The Barn theater space* ■ www.cowpokesno.com

68 **Cutter's** [MW,NH,WC] 504/948-4200 ■ 706 Franklin Ave (at Royal) ■ *3pm-3am*

69 **The Double Play** [M,NH,TG] 504/523-4517 ■ 439 Dauphine (at St Louis) ■ *24hrs*

70 **The Four Seasons** [★M,NH,E,K,DS,GO] 504/832-0659 ■ 3229 N Causeway Blvd (at 18th), Metairie ■ 3pm-close, also the Out Back Bar summers, patio

71 **The Friendly Bar** [★M,NH,WC] 504/943-8929 ■ 2301 Chartres St (at Marigny) ■ 11am-close

72 **Golden Lantern** [M,NH,DS,S] 504/529-2860 ■ 1239 Royal St (at Barracks) ■ 24hrs, [DS] Fri-Sun ■ heffie@bellsouth.net

73 **Good Friends Bar** [★M,NH,K,P,WC] 504/566-7191 ■ 740 Dauphine (at St Ann) ■ 1pm-2am, till 5am Fri-Sat, good cocktails; also Queens Head Pub upstairs Sun only, popular piano sing-along 4pm-8pm ■ www.goodfriendsbar.com

74 **Le Roundup** [M,NH,TG] 504/561-8340 ■ 819 St Louis St (at Dauphine) ■ 24hrs, very MTF-friendly crowd

75 **Masquerades Lounge** [MW,NH,F,K] 504/888-4101 ■ 3505 Division St, Metairie ■ noon-2am, till 3am Fri-Sat, from 5pm Sun; also Two Jokers Grill, 504/454-5101, 11am-8pm, till midnight Fri-Sat

76 **MRB** [★GS,NH] 504/524-2558 ■ 515 St Philip (at Decatur) ■ 10am-2am, patio

14 **Napoleon's Itch** [★M,E,NS] 504/371-5450 ■ 734 Bourbon (at St Ann, in Bourbon Orleans Hotel) ■ noon-2am, till 4am Fri-Sat, full-liquor wine & martini bar ■ www.napoleon-sitch.com

77 **Ninth Circle** [M,NH,TG] 504/524-7654 ■ 700 N Rampart (at St Peter) ■ 24hrs

78 **Orlando's Society Page Lounge** [M,NH,TG] 504/299-0156 ■ 542 N Rampart (at Toulouse) ■ 6pm-2am

25 **Phoenix** [★M,NH,B,L,F,GO] 504/945-9264 ■ 941 Elysian Fields Ave (at N Rampart) ■ 24hrs, cruise room, beer busts, also The Eagle [D] 9pm-5am

79 **Rawhide 2010** [★M,NH,D,A,B,L,K,V] 504/525-8106 ■ 740 Burgundy St (at St Ann) ■ 4pm-3am, 3pm-5am Fri-Sat, underground sound ■ www.rawhide2010.com

80 **The Sanctuary** [MW,NH,E,WC] 504/834-7979 ■ 2301 N Causeway Blvd (at 34th), Metairie ■ 5pm-close, monthly drag shows, live bands Sat

81 **Spotted Cat** [GF,E] 504/943-3887 ■ 623 Frenchmen St ■ 2pm-3am, excellent live jazz in the Faubourg Marigny

82 **Voodoo at Congo Square** [M,NH] 504/527-0703 ■ 718 N Rampart (at Orleans) ■ 24hrs

NIGHTCLUBS

22 **About Time** [M,D,E,DS,S] 504/948-1888 ■ 940 Elysian Fields Ave (at N Rampart) ■ 4pm-close, from noon wknds, 120" big screen for sporting events ■ www.moulinrouge-barneworleans.com

64 **Oz** [★M,D,E,DS,S,V,YC,WC] 504/593-9491 ■ 800 Bourbon St (at St Ann) ■ 24hrs ■ www.ozneworleans.com

83 **Starlight by the Park** [MW,NH,DS,WC] 504/561-8939 ■ 834 N Rampart (at Dumaine) ■ noon-2am, 24hrs Fri-Sun, also courtyard bar ■ www.starlightbythepark.com

CAFES

Cafe Rose Nicaud [WI] 504/949-3300 ■ 632 Frenchmen St (btwn Royal & Chartres) ■ 7am-7pm

CC's Coffee House [WI] 504/581-6996 ■ 941 Royal St ■ 7am-7pm

Croissants d'Or 504/524-4663 ■ 617 Ursulines St ■ 7am-2pm, clsd Mon-Tue, delicious pastries

Marigny Perks [MW,F] 504/948-7401 ■ 2401 Burgundy

Royal Blend Coffee & Tea House 504/523-2716 ■ 621 Royal St ■ 8am-5:30pm, on a quiet, hidden courtyard, also salads & sandwiches ■ www.royalblendcoffee.com

Z'otz [E] 504/861-2224 ■ 8210 Oak St ■ 24hrs, coffee shop & art space ■ mariaurbana23@hotmail.com

RESTAURANTS

13 Monaghan's [WC] 504/942-1345 ■ 517 Frenchmen St ■ 11am-4am, brkfst, lunch & dinner all the time, some veggie, full bar ■ www.13monaghan.com

Angeli on Decatur [WI] 504/566-0077 ■ 1141 Decatur St (at Gov Nicholls) ■ 11am-2am, till 4am Fri-Sat, pizza ■ www.angelipizza.com

Bluebird Cafe [★] 504/895-7166 ■ 3625 Prytania St (btwn Foucher & Antonine) ■ 7am-2pm, from 8am wknds, clsd Mon-Tue, great brkfsts, cash only

Bywater Bar-B-Que [GO] 504/944-4445, 504/947-0000 ■ 3162 Dauphine St (at Louisa) ■ 11am-9pm, clsd Wed; also Lorenzo's Pizzeria

Cafe Amelie 504/412-8965 ■ 912 Royal St (in Princess of Monaco Courtyard) ■ lunch & dinner, Sun brunch, clsd Mon-Tue, Creole

Cafe Negril 504/944-4744 ■ 606 Frenchman St (at Chartres St) ■ dinner, clsd Sun-Mon, Caribbean

Cafe Sbisa [E] 504/522-5565 ■ 1011 Decatur St ■ dinner nightly & Sun Jazz Brunch, French Creole, patio, live jazz ■ www.cafesbisa.com

Casamento's 504/895-9761 ■ 4330 Magazine St (at Napoleon Ave) ■ lunch, also dinner Fri-Sat, clsd Sun-Mon (also clsd June-Aug), best oyster loaf in city ■ www.casamentosrestaurant.com

Clover Grill [★] 504/598-1010 ■ 900 Bourbon St (at Dumaine) ■ 8am-midnight, 24hrs Th-Mon, diner fare ■ www.clovergrill.com

Commander's Palace [★R] 504/899-8221 ■ 1403 Washington Ave (at Coliseum St, in Garden District) ■ lunch & dinner Mon-Fri, upscale Creole & dress (jackets at dinner), jazz brunch wknds ■ www.commanderspalace.com

EAT New Orleans 504/522-7222 ■ 900 Dumaine St (at Dauphine) ■ lunch & dinner, wknd brunch, clsd Mon, Cajun/Creole, some veggie ■ www.nola.com

Feelings Cafe [P] 504/945-2222 ■ 2600 Chartres St (at Franklin Ave) ■ dinner Th-Sun, also Sun brunch, Creole, also piano bar ■ www.feelingscafe.com

Fiorella's Cafe 504/528-9566 ■ 45 French Market Pl (at Gov Nicholls & Ursulines) ■ noon-midnight, till 2am Fri, 11:30am-2am Sat, 11:30am-midnight Sun, homecooking

La Peniche 504/943-1460 ■ 1940 Dauphine St (at Touro St) ■ 8am-9pm, clsd Tue-Wed, Southern comfort foods, popular for brkfst

Lafitte's Restaurant 504/524-0581, 800/777-6193 ■ 2031 St Charles Ave (in Pontchartrain Hotel) ■ brkfst, lunch & dinner, Creole, the setting for part of Anne Rice's The Witching Hour ■ www.pontchartrainhotel.com/dining.html

Marigny Brasserie 504/945-4472 ■ 640 Frenchmen St ■ lunch Mon-Fri, dinner nightly, wknd brunch, French ■ www.marignybrasserie.com

Meauxbar Bistro 504/569-9979 ■ 942 N Rampart St ■ 6pm-10pm, clsd Sun-Mon

Mona Lisa [BW,GO] 504/522-6746 ■ 1212 Royal St (at Barracks) ■ 11am-10pm, from 5pm Tue-Wed, Italian, some veggie

Mona's 504/949-4115 ■ 504 Frenchmen St ■ 11am-10pm, till 11pm Fri-Sat, noon-9pm Sun, cheap Middle Eastern eats, some veggie

Moon Wok 504/523-6910 ■ 800 Dauphine St ■ 11am-9pm, till 10pm Fri-Sat, Chinese

Nola [WC] 504/522-6652 ■ 534 St Louis St (btwn Chartres & Decatur) ■ lunch Sat, dinner nightly, fusion Creole from Emeril Lagasse ■ www.emerils.com

Olivier's [WC] 504/525-7734 ■ 204 Decatur St ■ 5pm-10pm, clsd Wed, Creole

Orleans Grapevine 504/523-1930 ■ 718-720 Orleans Ave ■ 4pm-10:30pm, till 11:30pm Fri-Sat, wine bar & bistro ■ www.orleansgrapevine.com

Petunia's 504/522-6440 ■ 817 St Louis (at Bourbon) ■ 8am-3pm, till 10pm Th-Sun, Cajun/ Creole, full bar ■ www.petuniasrestaurant.com

Praline Connection [E] 504/943-3934 ■ 542 Frenchmen St (at Chartres) ■ 11am-10pm, soul food ■ www.pralineconnection.com

Quartermaster 504/529-1416 ■ 1100 Bourbon St ■ 24hrs, "The Nellie Deli," sandwiches & more

Sammy's Seafood 504/525-8442 ■ 627 Bourbon St (across from Pat O' Brien's) ■ 11am-11pm, Cajun/ Creole

The Upperline Restaurant 504/891-9822 ■ 1413 Upperline ■ dinner Wed-Sun, Creole, fine dining, full bar ■ www.upperline.com

Vera Cruz [WC] 504/866-1736 ■ 7537 Maple (at Hillard) ■ 5pm-11pm, Mexican

ENTERTAINMENT & RECREATION

Big Easy Rollergirls ■ New Orleans' female roller derby league, check web for upcoming events ■ www.bigeasyrollergirls.com

Cafe du Monde 504/587-0835, 800/772-2927 ■ 1039 Decatur St (Old Jackson Square) ■ till you've a had a beignet—fried dough, powdered w/ sugar, that melts in your mouth—you haven't been to New Orleans & this is "the" place to have them 24hrs a day ■ www.cafedumonde.com

French Quarter Ceremonies [WO] 504/588-2733 ■ ceremonies on land & sea, women-owned/ run ■ captainlynda@aol.com

Gay Heritage Tour 504/524-5222 (Alternatives' #) ■ 909 Bourbon St ■ call for details, departs from Alternatives giftshop

Haunted History Tour 504/861-2727, 888/644-6787 ■ guided 2-1/2-hour tours of New Orleans' most famous haunts, including Anne Rice's former home ■ www.hauntedhistorytours.com

Mardi Gras World 504/361-7821, 800/362-8213 ■ 233 Newton St ■ tour this year-round Mardi Gras float workshop, take the free ferry from the base of Canal St, tour costs $15 ■ www.mardigrasworld.com

Pat O'Brien's [GF,F] 504/525-4823, 800/597-4823 ■ 718 St Peter St (btwn Bourbon & Royal) ■ more than just a bar—come for the Hurricane, stay for the kitsch ■ www.patobriens.com

Preservation Hall [NS,$] 504/522-2841, 888/946-5299 ■ 726 Saint Peter St ■ 8pm-midnight, set begins at 8:30pm, $8 admission, come & hear the music that started jazz: New Orleans-style jazz! ■ www.preservationhall.com

St Charles Streetcar 504/248-3900 (RTA Rideline #) ■ Canal St (btwn Bourbon & Royal Sts) ■ it's not named Desire, but you should still ride it, Blanche, if you want to see the Garden District ■ www.norta.com

BOOKSTORES

Barnes & Noble [WC] 504/263-1146 ■ 1601 Westbank Expwy, Harvey ■ 9am-10pm, till 11pm Fri-Sat, 10am-9pm Sun

84 **FAB (Faubourg Marigny Art & Books)** 504/947-3700 ■ 600 Frenchmen St (at Chartres) ■ noon-10pm, LGBT

Garden District Book Shop 504/895-2266 ■ 2727 Prytania St ■ 10am-6pm, till 4pm Sun, independent ■ www.gardendistrictbookshop.com

Kitchen Witch Cook Books [GF] 504/528-8382 ■ 631 Toulouse St (at Royal St) ■ kwitchen1@aol.com

RETAIL SHOPS

85 **Alternatives** 504/524-5222 ■ 909 Bourbon St (at Dumaine) ■ 11am-6pm, LGBT cards, gifts

Dress to Kill 504/587-7012 ■ 227 Dauphine ■ 10am-10pm, till 11pm Wed-Sat, sexy footwear (up to size 14)

Hit Parade [★] 504/524-7700 ■ 741 Bourbon St ■ 3pm-11pm, 11am-2am Fri-Sat, 11am-midnight Sun, LGBT books, designer circuit clothing & more ■ www.hitparadeonline.com

NOLA Tattoo 504/524-6147 ■ 1820 Hampson St (Uptown, at Riverbend) ■ tattoos & piercing ■ www.nolatattoo.com

Queen Fashions 504/524-4335, 866/444-3357 ■ 808 N Rampart ■ 9am-5pm, clsd wknds, sexy footwear (up to size 17), clothing & accessories ■ www.queenfashions.com

Rab-Dab 504/525-6662 ■ 918 Royal St ■ noon-6pm, men's clothing/ clubwear & gifts ■ rabdabno@aol.com

Second Skin Leather 504/561-8167 ■ 521 St Philip St (btwn Decatur & Chartres) ■ noon-8pm, till 10pm Fri-Sat

Wicked Orleans 504/529-4384, 866/297-9207 (outside LA) ■ 1201 Decatur St (at Gov Nicholls) ■ 11am-6pm, leather & goth clothes ■ www.wickedorleans.com

PUBLICATIONS

Ambush Mag 504/522-8049 ■ LGBT newspaper for the Gulf South (TX through FL) ■ www.ambushmag.com

Southern Voice 404/876-1819 ■ weekly LGBT newspaper for AL, FL (panhandle), GA, LA, MS, TN w/ resource listings ■ www.southernvoice.com

MEN'S CLUBS

The Club New Orleans [★18+,PC] 504/581-2402 ■ 515 Toulouse St (at Decatur) ■ 24hrs, 5 levels, gym, sauna & steam room, rooftop sundeck ■ www.the-clubs.com

Flex—New Orleans [V] 504/598-3539 ■ 700 Baronne St ■ 24hrs, 5 flrs, gym, sauna & steam room ■ www.flex-baths.com

EROTICA

Airline Adult Books 504/468-2931 ■ 1404 26th St (off Bainbridge), Kenner ■ 24hrs, super-arcade

Bourbon-Strip Tease 504/581-6633 ■ 205 Bourbon St ■ 10am-1am, erotic lingerie, dancewear, adult novelties ■ www.bourbontease.com

Chartres St Conxxxion 504/586-8006 ■ 107 Chartres St (off Canal St) ■ 24hrs

Panda Bear [WC] 504/529-3593 ■ 415 Bourbon St (at St Louis) ■ leather & toys

Paradise Adult Video [WC] 504/461-0000 ■ 41 W 24th St (at Crestview), Kenner ■ 8am-4am wknds, till 2am weekdays, arcade

MARYLAND

Baltimore

ACCOMMODATIONS

1 **Abacrombie Fine Food & Accommodations** [GS,NS] 410/244-7227, 888/922-3437 ■ 58 W Biddle St (at Cathedral) ■ *1880s town house, also restaurant* ■ www.abacrombie.net

2 **Biltmore Suites** [GF] 410/728-6550, 800/868-5064 ■ 205 W Madison St (at Park) ■ *Victorian hotel* ■ www.biltmoresuites.com

Embassy Suites Hotel Baltimore at BWI [GF,SW,WI,WC] 410/850-0747, 800/362-2779 ■ 1300 Concourse Dr, Linthicum ■ *full-service hotel near Inner Harbor, full brkfst, kids ok* ■ www.embassysuites.com

3 **Harbor Inn Pier 5** [GS,F,WI,WC] 410/539-2000, 866/583-4162 ■ 711 Eastern Ave (at President) ■ *boutique hotel on waterfront, full brkfst, restaurant, cigar bar* ■ www.thepier5.com

4 **Park Avenue B&B** [GS,NS,GO] 410/523-2625 ■ 2018 Park Avenue (at Reservoir St) ■ *in historic Reservoir Hill, hot tub* ■ www.parkavenuebedandbreakfast.com

5 **Tremont Park Hotel** [GS,WC] 410/576-1200, 800/873-6668 ■ 8 E Pleasant St ■ www.tremontsuitehotels.com

BARS

6 **Baltimore Eagle** [★M,L,WC] 443/524-3333 ■ 2022 N Charles St (enter on 21st) ■ *3pm-2am, leather store, video store, patio* ■ www.baltimore-eagle.com

Blue Parrot [MW,NH,F,K] 410/254-3785 ■ 5860 Belair Rd ■ *11am-2am* ■ www.blueparrotbar.com

7 **Club Bunns** [MW,D,MR,S] 410/234-2866 ■ 608 W Lexington St (at Greene St) ■ *4pm-2am, till midnight Mon-Tue, male strippers Wed, female strippers Sat*

8 **Club Gypsies** [MW,K] 410/522-1602 ■ 4020 E Lombard ■ *6pm-2am* ■ www.clubgypsies.com

9 **Club Phoenix** [MW,D,MR,F,K,DS,V] 410/837-3906 ■ 1 W Biddle St ■ *4pm-2am, from noon Sun* ■ baltimorephoenix.com

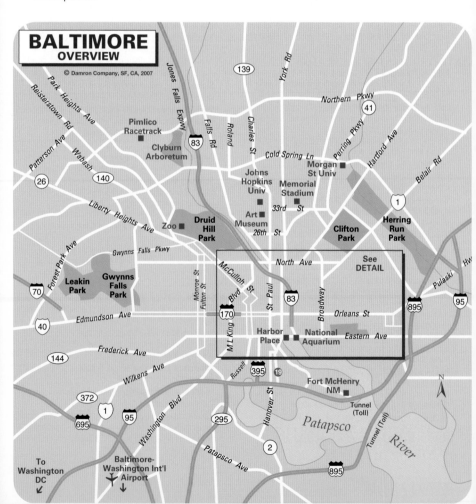

10 **Coconuts Cafe** [★W,D,F,E,K,WC,GO] 410/383-6064 ■ 311 W Madison (at Eutaw) ■ *5pm-2am, from 6pm Sat, hours vary Sun, lesbian-owned* ■ www.coconutscafe.com

11 **The Drinkery** [M,NH,K] 410/225-3100 ■ 203-207 W Read St (at Park) ■ *4pm-2am* ■ www.drinkery.net

12 **Eden's Lounge** [GF] 410/244-0405 ■ 15 W Eager St ■ *5pm-2am, tapas bar, live music, DJs* ■ www.edenslounge.com

13 **Gallagher's** [W,NH,F,K,DS] 410/327-3966 ■ 940 S Conkling St (at Dylan), Canton ■ *10am-2am, from 6pm Sat, from noon Sun* ■ www.gallaghersbar.com

14 **The Gallery Bar & Studio Restaurant** [MW,WC] 410/539-6965 ■ 1735 Maryland Ave (at Lafayette) ■ *2pm-1:30am, dinner Mon-Sat*

15 **Grand Central** [★MW,D,F,K,DS,V,18+] 410/752-7133 ■ 1001 N Charles St (at Eager) ■ *4pm-close, from 3pm Sun, 2 bars, also La Tijuana Cantina restaurant* ■ www.central-stationpub.com

16 **Hippo** [★MW,D,TG,E,K,DS,P,V,WC] 410/547-0069, 410/576-0018 ■ 1 W Eager St (at Charles) ■ *4pm-2am, 3 bars, more women 1st Sun for T-dance* ■ www.club-hippo.com

11 **Jay's on Read** [M,P] 410/225-0188 ■ 225 W Read St ■ *4pm-1am, clsd Sun*

BALTIMORE

Day Trips: Washington, DC
Washington, DC is an obvious choice, being only 39 miles away. The nation's capital has endless museums and historical sites to visit, not to mention a thriving gay scene of its own.

For something slightly different, check out Annapolis, Maryland's state capital. Home to the US Naval Academy, this town bustles with cute recruits in sparkling white uniforms. Rent a boat if you're feeling adventurous, or enjoy a water-based tour of the Chesapeake Bay. A walking tour will acquaint you with the rich history of the area, along with all the wonderful shopping and dining Annapolis has to offer.

Chocoholics might want to make the 90-mile drive to Hershey, PA, the "sweetest place on earth." With Hershey Park and Chocolate World to visit, look for lots of kids, a little kitsch, and a free sample or two.

Local Food:
While any kind of seafood is bound to be fresh and tasty here, crab is the local specialty. Crab cakes are everywhere, and the daring should check out a crab feast, where fresh crab in the shell are served by the dozen—half the fun is using nut crackers and mallets to release the sweet meat. Not for the faint of heart, and don't wear your Sunday best!

Tourist Info

AIRPORT DIRECTIONS
Baltimore/Washington International. To get to downtown area, take 295 North approximately 8 miles.

PUBLIC TRANSIT & TAXIS
Yellow Cab 410/685-1212.
Baltimore Airport Shuttle 410/821-5387, web: www.baltimoreeconomyshuttle.com.
MTA Transit 410/539-5000, web: www.mtamaryland.com.

TOURIST SPOTS & INFO
Baltimore Museum of Art 443/573-1700, web: www.artbma.org.
Fort McHenry 410/962-4290.
Harborplace.
Lexington Market.
National Aquarium 410/576-3800, web: www.aqua.org.
Poe House & Museum 410/396-7932.
Walters Art Museum 410/547-9000, web: www.thewalters.org.
Visitor's Center: Maryland Office of Tourism 866/639-3526, web: www.mdwelcome.org.

Weather
A temperate and, at times, temperamental climate. Spring brings great temperatures (50°-70°s) and unpredictable rains and heavy winds. In summer, the weather can be hot (90°s) and sticky. Fall cools off with an occasional "Indian Summer" in October. Winter brings cool days and colder nights, along with snow and ice.

Best Views
Top of the World Trade Center at the Inner Harbor. 401 E Pratt, 410/837-8439, web: www.viewbaltimore.org.

City Calendar
LGBT PRIDE
June. 410/837-5445 (GLCC #).

Queer Resources
COMMUNITY INFO
Gay/Lesbian Community Center 410/837-5445. 241 W Chase St, call for hours, web: www.glccb.org.
AA Gay/Lesbian 410/663-1922.
AIDS Action Baltimore 410/837-2437.

17 **Leon's** [M,NH,F,WC] 410/539-4993, 410/539-4850 ■ 870 Park Ave (at Chase) ■ *11am-2am, also Tyson's Place restaurant, Sun brunch* ■ leonsbaltimore.tripod.com

18 **The Quest** [M,NH] 410/563-2617 ■ 3607 Fleet St (at Conkling) ■ *4pm-2am*

19 **The Rowan Tree** [GS,K] 410/468-0550 ■ 1633 S Charles St ■ *4pm-2am, from 2pm Sat, from noon Sun, "Where diversity is our name"* ■ www.therowantree.net

NIGHTCLUBS

20 **Club 1722** [GS,D,MR,18+,PC] 410/547-8423 ■ 1722 N Charles St (at Lafayette) ■ *Sugar from midnight Fri, dress code* ■ www.club1722.com

21 **The Paradox** [★GS,D,MR,F,E,V,WC] 410/837-9110 ■ 1310 Russell St (at 13th) ■ *11pm-5am, midnight-6am Sat, more gay Sat* ■ www.thedox.com

22 **Sonar** [GS,D,E] 410/327-8333 ■ 407 E Saratoga St (at Holiday) ■ *live music venue* ■ www.sonarlounge.com

23 **Spectrum** [M,S] 410/563-2482 ■ 2000 Eastern Ave ■ *7pm-1am Th-Sat only* ■ www.spectrummen.com

CAFES

Donna's Coffee Bar [BW] 410/385-0180 ■ 2 W Madison (at Charles) ■ *7:30am-9pm, till 10pm Fri-Sat*

RESTAURANTS

Alonso's [NS,WC] 410/235-3433 ■ 415 W Cold Spring Lake (at Keswick Rd) ■ *10:30am-10pm, pizza & burgers, full bar* ■ www.alonsos.com

Cafe Hon [WC] 410/243-1230 ■ 1002 W 36th St (at Roland) ■ *7am-9pm, from 9am wknds* ■ www.cafehon.com

Loco Hombre 410/889-2233 ■ 413 W Cold Spring Ln (at Roland) ■ *11am-10pm, till 11pm Fri-Sat, wknd brunch* ■ www.locohombre.com

Mount Vernon Stable & Saloon 410/685-7427 ■ 909 N Charles St (btwn Eager & Read) ■ *11am-midnight, from 10am wknds, some veggie, also bar* ■ www.mvstable.com

Neo Viccino 410/347-0349 ■ 1317 N Charles St ■ *11am-11pm, till 9pm Sun, New American, full bar* ■ www.viccino.com

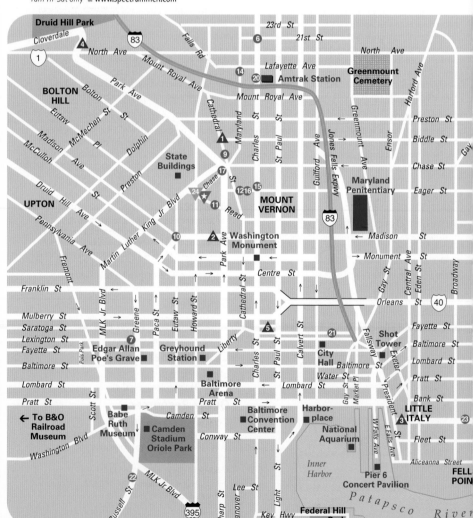

ENTERTAINMENT & RECREATION

The Charm City Kitty Club 410/276-1651 ■ 3134 Eastern Ave (at Creative Alliance) ■ *performing arts cabaret for lesbian, dyke, bisexual, trans women & allies* ■ www.charmcitykittyclub.com

Charm City Roller Girls 8025 Belair Rd (at Putty Hill Skateland) ■ *Baltimore's own female roller derby league, check web for events* ■ www.charmcityrollergirls.com

BOOKSTORES

24 Lambda Rising [WC] 410/234-0069 ■ 241 W Chase St (at Read) ■ *10am-10pm, LGBT* ■ www.lambdarising.com

Read Street Books 410/669-4103 ■ 229 W Read St ■ *noon-8pm, 10am-8pm wknds, women's bookstore, also cafe* ■ www.readstreetbooks.com

PUBLICATIONS

Baltimore OUTloud 410/244-6780 ■ www.baltimore-outloud.com

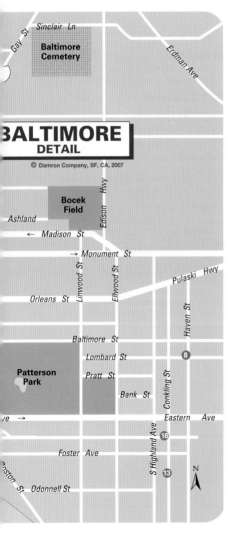

EXP Magazine 302/227-5787, 877/397-6244 ■ *bi-weekly gay magazine for Mid-Atlantic* ■ www.expmagazine.com

Gay Life 410/837-7748 ■ *LGBT newspaper* ■ www.baltimoregaylife.com

EROTICA

Big Top Books 410/547-2495 ■ 429 E Baltimore ■ *8am-midnight*

Chained Desires 410/528-8441 ■ 136 W Read St ■ *custom leather crafts & apparel, adult toys* ■ www.chaineddesires.com

Greenmount Books, Inc 410/467-0403 ■ 3222 Greenmount Ave (at 33rd St) ■ *10am-midnight, from noon Sun*

MASSACHUSETTS

Boston

ACCOMMODATIONS

1   463 Beacon St Guest House [GS,NS,WI,GO] 617/536-1302 ■ 463 Beacon St ■ *residential area, minutes from Boston's heart* ■ www.463beacon.com

2   Appleton Studio [GF,NS,WI,GO] 617/720-0522, 800/347-5088 ■ 30 Appleton St (at Berkely) ■ *spacious studio apt, also weekly/ monthly rentals* ■ www.bnbboston.com/boston-bnbs/b&tbs_5b.htm

3   Carolyn's B&B [GF,NS] 617/864-7042 ■ 102 Holworthy St (at Huron Ave), Cambridge ■ *near Harvard Square* ■ www.bbonline.com/ma/carolyns/index.html

4   Chandler Inn [GF,WI] 617/482-3450, 800/842-3450 ■ 26 Chandler St ■ *European-style hotel, centrally located* ■ www.chandlerinn.com

5   The Charles Street Inn [GS,NS,WC,GO] 617/314-8900, 877/772-8900 ■ 94 Charles St (at Mount Vernon, Beacon Hill) ■ *B&B, jacuzzi* ■ www.charlesstreetinn.com

6   Clarendon Square Inn [GS,NS,WI,GO] 617/536-2229 ■ 198 W Brookline St (btwn Tremont & Columbus) ■ *restored Victorian town house, hot tub* ■ www.clarendonsquare.com

7   The College Club [GF,NS,WI,WC] 617/536-9510 ■ 44 Commonwealth Ave (at Arlington St) ■ www.thecollege-clubofboston.com

8   Encore B&B [GF,NS,GO] 617/247-3425 ■ 116 W Newton St (at Tremont) ■ *19th-c town house in Boston's historic South End* ■ www.encorebandb.com

9   Holiday Inn Select Boston Government Center [GF,SW,WI,WC] 617/742-7630 ■ 5 Blossom St (Cambridge St) ■ *proximity to shops, restaurants & entertainment, full brkfst*

10 Hotel 140 [GS,NS,WC] 617/585-5600 ■ 140 Clarendon St (at Stuart St) ■ *boutique hotel, close to South End* ■ www.hotel140.com

The Liberty Hotel [GF,NS,WI,WC] 617/224-4000 ■ 215 Charles St (at Cambridge St) ■ *in the former Charles St Jail* ■ www.libertyhotel.com

11 Oasis Guest House [★GS,NS,WC,GO] 617/267-2262, 800/230-0105 ■ 22 Edgerly Rd ■ *Back Bay location, some shared baths* ■ www.oasisgh.com

12 Rutland Square House B&B [GS,NS,GO] 617/247-0018 ■ 56 Rutland Square ■ *Victorian town house* ■ www.rutlandsquarebandb.com

13 **Taylor House B&B** [GS,NS,WI,GO] 617/983-9334,
888/228-2956 ■ 50 Burroughs St, Jamaica Plain
■ *Italianate Victorian* ■ **www.taylorhouse.com**
14 <u>Victorian B&B</u> [WO,NS,GO] 617/536-3285 ■ *full brkfst,
lesbian-owned* ■ **mybuddysl@verizon.net**

BARS
15 **The Alley** [★M,NH,D,B,L,WC,GO] 617/263-1449 ■ 14 Pi
Alley (at 275 Washington St) ■ *2pm-2am, from noon wknds,
cruisy* ■ **www.TheAlleyBar.com**
16 **Boston Eagle** [M,NH] 617/542-4494 ■ 520 Tremont St
(near Berkeley) ■ *3pm-2am, from noon Sun*

BOSTON

Day Trips:
It's a short broomstick ride up to Salem, where witches and their admirers can examine the facts and fictions surrounding the Witch Trials of 1692. Fascinating historical sites and tours abound, and modern-day witches have a strong presence in this town, working to promote tolerance and religious acceptance among all people. For more info, visit www.salemweb.com.

Local Food:
Baked beans may come to mind first, but Italian food in Boston can't be beat. Make your stomach go bada-bing with a trip to the summer weekend festivals held in the North End.

Tourist Info

AIRPORT DIRECTIONS
Logan International. To get to the South End, take I-90 west through the Ted Williams Tunnel. Merge onto I-93 south and take the Albany Street exit. (Damron suggests not driving in Boston. Instead, take a shuttle, taxi, or the "T.")

PUBLIC TRANSIT & TAXIS
Boston Cab 617/536-5010, 617/262-2227. Instyle Transportation limo service 617/ 641-2400 or 877/ 64-STYLE. MBTA (the "T") 800/392-6100, web: www.mbta.com.

TOURIST SPOTS & INFO
Beacon Hill, web: www.beaconhillonline.com. Black Heritage Trail, web: www.afroammuseum.org/trail.htm. Boston Common. Faneuil Hall, web: www.faneuilhall.com. Freedom Trail 617/242-5642, web: www.thefree-domtrail.org. Harvard University, web: www.harvard.edu. Isabella Stewart Gardner Museum 617/566-1401, web: www.gardnermuseum.org. Museum of African American History 617/725-0022, web: www.afroammuseum.org. Museum of Fine Arts 617/267-9300, web: www.mfa.org. Museum of Science 617/723-2500, web: www.mos.org. New England Aquarium 617/973-5200, web: www.neaq.org. Old North Church 617/523-6676, web: www.oldnorth.com. Walden Pond, web: www.mass.gov/dcr/parks/northeast/wldn.htm. Visitor's Center: Greater Boston Convention & Visitors Bureau 888/733-2678, web: www.bostonusa.com.

Weather
Extreme—from freezing winters to boiling summers with a beautiful spring and fall.

City Calendar
LGBT PRIDE
June. 617/262-9405, web: www.bostonpride.org.

ENTERTAINMENT
Gay Men's Chorus 617/542-7464, web: www.bgmc.org. The Theatre Offensive 617/621-6090, web: www.thetheateroffensive.org.

ANNUAL EVENTS
May - Gay & Lesbian Film/Video Festival 617/369-3300 (Museum of Fine Arts #).

Queer Resources
COMMUNITY INFO
LGBT Helpline 617/267-9001. 6pm-11pm. Cambridge Women's Center 617/354-8807, web: www.cambridgewomenscenter.org. Edge Boston, web: www.edgeboston.com AA 617/426-9444. AIDS Action Committee 800/235-2331 web: www.aac.org.

17 **Boston Ramrod** [★M,D,B,L,WC] 617/266-2986 ■ 1254 Boylston St (at Ipswich, 1 block from Fenway Park) ■ *noon-2am* ■ www.ramrodboston.com

18 **Club Cafe Lounge & Video Bar** [★MW,F,E,K,P,V,WC] 617/536-0966 ■ 209 Columbus (at Berkeley) ■ *11:30am-2am, Sun brunch from 10:30am, 3 bars including Moonshine [V], also restaurant* ■ www.clubcafe.com

Dyke Night Productions [W,NH,D,E,YC,WC] ■ *special events in various locations, check website for events & locations* ■ www.dykenight.com

4 **Fritz** [★M,NH] 617/482-4428 ■ 26 Chandler St (in the Chandler Inn) ■ *noon-2am, sports bar, Sat & Sun brunch* ■ www.fritzboston.com

19 **Grrl Rush Mondays** [W,E] 617/783-5085 ■ 334 Massachusetts Ave (at All Asia), Cambridge ■ *7pm Mon only, live music for & by women* ■ www.cncmusicproductions.com

20 **Jacque's** [★M,TG,C,DS,$] 617/426-8902 ■ 79 Broadway (at Stuart) ■ *11am-midnight, from noon Sun, drag cabaret* ■ www.jacquescabaret.com

Johnny D's Restaurant & Music Club [D,E] 617/776-2004 ■ 17 Holland St (in Davis Square), Somerville ■ *12:30pm-1am, from 9am wknds, Southern, plenty veggie, live music nightly* ■ www.johnnydsuptown.com

21 **Milky Way Lounge & Lanes** [GS,F,E,K] 617/524-3740 ■ 403 Centre St, Jamaica Plain ■ *6pm-1am, live music, poetry readings, bowling, also restaurant* ■ www.milkywayjp.com

22 **Paradise** [M,D,S,V] 617/868-3000 ■ 180 Massachusetts Ave, Cambridge ■ *7pm-1am, till 2am Th-Sat* ■ www.paradisecambridge.com

23 **Rumor/ Venu** [M,D,P] 617/338-8061 ■ 100-101 Warrenton St (at Stuart) ■ *Church Sun T-dance at Rumor, Latin Wed at Venu* ■ www.gaymafiaboston.com

24 **Ryles** [GS,F,E] 617/876-9330 ■ 212 Hampshire St (at Cambridge St, in Inman Square), Cambridge ■ *great wknd jazz brunch* ■ www.rylesjazz.com

NIGHTCLUBS

25 **Avalon** [★GS,D,YC,$] 617/262-2424 ■ 15 Lansdowne St ■ *10pm-2am Th-Sun, 19+ Sat, [MW] Sun* ■ www.avalon-boston.com

26 **Buzz** [M,D,S,$] 617/338-7080 ■ 246 Tremont St (below Wilbur Theatre) ■ *11pm Wed only* ■ www.buzzboston.com

27 **DBar** [GS] 617/265-4490 ■ 1236 Dorchester Ave, Dorchester ■ *also restaurant, dinner nightly* ■ www.dbar-boston.com

28 **Dyke Night Productions** [W,D,E,WC] 617/623-9211 ■ 70 Union Sq (at Pleasant St), Somerville ■ www.dykenight.com

25 **The Glamorous Life** [MW,D,19+,$] 617/536-2100 ■ 36 Lansdowne St (at Embassy/ Modern) ■ *Th only, hip-hop* ■ www.shuttavac.com/themodern

29 **Hot Lunch** [MW,D,TG,S] 617/783-3222 ■ 1222 Commonwealth Ave (at Great Scott), Allston ■ hotlunchboston@gmail.com

17 **Machine** [★M,D,V,S,YC,WC] 617/536-1950 ■ 1256 Boylston St (below Boston Ramrod) ■ *10pm-2am* ■ www.machineboston.com

30 **The Middle East** [GF,A,F,E,YC,$] 617/497-0576 ■ 472 Massachusetts Ave (in Central Square), Cambridge ■ *11am-1am, till 2am wknds, live music, also restaurant* ■ www.mideastclub.com

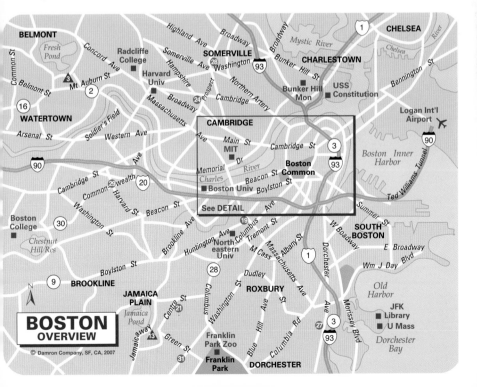

© Damron Company, SF, CA, 2007

BOSTON OVERVIEW

31 Midway Cafe [GS,D,E,K] 617/524-9038 ■ 3496 Washington St, Jamaica Plain ■ *mostly women Th* ■ www.midwaycafe.com

31 The Neighborhood [GS,D,E] 617/524-9038 ■ 3496 Washington St, Jamaica Plain ■ *mostly women Th* ■ www.myspace.com/theneighborhoodjp

32 Rise [GS,D,PC] 617/423-7473 ■ 306 Stuart St (btwn Berkeley & Arlington) ■ *1:30am-6:30am Fri-Sat & holiday Sun only, straight Fri* ■ www.riseclub.us

25 Static [MW,D,S,19+,$] 617/262-2437 ■ 13 Lansdowne St (at Axis) ■ *10pm-2am Mon* ■ www.bostonaxis.com

28 Toast [MW,D] 617/623-9211 ■ 70 Union Square, Somerville ■ *9pm-1am Wed, 5:30pm-1am Fri, 9pm-2am Sat, theme nights, mostly lesbians Fri for Dyke Night* ■ www.toast-lounge.com

33 Tribe at Felt [WO,D,MR,TG,F,YC] 617/350-5555 ■ 533 Washington (at Club Felt) ■ *9pm-2am Th only* ■ www.tribenightclub.com

34 Tribe at Vinalia 617/737-1777 ■ 101 Arch St (enter at 34 Summer St) ■ *10pm-2am Sat only* ■ www.tribenightclub.com

CAFES

1369 Cafe 617/576-4600 ■ 757 Massachusetts Ave (in Central Square), Cambridge ■ *7am-11pm, from 8am wknds, till 10pm Sun, coffee & baked goods; also 1369 Cambridge St (Inman Square), 617/576-1369* ■ www.1369coffeehouse.com

Berkeley Perk [F,GO] 617/426-7375 ■ 69 Berkeley St (at Chandler) ■ *6am-5pm, 7:30am-4pm Sat, 8am-noon Sun, clsd Sun summers*

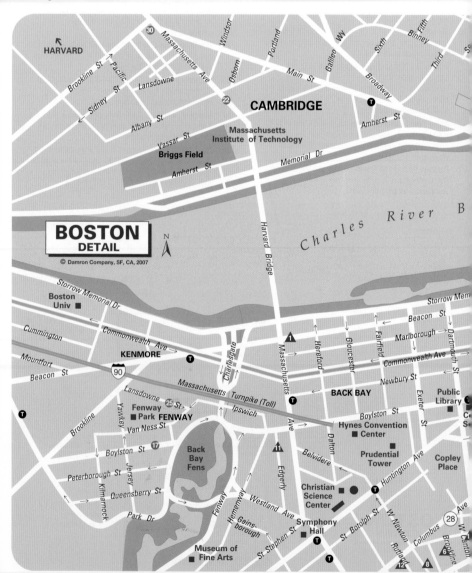

Diesel Cafe [GO] 617/629-8717 ■ 257 Elm St (in Davis Square), Somerville ■ 7am-midnight, till 1am Fri-Sat, from 8am wknds, plenty veggie, lesbian-owned ■ www.diesel-cafe.com

Fiore's Bakery [GO] 617/524-9200 ■ 55 South St, Jamaica Plain ■ 7am-7pm, 8am-6pm wknds, bakery & organic coffees

Francesca's [★MW,WC] 617/482-9026 ■ 564 Tremont St (at Clarendon) ■ 8am-11pm, till midnight Fri-Sat, pastries

JP Licks [★] 617/236-1666 ■ 352 Newbury St ■ "homemade ice cream cafe"—and yes, they serve coffee too ■ www.jplicks.com

June Bug Cafe [WI,GO] 617/522-2393 ■ 403A Centre St, Jamaica Plain ■ 8am-11pm, from 9am Sat-Sun, also sandwiches, lesbian-owned ■ june@junebugcafe.com

True Grounds [E] 617/591-9559 ■ 717 Broadway, Somerville ■ 7am-7pm, from 8am wknds, brkfst, lunch ■ www.truegrounds.com

RESTAURANTS

209 Boston [★E,P,V,WC] 617/536-0972 ■ 209 Columbus (adjacent to Club Cafe) ■ dinner & wknd brunch, also 3 bars ■ www.209boston.com

33 Restaurant & Lounge 617/572-3311 ■ 33 Stanhope St ■ dinner nightly, Sun brunch, French/ Italian, patio ■ www.33restaurant.com

BarLola 617/266-1122 ■ 160 Commonwealth Ave (at Dartmouth) ■ 4pm-1:30am, from 10am wknds, Spanish tapas lounge ■ www.barlola.com

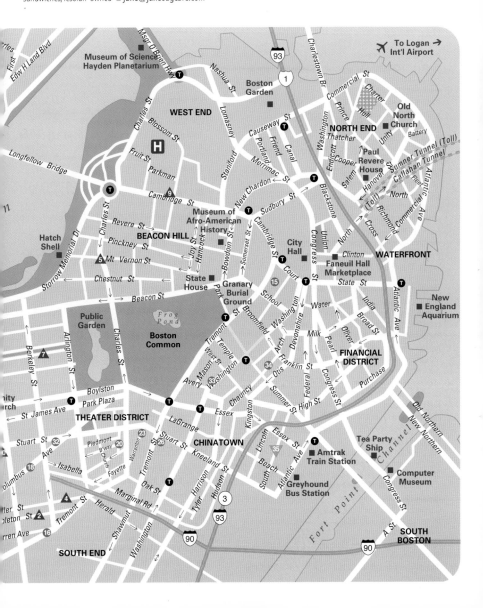

Bob's 617/536-0907 ■ 604 Columbus Ave ■ *dinner nightly, wknd brunch, jazz Sun, Southern bistro* ■ www.bobthechefs.com

Bomboa 617/236-6363 ■ 35 Stanhope St ■ *dinner nightly, French/ Latin, patio* ■ www.bomboaboston.com

Buddha's Delight 617/451-2395 ■ 3 Beach St, 2nd flr ■ *11am-10pm, till 11pm Fri-Sat, Chinese, vegetarian*

Casa Romero 617/536-4341 ■ 30 Gloucester St ■ *dinner, Mexican* ■ www.casaromero.com

City Girl Cafe [BW,GO] 617/864-2809 ■ 204 Hampshire St (at Prospect), Cambridge ■ *11am-9pm, from 10am Sat, till 4pm Sun, clsd Mon, Italian, plenty veggie, great sandwiches, lesbian-owned* ■ www.citygirlcafe.com

Icarus [E] 617/426-1790 ■ 3 Appleton St (off Tremont) ■ *dinner only, New American, jazz Fri* ■ www.icarusrestaurant.com

Laurel 617/424-6711 ■ 142 Berkeley St (at Columbus) ■ *lunch weekdays & dinner nightly, Sun brunch* ■ www.laurelgrillandbar.com

Om 617/576-2800 ■ 92 Winthrop, Cambridge ■ *noon-3pm & 5pm-1am Mon-Fri, 5pm-2am only Th-Sat, American* ■ www.omrestaurant.com

Rabia's [WC] 617/227-6637 ■ 73 Salem St (at Cross St) ■ *11am-10:30pm, fine Italian, some veggie* ■ www.rabias.com

Ristorante Lucia 617/367-2353 ■ 415 Hanover St ■ *lunch & dinner, great North End pasta, some veggie* ■ www.lucia-boston.com

Shine [GO] 617/621-9500 ■ 1 Kendall Sq (building 300), Cambridge ■ www.shinerestaurant.com

Sorellina [R] 617/412-4600 ■ 1 Huntington Ave ■ *5:30pm-10:30pm, till 11pm Fri-Sat, till 10pm Sun, Italian* ■ www.sorellinaboston.com

Trattoria Pulcinella 617/491-6336 ■ 147 Huron Ave (at Concord), Cambridge ■ *5pm-10pm, fine Italian* ■ www.trattoriapulcinella.net

Veggie Planet 617/661-1513 ■ 47 Palmer St (at Club Passim), Cambridge ■ *11:30am-10:30pm, vegetarian, also live music venue* ■ www.veggieplanet.net

ENTERTAINMENT & RECREATION

Boston Derby Dames ■ *Boston's female roller derby league, check web for upcoming events* ■ www.bostonderbydames.com

Boston Gay Men's Chorus 617/542-7464 ■ *diverse array of classical & pop, concerts usually held in Dec, March & June* ■ www.bgmc.org

Center for New Words [MR] 617/876-5310 ■ 7 Temple St ■ *cultural & political events for women* ■ www.centerfornewwords.org

Club Passim 617/492-5300 ■ 47 Palmer St, Cambridge ■ *folk music & cultural center* ■ www.passimcenter.org

Freedom Trail 617/357-8300 ■ *start at the Visitor Information Center in Boston Common (at Tremont & West Sts), the most famous cow pasture & oldest public park in the US, then follow the red line to some of Boston's most famous sites* ■ www.thefreedomtrail.org

Gender Crash [MW,MR,TG] 45 Danforth St (at Spontaneous Celebrations), Jamaica Plain ■ *7:30pm 2nd Th only, spoken word & performance for LGBT/ tranny/ queer community* ■ www.gendercrash.com

Isabella Stewart Gardner Museum 617/566-1401 ■ 280 The Fenway ■ *Venetian palazzo filled w/ Old Masters to Impressionists, gorgeous courtyard, clsd Mon* ■ www.gardnermuseum.org

Jamaica Pond ■ *great girl-watching*

The Mapparium 617/450-7000 ■ 200 Massachusetts Ave (in Mary Baker Eddy Library) ■ *10am-4pm, clsd Mon, the map's out of date, but where else can you walk through a 30-ft stained-glass globe?* ■ www.marybakereddylibrary.org/exhibits/mapparium.jhtml

Museum of African American History/ Black Heritage Trail 617/725-0022 ■ 46 Joy St (at Smith Ct, on Beacon Hill) ■ *10am-4pm, clsd Sun, exhibits in the Abiel Smith School, the nation's first public school for black children* ■ www.afroammuseum.org

The Theater Offensive 617/621-6090 ■ *"New England's premier presenter of LGBT theater," also Out on the Edge festival in Oct* ■ www.thetheateroffensive.org

Urban Adventours 617/233-7595 ■ PO Box 180033 02118 ■ *guided bike tours of Boston* ■ www.urbanadventours.com

BOOKSTORES

35 **Calamus Bookstore** [★] 617/338-1931, 888/800-7300 ■ 92-B South St ■ *9am-7pm, noon-6pm, LGBT, also cards, music, jewelry, videos, magazines* ■ www.calamusbooks.com

The Globe Corner Bookstore 617/497-6277, 800/358-6013 ■ 90 Mt Auburn (Harvard Square), Cambridge ■ www.globecorner.com

Trident Booksellers & Cafe [F,BW,WC] 617/267-8688 ■ 338 Newbury St (off Mass Ave) ■ *9am-midnight, good magazine browsing, also restaurant* ■ www.tridentbookscafe.com

PUBLICATIONS

Bay Windows 617/266-6670 ■ *LGBT newspaper* ■ www.baywindows.com

In Newsweekly 617/426-8246 ■ *New England's largest LGBT newspaper* ■ www.innewsweekly.com

GYMS & HEALTH CLUBS

Columbus Athletic Club [GF] 617/536-3006 ■ 209 Columbus ■ www.bostonfitness.com

EROTICA

Amazing Express 617/859-8911 ■ 1258 Boylston St (at Ipswich) ■ *also 57 Stuart St, 617/338-1252*

Eros Boutique 617/425-0345 ■ 581-A Tremont St, 2nd flr ■ *10am-10pm, fetishwear & toys* ■ www.erosboutique.com

Good Vibrations [★WC] 617/264-4400 ■ 308 Harvard St, Brookline ■ *noon-7pm, till 8pm Th-Sat, clean, well-lighted sex toy store, also mail order, workshops & events* ■ www.goodvibes.com

Hubba Hubba 617/492-9082 ■ 534 Massachusetts Ave (at Brookline, in Central Square), Cambridge ■ *noon-8pm, clsd Sun, fetish gear* ■ www.hubbahubba.com

Marquis de Sade 617/426-2120 ■ 92 South St ■ *10am-11pm*

Provincetown

ACCOMMODATIONS

1 **1807 House** [MW,NS,WI,GO] 508/487-2173, 888/522-1807 ■ 54 Commercial St (btwn W Vine & Point St) ■ *50 ft from beach* ■ www.1807House.com

2 **Admiral's Landing Guest House** [M,NS,WI,GO] 508/487-9665, 800/934-0925 ■ 158 Bradford St (btwn Conwell & Pearl) ■ *1840s Greek Revival home & studio efficiencies* ■ www.admiralslanding.com

3 **Aerie House & Beach Club** [MW,WI,GO] 508/487-1197, 800/487-1197 ■ 184 Bradford St (at Miller Hill) ■ *bay views, hot tub, sundeck* ■ www.aeriehouse.com

4   **Ampersand Guesthouse** [M,NS,GO] 508/487-0959, 800/574-9645 ■ 6 Cottage St ■ *1880s Greek Revival, sundeck* ■ www.ampersandguesthouse.com

5   **Anchor Inn Beach House** [★GS,NS,WC] 508/487-0432, 800/858-2657 ■ 175 Commercial St ■ *private beach, harbor view* ■ www.anchorinnbeachhouse.com

6   **Bayberry Accommodations** [MW,NS,WI,GO] 508/487-4605, 800/422-4605 ■ 16 Winthrop St ■ *newly renovated, award-winning home, hot tub* ■ www.bayberry-accommodations.com

7   **Bayshore** [GS,WI,GO] 508/487-9133 ■ 493 Commercial St (at Howland) ■ *apts, private beach, lesbian-owned* ■ www.bayshorechandler.com

    Beachfront Realty 508/487-1397 ■ 139 Commercial St ■ *vacation rentals* ■ www.beachfront-realty.com

8   **Beaconlight Guest House** [★M,NS,WI,GO] 508/487-9603, 800/696-9603 ■ 12 Winthrop St ■ *award-winning guesthouse, hot tub, sundecks, parking* ■ www.beaconlightguesthouse.com

9   **Benchmark Inn & Central** [MW,SW,NS,WI,WC,GO] 508/487-7440, 888/487-7440 ■ 6-8 Dyer St ■ *hot tub, sauna, fireplaces, harbor views, sundeck* ■ www.benchmarkinn.com

10 **The Black Pearl Inn** [MW,GO] 508/487-0302, 800/761-1016 ■ 11 & 18 Pearl St ■ *renovated 19th-c sea captain's home, hot tub, "friends of Bill welcome"* ■ www.theblackpearlinn.com

11 **Boatslip Resort** [★M,SW,GO] 508/487-1669, 877/786-9662 ■ 161 Commercial St (at Atlantic) ■ *seasonal, also several bars & popular T-dance* ■ www.boatsliprresort.com

12 **The Bradford Carver House** [MW,NS,GO] 508/487-4966, 800/826-9083 ■ 70 Bradford St ■ *restored mid-19th-c home, centrally located* ■ www.bradfordcarver.com

13 **Bradford House & Motel** [GF,WC] 508/487-0173 ■ 41 Bradford St ■ *near town center, 1 block from the beach* ■ www.bradfordhousemotel.com

14 **Brass Key Guesthouse** [★M,SW,NS,WI,WC,GO] 508/487-9005, 800/842-9858 ■ 67 Bradford St (at Carver) ■ *luxury inn w/ hot tub* ■ www.brasskey.com

15 **Burch House** [GS] 508/487-9170 ■ 116 Bradford St ■ *seasonal, studios, some shared baths, kids/ pets ok* ■ www.burchhouse.com

    Cape Inn [GS,SW,NS,WC] 508/487-1711, 800/422-4224 ■ *also restaurant & lounge* ■ www.capeinn.com

16 **Captain's House B&B** [M,B,NS,GO] 508/487-9353, 800/457-8885 ■ 350-A Commercial St (at Center) ■ *hot tub, patio* ■ www.captainshouseptown.com

17 **Carl's Guest House** [MO,N,NS,GO] 508/487-1650, 800/348-2275 ■ 68 Bradford St (at Court St) ■ *some shared baths, sundeck* ■ www.carlsguesthouse.com

18 **Carpe Diem Guesthouse** [MW,NS,WI,GO] 508/487-4242, 800/487-0132 ■ 12 Johnson St ■ *also cottage, full German brkfst, hot tub* ■ www.carpediemguesthouse.com

19 **The Carriage House Guesthouse** [GS,GO] 508/487-8855, 800/309-0248 ■ 7 Central St ■ *1700s guesthouse, hot tub* ■ www.ProvincetownGuesthouse.com

20 **Chicago House** [MW,NS,WI,GO] 508/487-0537, 800/733-7869 ■ 6 Winslow St (at Bradford) ■ *rooms & apts, hot tub* ■ www.chicagohse.com

18 **Christopher's by the Bay** [MW,NS,WI,GO] 508/487-9263, 877/487-9263 ■ 8 Johnson St (at Bradford) ■ *Victorian guesthouse, full brkfst, some shared baths, patio* ■ www.christophersbythebay.com

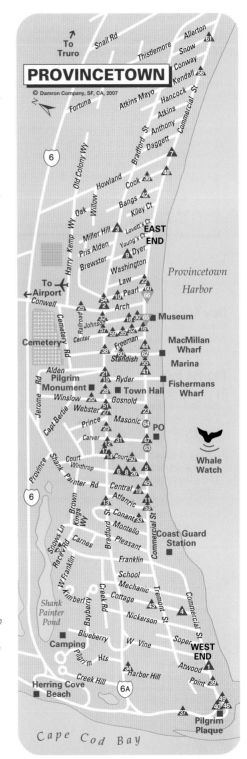

21 **The Clarendon House** [GS,NS] 508/487-1645, 800/669-8229 ■ 118 Bradford St (btwn Ryder & Alden) ■ *also cottage, hot tub, roof deck* ■ www.clarendonhse.com

22 **The Commons Guest House & Bistro** [GS,GO] 508/487-7800, 800/487-0784 ■ 386 Commercial St (at Pearl) ■ *deck w/ full bar, also restaurant* ■ www.commons-ghb.com

23 **Crown & Anchor** [MW,SW,NS,WI,GO] 508/487-1430 ■ 247 Commercial St ■ *also cabaret & poolside bars* ■ www.onlyatthecrown.com

24 **Crowne Pointe Historic Inn** [MW,SW,NS,WI,WC,GO] 508/487-6767, 877/276-9631 ■ 82 Bradford St ■ *luxurious inn, full brkfst, 2 large jacuzzis, spa, restaurant* ■ www.crownepointe.com

16 **Designer's Dock** [GS,WI,GO] 508/487-0385, 800/724-9888 ■ 349 Commercial St ■ *weekly condos in town & on beach, seasonal* ■ www.DesignersDock.com

25 **Dexter's Inn** [MW,NS,GO] 508/487-1911, 888/521-1999 ■ 6 Conwell St (at Railroad) ■ *sundeck* ■ www.ptowndextersinn.com

26 **Dyer's Antique Barn Guest Suites** [MW,SW] 508/487-2061 ■ 9 Winthrop St (at Commercial) ■ *seasonal, self-catering units* ■ www.provincetowngetaway.com

5 **Enzo** [GS] 508/487-7555, 888/873-5001 ■ 186 Commercial St ■ *Italian restaurant & piano bar on premises* ■ www.enzolives.com

27 Fairbanks Inn [★MW,NS,WI,GO] 508/487-0386, 800/324-7265 ■ 90 Bradford St ■ *kids ok, lesbian-owned* ■ www.fairbanksinn.com

28 **Four Gables** [GS,GO] 866/487-2427 ■ 15 Race Rd ■ www.fourgables.com

29 Gabriel's Apartments & Guest Rooms [★W,NS,WI,GO] 508/487-3232, 800/969-2643 ■ 102 Bradford St ■ *full brkfst, hot tub, sundecks, gym* ■ www.gabriels.com

30 **The Gallery Inn** [M] 508/487-3010, 800/676-3010 ■ 3 Johnson St ■ *seasonal* ■ www.galleryinnptown.com

31 **Gifford House Inn** [MW,GO] 508/487-0688, 800/434-0130 ■ 9 Carver St ■ *seasonal, also several bars & 11 Carver restaurant (dinner only, seafood)* ■ www.gifford-house.com

PROVINCETOWN

Day Trips: Why leave the country's largest lesbian and gay resort at all? Though it is the sleepy, quintessential New England whaling village in the winter months, Provincetown swarms with lesbian and gay tourists from Memorial Day through Labor Day weekend. A car is almost a liability on the crowded streets; bicycle rentals are a better choice. Explore all day on bike, go whale-watching, then get prepped and ready to dance the night away!

Tourist Info

AIRPORT DIRECTIONS

Provincetown Airport (508/487-0241) handles Cape Air flights from Logan Int'l in Boston. It is appproximately a 3-hour drive from Logan in Boston or TF Green Int'l Airport in Providence.

PUBLIC TRANSIT & TAXIS

Cape Cab 508/487-2222.
Queen Cab Co 508/487-5500, web: www.queen-cabco.com.
Ferry: Bay State Cruise Company (from Commonwealth/World Trade Center Pier in Boston, during summer) 617/748-1428, 877-783-3770, web: www.baystatecruisecompany.com.
Air: Cape Air 800/352-0714, web: www.flycapeair.com.

TOURIST SPOTS & INFO

The beach.
Galleries.
Herring Cove Beach.
Pilgrim Monument.
Provincetown Museum 508/487-1310, web: www.pilgrim-monument.org.
Whale-watching.
Visitor's Center: Provincetown Business Guild 508/487-2313, 800/637-8696, web: www.ptown.org.

Weather

New England weather is unpredictable. Be prepared for rain, snow, or extreme heat! Otherwise, the weather during the season consists of warm days and cooler nights.

Best Views

People-watching from an outdoor cafe or on the beach.

City Calendar

LGBT PRIDE

August - Provincetown Carnival.

ANNUAL EVENTS

June - Golden Threads. Gathering for lesbians over 50 & their admirers, at the Provincetown Inn, web: www.goldenthreadsptown.org.
August - Provincetown Carnival 800/637-8696.
October - Fantasia Fair - for trannies & their admirers, web: www.fantasiafair.org.
October - Women's Week 800/637-8696, web: www.womeninnkepers.com. It's very popular, so make your reservations early!
December - Holly Folly, web: www.ptown.org. Gay & Lesbian Holiday Festival.

Queer Resources

COMMUNITY INFO

Provincetown Business Guild 508/487-2313, 800/637-8696, web: www.ptown.org.
508/487-9445, web: www.asgcc.org.

32 Gracie House [MW,NS,GO] 508/487-4808 ■ 152 Bradford St (at Conwell) ■ historic, restored Queen Anne, lesbian-owned ■ home.att.net/~graciehouse

33 Grand View Inn [MW,NS,GO] 508/487-9193, 888/268-9169 ■ 4 Conant St ■ decks ■ www.grandviewinn.com

34 Harbor Hill at Provincetown [GF,GO] 508/487-0541 ■ 4 Harbor Hill Rd ■ condo resort in West End, 500 yds from Nat'l Seashore ■ www.harborhill.com

35 Heritage House [MW,GO] 508/487-3692 ■ 7 Center St ■ shared baths, lesbian-owned ■ www.heritageh.com

36 The Inn at Cook Street [GF,NS,GO] 508/487-3894, 888/266-5655 ■ 7 Cook St ■ intimate & quiet ■ www.innatcookstreet.com

37 Inn at the Moors [GF,SW,NS,WI,GO] 508/487-1342, 800/842-6379 ■ 59 Provincelands Rd ■ motel, across from Nat'l Seashore Province Lands, seasonal ■ www.innatthemoors.com

38 John Randall House [MW,NS,GO] 508/487-3533, 800/573-6700 ■ 140 Bradford St (at Standish) ■ open yr-round ■ www.johnrandallhouse.com

39 Labrador Landing [MW,GO] 917/597-1500 ■ 47 Commercial St ■ luxury cottages on West End, kids/ pets ok ■ www.labradorlanding.com

40 Land's End Inn [GS,NS,GO] 508/487-0706, 800/276-7088 ■ 22 Commercial St ■ seasonal ■ www.landsendinn.com

41 Lotus Guest House [MW,GO] 508/487-4644, 888/508-4644 ■ 296 Commercial St (at Standish) ■ seasonal, decks, garden ■ www.provincetown.com/lotus

42 Mayflower Apartments & Cottages [GF] 508/487-1916 ■ 6 Bangs St (at Commercial St) ■ kitchens

41 Moffett House [MW,GO] 508/487-6615, 800/990-8865 ■ 296-A Commercial St ■ seasonal, levi/ leather-friendly, women very welcome ■ www.moffetthouse.com

43 The Oxford [MW,NS,WI,GO] 508/487-9103, 888/456-9103 ■ 8 Cottage St ■ newly renovated 1850 Revival, parking ■ www.oxfordguesthouse.com

44 Pilgrim House Hotel [W,WC] 508/487-6424 ■ 336 Commercial St ■ seasonal, kids ok, also Vixen bar/ dance club, also wine bar ■ www.thepilgrimhouse.com

45 The Prince Albert Guest House [M,NS,GO] 508/487-1850, 800/400-2278 ■ 166 Commercial St ■ Victorian ■ www.provincetownvacations.com

46 Provincetown Inn [GS,SW,WC] 508/487-9500, 800/942-5388 ■ 1 Commercial St (at Rotary) ■ waterfront, private beach, poolside bar & grill, theater ■ provincetown-inn.com

47 The Ranch Guestlodge [MO,NS,WI,GO] 508/487-1542, 800/942-1542 ■ 198 Commercial St ■ shared baths, sundeck, also bar ■ www.theranch.ws

48 Ravenwood Guest House [MW,NS,WC,GO] 508/487-3203 ■ 462 Commercial St (at Cook) ■ 1830 Greek Revival, also apts & cottage, patio, private beach, lesbian-owned ■ www.provincetown.com/ravenwood/

49 The Red Inn [GF,NS,WC,GO] 508/487-7334, 866/473-3466 ■ 15 Commercial St (at Point) ■ www.theredinn.com

50 Revere Guesthouse [MW,NS,GO] 508/487-2292, 800/487-2292 ■ 14 Court St (btwn Commercial & Bradford) ■ restored 1820s captain's home, also apt ■ www.reverehouse.com

51 Romeo's Holiday [MW,N,WI,GO] 508/487-6636, 877/697-6636 ■ 97 Bradford St (btwn Gosnold & Masonic) ■ hot tub ■ www.romeosholiday.com

52 Rose Acre [WO,NS,WI] 508/487-2347 ■ 5 Center St (at Commercial) ■ also apts & cottage, decks, gardens ■ roseacreguests.com

53 Rose & Crown Guest House [GS,GO] 508/487-3332 ■ 158 Commercial St ■ also cottage, lavish gardens, lesbian-owned ■ www.provincetown.com/rosecrown

Sandbars [GS] 800/223-0088 x160 ■ 570 Shore Rd, Beach Pt, North Truro ■ seasonal, all oceanfront rooms, private beach ■ www.sandbars.com

54 Seasons, An Inn for All [MW,NS,GO] 508/487-2283, 800/563-0113 ■ 160 Bradford St (at Pearl) ■ Victorian B&B, full brkfst ■ www.provincetownseasons.com

55 The Secret Garden Inn [MW,NS] 508/487-9027, 866/786-9646 ■ 300-A Commercial St ■ shared baths, sundeck, garden ■ www.secretgardenptown.com

3 Snug Cottage [GS,NS,WI,GO] 508/487-1616, 800/432-2334 ■ 178 Bradford St ■ boutique B&B ■ www.snugcottage.com

56 Somerset House [MW,NS,WI,GO] 508/487-0383, 800/575-1850 ■ 378 Commercial St (at Pearl) ■ Victorian mansion, "Provincetown's only hip & trendy boutique-style guesthouse" ■ www.somersethouseinn.com

Sunny West End Guest Apartment [MW,NS,GO] 508/487-9055 ■ sunny rental apt, balconies, jacuzzi, lesbian-owned ■ thatrabbittgirl@verizon.net

57 Sunset Inn [MW,N,NS,GO] 508/487-9810, 800/965-1801 ■ 142 Bradford St (at Center) ■ seasonal, some shared baths ■ www.sunsetinnptown.com

58 Surfside Hotel & Suites [GS,SW] 508/487-1726, 800/421-1726 ■ 543 Commercial St (at Kendall Ln) ■ seasonal, waterfront hotel w/ lots of amenities, private beach ■ www.surfsideinn.cc

59 The Tucker Inn [MW,NS,WI,GO] 508/487-0381, 800/477-1867 ■ 12 Center St ■ 1870s guesthouse & 1 cottage ■ www.thetuckerinn.com

60 Victoria House [MW,GO] 508/487-4455, 877/867-8696 ■ 5 Standish St ■ www.victoriahouseprovincetown.com

61 Watermark Inn [GS,NS] 508/487-0165 ■ 603 Commercial St ■ suites w/ kitchens, beachside ■ watermark-inn.com

26 Watership Inn [★M,WI,GO] 508/487-0094, 800/330-9413 ■ 7 Winthrop St ■ sundeck ■ www.watershipinn.com

39 West End Inn [GF,GO] 508/487-9555, 800/559-1220 ■ 44 Commercial St ■ seasonal ■ www.westendinn.com

Westville Cottage [GS,NS,WI,GO] 203/710-5733 ■ Pleasant St (at Kings Wy) ■ private condo for 2 ■ domathome-damron@yahoo.com

5 White Wind Inn [MW,NS,GO] 508/487-1526, 888/449-9463 ■ 174 Commercial St (at Winthrop) ■ well-appointed Provincetown landmark ■ www.whitewindinn.com

BARS

62 The Alibi [★GS,NH] 508/487-2890 ■ 291 Commercial St (at Rider) ■ noon-1am, from 10am summers, local favorite ■ ptownalibi.net

11 The Boatslip Beach Resort [★MW,D,F,YC] 508/487-1669, 877/786-9662 ■ 161 Commercial St (at Central) ■ seasonal, popular T-dance 4pm daily, special events, outdoor/ waterfront grill ■ www.boatslipresort.com

62 **Governor Bradford** [GF,F,E,K,DS] 508/487-2781 ■ 312 Commercial St (at Standish) ■ *11am-1am, from noon Sun, "drag karaoke" Sat (nightly in season), also restaurant in summer*

63 **PiedBar** [★MW,D,F,E,P,S,WC] 508/487-1527 ■ 193-A Commercial St (at Court St) ■ *seasonal May-Oct, noon-1am, more women Fri-Sat* ■ www.piedbar.com

31 **Porchside Lounge** [M,NH,P] 508/487-0688 ■ 11 Carver St (in the Gifford House) ■ *5pm-1am, Lobby Bar from 10pm, also restaurant* ■ www.giffordhouse.com

23 **Vault** [MO,B,L] 508/487-1430 ■ 247 Commercial St (downstairs in the Crown & Anchor) ■ *9pm-1am Fri-Sat only* ■ www.onlyatthecrown.com

44 **Vixen** [W,D,F,E,WC] 508/487-6424 ■ 336 Commercial St (at Pilgrim House Inn) ■ *noon-1am , late night food, also wine bar* ■ www.ptownvixen.com

23 **Wave Video Bar** [MW,NH,K] 508/487-1430 ■ 247 Commercial St (in the Crown & Anchor) ■ *6pm-1am, from noon in season, [K] Wed, more women Mon for G-Spot from 9pm in season, T-dance Sun from 6pm* ■ www.onlyatthecrown.com

NIGHTCLUBS

64 **Atlantic House (The "A-House")** [★M,D] 508/487-3169 ■ 6 Masonic Pl ■ *10pm-1am, 3 bars, weekly theme parties, also The Little Bar from noon [M,NH] & the Macho Bar [M,L]* ■ www.ahouse.com

31 **Club Purgatory** [MW,D,L] 508/487-8442 ■ 9-11 Carver St (at Bradford St, in the Gifford House) ■ *5pm-1am, theme nights, popular leather night Sun* ■ www.giffordhouse.com

63 **Girl Power** [W,D] 508/487-1527 ■ 193-A Commercial St (at The PiedBar) ■ *9:30-close, Fri-Sat only, seasonal* ■ www.girlpowerevents.com

23 **Paramount** [★MW,D,E,C,DS,$] 508/487-1430 ■ in the Crown & Anchor ■ *10pm-1am wknds, seasonal, Power T 6pm-9pm Sun (no cover Sun)* ■ www.onlyatthecrown.com

CAFES

Cicchetti's Espresso Bar 508/487-0036 ■ 353 Commercial St (at Angel's Landing) ■ *from 7am, seasonal, serves fair trade coffees (hot & frozen) & baked goods, women-owned*

Joe's 508/487-6656 ■ 148-A Commercial St (btwn Atlantic & Conant) ■ *7:30am-close, great coffee w/ a view*

Post Office Cafe Cabaret [MW,E] 508/487-3892 ■ 303 Commercial St (upstairs) ■ *8am-11pm (brkfst till 1pm), seasonal hours, some veggie*

RESTAURANTS

Bayside Betsy's [WC] 508/487-6566 ■ 177 Commercial St ■ *brkfst, lunch & dinner on waterfront, clsd Tue-Wed, bar till 10pm* ■ www.baysidebetsys.com

Big Daddy's Burritos 508/487-4432 ■ 205 Commercial St ■ *11am-10pm (May-Oct), Tex-Mex, burritos, veggie wraps, salads & nachos* ■ www.bigdaddysburritos.com

Bubala's by the Bay [★] 508/487-0773 ■ 183-185 Commercial ■ *seasonal, 8am-11pm, bar till 1am, patio* ■ www.bubalas.com

Chester [★] 508/487-8200 ■ 404 Commercial St ■ *dinner from 6pm, seasonal hours, upscale* ■ www.chesterrestaurant.com

Ciro & Sal's [R] 508/487-6444 ■ 4 Kiley Ct (btwn Bangs St & Lovett's Ct) ■ *dinner from 5:30pm, bar from 5pm, Northern Italian* ■ www.ciroandsals.com

Clem & Ursie's [BW] 508/487-2333 ■ 89 Shank Painter Rd ■ *11am-10pm, affordable outdoor dining, cuisine theme nights, also fish market, deli & grocery* ■ www.clemandursies.com

Fanizzi's [★WC] 508/487-1964 ■ 539 Commercial St (at Kendall Lane) ■ *open daily year round, lunch & dinner, some veggie, full bar, on the water* ■ www.fanizzisrestaurant.com

Front Street Restaurant [BW] 508/487-9715 ■ 230 Commercial St ■ *seasonal, 6pm-10:30pm, bistro, bar till 1am* ■ www.frontstreetrestaurant.com

Grand Central Cafe [★] 508/487-7599 ■ 5 Masonic Pl ■ *dinner, seasonal, full bar*

L'Uva Restaurant 508/487-2010 ■ 133 Bradford St ■ *classic Mediterranean/ New American, outdoor garden & full bar* ■ www.luvarestaurant.com

Lobster Pot [WC] 508/487-0842 ■ harborside (at 321 Commercial St) ■ *11:30am-10pm (April-Nov), seafood, some veggie, "a Provincetown tradition"* ■ www.ptownlobster-pot.com

Lorraine's [★MW,BW,GO] 508/487-6074 ■ 133 Commercial St ■ *dinner, clsd Th-Sun off-season, Mexican* ■ www.lorrainesrestaurant.com

Martin House [WC] 508/487-1327 ■ 157 Commercial St (at Atlantic Street Landing) ■ *6pm-close, clsd Wed, clsd Jan, outdoor dining (summers), full bar* ■ www.themartinhouse.com

The Mews Restaurant & Cafe [★E,WC] 508/487-1500 ■ 429 Commercial St (btwn Lovett's & Kiley) ■ *dinner, Sun brunch, also Cafe Mews upstairs, waterfront dining* ■ www.mews.com

Napi's Restaurant [WC] 508/487-1145, 800/571-6274 ■ 7 Freeman St ■ *dinner (lunch Oct-April), int'l/ seafood, plenty veggie* ■ www.napis-restaurant.com

Sal's Place [★] 508/487-1279 ■ 99 Commercial St ■ *seasonal, seafood/ Italian (publisher's choice: cheese & butter pasta), deck, on the water* ■ Salsplace@mindspring.com

Spiritus Pizza [★] 508/487-2808 ■ 190 Commercial St ■ *noon-2am, great espresso shakes & late-night hangout for a slice* ■ www.spirituspizza.com

ENTERTAINMENT & RECREATION

Art's Dune Tours [GO] 508/487-1950, 800/894-1951 ■ 4 Standish St ■ *day trips, sunset tours & charters through historic sand dunes & Nat'l Seashore Park* ■ www.artsdunetours.com

Ptown Bikes [GO] 508/487-8735 ■ 42 Bradford ■ *rentals* ■ www.ptownbikes.com

Spaghetti Strip ■ *nude beach, 1.5 miles S of Race Point Beach*

BOOKSTORES

65 **Now, Voyager Bookstore & Gallery** 508/487-0848 ■ 357 Commercial St ■ *10am-10pm (summers), LGBT & general books, cards* ■ www.nowvoyagerbooks.com

Provincetown Bookshop 508/487-0964 ■ 246 Commercial St ■ *10am-11pm (till 4:30pm off-season)*

RETAIL SHOPS

Don't Panic 508/487-1280 ■ 200 Commercial St ■ *seasonal, 10am-10pm, LGBT gifts* ■ www.dont-panic.com

Piercings by the Bearded Lady [GO] 508/487-7979 ■ 336 Commercial St #4

Recovering Hearts [WC] 508/487-4875 ■ 2-4 Standish St ■ *10am-11pm (in summer), call for off-season hours, recovery, LGBT & New Age titles*

66 **Womencrafts** 508/487-2501 ■ 376 Commercial St (at Pearl St) ■ *11am-10pm (in summer), call for off-season hours, jewelry, pottery, books, music, gifts, etc* ■ www.womencrafts.com

PUBLICATIONS

In Newsweekly 617/426-8246 ■ *New England's largest LGBT newspaper* ■ www.innewsweekly.com

Provincetown Banner 508/487-7400 ■ *newspaper* ■ www.provincetownbanner.com/articles/

Provincetown Magazine 508/487-1000 ■ *seasonal, Provincetown's oldest weekly magazine* ■ www.province-town.com

GYMS & HEALTH CLUBS

Mussel Beach Health Club [MW] 508/487-0001 ■ 35 Bradford St (btwn Montello & Conant) ■ *6am-9pm, till 8pm in winter* ■ www.musselbeach.net

Provincetown Gym [MW] 508/487-2776 ■ 82 Shank Painter Rd (at Winthrop) ■ *6am-9pm, 7am-7pm wknds (till 9pm in season)* ■ www.ptowngym.com

EROTICA

<u>MG Leather Inc</u> [GO] 508/487-4036 ■ 338 Commercial St (at Standish St) ■ *leather, fetish, toys, gifts* ■ www.mgleather.com

<u>Wild Hearts</u> 508/487-8933 ■ 244 Commercial St ■ *11am-11pm (in summer), noon-5pm (off-season), toys for women* ■ www.wildhearts.com

Detroit

ACCOMMODATIONS

1 **The Atheneum Suite Hotel** [GF,WC] 313/962-2323, 800/772-2323 ■ 1000 Brush St (at Lafayette) ■ *luxury all-suite hotel, restaurant & lounge, gym* ■ www.atheneum-suites.com

2 **Milner Hotel** [GF] 313/963-3950, 877/645-6377 ■ 1526 Centre St ■ *downtown* ■ www.milner-hotels.com

3 **Shorecrest Motor Inn** [GF,WC] 313/568-3000, 800/992-9616 ■ 1316 E Jefferson Ave ■ *downtown, also restaurant* ■ www.shorecrestmi.com

4 **Woodbridge Star B&B** [GS,NS,GO] 313/831-9668 ■ 3985 Trumbull Ave ■ *in Victorian home, full brkfst, hot tub* ■ www.woodbridgestar.com

BARS

5 **Adam's Apple** [M,NH] 313/240-8482 ■ 18937 W Warren (at Artesian) ■ *3pm-2am, from noon wknds*

DETROIT

Tourist Info

AIRPORT DIRECTIONS

Detroit International. To get downtown, take I-94 East into Detroit. Take the exit for Federal Hwy 10 and head south until Hwy 10 runs into I-75 and East Jefferson Ave.

PUBLIC TRANSIT & TAXIS

Checker Cab 313/963-7000, web: www.checkersedan.com.

Dynasty 800/445-5418, web: www.dynastyservices.com.

DOT bus service 313/933-1300 & 888/336-8287 (outside 313 area code), web: www.ci.detroit.mi.us/ddot.

Detroit People Mover 313/962-7245, web: www.thepeoplemover.com.

TOURIST SPOTS & INFO

Belle Isle Park 313/852-4075.
Detroit Institute of Arts 313/833-7900, web: www.dia.org.
Ford Detroit International Jazz Festival, web: www.detroitjazzfest.com.
Greektown.
Motown Historical Museum 313/875-2264, web: www.motownmuseum.com.
Museum of African American History 313/494-5800, web: www.maah-detroit.org.
North American Black Historical Museum in Windsor, Ontario, 800/713-6336, web: www.blackhistoricalmuseum.com.
Renaissance Center 313/259-5400, web: www.detroitrenaissance.com.
Visitor's Center: 313/202-1800 or 800/338-7648, web: www.visitdetroit.com.

Weather

Be prepared for hot, humid summers and cold, dry winters.

Best Views

From the top of the 73-story Marriott Hotel at the Renaissance Center.

City Calendar

LGBT PRIDE

June. 313/537-3323 (Triangle Foundation #), web: www.pridefest.net.
July. Hotter Than July, web: www.hotterthanjuly.com. "The Midwest's oldest black lesbian, gay, bi-affectionate and transgender pride celebration."

ANNUAL EVENTS

January - Reel Pride Michigan Film Festival 313/537-3323 x103, web: www.reelpridemichigan.com.
End of April/early May - London Lesbian Film Festival 519/434-0246, web: www.www.llff.ca. Held in London, Ontario, Canada, but worth the trip. Women only.
August - Michigan Womyn's Music Festival 231/757-4766, web: www.michfest.com. One of the biggest annual gatherings of lesbians on the continent, in Walhalla.

Queer Resources

COMMUNITY INFO

Affirmations Lesbian/Gay Community Center 248/398-7105. 195 W 9 Mile Rd, Ferndale, 9am-9pm, till 11pm Fri-Sat, clsd Sun, web: www.goaffirmations.org.
Lesbian/Gay Switchboard 800/398-4297. 4pm-9pm, till 11pm Fri-Sat.

6 **Club Gold Coast** [★M,D,DS,S,WC] 313/366-6135 ■ 2971 E 7 Mile Rd (at Conant) ■ 7pm-2am, till 5am Fri-Sat, male dancers nightly ■ www.detroitsclubgoldcoast.com

7 **Detroit Eagle** [★M,D,L,WC] 313/873-6969 ■ 1501 Holden (at Trumbull) ■ 8pm-2am, from 5pm Fri, clsd Mon-Tue, patio ■ www.detroiteagle.com

8 **Diamond Jim's Saloon** [M,NH,D,CW,B,L,MR,F,K,GO] 313/336-8680 ■ 19650 Warren (1 block E of Evergreen) ■ noon-2am, dance lessons, also Round Up Grill ■ www.diamondjimssaloon.com

9 **Gigi's** [M,D,TG,K,DS,S,GO] 313/584-6525 ■ 16920 W Warren (at Clayburn, enter rear) ■ noon-2am, from 2pm wknds, dancers ■ www.gigisbar.com

10 **Hayloft Saloon** [M,NH,B,L,OC,WC] 313/581-8913 ■ 8070 Greenfield Rd (S of Joy Rd) ■ 3pm-2am, cruise bar for leathermen, bears, daddies, mature men ■ www.hayloftsaloon.com

11 **Male Box Bar** [M,NH,D,K,18+,GO] 313/892-5420 ■ 3537 E 7 Mile Rd (btwn Conant & Ryan) ■ 2pm-2:30am, [CW] Wed, T-dance Sun ■ www.maleboxbar.com

12 **Menjo's** [★M,D,V,YC] 313/863-3934 ■ 928 W McNichols (at Hamilton) ■ 1pm-2am, till 10pm Mon-Wed, popular happy hour

13 **Pronto** [★MW,F,V] 248/544-7900 ■ 608 S Washington (at 6th St), Royal Oak ■ 11am-2am Wed-Sat, till midnight Sun-Tue, patio, also restaurant ■ www.prontorestaurant.com

14 **R&R Saloon** [M,NH,D,L,F] 313/849-2751 ■ 7330 Michigan Ave (at Central) ■ 2pm-2am

15 **Soho** [M] 248/542-7646 ■ 205 W 9 Mile (at Woodward), Ferndale ■ 4pm-close, from 6pm wknds ■ www.qferndale.com/soho/soho.html

16 **Stingers Lounge** [MW,NH,F,DS,GO] 313/892-1765 ■ 19404 Sherwood (at 7 Mile) ■ 6pm-5am, from 8pm wknds

17 **The Woodward Bar & Grill** [★M,D,MR,F,K] 313/872-0166 ■ 6426 Woodward Ave (at Milwaukee, rear entrance) ■ 2pm-2am, lounge, DJ Th-Sun

18 **The Works Detroit** [GS,D,V] 313/961-1742 ■ 1846 Michigan Ave (at Rosa Parks) ■ 10pm-3am Th, till 5am Fri, till 6am Sat, mostly gay men Sat ■ www.theworksdetroit.com

NIGHTCLUBS

19 **Backstreet** [★M,D,18+,WC,$] 313/838-6699 ■ 15606 Joy Rd (at Greenfield) ■ 9pm-2am Wed, Fri-Sat, 5 levels ■ www.boysonjoy.com

20 **Ice** [M,D] 313/365-1446 ■ 1142 Joseph Campau St, Hamtramck ■ gay Sat only ■ www.icedetroit.net

21 **Inuendo** [MW,D,K,DS] 313/891-5798 ■ 744 E Savannah (at 6 1/2 Mile & I-75), Highland Park ■ 10pm-5am, till 2am Sun-Wed, clsd Mon ■ inuendodet@aol.com

22 **Leland City Club/ The Labyrinth** [GF,D,A,18+] 400 Bagley St (enter through unmarked door on First St side of Ramada Hotel building; club at top of stairwell) ■ 10pm-4:30am Fri-Sat, goth/ alternative crowd ■ www.lelandcityclub.net

Luna [GF,D,A] 248/589-3344 ■ 1815 N Main St (at 12 Mile), Royal Oak ■ from 9pm, clsd Sun-Mon, goth/alternative crowd, theme nights ■ www.lunaroyaloak.com

23 **Pandora's Box** [★MW,D,MR-AF,K,DS,S,WC] 313/892-8120 ■ 6221 E Davison (at Mound) ■ 9pm-2am Th-Sat, more women Sat

24 **Pink** [W,D,E] 313/521-8433 ■ 19910 Hoover Rd

25 **The Rainbow Room** [MW,D,K,DS,18+] 313/891-1020 ■ 6640 E 8 Mile Rd (btwn Mound Rd & Van Dyke Ave) ■ 7pm-2am Wed-Sun ■ www.clubrainbowroom.com

Stiletto's [W,D,E,K] 734/729-8980 ■ 1641 Middlebelt Rd (btwn Michigan Ave & Cherry Hill Rd), Inkster ■ 8pm-2am Th-Sun ■ clubs.yahoo.com/clubs/stilettos

26 **Temple** [GS,D,MR-AF,TG,WC] 313/832-2822 ■ 2906 Cass Ave (btwn Charlotte & Temple) ■ 11am-2am, popular wknds ■ thetemplebar@aol.com

CAFES

Avalon International Breads [GO] 313/832-0008 ■ 422 W Willis (at Cass) ■ 6am-6pm, clsd Sun-Mon, lesbian-owned

Coffee Beanery Cafe 248/543-9434 ■ 22871 S Woodward Ave (at 9 Mile), Ferndale ■ 7am-11pm

Meetery Eatery [MR,F] 313/758-0136 ■ 5408 Woodward Ave ■ www.meeteryeatery.com

Trixie's Cafe [E] 586/776-9002 ■ 25925 Gratiot Ave, Roseville ■ 10am-1am, from 6pm Sun, hosts open mics ■ trixiescoffee.com

RESTAURANTS

Amici's Living Room 248/544-4100 ■ 3249 12 Mile Rd, Berkley ■ gourmet pizza & martinis ■ www.amicispizza.com

Cass Cafe [WI] 313/831-1400 ■ 4620 Cass Ave (at Forest) ■ 11am-2am, 5pm-midnight Sun, full bar ■ www.casscafe.com

Como's [WC] 248/548-5005 ■ 22812 Woodward (at 9 Mile), Ferndale ■ 11am-2am, till 3:30am Th-Sat, Italian, Sun brunch, full bar, patio ■ www.comospizza.com

Inn Season 248/547-7916 ■ 500 E 4th St, Royal Oak ■ vegetarian

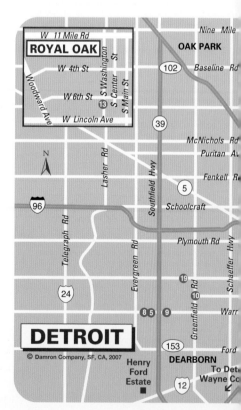

La Dolce Vita [MW,WC] 313/865-0331 ■ 17546 Woodward Ave (at McNichols) ■ *lunch & dinner, Sun brunch, clsd Mon, Italian, patio, full bar*

Pronto [★MW] 248/544-7900 ■ 608 S Washington (at 6th St), Royal Oak ■ *11am-10pm, till midnight Fri, 9am-10pm Sat, patio, also video bar* ■ www.prontorestaurant.com

Starving Artist [GO] 248/545-5650 ■ 212 W 9 Mile (1/2 block W of Woodward), Ferndale ■ *lunch & dinner, clsd Sun-Mon, plenty veggie, full bar* ■ info@starvingartistferndale.com

Sweet Lorraine's Cafe & Bar [★WC] 248/559-5985 ■ 29101 Greenfield Rd (at 12 Mile), Southfield ■ *11am-10pm, till 11pm Fri-Sat, till 9:30pm Sun, modern American, some veggie* ■ www.sweetlorraines.com

Traffic Jam & Snug 313/831-9470 ■ 511 W Canfield St (at SE corner of 2nd Ave) ■ *11am-10:30pm, till midnight Fri, from noon Sat, till 8pm Sun, eclectic, plenty veggie, also full bar, bakery, dairy & brewery* ■ www.traffic-jam.com

Vivio's 313/393-1711 ■ 2460 Market St (btwn Gratiot & Russell) ■ *lunch & dinner, clsd Sun, Italian, some veggie*

ENTERTAINMENT & RECREATION

Charles H Wright Museum of African American History 313/494-5800 ■ 315 E Warren Ave (at Brush) ■ www.maah-detroit.org

Detroit Derby Girls ■ *Detroit's female roller derby league, check web for upcoming events* ■ www.detroitrollerderby.com

Detroit Shock Palace of Auburn Hills, Auburn Hills ■ *check out the Women's National Basketball Association while you're in Detroit* ■ www.wnba.com/shock

Detroit Together Men's Chorus 248/544-3872 ■ 2441 Pinecrest, Ferndale ■ www.dtmc.org

Element [GS,MR,E] 35 W Grand River (at Woodward) ■ *live music, poetry readings, hip hop, house music & more* ■ elementcafe@gmail.com

Motown Historical Museum 313/875-2264 ■ 2648 W Grand Blvd ■ www.motownmuseum.com

BOOKSTORES

27 **Chosen Books** [WC] 248/543-5758, 800/453-5758 ■ 1956 Hilton (at E 9 Mile), Ferndale ■ *noon-10pm, LGBT*

28 **Just 4 Us** [GO] 248/547-5878 ■ 211 W 9 Mile Rd (at Woodward), Ferndale ■ *noon-8pm, till 10pm Th-Fri, 10am-8pm Sat, 11am-5pm Sun, also cafe* ■ www.just4usmi.com

RETAIL SHOPS

Royal Oak Tattoo 248/398-0052 ■ 820 S Washington St, Royal Oak ■ *noon-8pm, till 9pm Fri-Sat, clsd Sun, tattoo & piercing studio* ■ www.royaloaktattoo.com

PUBLICATIONS

Between the Lines 734/293-7200, 888/615-7003 ■ *statewide LGBT weekly* ■ www.pridesource.com

Metra Magazine 248/543-3500 ■ *covers IN, IL, MI, OH, PA, WI & Ontario, Canada* ■ www.metramagazine.com

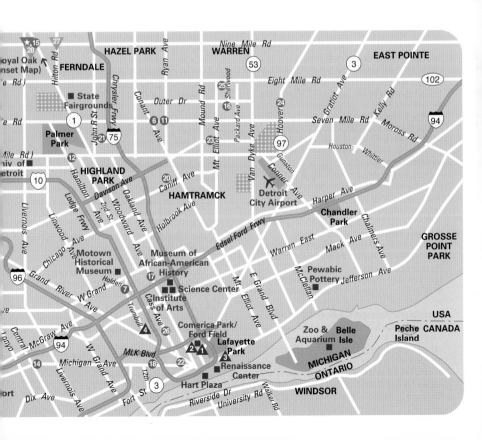

MEN'S CLUBS

Body Zone Health Club [★MO,V,18+,PC,GO]
313/366-9663 ■ 1617 E McNichols (at I-75) ■ *24hrs, gym & steam, sauna & tanning, day passes, "Detroit's busiest gay health club"* ■ bodyzonedetroit.com

TNT Health Club [★MO,V,18+,PC,GO,$] 313/341-5322
■ 13333 W 8 Mile Rd (at Schaefer, enter rear) ■ *24hrs*

EROTICA

24hr Video 313/869-2955 ■ 17438 Woodward Ave (N of McNichols Rd) ■ *11am-4am* ■ xxx24hourvideo@aol.com

Blue Moon Video 313/340-1730 ■ 7041 W 8 Mile Rd (2 blocks W of Livernois) ■ *11am-1am, till 10pm Sun* ■ www.bluemoonvideodvd.com

Escape Adult Bookstore 313/336-6558 ■ 18728 W Warren Ave (8 blocks W of Southfield)

Fifth Wheel Adult Books 313/846-8613 ■ 9320 Michigan Ave (at Wyoming)

Noir Leather [WC] 248/541-3979 ■ 124 W 4th St (at S Center St), Royal Oak ■ *11am-9pm, till 7pm Fri-Sat, noon-7pm Sun, leather, S&M gear, toys, fetishwear* ■ www.noir-leather.com

Uptown Book Store 313/869-9477 ■ 16541 Woodward Ave (at 6 Mile Rd)

Saugatuck

ACCOMMODATIONS

Beechwood Manor Inn [GS,NS,WI,GO] 269/857-1587, 877/857-1587 ■ 736 Pleasant St ■ *upscale inn, full brkfst* ■ www.beechwoodmanorinn.com

1 **The Belvedere Inn & Restaurant** [GF,NS,GO]
269/857-5777 ■ 3656 63rd St ■ *boutique inn in 1913 mansion, full gourmet brkfrst* ■ www.thebelvedereinn.com

2 **Bird Center Resort** [GF,WI] 269/857-3900,
269/857-1750 ■ 584-586 Lake St ■ *3 cottages across from Sautatuck Harbor, 2 w/ hot tubs* ■ www.quaintcottages.com

The Bunkhouse B&B [MW,SW,NS,WI,GO] 269/543-4335, 877/226-7481 ■ *access to Campit Resort amenities (see below)* ■ www.campitresort.com

Campit Outdoor Resort [MW,SW,WI,GO] 269/543-4335, 877/226-7481 ■ 6635 118th Ave, Fennville ■ *seasonal, campsites & RV hookups, also B&B* ■ www.campitresort.com

Deerpath Lodge [WO,SW] 269/857-DEER, 888/DEERPATH ■ *deluxe private suites on 40 waterfront acres, hot tub, kayaks*

3 **Douglas House B&B** [GS,NS,GO] 269/857-1119, 248/478-9392 (winter) ■ 41 Spring St, Douglas ■ *near gay beach*

4 **The Dunes Resort** [MW,D,TG,F,E,DS,SW,WC,GO]
269/857-1401 ■ 333 Blue Star Hwy, Douglas ■ *motel & cottages, open year-round* ■ www.dunesresort.com

The Glenn Country Inn [GS,GO] 269/227-3045, 888/237-3009 ■ 1286 64th St (at 113th Ave), Fennville ■ *"SW Michigan's #1 pet-friendly B&B"* ■ www.glenncountryinn.com

5 **Hidden Garden Cottages & Suites** [GF,NS,WI]
269/857-8109, 888/857-8109 ■ 247 Butler St ■ *cottages & suites for 2* ■ www.hiddengardencottages.com

Hillby Thatch Cottages [GS,NS] 847/864-3553 ■ 71st St, Glenn ■ *15 minutes from Saugatuck, kids ok, woman-owned* ■ www.hillbythatch.com

Hooten Inn [GS] 269/857-1039 ■ 6541 Blue Star Hwy (at Washinton) ■ *boutique motel* ■ www.HootenInn.com

6 **The Hunter's Lodge** [GS,NS] 269/857-5402 ■ 2790 Blue Star Hwy (at US 31), Douglas ■ *motel in rustic lodge, kids/pets ok* ■ www.thehunterslodge.com

J Paules Fenn Inn [GF,NS] 269/561-2836, 877/561-2836 ■ 2254 S 58th St, Fennville ■ www.jpaulesfenninn.org

The Kingsley House B&B [GF,NS,WI,GO] 269/561-6425, 866/561-6425 ■ 626 West Main St, Fennville ■ *B&B in Victorian Queen Anne mansion, full brkfst* ■ www.kingsley-house.com

7 **Kirby House** [GS,SW,NS,WI,GO] 269/857-2904, 800/521-6473 ■ 294 W Center (at Blue Star Hwy) ■ *Queen Anne Victorian* ■ www.kirbyhouse.com

8 **Lake Street Commons** [GF,NS,WI,GO] 269/857-1680 ■ 790 Lake St ■ *suites w/ kitchen & private decks, jacuzzi* ■ www.lakestreetcommons.com

9 **Maple Ridge Cottages** [GS,NS,GO] 269/857-5211 (Pines #) ■ 713-719 Maple ■ *quaint 2-brdm & 1-bath cottages w/ private hot tubs* ■ www.thepinesmotorlodge.com

10 **Mason Street B&B & Suites** [GF,NS,GO] 866/857-5553 ■ 320 Mason St ■ *kitchenettes in suites, full brkfst in B&B, open year-round* ■ www.homestead.com/masonstreet-suites

11 **Moore's Creek Inn** [GF,NS] 269/857-5241 ■ 820 Holland St (at Lucy) ■ *old-fashioned farmhouse* ■ www.moore-screekinn.com

12 **The Newnham SunCatcher Inn** [GF,SW,NS,GO]
269/857-4249 ■ 131 Griffith (at Mason) ■ *full brkfst, hot tub, lesbian-owned* ■ www.suncatcherinn.com

13 **The Park House Inn B&B** [GF,NS,WI] 269/857-4535, 866/321-4535 ■ 888 Holland St ■ *B&B in one of Saugatuck's oldest residences, full brkfst, also cottages* ■ www.parkhouseinn.com

14 **The Pines Motor Lodge** [GS,NS,GO] 269/857-5211 ■ 56 Blue Star Hwy (at Center St), Douglas ■ *boutique retro motel, also retro gift gallery* ■ www.thepinesmotorlodge.com

15 **The Spruce Cutter's Cottage** [GS,GO] 269/543-4285, 800/493-5888 ■ 6670 126th Ave (at Blue Star Hwy & M-89), Fennville ■ *full brkfst* ■ www.sprucecutters.com

16 **Timber Bluff** [NS] 269/857-2586 ■ 2731 Lakeshore Dr, Fennville ■ *cottages on Lake Michigan* ■ timberbluff.net

17 **The Timberline Motel** [GF,SW] 269/857-2147, 800/257-2147 ■ 3353 Blue Star Hwy ■ *open year-round, jacuzzi* ■ www.timberlinemotel.com

BARS

4 **Dunes Disco** [★MW,D,TG,E,C,DS,GO] 269/857-1401 ■ 333 Blue Star Hwy (at the Dunes Resort) ■ *9am-2am, 6 bars, T-dance, patio* ■ www.dunesresort.com

CAFES

Uncommon Grounds 269/857-3333 ■ 127 Hoffman (at Water) ■ *7am-9pm, organic coffee & juice bar* ■ www.uncommongroundscafe.com

The Yum Yum Gourmet Cafe & Gelateria [GS,GO] 269/857-4567 ■ 98 Center St, lower level (at Union St), Douglas ■ *also paninis, soup, salad*

RESTAURANTS

Back Alley Pizza Joint 269/857-7277 ■ 22 Main St, Douglas ■ *11am-9pm, till 10pm Fri-Sun, fresh grinder bread daily*

Blue Frog [MW] 269/857-1401 x143 ■ in the Dunes Resort ■ *11am-5pm, clsd Tue, open May-Oct only, take-out only* ■ www.dunesresort.com

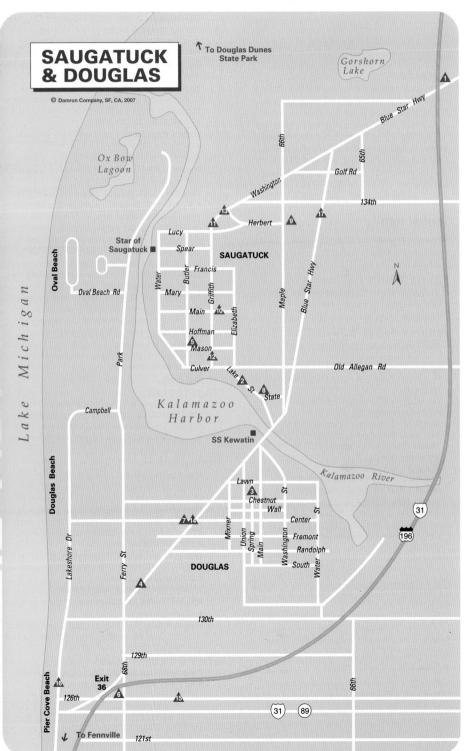

SAUGATUCK & DOUGLAS

© Damron Company, SF, CA, 2007

To Douglas Dunes State Park

Gorshorn Lake

Ox Bow Lagoon

Blue Star Hwy

66th

65th

Golf Rd

134th

Washington

Herbert

SAUGATUCK

Lucy

Spear

Star of Saugatuck

Francis

Butler

Water

Griffith

Mary

Main

Hoffman

Mason

Culver

Elizabeth

Maple

Blue Star Hwy

Old Allegan Rd

N

Lake St

State

Oval Beach

Oval Beach Rd

Park

Campbell

Lake Michigan

Kalamazoo Harbor

SS Kewatin

Kalamazoo River

Lawn

Chestnut

Wall

Center

Fremont

Randolph

South

Mixner

Union

Spring

Main

Washington

Water

St

St

Douglas Beach

DOUGLAS

Lakeshore Dr

Ferry St

130th

129th

68th

Exit 36

126th

To Fennville

121st

Pier Cove Beach

31

196

31

31

89

SAUGATUCK

Local Food:
Here's a tip from a local: you will find the most AWESOME blueberries in west Michigan during their season, which begins in late July. If you can't find a U-Pick farm or orchard nearby, search these blue beauties out at the local farmers market. Western Michigan is part of the "fruit belt" that surrounds Lake Michigan, so you will also find strawberries, cherries, and apples in abundance during the summer and early fall.

Tourist Info

AIRPORT DIRECTIONS
Kent County Airport in Grand Rapids, Michigan. 2 hours from Chicago.

PUBLIC TRANSIT & TAXIS
Saugatuck Douglas Taxi Service 269/543-3355, web: www.saugatuckdouglas.com.
Interurban Transit Authority 269/857-1418.

TOURIST SPOTS & INFO
Fenn Valley Wineries 269/561-2396, web: www.fennvalley.com.
Galleries.
Historical Holland (home of the Wooden Shoe Factory).
Lakeshore Jazz Connection, web: www.lakeshore-jazzconnection.org.
Mason Street Warehouse (theatre) 269/857-4898, web: www.masonstreetwarehouse.org.
Saugatuck Center for the Arts 269/857-2399, web: www.sc4a.org.
Saugatuck Dunes State Park.
Saugatuck-Douglas Historical Society Museum 269/857-7900, web: www.sdhistory.com.
Visitor's Center: Saugatuck-Douglas Convention & Visitors Bureau 269/857-1701, web: www.saugatuck.com.
City of the Village of Douglas, web: www.douglas-michigan.com.
Holland Chamber of Commerce 616/392-2389, web: www.holland-chamber.org.

City Calendar

ANNUAL EVENTS
May - Tulip Time Festival, Holland 800/822-2770, web: www.tuliptime.org.
June - Waterfront Film Festival 269/857-8351, web: www.waterfrontfilm.com.
August - Michigan Womyn's Music Festival 231/757-4766, web: www.michfest.com. One of the biggest annual gatherings of lesbians on the continent, in Walhalla.
August - Camp Trans, web: www.camp-trans.org.

Blue Moon Bar & Grille 269/857-8686 ■ 310 Blue Star Hwy (corner of Wiley Rd), Douglas ■ *11am-11pm, contemporary cuisine w/ int'l flair, full bar* ■ www.blue-moonbarandgrille.com

The Boathouse [E] 269/857-2888 ■ 449 Water St ■ *dinner nightly, live music wknds* ■ www.the-boathouse.net

Everyday People Cafe [E] 269/857-4240 ■ 11 Center St, Douglas ■ *brunch wknds, dinner Th-Tue, clsd Wed, live jazz in patio wine garden Th-Sun till 1am, eclectic comfort food* ■ www.everydaypeoplecafe.com

Kalico Kitchen 269/857-2678 ■ 312 Ferry St, Douglas ■ *6am-9pm winter, till midnight summer, American* ■ www.kalicokitchenrestaurant.com

Monroe's Cafe-Grille [NS] 269/857-1242 ■ 302 Culver St ■ *9am-3pm, 8am-9pm Fri-Sun, clsd Th, ribs*

Phil's Bar & Grille 269/857-1555 ■ 215 Butler St ■ *11:30am-10pm, till 11pm Fri-Sat, noon-10pm Sun, patio*

Pumpernickel's 269/857-1196 ■ 202 Butler St (at Mason) ■ *seasonal, brkfst, lunch & dinner, sandwiches & fresh breads, some veggie* ■ www.pumpernickelssaugatuck.com

Restaurant Toulouse [R,WC] 269/857-1561 ■ 248 Culver St (at Griffith) ■ *dinner nightly, lunch wknds (dinner only, clsd Mon-Wed winters), country French, some veggie, full bar* ■ www.restauranttoulouse.com

The White House Bistro [E] 269/857-3240 ■ corner of Mason & Griffith ■ *4pm-9:30pm, 9am-midnight Sat, 9am-9pm Sun, live music* ■ www.whitehousebistro.com

ENTERTAINMENT & RECREATION
Earl's Farm Market 269/543-3156 ■ 1630 Blue Star Hwy, Fennville ■ *8am-9pm May-Oct only, pick your own berries!* ■ www.earlsberries.com

Oval Beach

BOOKSTORES
Open Door Music & Books 269/857-4565, 888/613-8570 ■ 403 Water St ■ *New Age books, cards, gifts, CDs* ■ www.opendoormusicandbooks.com

Singapore Bank Bookstore 269/857-3785 ■ 317 Butler St (upstairs) ■ *general, new & used*

RETAIL SHOPS
Amaru Leather 269/857-3745 ■ 322 Griffith St ■ *"original & custom creations in leather by two resident designers"*

Circa Antiques, Arts & Accessories [GO] 269/857-7676 ■ 98 Center St (at Union St), Douglas ■ *10am-5pm, antiques, art, furnishings & accessories from a range of periods* ■ www.circahousewares.com

Groovy! Groovy! Retro Gift Gallery [GO] 269/857-2171 ■ 56 Blue Star Hwy (at Center St), Douglas ■ *seasonal hours, antiques, funky gifts & goods* ■ www.thepinesmotorlodge.com/groovy.htm

Hoopdee Scootee 269/857-4141 ■ 133 Mason (at Butler) ■ *seasonal, clothing, gifts*

Saugatuck Drug Store 269/857-2300 ■ 201 Butler St ■ *seasonal, old-fashioned corner drug store, including actual soda fountain!*

GYMS & HEALTH CLUBS
Pump House Gym 269/857-7867 ■ 6492 Blue Star Hwy ■ *day passes* ■ www.pumphousegym.info

MINNESOTA

Minneapolis/ St Paul

ACCOMMODATIONS

1   **The Chambers** [GF,WI,WC] 612/767-6900 ■ 901 Hennepin Ave, Minneapolis ■ *chic, art-filled hotel; also restaurant* ■ www.chambersminneapolis.com

Cover Park Manor [GF,NS] 651/430-9292, 877/430-9292 ■ 15330 58th St N (at Peller), Stillwater ■ *full brkfst, in-room jacuzzi & fireplace, kids ok* ■ www.coverpark.com

2   **Hotel Amsterdam** [M,WI,GO] 612/288-0459 ■ 828 Hennepin Ave (btwn 8th & 9th), Minneapolis ■ *shared baths, above The Saloon Bar* ■ www.gaympls.com

3   **Millennium Hotel Minneapolis** [GF,F,SW,WI,WC] 612/332-6000, 866/866-8086 ■ 1313 Nicollet Mall (btwn W Grant & 13th St), Minneapolis ■ *also restaurant & bar* ■ www.millennium-hotels.com

4   **Nan's B&tB** [GF,NS] 612/377-5118 ■ 2304 Fremont Ave S (at 22nd), Minneapolis ■ *1895 Victorian family home, full brkfst, shared bath* ■ www.virtualcities.com/mn/nan.htm

Quill & Quilt [GF,NS,WI,GO] 507/263-5507, 800/488-3849 ■ 615 Hoffman St W (at Hwy 52 & Hwy 19), Cannon Falls ■ www.quilllandquilt.com

BARS

5   **19 Bar** [M,NH,WC] 612/871-5553 ■ 19 W 15th St (at La Salle), Minneapolis ■ *3pm-2am*

6   **Bev's Wine Bar** [GF] 612/337-0102 ■ 250 3rd Ave N (at Washington Ave), Minneapolis ■ *4:30pm-1am, from 6:30pm Sat, clsd Sun-Mon, patio*

7   **Brass Rail** [★M,E,K,DS,P,S,V,WC] 612/333-3016 ■ 422 Hennepin Ave (at 4th), Minneapolis ■ *2pm-2am, dancers Th-Sat* ■ www.gaympls.com

8   **Bryant Lake Bowl** [GF,A,F,E,WC] 612/825-3737 ■ 810 W Lake St (near Bryant), Minneapolis ■ *8am-2am, bar, theater, restaurant & bowling alley* ■ www.bryantlakebowl.com

9   **The Independent** [GS,F] 612/378-1905 ■ 3001 Hennepin Ave (in Calhoun Square, upstairs), Minneapolis ■ *11am-2am, Sun brunch, great martini selection* ■ www.theindependent-uptown.com

10   **Jetset** [MW,NS] 612/339-3933 ■ 115 N First St (at 1st Ave N), Minneapolis ■ *5pm-close, from 6pm Sat, clsd Sun-Mon, upscale*

11   **Minneapolis Eagle** [M,B,L,F] 612/338-4214 ■ 515 Washington Ave S (btwn Portland & 5th Ave), Minneapolis ■ *4pm-2am, till 3am Fri-Sat, from noon wknds, patio, dress code encouraged Fri-Sat, beer bust Sun, Bear Night 2nd Th* ■ www.minneapoliseagle.com

12   **Times Bar/ Jitters** [GF,E,C] 612/617-8098 ■ 201 E Hennepin Ave (at 2nd St NE), Minneapolis ■ *11am-1am, 10am-11pm Sun (jazz brunch), also cafe & restaurant* ■ www.timesbarandcafe.com

13   **The Town House** [★MW,D,E,K,C,DS,P] 651/646-7087 ■ 1415 University Ave W (at Elbert), St Paul ■ *3pm-2am, from noon wknds, theme nights* ■ www.townhousebar.com

NIGHTCLUBS

11   **The Bolt** [M,D,MR,F,V,WC,GO] 612/338-0896 ■ 513 Washington Ave S (at Portland), Minneapolis ■ *7pm-2:30am, from 5pm Fri, from 4pm Sun* ■ www.boltbar.com

Diva Riot [W,D] Minneapolis ■ *monthly women's dance parties, check www.divariot.com for details* ■ www.divariot.com

14   **Gay 90s** [★MW,D,MR,F,E,K,DS,18+,WC] 612/333-7755 ■ 408 Hennepin Ave (at 4th), Minneapolis ■ *8am-2am (dinner nightly 5pm-9:30pm), 9-bar complex, also Men's Room [MO,L]* ■ www.gay90s.com

15   **Ground Zero/ The Front** [★GS,D,A,S,WC] 612/378-5115 ■ 15 NE 4th St (at Hennepin), Minneapolis ■ *10pm-2am Th-Sat only, more gay Th for Bondage-A-Go-Go, also The Front lounge from 9pm* ■ grndzero@attibi.com

16   **Krave** [M,D] 612/340-1100 ■ 315 1st Ave N (at 3rd St N, in Karma), Minneapolis ■ *seasonal monthly party, call for info* ■ www.kravempls.com

17   **The Saloon** [★M,D,F,S,YC,WC,GO] 612/332-0835 ■ 830 Hennepin Ave (at 9th), Minneapolis ■ *10pm-close, grill open from 5pm Mon-Sat, theme nights, [18+] Mon & Th* ■ www.gaympls.com

CAFES

Anodyne at 43rd [F,E,WC] 612/824-4300 ■ 4301 Nicollet Ave S (at 43rd), Minneapolis ■ *6:30am-10pm, till 11pm Fri-Sat, from 7am Sat, 7:30am-9pm Sun* ■ www.anodynecoffeehouse.com

Black Dog Coffee & Wine Bar [F] 651/228-9274 ■ 308 Prince St (at Broadway), St Paul ■ *7am-10pm, till 11pm Fri-Sat, 8am-8pm Sun* ■ www.blackdogstpaul.com

Blue Moon 612/721-9230 ■ 3822 E Lake St, Minneapolis ■ *7am-11pm, from 8am Sun* ■ www.drinkbluemoon.com

Cahoots 651/644-6778 ■ 1562 Selby Ave (at Snelling), St Paul ■ *6:30am-10:30pm, from 7am wknds, coffee bar*

Dunn Bros Coffee [WI] 612/822-3292 ■ 3348 Hennepin Ave S, Minneapolis ■ *6:30am-10pm, patio* ■ www.dunnbroscoffee.com

Moose & Sadie's 612/371-0464 ■ 212 3rd Ave N (at 2nd St), Minneapolis ■ *7am-8pm, 9am-2pm wknds*

Sisu Coffee & Cafe 651/695-1960 ■ 649 Snelling Ave S, St Paul ■ *7am-3pm, from 8am Sun* ■ www.sisucoffee.com

Uncommon Grounds [GS] 612/872-4811 ■ 2809 Hennepin Ave (at 28th Ave), Minneapolis ■ *5pm-1am, from noon wknds, outdoor seating* ■ www.uncommongroundscoffeehouse.com

The Urban Bean 612/824-6611 ■ 3255 Bryant Ave S (at 33rd), Minneapolis ■ *6:30am-11pm, from 7am Sun, patio*

Vera's Cafe 612/822-3871 ■ 2901 Lyndale Ave S (at 29th St W), Minneapolis ■ *7am-11pm, cozy coffeehouse w/ baked goods & light meals* ■ www.verascafe.com

Wilde Roast Cafe [BW,WC,GO] 612/331-4544 ■ 518 Hennepin Ave E (at Central), Minneapolis ■ *7am-11pm, till 1am Fri-Sat, shares entrance w/ LGBT bookstore* ■ www.wilderoastcafe.com

RESTAURANTS

Al's Breakfast [★] 612/331-9991 ■ 413 14th Ave SE (at 4th), Minneapolis ■ *6am-1pm, from 9am Sun, great hash* ■ www.tholt.com/als.html

Azia 612/813-1200 ■ 2550 Nicollet Ave S, Minneapolis ■ *11am-2am, from 3pm Sun, Asian fusion, full bar* ■ www.aziarestaurant.com

Birchwood Cafe 612/722-4474 ■ 3311 E 25th St, Minneapolis ■ www.birchwoodcafe.com

Cafe Barbette [MW,BW] 612/827-5710 ■ 1600 W Lake St (at Irving), Minneapolis ■ *8am-1am, till 2am Fri-Sat, French/ American* ■ www.barbette.com

Cafe Brenda [NS] 612/342-9230 ■ 300 1st Ave N (at 3rd), Minneapolis ■ *lunch Mon-Fri, dinner Mon-Sat, clsd Sun, vegetarian & seafood* ■ www.cafebrenda.com

Campiello 612/825-2222 ■ 1320 W Lake St (at Hennepin), Minneapolis ■ *dinner & Sun brunch, Italian* ■ campiello.damico.com

D'Amico Cucina [E] 612/338-2401 ■ 100 N 6th St (btwn 1st & 2nd Aves), Minneapolis ■ *dinner nightly, clsd Sun, full bar, live music Fri-Sat* ■ www.damico.com

Figlio 612/822-1688 ■ 3001 Hennepin Ave S (in Calhoun Square Mall), Minneapolis ■ *lunch & dinner, bar till 2am* ■ www.figlio.com

Joe's Garage 612/904-1163 ■ 1610 Harmon Pl, Minneapolis ■ *lunch & dinner, full bar till 1am, rooftop seating* ■ www.joes-garage.com

Lucia's Restaurant & Wine Bar [GS] 612/825-1572 ■ 1432 W 31st St, Minneapolis ■ *lunch & dinner, clsd Mon, American bistro* ■ www.lucias.com

Monte Carlo 612/333-5900 ■ 219 3rd Ave N, Minneapolis ■ *lunch & dinner, bar till 1am*

Murray's 612/339-0909 ■ 26 S 6th St (at Hennepin), Minneapolis ■ *lunch Mon-Fri, dinner nightly, steak & seafood* ■ www.murraysrestaurant.com

Nye's Polonaise [E,P] 612/379-2021 ■ 112 E Hennepin Ave, Minneapolis ■ *11am-2am, from 4pm Sun, prime rib, piano bar, live polka & bands, full bar* ■ nyespolonaise.com

Palomino Euro Bistro 612/339-3800 ■ 825 Hennepin Ave (at 9th St), Minneapolis ■ *lunch Mon-Sat, dinner nightly, Italian/ Mediterranean* ■ www.palomino.com

Psycho Suzi's 612/788-9069 ■ 2519 Marshall St NE, Minneapolis ■ *11am-2am, tiki lounge* ■ www.psychosuzis.com

Punch Neapolitan Pizza 651/696-1066 ■ 704 Cleveland Ave S, St Paul ■ *11am-9:30pm, till 10pm Fri-Sat*

Royal Orchid [TG] 651/639-9999 ■ 2401 Fairview Ave N, St Paul ■ *11am-9pm, from noon Sat, clsd Sun, Thai*

Rudolph's Bar-B-Que [WC] 612/871-8969 ■ 1933 Lyndale (at Franklin), Minneapolis ■ *11am-2am, till 1am Sun, full bar* ■ www.rudolphsbbq.com

Seward Cafe 612/332-1011 ■ 2129 E Franklin Ave, Minneapolis ■ *7am-3pm, 8am-4pm wknds, vegetarian cafe*

Trattoria da Vinci 651/222-4050 ■ 400 Sibley St, St Paul ■ *11am-9pm, till 10pm Fri, 5pm-10pm Sat, clsd Sun, Italian* ■ www.trattoriadavinci.com

ENTERTAINMENT & RECREATION

Calhoun 32nd Beach [GS] E side of Lake Calhoun (33rd & Calhoun Blvd), Minneapolis

Fresh Fruit 612/341-0980 (on-air studio), 612/341-3144 (office) ■ KFAI 90.3 FM, Minneapolis ■ *7pm-8pm Th, gay radio program, also a variety of LGBT programs 9pm-11pm Sun* ■ www.kfai.org

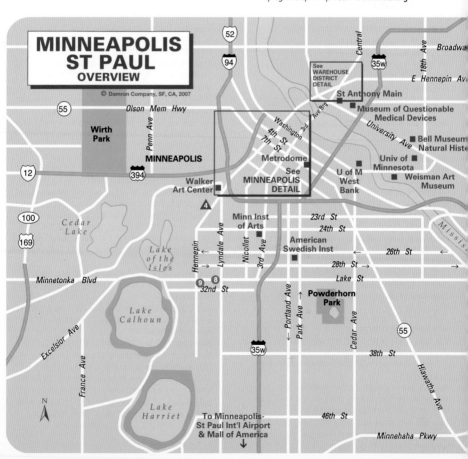

genderBLUR [TG] 612/823-1152 ■ 3010 Minnehaha Ave S (at Patrick's Cabaret), Minneapolis ■ *events for trans, genderqueer & allied communities* ■ www.genderblur.org

Illusion Theater 612/339-4944 ■ 528 Hennepin Ave (8th floor), Minneapolis ■ *some LGBT-themed productions* ■ www.illusiontheater.org

Minnesota Lynx 612/673-8400, 877/962-2849 ■ Target Center, Minneapolis ■ *check out the Women's National Basketball Association while you're in Minneapolis* ■ www.wnba.com/lynx

Minnesota RollerGirls 612/296-4743 ■ *MN's female roller derby league, check web for upcoming events* ■ www.mnrollergirls.com

One Voice Mixed Chorus 612/332-1302 ■ *LGBT community chorus* ■ www.ovmc.org

Outward Spiral Theater 612/729-1520 ■ *"theater from a Queer point of view"* ■ www.outwardspiral.org

Patrick's Cabaret [GS] 612/724-6273, 612/721-3595 ■ 3010 Minnehaha Ave S, Minneapolis ■ *informal performance space w/ bi-weekly shows* ■ www.patrickscabaret.org

Suburban World Theater [F] 612/822-9000 ■ 3022 Hennepin Ave S ■ www.suburbanworldtheater.com

Theatre de la Jeune Lune 612/333-6200, 612/332-3968 ■ 105 N First St, Minneapolis ■ www.jeunelune.org

Twin Cities Gay Men's Chorus 612/339-7664 ■ 528 Hennepin Avenue #307, Minneapolis ■ www.tcgmc.org

BOOKSTORES

18 **Amazon Bookstore Co-operative** 612/821-9630 ■ 4755 Chicago Ave S, Minneapolis ■ *10am-8pm, till 6pm Sat, noon-5pm Sun, feminist bookstore since 1970 (no relation to Seattle's amazon.com), women-owned/ run* ■ www.amazonbookstorecoop.com

Birchbark Books 612/374-4023 ■ 2115 W 21st St, Minneapolis ■ *8am-7pm, 10am-5pm wknds, specializes in Native American art & literature, owned by Louise Erdrich* ■ www.birchbarkbooks.com

Magus Books, Ltd 612/379-7669, 800/996-2387 ■ 1309 1/2 SE 4th St (at 13th/ 14th), Minneapolis ■ *10am-9pm, till 6pm wknds, from noon Sun, alternative spirituality books & supplies, also mail order* ■ www.magusbooks.com

RETAIL SHOPS

The Rainbow Road [WC] 612/872-8448 ■ 109 W Grant (at LaSalle), Minneapolis ■ *10am-10pm, LGBT retail & video*

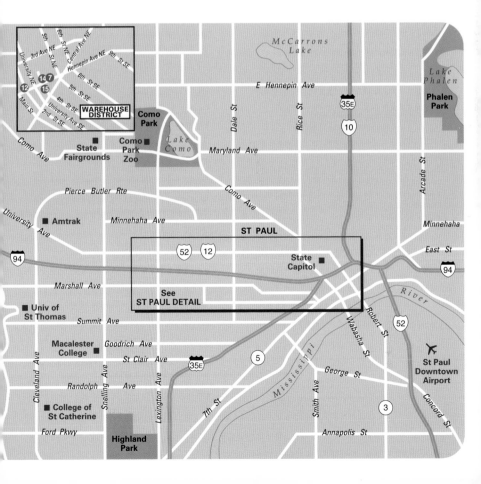

MINNEAPOLIS/ST PAUL

Day Trips: Grand Rounds Scenic Byway & The Mall of America

Nature-lovers and city-slickers alike will enjoy a spin around Minneapolis' Grand Rounds Scenic Byway. Like the city herself, this 53-mile jaunt incorporates lush natural beauty and stunning human accomplishment by taking you through the Chain of Lakes, Nokomis-Hiawatha Park, and Minnehana Falls, as well as by the Walker Art Center Sculpture Garden, and the historic Stone Arch Bridge.

Those looking to shop till they drop should not miss Mall of America (www.mallofamerica.com). The size of 7 Yankee Stadiums, it also houses a bowling alley, an aquarium, a movie theater, and a kids' theme park.

Local Food:

It's no surprise that the fresh fish is excellent here in the land of 10,000 lakes. Wild rice and morel mushrooms are also local delicacies.

Tourist Info

AIRPORT DIRECTIONS

Minneapolis/St Paul International. To get to downtown Minneapolis, get on I-494 West to I-35W North. Follow I-35W until you come to the downtown exits.
To get to the State Capitol in St Paul, take I-494 East to I-35E North. Follow I-35E to the Kellogg Blvd exit. Take Kellogg Blvd to West 7th St and turn left. Follow West 7th to 8th St and Robert, turn left and follow to University Ave. Turn left on University.

PUBLIC TRANSIT & TAXIS

Yellow Cab (Minn) 612/824-4444.
Yellow Cab (St Paul) 651/647-3000.
Super Shuttle 612/827-7777.
MTC 612/373-3333, web: www.metrotransit.org.

TOURIST SPOTS & INFO

American Swedish Institute 612/871-4907, web: www.americanswedishinst.org.
Mall of America (the largest mall in the US w/indoor theme park) 952/883-8800, web: www.mallofamerica.com.
Minneapolis American Indian Center 612/879-1700, web: www.maicnet.org.
Minneapolis Institute of Arts 612/870-3131, web: www.artsmia.org.
Collection of Questionable Medical Devices at The Science Museum of Minnesota 651/221-9444, web: www.smm.org.
Walker Art Center/Minneapolis Sculpture Garden 612/375-7600, web: www.walkerart.org.
Frederick R Weisman Art Museum 612/625-9494, web: www.weisman.umn.edu.
Visitor's Center: 888/676-6757, web: www.minneapolis.org.

Weather

Winters are harsh. If driving, carry extra blankets and supplies. The average temperature is 19°, and it can easily drop well below 0°, and then there's the wind chill! Summer temperatures are usually in the upper-80°s to mid-90°s and HUMID.

Best Views

Observation deck of the 32nd story of Foshay Tower, 821 Marquette Ave (closed in winter).

City Calendar

LGBT PRIDE

June. 612/305-6900, web: www.tcpride.com.

ANNUAL EVENTS

March - Diva (fashion show benefiting HIV/AIDS service organizations) 952/544-6599, web: www.divamn.org.
May - Minnesota AIDS Walk 612/373-2411, web: www.minnesotaaidswalk.org.
August - Minnesota Fringe Festival 612/872-1212, web: www.fringefestival.org.
November - Flaming Film Festival 612/839-3189, web: www.flamingfilmfestival.com.

Queer Resources

COMMUNITY INFO

OutFront Minnesota 612/822-0127 or 800/800-0350, 24-hour info line, web: www.outfront.org.
Chrysalis Women's Center 612/871-0118. 4432 Chicago Ave S, 9am-8:30pm, till 5pm Fri, clsd wknds, web: www.chrysaliswomen.org.
Quatrefoil Library, LGBT Library & Resource Center 651/641-0969. 1619 Dayton Ave, St Paul, web: www.QuatrefoilLibrary.org.
AA Intergroup 952/922-0880, web: www.aaminneapolis.org.
The Aliveness Project 612/822-7946, web: www.aliveness.org.
Minnesota AIDS Project 612/341-2060, web: www.mnaidsproject.org.

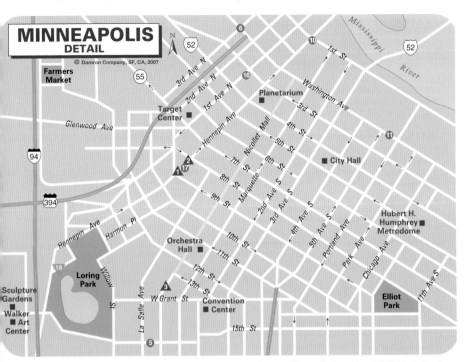

PUBLICATIONS

Lavender Magazine 612/436-4660, 877/515-9969 ■ *LGBT newsmagazine for MN, WI, IA, ND, SD* ■ www.lavendermagazine.com

Minnesota Women's Press 651/646-3968 ■ 771 Raymond Ave, St Paul ■ *newspaper* ■ www.womenspress.com

EROTICA

Denmark Books 651/222-2928 ■ 459 W 7th St, St Paul ■ *10am-midnight*

Fantasy Gifts 952/922-0838 ■ 1437 University Ave, St Paul ■ *10am-10pm, noon-6pm Sun, adult gifts* ■ www.fantasygifts.com

Lickety Split 612/333-0599 ■ 251 3rd Ave S, Minneapolis ■ *24hrs*

SexWorld 612/672-0556 ■ 241 2nd Ave N (at Washington), Minneapolis ■ *24hrs*

The Smitten Kitten [TG,GO] 612/721-6088, 888/751-0523 ■ 3010 Lyndale Ave S, Minneapolis ■ *11am-7pm, till 8pm Fri-Sat, till 6pm Sun, clsd Mon, woman-centered sex toy store, lesbian-owned* ■ www.smittenkittenonline.com

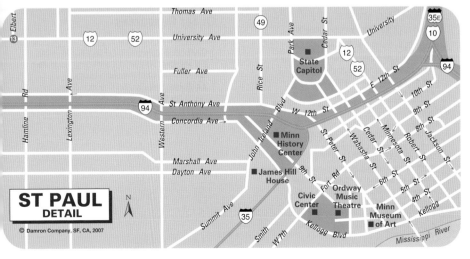

MISSOURI

Kansas City

ACCOMMODATIONS

1   **40th St Inn** [NS,WI,GO] 816/561-7575 ▪ 1007 E 40th St ▪ www.40thstreetinn.com

2   **The Concourse Park B&B** [M,GO] 816/231-1196 ▪ 300 Benton Blvd (at Anderson) ▪ austindue@sbcglobal.net

     Hydes Guesthouse [M,NS,WI,GO] 816/561-1010 ▪ in historic Hyde Park ▪ www.hydeskc.com

3   **Ken's Place** [MW,SW,N,GO] 816/753-0533 ▪ 18 W 38th St (at Baltimore) ▪ some shared baths, near gay bars ▪ machogene@netscape.net

     The Porch Swing Inn [GF,WI,GO] 816/587-6282, 866/587-6282 ▪ 702 East St, Parkville ▪ B&B, full brkfst, kids/ pets ok, lesbian-owned ▪ www.theporchswinginn.com

5   **Quarterage Hotel** [GF,WI,WC] 816/931-0001, 800/942-4233 ▪ 560 Westport Rd (at Mill St) ▪ in Westport district, whirlpool, dry spa ▪ www.quarteragehotel.com

     Sleep Inn [GF,SW,WI,WC] 816/891-0111 ▪ 7611 NW 97th Terrace (at Tiffany Springs Rd) ▪ hotel, kids/ pets ok ▪ www.choicehotels.com

6   **Southmoreland on the Plaza** [GF,NS,WC] 816/531-7979 ▪ 116 E 46th St ▪ 1913 B&B, full brkfst, veranda ▪ www.southmoreland.com

     Su Casa B&B [GF,SW,NS] 816/965-5647, 816/916-3444 (cell) ▪ 9004 E 92nd St ▪ Southwest-style home, full brkfst wknds ▪ www.sucasabb.com

BARS

7   **Balanca's** [GS,D,MR,F,E] 816/474-6369 ▪ 1809 Grand Ave ▪ 9pm-3am, from 6pm Fri-Sat, clsd Sun-Mon, 2 flrs ▪ www.balancaskc.com

8   **Bar Natasha** [GS,F,E,C,P] 816/472-5300 ▪ 1911 Main St (at 20th) ▪ 5pm-1:30am, clsd Sun ▪ www.barnatasha.com

KANSAS CITY

Day Trips: Parkville, MO

For a change of pace that's just a short drive away, head north to the beautiful little turn-of-the-century town of Parkville. Here, on the Missouri River, amidst an abundance of trees, you will find a slower pace, some great restaurants, shops, and a wonderful farmer's market.

Local Food:

Merging savory influences from the South and Texas, Kansas City is called the "melting pot" of barbecue. Even if you miss the annual American Royal Barbecue Contest in October, your urge for 'cue can be satisfied at one of the more than 70 barbecue joints in town.

Tourist Info

AIRPORT DIRECTIONS

Kansas City International. To get downtown, take I-29 approximately 20 miles south.

PUBLIC TRANSIT & TAXIS

Yellow Cab 816/471-5000.
KCI Shuttle 816/ 243-5000.
Metro 816/221-0660, web: www.cata.org.

TOURIST SPOTS & INFO

American Jazz Museum 816/474-8463, web: www.americanjazzmuseum.com.
Black Archives of Mid-America, web: www.blackarchives.org.
Historic 18th & Vine District (includes Kansas City Jazz Museum & the Negro Leagues Baseball Museum).
Nelson-Atkins Museum of Art 816/751-1278, web: www.nelson-atkins.org.
Thomas Hart Benton Home & Studio 816/931-5722, web: www.mostateparks.com/benton.htm.
Harry S Truman Nat'l Historical Site (in Independence, MO) 816/254-9929, web: www.nps.gov/hstr.

Visitor's Center: Convention & Visitors Bureau 816/221-5242, web: www.visitkc.com.

City Calendar

LGBT PRIDE

June. web: www.kansascitygaypride.org.

ANNUAL EVENTS

April - AIDS Walk 816/931-0959, web: www.aidswalkkansascity.org.

Queer Resources

COMMUNITY INFO

Gay/Lesbian Community Center 816/931-4420. 207 Westport Rd, Ste 218, 6pm-9pm, noon-3pm Sat, clsd Sun, web: www.lgcc-kc.org.
AA Central Office 816/471-7229.
Live & Let Live AA 816/531-9668.
816/931-0959.

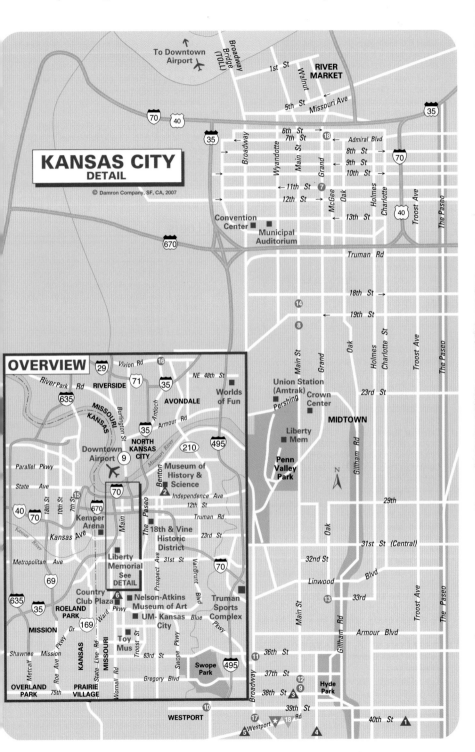

KANSAS CITY
DETAIL

© Damron Company, SF, CA, 2007

To Downtown Airport
Broadway Bridge (TOLL)
1st St
Walnut
RIVER MARKET
5th St
Missouri Ave
6th St
7th St
Broadway
Wyandotte
Main St
Grand
Admiral Blvd
8th St
9th St
10th St
11th St
12th St
McGee
Oak
Holmes
Charlotte
13th St
Troost Ave
The Paseo
Convention Center
Municipal Auditorium
Truman Rd
18th St
19th St
Oak
Holmes
Charlotte St
Troost Ave
The Paseo
Main St
Grand
Union Station (Amtrak)
Pershing
Crown Center
23rd St
MIDTOWN
Liberty Mem
Penn Valley Park
N
Gillham Rd
29th
31st St (Central)
32nd St
Linwood
Blvd
33rd
13
Main St
Oak
Gillham Rd
Troost Ave
The Paseo
Armour Blvd
36th St
37th St
38th St
39th St
40th St
Hyde Park

OVERVIEW

Vivion Rd
29
16
River Park Rd
RIVERSIDE
71
35
NE 48th St
635
MISSOURI
KANSAS
Burlington St
Antioch
AVONDALE
Worlds of Fun
Armour Rd
NORTH KANSAS CITY
Downtown Airport
9
210
495
Parallel Pkwy
State Ave
Missouri River
Benton
Museum of History & Science
2
Independence Ave
12th St
Truman Rd
15
70
18th St
10th St
7th St
40
70
670
Kemper Arena
Kansas Ave
Main
The Paseo
18th & Vine Historic District
23rd St
Kansas River
Metropolitan Ave
Liberty Memorial See DETAIL
Prospect Ave
31st St
VanBrunt
70
69
Country Club Plaza
6
Nelson-Atkins Museum of Art
UM- Kansas City
Blvd
Truman Sports Complex
Blue Pkwy
635
35
ROELAND PARK
169
Ward Pkwy
MISSION
KANSAS
MISSOURI
State Line Rd
Dr
Toy Mus
Troost St
63rd St
Swope Pkwy
Swope Park
495
11
Broadway
36th St
37th St
38th St
12
9
Shawnee Mission
Metcalf
Roe Ave
75th
Wornall Rd
Gregory Blvd
10
17
Westport
18
4
WESTPORT
5
39th Rd
OVERLAND PARK
PRAIRIE VILLAGE
8
14
7
18

9 **Buddie's** [M,NH] 816/561-2600 ■ 3715 Main St (at 37th) ■ 6pm-3am, clsd Sun ■ www.buddieslounge.com

10 **Missie B's/ Bootleggers** [MW,NH,D,L,TG,K,DS,S] 816/561-0625 ■ 805 W 39th St (at SW Trafficway) ■ noon-3am, clsd Sun, 2 flrs ■ www.missiebs.com

11 **OutaBounds** [M] 816/756-2577 ■ 3601 Broadway ■ 11am-1:30am, sports bar

12 **Sidekicks** [MW,D,CW,DS,WC] 816/931-1430 ■ 3707 Main St (at 37th) ■ 2pm-3am, from 4pm Sun

13 **Sidestreet Bar** [M,NH,GO] 816/531-1775 ■ 413 E 33rd St (at Gilliam) ■ 10am-3am, from 6am Fri-Sat, clsd Sun

14 **Tootsie's New Place** [W,D,F,K,DS,WC] 816/471-7704 ■ 1822 Main (at 18th) ■ 10am-3am, from 5pm Wed & Sat ■ www.myspace.com/tootsiesbar

15 **The View on the Hill** [M,NH,GO] 913/281-0833 ■ 204 Orchard St, KS ■ 4pm-2am, from noon Sun, clsd Mon

16 **Wetherbee's** [GS,D,F,E,WC] 816/454-2455 ■ 2510 NE Vivion Rd (at Antioch) ■ 6pm-3am

NIGHTCLUBS

17 **The Hurricane** [GF,D,E,WC] 816/268-4781 ■ 4048 Broadway (at Westport Rd) ■ 5pm-3am, live bands ■ www.hurricanekc.com

17 **NV** [GF,E,D,V,WC] 816/421-6852 ■ 220 Admiral Blvd (at Grand Blvd) ■ 8pm-3am Th-Sun only ■ www.nv-kc.com

CAFES

Broadway Cafe [F,NS] 816/531-2432 ■ 4106 Broadway (at Westport) ■ 7am-11pm, till midnight Fri-Sat, from 8am Sat-Sun; also 301 Westport Rd, 816/931-9955 ■ www.broadwaycafeandroastery.com

Planet Cafe [★E,GO] 816/561-7287 ■ 3535 Broadway Blvd (at 35th) ■ 8am-10pm, till midnight Fri-Sat, from 9am wknds ■ myspace.com/theplanetcafe

RESTAURANTS

Bistro 303 816/753-2303 ■ 303 Westport Rd ■ also martini bar

Cafe Trio/ Starlet Lounge [P,GO] 816/756-3227 ■ 3535 Broadway (at Knickerbocker Pl) ■ 4:30pm-11pm, clsd Sun, New American ■ kansascitymenus.com/cafetrio

Classic Cup Cafe [WC] 816/753-1840 ■ 301 W 47th St (at Central) ■ brkfst, lunch, dinner, Sun brunch, great appetizers ■ www.classiccup.com

The Corner Restaurant [WC] 816/931-6630 ■ 4059 Broadway (at Main) ■ 7am-7pm, till 5pm Sun, lots of veggie

Hereford House 816/842-1080 ■ 2 E 20th St (at Main) ■ 11am-9pm, till 10pm Fri-Sat, from 4pm wknds, steak ■ www.herefordhouse.com

Sharp's 63rd St Grill [WC] 816/333-4355 ■ 128 W 63rd St ■ 7am-10pm, from 8am wknds, full bar ■ www.sharpsgrill.com

YJ's Snack Bar 816/472-5533 ■ 128 W 18th St ■ 8am-10pm, 24hrs Th-Sat, eclectic menu, inexpensive

Zin 816/527-0120 ■ 1900 Main St ■ dinner, clsd Mon, contemporary ■ www.zinkc.com

ENTERTAINMENT & RECREATION

Heartland Men's Chorus 816/931-3338 ■ www.hmckc.org

Kansas City Roller Warriors ■ KC's female roller derby league, check web for upcoming events ■ kcrollerwarriors.com

Unicorn Theatre 816/531-7529 ■ 3828 Main St (at 39th St) ■ contemporary American theater ■ www.unicorntheatre.org

RETAIL SHOPS

18 **Out There** 816/753-4757 ■ 205 Westport Rd (btwn Main & Broadway) ■ 10am-7pm, till 6:30pm Sat, noon-5pm Sun, LGBT ■ out.there@sbcglobal.net

PUBLICATIONS

EXP Magazine 314/367-0397, 877/397-6244 ■ bi-weekly gay magazine for MO, KS & IL ■ www.expmagazine.com

MEN'S CLUBS

Hydes KC Gym & Guesthouse 816/561-1010 ■ hours vary, call for location ■ www.hydeskc.com

EROTICA

Erotic City 816/252-3370 ■ 8401 E Truman Rd (at I-435) ■ 24hrs, arcade

Hollywood at Home 913/649-9666 ■ 9063 Metcalf (at 91st), Overland Park, KS ■ 10am-11pm ■ hollywoodathome.tv

St Louis

ACCOMMODATIONS

1 **A St Louis Guesthouse** [M,N,NS,WI,GO] 314/773-1016 ■ 1032-38 Allen Ave (at Menard) ■ in historic Soulard district, hot tub ■ www.stlouisguesthouse.com

2 **Brewers House B&B** [MW,NS,WI,GO] 314/771-1542, 888/767-4665 ■ 1829 Lami St (at Lemp) ■ 1860s home, jacuzzi ■ www.brewershouse.com

3 **Dwell 912 B&B** [GF,NS,WI,GO] 314/599-3100 ■ 912 Hickory St (at Choteau) ■ www.dwell912.com

4 **Lafayette Park B&B** [GS,NS,WI,GO] 314/771-9700, 866/338-1415 ■ 1415 Missouri Ave (at Park) ■ elegant B&B in historic neighborhood w/ decks & garden ■ lafayetteparkbedandbreakfast.com

5 **Napoleon's Retreat B&B** [GS,NS,WI,GO] 314/772-6979, 800/700-9980 ■ 1815 Lafayette Ave (at Mississippi) ■ restored 1880s town house, full brkfst ■ www.napoleonsretreat.com

6 **Park Avenue Mansion—A B&B Guesthouse** [GS,WI] 314/588-9004, 866/588-9004 ■ 2007 Park Ave (at Mississippi) ■ B&B inn, full brkfst, jacuzzi ■ www.parkavenuebandb.com

BARS

7 **Absolutli Goosed Martini Bar, Etc** [MW,NH,GO] 314/772-0400 ■ 3196 S Grand (4 blocks S of Tower Grove Park) ■ 4pm-midnight, till 1am Fri, 5pm-1am Sat, clsd Mon, also desserts, appetizers, lesbian-owned ■ www.absolutligoosed.com

8 **AMP (Alternative Music Pub)** [MW,NH] 314/652-5267 ■ 4199 Manchester Ave (at Boyle) ■ 6pm-3am, from 8pm Sat, clsd Sun

9 **Bad Dog Saloon** [M,NH,B,L,GO] 314/652-0011 ■ 17 S Vandeventer ■ 4pm-1:30am, from 1pm Sat, clsd Sun ■ www.baddogsaloonstl.com

10 **Cicero's** [GS,E] 314/862-0009 ■ 6691 Delmar, University City ■ 11am-12:30am, till 11pm Sun, Italian restaurant, tavern, live music venue ■ www.ciceros-stl.com

11 **Clementine's** [★M,NH,L,F,WC] 314/664-7869 ■ 2001 Menard (at Allen) ■ 10am-1:30am, 11am-midnight Sun, patio ■ www.clementinesbar.com

Club Escapades [MW,D,K,S] 618/222-9597 ■ 133 W Main St, Belleville, IL ■ 6pm-2am

12 **Freddie's** [MW,NH,D,K,V] 314/371-1333 ■ 4112 Manchester Ave ■ 3pm-1:30am, noon-midnight Sun ■ www.freddiesbar.com

8   **Grandma's Politician Lounge** [MW] 314/800-4486 ■ 4170 Manchester ■ 9am-1:30am

13   **Grey Fox Pub** [MW,NH,TG,DS,S] 314/772-2150 ■ 3503 S Spring (at Potomac) ■ 2pm-1:30am, noon-midnight Sun, patio ■ www.greyfoxstl.com

14   **JJ's Clubhouse & Bar** [M,NH,B,L,WC] 314/535-4100 ■ 3858 Market St (at Vandeventer) ■ 3pm-3am ■ www.jjsclubhouse.com

      Korner's Bar [MW,D,DS] 314/352-3088 ■ 7101 S Broadway (at Blow St) ■ 4pm-1:30am, clsd Sun-Mon ■ korners-stl.com

15   **Loading Zone** [★MW,V,WC,GO] 314/361-4119 ■ 16 S Euclid (at Forest Park Pkwy) ■ 2:30pm-1:30am, show tunes Tue ■ www.zonestl.com

12   **Novak's Bar & Grill** [W,D,F,E,K,S,WC] 314/531-3699 ■ 4121 Manchester ■ 4pm-3am, from noon Sun, dancers Wed & Fri, patio ■ www.novaksbar.com

16   **Soulard Bastille** [M,NH,F] 314/664-4408 ■ 1027 Russell (at Menard) ■ 11am-1:30am ■ www.soulardbastille.com

17   **Van Goghz** [GS,F,E] 314/865-3345 ■ 3200 Shenandoah ■ 4pm-11pm, till 1:30am Fri-Sat, clsd Sun-Mon, live music ■ www.vangoghz.com

NIGHTCLUBS

8   **Atomic Cowboy** [GS,F,W] 314/775-0775 ■ 4140 Manchester ■ 5pm-3am, 9pm-close Mon-Tue, also Fresh-Mex Mayan grill, patio ■ www.atomic-cowboy.com

12   **Attitudes** [MW,D] 314/534-0044 ■ 4100 Manchester ■ 7pm-3am, clsd Sun-Mon

Bubby & Sissy's [MW,D,E,K,DS,V,WC] 618/465-4773 ■ 602 Belle St (at 6th St), Alton, IL ■ 3pm-2am, till 3am Fri-Sat ■ www.bubbyandsissys.com

18   **The Complex Nightclub & Restaurant** [★MW,D,F,DS,V,WC] 314/772-2645 ■ 3515 Chouteau Ave (at Grand) ■ 9pm-3am, clsd Mon-Tue, 5 bars, patio ■ www.complexnightclub.com

19   **Faces on Fourth Street** [MW,D,F,E,C,DS,V,WI,18+] 618/271-7410 ■ 132 Collinsville Ave (btwn Missouri & Riverpark Dr), East St Louis, IL ■ 11pm-6am, from 10pm Wed & Sun, clsd Mon-Tue, 3 levels, also cruise bar Fri-Sun, patio ■ www.facesnolimits.com

CAFES

Coffee Cartel [★WI] 314/454-0000 ■ 2 Maryland Plaza (at Euclid) ■ 24hrs ■ www.cwecartel.com

MoKaBe's [★E,WC] 314/865-2009 ■ 3606 Arsenal (at S Grand) ■ 8am-midnight, from 9am Sun, plenty veggie, shows wknds ■ www.mokabes.com

Soulard Coffee Garden Cafe [F] 314/241-1464 ■ 910 Geyer St ■ 6:30am-4pm

RESTAURANTS

After Diner [MW,GO] 314/652-4800 ■ 4146 Manchester Ave ■ 24hrs ■ www.afterdiner.com

Billie's Diner 314/621-0848 ■ 1802 S Broadway ■ 5am-2:30pm, midnight-1:30pm wknds

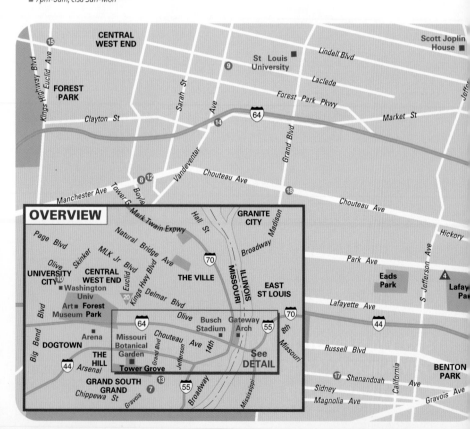

Cafe Balaban [★WC] 314/361-8085 ■ 405 N Euclid Ave (at McPherson) ■ *lunch, dinner, Sun brunch, full bar, live jazz Tue, contemporary live music Sun, also upscale dining room for dinner only, full bar, private dining room seating up to 50* ■ www.cafebalaban.com

Chez Leon [GO] 314/361-1589 ■ 4580 Laclede Ave (at Euclid) ■ *5:30pm-10pm, till 11pm Fri-Sat, 5pm-9pm Sun, clsd Mon, French bistro, full bar* ■ www.chezleon.com

City Diner 314/772-6100 ■ 3139 S Grand ■ *7am-11pm, 24hrs Fri-Sat, till 10pm Sun* ■ www.citydiner.us

Dressel's [E] 314/361-1060 ■ 419 N Euclid (at McPherson) ■ *11:30am-1:30am, till midnight Sun, great Welsh pub food, full bar*

Duff's [WC] 314/361-0522 ■ 392 N Euclid Ave (at McPherson) ■ *lunch & dinner, clsd Mon, brunch Sat-Sun, fine dining, full bar* ■ www.dineatduffs.com

Eternity 314/454-1851 ■ 11 S Euclid ■ *11am-9pm, till 10pm Fri-Sat, clsd Sun, vegetarian deli* ■ www.eternitydeli.com

Majestic Cafe 314/361-2011 ■ 4900 Laclede (at Euclid) ■ *6am-midnight, Greek-American diner fare*

Rue 13 [D,C] 314/588-7070 ■ 1313 Washington ■ *5pm-3am, from 7pm Sat, clsd Sun, sushi, full bar* ■ www.rue13stl.com

Ted Drewes Frozen Custard [★WC] 314/481-2652, 314/481-2124 ■ 6726 Chippewa (at Jameson) ■ *11am-10pm, seasonal, a St Louis landmark; also 4224 S Grand Blvd, 314/352-7376* ■ www.teddrewes.com

Tomatillo Mexican Grill 314/726-1005 ■ 6333 Delmar Blvd ■ *11am-10pm, till midnight Fri-Sat; also 9641 Olive Blvd, 314/991-4995*

Tony's [R] 314/231-7007 ■ 410 Market St (at Broadway) ■ *dinner only, clsd Sun, Italian fine dining* ■ www.tonysstlouis.com

The Wild Flower Restaurant & Bar 314/367-9888 ■ 4590 Laclede Ave ■ *lunch & dinner, bar till 1:30am, clsd Tue, Sun brunch* ■ www.wildflowerdining.com

Zinnia 314/962-0572 ■ 7491 Big Bend Blvd (at Shrewsbury), Webster Groves ■ *lunch Tue-Th, dinner Tue-Sun, clsd Mon, California-style bistro* ■ www.zinnia-stl.com

ENTERTAINMENT & RECREATION

Anheuser-Busch Brewery Tours/ Grant's Farm 314/577-2626, 314/843-1700 (Grant's Farm) ■ 12th & Lynch ■ *all-American kitsch: see the Clydesdales in their air-conditioned stables, or visit the Busch family estate that was once the home of Ulysses S Grant, www.grantsfarm.com* ■ www.budweisertours.com

Int'l Bowling Museum & Hall of Fame 314/231-6340 ■ 111 Stadium Plaza (across from Busch Stadium) ■ *5,000 years of bowling history (!) & 4 free frames* ■ www.bowling-museum.com

Opera Theatre of Saint Louis [WC] 314/961-0644 (box office) ■ 430 Hazel Ave (at Edgar & Big Bend) ■ *intimate theater w/ operas sung in English* ■ www.opera-stl.org

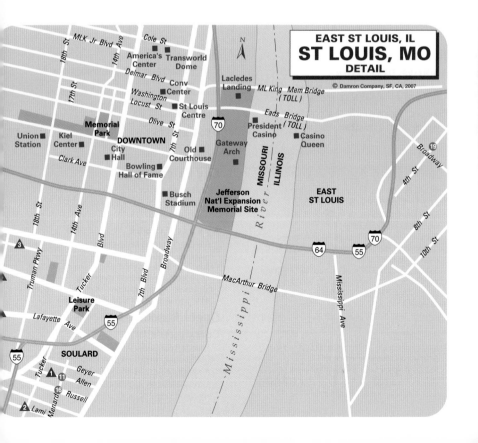

BOOKSTORES

20   **Left Bank Books** [★] 314/367-6731 ■ 399 N Euclid Ave (at McPherson) ■ *10am-10pm, 11am-6pm Sun, feminist & LGBT titles* ■ www.left-bank.com

RETAIL SHOPS

➤ **Boxers** 314/454-0209 ■ 1305 Washington Ave ■ *11am-6pm, clsd Sun, men's underwear* ■ www.mensunderwear-store.com

CheapTRX 314/664-4011 ■ 3211 S Grand Blvd ■ *alternative shopping, body piercing, tattoos* ■ www.cheaptrx.com

PUBLICATIONS

EXP Magazine 314/367-0397, 877/397-6244 ■ *bi-weekly gay magazine for MO, KS, & IL* ■ www.expmagazine.com

Vital Voice 314/289-9666 ■ *bi-weekly news & feature publication* ■ www.thevitalvoice.com

Women's Yellow Pages of Greater St Louis 314/997-6262 ■ www.wypstlouis.com

MEN'S CLUBS

Club St Louis [PC,SW,18+] 314/533-3666 ■ 2625 Samuel Shepard Dr (at Jefferson) ■ *24hrs* ■ www.theclubs.com

EROTICA

Friends & Luvers 314/771-9405 ■ 3550 Gravois (at Grand) ■ *10am-10pm, noon-7pm Sun, fetish clothes, toys, videos, dating service* ■ www.friends-luvers.com

ST LOUIS

Day Trips: Bonne Terre & Missouri River Valley

Scuba divers can take the plunge at Bonne Terre, the largest freshwater dive resort in the world. Landlubbers will enjoy the walking and boat tours of this billion-gallon underground lake, on the site of an abandoned lead mine. Unwavering, moderate temperatures (58° for the water and 62° for the air) make this a suitable place to visit year-round. For more info, visit www.2dive.com.

The Missouri River Valley, "America's first wine district," about 90 miles west of St Louis, boasts an astonishing number of wineries. Take a drive to the town of Hermann, where many are located, and sample the fruits of a culture imported in the 1830s by German immigrants from the Rhine River Valley. Visit www.missouriwine.org to learn more.

Tourist Info

AIRPORT DIRECTIONS

Lambert-St Louis International. To get downtown, take I-70 approximately 17 miles east.

PUBLIC TRANSIT & TAXIS

County Cab 314/993-8294, web: www.stlouis-countycab.com.
TransExpress 314/428-7799, web: www.transex-press-stl.com.
MetroBus 314/231-2345, web: www.metrost-louis.org.

TOURIST SPOTS & INFO

Anheuser-Busch Brewery 314/577-2626, web: www.budweisertours.com.
Cathedral Basilica of St Louis (world's largest collection of mosaic art) 314/738-8200, web: www.cathedralstl.org.
Gateway Arch 877/982-1410, web: www.gateway-arch.com.
Grant's Farm 314/843-1700, web: www.grants-farm.com.
Soulard, the "French Quarter of St Louis."
St Louis Art Museum 314/721-0072, web: www.slam.org.
Stone Hill Winery (in Hermann) 800/909-9463, web: www.stonehillwinery.com.
The extremely quaint town of St Charles.
Visitor's Center: 314/421-1023 or 800/ 888-3861, web: www.explorestlouis.com.

Weather

100% midwestern. Cold winters—little snow and the temperatures can drop below 0°. Hot, muggy summers raise temperatures back up into the 100's. Spring and fall bring out the best in Mother Nature.

Best Views

Where else? Top of the Gateway Arch in the Observation Room, web: www.gatewayarch.com.

City Calendar

LGBT PRIDE

June. PrideFest 314/772-8888, web: www.pridestl.org.

ANNUAL EVENTS

February - Soulard Mardi Gras 314/771-5110, web: www.mardigrasinc.com.
July - Fair St Louis & LIVE on the Levee 314/434-3434, web: www.celebratestlouis.org.
September - The Great Forest Park Balloon Race, web: www.greatforestparkballoonrace.com.

Queer Resources

COMMUNITY INFO

Pride St. Louis, web: www.pridestl.org.
Gay St. Louis, web: www.gaystlouis.org.
AA 314/647-3677, web: www.aastl.org.
St Louis Effort for AIDS 314/645-6451, web: www.stlefa.org.

NEVADA

Las Vegas

ACCOMMODATIONS

1   **Blue Moon Resort** [MO,SW,N,WI,WC,GO] 702/361-9099, 866/798-9194 ■ 2651 Westwood Dr ■ *hot tub* ■ www.bluemoonlasvegas.com

Lucky You B&B [M,SW,N,GO] 702/384-1129 ■ *hot tub, sauna, shared baths* ■ haven00069@aol.com

BARS

2   **8 1/2 Ultra Lounge/ Piranha** [MW,NH,V,WC] 702/791-0100 ■ 4633 Paradise Rd (at Naples) ■ *ladies night Wed* ■ www.gipsylv.net

3   **Backdoor Lounge** [MW,NH,D,MR-L,WC] 702/385-2018 ■ 1415 E Charleston (near Maryland Pkwy) ■ *24hrs, patio*

4   **Badlands Saloon** [M,NH,D,CW,WC,GO] 702/792-9262 ■ 953 E Sahara #22 (in Commercial Center) ■ *24hrs*

5   **The Buffalo** [★M,B,L,V,WC] 702/733-8355 ■ 4640 Paradise Rd #11 (at Naples) ■ *24hrs*

6   **Charlie's Las Vegas** [★M,D,CW,WC] 702/876-1844 ■ 5012 S Arville St (at Tropicana) ■ *24hrs, dance lessons 7pm-9pm Mon, Th-Sat* ■ www.charlieslasvegas.com

7   **Escape Lounge** [M,NH] 702/364-1167 ■ 4213 W Sahara Ave ■ *24hrs*

8   **Flex** [MW,D,DS,S] 702/385-3539 ■ 4347 W Charleston (at Arville) ■ *24hrs* ■ www.flexlasvegas.com

9   **Freezone** [MW,NH,D,TG,F,K,DS,S,YC,GO] 702/794-2300 ■ 610 E Naples ■ *24hrs, women's night Tue, also restaurant* ■ www.freezonelv.com

10 **Goodtimes** [M,NH,D,WC] 702/736-9494 ■ 1775 E Tropicana Ave (at Spencer, in Liberace Plaza) ■ *24hrs, DJ Mon & after-hours Fri-Sat, [K] Wed* ■ www.goodtimeslv.com

11 **The Las Vegas Eagle** [M,L] 702/458-8662 ■ 3430 E Tropicana (at Pecos) ■ *24hrs, DJ Wed, Fri-Sat*

12 **Las Vegas Lounge** [GF,NH,TG,DS,S] 702/737-9350 ■ 900 E Karen Ave (at Maryland Pkwy) ■ *24hrs*

12 **Ramrod LV** [M,L,F,S,V,YC,GO] 702/735-0885 ■ 900 E Karen Ave #H-102 (in Commercial Center) ■ *noon-4am, strippers* ■ www.ramrodlv.com

13 **Snick's Place** [MO,NH] 702/385-9298 ■ 1402 S 3rd St (at Imperial) ■ *24hrs* ■ www.snicksplace.com

14 **The Spotlight Lounge** [★M,NH,D,E] 702/696-0202 ■ 957 E Sahara (at Commerical Center's entrance) ■ *24hrs, theme nights* ■ www.spotlightlv.com

NIGHTCLUBS

15 **Barcode** [GS,D,F] 702/221-5150 ■ 5150 Spring Mtn Rd (at Decatur) ■ *10pm-close Mon & Fri-Sat, from 7:30pm Wed-Th* ■ www.barcodelv.com

16 **The Gipsy** [★M,D,S,V,YC] 702/731-1919 ■ 4605 S Paradise Rd (at Naples) ■ *9pm-close, go-go boys* ■ www.gipsylv.net

17 <u>**Girl Bar at Krave**</u> [★W,D,MR] 702/836-0830 ■ 3663 S Las Vegas Blvd (at Harmon, next to the Aladdin) ■ *9pm-3am Sat only* ■ www.kravelasvegas.com

   House of Blues [GF,D,F,S,$] 702/632-7600 ■ 3950 Las Vegas Blvd S (at Hacienda Ave, in Mandalay Bay) ■ www.hob.com

17 **Krave** [★M,D,MR,TG,DS,S] 702/836-0830 ■ 3663 S Las Vegas Blvd (at Harmon, next to the Aladdin) ■ *11pm-close, clsd Sun* ■ www.kravelasvegas.com

   Lure [GS] 702/770-3633 ■ 3131 S Las Vegas Blvd (at Wynn) ■ *9pm-3am, clsd Sun-Mon, ultralounge, [$] Wed & Fri-Sat* ■ www.wynnlasvegas.com

   Pure Nightclub [GS,D,$] 702/731-7873 ■ 3570 S Las Vegas Blvd (at Caesar's Palace) ■ *10pm-4am, clsd Mon & Wed-Th, upscale, top DJs* ■ www.purethenightclub.com

5 **Suede Bar & Restaurant** [M,TG,F,E,K,C,DS,P,OC,GO] 702/791-3463 ■ 4640 Paradise Rd, #4 (at Naples) ■ *6pm-3am, till 5am Fri-Sun, clsd Mon*

LAS VEGAS

Day Trips: Area 51/ The Extraterrestrial Hwy & Hoover Dam

Government cover-up? UFO hotspot? You decide. This stretch of highway about 90 miles northeast of Vegas, dubbed "Area 51" after the secret military aircraft test site nearby, attracts visitors who are hoping to find the truth, or at least a good story. Pop in over at the bar and restaurant at Little A 'Le 'Inn for the latest scoop and memorabilia.

While you may or may not see aliens, there is no mistaking the presence of the Hoover Dam. Take a tour of the inner workings of the dam and power plant, or just relish in the view. Be sure to arrive by 3pm if you want to have enough time to do it all! For more info, visit www.usbr.gov/lc/hooverdam.

City Calendar

LGBT PRIDE

May. 702/615-9429 (NVAPI Hotline), web: www.lasvegaspride.org.

ANNUAL EVENTS

Sept - NGRA (Nevada Gay Rodeo Assn) Bighorn Rodeo 888/643-6472, web: www.ngra.com.

Queer Resources

COMMUNITY INFO

Gay/Lesbian Community Center 702/733-9800. 953 E Sahara Ave, Ste B-31, 11am-7pm, 10am-3pm Sat, clsd Sun, web: www.thecenter-lasvegas.com.

Alcoholics Together 702/737-0035. 900 E Karen, 2nd flr #A-202, noon & 8pm daily.

Aid for AIDS of Nevada 702/382-2326, web: www.afanlv.org

Tourist Infos

AIRPORT DIRECTIONS

McCarran International. To get to the bars, take Swenson St to Tropicana Ave. Turn left on Tropicana. At Paradise Rd, turn right. Take Paradise to Sahara Ave or to Las Vegas Blvd (The Strip).

PUBLIC TRANSIT & TAXIS

Western Cab 702/736-8000.
Lucky Cab 702/477-7555.
Various resorts have their own shuttle service.
CAT (Citizens Area Transit) 702/228-7433, web: www.rtcsouthernnevada.com.

TOURIST SPOTS & INFO

Bellagio Art Gallery 702/693-7871, web: www.bellagio.com.

Fremont Street Experience, web: www.vegasexperience.com.

Guggenheim Hermitage Museum, 702/414-2440, web: guggenheimlasvegas.com.

Hoover Dam & Museum, 702/294-1988, web: www.bcmha.org & www.usbr.gov/lc/hooverdam.

Imperial Palace Auto Collection 702/794-3174, web: www.imperialpalace.com.

King Tut Museum (at the Luxor) 702/262-4000, web: www.luxor.com.

La Cage at the Rivieria 877/892-7469, web: www.rivierahotel.com.

Las Vegas Art Museum 702/360-8000, web: www.lasvegasartmuseum.org.

Liberace Museum 702/798-5595, web: www.liberace.org.

Museum of Natural History 702/384-3466, web: www.lvnhm.org.

StarTrek: The Experience (at the Hilton) 888/462-6535, web: www.startrekexp.com.

Visitor's Center: Convention & Visitors Authority 702/892-0711, web: www.vegasfreedom.com. Also www.lasvegas.com.

Weather

It's in the desert. What do you think?

Best Views

Top of the Stratosphere. Or hurtling through the loops of the rollercoaster atop the New York New York Hotel. (Note: Do not ride immediately after the buffet.)

RESTAURANTS

Bootlegger Bistro 702/736-4939 ■ 7700 S Las Vegas Blvd ■ 24hrs, a Vegas classic, Italian, musical entertainment nightly ■ www.bootleggerlasvegas.com

Cravings 800/627-6667 ■ 3400 Las Vegas Blvd (at The Mirage) ■ buffet, Sat-Sun brunch ■ www.themirage.com

Go Raw 702/450-9007 ■ 2381 Windmill Ln ■ 10am-9pm, 11am-6pm Sun, organic vegan, also juice bar; also at 2910 Lake East Dr, 702/254-5382 ■ www.gorawcafe.com

Guy Savoy [R] 877/346-4642 ■ 3570 Las Vegas Blvd (at Caesar's Palace) ■ 5pm-10:30pm, clsd Mon-Tue, French

Joël Robuchon [R] 702/891-7925 ■ 3799 Las Vegas Blvd S (at MGM Grand Hotel) ■ 5:30pm-10pm, till 10:30pm Fri-Sat, French ■ www.mgmgrand.com

Mama Jo's 702/869-8099 ■ 3655 S Durango ■ lunch & dinner, dinner only Sun, Italian

Sushi Boy Desu 702/736-8234 ■ 4632 S Maryland Pkwy #12 ■ 11:30am-10pm

Wichcraft 877/891-7777 ■ at MGM Grand ■ 10am-6pm, till 8pm Fri-Sat, creative sandwiches, eat-in or take-out ■ www.mgmgrand.com

ENTERTAINMENT & RECREATION

Cupid's Wedding Chapel [GS] 702/598-4444, 800/543-2933 ■ 827 Las Vegas Blvd S (1 block N of Charleston) ■ commitment ceremonies, "Have the Vegas wedding you've always dreamed of!" ■ www.cupidswedding.com

The Forum Shops at Caesars 3570 Las Vegas Blvd S (in Caesars Palace) ■ you saw it in Showgirls & many other movies, now come shop for yourself

Kà by Cirque du Soleil 702/891-7777, 877/880-0880 ■ at MGM Grand ■ 6:30pm & 9:30pm Tue-Sat ■ www.ka.com

King Tutankhamun's Tomb & Museum 702/262-4555 ■ 3900 Las Vegas Blvd S (in the Luxor Las Vegas) ■ exact replica of the tomb when Howard Carter opened it in 1922 ■ www.luxor.com

La Cage 702/794-9433 ■ 2901 Las Vegas Blvd (at the Riviera) ■ show at 7:30pm, clsd Tue, the biggest drag show in town: Frank Marino & friends impersonate the divas, from Joan Rivers to Tina Turner ■ www.theriviera.com

Liberace Museum 702/798-5595 ■ 1775 E Tropicana Ave (at Spencer Ave) ■ this is one queen's closet you have to look into— especially if you love your pianos, clothes & cars covered w/ diamonds ■ www.liberace.org

Mystère by Cirque du Soleil 702/796-9999, 800/392-1999 ■ at Treasure Island ■ 7:30pm & 10:30pm Wed-Sat, 4:30pm & 7:30pm Sun ■ www.cirquedusoleil.com

O by Cirque du Soleil 702/796-9999, 888/488-7111 (reservations only) ■ at the Bellagio ■ 7:30pm & 10:30pm Wed-Sun, showstopper in a specially constructed aquatic theater (pricey tickets but more fun than losing your shirt in the casino) ■ www.cirquedusoleil.com

Sin City Rollergirls ■ Vegas' female roller derby league, check web for upcoming events ■ www.sincityrollergirls.com

Zumanity [18+] 702/740-6815, 866/606-7111 ■ at New York–New York Hotel & Casino ■ 7:30pm & 10:30pm Wed-Sun, explores human sexuality in an intimate, cabaret-style setting ■ www.zumanity.com

BOOKSTORES

Borders [WC] 702/258-0999 ■ 2323 S Decatur (at Sahara) ■ 9am-11pm, till 9pm Sun, LGBT section, cafe

5   **Get Booked** 702/737-7780 ■ 4640 Paradise #15 (at Naples) ■ 10am-midnight, till 2am Fri-Sat, LGBT ■ www.getbooked.com

RETAIL SHOPS

Glamour Boutique II 702/697-1800, 866/692-1800 ■ 714 E Sahara Ave #250 ■ clsd Sun, large-size dresses, wigs, etc ■ www.glamourboutiquewest.com

Male Bag 702/474-6253 ■ 610 E Sahara (at 6th) ■ www.themalebagvegas.com

The Rack 702/732-7225 ■ 953 E Sahara Ave, Ste 101, Bldg 16 (in Commercial Center) ■ leather, fetish

Sin City 702/387-6969 ■ 1013 E Charleston Blvd (at S 10th St) ■ 10:30am-2am, piercing & tattoo studio

PUBLICATIONS

Las Vegas Night Beat 702/369-8441 ■ LVNightBeat@aol.com

Out Las Vegas 702/650-0636 ■ monthly LGBT entertainment newspaper ■ www.outlasvegas.com

QVegas 702/650-0636 ■ monthly LGBT news & entertainment magazine ■ www.QVegas.com

GYMS & HEALTH CLUBS

Hands On Therapeutic Massage 702/458-8777 ■ 8335 S Las Vegas Blvd (at Cancun Resort) ■ licensed massage therapists visit home or hotel room, "open to all men & women," mention Damron for discount ■ www.handson-massagelv.com

The Las Vegas Athletic Club [GF] 702/734-5822 ■ 2655 S Maryland Pkwy ■ 5am-midnight, 7am-8pm wknds, day passes ■ www.lvac.com

MEN'S CLUBS

Apollo Spa & Health Club [MO,SW] 702/650-9191 ■ 953 E Sahara Ave #A19 (near Paradise & Maryland, at Commercial Center entrance) ■ 24hrs ■ www.apollospa.com

Hawks Gym [MO,OC,PC,AYOR,GO,$] 702/731-4295 ■ 953 E Sahara (at SE corner of Commercial Center) ■ 24hrs wknds ■ www.hawksgymlv.com

EROTICA

Adult World/ Mini Theaters [V] 702/579-9735 ■ 3781 Meade Ave (at Valley View) ■ 24hrs

Bare Essentials Fantasy Fashions [GO] 702/247-4711 ■ 4029 W Sahara Ave (near Valley View Blvd) ■ exotic/ intimate apparel for men & women, toys ■ bareessentialsvegas.com

Desert Adult Books 702/643-7982 ■ 4350 N Las Vegas Blvd (at Craig Rd) ■ 24hrs

Fantasy World Arcade/ Theaters 702/433-6311 ■ 6760 Boulder Hwy (btwn Sunset & Russell) ■ 24hrs

Industrial Road Adult Books 702/734-7667 ■ 3427 Industrial Rd (at Spring Mtn) ■ 24hrs

Onyx Theater 702/732-7225 ■ 953 E Sahara Ave, Bldg 16

Price Video 702/734-1342 ■ 700 E Naples Dr #102 (at Swenson) ■ 10am-10pm

Rancho Adult Entertainment Center 702/645-6104 ■ 4820 N Rancho #D (at Lone Mtn) ■ 24hrs

Romantix Adult Superstore 702/892-0699 ■ 2923 S Industrial Rd (behind Circus Circus) ■ www.romantixon-line.com

Tropicana Book & Video/ Adult Super Store 702/798-0144 ■ 3850 W Tropicana (at Valley View) ■ 24hrs, cruisy theaters

Video West [GO] 702/248-7055 ■ 5785 W Tropicana (at Jones) ■ also 4637 S Paradise Rd, 702/735-1469

Reno

ACCOMMODATIONS

1   **Holiday Inn & Diamonds Casino** [GF,SW,WI,WC]
     775/786-5151 ■ 1000 E 6th St (at Wells Ave) ■ *restaurant*
     ■ www.holidayinnreno.com

2   **Sands Regency Casino Hotel Downtown Reno** [GF,E]
     775/348-2200, 866/386-7829 ■ 345 N Arlington Ave ■
     www.sandsregency.com

BARS

3   **1099 Club** [★MW,NH,S,V,WC] 775/329-1099 ■ 1099 S
     Virginia St (at Vassar) ■ *10am-2am, patio* ■
     www.ten99club.com

4   **Carl's Pub** [M,NH,D,L] 775/829-8886 ■ 3310 S Virginia St
     (at Moana) ■ *1pm-3am, patio* ■
     www.renodean.com/carlspub

5   **Five Star Saloon** [M,NH,D,WC] 775/329-2878 ■ 132 West
     St (at 1st) ■ *24hrs*

6   **The Patio** [MW,NH] 775/323-6565 ■ 600 W 5th St (btwn
     Washington & Ralston) ■ *11am-2am* ■
     www.thepatiobar.com

7   Reflections [MW,D,WI] 775/322-3001 ■ 3001 W 4th St
     ■ *noon-9pm, till 3am Fri-Sat, till 8pm Sun* ■ www.reflec-
     tionsreno.com

NIGHTCLUBS

8   **Neutron** [★GS,D,YC] 775/786-2121 ■ 340 Kietzke Ln (btwn
     Glendale & Mill) ■ *2pm-close*

8   **Tronix** [★MW,D,MR,TG,S,V,YC,WC,GO] 775/333-9696 ■ 303
     Kietzke Ln (at E 2nd St) ■ *10am-3am* ■
     www.tronixreno.com

RESTAURANTS

Pneumatic Diner 775/786-8888 x106 ■ 501 W 1st St (in
Truckee River Apts, 2nd flr) ■ *11am-11pm, from 9am Sat,
from 8am Sun, vegetarian*

ENTERTAINMENT & RECREATION

Brüka Theatre 775/323-3221 ■ 99 N Virginia St
■ *alternative theater & performance space* ■ www.bruka-
land.com

BOOKSTORES

Borders 775/448-9999 ■ 4995 S Virginia St (at Kietzke)
■ *9am-10pm, till 11pm Fri-Sat, till 9pm Sun*

Dharma Books 775/786-8667 ■ 11 N Sierra St #107
■ *11am-7pm, noon-5pm Sun, clsd Mon, used & rare books* ■
www.dharmabooks.biz

9   **Heart Spot Gallery & Books** 775/348-9888 ■ 900 1st St
     (at Vine) ■ *9am-6pm, clsd wknds, gallery & bookstore
     benefiting Nevada AIDS Foundation* ■
     www.nvaf.net/heartspot.html

RENO

Day Trips: Truckee, CA

    Whatever the season, Truckee is a great little town with lots of activities to keep you entertained. So close to
great skiing in winter; rock-climbing, hiking, and sight-seeing in warmer weather; and with plenty of cute little
shops, there is something for everyone. Check out The Sports Exchange (www.truckeesportsexchange.com) for
sporting gear and their great little indoor climbing gym. It's a blast!

Tourist Info

AIRPORT DIRECTIONS

Reno-Tahoe International Airport. To get
dowtown, take Plumb Ln from terminal to
Virginia St. Turn right on Virginia and head north.

PUBLIC TRANSIT & TAXIS

Bell Limo 775/786-3700.
Reno/Sparks Cab 775/333-3333.
City Fare (bus) 775/348-7433.

TOURIST SPOTS & INFO

Casinos.
Lake Tahoe.
National Automobile Museum 775/333-9300,
web: www.automuseum.org.
Nevada Museum of Art 775/329-3333, web:
www.nevadaart.org.
Sierra Safari Zoo 775/677-1101, web: www.sier-
rasafarizoo.org.
Virginia City.
Visitor's Center: Reno-Sparks Chamber of
Commerce 775/337-3030, web: www.reno-
sparkschamber.org.
Reno/Sparks Convention & Visitors Authority
800/FOR-RENO, web: www.visitrenotahoe.com.

City Calendar

LGBT PRIDE

August, web: www.renogaypride.com

ANNUAL EVENTS

March - Lake Tahoe WinterFest. LGBT ski week
west of Reno, web:
www.laketahoewinterfest.com.
Aug-Sept - Burning Man. Artsy freakfest in the
Black Rock Desert, north of Reno 415/863-5263,
web: www.burningman.com.

Queer Resources

COMMUNITY INFO

A Rainbow Place 775/789-1780. 2890 Vassar St,
LGBT center, web: www.arainbowplace.org.
AA Central Office 775/355-1151, web:
www.nnig.org.
Nevada AIDS Foundation 775/348-9888, web:
www.nvaf.net.

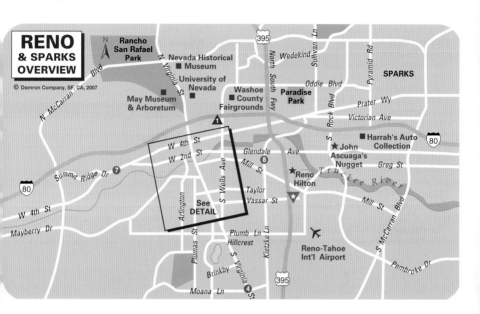

RENO & SPARKS OVERVIEW

© Damron Company, SF, CA, 2007

Rancho San Rafael Park

Nevada Historical ■ Museum

University of Nevada

May Museum & Arboretum

Washoe ■ County Fairgrounds

Paradise Park

SPARKS

Wedekind

Oddie Blvd

Prater Wy

Victorian Ave

Harrah's Auto ■ Collection

★ John Ascuaga's Nugget

Greg St

★ Reno Hilton

Glendale   Ave

Taylor

Vassar St

Truckee River

Mill St

W 4th St

W 2nd St

See DETAIL

Summit Ridge Dr

W 4th St

Mayberry Dr

Plumb Ln

Hillcrest

Brinkby

Moana Ln

Reno-Tahoe Int'l Airport

Pembroke Dr

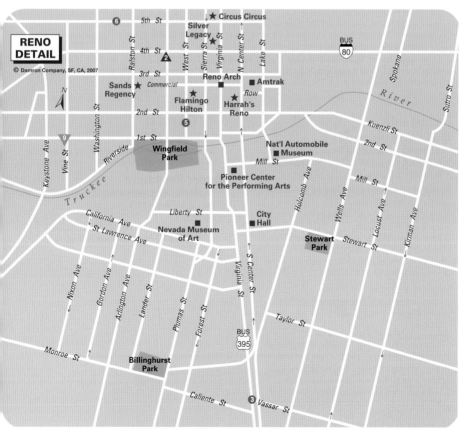

RENO DETAIL

© Damron Company, SF, CA, 2007

5th St

★ Circus Circus

Silver Legacy

4th St

3rd St

Reno Arch

★ Amtrak

Sands ★ Commercial Regency

Flamingo Hilton

★ Harrah's Reno

Row

2nd St

1st St

Wingfield Park

Nat'l Automobile ■ Museum

Mill St

Pioneer Center for the Performing Arts

BUS 80

River

Kuenzli St

2nd St

Mill St

Wells Ave

Spokane

Sutro St

Liberty St

California Ave

St Lawrence Ave

Nevada Museum of Art

City ■ Hall

Stewart Park

Stewart St

Locust Ave

Kirman Ave

Holcomb Ave

Nixon Ave

Gordon Ave

Arlington Ave

Lander St

Plumas St

Forest St

Monroe St

Billinghurst Park

Caliente St

Vassar St

BUS 395

Taylor St

S Center St

Virginia St

Sundance Books 775/786-1188 ■ 1155 W 4th St #106 (at Keystone) ■ *9am-9pm, 10am-6pm wknds, independent* ■ www.sundancebookstore.com

RETAIL SHOPS
The Hidden Woman [TG] 775/329-8050 ■ 1507 S Wells Ave #100 (at E Pueblo St) ■ *10am-6pm, 11am-5pm Sat, specializes in transgender/ MTF clothing & accessories, also men's lingerie & clubwear* ■ www.hiddenwoman.com

PUBLICATIONS
The Outlands 775/324-7866 ■ *calendar, resources, features, classifieds, listings* ■ www.OutlandsMagazine.com
Sierra Voice 775/322-7866 ■ *monthly, bar & resource listings, community events, arts & entertainment* ■ www.sierravoice.com

MEN'S CLUBS
Steve's [PC] 775/323-8770 ■ 1030 W 2nd St (at Keystone) ■ *24hrs, spa* ■ www.stevesbathhousereno.com

EROTICA
The Chocolate Walrus 775/825-2267 ■ 1278 S Virginia St ■ *10am-8pm, noon-5pm Sun*

Fantasy Faire 775/323-6969 ■ 1298 S Virginia (at Arroyo) ■ *toys, fetish gear*
G Spot [★GO] 775/333-6969 ■ 138 West St (btwn 1st & 2nd) ■ *10am-10pm, till midnight Fri-Sat*
Suzie's 775/786-8557 ■ 195 Kietzke Ln (at E 2nd St) ■ *24hrs*

NEW JERSEY

Atlantic City

ACCOMMODATIONS
The Carisbrooke Inn [GF,NS,WI] 609/822-6392 ■ 105 S Little Rock Ave, Ventnor ■ *on a beach block 1 mile from Atlantic City* ■ www.carisbrookeinn.com
1   Ocean House [MO,V,SW,N,GO] 609/345-8203 ■ 127 S Ocean Ave ■ *intimate atmosphere* ■ oceanhouseatlanticcity.com

ATLANTIC CITY

Day Trips: Jersey Shore & Cape May
There are plenty of towns to visit along the shore, and miles of beach. Just north, across the bridge from Atlantic City you might find your fortune—buried in the sand. It has been said that Blackbeard and Captain Kidd buried booty on the island, and it has yet to be found!
Other treasures are to be found in Cape May, at the southern tip of New Jersey, in the form of beautifully restored Victorians, great dining and shopping, and fabulous sunsets. For more info about towns on the shore, visit: www.jerseyshore-online.com.

Tourist Info
AIRPORT DIRECTIONS
Atlantic City International. To get to the Boardwalk, simply take Atlantic City Expressway to Atlantic or Pacific.

PUBLIC TRANSIT & TAXIS
Yellow Cab 609/344-1221.
Airport Chariot 609/748-3506, web: www.airportchariot.com.
Royal Airport Shuttle 888/824-7767, web: www.royalairportshuttle.com.
New Jersey Transit 800/772-2222, web: www.njtransit.com.

TOURIST SPOTS & INFO
Absecon Lighthouse 609/449-1360, web: www.abseconlighthouse.org.
Casinos.
Ripley's Believe It Or Not! Museum 609/347-2001, web: www.ripleysatlanticcity.com. Just what you'd expect to find here and then some, including a lock of George Washington's hair.
Visitor's Center: Convention & Visitors Authority 888/228-4748, web: www.atlanticcitynj.com.
Chamber of Commerce 609/345-4524, web: www.atlanticcitychamber.com.

City Calendar
LGBT PRIDE
Jersey Pride, web: www.jerseypride.org. Statewide Pride festival held in Asbury Park.

Queer Resources
AA 609/641-8855, web: www.caigrp.org.
New Jersey AIDS/STD Hotline, 800/624-2377 (NJ only).
New Jersey Women & AIDS Network 732/846-4462 & 800/747-1108, web: www.njwan.org.

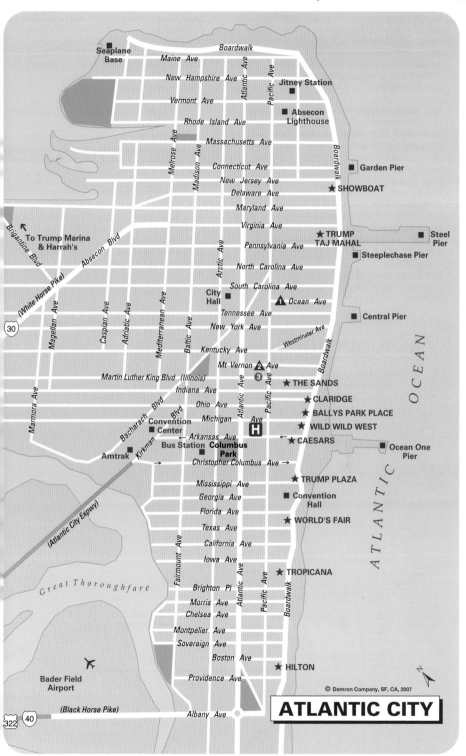

Seaplane Base

Boardwalk

Maine Ave

New Hampshire Ave

Vermont Ave

Rhode Island Ave

Massachusetts Ave

Connecticut Ave

New Jersey Ave

Delaware Ave

Maryland Ave

Virginia Ave

Pennsylvania Ave

North Carolina Ave

South Carolina Ave

City Hall

Ocean Ave

Tennessee Ave

New York Ave

Kentucky Ave

Mt Vernon Ave

Martin Luther King Blvd (Illinois)

Indiana Ave

Ohio Ave

Convention Center

Michigan Ave

Arkansas Ave

Bus Station

Columbus Park

Amtrak

Christopher Columbus Ave →

Mississippi Ave

Georgia Ave

Florida Ave

Texas Ave

California Ave

Iowa Ave

Brighton Pl

Morris Ave

Chelsea Ave

Montpelier Ave

Sovereign Ave

Boston Ave

Providence Ave

Albany Ave

Atlantic Ave

Pacific Ave

Jitney Station

Absecon Lighthouse

Boardwalk

Garden Pier

★ SHOWBOAT

★ TRUMP TAJ MAHAL

Steel Pier

Steeplechase Pier

Central Pier

Westminster Ave

Boardwalk

★ THE SANDS

★ CLARIDGE

★ BALLYS PARK PLACE

★ WILD WILD WEST

★ CAESARS

Ocean One Pier

★ TRUMP PLAZA

Convention Hall

★ WORLD'S FAIR

★ TROPICANA

★ HILTON

To Trump Marina & Harrah's

Brigantine Blvd

Absecon Blvd

(White Horse Pike)

30

Magellan Ave

Marmora Ave

Caspian Ave

Adriatic Ave

Melrose Ave

Madison Ave

Mediterranean Ave

Baltic Ave

Bacharach Blvd

Kirkman Blvd

Arctic Ave

Atlantic Ave

Pacific Ave

Fairmount Ave

Atlantic Ave

Pacific Ave

Boardwalk

(Atlantic City Expwy)

Great Thoroughfare

Bader Field Airport

(Black Horse Pike)

322 40

OCEAN

ATLANTIC

© Damron Company, SF, CA, 2007

ATLANTIC CITY

2 **Surfside Resort Hotel** [GS,21+,SW,GO] 609/347-7873, 888/277-7873 ■ 18 S Mt Vernon Ave (at Pacific, at Club Tru/ Studio Six Complex) ■ *small, upscale straight-friendly hotel, sundeck* ■ www.surfsideresorthotel.com
Tropicana Casino & Resort [GF,SW] 609/340-4000, 800/345-8767 ■ Brighton & The Boardwalk ■ www.tropicana.net

BARS

2 **Brass Rail Bar & Grill** [★GS,NH,F,K,S,GO] 609/347-0808 ■ 12 S Mt Vernon Ave (at Club Tru/ Studio Six Complex) ■ *24hrs, [K] Fri-Sat, go-go boys Sun* ■ www.clubtru.com

2 **Oak Room** [GF,P,GO] 609/347-7873 ■ at Surfside Resort Hotel ■ *24hrs Fri-Sun, seasonal, upscale piano lounge* ■ www.clubtru.com

NIGHTCLUBS

3 **Club Tru** [★GS,D] 609/344-2222 ■ 9 S Martin Luther King Jr Blvd (btwn Atlantic & Pacific Aves) ■ *10pm-6am, 11pm-noon wknds, several bars* ■ www.clubtru.com

2 **Studio Six Video Dance Club** [★MW,D,E,V] 609/348-3310 ■ 18 S Mt Vernon Ave (near Kentucky) ■ *10pm-close, 5 bars, go-go boys* ■ www.studiosix.com

RESTAURANTS

Dock's Oyster House [WC] 609/345-0092 ■ 2405 Atlantic Ave ■ *5pm-10pm, till 11pm Fri-Sat* ■ www.docksoysterhouse.com

White House Sub Shop 609/345-1564 ■ 2301 Arctic Ave (at Mississippi) ■ *10am-10pm, till 11pm Fri-Sat, from 11am Sun*

PUBLICATIONS
EXP Magazine 302/227-5787, 877/397-6244 ■ *bi-weekly gay magazine for Mid-Atlantic* ■ www.expmagazine.com

EROTICA
Atlantic City News 609/344-9444 ■ 101 S Martin Luther King Jr Blvd (at Pacific) ■ *24hrs*

NEW MEXICO

Albuquerque

ACCOMMODATIONS
1 **Adobe Nido** [GF,NS,WI] 505/344-1310, 866/435-6436 ■ 1124 Major Ave NW ■ *B&B, also aviary* ■ www.adobenido.com

2 **Bottger Mansion of Old Town** [GF,TG,WI] 505/243-3639, 800/758-3639 ■ 110 San Felipe ■ *B&B* ■ www.bottger.com

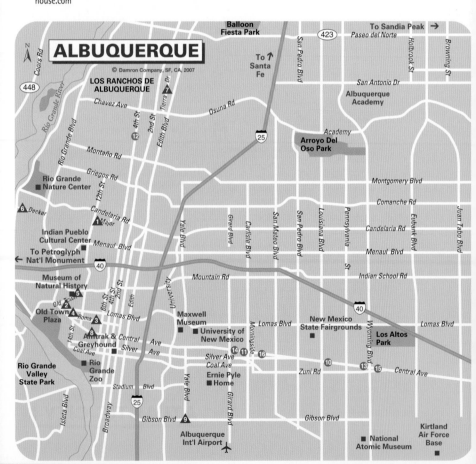

3 **Brittania & W E Mauger Estate B&B** [GF,NS,WI] 505/242-8755, 800/719-9189 ■ 701 Roma Ave NW (at 7th) ■ *intimate Queen Anne house, full brkfst* ■ www.maugerbb.com

4 **La Casita B&B** [GF,NS,WI] 505/242-0173 ■ 317 16th St NW ■ *adobe guesthouse* ■ www.lacasitabb.com

5 **Casitas at Old Town** [GS,NS,GO] 505/843-7479 ■ 1604 Old Town Rd NW ■ *suites in a classic adobe bldg, private patios* ■ www.oldtowncasitas.com

   El Peñasco [W,NS,GO] 505/771-8909, 888/576-2726 ■ *private historic adobe guesthouse, halfway btwn Albuquerque & Santa Fe, lesbian-owned* ■ www.purpleroofs.com/listingpictures/e/elpenasco-nm.html

6 Golden Guesthouses [MW,NS,GO] 505/344-9205, 888/513-GOLD ■ 2645 Decker NW ■ *individual & shared units, lesbian-owned* ■ www.goldenguesthouses.com

7 **Hacienda Antigua B&B** [GS,SW,NS] 505/345-5399, 800/201-2986 ■ 6708 Tierra Dr NW (close to corner of 2nd & Osuna) ■ *full brkfst, hot tub* ■ www.haciendantigua.com

ALBUQUERQUE

Day Trips: Turquoise Trail

Head east out of town on I-40 (the modern incarnation of the famous Route 66), and hang a left onto the Turquoise Trail, which begins in the dusty town of Tijeras. Ancient Pueblo dwellings, ghost mining towns, and cultural treasures from New Mexico's rich past await you on this 52-mile road to Santa Fe. If you don't have time for the drive, at least take the Sandia Peak Tramway up to the top of Sandia Peak, where you will be amazed by the awesome, hundred-mile vistas. Visit www.turquoisetrail.org to learn more.

Local Food:

More than just "Southwestern," New Mexican cuisine is actually a delicious hybrid of Mexican and Native American cultures, with a nod to the Spanish for the vegetables they brought from Europe. Corn, pinto beans, and of course the versatile chile pepper are the basics for a wide range of hearty, tasty fare. The chile pepper grows in some 2,000 varieties, and can be prepared in almost as many ways. Color, size, and spiciness vary, so go slow if you are a beginner. Note: If you find your tongue burning from the heat of a pepper, dairy products are the quickest remedy to quash the flames, so heap on the sour cream!

Tourist Info

TOURIST SPOTS & INFO
Albuquerque Museum 505/243-7255, web: www.albuquerquemuseum.com.
Indian Pueblo Cultural Center 505/843-7270 or 866/855-7902 (outside NM), web: www.indian-pueblo.org.
New Mexico Museum of Natural History & Science 505/841-2800, web: www.nmnaturalhistory.org. Old Town.
Petroglyph National Monument 505/899-0205, web: www.nps.gov/petr/.
Rattlesnake Museum 505/242-6569, web: www.rattlesnakes.com.
Sandia Peak Tramway 505/856-7325, web: www.sandiapeak.com.
Wildlife West Nature Park 505/281-7655, web: www.wildlifewest.org
Visitor's Center: 800/284-2282, web: www.abqcvb.org.

Weather
Sunny and temperate. Warm days and cool nights in summer, with average temperatures from 65° to 95°. Winter is cooler, from 28° to 57°.

Best Views
Sandia Peak Tramway (505/856-7325) at sunset.

City Calendar

LGBT PRIDE
June. 505/873-8084, web: www.abqpride.com.

ENTERTAINMENT
New Mexico Gay Rodeo Association www.nmgra.com.

ANNUAL EVENTS
September - Closet Cinema, LGBT film festival 505/243-1870, web: www.closetcinema.org.
October - Albuquerque Int'l Balloon Fiesta 505/821-1000 or 888/422-7277, web: www.balloonfiesta.com.

Queer Resources

COMMUNITY INFO
Common Bond Info Line 505/891-3647, web: members.aol.com/gayinformation/.
AA Gay/Lesbian 505/266-1900 (AA#). 505/938-7100, web: www.nmas.net.

8   **Silver Moon Lodge** [GF,WI,WC] 505/243-1773, 866/425-8085 ■ 918 Central Ave W ■ *central location, also restaurant* ■ www.silver-moon-lodge.com

9   **Wyndham Albuquerque Hotel** [GF,SW] 505/843-7000, 800/227-1117 ■ 2910 Yale Blvd SE (at Gibson) ■ *4-star hotel, also Rojo Grille restaurant* ■ www.wyndhamhotels.com/abqap

BARS

10 **Albuquerque Mining Co (AMC)** [★M,D,S,V,WC,GO] 505/255-4022 ■ 7209 Central Ave NE (at Louisiana) ■ *6pm-2am, till midnight Sun, clsd Mon-Tue, also Pit Bar*

11 **Albuquerque Social Club** [★MW,D,PC] 505/255-0887 ■ 4021 Central Ave NE (enter rear) ■ *3pm-midnight, till 2am Fri-Sat, noon-midnight Sun* ■ albsocclub@aol.com

12 **Exhale** [W,NH,D,F,K] 505/342-0049 ■ 6132 4th NW (near Osuna) ■ *6pm-close, from 4:30pm Sun, clsd Mon-Tue* ■ www.exhaleabq.com

13 **Foxes Lounge** [MW,D,DS] 505/255-3060 ■ 8521 Central Ave NE (btwn Wisconsin & Wyoming) ■ *10am-2am, noon-midnight Sun, home bar of the Royal Court*

14 **Gulp** [GS,F,GO] 505/268-4729 ■ 3128 Central SE ■ *11am-2am, 4pm-midnight Sun, patio* ■ www.grazeabq.com

15 **Sidewinders Ranch** [M,D,CW,B,L,K,WC] 505/275-1616 ■ 8900 Central SE (at Wyoming) ■ *noon-2am, till midnight Sun* ■ www.sidewindersranch.com

NIGHTCLUBS

Fire [WO,D] ■ *monthly dance party, check local listings or website for location* ■ www.firewomyn.com

16 **Pulse/ Blu** [★M,D,E,$] 505/255-3334 ■ 4100 Central Ave SE (at Montclaire, in Nob Hill) ■ *9pm-2am, clsd Sun-Tue* ■ www.pulseandblu.com

CAFES

Java Joe's 505/765-1514 ■ 906 Park Ave SW ■ *6:30am-3:30pm, coffee & pastries, monthly art shows* ■ www.downtownjavajoes.com

RESTAURANTS

Artichoke Cafe 505/243-0200 ■ 424 Central Ave ■ *lunch Mon-Fri, dinner nightly, bistro, plenty veggie* ■ artichoke-cafe.com

Cafe Cubano at Laru Ni Hati [GO] 505/255-1575 ■ 3413 Central Ave NE ■ *9am-9pm Tue-Sat, 10am-5pm Sun, clsd Mon, cigars & cheap Cuban food, also unisex hair salon*

Chef du Jour [WC] 505/247-8998 ■ 119 San Pasquale SW (at Central) ■ *lunch Tue-Fri, dinner Th-Sat, plenty veggie*

District Bar and Grill [E] 505/243-0003 ■ 115 4th St NW (downtown) ■ *5pm-2am, clsd Sun, New Mexican, live bands* ■ www.districtbar.com

El Patio [★YC,BW] 505/268-4245 ■ 142 Harvard St SE ■ *11am-9pm, from noon Sun, plenty veggie*

Flying Star Cafe [WC] 505/255-6633 ■ 3416 Central SE (2 blocks W of Carlisle) ■ *6am-11:30pm, till midnight Fri-Sat, plenty veggie* ■ www.flyingstarcafe.com

Frontier 505/266-0550 ■ 2400 Central SE (at Cornell) ■ *24hrs, good brkfst burritos*

Martini Grille 505/255-4111 ■ 4200 Central Ave NE ■ *4pm-2am, from 5pm Sat, clsd Sun, swank* ■ www.nmrestaurants.com/martinigrille/

Romano's Macaroni Grill 505/881-3400 ■ 2100 Louisiana NE (at Winrock Mall) ■ *11am-10pm, Italian* ■ macaronigrill.com

Sadie's Cocinita [★] 505/345-5339 ■ 6230 4th St NW (near Osuna) ■ *11am-10pm, 1am-9pm Sun, New Mexican* ■ www.sadiesofnewmexico.com

Zinc Wine Bar & Bistro [E,R] 505/254-9462 ■ 3009 Central Ave NE ■ *lunch & dinner, brunch Sun, also Blues Cellar till 1am Mon-Sat, live jazz Th & Sat-Sun* ■ www.zincabq.com

ENTERTAINMENT & RECREATION

Duke City Derby ■ *Albuquerque's female roller derby league, check web for upcoming events* ■ www.dukecityderby.com

New Mexico Gay Men's Chorus 505/268-6995 ■ www.nmgmc.org

Rainbow Ryders [GF] 505/823-1111, 800/725-2477 ■ 11520 San Bernardino NE ■ *scenic balloon rides* ■ www.rainbowryders.com

WIMIN (Women in Movement in New Mexico) 505/899-3627 ■ *production company promoting women's music, art & culture, w/ events throughout year* ■ www.wiminfest.org

BOOKSTORES

Bird Song 505/268-7204 ■ 1708 Central SE ■ *11am-7pm, clsd Mon, used, LGBT section* ■ www.birdsongusedbooks.com

Page One 505/294-2026, 800/521-4122 ■ 11018 Montgomery NE ■ *9am-10pm, till 8pm Sun, "New Mexico's largest independent bookstore"* ■ www.page1book.com

RETAIL SHOPS

Newsland 505/242-0694 ■ 2122 Central Ave SE (at Yale) ■ *8am-9pm, till 8pm Sun, some LGBT magazines*

GYMS & HEALTH CLUBS

Betty's Bath & Day Spa 505/341-3456 ■ 1835 Candelaria NW ■ *full-service spa w/ separate women-only hot tub* ■ www.bettysbath.com

Pride Gym [★MO,18+,PC] 505/242-7810 ■ 1803 3rd St NW (4 blocks S of I-40, exit 158) ■ *sundeck, parties, day passes available* ■ www.pride-gym.com

EROTICA

Castle Superstore 505/262-2266 ■ 5110 Central Ave SE (at San Mateo)

Video Maxxx 505/341-4000 ■ 810 Comanche NE (at I-25) ■ *leather, novelties, books, etc*

Viewpoint [★] 505/268-6373 ■ 6406 Central Ave SE (at San Pedro) ■ *24hrs*

NEW YORK

Fire Island

ACCOMMODATIONS

A Summer Place Realty [MW,GO] 631/597-6140 ■ Bayview Walk (at Main Walk), Cherry Grove ■ *rentals, private homes & apts, also sales* ■ www.asummerplacerealty.com

Belvedere Hotel [MO,SW,WC,GO] 631/597-6448 ■ *Venetian-style palace, hot tub, jacuzzi, gym* ■ www.belvederefireisland.com

Bob Howard Real Estate 631/597-9400, 212/819-9400 ■ The Pines ■ *great source for rentals* ■ www.fireisland-pineshomes.com

D Katen Fire Island Properties, Ltd [GO] 631/597-7000 ■ 42 Harbor, The Pines ■ *weekly, monthly & seasonal rentals & sales* ■ www.fireislandpines.com

Dune Point Guesthouse [GF,NS,WC] 631/597-6261, 631/560-2200 (cell) ■ *hot tub* ■ www.dunepointfireisland.com

GroveHotel [M,SW,N,WC,GO] 631/597-6600 ■ Dock Walk, Cherry Grove ■ *4 bars on premises* ■ www.grovehotel.com

Hotel Ciel [M,F,SW,WC] 631/597-6500 ■ The Pines ■ *also restaurant* ■ www.thepinesfireisland.com

Island Properties of the Pines, Inc. [GO] 631/597-6900 ■ 37 Fire Island Blvd, The Pines ■ *weekly, monthly & seasonal rentals* ■ www.thepines.us

The Madison Fire Island Pines [M,SW,NS,WI,GO] 631/597-6061 ■ *new guesthouse w/ full amenities, near beach, roof deck, hot tub* ■ www.themadisonfi.com

Pines Harbor Realty [GO] 631/597-7575 ■ *seasonal rentals* ■ www.pinesharbor.com

BARS

Blue Whale [★MW,D,F,WC] 631/597-6500 ■ Fire Island Blvd, The Pines ■ *seasonal, noon-8am, popular High Tea dance* ■ www.thepinesfireisland.com

Cherry's [★MW,F,E,DS,P] 631/597-6820 ■ 158 Bayview Walk, Cherry Grove ■ *seasonal, noon-4am, patio, also restaurant*

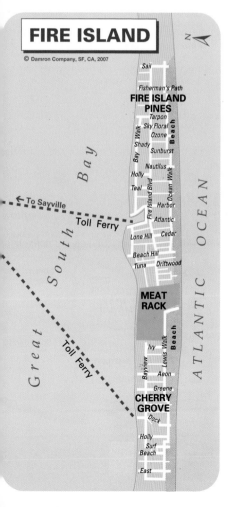

FIRE ISLAND

© Damron Company, SF, CA, 2007

N

Sail

Fisherman's Path

FIRE ISLAND PINES

Tarpon
Sky Floral
Ozone
Shady
Sunburst
Nautilus
Holly
Teal

Walk
Bay
Fire Island Blvd
Ocean Walk
Beach

South Bay

←To Sayville

Toll Ferry

Harbor
Atlantic
Lone Hill   Cedar
Beach Hill
Tuna   Driftwood

Great South Bay

Toll Ferry

MEAT RACK

Ivy   Lewis Walk
Bayview
Aeon
Greene

CHERRY GROVE

Dock
Holly
Surf
Beach
East

ATLANTIC OCEAN

FIRE ISLAND

Tourist Info

AIRPORT DIRECTIONS

Long Island Airport in Islip. Service from NYC and other US cities, then taxi to Sayville ferry.

PUBLIC TRANSIT & TAXIS

Fire Island Ferry Water Taxi 631/665-8885, web: www.fireislandwatertaxi.com. Service from Sayville to Fire Island.

Colonial Taxi 631/ 589-3500. Service between ferry and train station, airport, or other Long Island destinations.

Ferry service to The Pines and Cherry Grove from Sayville takes 20 minutes. Call for schedule 631/665-8885, web: www.fireislandferries.com.

By car: go east on the Long Island Expressway to exit 59 to Ocean Ave, then head south to Lakeland Ave and the town of Sayville. The ferry is located on River Rd.

By train: Long Island Railroad service from Penn Stn in NYC to Sayville (shuttle or taxi to ferry). 90 minutes, $10-13 one way. 631/-231-5477.

TOURIST SPOTS & INFO

Sunken Forest
Fire Island Lighthouse, web: www.fireislandlighthouse.com.

City Calendar

ANNUAL EVENTS

4th of July - Invasion of the Pines, web: www.fireislandinvasion.com. Hundreds of men & women in drag ferry over from Cherry Grove for this historic event stemming from the past rivalry between the two communities.

Queer Resources

COMMUNITY INFO

Gay & Lesbian Switchboard of Long Island (GLSB of LI) 631/665-3700.
Fire Island Community News, web: www.fireislandqnews.com.
AA 631/669-1124, web: www.suffolkny-aa.org.

The Tides [M,D,E,C,S] 631/597-3744 ■ 177 Ocean Walk, Cherry Grove ■ www.tidescherrygrove.com

NIGHTCLUBS

Ice Palace [MW,Ð,DS,WC] 631/597-6600 ■ Bayview Walk, Cherry Grove ■ *hours vary* ■ www.grovehotel.com

The Pavilion [★MW,D,WC] 631/597-6500 ■ Fire Island Blvd, The Pines ■ *seasonal, noon-8am Fri-Sun only, popular High Tea dance* ■ www.thepinesfireisland.com

RESTAURANTS

Cherry Grove Pizza 631/597-6766 ■ Dock Walk (under the GroveHotel), Cherry Grove ■ *11am-11pm, till 1am Fri-Sat*

Jumpin' Jack's Seafood Shack 631/597-4174 ■ Ocean Walk, Cherry Grove ■ *lunch & dinner, also piano bar*

Marina Meat Market 631/597-6588 ■ Harbor Park, The Pines ■ *brkfst, lunch & dinner, take-out available all day* ■ www.petersmeatmarket.com

ENTERTAINMENT & RECREATION

Invasion of the Pines The Pines dock (July 4th wknd) ■ *come & enjoy the annual fun as boatloads of drag queens from Cherry Grove arrive to terrorize the posh Pines* ■ www.fireislandinvasion.com

RETAIL SHOPS

All American Boy 631/597-7758 ■ 36 Fire Island Blvd, The Pines ■ *seasonal, call for hours, clothing*

Long Island

Long Island is divided into 2 geographical areas:
Long Island—Nassau
Long Island—Suffolk/ Hamptons

Long Island—Nassau

BARS

Beenzy's Bar & Grill [MW,NH,D,F] 516/679-5456 ■ 2955 Merrick Rd, Wantagh ■ *3pm-4am, from 12:30pm wknds* ■ www.beenzysbar.com

Blanche [M,NH,E,S] 516/694-6906 ■ 47-2 Boundary Ave, South Farmingdale ■ *5pm-close, from 3pm Sun, [S] Fri-Sat* ■ blanchesli@aol.com

Zen Lounge [M,D,K,GO] 516/489-1976 ■ 121 Woodfield Rd, West Hempstead ■ *8pm-4am, from 5pm Sat, clsd Mon* ■ www.zenlounge.us

NIGHTCLUBS

Deluxe [MW,D] 516/520-1332 ■ 2686 Hempstead Tpke (at Club 2686), Levittown ■ *9pm-4am Wed only*

RESTAURANTS

RS Jones 516/378-7177 ■ 153 Merrick Ave (off Sunrise), Merrick ■ *dinner, clsd Mon, Tex-Mex* ■ rsjones.com

ENTERTAINMENT & RECREATION

Jones Beach Field #6

Pride for Youth Coffeehouse [MW,D] 516/679-9000 ■ 2050 Bellmore Ave, Bellmore ■ www.prideforyouth.org

PUBLICATIONS

PM Entertainment Magazine 516/845-0759 ■ *events, listings, classifieds & more for Long Island, NJ & NYC* ■ www.pmentertainmentonline.com

Long Island—Suffolk/ Hamptons

ACCOMMODATIONS

By the Sea [WO,SW,NS] 631/725-4952 ■ lstherapy@optonline.net

Comfort Inn [GF,SW,WC] 631/654-3000, 800/626-7779 (out-of-state reservations only) ■ 2695 Rte 112 (exit 64 off LI Expwy), Medford ■ *also Gateway Lounge [F]* ■ www.choicehotels.com

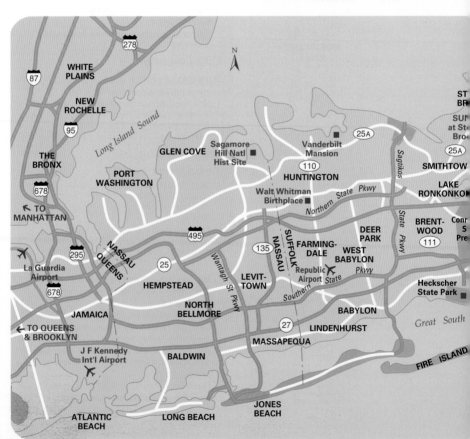

The Country Place [GS,NS] 631/324-4125 ■ 29 Hands Creek Rd, East Hampton ■ *B&B on 3 acres w/ pond, private entrances, minutes to beach* ■ www.webhampton.com/thecountryplace

Cozy Cottages [GS] 631/537-1160 ■ 395 Montauk Hwy, East Hampton ■ *hot tub, sundeck* ■ hamptsonescape@aol.com

East Hampton Village B&B [GS,NS] 631/324-1858 ■ 172 Newtown Ln (at McGuirk St), East Hampton ■ *lovely turn-of-the-century home* ■ www.easthamptonvillagebandb.com

EconoLodge–Bay Shore [GS] 631/666-6000, 800/553-2666 ■ 501 E Main St (at Saxon Ave), Bay Shore ■ *comfortable budget motel, close to beaches & ferries to Fire Island* ■ www.econolodge.com/hotel/ny267

EconoLodge–MacArthur Airport [GF,NS,WC] 631/588-6800, 800/553-2666 ■ 3055 Rte 454, Ronkonkoma ■ *budget motel* ■ www.econolodge.com/hotel/ny173

EconoLodge–Smithtown/ Hauppauge [GF] 631/724-9000, 800/553-2666 ■ 755 Rte 347 (at Terry Rd), Smithtown ■ www.econolodge.com/hotel/ny174

Hampton Resorts & Hospitality [GF,SW,WC] 631/283-6100 ■ 1655 Country Rd 39, Southampton ■ *boutique hotels, jacuzzi* ■ www.hrhresorts.com

Mill House Inn [GF,NS,WI,WC] 631/324-9766 ■ 31 N Main St (at Newtown Lane), East Hampton ■ www.millhouse-inn.com

Stirling House B&B [GF,NS,GO] 631/477-0654, 800/551-0654 ■ 104 Bay Ave, Greenport ■ *full brkfst, jacuzzi* ■ www.stirlinghousebandb.com

Sunset Beach [GF,F] 631/749-2001 ■ 35 Shore Rd, Shelter Island ■ *seasonal* ■ www.sunsetbeachli.com

BARS

Club 422 [MW,D,F] 631/588-4632 ■ 422 Smithtown Blvd (at Bavarian Inn), Lake Ronkoroma

Club 608 [MW,NH,GO] 631/661-9580 ■ 608 Sunrise Hwy (at Belmont Ave), West Babylon ■ *8pm-4am* ■ www.club608.com

The Long Island Eagle [M,NH,L] 631/968-2750 ■ 94 N Clinton St (at Union Blvd), Bay Shore ■ *9pm-4am, from 4pm Sun* ■ lieagle@aol.com

One More Shot [MW,NH,D] 631/226-6690 ■ 841 N Broome Ave, Lindenhurst ■ *7pm-4am, from 4pm Sun, clsd Mon* ■ www.onemoreshot.net

NIGHTCLUBS

Boi Wonder [M,D] 631/424-7757 ■ 70 Gerard St (at Indigo), Huntington Village ■ *11pm Sat only* ■ www.boiwonderli.com

Bunkhouse [★M,D,K,S,WC,GO] 631/567-2865 ■ 192 N Main St/ Montauk Hwy (at Foster Ave), Sayville ■ *7pm-4am*

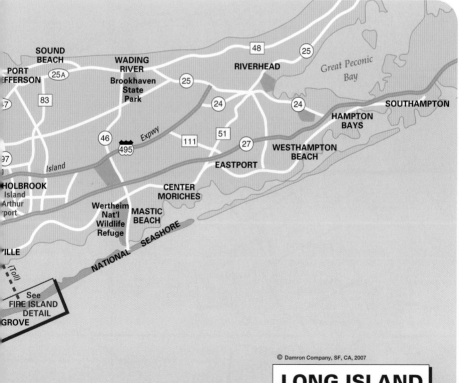

Ladies Club Saturdays [W,D] 631/585-0151 ■ 33 Railroad Ave, Ronkonkoma ■ *Sat only* ■ www.ladiesclubsaturdays.com

Skin Fridays [★M,D,18+] 631/425-7575 ■ 508 Rte 110 (at City Lounge), Melville ■ *Fri only* ■ www.thunders.com

RESTAURANTS

Babette's 631/329-5377 ■ 66 Newtown Ln, East Hampton ■ *brkfst, lunch & dinner, healthy*

ENTERTAINMENT & RECREATION

Fowler Beach Southampton

PUBLICATIONS

PM Entertainment Magazine 516/845-0759 ■ *events, listings, classifieds & more for Long Island, NJ & NYC* ■ www.pmentertainmentonline.com

EROTICA

Heaven Sent Me 631/567-6600 ■ 1601 Arctic Ave, Bohemia

New York City

New York City is divided into 8 geographical areas:
NYC—Overview
NYC—Soho, Greenwich & Chelsea
NYC—Midtown
NYC—Uptown
NYC—Bronx
NYC—Downtown
NYC—Queens
NYC—Staten Island
NYC—Brooklyn

NYC—Overview

ACCOMMODATIONS

Manhattan Getaways [GS] 212/956-2010 ■ *B&B rooms & private apts throughout Manhattan* ■ www.manhattangetaways.com

ENTERTAINMENT & RECREATION

Before Stonewall: A Lesbian & Gay History Tour 212/439-1090 ■ meet: Washington Square Arch (at Big Onion Walking Tours) ■ www.bigonion.com

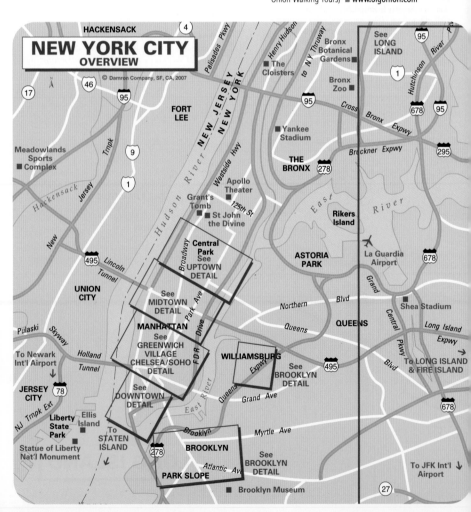

NEW YORK CITY

Day Trips: Cheap rents and cultural diversity make Brooklyn fertile ground for projects off the beaten path. Artsy types check out experimental queer performance at the Dumba Collective or the Elizabeth A. Sackler Center for Feminist Art at the Brooklyn Museum. In the spring, watch the cherry trees blossom in the Brooklyn Botanic Garden before grabbing a drink with the young lesbians at Cattyshack. Hipsters flock to Williamsburg, where many bars lure young folks with free pizza and ironic theme nights.

Tourist Info

AIRPORT DIRECTIONS
John F Kennedy International. 1 hr ($45+ taxi ride) to Manhattan.
LaGuardia: 45 minutes ($35+ taxi ride).

PUBLIC TRANSIT & TAXIS
Wave an arm on any streetcorner for a taxi.
Public transit MTA 718/330-1234, web: www.mta.info.

TOURIST SPOTS & INFO
American Museum of Natural History 212/769-5100, web: www.amnh.org.
Broadway.
Brooklyn Botanic Garden 718/623-7200, web: www.bbg.org.
Carnegie Hall 212/247-7800, web: www.carnegiehall.org.
Central Park.
Ellis Island, web: www.ellisisland.org.
Empire State Building 212/736-3100, web: www.esbnyc.com.
Greenwich Village.
Guggenheim Museum 212/423-3500, web: www.guggenheim.org.
International Center of Photography 212/857-0000, web: www.icp.org.
Lincoln Center 212/875-5000, web: www.lincoln-center.org.
Metropolitan Museum of Art 212/535-7710, web: www.metmuseum.org.
Museum of Modern Art 212/708-9400, web: www.moma.org.
Radio City Music Hall 212/307-7171, web: www.radiocity.com.
Rockefeller Center.
Statue of Liberty 866/782-8834.
Times Square.
United Nations 212/963-8687, web: www.un.org.
Wall Street.
World Trade Center Memorial.
Visitor's Center: 212/484-1200.
nycvisit.com

Weather
A spectrum of extremes with pleasant moments thrown in. Spring and fall are the best times to visit.

Best Views
Coming over any of the bridges into New York or from the Empire State Building.

City Calendar

LGBT PRIDE
Last Sunday in June. 212/807-7433, web: www.hopinc.org.
Brooklyn Pride - June. 718/670-3337, web: www.brooklynpride.org.

ANNUAL EVENTS
March - Saint-at-Large Black Party, web: www.saintatlarge.com.
May - AIDS Walk 212/807-9255, web: www.aidswalk.net/newyork.
May/June - NewFest: NY LGBT Film Festival 212/571-2170, web: www.newfestival.org.
June - Mermaid Parade, web: www.coneyisland.com/mermaid.shtml.
July - Siren Music Festival, web: www.villagevoice.com/siren.
September - Wigstock. Outrageous wig/drag/performance festival in Tompkins Square Park in the East Village 212/243-3143, web: www.wigstock.nu.
November - New York Lesbian/Gay Experimental Film/Video Fest 212/742-8880, web: www.mixnyc.org. Film, videos, installations & media performances.

Queer Resources

COMMUNITY INFO
Lesbian & Gay Community Services Center 212/620-7310. 208 W 13th, 9am-11pm, web: www.gaycenter.org.
Lesbian & Gay Switchboard of NY 212/989-0999, web: glbtnationalhelpcenter.org.
Audre Lorde Project 718/596-0342. 85 S Oxford St, Brooklyn, LGBT center for people of color, web: www.alp.org.
Intergroup Gay AA 212/647-1680, web: www.nyintergroup.org.
Crystal Meth Anonymous 212/642-5029, web: www.nycma.org.
Gay Men's Health Crisis 212/367-1000, web: www.gmhc.org.

Dyke TV 718/230-4770 ■ "only nat'l TV show by & for lesbians," also video workshops ■ dyketv.org

Gotham Girls Roller Derby 646/405-9803 ■ NYC's female roller derby league, check web for upcoming events ■ gothamgirlsrollerderby.com

New York Liberty 212/564-9622 ■ Madison Square Garden, New York ■ check out the Women's National Basketball Association while you're in New York ■ www.wnba.com/liberty

Townhouse Tours 347/693-1484 ■ walking tours of New York's gay history before & after Stonewall ■ www.townhousetours.com

Urban Outings 212/505-9985 x213, 800/495-7091 x213 (outside NYC) ■ social activity club for gay men, membership req'd ■ www.urbanoutings.com

PUBLICATIONS

Gay City News 646/452-2500 ■ LGBT newspaper, weekly ■ www.gaycitynews.com

GO NYC 888/466-9244 ■ "cultural road map for the city girl," listings, features, entertainment, style, fitness & more ■ www.gonycmagazine.com

HX Magazine 212/352-3535 ■ complete weekly guide to gay New York at night ■ www.hx.com

MetroSource 212/691-5127 ■ 180 Varick St, 5th flr ■ LGBT lifestyle magazine & resource directory ■ www.metrosource.com

New York Blade News 212/352-3535 ■ weekly LGBT newspaper ■ www.nyblade.com

Next 212/627-0165 ■ party paper ■ www.nextmagazine.net

PM Entertainment Magazine 516/845-0759 ■ events, listings, classifieds & more for Long Island, NJ & NYC ■ www.pmentertainmentonline.com

Velvetpark Magazine 347/881-1025, 888/616-1989 ■ quarterly lesbian/ feminist glossy w/ focus on the arts ■ www.velvetparkmagazine.com

NYC—Soho, Greenwich & Chelsea

ACCOMMODATIONS

1　**Abingdon Guesthouse** [GS,NS,WC] 212/243-5384 ■ 21 8th Ave (at W 12th St) ■ quiet, mature clientele ■ www.abingdonguesthouse.com

2　**The Bank St B&B** [W,NS,GO] 212/645-4611 ■ 1837 brownstone in West Village, roofdeck, lesbian-owned ■ adouglas7@nyc.rr.com

　Chelsea 18th Street B&B [M,NS,WI,GO] 646/416-4176 ■ modern studio apts on 18th St in heart of gay Chelsea, kitchens ■ chelseanycbb@aol.com

3　**Chelsea Inn** [GF] 212/645-8989, 800/640-6469 ■ 46 W 17th St (btwn 5th & 6th Aves) ■ European-style inn ■ www.chelseainn.com

4　**Chelsea Mews Guest House** [MO,NS,GO] 212/255-9174 ■ 344 W 15th St (btwn 8th & 9th Aves) ■ some shared baths

5　►**Chelsea Pines Inn** [MW,WI,GO] 212/929-1023, 888/546-2700 ■ 317 W 14th St (btwn 8th & 9th Aves) ■ some shared baths ■ www.chelseapinesinn.com

6　**The Chelsea Savoy Hotel** [GS,WI,WC] 212/929-9353, 866/929-9353 ■ 204 W 23rd St (at 7th Ave) ■ kids ok ■ www.chelseasavoyNYC.com

7　**Colonial House Inn** [MW,N,GO] 212/243-9669, 800/689-3779 ■ 318 W 22nd St (btwn 8th & 9th Aves) ■ 1850 brownstone in Chelsea, rooftop patio ■ www.colonialhouseinn.com

8　**Gershwin Hotel** [GF,WI] 212/545-8000 ■ 7 E 27th St (at 5th Ave) ■ artsy, seedy hotel w/ model's floor dorms & rooms, art gallery ■ www.gershwinhotel.com

　Greenwich Village Home [MW,GO] 877/878-2263 ■ B&B in private town house, lesbian-owned ■ www.greenwichvillagehome.com

9　**Holiday Inn Downtown** [GF,F,WI] 212/966-8898 ■ 138 Lafayette St (btwn Canal & Howard, in Chinatown) ■ located at the crossroads of SoHo, Chinatown & Little Italy, convenient to subway, shopping & restaurants ■ www.hidowntownnyc.com

10　**Hotel 17** [GF] 212/475-2845 ■ 225 E 17th St ■ "East Village chic" budget hotel, shared baths ■ www.hotel17ny.com

11　**Incentra Village House** [MW,NS,WI,GO] 212/206-0007 ■ 32 8th Ave (at W 12th St) ■ in 2 red-brick buildings built in 1841 ■ www.incentravillage.com

12　**Lambda Mews** [MW,WI,GO] 212/213-8798 ■ 24 W 30th St (at 5th Ave & Broadway) ■ www.urbanlegendny.com

13　**Soho Grand Hotel** [GF,WI,WC] 212/965-3000 ■ 310 W Broadway (at Canal St) ■ big, glossy, over-the-top hotel ■ www.sohogrand.com

14　**Tribeca Grand** [GS,WI] 212/519-6600 ■ 2 Ave of the Americas ■ www.tribecagrand.com

15　**W New York—Union Square** [GS,WI,WC] 212/253-9119, 877/WHOTELS (reservations only) ■ 201 Park Ave S ■ also restaurant & bar ■ www.whotels.com/unionsquare

16　**Washington Square Hotel** [GF,F,WI] 212/777-9515, 800/222-0418 ■ 103 Waverly Pl (at MacDougal St) ■ renovated 100-year-old hotel, also North Square restaurant & lounge ■ www.washingtonsquarehotel.com

BARS

17　**Barracuda** [★M,S] 212/645-8613 ■ 275 W 22nd St (at 8th Ave) ■ 4pm-4am, live DJs

18　**Beauty Bar** [GS,D,E] 212/539-1389 ■ 213 E 14th St (at 3rd Ave) ■ 5pm-4am, from 7pm wknds, Drop Dead Gorgeous beauty pageant 1st Sun ■ www.beautybar.com

19　**Big Lug** [M,D,B] 212/673-1775 ■ 85 Ave A (btwn 5th & 6th) ■ 4pm-close, theme nights ■ www.biglugnyc.com

20　**The Boiler Room** [★M,NH] 212/254-7536 ■ 86 E 4th St (at 2nd Ave) ■ 4pm-4am

21　**Brite Bar** [GS] 212/279-9706 ■ 297 10th Ave (at 27th St) ■ 5:30pm-3am, from 8pm Sat, clsd Sun-Mon, swank ■ britebar.com

22　**Chi Chiz** [M,MR,MR-AF,F,K,S] 212/462-0027 ■ 135 Christopher St (at Hudson) ■ 6pm-4am

23　**Climaxx** [M,NH] 212/929-9684 ■ 76 Christopher St (at 7th Ave S) ■ noon-4am ■ www.climaxx.bz

24　**The Cock** [M,K,S,$] 29 2nd Ave (1 blk above Houston) ■ 10pm-4am, a "sleazy rock 'n' roll bar," live DJs

25　**Cornhole County** [MW,CW] 212/228-2240 ■ 538 E 14th (at Otto's Shrunken Head) ■ from 7pm Wed only ■ www.ottosshrunkenhead.com

26　**Cubbyhole** [MW,NH] 212/243-9041 ■ 281 W 12th St (at 4th St) ■ 4pm-4am, from 2pm wknds

27　**Dick's Bar** [M] 212/475-2071 ■ 192 2nd Ave (at 12th St) ■ 2pm-4am, porno nights Tue & Th, digital jukebox

28　**The Dugout** [M,NH,B,WC] 212/242-9113 ■ 185 Christopher St (at Weehawken St) ■ noon-close, from 1pm Sun, bear/ sports bar ■ www.thedugouty.net

29　**Duplex** [GF,C,P,$] 212/255-5438 ■ 61 Christopher St (at 7th Ave) ■ 4pm-4am, piano bar from 9pm, cover charge + 2 drink minimum ■ www.theduplex.com

30 **Dusk** [GS] **212/924-4490** ■ 147 W 24th St (btwn 6th & 7th) ■ *5:30pm-close, from 7:30pm Sat, clsd Sun* ■ www.dusklounge.com

31 **The Eagle** [★M,L] **646/473-1866** ■ 554 W 28th St (btwn 10th & 11th) ■ *10pm-4am* ■ www.eaglenyc.com

32 **Eastern Bloc** [★MW,D,S,WC] **212/777-2555** ■ 505 E 6th St (at Ave A) ■ *7pm-4am, trendy lounge w/ DJ* ■ www.easternblocnyc.com

33 **G Lounge** [★M,GO] **212/929-1085** ■ 225 W 19th St (at 7th Ave) ■ *4pm-4am, lounge, live DJs* ■ www.glounge.com

34 **Gym Sports Bar** [M,NH] **212/337-2439** ■ 167 8th Ave (btwn 18th & 19th) ■ *4pm-close, from 1pm wknds, neighborhood sports bar* ■ www.gymsportsbar.com

35 **The Hangar** [M,DS,S] **212/627-2044** ■ 115 Christopher St (at Bleecker) ■ *3pm-4am, live DJs* ■ HangarBar@yahoo.com

36 **Helen's** [M,F,E,C,P] **212/206-0609** ■ 169 8th Ave (at 18th St) ■ *4pm-4am, from noon wknds* ■ helensnyc.com

37 **Henrietta Hudson** [W,NH,D,WC] **212/924-3347** ■ 438 Hudson (at Morton) ■ *4pm-4am, from 2pm wknds* ■ www.henriettahudsons.com

38 **Kanvas** [GS,F,WC] **212/727-2616** ■ 219 9th Ave (at 23rd St) ■ *4pm-midnight, till 1am Wed, till 2am Th, till 4am Fri-Sat, clsd Sun, ladies night Wed, rotating collection of artwork* ■ www.kanvasnyc.com

39 **Luke & Leroy** [GS,D,F,K] **212/929-8356** ■ 21 7th Ave S (at Leroy) ■ *5pm-4am, also restaurant* ■ www.lukeandleroy.com

40 **Marie's Crisis** [MW,P] **212/243-9323** ■ 59 Grove St (at 7th Ave) ■ *4pm-4am, piano bar from 9:30pm (from 5pm Fri-Sun)*

41 **The Monster** [★M,D,C,P,WC] **212/924-3558** ■ 80 Grove St (at W 4th St, Sheridan Square) ■ *4pm-4am, from 2pm wknds, piano bar, Sabor Latino Mon, disco Tue, T-dance Sun* ■ www.manhattan-monster.com

42 **Mr Black** [★M,D] **212/253-2560** ■ 643 Broadway (at Bleecker) ■ *call for events, publisher's choice Sun night* ■ www.mrblacknyc.com

43 **Nowhere** [MW,NH] **212/477-4744** ■ 322 E 14th St (btwn 1st & 2nd) ■ *3pm-4am, women's night Th* ■ gaybarsnyc.com

44 **Orchid Lounge** [GS] **212/254-4090** ■ 500 E 11th St (at Ave A) ■ *9pm-close, big lesbian following, specializes in vodka infusions*

45 **Phoenix** [MW,NH] **212/477-9979** ■ 447 E 13th (at Ave A) ■ *4pm-4am, patio* ■ gaybarsnyc.com

46 **Pieces** [M,NH,D,K,C] **212/929-9291** ■ 8 Christopher St (btwn 6th & 7th) ■ *2pm-4am, [K] Tue, [C] Th, DJ Th-Sat* ■ www.piecesbar.com

47 **Rawhide NYC** [M,L,S] **212/242-9332** ■ 212 8th Ave (at 21st) ■ *10am-4am, from noon Sun, leather/ levi cruise bar, go-go men, beer blast wknds*

48 **Rose's Turn** [M,C,P] **212/366-5438** ■ 55 Grove St (btwn 7th & Bleecker) ■ *4pm-4am* ■ www.rosesturn.com

49 **Rubyfruit Bar & Grill** [W,F,E] **212/929-3343** ■ 531 Hudson St (at Charles St) ■ *3pm-2am, till 4am Fri-Sat, full menu served 5pm-11pm, till midnight Fri-Sat, Sun brunch, bingo Tue* ■ www.rubyfruitnyc.com

50 **Secret** [M] **212/268-5580** ■ 525 W 29th St (at 10th Ave) ■ *7pm-4am, clsd Sun-Wed, lounge*

51 **Splash** [★MO,D,S,V,YC] **212/691-0073** ■ 50 W 17th St (at 6th Ave) ■ *4pm-5am* ■ www.splashbar.com

52   <u>Star Six Seven</u> [W] 212/529–2153 ■ 167 Ludlow St (btwn Rivington & Stanton, at Libation) ■ *women's party Th only* ■ star6seven.com

53   **Starbar** [MW] 218 Ave A (btwn 13th & 14th)

54   **Tea-ze Me** [M,D,F] 212/929–7515 ■ 559 W 22nd St (at 11th Ave, at Opus 22) ■ *3pm Sun, T-dance* ■ www.opus22nyc.com

55   **Ty's** [M,NH,L,GO] 212/741–9641 ■ 114 Christopher St (btwn Bleecker & Hudson) ■ *2pm-4am* ■ www.citysearch.com/nyc/tys

21   **Urge** [M,NH,F,S] 212/533–5757 ■ 33 2nd Ave (at 2nd St) ■ *4pm-4am, cruisy lounge, go-go boys* ■ www.theurgenyc.com

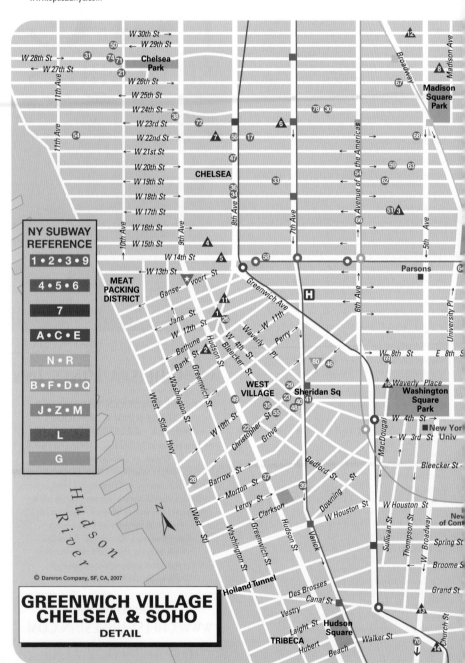

NY SUBWAY REFERENCE

1 • 2 • 3 • 9
4 • 5 • 6
7
A • C • E
N • R
B • F • D • Q
J • Z • M
L
G

MEAT PACKING DISTRICT

CHELSEA

WEST VILLAGE

Sheridan Sq

Washington Square Park

Madison Square Park

Chelsea Park

Hudson River

© Damron Company, SF, CA, 2007

GREENWICH VILLAGE CHELSEA & SOHO
DETAIL

TRIBECA

Holland Tunnel

Hudson Square

56 **View Bar** [★M,V] 212/929-2243 ■ 232 8th Ave (at 22nd St) ■ *4pm-4am, from 1pm wknds, theme nights* ■ www.viewbarnyc.com

NIGHTCLUBS

Alegria [★M,D] ■ *8 parties a year, during holiday wknds & Black Party in March* ■ www.alegriaevents.com

58 **Asseteria** [M,D,S] 246 W 14th St (btwn 7th & 8th, at Plumm) ■ *11pm Sun only* ■ www.asseteria.com

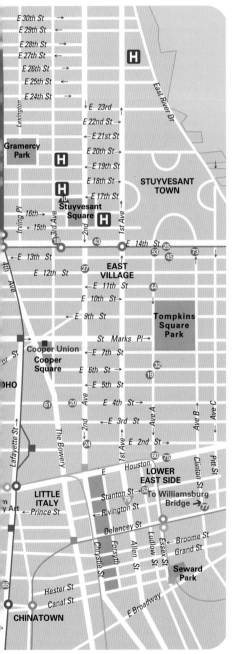

59 **Avalon** [GS,D] 212/807-7780 ■ 47 W 20th St (at 6th Ave, club entrance on 6th) ■ *gay wknds*

60 **Bank** [M,D] 212/254-2200 ■ 225 E Houston (at Ave A, at Element) ■ *Sat only* ■ www.elementny.com

61 **Beige** [GS] 212/475-2220 ■ 40 E 4th St (at Bowery, at B-Bar) ■ *11pm Tue only, swank lounge, garden* ■ www.bbarandgrill.com

62 **Big Apple Ranch** [MW,D,CW,BW,$] 212/358-5752 ■ 39 W 19th St, 5th flr (btwn 5th & 6th, at Dance Manhattan) ■ *8pm-1am Sat only, two-step lessons* ■ www.bigapplerranch.com

43 **Catfight** [W,D,S] 212/477-4744 ■ 322 E 14th St (at Nowhere Bar) ■ *10pm-close Wed only* ■ www.myspace.com/catfightnyc

63 **Club 20** [M,S,$] 212/633-1199 ■ 20 W 20th St (btwn 5th & 6th Ave, at VIP) ■ *Sun only, male revue* ■ www.vipny.com

66 **Club Rush** [W,D,S] 646/351-7174 ■ 579 6th Ave (off 16th St, at Heaven) ■ *10pm-4am Fri only* ■ www.lpeventsnyc.com

64 **Detention** [M,D,S,18+] 212/979-6677 ■ 35 E 13th St (at University, at Bar 13) ■ *Th only* ■ detentionnyc.com

65 **Eros** [M,D,S] 212/219-4006 ■ 157 Lafayette St (at Canal St, at Moomia Bar) ■ *Wed only* ■ www.moomianyc.com

66 **Gay College Party** [M,D,18+] 212/243-6100 ■ 579 6th Ave (off 16th St, at Heaven) ■ www.gaycollegeparty.com

66 **Heaven** [MW,D,MR,S,GO] 212/243-6100 ■ 579 6th Ave (off 16th St) ■ *5pm-4am Wed & Fri-Sun [W,D,MR], mostly women Wed & Fri, Gay College Party Sat [M,D,18+]* ■ heavenchelsea@aol.com

67 **Inter.Nation** [GS,D] 212/725-3860 ■ 37 W 26th St (at Ultra) ■ *10pm-close Th only* ■ www.theultranyc.com

68 **Krash/ Freaky Friday** [MW,D,MR] 212/229-0585 ■ 16 W 22nd St (btwn 5th & 6th, at Deep) ■ *popular Fri party* ■ krashnyc.com

69 **Love** [GS,D,E] 212/477-5683 ■ 179 MacDougal St (at W 8th St) ■ *9pm-close Th-Sun only (call to confirm), live art & music, more gay for monthly Ritmo party* ■ www.musicislove.net

70 **LoverGirl NYC** [W,D,S,$] 212/252-3397 ■ 83 Worth St (btwn Church & Broadway, at The Millionaire's Club) ■ *10:30pm-4am Sat* ■ www.lovergirlnyc.com

Moments [W,E,S] 917/608-5647 ■ 116 MacDougal St (at Alibi, btwn 3rd & Bleecker) ■ *9pm-3am Mon only* ■ www.alibiny.com

71 **Myst Sundays** [M,D] 212/268-5105 ■ 511 W 28th St (btwn 10th & 11th Aves) ■ *10pm Sun* ■ www.jblair.com

67 **Press Play** [M,D] 212/725-3860 ■ 37 W 26th St (at Ultra) ■ *10pm-close Wed only* ■ www.theultranyc.com

Saint-At-Large [★M,D] 212/674-8541 ■ *producers of the Black Party in March* ■ www.saintatlarge.com

Sea Tea [M,D,MR,F,P,S,GO,$] 212/675-4357 ■ *leaves from Pier 40 (at Christopher St) ■ 6pm-10pm Sun (June-Oct)* ■ www.seatea.com

Shescape [WO,D] ■ *women's dance parties in various locations, see web for info* ■ www.shescape.com

64 **Snapshot** [MW,D,YC] 212/979-6677 ■ 35 E 13th St (at Bar 13, University Pl) ■ *Tue only* ■ www.snapshotnyc.com

72 **Snaxx** [M,D] 212/366-3738 ■ 360 W 23rd St (at 9th, in basement of Westside Tavern) ■ *11pm-close Fri only*

73 ►**Spit** [M,B,L] 212/979-8506 ■ 225 Ave B, 2nd flr (btwn 13th & 14th Sts, at Uncle Ming's) ■ *10pm 4th Wed* ■ www.spitny.com

74 **Studio Mezmor** [GS,D] 212/629-9000 ■ 530 W 28th St (btwn 10th & 11th) ■ www.studiomezmor.com

75 **Temperamental** [W,D] 212/982-3532 ■ 244 E Houston (btwn Aves A & B, at Stay) ■ *9pm-3am Tue only* ■ www.stay-nyc.com

76 **Tuesdays at Room Service** [GS,D,S] 212/254-5709 ■ 35 E 21st St (at Broadway) ■ *10:30pm Tue only, wild & colorful party* ■ www.roomservicenyc.com

77 **Unisex Salon** [MW,D,TG,E] 212/254-9920 ■ 168 Delancey St (at Clinton St, at The Delancey) ■ *10pm-4am Th only; live, strange, over-the-top performances* ■ www.scenedown-town.com

68 **Venue** [M,D] 16 W 22nd St (btwn 5th & 6th, at Deep) ■ *10pm Sat*

78 **XES Lounge** [★M,D,K,C,V,GO] 212/604-0212 ■ 157 W 24th St (at 7th Ave) ■ *4pm-4am, smoking patio* ■ www.xesnyc.com

CAFES

Brown Cup Cafe 212/675-7765 ■ 334 8th Ave (at 27th St) ■ *7am-7pm, 8am-6pm Sat, clsd Sun*

Factory Cafe 212/807-6900 ■ 104 Christopher St ■ *7am-midnight*

RESTAURANTS

7A [★] 212/673-6583 ■ 109 Ave A (at 7th St) ■ *24hrs* ■ www.7acafe.com

Agave 212/989-2100 ■ 140 Seventh Ave (btwn 10th St & Charles) ■ *noon-close, Southwestern, popular brunch* ■ www.agaveny.com

Angelica Kitchen 212/228-2909 ■ 300 E 12th St (at 1st Ave) ■ *11:30am-10:30pm, vegetarian/ vegan* ■ angelicak-itchen.com

Angon 212/260-8229 ■ 320 E 6th (btwn 1st & 2nd Aves) ■ *noon-11pm, Indian* ■ www.angon.biz

Antica Venezia 212/229-0606 ■ 396 West St (at W 10th St) ■ *dinner nightly, Italian* ■ www.avnyc.com

Around the Clock 212/598-0402 ■ 8 3rd Ave (at 9th St) ■ *8am-3am, 24hrs wknds*

ArtePasta 212/229-0234 ■ 81 Greenwich Ave (at Bank St) ■ *dinner nightly, Sun brunch, Italian* ■ www.artepastanyc.com

Awash 212/982-9589 ■ 338 E 6th (btwn 1st & 2nd Aves) ■ *11am-11pm, Ethiopian* ■ www.awashnyc.com

Bayard's House Bar & Grill 212/989-0313 ■ 533 Hudson (at Charles) ■ *lunch & dinner, Cajun, full bar*

Benny's Burritos 212/254-2054 ■ 93 Ave A (at 6th St) ■ *11am-midnight, till 1am Fri-Sat, cheap & huge; also* 113 Greenwich (at Jane), 212/727-0584

Better Burger 212/989-6688 ■ 178 Eighth Ave (at 19th St) ■ *11am-midnight, burgers, hot dogs, salads & more, plenty veggie* ■ www.betterburgernyc.com

Blossom 212/627-1144 ■ 187 9th Ave (at 21st) ■ *lunch Fri-Sun, dinner nightly, gourmet vegan* ■ www.blossomnyc.com

Blue Ribbon [WC] 212/274-0404 ■ 97 Sullivan St (at Spring St) ■ *4pm-4am, cont'l/ American, chef hangout* ■ www.blueribbonrestaurants.com

Bone Lick Park [WC,GO] 212/647-9600 ■ 75 Greenwich Ave (at 7th Ave) ■ *BBQ, full bar* ■ bonelickpark@aol.com

Cola's [★] 212/633-8020 ■ 148 8th Ave (at 17th St) ■ *lunch & dinner, affordable Italian*

Counter [BW,GO] 212/982-5870 ■ 105 1st Ave (at 7th St) ■ *4pm-midnight, 11am-1am wknds, vegan, '50s retro wine & martini bar, lesbian-owned* ■ counterrestaurant.com

Cowgirl Hall of Fame 212/633-1133 ■ 519 Hudson St (at W 10th) ■ *lunch, dinner, wknd brunch* ■ cowgirlnyc.com

Deborah Stanton [MW,GO] 212/242-2606 ■ 43 Carmine St (near Beford St) ■ *lunch & dinner, clsd Mon* ■ deborahlifelovefood.com

The Dish 212/352-9800, 212/352-3003 ■ 201 8th Ave (btwn 20th & 21st) ■ *brkfst, lunch & dinner, also bar*

East of Eighth 212/352-0075 ■ 254 W 23rd St (at 8th) ■ *lunch & dinner, bar open late* ■ www.eastofeighth.com

Elmo 212/337-8000 ■ 156 7th Ave (at 20th St) ■ *lunch & dinner, also lounge* ■ elmorestaurant.com

Empire Diner 212/243-2736 ■ 210 10th Ave (at 22nd St) ■ *24hrs*

Florent [★] 212/989-5779 ■ 69 Gansevoort St (at Washington) ■ *24hrs, French diner* ■ www.restaurantflo-rent.com

Food Bar 212/243-2020 ■ 149 8th Ave (at 17th St) ■ *11am-midnight, Mediterranean*

Garage [E] 212/645-0600 ■ 99 7th Ave S (at Grove St) ■ *noon-3am, contemporary American, plenty veggie, live jazz* ■ www.garagerest.com

Gobo 212/255-3242 ■ 401 Ave of the Americas (at W 8th) ■ *11:30am-11pm, vegetarian/ vegan* ■ www.goborestau-rant.com

Gonzo [★] 212/645-4606 ■ 140 W 13th St (btwn 6th & 7th Aves) ■ *5pm-11pm, till midnight Fri-Sat, till 10:30pm Sun, great Tuscan menu, over 60 wines by the glass, full bar*

I Coppi 212/254-2263 ■ 432 E 9th St (at 1st Ave) ■ *5pm-11pm, 11am-3pm Sat-Sun* ■ www.lcoppinyc.com

Intermezzo 212/929-3433 ■ 202 8th Ave (at 21st St) ■ *noon-midnight, Italian, great wknd brunch* ■ www.inter-mezzony.com

Kate's Joint 212/777-7059 ■ 58 Ave B (at 4th St) ■ *11am-11pm, till 1am Fri-Sat, from 10am wknds, supercool vegetarian*

LaVagna 212/979-1005 ■ 545 E 5th St (btwn Aves A & B) ■ *dinner only, affordable Italian* ■ www.lavagnanyc.com

Life Cafe 212/477-8791 ■ 343 E 10th St (at Ave B)
■ 10am-midnight, till 2am Fri-Sat, full bar, plenty veggie,
artist hangout ■ www.lifecafe.com

Lips [DS] 212/675-7710 ■ 2 Bank St (at Greenwich)
■ 6pm-midnight, till 1:30am Fri-Sat, Disco Fever Brunch
noon-6pm Sun, "the Hard Rock Cafe of drag," Italian/
American served by queens ■ www.lipsnyc.com

Lucky Cheng's [★K,DS] 212/995-5500, 212/473-0516
■ 24 1st Ave (at 2nd St) ■ 5:30pm-midnight, also drag
lounge from 9pm ■ www.planetluckychengs.com

Marion's Continental 212/475-7621 ■ 354 Bowery St
(btwn E 3rd & E 4th Sts) ■ www.marionsnyc.com

Mo Pitkin's [GS,E,C] 34 Ave A (at 2nd St) ■ American, also
full bar, bingo Mon ■ www.mopitkins.com

The Noho Star 212/925-0070 ■ 330 Lafayette St (at
Bleecker) ■ 8am-midnight, from 10:30am wknds, eclectic
European & Chinese ■ www.nohostar.com

O Mai 212/633-0550 ■ 158 9th Ave (at 19th St) ■ dinner
nightly, Vietnamese ■ omainyc.com

The Pink Tea Cup 212/807-6755 ■ 42 Grove St (btwn
Bleecker & Bedford) ■ 8am-midnight, till 1am Fri-Sat,
Southern homestyle ■ www.thepinkteacup.com

Sacred Chow [WC] 212/337-0863 ■ 227 Sullivan St (at W
3rd St) ■ 11am-10pm, till 11pm Fri-Sat, gourmet vegan, juice
& smoothie bar, baked goods ■ www.sacredchow.com

Sapa 212/929-1800 ■ 43 W 24th St (btwn 6th Ave &
Broadway) ■ lunch & dinner, Sun brunch, French/ Vietnamese
■ sapanyc.com

Shag [M] 212/242-0220 ■ 11 Abingdon Sq (at Bleecker St)
■ 5:30pm-2am, till 4am Th-Sat, also full bar, American ■
www.shagbar.com

Sigiri 212/614-9333 ■ 91 1st Ave (btwn E 1st & E 2nd Sts)
■ lunch & dinner, Sri Lankan ■ www.sigirinyc.com

Summers 212/260-7080 ■ 49 Clinton St (btwn Stanton &
Rivington) ■ 6pm-close, wknd brunch, clsd Mon, full bar till
late, American, more gay Wed for Retro Electro Bingo ■
www.summersnyc.com

Trattoria Pesce Pasta 212/645-2993 ■ 262 Bleecker St
(at 6th Ave) ■ noon-midnight ■ www.pescepasta.com

Tribeca Grill [★R] 212/941-3900 ■ 375 Greenwich St
(btwn N Moore & Franklin) ■ lunch Sun-Fri, dinner nightly,
chic neighborhood restaurant co-owned by Robert DeNiro,
full bar, extensive wine list ■ www.tribecagrill.com

Veselka 212/228-9682 ■ 144 2nd Ave (at 9th St) ■ 24hrs,
Ukrainian, great pierogi ■ www.veselka.com

The Viceroy [★] 212/633-8484 ■ 160 8th Ave (at 18th St)
■ 11am-midnight, from 9am wknds, till 1am Sat, fusion, full
bar

Waikiki Wally's [E] 212/673-8908 ■ 101 E 2nd St (at 1st
Ave) ■ 6pm-2am, till 4am Fri-Sat, tiki bar open later, new
Polynesian, fun island atmosphere ■
www.waikikiwallys.com

ENTERTAINMENT & RECREATION

Leslie/ Lohman Gay Art Foundation & Gallery
212/673-7007, 212/431-2609 ■ 26 Wooster St ■ noon-
6pm, clsd Sun-Mon ■ www.leslielohman.org

PS 122 212/477-5288, 212/477-5829 ■ 150 1st Ave (at
E 9th St) ■ it's rough, it's raw, it's real New York performance
art ■ www.ps122.org

WOW Cafe Theatre 212/777-4280 ■ 59 E 4th St, 4th flr
(btwn 2nd Ave & Bowery) ■ open Th-Sat, women's theater ■
www.wowcafe.org

BOOKSTORES

79 **Bluestockings Women's Bookstore** [E] 212/777-6028
■ 172 Allen St (btwn Stanton & Rivington) ■ noon-10pm,
from 10am wknds, also cafe ■ www.bluestockings.com

80 **Oscar Wilde Bookshop** [★] 212/255-8097 ■ 15
Christopher St (at 6th Ave) ■ 11am-7pm, world's oldest LGBT
bookshop ■ www.oscarwildebooks.com

RETAIL SHOPS

Condomania 212/691-9442 ■ 351 Bleecker St ■
www.condomania.com

DeMask 212/466-0814 ■ 144 Orchard St ■ European
fetish fashion ■ www.demask.com

Flight 001 212/989-0001, 877/354-4481 ■ 96
Greenwich Ave (btwn Jane & 12th) ■ 11am-8pm, noon-6pm
Sun, way cool travel gear ■ www.flight001.com

Rainbows & Triangles 212/627-2166 ■ 192 8th Ave (at
19th St) ■ 11am-10pm, noon-9pm Sun, LGBT cards, books,
gifts & more

Universal Gear 212/206-9119 ■ 140 8th Ave (btwn 16th
& 17th) ■ casual, club, athletic & designer clothing ■
www.universalgear.com

GYMS & HEALTH CLUBS

19th St Gym [MW] 212/414-5800 ■ 22 W 19th St (btwn
5th & 6th) ■ day passes available

New York Sports Club [M] 212/627-0065 ■ 128 8th Ave
(btwn 16th & 17th) ■ 6am-midnight ■ www.mysports-
clubs.com

MEN'S CLUBS

West Side Club [★M,PC] 212/691-2700 ■ 27 W 20th St,
2nd flr (at 6th Ave) ■ 24hrs

SEX CLUBS

Submit [WO,$] 718/789-4053 ■ 253 E Houston (btwn Aves
A & B, at Studio 253) ■ monthly, women-only play party, call
for dates ■ www.SubmitParty.com

EROTICA

Babeland 212/375-1701 ■ 94 Rivington (btwn Orchard &
Ludlow) ■ noon-10pm, till 11pm Wed-Sat ■
www.babeland.com

Blue Door Video 212/995-2248 ■ 87 1st Ave (at 5th St)
■ gay movie theater

Leather Man 212/243-5339 ■ 111 Christopher St (at
Bleecker) ■ theleatherman.com

The Noose 212/807-1789 ■ 261 W 19th St (at 8th Ave)

Pleasure Chest 212/242-2158 ■ 156 7th Ave S (at
Charles) ■ adulttoyexpress.com

Purple Passion [GO] 212/807-0486 ■ 211 W 20th St (at
7th Ave) ■ fetishwear

Unicorn 212/924-2921 ■ 277-C W 22nd St (at 8th Ave)

NYC—Midtown

ACCOMMODATIONS

1   **The Algonquin Hotel** [GF,WI,WC] 212/840-6800, 888/304-2047 ■ 59 W 44th St (btwn 5th & 6th Aves) ■ *totally renovated luxury hotel* ■ www.algonquinhotel.com

2   **Belvedere Hotel** [GF,WI] 212/245-7000, 888/468-3558 ■ 319 W 48th St (at 8th Ave) ■ *"New York Art Deco monument,"* kitchenettes ■ www.belvederehotelnyc.com

3   **Buckingham Hotel** [GF] 212/246-1500, 888/511-1900 ■ 101 W 57th St (at 6th Ave) ■ *studios & 1-bdrm suites, concierge, fitness center* ■ www.buckinghamhotel.com

4   **Doubletree Guest Suites® Times Square-New York City** [NS,WI,WC] 212/719-1600, 877/692-4458 ■ 1568 Broadway ■ *all-suite hotel in heart of Times Square* ■ www.hiltonfamilynewyork.com/Damron

5   **Hilton New York** [NS,WC] 212/586-7000, 877/692-4458 ■ 1335 Ave of the Americas ■ *also 2 restaurants* ■ www.hiltonfamilynewyork.com/Damron

6   **Hilton Times Square** [NS,WC] 212/840-8222, 877/692-4458 ■ 234 W 42nd St (btwn 7th & 8th Aves) ■ *hotel located on 42nd St near Times Square & Broadway* ■ www.hiltonfamilynewyork.com/Damron

7   **Hotel 57** [GF,NS,WI,WC] 212/753-8841, 800/497-6028 ■ 130 E 57th St (at Lexington) ■ *upscale* ■ www.hotel57.com

8   **The Hotel Metro** [GF,WI,WC] 212/947-2500, 800/356-3870 ■ 45 W 35th St (at 5th Ave) ■ *art deco hotel, 1 block from Empire State Bldg* ■ www.hotel-metronyc.com

    Hotel Roger Williams 212/448-7000, 888/448-7788 ■ 131 Madison Ave (at 31st St) ■ *cozy & sophisticated* ■ www.hotelrogerwilliams.com

9   **Hudson Hotel** [GF,WI,WC] 512/554-6000, 800/697-1791 ■ 356 W 58th St ■ *magical hotel w/ trendy bars* ■ www.hudsonhotel.com

10 **Ivy Terrace** [NS] 516/662-6862 ■ 230 E 58th St ■ *private studio rental w/ terrace* ■ www.ivyterrace.com

11 **Park Central Hotel** [GF,WC] 212/247-8000, 800/346-1359 ■ 870 7th Ave (at 56th St) ■ *also restaurant* ■ www.parkcentralny.com

12 **Radisson Martinique** [GS,WI] 212/736-3800 ■ 49 W 32nd St (btwn Broadway & 5th) ■ *also restaurant, cafe & cocktail lounge* ■ www.radisson.com/martinique

13 **Travel Inn** [GF,SW,WC] 212/695-7171, 800/869-4630 ■ 515 W 42nd St (at 10th Ave) ■ *fitness center* ■ www.thetravelinnhotel.com

14 **W New York–The Tuscany** [GS,WI,WC] 212/686-1600, 877/WHOTELS (reservations only) ■ 120 E 39th St ■ *also Parisian-style cafe-bar* ■ www.whotels.com/thetuscany

15 **The Waldorf=Astoria®** [WI,WC] 212/355-3000, 877/692-4458 ■ 301 Park Ave ■ *legendary luxury landmark on Park Ave, also restaurants & bar* ■ www.hiltonfamilynewyork.com/Damron

BARS

16 **9th Avenue Saloon** [M,NH] 212/307-1503 ■ 656 9th Ave (at 46th St) ■ *11am-4am, from noon Sun*

17 **Barrage** [M] 212/586-9390 ■ 401 W 47th St (at 9th Ave) ■ *5pm-4am*

18 **Cosmo** [M,WC] 212/582-2200 ■ 359 W 54th St (btwn 8th & 9th) ■ *6pm-4am, also downstairs lounge* ■ www.cosmo-bar.com

19 **Don't Tell Mama** [★GF,C,P,YC,$] 212/757-0788 ■ 343 W 46th St (at 9th Ave) ■ *4pm-4am, cover + 2 drink minimum for [C], call for shows* ■ www.donttellmama.com

20 **OW Bar** [M,E,DS,S,V,GO] 212/355-3395 ■ 221 E 58th St (at 2nd Ave) ■ *4pm-4am, from 2pm Sun, digital jukebox, go-go dancers, patio* ■ www.owbar.com

21 **Posh** [M,NH] 212/957-2222 ■ 405 W 51st St (at 9th Ave) ■ *4pm-4am, popular happy hour, theme nights, DJ Fri-Sun* ■ poshlounge@aol.com

22 **The Ritz** [M,D] 212/333-2554 ■ 369 W 46th St (btwn 8th & 9th Aves)

23 **Therapy** [MW,F,E,C] 212/397-1700 ■ 348 W 52nd St (at 9th) ■ *5pm-4am* ■ www.therapy-nyc.com

24 **Townhouse Bar** [M,E,C,P] 212/754-4649 ■ 236 E 58th St (btwn 2nd Ave & 3rd Ave) ■ *4pm-3am, till 4am Fri-Sat, upscale, dress code* ■ www.townhouseny.com

25 **Vlada** [M] 212/974-8030 ■ 331 W 51st St ■ *4pm-3am, clsd Mon, slick gay lounge* ■ vladabar.com

26 **The Web** [M,D,MR-A,S] 212/308-1546 ■ 40 E 58th St (at Madison) ■ *4pm-close, from 8pm wknds, theme nights, [K] Sat, go-go boys* ■ www.thewebnewyork.com

27 **Xth Ave Lounge** [M,F] 212/245-9088 ■ 642 10th Ave (at 45th St) ■ *6pm-4am, DJ Th-Sat, lounge*

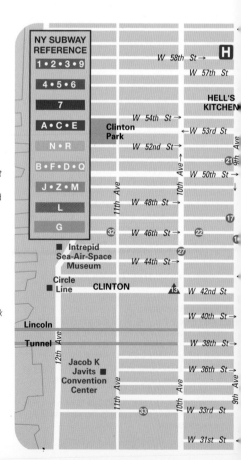

NIGHTCLUBS

28 **Escuelita** [M,D,MR-L,TG,DS,S,18+,$] 212/631-0588 ■ 301 W 39th St (at 8th Ave) ■ *10pm-5am Th-Sun, more women Fri for Secret Fri* ■ www.escuelita.com

29 <u>**Girlnation**</u> [W,D,F] 212/391-8053 ■ 12 W 45th St (btwn 5th & 6th Ave) ■ *10pm Sat only, also restaurant*

30 **Jim Caruso's Cast Party** [★GS,E,C] 212/581-3080 ■ 315 W 44th St (btwn 8th & 9th Aves, at Birdland) ■ www.CastPartyNYC.com

31 **Night Life** [M,D,MR-AF] 212/835-9600 ■ 132 W 45th St (btwn 6th & 7th Aves, at Night Hotel Lounge) ■ *9pm-close Sat only*

32 **Pacha** [GS] 212/209-7500 ■ 618 W 46th St ■ *10pm-close Fri-Sat only* ■ www.pachanyc.com

33 **Stereo** [GS,D] 555 W 33rd St (btwn 10th & 11th)

RESTAURANTS

44 & X Hell's Kitchen [WC,GO] 212/977-1170 ■ 626 10th Ave (at 44th St) ■ *5:30pm-close, brunch wknds, American comfort food* ■ 44andX.com

A Voce [R] 212/545-8555 ■ 41 Madison Ave (at 26th), New York ■ *lunch Mon-Sat, dinner nightly, Sun brunch, Italian* ■ www.avocerestaurant.com

Bamboo 52 212/315-2777 ■ 344 W 52nd St (btwn 8th & 9th Aves) ■ *noon-4am, from 4pm Sun, sushi, more gay Sun for Raw Joke-e-okie* ■ www.bamboo52nyc.com

Bann 212/582-4446 ■ 350 W 50th St (btwn 8th & 9th Aves) ■ *lunch Mon-Fri, dinner nightly, Korean* ■ www.bannrestaurant.com

Beacon 212/332-0500 ■ 25 W 56th St (btwn 5th & 6th) ■ *lunch & dinner, wknd brunch, open-fire cooking, also bar* ■ beaconnyc.com

Cafe Un Deux Trois [★] 212/354-4148 ■ 123 W 44th St (at Broadway) ■ *noon-midnight, brunch wknds, bistro* ■ www.cafeundeuxtrois.biz

Country [R] 212/889-7100 ■ 90 Madison Ave (at 29th St), New York ■ *brkfst, lunch & dinner, upscale American* ■ www.countryinnewyork.com

Dona [R] 212/308-0830 ■ 208 E 52nd St (at 3rd Ave), New York ■ *noon-2:30pm Mon-Fri & 5pm-11pm Mon-Sat, clsd Sun, Italian*

Mangia e Bevi 212/956-3976 ■ 800 9th Ave (at W 53rd St) ■ *noon-midnight, Italian* ■ www.mangiaebevirestaurant.com

Rice 'N' Beans [BW] 212/265-4444 ■ 744 9th Ave (at 50th St) ■ *11am-10pm, till 11pm Fri-Sat, Latin/ Brazilian, plenty veggie* ■ www.ricenbeansrestaurant.com

Sofia 58 [★MW] 212/826-6241 ■ 206 E 58th St (at 3rd Ave) ■ *lunch & dinner, Sun brunch, open late wknds, Italian, plenty veggie*

Vynl 212/974-2003 ■ 754 9th Ave (at 51st St) ■ *11am-11pm, also bar* ■ www.vynl-nyc.com

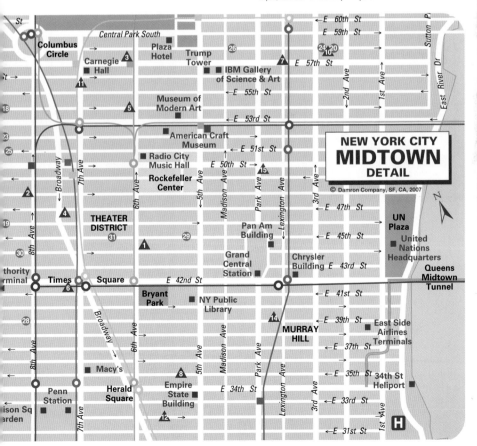

ENTERTAINMENT & RECREATION

Sex and the City Tour [R] 212/209-3370 ■ 5th Ave, in front of Pulitzer Fountain (at 58th St) ■ *3 hours, reservations a must!* ■ www.sceneontv.com

GYMS & HEALTH CLUBS

Club H Fitness 888/640-2582 ■ 423 W 55th St (at 9th Ave) ■ www.clubhfitness.com

MEN'S CLUBS

East Side Club [★PC] 212/753-2222, 212/888-1884 ■ 227 E 56th St, 6th flr (btwn 2nd & 3rd) ■ *24hrs, day passes available*

EROTICA

Come Again 212/308-9394 ■ 353 E 53rd St (at 2nd Ave) ■ *clsd Sun, woman-owned erotica store*

Eve's Garden 800/848-3837 ■ 119 W 57th St #1201 (btwn 6th & 7th) ■ *11am-6:30pm, clsd Sun, women's sexuality boutique, men must be escorted by a woman* ■ www.evesgarden.com

NYC—Uptown

ACCOMMODATIONS

BB Lodges [GS,NS,WI,GO] 917/345-7914 ■ 1598 Lexington Ave (btwn 101st & 102nd), New York ■ *private rooms w/ private kitchens* ■ www.bblodges.com

1 **The Carlyle** [GF,WC] 212/744-1600, 888/767-3966 ■ 35 E 76th St (at Madison Ave) ■ *sauna, massage, full brkfst* ■ www.thecarlyle.com

Country Inn the City [GF,NS] 212/580-4183 ■ W 77th St (at Broadway) ■ *studio apts in restored 1891 town house* ■ www.countryinnthecity.com

The Harlem Flophouse [NS,WI] 212/662-0678 ■ *guesthouse, near Apollo Theatre* ■ www.harlemflophouse.com

2 **Hotel Newton** [GS,NS,WC] 212/678-6500, 800/643-5553 ■ 2528 Broadway ■ www.newyorkhotel.com

BARS

3   **Brandy's Piano Bar** [MW,P] 212/650-1944 ■ 235 E 84th St (at 2nd Ave) ■ *4pm-4am* ■ www.brandysnyc.com

    Suite [M,NH,K,DS] 212/222-4600 ■ 992 Amsterdam (at 109th St) ■ *4pm-4am* ■ suitenyc.com

4   **Tool Box** [M,NH,V] 212/348-1288 ■ 1742 2nd Ave (at 91st St) ■ *5pm-4am, cruisy*

RESTAURANTS

    Billie's Black [E,GO] 212/280-2248 ■ 271 W 119th St (btwn St Nicholas Ave & Frederick Douglass Blvd) ■ *noon-midnight, till 4am Fri-Sat, soul food, also full bar, live music Th-Fri* ■ www.billiesblack.com

EROTICA

    Les Hommes 212/580-2445 ■ 217-B W 80th St, 2nd flr (at Broadway)

NYC—Bronx

BARS

    No Parking [MW] 212/923-8700 ■ 4168 Broadway (at 177th St) ■ *5pm-4am, swank lounge* ■ www.noparkinglouge.com

NIGHTCLUBS

    Get Wet [MW,D] 917/569-8929, 718/518-0986 ■ 923 Castle Hill Ave (at Candela Lounge) ■ *10pm-4am Wed only* ■ www.candelalounge.net

    Passion Piano Bar [GS,D] 718/299-7622 ■ 709 E Tremont Ave (at Crotona Ave) ■ *noon-4am, more gay Fri for Gay Night & Sun for Super Soaked Sundays* ■ www.passionpianobar.com

    Taboo [W,D] 718/518-0986 ■ 923 Castle Hill Ave (at Candela Lounge) ■ *9pm-4am* ■ www.candelalounge.net

    Top or Bottom [M,D] 718/822-9274 ■ 1306 Union Port Rd (at Mi Gente Cafe) ■ *9pm Tue only* ■ migentecafe.com

NYC—Downtown

ACCOMMODATIONS

1   **Embassy Suites Hotel® New York City** [WC] 212/945-0100, 877/692-4458 ■ 102 North End Ave ■ *upscale all-suite hotel located on water in downtown Manhattan* ■ www.hiltonfamilynewyork.com/Damron

2   **Millenium Hilton** [SW,WC] 212/693-2001, 877/692-4458 ■ 55 Church St ■ *hotel close to all lower Manhattan's finest* ■ www.hiltonfamilynewyork.com/Damron

3   **Wall Street District Hotel** [GS,WC] 212/232-7700, 212/232-7800 (reservations) ■ 15 Gold St (at Platt) ■ *high-tech boutique hotel, also restaurant & lounge* ■ wallstreetdistrict.com

NIGHTCLUBS

4   Ife's Monthly Dance Party [W,D,MR] 917/312-3090 (promoter #), 212/267-5252 (Club Remix) ■ 27 Park Pl (at Church, at Club Remix) ■ *2nd Sat only* ■ www.ifestouch.com

4   After Work/ Flava [W,D,K] 718/598-4137, 646/691-4187 ■ 27 Park Pl (at Club Remix) ■ *7pm-3am Wed* ■ www.girlzparty.com

    Sholay Productions/ Desilicious [MW,D,MR] 212/713-5111 ■ 95 Leonard (at Broadway) ■ *monthly party, Bollywood, bhangra & house music, call for dates* ■ www.sholayevents.com

RETAIL SHOPS

    David Menkes Leather 212/989-3706 ■ 114 Fifth Ave #3 ■ *custom-made leather- & bondagewear, by appt only* ■ www.davidmenkesleather.com

NYC—Queens

BARS

    Albatross [GS,NH,GO] 718/204-9045 ■ 36-19 24th Ave (at 37th), Astoria ■ *6pm-4am, more gay wknds* ■ albatrossbar.com

    Bungalo [GS,F] 718/204-7010 ■ 32-03 Broadway (at 32nd St) ■ *11am-4am, gay night Wed, dress code* ■ www.bungaloastoria.com

    Chueca [W,MR-L,GO] 718/424-1171 ■ 69-04 Woodside Ave (at 69th St), Woodside ■ *6pm-4am, clsd Mon-Tue, [K] Th, special events Fri, gay men welcome, lesbian-owned* ■ www.chuecabar.com

    Friend's Tavern [M,NH,MR-L] 718/397-7256 ■ 78-11 Roosevelt Ave, Jackson Hts ■ *4pm-4am, DJ Wed-Sun*

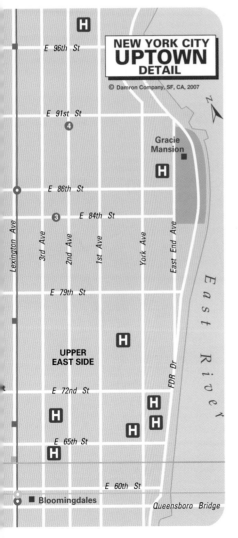

NEW YORK CITY
UPTOWN
DETAIL

© Damron Company, SF, CA, 2007

E 96th St

E 91st St

Gracie Mansion

E 86th St

E 84th St

Lexington Ave — 3rd Ave — 2nd Ave — 1st Ave — York Ave — East End Ave

E 79th St

East River

UPPER EAST SIDE

E 72nd St

FDR Dr

E 65th St

E 60th St

■ Bloomingdales   Queensboro Bridge

Hell Gate Social [GS,D] 718/204-8313 ■ 12-21 Astoria Blvd (at 14th St) ■ *7pm-4am* ■ www.hellgatesocial.com

Music Box [M,MR-LDS] 718/457-5306 ■ 40-08 74th St (at Roosevelt Ave), Jackson Hts ■ *4pm-4am, [DS] Sun*

NIGHTCLUBS

The Cave [M,D,18+] 212/714-8149 ■ 31-11 Broadway (at 31st St) ■ *10pm-close Fri only* ■ www.thecaveinastoria.com

Club Atlantis [MW,D,MR-LDS] 718/457-3939 ■ 76-19 Roosevelt Ave (at 77th St), Jackson Hts ■ *10pm-4am Fri-Sun only* ■ www.myspace.com/clubatlantis

RESTAURANTS

Mezzo Mezzo 718/278-0444 ■ 31-29 Ditmars Blvd ■ *11am-1am, till 2am Th-Sun, Greek* ■ www.mezzomezzony.com

Mundo Cafe 718/777-2829 ■ 31-18E Broadway (at 32nd St), Astoria ■ *5pm-11:30pm, Mediterranean/ Turkish, plenty veggie* ■ mundoastoria.com

MEN'S CLUBS

Northern Men's Sauna [PC] 718/445-9775 ■ 3365 Farrington St, Flushing

NYC—Staten Island

BARS

Hush [M,D,S] 718/227-1500 ■ 20 Ellis St, New York ■ *10pm-close Sat only* ■ www.scoobproductions.com

Krave [M,D] 718/720-3158 ■ 1389 Bay St ■ *9pm-4am, clsd Mon-Wed*

NYC—Brooklyn

ACCOMMODATIONS

The Loralei B&B [GS,NS,WI,GO] 646/228-4656 ■ 667 Argyle Rd (at Foster Ave) ■ www.loraleinyc.com

BARS

1   **The Abbey** [GS,NH,D] 718/599-4400 ■ 536 Driggs Ave (btwn N 7th & 8th), Williamsburg ■ *3pm-4am*

2   **Alligator Lounge** [GS,F,K] 718/599-4440 ■ 600 Metropolitan Ave (at Lorimer) ■ *3pm-4am, more gay Sat for (Not Straight) Outta Compton, free pizza from 6pm* ■ www.alligatorlounge.com

3   **Bar 4** [GS,NH,E] 718/832-9800 ■ 444 7th Ave (at 15th St, in Park Slope) ■ *6pm-4am, DJ Fri-Sat* ■ www.bar4.net

4   **Capone's** [GS,D,F] 718/599-4044 ■ 221 N 9th St (at Driggs Ave) ■ *3pm-4am, more gay Fri-Sat for The Beat Club/ All Disco, free pizza* ■ www.caponesbar.com

5   **Excelsior** [MW] 718/832-1599 ■ 390 5th Ave (btwn 6th & 7th) ■ *6pm-4am, from 2pm wknds, patio*

6   **Foot Friends** [M,$] 212/760-5952 ■ 778 Bergen St (at Grand Space) ■ *Breathe 9pm-3am most Fri, Touch 4pm-11pm most Sun, massage parties* ■ www.footfriends.com

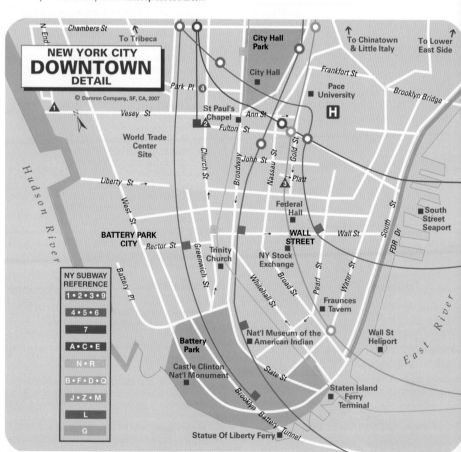

7   Ginger's Bar [MW,NH,E] 718/788-0924 ■ 363 5th Ave
    (btwn 5th & 6th Sts, in Park Slope) ■ *5pm-4am, from 2pm
    wknds, occasional live entertainment, patio*

8   Kili [★GS,NH,E] 718/855-5574 ■ 81 Hoyt St (btwn State &
    Atlantic) ■ *5pm-4am, funky local bar*

9   Metropolitan [MW,NH,D] 718/599-4444 ■ 559 Lorimer St
    (at Metropolitan), Williamsburg ■ *3pm-4am, comfy bar w/ 2
    fireplaces, more women Wed*

10 Outpost [MW,YC] 718/636-1260 ■ 1014 Fulton St ■ *8am-
    10:30pm, from 9am wknds, coffee, lounge, art gallery* ■
    www.outpostlounge.com

11 R Bar [GF,NH] 646/523-1813 ■ 451 Meeker Ave (Graham
    Ave) ■ *5pm-close, more gay Tue*

12 Superfine [GS,E,GO] 718/243-9005 ■ 126 Front St
    ■ *11:30am-4am, clsd Mon, popular among hip lesbians, also
    restaurant, relaxed atmosphere, lesbian-owned*

NIGHTCLUBS

13 Cattyshack [W,D,MR,E,K] 718/230-5740 ■ 249 4th Ave
    (btwn President & Carroll) ■ *theme nights* ■
    www.cattyshackbklyn.com

13 Cirrah [WO,D,MR] 718/230-5740 ■ 249 4th Ave (at
    Cattyshack) ■ *10pm-4am Fri only* ■ cirrah.com

14 Last Monday [MW] 718/858-5810 ■ 131 Atlantic Ave (at
    Henry St, at Floyd) ■ *last Mon only* ■ www.lastmonday.info

13 Oink! [M,D,S,V] 718/230-5740 ■ 249 4th Ave (at
    Cattyshack) ■ *10pm-3am Wed only, go-go boys, piggie films*
    ■ www.cattyshackbklyn.com

    Secrets [MW,NH,D,K] 718/368-9547 ■ 1321 Ave Z (at E
    14th St) ■ *noon-4am, more women Th* ■ secretsbklyn.com

15 Sinsations [W,D,MR-AF] 646/691-4187, 718/773-1761x4
    ■ 1428 Fulton (at The Lab) ■ *10pm Fri only* ■ www.girlz-
    party.com

CAFES

The Chocolate Monkey [E] 718/789-7896 ■ 329 Flatbush
Ave (at 7th Ave) ■ *more gay Tue for Adam's Apple, coffee &
chocolate, also lounge*

Jacques Torres 718/875-9772 ■ 66 Water St ■ *9am-7pm,
10am-6pm Sun, chocolatier* ■ www.mrchocolate.com

Tea Lounge [★] 718/768-4966 ■ 350 7th Ave ■ *7am-
1am, till 2am Fri-Sat, from 8am wknds, full bar, popular
hangout for dykes w/ tykes* ■ www.tealoungeny.com

RESTAURANTS

200 Fifth [E] 718/638-0023, 718/638-2925 ■ 200 5th
Ave (btwn Union & Sackett) ■ *4pm-close, from 11am Fri-Sat,
eclectic, full bar*

Alma 718/643-5400 ■ 187 Columbia St (at Degraw)
■ *dinner nightly, wknd brunch, upscale Mexican, outdoor
rooftop seating w/ view of Manhattan, also B61 Bar
downstairs* ■ www.almarestaurant.com

Aunt Suzie [E] 718/788-2868 ■ 247 5th Ave (at Garfield
Pl) ■ *dinner only, Italian* ■ www.auntsuzie.com

ChipShop/ The Curry Shop [★] 718/244-7746 ■ 383 5th
Ave (at 6th St) ■ *noon-10pm, till 11pm Th-Sat, from 11am
wknds, English/ Indian, home of the famous fried Twinkie!* ■
www.chipshopnyc.com

Faan 718/694-2277 ■ 209 Smith St (at Baltic) ■ *lunch &
dinner, pan-Asian, also bar downstairs*

Johnny Mack's [E] 718/832-7961 ■ 1114 8th Ave (btwn
11th & 12th) ■ *4pm-11pm, till midnight Fri-Sat, Sun brunch*

Red Hot 718/369-0700 ■ 349 7th Ave (at 10th St, in Park
Slope) ■ *lunch & dinner, delicious Chinese, plenty veggie*

Santa Fe Grill 718/636-0279 ■ 62 7th Ave (at Lincoln)
■ *5pm-close, from noon wknds, also bar*

ENTERTAINMENT & RECREATION

Dumba Collective [MW,TG] 718/858-4886 ■ 57 Jay St (at
Water St) ■ www.myspace.com/dumbacollective

Gloria Kennedy Gallery [GO] 718/858-5254 ■ 111 Front
St Gallery 222 (at Washington, in D.U.M.B.O.) ■ *1pm-6pm
Wed-Sat, till 8pm Th, contemporary art gallery, lesbian-owned*
■ www.gkgart.com

EROTICA

Pink Pussy Cat Boutique 718/369-0088 ■ 355 5th Ave
■ www.pinkpussycat.com

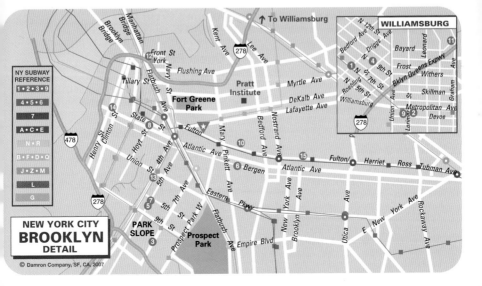

NORTH CAROLINA

Charlotte

ACCOMMODATIONS

Doubletree Guest Suites Charlotte/ South Park [GF,SW] 704/364-2400, 800/222-8733 ■ 6300 Morrison Blvd ■ *all-suite hotel* ■ www.doubletree.com

1 **Four Points by Sheraton** [GS,SW,WI,GO] 704/522-0852 ■ 315 E Woodlawn Rd ■ *close to Charlotte Eagle* ■ www.sheraton.com

2 **The Morehead Inn** [GF,WI,WC] 704/376-3357, 888/667-3432 ■ 1122 E Morehead St ■ *antique-filled suites in historic neighborhood, full brkfst* ■ www.moreheadinn.com

3 **VanLandingham Estate** [GF,NS,WI,GO] 704/334-8909, 888/524-2020 ■ 2010 The Plaza ■ *bungalow-style estate on 4 acres of gardens, on National Historic Register, full brkfst* ■ www.vanlandinghamestate.com

BARS

4 **The Cell Block** [M,NH,E] 704/347-6826 ■ 1704 Shamrock Dr ■ *5pm-2:30am, patio* ■ www.thecellblocknc.com

5 **Charlotte Eagle** [★M,D,CW,B,L,V,GO] 704/679-9901 ■ 4544-H South Blvd (at Woodlawn) ■ *8pm-2am, from 3pm Sun, theme nights* ■ www.CharlotteEagle.com

6 **Hartigan's Irish Pub** [★GS,NH,D,CW,F,E,GO] 704/347-1841 ■ 601 S Cedar St ■ *11am-10pm, till 2am wknds, from 5pm Sun, lesbian hangout* ■ www.hartigans.com

7 **Liaisons** [★MW,NH,F,V,PC] 704/376-1617 ■ 316 Rensselaer Ave (at South Blvd) ■ *5pm-1am, restaurant Wed-Sun, 2 flrs* ■ www.pinkhousenc.com

8 **Morehead Street Tavern** [GF,NH,D,F,E] 704/334-2655 ■ 300 E Morehead St (btwn South Blvd & S Tryon) ■ *11:30am-2am, from 5pm Sun, [18+] Sat* ■ www.moreheadstreettavern.com

9 **The Woodshed** [M,NH,B,L,F,PC,WC] 704/394-1712 ■ 4000 Queen City Dr (at Little Rock) ■ *5pm-2am, from 3pm Sun, also patio bar* ■ www.woodshedlounge.com

NIGHTCLUBS

10 **Chaser's** [M,D,S,V,PC,WC] 704/339-0500 ■ 3217 The Plaza (at 36th) ■ *5pm-2am* ■ www.scorpios.com

11 **Club Myxx** [MW,D,MR-AF,S,PC] 704/525-5001 ■ 3110 S Tryon St ■ *10:30pm-close Sat only*

12 **Scorpio's** [MW,D,MR,DS,V,18+,PC,WC] 704/373-9124 ■ 2301 Freedom Dr ■ *9pm-3am Wed & Sun, also Diva's show bar* ■ www.scorpios.com

---

CHARLOTTE

Local Food:

Hearty Southern classics are sure to satisfy any appetite. Cornbread, biscuits and gravy, and sweet cobbler shouldn't be missed, but the main event in North Carolina is the barbecued pork. Enjoy it by the plate or tucked into a sandwich, accompanied by zesty slaw and a pile of crisp-tender hushpuppies.

Tourist Info

AIRPORT DIRECTIONS

Charlotte-Douglas International. To get downtown, take Hwy 74/29 east to I-277.

PUBLIC TRANSIT & TAXIS

Yellow Cab 704/332-6161.
Various hotels have their own shuttles.
Charlotte Transit 704/336-7433.

TOURIST SPOTS & INFO

Blumenthal Performing Arts Center 704/372-1000, web: www.blumenthalcenter.org.
Daniel Stowe Botanical Gardens 704/825-4490, web: www.dsbg.org.
Discovery Place 704/372-6261, web: www.discoveryplace.org.
Lowes Motor Speedway 800/455-3267, web: www.lowesmotorspeedway.com.
Mint Museum of Art 704/337-2000, web: www.themintmuseums.org.
Paramount's Carowinds Amusement Park 704/588-2600, web: www.carowinds.com.
Visitor's Center: Convention & Visitors Bureau 704/334-2282 or 800/722-1994, web: www.charlottecvb.org.

City Calendar

LGBT PRIDE

Fall. 704/333-0144, web: www.pridecharlotte.com.

ANNUAL EVENTS

May - AIDS Walk 704/372-7246 x 161, web: www.aidswalkcharlotte.org.

Queer Resources

COMMUNITY INFO

The Lesbian/Gay Community Center 704/333-0144. 1401 Central Ave, 5pm-8pm, 10am-2pm Sat, clsd Fri & Sun-Mon, web: www.gaycharlotte.com.
Gay/Lesbian Switchboard 704/535-6277. 6:30pm-9:30pm Sun-Th.
AA Central Office 704/332-4387, web: www.charlotteaa.org.
Metrolina AIDS Project 704/333-1435, web: www.metrolinaaidsproject.org.

<u>Studio Diesel</u> [W,D,E,DS] in University Area (just off I-85) ■ 4pm-close, from 2pm Sun, clsd Mon ■ www.mystudiodiesel.com

13 Tremont Music Hall [GF,E] 704/343-9494 ■ 400 W Tremont Ave ■ live music venue ■ www.tremontmusichall.com

14 Velocity [★M,D,C,18+,PC,WC] 704/333-0060 ■ 935 S Summit Ave (at Morehead St) ■ 10pm-3:30am Fri, 9pm-2:30am Sat, clsd Sun-Th ■ www.velocitync.com

CAFES

Caribou Coffee [WI] 704/334-3570 ■ 1531 East Blvd (near Scott) ■ 6am-11pm, from 7am Sat-Sun, till midnight Fri-Sat, popular gay hangout Wed nights ■ www.cariboucoffee.com

Smelly Cat Coffee [GF] 704/374-9656 ■ 514 E 36th St ■ 7am-8pm, till 10pm Th, till midnight Fri-Sat, 8am-5pm Sun ■ www.smellycatcoffee.com

Tic Toc Coffeeshop 704/375-5750 ■ 512 N Tryon St (btwn 8th & 9th) ■ 7am-3pm, clsd wknds, plenty veggie

RESTAURANTS

300 East [WC] 704/332-6507 ■ 300 East Blvd (at Cleveland) ■ 11am-10pm, till 11pm Fri-Sat, 10am-10pm Sun, eclectic fusion, some veggie, full bar ■ www.300east.net

Alexander Michael's [WC] 704/332-6789 ■ 401 W 9th St (at Pine) ■ lunch & dinner, clsd Sun, pub fare, full bar

Catalunya Cafe [WC,GO] 704/335-3700 ■ 1408 E Blvd Ste A-1 ■ 8am-11pm, Catal-style cafe ■ www.catalunyacafe.com

Cosmos Cafe 704/372-3553 ■ 300 N College (at 6th) ■ 11am-2am, from 5pm Sat, clsd Sun, some veggie, also martini lounge ■ www.cosmoscafe.com

Lupie's Cafe [★] 704/374-1232 ■ 2718 Monroe Rd (near 5th St) ■ 11am-10pm, from noon Sat, clsd Sun, homestyle cookin', worth the wait ■ www.lupiescafe.com

The Pewter Rose Bistro [D,E] 704/332-8149 ■ 1820 S Blvd (near E Blvd) ■ dinner nightly, lunch Mon-Fri, wknd brunch, int'l/ american cuisine, outdoor dining, also nightclub ■ www.pewterrose.com

ENTERTAINMENT & RECREATION

<u>Charlotte Sting</u> 877/962-2849, 704/424-9622 ■ Bobcat's Arena ■ check out the Women's National Basketball Association while you're in Charlotte ■ www.wnba.com/sting

One Voice Chorus [GO] 704/716-1129 ■ PO Box 9241 28299 ■ www.onevoicechorus.com

BOOKSTORES

Paper Skyscraper [WC] 704/333-7130 ■ 330 East Blvd (at Euclid Ave) ■ 10am-7pm, till 6pm Sat, noon-5pm Sun, books & funky gifts ■ www.paperskyscraper.com

Rainbow Path Metaphysical Bookstore 704/332-3404, 800/294-8896 ■ 1412 E Blvd, Ste F (near Scott Ave) ■ 10am-6pm, 1pm-5pm Sun, 10am-5pm Mon, gifts, books, music, health products ■ www.rainbowpath.net

15 White Rabbit Books & Things 704/377-4067 ■ 1401 Central Ave (at Clement Ave) ■ 10am-9pm, noon-6pm Sun, LGBT, also magazines, T-shirts & gifts ■ www.whiterabbitbooks.com

RETAIL SHOPS

Charlotte Leather Company 704/527-1126 ■ 4544-H South Blvd (in Charlotte Eagle) ■ 8pm-2am Wed-Sat, leather, fetish ■ www.charlotteleathercompany.com

Heritage Antiques 704/644-2799 ■ 2000 South Blvd, Ste 200 (Interiors Marketplace) ■ English, European & garden antiques ■ www.heritageantiques.us

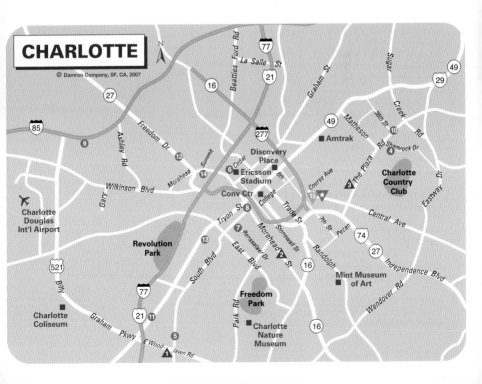

PUBLICATIONS

OIA 828/687-7237 ■ www.outinasheville.com

Q Notes 704/531-9988 ■ *bi-weekly LGBT newspaper for the Carolinas* ■ www.q-notes.com

EROTICA

Carolina Video Source 704/566-9993 ■ 8829 E Harris Blvd (at Albemarle Rd)

Hwy 74 Video & News 704/399-7907 ■ 3514 Barry Dr (at Wilkinson Blvd)

Independence News 704/332-8430 ■ 3205 The Plaza (at 36th)

Raleigh/Durham/Chapel Hill

ACCOMMODATIONS

1 **Carol's Garden Inn** [GF,NS,WI] 919/740-1240, 877/922-6777 ■ 2412 S Alston Ave, Durham ■ *on 3 acres, whirlpools in 2 rms* ■ www.carolsgardeninn.com

Fickle Creek Farm B&B [GS,GO] 919/304-6287 ■ home.mebtel.net/~ficklecreek

2 **Morehead Manor B&B** [GS,NS,WI] 919/687-4366, 888/437-6333 ■ 914 Vickers Ave (at Morehead), Durham ■ *splendid colonial home, full brkfst* ■ www.morehead-manor.com

3 **The Oakwood Inn B&B** [GF,NS,WI] 919/832-9712, 800/267-9712 ■ 411 N Bloodworth St (at Oakwood), Raleigh ■ *full brkfst* ■ www.oakwoodinnbb.com

BARS

Blend [GS,D,E] 919/338-2746 ■ 157 E Rosemary St, Chapel Hill ■ *8am-2:30am, also coffee shop, more gay Fri for Firefly* ■ www.blendchapelhill.com

4 **Blue Martini** [GS,F,WI] 919/899-6464 ■ 116 N West St, Raleigh ■ *4pm-2am, tapas, martini bar* ■ www.bluemartini-raleigh.com

5 **Flex** [★M,B,L,E,S,PC] 919/832-8855 ■ 2 S West St (at Hillsborough), Raleigh ■ *5pm-close, from 2pm Sun, [18+] Th* ■ www.flex-club.com

6 **Hibernian Restaurant & Pub** [GF,F,E] 919/833-2258 ■ 311 Glenwood Ave (at W Lane St), Raleigh ■ *11am-2am daily* ■ www.hibernianpub.com

NIGHTCLUBS

7 **The Capital Corral (CC)** [M,D,MR,P,18+,WI,PC,WC] 919/755-9599 ■ 313 W Hargett St (at Harrington), Raleigh ■ *8pm-close, from 6pm Sun, also piano bar, more diverse Th* ■ www.cc-raleigh.com

Cat's Cradle [GF,A,E] 919/967-9053 ■ 300 E Main St, Carrboro ■ www.catscradle.com

8 **Club Black Tie** [GS,D,E,GO] 919/255-1314 ■ 3201 New Bern Ave (at Milburnie), Raleigh ■ *7pm-3am, from 8pm wknds, patio, [18+] Wed* ■ www.clubblacktie.com

9 **Legends** [MW,D,DS,S,YC,PC,WC] 919/831-8888 ■ 330 W Hargett St, Raleigh ■ *5pm-close, clsd Wed, theme nights, deck* ■ www.legends-club.com

10 **The Office** [GF,D,YC,PC] 919/828-9994 ■ 310 S West St, Raleigh ■ *Fri-Sun only, preppy dance club, [18+] Fri* ■ www.theofficenightclub.com

11 **Ringside** [GS,D,PC] 919/680-2100 ■ 308 W Main St (at Market St), Durham

12 **Visions** [W,D,E,PC] 919/688-3002 ■ 711 Rigsbee Ave, Durham ■ *9pm-close Fri-Sat only, drag king shows, deck* ■ visionsemail@aol.com

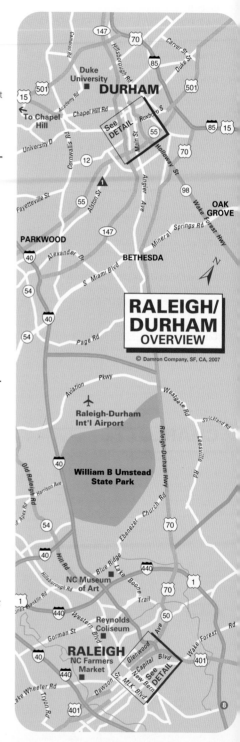

© Damron Company, SF, CA, 2007

RALEIGH/ DURHAM
OVERVIEW

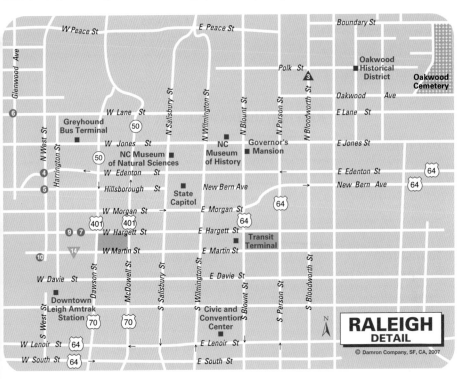

RALEIGH DETAIL

W Peace St
E Peace St
Boundary St
Glenwood Ave
Polk St
Oakwood Historical District
Oakwood Cemetery
Oakwood Ave
W Lane St
E Lane St
Greyhound Bus Terminal
N West St
Harrington St
N Salisbury St
N Wilmington St
N Blount St
N Person St
N Bloodworth St
E Jones St
W Jones St
NC Museum of Natural Sciences
NC Museum of History
Governor's Mansion
E Edenton St
W Edenton St
Hillsborough St
State Capitol
New Bern Ave
New Bern Ave
W Morgan St
E Morgan St
W Hargett St
E Hargett St
Transit Terminal
W Martin St
E Martin St
Dawson St
McDowell St
S Salisbury St
S Wilmington St
W Davie St
E Davie St
S Blount St
S Person St
S Bloodworth St
Downtown Leigh Amtrak Station
Civic and Convention Center
W Lenoir St
E Lenoir St
W South St
E South St
© Damron Company, SF, CA, 2007

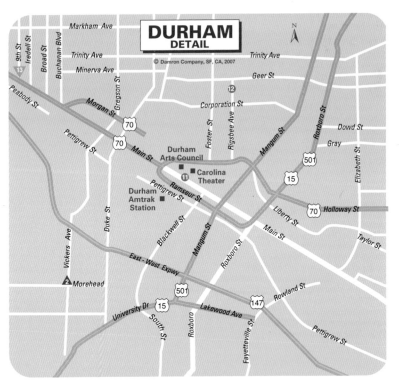

DURHAM DETAIL
© Damron Company, SF, CA, 2007

9th St
Iredell St
Broad St
Buchanan Blvd
Markham Ave
Trinity Ave
Trinity Ave
Minerva Ave
Geer St
Peabody St
Gregson St
Morgan St
Corporation St
Foster St
Rigsbee Ave
Mangum St
Roxboro St
Dowd St
Gray
Pettigrew St
Main St
Durham Arts Council
Carolina Theater
Ramseur St
Pettigrew St
Liberty St
Holloway St
Durham Amtrak Station
Elizabeth St
Duke St
Blackwell St
Mangum St
Roxboro St
Main St
Taylor St
Vickers Ave
East - West Expwy
Morehead
Rowland St
University Dr
South St
Lakewood Ave
Fayetteville St
Roxboro
Pettigrew St

CAFES

Caribou Coffee 919/933-5404 ■ 110 West Franklin St (at N Columbia St), Chapel Hill ■ *7am-11pm, till midnight Fri-Sat, from 8am Sun* ■ **www.cariboucoffee.com**

Reverie: A Coffee Den [GO] 919/839-2233 ■ 2522 Hillsborough St (at Pogue), Raleigh

RESTAURANTS

Crooks Corner [WC] 919/929-7643 ■ 610 Franklin St (at Merritt Mill Rd), Chapel Hill ■ *dinner nightly, clsd Mon, Southern cooking, full bar* ■ **www.crookscorner.com**

RALEIGH/DURHAM/CHAPEL HILL

Day Trips: North Carolina is rich with African American history, and the city of Durham has compiled an African American tour to highlight the city's places of interest. Spend a day exploring the historical sites mapped out on the African American Heritage Map, available from the Durham Convention and Visitors Bureau. Check out www.durham-nc.com for more info.

Those looking to take a walk on the wild side should don some comfy shoes and head for the North Carolina Zoological Park (www.nczoo.org), in Asheboro, NC. With over 500 acres of (sometimes very hilly) terrain, it's the country's largest natural-habitat zoo.

Tourist Info

AIRPORT DIRECTIONS

Raleigh-Durham International. Take US 40 toward Raleigh and use the Wade Ave exit. At Capital Ave (US 1), turn right. Head south toward downtown. The street will change to Dawson at W Martin. Turn right here. Take US 40 toward Durham to 147 North (Durham Fwy). Take Swift Ave exit toward Duke east Campus. Go right, it turns into Broad St, which will lead you to Main St.

PUBLIC TRANSIT & TAXIS

Regional Transit Information 919/549-9999, web: www.gotriangle.org.

TOURIST SPOTS & INFO

Ackland Art Museum, Chapel Hill 919/966-5736, web: www.ackland.org.
African-American Dance Ensemble, Durham 919/560-2729, web: www.africanamerican-danceensemble.org.
African-American Cultural Complex, Raleigh 919/250-9336, web: www.aaccmuseum.org.
City Market, Raleigh.
Duke University, Durham.
Exploris (interactive global learning center), Raleigh 919/834-4040, web: www.exploris.org.
Morehead Planetarium & Science Center 919/549-6863, web: www.moreheadplanetarium.org.
NC Botanical Garden, Chapel Hill 919/962-0522, web: www.ncbg.unc.edu.
NC Museum of Art, Raleigh 919/839-6262, web: www.ncartmuseum.org.
NC Museum of Life & Science, Durham 919/220-5429, web: www.ncmls.org.
Oakwood Historic District, Raleigh.
University of North Carolina, Chapel Hill.
W. Franklin St. in Chapel Hill, south of UNC and into Carrboro—charming and hip shopping area.
Visitor's Center: 919/834-5900 or 800/849-8499, web: www.visitraleigh.com.
Chapel Hill/Orange County Visitors Bureau 888/968-2060, web: www.chocvb.org.

City Calendar

LGBT PRIDE

September, Durham. web: www.ncpride.org.

ANNUAL EVENTS

August - North Carolina Gay and Lesbian Film Festival, web: www.carolinatheatre.org/ncglff.

Queer Resources

COMMUNITY INFO

Gay & Lesbian Helpline of Wake County 919/821-0055. 6:30pm-9:30pm Sun-Th.
Orange County Women's Center 919/968-4610. 210 Henderson, Chapel Hill, 9am-5pm Mon-Tue, till 6pm Wed, till 7pm Th, till 2pm Fri, clsd wknds, web: www.womenspace.org.
AA Raleigh 919/783-6144, web: www.nctriaa.org.
AA Durham 919/286-9499. web: www.aanc32.org.
Alliance of AIDS Services 919/834-2437.

Elmo's Diner 919/416-3823 ■ 776 9th St (in the Carr Mill Mall), Durham ■ 6:30am-10pm, till 11pm Fri-Sat, some veggie ■ www.elmosdiner.com

Irregardless Cafe [E] 919/833-8898 ■ 901 W Morgan St (at Hillsborough), Raleigh ■ lunch Tue-Fri, dinner Tue-Sat, Sun brunch, clsd Mon, plenty veggie, dancing Saturday night ■ www.irregardless.com

Magnolia Grill [WC] 919/286-3609 ■ 1002 9th St (at Knox), Durham ■ dinner, clsd Sun-Mon, upscale Southern, full bar

Spotted Dog 919/933-1117 ■ 111 E Main St, Carrboro ■ 11:30am-midnight, clsd Mon, some veggie ■ www.spotteddog.biz

Weathervane Cafe [E,WC] 919/929-9466 ■ 201 S Estes Dr (in the University Mall), Chapel Hill ■ 7am-9pm, till 10pm Fri-Sat, 10:30am-6pm Sun, patio, full bar, great brunch ■ www.southernseason.com

ENTERTAINMENT & RECREATION

Carolina Rollergirls ■ NC's female roller derby league, check web for upcoming events ■ www.carolinarollergirls.com

BOOKSTORES

Internationalist Books & Community Center 919/942-1740 ■ 405 W Franklin St (at Kenan St), Chapel Hill ■ 11am-8pm, noon-6pm Sun, progressive/ alternative, cooperatively run, nonprofit, literature readings & events ■ www.internationalistbooks.org

Quail Ridge Books 919/828-1588, 800/672-6789 ■ 3522 Wade Ave (at Ridgewood Center), Raleigh ■ 9am-9pm, LGBT section ■ www.quailridgebooks.com

Reader's Corner 919/828-7024 ■ 3201 Hillsborough St (at Rosemary), Raleigh ■ 10am-8pm, till 6pm Sat, noon-6pm Sun, used books

13 **The Regulator Bookshop** 919/286-2700 ■ 720 9th St (btwn Hillsborough & Perry), Durham ■ 9am-9pm, 10am-6pm Sun ■ www.regbook.com

14 **White Rabbit Raleigh** [WC] 919/856-1429 ■ 309 W Martin St (btwn Dawson & Harrington), Raleigh ■ 11am-9pm, noon-7pm Sun, LGBT, music, movies, cards & gifts ■ www.whiterabbitbooks.com

EROTICA

Capitol Blvd News 919/831-1400 ■ 2236 Capitol Blvd, Raleigh ■ 24hrs, DVDs & videos, arcade, toys

Castle Video & News 919/836-9189 ■ 1210 Capitol Blvd, Raleigh ■ 24hrs

Eagles/ Videos for the Mature 919/787-0016 ■ 9016 Glenwood Ave, Raleigh ■ 24hrs

Our Place 919/833-8968 ■ 327 W Hargett (at Harrington), Raleigh ■ 24hrs

---

OHIO

Cincinnati

ACCOMMODATIONS

1 **Cincinnatian Hotel** [GF,WI,WC] 513/381-3000, 800/942-9000 ■ 601 Vine St (at 6th St) ■ restaurant & lounge ■ www.cincinnatianhotel.com

Crowne Plaza [GF,SW,WI,WC] 513/793-4500 ■ 5901 Pfeiffer Rd (at I-71) ■ www.ClarionCincinnati.com

First Farm Inn [GF,NS,WC] 859/586-0199 ■ 2510 Stevens Rd, Idlewild, KY ■ 1800s farmhouse B&B, full brkfst, 20 minutes from Cincinnati ■ www.firstfarminn.com

2 **Millennium Hotel Cincinnati** [GF,SW,WI,WC] 513/352-2100, 800/876-2100 ■ 141 W Sixth St ■ centrally located hotel near gay bars & clubs & all of the city's major attractions, w/ city's only outdoor rooftop pool & sundeck, also 24hr business & fitness cetner ■ www.millenniumhotels.com/cincinnati

3 **The Vernon Manor Hotel** [GF,WI,WC] 513/281-3300, 800/543-3999 ■ 400 Oak St ■ restaurant, pub, gym ■ www.vernon-manor.com

4 **Weller Haus B&B** [GF,NS,WI] 859/431-6829, 800/431-4287 ■ 319 Poplar St, Newport, KY ■ B&B in 2 side-by-side historic homes, 2 jacuzzis

BARS

5 Bullfishes [W,NH,D,E,K] 513/541-9220 ■ 4023 Hamilton Ave (at Blue Rock) ■ 8pm-2:30am, clsd Sun-Mon ■ www.bullfishes.com

6 **Crazy Fox Saloon** [GS,NH] 859/261-2143 ■ 901 Washington Ave (at 9th), Newport, KY ■ 3pm-2:30am

7 **Golden Lion** [M,NH,D,K,S] 513/281-4179 ■ 340 Ludlow (at Telford), Clifton ■ 11am-2:30am, from 1pm Sun, dive bar

8 **Junkers Tavern** [GF,NH] 513/541-5470 ■ 4156 Langland (at Pullan) ■ 7:30am-1am

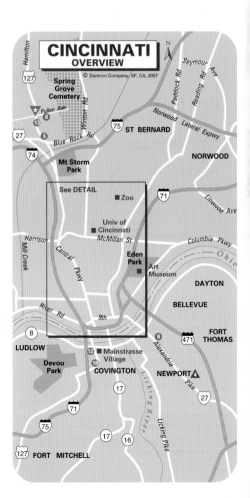

9 **"Little Bit" Bar** [MW,NH,D,K,DS,V,WC] 513/721-8484 ■ 2401 Vine St (at Hollister, Clifton Heights) ■ *7pm-2:30am, clsd Mon, ladies night Sat* ■ **www.freewebs.com/littlebitbar**

10 **Milton's** [GF,NH] 513/784-9938 ■ 301 Milton St (at Sycamore) ■ *4pm-2:30am*

11 **On Broadway** [M,NH,CW,B,L,K,DS,V,GO] 513/421-2555 ■ 817 Broadway ■ **www.onbroadwaybaronline.com**

12 **Rosie's Tavern** [GS,NH,GO] 859/291-9707 ■ 643 Bakewell St (at 7th St), Covington, KY ■ *3pm-2:30am* ■ **rosiestav@aol.com**

13 **The Serpent** [M,L] 513/681-6969 ■ 4042 Hamilton Ave (at Blue Rock) ■ *9pm-2:30am, dress code Fri-Sat* ■ **www.serpentbar.com**

14 **Shooters** [M,D,CW,K,S] 513/381-9900 ■ 927 Race St (at Court) ■ *4pm-2:30am, [K] Wed, more women Th*

15 **Simon Says** [★M,NH,P,WC] 513/381-7577 ■ 428 Walnut St (at 5th) ■ *11am-2:30am, from 1pm Sun* ■ **www.simons-dtcincy.com**

16 **The Subway** [M,NH,D,F,S] 513/421-1294 ■ 609 Walnut St (at 6th) ■ *5:30am-2:30am, from noon Sun*

17 **Univeral Grille** [★MW,D,K,DS,WC] 513/381-6279 ■ 909 Vine St (at 9th St) ■ *11am-10pm, till midnight Fri-Sat, bar open till 2:30am* ■ **www.myuniversalgrille.com**

18 **Yadda Club** [MW,NH,MR,F,E,K,WC,GO] 859/491-5600 ■ 404 Pike St (at Main St), Covington, KY ■ *5pm-2:30am, from 7pm Sat, till 1am Sun, clsd Mon-Wed, T-dance Sun, patio, lesbian-owned* ■ **grdittoe1@aol.com**

NIGHTCLUBS

Adonis [MW,D,TG,K,DS] 513/871-1542 ■ 4601 Kellogg Ave ■ *9pm-2:30am, 1pm-7pm Sun, clsd Tue-Th* ■ **www.adonis-thenightclub.com**

5 **Bronz** [MW,D,E,K,V,WC,GO] 513/591-2100 ■ 4029 Hamilton Ave (at Blue Rock) ■ *5pm-2:30am*

19 **The Dock** [★MW,D,DS,S,19+,WC] 513/241-5623 ■ 603 W Pete Rose Wy (near Central) ■ *9pm-2:30am, till 4am wknds* ■ **www.thedockcomplex.com**

CAFES

College Hill Coffee Co. [E] 513/541-1243 ■ 6128 Hamilton Ave ■ *6:30am-6:30pm, till 10pm Fri, 8:30am-10pm Sat, 8:30am-4pm Sun, live music Sat*

Zen & Now 513/598-8999 ■ 4453 Bridgetown Rd ■ *7am-11pm, from 9am Sat, clsd Sun*

RESTAURANTS

Boca [WC] 513/542-2022 ■ 3200 Madison Rd, Oakley ■ *dinner Tue-Sat, nouvelle int'l, patio, full bar* ■ **boca-restaurant.com**

CINCINNATI

Local Food:

Cincinnati holds the distinction of having the largest number of chili parlors per capita in the world. "5-way" is how the locals like it: cheese, onions, and kidney beans layered over a healthy dose of meaty chili, all heaped onto a bed of spaghetti noodles.

Tourist Info

AIRPORT DIRECTIONS

Greater Cincinnati International (in Kentucky). To get to downtown, take I-275 East to I-75/I-71 North over the Ohio River. Follow I-75 North or I-71 East, and look for downtown exits.

PUBLIC TRANSIT & TAXIS

Yellow Cab 513/241-2100.
Queen City Metro 513/621-4455, web: www.sorta.com.

TOURIST SPOTS & INFO

The Beach waterpark (in Mason) 513/398-7946, web: www.thebeachwaterpark.com.
Carew Tower 513/241-3888.
Cincinnati Art Museum 513/639-2995, web: www.cincinnatiartmuseum.org.
Fountain Square.
Krohn Conservatory 513/421-4086.
Museum Center at Union Terminal 513/287-7000, web: www.cincymuseum.org.
Paramount King's Island (24 miles N of Cincinnati) 513/754-5700, web: www.pki.com.
Visitor's Center: 513/621-2142 or 800/246-2987, web: www.cincyusa.com.

Best Views

Mt Adams & Eden Park.

City Calendar

LGBT PRIDE

June. 513/591-0200, web: www.prideisalive.com.

ANNUAL EVENTS

June - OUTReels LGBT film festival 513/591-0200, web: www.myspace.com/outreels.
August - TriState Womonfest 513/591-0200, web: www.tristate-womonfest.com.

Queer Resources

COMMUNITY INFO

Gay & Lesbian Community Center 513/591-0200. 4119 Hamilton Ave, 6pm-9pm, till 11pm Fri, noon-4pm Sat, clsd Sun & holidays, web: www.glbtcen-tercincinnati.com.
AA Lesbian/Gay 513/351-0422.
513/421-2437, web: www.avoc.org.

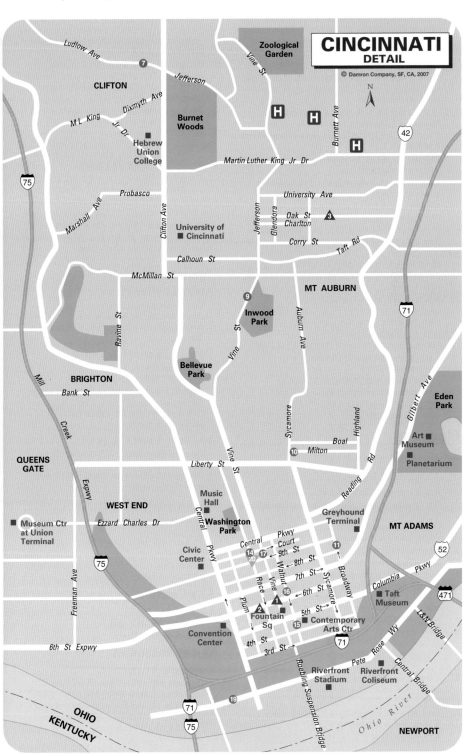

CINCINNATI
DETAIL
© Damron Company, SF, CA, 2007

Coach & Four 315/559-9900 ■ 2200 Victory Pkwy (at the Edgecliff) ■ *lunch Mon-Fri, dinner nightly, Sun brunch, clsd Mon, American* ■ www.coachandfourrestaurant.com

Kaldi's Cafe [E,WC] 513/241-3070 ■ 1204 Main St (at 12th) ■ *10am-midnight, till 2am Fri-Sat, plenty veggie*

Union Station Video Cafe [★MW,F,WC,GO] 513/651-2667 ■ 825 Main St (btwn 8th & 9th) ■ *11am-2am, from 5pm wknds* ■ www.usvc.com

Entertainment & Recreation

Alternating Currents 513/749-1444 (during show) ■ WAIF 88.3 FM ■ *3pm Sat, LGBT public affairs radio program* ■ waif883.org

Ensemble Theatre of Cincinnati 513/421-3555 ■ 1127 Vine St ■ www.cincyetc.com

Know Theatre 513/300-5669 ■ 1425 Sycamore St ■ *contemporary multicultural theater* ■ www.knowtheatre.com

Ohio Lesbian Archives 513/256-7695 ■ 3416 Clifton Ave (at Clifton United Methodist Church) ■ *call first for appt* ■ www.geocities.com/ohiolesbianarchives

Retail Shops

Elyse's Passion 513/541-0800 ■ 1569 Chase Ave (at Hamilton) ■ *noon-8pm, clsd Sun-Mon, spiritual/ erotic books, videos & more*

20 **Pink Pyramid** 513/621-7465 ■ 907 Race St (btwn 9th & Court) ■ *noon-10pm, till 11pm Fri-Sat, 1pm-7pm Sun, pride items, also leather*

Publications

EXP Magazine 314/367-0397, 877/397-6244 ■ *gay magazine serving Indiana, Ohio & Kentucky* ■ www.expmagazine.com

Greater Cincinnati GLBT News 513/241-7539 ■ www.greatercincinnatiglbtnews.com

Q City News PO Box 73003, Bellevue, KY 41073 ■ www.qcitynews.com

Cleveland

Accommodations

1 **Clifford House** [GS,NS,GO] 216/589-0121 ■ 1810 W 28th St (at Jay) ■ *1868 historic brick home, near downtown, fireplaces* ■ www.cliffordhouse.com

2 **Flex Cleveland** [M,SW,NS,WI,GO] 216/812-3304 ■ 2600 Hamilton Ave (at 26th) ■ *24hrs, in renovated art deco Greyhound bus station, steam room, sauna, gym & 20-man whirlpool* ■ www.flexbaths.com

3 **Glendennis B&B** [GS] 216/589-0663 ■ 2808 Bridge Ave (at 28th St) ■ *3-rm suite, full brkfst* ■ www.glendennis.com

4 **Radisson Hotel Cleveland—Gateway** [GF,WI,WC] 216/377-9000, 888/201-1718 ■ 651 Huron Rd ■ *full-service hotel in downtown Cleveland directly across from Jacobs Field & Q Arena, gym access, also restaurant* ■ www.radisson.com/clevelandoh_gateway

5 **Stone Gables B&B** [GS,WI,WC,GO] 216/961-4654, 877/215-4326 ■ 3806 Franklin Blvd (at W 38th) ■ *full brfkst, sauna, kids/ pets ok* ■ www.stonegables.net

Bars

6 **A Man's World** [M,D] 216/574-2203 ■ 2909 Detroit Ave (at 29th St) ■ *7am-2:30am, from noon Sun-Mon, DJ wknds, patio*

7 **Apex** [★MW,NH,E,K] 216/476-1970 ■ 11633 Lorain Ave (at W 117th St) ■ *5pm-2:30am, from 7pm Sat, from 2pm Sun* ■ www.apexnightclub.com

8 **Club Argos** [M,NH,D,B,MR,S,YC] 216/781-9191 ■ 2032 W 25th St (at Lorain & 24th) ■ *3pm-close, from noon wknds, alternative sports bar, more women Tue for Ladies Night* ■ www.club-argos.com

9 **Cocktails Cleveland** [★M,D,L,F,K,S,V] 216/961-3115 ■ 9208 Detroit Ave (at W 93rd St) ■ *3pm-2:30am, patio, "Cleveland's only Sun T-dance"* ■ www.cocktails-cleveland.comf

10 **The Edge** [MW,NH,D,K,DS,S] 216/221-8576 ■ 11213 Detroit Ave (at 112th St) ■ *3pm-2:30am, from 4pm Sun*

Cleveland

An historic industrial center, Cleveland also offers all the best in culture and nightlife. The riverfront area known as "The Flats" houses clubs and restaurants, while University Circle is home to the Cleveland Museum of Art and the Museum of Natural History, among many others.

Tourist Info

Airport Directions

Cleveland Hopkins International. To get downtown, take the Berea Freeway to I-71 and continue on until it merges with I-90 and follow into downtown.

Public Transit & Taxis

Yellow Cab 216/623-1500.
AmeriCab 216/881-1111.
Regional Transit Authority (RTA) 216/621-9500, web: www.gcrta.org.
Lolly the Trolley 216/771-4484, web: www.lollytrolley.com.

Tourist Spots & Info

Cleveland Metroparks Zoo 216/661-6500, web: www.clemetzoo.com.
Cleveland Museum of Art 216/421-7340, web: www.clemusart.com.
Coventry Road district.
Cuyahoga Valley National Recreation Area 216/524-1497.
The Flats.
Rock and Roll Hall of Fame 216/781-7625, web: www.rockhall.com.
Visitor's Center: 216/621-4110 or 800/321-1004, web: www.travelcleveland.com.

City Calendar

LGBT Pride

June. 216/371-0214, web: www.clevelandpride.org.

Queer Resources

Community Info

Cleveland Lesbian/Gay Community Center 216/651-5428. 6600 Detroit Ave, noon-10pm, 10am-6pm Sat, clsd Sun, web: www.lgcsc.org.
Women's Center 216/651-1450. 6209 Storer Ave, web: www.womensctr.org.

CLEVELAND
OVERVIEW
© Damron Company, SF, CA, 2007

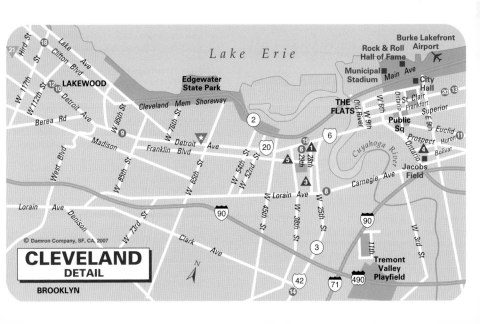

CLEVELAND
DETAIL

© Damron Company, SF, CA, 2007

BROOKLYN

11 **Hamilton's** [MW,D] 216/241-7721 ■ 1415 Euclid Ave (at E 14th) ■ *4pm-2:30am*

12 **The Hawk** [MW,NH,WC] 216/521-5443 ■ 11217 Detroit Ave (at 112th St) ■ *10am-2:30am, from 1pm Sun*

13 **Leather Stallion Saloon** [★M,NH,B,L,F,E] 216/589-8588 ■ 2205 St Clair Ave (near E 21st St) ■ *3pm-2am, DJ wknds, patio* ■ www.leatherstallion.com

14 **Muggs** [MW,NH,D,K] 216/398-7012 ■ 3194 W 25th St (near Clark) ■ *11am-2am* ■ www.muggs.freeservers.com

15 **The Nickel/ Five Cent Decision** [W,NH,D,CW,E,K] 216/661-1314 ■ 4365 State Rd (Rte 94, at Montclair) ■ *6pm-2am*

16 **Paradise Inn** [W,NH] 216/741-9819 ■ 4488 State Rd (Rte 94, at Rte 480) ■ *11am-2:30am*

17 **Rec Room** [W] 216/570-6580 ■ 15320 Brookpark Rd (at Smith Rd) ■ *6:30pm-2:30am, from 5pm Sun, clsd Mon-Wed*

18 **Twist** [★MW,NH,D,P] 216/221-2333 ■ 11633 Clifton (at 117th St) ■ *9am-2:30am, from 1pm Sun*

19 **Union Station Video Cafe** [★MW,F,V,GO] 216/357-2997 ■ 2814 Detroit Ave (at W 28th) ■ *5pm-2:30am, also Sun brunch; also Bounce [D,DS] Th-Sun* ■ www.clevelandcock-tails.com

NIGHTCLUBS

20 **The Grid** [★M,D,K,DS,S,V] 216/623-0113 ■ 1437 St Clair Ave ■ *9pm-2:30am, from 5pm Sun, till close Sat, more women Wed, also Orbit [D,18+]* ■ www.thegrid.com

6 **The Shed** [M,NH,D,CW,L,WC] 216/574-2203 ■ 2901-2909 Detroit Ave (enter on W 29th St) ■ *7pm-2:30am, cruise bar, CW Sun, also Crossover [MO,L] from 10pm Fri-Sat, dress code*

CAFES

Johnny Mango [NS,WC] 216/575-1919 ■ 3120 Bridge Ave (btwn Fulton & W 32nd) ■ *11am-10pm, 9am-11pm Fri-Sat, till 10pm Sun, healthy world food & juice bar, also full bar till 1am* ■ jmango.com

RESTAURANTS

Battiste & Dupree Cajun Grill & Bar 216/381-3341 ■ 1992 Warrensville Ctr Rd ■ *lunch & dinner, clsd Sun*

Cafe Limbo [E] 216/707-3333 ■ 12706 Larchmere Blvd ■ *8:30am-10pm, till midnight Fri-Sat, till 3pm Sun, till 4pm Tue, clsd Mon, vegetarian, live music Th-Sat, patio* ■ www.cafelimbo.com

Cafe Tandoor 216/371-8500, 216/371-8569 ■ 2096 S Taylor Rd (at Cedar), Cleveland Hts ■ *lunch & dinner, 3pm-9pm Sun, Indian, plenty veggie*

Hecks [★WC] 216/861-5464 ■ 2927 Bridge Ave (at W 30th) ■ *lunch & dinner, gourmet burgers* ■ www.heckscafe.com

The Inn on Coventry [WC] 216/371-1811 ■ 2785 Euclid Heights Blvd (at Coventry), Cleveland Hts ■ *7am-8:30pm, from 8:30am Sat-Mon, till 3pm Sun-Mon, homestyle, popular Bloody Marys*

Jimmy O'Neill's Tavern [GO] 216/321-1116 ■ 2195 Lee Rd, Cleveland Heights ■ *4:30pm-11pm, till midnight Th-Sat, bar till 2:30am*

My Friend's Deli & Restaurant 216/221-2575 ■ 11616 Detroit Ave ■ *24hrs*

ENTERTAINMENT & RECREATION

Rock & Roll Hall of Fame 216/781-ROCK ■ 1 Key Plaza (at E 9th & Lake Erie) ■ *even if you don't like rock, stop by & check out IM Pei's architectural gift to Cleveland* ■ www.rockhall.com

BOOKSTORES

Bookstore on W 25th St 216/566-8897 ■ 1921 W 25th St (at Lorain) ■ *11am-5pm, 10am-6pm Sat, clsd Sun, LGBT section*

Borders Bookshop & Espresso Bar 216/292-2660 ■ 2101 Richmond Rd (at Cedar, in LaPlace Mall), Beachwood ■ *9am-10pm, till 11pm Fri-Sat, till 9pm Sun*

RETAIL SHOPS

Big Fun 216/371-4386 ■ 1827 Coventry Rd ■ *11am-8pm, till 10pm Fri-Sat, till 6pm Sun, variety store*

City Dweller [GO] 216/221-4297 ■ 12005 Detroit Ave, Lakewood ■ *10am-6pm, 11am-6pm Sun, cards, gifts & home decorations* ■ www.citydweller.net

The Clifton Web 216/961-1120 ■ 11512 Clifton Blvd (at W 115th) ■ *11am-7pm, till 5pm Sun, cards & gifts*

21 **Diverse Universe** [WC,GO] 216/221-4297 ■ 12011 Detroit Ave (at Hopkins), Lakewood ■ *10am-9pm, 11am-6pm Sun, LGBT books, videos, music, clothing & pride gifts* ■ www.diverseuniverse.net

PUBLICATIONS

Erie Gay News 814/456-9833 ■ www.eriegaynews.com

Gay People's Chronicle 216/631-8646 ■ *Ohio's largest weekly LGBT newspaper w/ extensive listings* ■ www.gaypeopleschronicle.com

OUTlines Magazine 216/433-1280 ■ *free bi-weekly club magazine covering Akron, Cleveland, Columbus, Sandusky, Toledo & more* ■ www.outlinesmagazine.com

MEN'S CLUBS

The Club Cleveland [★PC] 216/961-2727 ■ 3219 Detroit Ave ■ *24hrs* ■ www.the-clubs.com

Flex [MR,SW,V,PC] 216/812-3304 ■ 2600 Hamilton Ave ■ *24hrs, in renovated art deco Greyhound bus station, steam room, sauna, gym & 20-man whirlpool* ■ www.flexbaths.com

EROTICA

Bank News 216/281-8777 ■ 4025 Clark Ave (at W 41st St)

Body Language 216/251-3330, 888/429-7733 ■ 11424 Lorain Ave (at W 115th St) ■ *11am-11pm, till 6pm Sun, "an educational store for adults in alternative lifestyles"* ■ www.body-language.com

Laws Leather Shop 216/344-9229 ■ 1418 W 29th St ■ *1pm-9pm Th, 1pm-8pm & 10pm-midnight Fri-Sat* ■ www.lawsleather.com

Rocky's Entertainment & Emporium [AYOR] 216/267-4659 ■ 13330 Brookpark Rd (at W 130th)

Columbus

ACCOMMODATIONS

1 **The Brewmaster's House** [MO,NS,WI,GO] 614/449-8298 ■ *full brkfst, historic house* ■ www.damron.com/home-pages/brewmastershouse/

2 **Courtyard by Marriott** [GF,SW,WI,WC] 614/228-3200, 800/321-2211 ■ 35 W Spring St (at Front St) ■ *hot tub* ■ www.marriott.com

BARS

3 **AWOL** [M,NH,K,WC] 614/621-8779 ■ 49 Parsons Ave (at Oak) ■ *noon-2:30am, from 1pm Sun*

4 **Blazer's Pub** [MW,NH,K] 614/299-1800 ■ 1205 N High St (at 5th) ■ *4pm-midnight, till 2am Th-Sat, clsd Sun* ■ www.blazerspub.biz

5 **The Closet** [MW,D,F,E,K] 614/443-4354 ■ 1295 Parsons Ave ■ *1pm-2:30am, from noon Sun, Sun brunch*

6   **Club 20** [M,NH,K] **614/261-9111** ■ 20 E Duncan (at High) ■ noon-2:30am, from 1pm Sun, patio

7   **Club Diversity** [MW,E,P] **614/224-4050** ■ 863 S High St ■ 4pm-midnight, till 2:30am Fri-Sat, piano bar, [E] Fri-Sat ■ www.clubdiversity.com

8   **Downtown Connection** [MW,D] **614/223-9600** ■ 894 W Broad St ■ 4pm-close, from 3pm wknds ■ www.dccolumbus.com

9   <u>The Far Side</u> [W,NH,F,E,K,OC,GO] **614/276-5817** ■ 1662 W Mound St (at Reed) ■ 5pm-close, from 6pm wknds, live bands wknds, lesbian-owned

10   **Garrett's Saloon** [M,K,S] **614/484-0048** ■ 1071 Parsons Ave (at E Stewart Ave) ■ 4pm-2:30am

11   **Havana Video Lounge** [★MW,NH,D,F,DS,S,V] **614/421-9697** ■ 862 N High (at 1st Ave) ■ 5pm-2:30am, martini lounge, male strippers Sun ■ www.columbus-nightlife.com

12   **The Pyramid II** [M,NH,DS,S] **614/228-6151** ■ 211 N 6th St ■ 4pm-2:30am, from 1pm wknds

13   **Q** [M,D,TG,K,S,V,GO] **614/222-2401** ■ 205 N 5th St (at Spring) ■ 4pm-2am, from 1pm wknds, patio ■ www.q-nation.com

14   <u>Slammer's</u> [W,D,F,E,WC] **614/469-7526** ■ 202 E Long St (at 5th St) ■ 11am-12:30am, till 2:30am Fri-Sat, from 6pm wknds, open mic Tue, patio ■ www.slammersbar.us

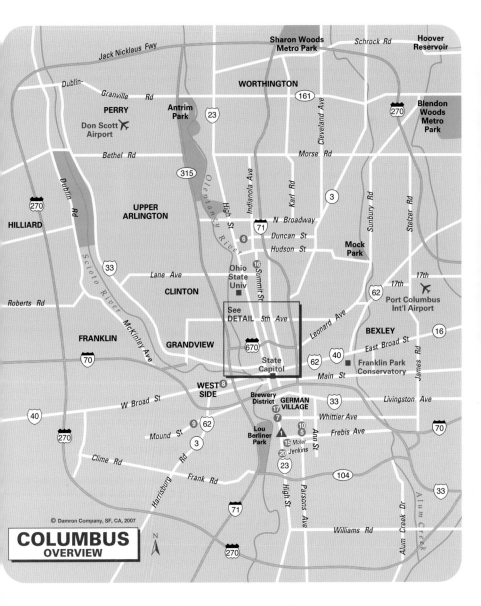

COLUMBUS OVERVIEW

© Damron Company, SF, CA, 2007

15   **Somewhere Else** [MW,F,E,K,DS,S] 614/443-4300 ■ 1312 S High St (at Moler) ■ 5pm-2:30am, from 7pm Sun-Mon, clsd Mon winters ■ www.somewhereelseclub.com

15   **The South Bend Tavern** [MW,NH,DS,WC] 614/444-3386 ■ 126 E Moler St (at 4th St) ■ noon-2:30am

16   **Summit Station** [W,NH,E,K,S] 614/261-9634 ■ 2210 Summit St (btwn Alden & Oakland) ■ 4pm-2:30am ■ www.summitstationbar.com

17   **Tremont II** [M,NH,OC] 614/445-9365 ■ 708 S High St (at Frankfort) ■ 1pm-2:30am

18   **Union Station Video Cafe** [★MW,F,V,WC] 614/228-3740 ■ 630 N High St (at Goodale) ■ 11am-11pm, video bar, internet access, also full menu ■ www.usvc.com

19   **The Vine Cocktails & Cafe** [MW,F,K,DS,V,WC] 614/221-8463 ■ 73 E Gay St (at 3rd St) ■ 5pm-1am, Sun brunch from 11am, full martini menu ■ vineonline.biz

20   **WOOFs Bar & Grill** [M,NH,D,CW,B,L,K,S] 614/237-3539 ■ 2063 E Livingston Ave (at College) ■ 10am-2:30am, clsd Sun ■ www.WOOFsColumbus.com

NIGHTCLUBS

21   **Axis** [★M,D,C,DS,S,18+,WC,GO] 614/291-4008 ■ 775 N High St (at Hubbard) ■ 10pm-2:30am Fri-Sat only, also Pump lounge, go-go boys ■ www.columbusnightlife.com

22   **Tradewinds II** [M,D,B,L,V,WC] 614/461-4110 ■ 117 E Chestnut (at 3rd St) ■ 4pm-2:30am, clsd Mon, 3 bars & restaurant ■ www.tradewindsII.com

23   **Wall Street** [★MW,D,CW,DS,P,YC,WC] 614/464-2800 ■ 144 N Wall St (at Long) ■ 9pm-2:30am, from 10pm Wed, 8pm-midnight Th, clsd Mon-Tue, more women Fri, TGIF party 1st Fri, [CW] Th ■ www.wallstreetnightclub.com

CAFES

The Coffee Table [MW] 614/297-1177 ■ 731 N High St (at Buttles) ■ 7am-10pm, till 11pm Fri-Sat, 8am-11pm Sun

Cup-O-Joe Cafe [F] 614/221-1563 ■ 627 3rd St (at Sycamore) ■ 6am-10:30pm, till 11pm Fri-Sat, from 7am wknds, till 10pm Sun

RESTAURANTS

Cap City Diner 614/291-3663 ■ 1299 Olentangy River Rd ■ 11am-10pm, till 11pm Fri-Sat, till 9pm Sun ■ www.capcityfinediner.com

L'Antibes [WC,GO] 614/291-1666 ■ 772 N High St #106 (at Warren) ■ 5pm-close, clsd Sun-Mon, French ■ www.lantibes.com

Lemon Grass [★R] 614/224-1414 ■ 641 N High (at Russell) ■ lunch weekdays & dinner nightly, Asian cuisine ■ www.lemongrassfusion.com

COLUMBUS

Columbus is both Ohio's largest city and its capital. It offers a wide variety of attractions, from the Columbus Jazz Orchestra to the Brewery District. The Short North, the area on High Street just north of downtown, hosts the very popular "Gallery Hop" on the first Saturday of the month.

Tourist Info

AIRPORT DIRECTIONS

Port Columbus International. To get to downtown, take 17th Ave to Hwy 62 South. Follow Hwy 62 until it comes to Hwy 40 West. Follow 40 West as it runs right through downtown.

PUBLIC TRANSIT & TAXIS

Yellow Cab 614/444-4444.
Acme Taxi 614/299-9990.
Central Ohio Transit Authority (COTA) 614/228-1776, web: www.cota.com.

TOURIST SPOTS & INFO

Brewery District.
Columbus Jazz Orchestra 614/294-5200, web: www.columbusjazzorchestra.com.
Columbus Museum of Modern Art 614/221-6801, web: www.columbusmuseum.org.
Columbus Zoo 614/645-3550, web: www.colszoo.org.
Franklin Park Conservatory 614/645-8733, web: www.fpconservatory.org.
German Village district.
The Short North neighborhood (popular "Gallery Hop" 1st Sat), web:www.shortnorth.org.
Wexner Center for the Arts 614/292-3535, web: www.wexarts.org.
Visitor's Center: 800/282-5393, web: www.ohiotourism.com.

Weather

Truly midwestern. Winters are cold, summers are hot.

City Calendar

LGBT PRIDE

June. 614/299-7764 (Stonewall #).

ANNUAL EVENTS

June - Pagan Spirit Gathering in Athens campground, 1.5 hours south of Columbus 608/924-2216 (Wisconsin office), web: circlesanctuary.org/psg/site.
June - Columbus Arts Festival 614/224-2606, web: www.gcac.org.
August - Ohio State Fair 888/646-3976, web: www.ohioexpocenter.com.
September - Ohio Lesbian Festival, web: www.ohiolba.org.

Queer Resources

COMMUNITY INFO

Stonewall Columbus Hotline/Community Center 614/299-7764. 1160 N High St (at E 4th Ave), 9am-7pm, clsd wknds, web: www.stonewallcolumbus.org.
Drummer's Group AA 614/253-8501, web: www.aacentralohio.org.
Columbus AIDS Task Force 614/299-2437, web: www.catf.net.

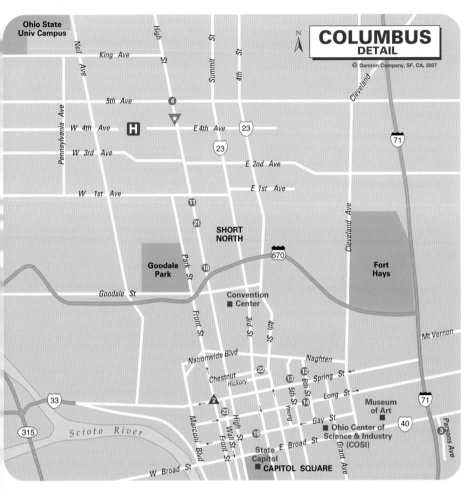

ENTERTAINMENT & RECREATION

Ohio Roller Girls ■ *Columbus' female roller derby league, check web for upcoming events* ■ www.ohiorollergirls.com

BOOKSTORES

The Book Loft of German Village 614/464-1774 ■ 631 S 3rd St (at Sycamore) ■ *10am-11pm, till midnight Fri-Sat, LGBT section* ■ www.bookloft.com

RETAIL SHOPS

Columbus Leather Company 614/224-8989 ■ 642 N High St, Ste B (in Short North) ■ *leather, fetish* ■ www.columbusleathercompany.com

Hausfrau Haven 614/443-3680 ■ 769 S 3rd St (at Columbus) ■ *10am-7pm, noon-5pm Sun, greeting cards, wine & gifts*

Piercology [GO] 614/297-4743 ■ 190 W 2nd Ave ■ *noon-10pm, 1pm-7pm Sun, body-piercing studio* ■ www.piercology.com

Torso 614/421-7663 ■ 772 N High St (at Warren) ■ *11am-8pm, till 9pm Fri-Sat, clsd Mon, clothing* ■ www.torsoonline.com

PUBLICATIONS

OUTlines Magazine 216/433-1280 ■ *free bi-weekly club magazine covering Akron, Cleveland, Columbus, Sandusky, Toledo & more* ■ www.outlinesmagazine.com

Outlook Weekly 614/268-8525 ■ *statewide LGBT weekly, good resource pages* ■ www.outlooknews.com

MEN'S CLUBS

➤The Club Columbus [SW] 614/291-0049 ■ 795 W 5th Ave (at Olentangy Rd) ■ *gym, steam, sauna* ■ www.theclubs.com

Flex Columbus [V,PC] 614/252-0730 ■ 1567 E Livingston Ave (at Geers Ave) ■ *24hrs, lounge, steam room, glory room, dungeon, dry sauna, guest memberships* ■ www.flexbaths.com

EROTICA

The Garden 614/294-2869 ■ 1174 N High St (btwn 4th & 5th Ave) ■ *11am-3am, noon-midnight Sun, adult toys* ■ www.thegardencolumbus.com

The Lion's Den Adult Superstore 614/475-1943 ■ 3015 Morse Rd ■ *24hrs* ■ www.lionsdenadult.com

The Lion's Den Adult Superstore 614/861-6770 ■ 4315 Kimberly Pkwy (off Hamilton Rd) ■ *24hrs* ■ www.lionsdenadult.com

North Campus Video 614/268-4021 ■ 2465 N High St (at Hudson) ■ *24hrs*

OKLAHOMA

Oklahoma City

ACCOMMODATIONS

America's Crossroads B&B [M,SW,WI,GO] 405/495-1111 ■ *reservation service for private homes* ■ www.inntravels.com/usa/ok/rdac.html

1 Days Inn Oklahoma City Northwest [GF,SW,WI] 405/946-0741 ■ 2801 NW 39th St (at I-44 & May Ave, Exit 124) ■ www.daysinn.com

2 ➤Habana Inn [★MW,SW,NS,WC] 405/528-2221, 800/988-2221 (reservations only) ■ 2200 NW 39th St (at Youngs) ■ *LGBT resort, also 3 bars, restaurant, gift shop* ■ www.habanainn.com

3 Hawthorn Suites [GF,SW] 405/840-1440, 800/527-1133 (reservations) ■ 1600 NW Expy (Richmond Square) ■ *all suites, full brkfst* ■ www.hawthorn.com

4 The Hollywood Hotel & Suites [M,SW] 405/947-2351 ■ 3535 NW 39th St (at Portland) ■ *also 4 bars & restaurant* ■ www.hollywoodhotelokc.com

5 Waterford Marriott [GF,SW,NS,WI] 405/848-4782, 800/228-9290 ■ 6300 Waterford Blvd ■ *boutique hotel, also restaurant & bar* ■ www.marriott.com

BARS

6 Alibi's [GS,NH,TG,K,GO] 405/605-3795 ■ 1200 N Pennsylvania (at NW 11th) ■ *3pm-2am, from noon wknds* ■ www.alibisandexcuses.com

7 Bearz 3020 [GS,NH,K] 405/524-9306 ■ 3020 N Pennsylvania (at NW 29th St) ■ *2pm-2am, [K] Th & Sat*

8 The Boom [MW,NH,K,DS,S,WI,WC] 405/601-7200 ■ 2807 NW 36th St (at May Ave) ■ *4pm-2am, [K] Tue & [DS] Wed, Fri-Sat, patio* ■ www.myspace.com/boomokc

9 Excuses [W,NH,D,WC] 405/525-3734 ■ 2024 NW 11th (at Pennsylvania) ■ *3pm-2am, from 6pm Sat, clsd Mon, beer bar, patio*

2 ➤The Finishline [MW,NH,D,CW,WC] 405/525-2900 ■ at Habana Inn ■ *noon-2am, CW lessons 7pm Tue, poolside bar* ■ www.habanainn.com/hifinishline.htm

10 Hi-Lo Club [MW,NH,D,E,DS] 405/843-1722 ■ 1221 NW 50th St (btwn Western & Classen) ■ *noon-2am, live bands weekly* ■ www.hi-loclub.com

2 ➤The Ledo [MW,F,K,NS,WC] 405/525-0730 ■ at Habana Inn ■ *4pm-10:30pm, till 2am Fri-Sat, martini lounge, [K] Th* ■ www.habanainn.com

8 Partners [★W,NH,D,E,K,WC] 405/942-2199 ■ 2805 NW 36th St (at May Ave) ■ *6pm-close, from 7pm Fri-Sat, clsd Mon-Tue, patio* ■ www.partners4club.com

4 Pecs [M,B,L] 405/947-2351 ■ 3535 NW 39th St (at Hollywood Hotel & Suites) ■ *7pm-2am Tues-Th & Sun, levi/leather bar* ■ www.hollywoodhotelokc.com/pecs.html

11 Phoenix Rising [M,NH,D,CW,B,L,GO] 405/601-3711 ■ 2120 NW 39th St (at Pennsylvania Ave) ■ *4pm-2am, patio*

4 Rudy's [MW] 405/947-2351 ■ 3535 NW 39 Expwy (at Hollywood Hotel & Suites) ■ *5pm-3am, clsd Sun, cocktail lounge, [P] Wed, Fri-Sat* ■ www.hollywoodhotelokc.com/rudys.html

12 Tramps [★M,D,S,WC] 405/521-9888 ■ 2201 NW 39th St (at Barnes) ■ *noon-2am, from 10am wknds*

NIGHTCLUBS

4 Club Rox [MW,D,DS,S,GO] 405/947-2351 ■ 3535 NW 39 Expwy (at Hollywood Hotel & Suites) ■ *4pm-2am* ■ www.hollywoodhotelokc.com/rox.html

2 ➤The Copa [MW,D,E,DS,S,WC] 405/525-0730 ■ at Habana Inn ■ *9pm-2am, clsd Mon, theme nights, male dancers Fri-Sat* ■ www.habanainn.com/copa.html

13 The Park [M,D,S,V,WC] 405/528-4690 ■ 2125 NW 39th St (at Barnes/ Pennsylvania) ■ *5pm-2am, from 3pm Sun, patio, cruisy* ■ www.anglesclub.com

14 Wreck Room [★MW,D,DS,S,YC] 405/525-7610 ■ 2127 NW 39th St (at Pennsylvania) ■ *10pm-close Fri-Sat only, [18+] after 1am* ■ www.anglesclub.com

CAFES

The Red Cup [F,E,NS,WI] 405/525-3430 ■ 3122 N Classen Blvd (at NW 30th St) ■ *7am-3:30pm, till 10pm Wed-Fri, 9am-10pm Sat, till 7pm Sun, coffeehouse, also sandwiches* ■ www.redcupok.com

RESTAURANTS

Bricktown Brewery Restaurant [E] 405/232-2739 ■ 1 N Oklahoma Ave (at Sheridan) ■ 11am-10pm, till midnight wknds, noon-8pm Sun, live bands wknds, full bar ■ www.bricktownbrewery.com

Cheever's Cafe [R] 405/525-7007 ■ 2409 N Hudson Ave (at NW 23rd) ■ 11am-9:30pm, till 10:30pm Fri-Sat, from 5pm Sat, clsd Sun, contemporary comfort food ■ www.cheever-scafe.com

Earl's Rib Palace 405/272-9898 ■ 216 Johnny Bench Dr, Ste BBQ (in Bricktown) ■ 11am-9pm, till 10pm Fri-Sat, noon-5pm Sun, BBQ, several locations in OKC ■ www.earlsrib-palace.com

Galileo [E] 405/415-7827 ■ 3009 Paseo (at NW 29th St) ■ 11am-2am, from 4pm Sun, clsd Mon, full bar ■ www.galileo-okc.com

Gusher's [WC] 405/525-0730 ■ at Habana Inn ■ 11am-10:30pm, from 9am wknds, till 3:30am Fri-Sat for after-hours brkfst ■ www.habanainn.com

▶**Ingrid's Kitchen** 405/946-8444 ■ 3701 N Youngs (btwn Penn & May, on NW 36th) ■ 7am-6:30pm, till 5pm Sat, 11am-2pm Sun, German/ American bakery, delicatessen, restaurant ■ www.ingridskitchen.com

La Luna Mexican Cafe 405/235-9596 ■ 409 W Reno Ave (at Walker) ■ full bar ■ www.lalunamexicancafe.com

Rococo Restaurant & Fine Wine 405/528-2824 ■ 2824 N Pennsylvania (at NW 27th St) ■ lunch Mon-Fri, dinner nightly, Sun jazz brunch ■ www.rococo-restaurant.com

The Rose Garden Tea Room 405/495-2252 ■ 4413 N Meridian Ave (next to Antique House) ■ 11am-2pm, clsd Sat-Sun, homemade soups, salads, sandwiches, dessert, Victorian decor

Someplace Else Deli & Bakery [★] 405/524-0887 ■ 2310 N Western Ave ■ 7am-6:30pm, 9:30am-4pm Sat, clsd Sun, soups, salads, sandwiches

Sushi Neko 405/528-8862 ■ 4318 N Western (btwn 42nd & 43rd) ■ 11am-11pm, till midnight Fri-Sat, clsd Sun ■ www.sushineko.com

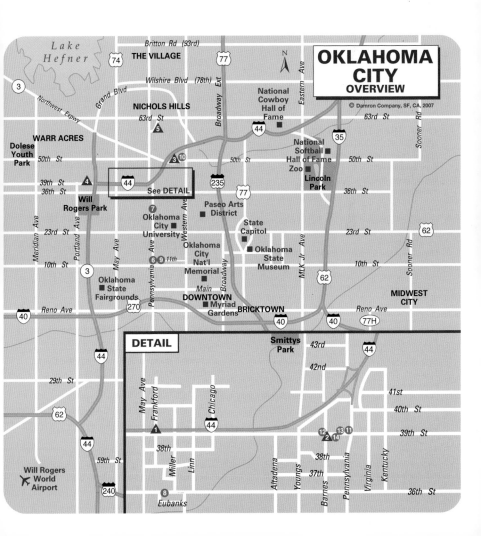

Topanga Bar & Grill [MW,GO] 405/947-2351 ■ 3535 NW 39 Expwy (at Hollywood Hotel & Suites) ■ *4pm-11pm, till 3am Fri-Sat, 11am-2pm Sun (champagne brunch) & 4pm-11pm, Southwestern, full bar* ■ hollywoodhotelokc.com/topanga.html

ENTERTAINMENT & RECREATION

Carpenter Square Theater 405/232-6500 ■ 400 W Sheridan (at Stage Center) ■ *occasional gay-themed material* ■ www.carpentersquare.com

First Friday Gallery Walk 405/525-2688 ■ from 28th at N Walker to 30th at N Dewey ■ *open tour of Paseo Arts District galleries, first Fri & Sat* ■ www.thepaseo.com

BOOKSTORES

Full Circle Bookstore [F] 405/842-2900, 800/683-7323 ■ 50 Penn Pl, 1900 NW Expwy (in NE corner of 1st level) ■ *10am-9pm, till 10pm Fri-Sat, noon-5pm Sun, independent, readings, also cafe & coffee bar* ■ **www.fullcirclebooks.com**

Nature's Treasures 405/741-4322 ■ 6223 SE 15th St (btwn Sooner & Air Depot Blvd), Midwest City ■ *10am-7pm, till 6pm Sat, from noon Sun, New Age books, crystals, gifts, also classes*

RETAIL SHOPS

23rd St Body Piercing 405/524-6824 ■ 411 NW 23rd St (btwn Hudson & Walker) ■ *noon-9pm, 1pm-6pm Sun* ■ www.23rdstreetbodypiercing.com

➤ **Jungle Red** [WC] 405/524-5733 ■ at Habana Inn ■ *1pm-close, novelties, leather, gifts* ■ www.habanainn.com

OKLAHOMA CITY

First settled in 1889, Oklahoma City maintains its "Old West" roots. In keeping with its history of rugged individualism and invention, Oklahoma City is home to the National Cowboy and Western Heritage Museum...and to a monument commemorating the inventor of the shopping cart, OKC resident Sylvan Goldman.

Tourist Info

AIRPORT DIRECTIONS

Will Rogers World Airport. To get to the area within the detail map, take I-44 North. Exit on Pennsylvania Ave.

PUBLIC TRANSIT & TAXIS

Yellow Cab 405/232-6161.

Airport Express 405/681-3311, web: www.taxivan.com.

Metro Transit 405/235-7433, web: www.gometro.org.

TOURIST SPOTS & INFO

Bricktown—renovated nightlife district with canal.
Historic Paseo Arts District, web: www.thepaseo.com.
Myriad Gardens' Crystal Bridge 405/297-3995, web: www.myriadgardens.com.
National Cowboy and Western Heritage Museum 405/478-2250, web: www.nationalcowboymuseum.org.
National Softball Hall of Fame 405/424-5266, web: www.softball.org.
Oklahoma City Museum of Art 405/236-3100, web: www.okcmoa.com.
Oklahoma City National Memorial 405/235-3313, web: www.oklahomacitynationalmemorial.org.
Oklahoma City Zoo 405,424-3344, web: www.okczoo.com.
Omniplex 405/602-6664, web: www.omniplex.org.
State Capitol: only one in country with its own active oil well.
Sylvan Goldman monument (inventor of the shopping cart).
Will Rogers Park.
Visitor's Center: 405/297-8912 & 800/225-5652, web: www.okccvb.org.

Weather

Spring brings out the best of Oklahoma—blue skies for miles and the dogwood, redbud, and azaleas in bloom. (It's also the start of tornado season.) Summer gets mighty hot (90's-100's), with thunderstorms thrown in for relief. Fall is the time to head east to the hills of "Green Country" and watch the leaves change. Winters bring cold temps (20's-30's), gray skies, a brown landscape, and the occasional dusting of snow and the even rarer but more serious ice storm.

Best Views

From a water taxi on the Bricktown Canal (www.watertaxi.com/Oklahoma/OKCHome.Asp). Or anywhere in Myriad Gardens.

City Calendar

LGBT PRIDE

June, web: www.okcpride.com.

ANNUAL EVENTS

May - Herland Spring Retreat 405/521-9696. Music, workshops, web: www.herlandsisters.org.
May - Paseo Arts Festival 405/525-2688, web: www.thepaseo.com.
September - Herland Fall Retreat.
October - Oklahoma GLBT Int'l Film Festival, web: www.out-ok.com.

Queer Resources

COMMUNITY INFO

Gay OKC, web: www.gayokc.com
Herland Sister Resources 405/521-9696, web: www.herlandsisters.org.
OKC Lesbian, web: www.okclesbian.com.
Live & Let Live AA 405/842-1200, web: www.aaoklahoma.org.
RAIN-OK 405/232-2437, web: www.rainoklahoma.org.

PUBLICATIONS

The Herland Voice 405/521-9696 ■ *monthly newsletter for OKC women's community* ■ www.herlandsisters.org

Oklahoma Gazette 405/528-6000 ■ *"Metro OKC's independent weekly"* ■ www.okgazette.com

Standout Magazine [GO] 405/473-7891 ■ *LGBT* ■ www.standout-online.com

EROTICA

Christie's Toy Box 405/946-4438 ■ 3126 N May Ave (at 30th) ■ *multiple locations in OKC* ■ www.christiestoybox.com

Naughty & Nice 405/681-5044 ■ 3121 SW 29th St (at I-44) ■ *24hrs* ■ naughtyandnicellc.com

Priscilla's 405/755-8600 ■ 615 E Memorial ■ *toys, lingerie* ■ www.priscillas.com

OREGON

Portland

ACCOMMODATIONS

1 **The Ace Hotel** [GS,NS,WI,WC] 503/228-2277 ■ 1022 SW Stark St (at 11th) ■ *hip hotel for "cultural influencers & opinion leaders on a budget"* ■ www.theacehotel.com

2 **Fifth Avenue Suites Hotel** [GF,WI] 503/222-0001, 888/207-2201 ■ 506 SW Washington (at 5th Ave) ■ *also restaurant, gym* ■ www.5thavenuesuites.com

Forest Springs B&B [GS,NS,GO] 503/674-8992, 877/674-9282 ■ 3680 SW Towle Ave, Gresham ■ *full brkfst* ■ www.ForestSpring.com

3 **The Grand Ronde Place** [GS,NS,GO] 503/808-9048, 866/330-7245 ■ 250 NE Tomahawk Island Dr, Slip A-15 (I-5, at north exit 308) ■ *B&B, 34-ft yacht, also private charter cruises* ■ www.thegrandrondeplace.com

4 **Hotel Vintage Plaza** [★GF,WI,WC] 503/228-1212, 800/263-2305 ■ 422 SW Broadway ■ *upscale hotel, also restaurant & lounge* ■ www.vintageplaza.com

5 **Jupiter Hotel** [★GF,NS,WI,WC] 503/230-9200, 877/800-0004 ■ 800 E Burnside ■ *upscale hotel, also restaurant & lounge (7am-4am daily)* ■ www.jupiterhotel.com

6 **The Kinley Manor Coach House** [GS,NS,WI,GO] 503/249-7270 ■ 924 NE Schuyler ■ *rental home, fully equipped kitchen, laundry facilities, no partiers* ■ www.kinleymanor.com

7 **The Lion & the Rose** [GS,NS,WI,GO] 503/287-9245, 800/955-1647 ■ 1810 NE 15th Ave ■ *in 1906 Queen Anne mansion* ■ www.lionrose.com

8 **MacMaster House** [GF,NS] 503/223-7362, 800/774-9523 ■ 1041 SW Vista Ave (at Park Pl) ■ *historic inn near Rose Gardens* ■ www.macmaster.com

9 **The Mark Spencer Hotel** [GF,NS] 503/224-3293, 800/548-3934 ■ 409 SW Eleventh Ave (near Stark) ■ www.markspencer.com

10 **Portland's White House B&B** [GS,NS,WI,GO] 503/287-7131, 800/272-7131 ■ 1914 NE 22nd Ave ■ *in 1911 Greek Revival mansion* ■ www.portlandswhitehouse.com

11 **Sullivan's Gulch B&B** [GS,NS,GO] 503/331-1104 ■ 1744 NE Clackamas St (at 17th) ■ *1907 Portland home, decks* ■ www.sullivansgulch.com

BARS

12 **Booty** [MW,D] 503/230-9020 ■ 1305 SE 8th Ave (at Acme) ■ *9pm-2am Th only, "Portland's queer party for the piratecore"* ■ www.bootypdx.com

13 **Boxxes** [★M,D,K,V,WI,WC] 503/226-4171 ■ 1035 SW Stark (at SW 11th Ave) ■ *5pm-close, also Brig [MW,D], also Red Cap Garage* ■ www.boxxes.com

14 **Brazen Bean** [GS,F,E,WC] 503/294-0636 ■ 2075 NW Glisan St (at 21st Ave) ■ *5pm-midnight, till 1am Fri-Sat, clsd Sun, swank cigar & martini bar*

15 **Candlelight Cafe & Bar** [GF,F,E] 503/222-3378 ■ 2032 SW 5th (at Lincoln) ■ *11am-2:30am, live blues, hamburgers* ■ www.candlelightcafebar.com

16 **CC Slaughter's** [★M,D,CW,F,K,V,WC] 503/248-9135 ■ 219 NW Davis (at 3rd) ■ *3pm-2am, [K] Tue, also martini lounge, Bear Night 4th Fri* ■ www.ccslaughterspdx.com

17 **Chopsticks Express** [GS,F,K,YC,WC] 503/234-6171 ■ 2651 E Burnside St (at SE 26th) ■ *11am-2am, karaoke venue*

18 **Crush** [GS,F] 503/235-8150 ■ 1400 SE Morrison (at SE 14th) ■ *4:30pm-2am, from 6pm Sat, 9am-midnight Sun, clsd Mon, wine & martini bar* ■ crushbar.com

19 **Darcelle XV** [GS,D,F,C,DS,S,WC] 503/222-5338 ■ 208 NW 3rd Ave (at NW Davis St) ■ *6pm-11pm, till 2am Fri-Sat, clsd Sun-Tue* ■ www.darcellexv.com

20 **Dirty Duck Tavern** [M,NH,B,L,OC,BW,WC] 503/224-8446 ■ 439 NW 3rd (at Glisan) ■ *3pm-1am, 2pm-2am Fri, 3pm-2am Sat, noon-1am Sun, "home of the bears," hanky night & leather social 1st & 3rd Fri* ■ www.dirtyducktavern.com

21 **Doug Fir** [★GF,F,E] 503/231-9663 ■ 830 E Burnside (at NE 9th) ■ *7am-3am, hipster log cabin lounge, also restaurant, live music* ■ www.dougfirlounge.com

22 **Eagle PDX** [M,L,V,WC] 503/241-0105 ■ 1300 W Burnside (at 13th Ave) ■ *4pm-2am* ■ www.portlandeagle.com

43 **Eagle Portland** [M,B,L,N] 503/283-9734 ■ 835 N Lombard (at Albina) ■ *11am-2:30am, naked pool Tue* ■ www.eagle-portland.com

23 **The Egyptian Club** [★W,D,F,K,S,WC,GO] 503/236-8689 ■ 3701 SE Division St (at SE 37th Ave) ■ *1pm-2:30am, from 4pm wknds, lesbian-owned* ■ www.eroompdx.com

13 **Flirt** [★M,D,MR-AF,V,WC] 503/226-4171 ■ 1035 SW Stark (at SW 11th Ave, at Boxxes) ■ *9pm Tue, hip-hop, also Brig [MW,D], also Red Cap Garage* ■ www.boxxes.com

24 **Fox & Hound** [★M,K,WC] 503/243-5530 ■ 217 NW 2nd Ave (btwn Everett & Davis) ■ *9am-2am, from 8:30am wknds, also restaurant, brunch Sun*

25 **Hobo's** [GS,P,WC] 503/224-3285 ■ 120 NW 3rd Ave (btwn Davis & Couch) ■ *4pm-2:30am, piano bar, also restaurant, some veggie* ■ www.hobospdx.com

26 **JOQ's Tavern** [M,NH,F,WC] 503/287-4210 ■ 2512 NE Broadway (at NE 24th Ave) ■ *11am-2am* ■ www.joqspdx.com

27 **Moonstar** [GS,D] 503/285-1230 ■ 7410 NE Martin Luther King Jr Blvd (btwn NE Knott & NE Graham) ■ *11am-2:30am*

Northbank [MW,D,F,K,NS,WC] 360/695-3862 ■ 106 W 6th St (at Main), Vancouver, WA ■ *2pm-2am* ■ www.thenorthbank.com

28 **Salon Q** [MW,NS] 503/445-8331 ■ 1135 SW Washington St (at Bettie Ford Lounge) ■ *7pm 2nd Tue only* ■ www.bettiefordlounge.com

29 **Scandals Tavern** [M,NH,F,WC,GO] 503/227-5887 ■ 1125 SW Stark St (at 12th) ■ *noon-2am, friendly bar, also Other Side Lounge* ■ www.scandalspdx.com

30 **Shanghai Steakery** [GS,TG,WC] 503/228-9325 ■ 16 NW Broadway ■ *7am-2am*

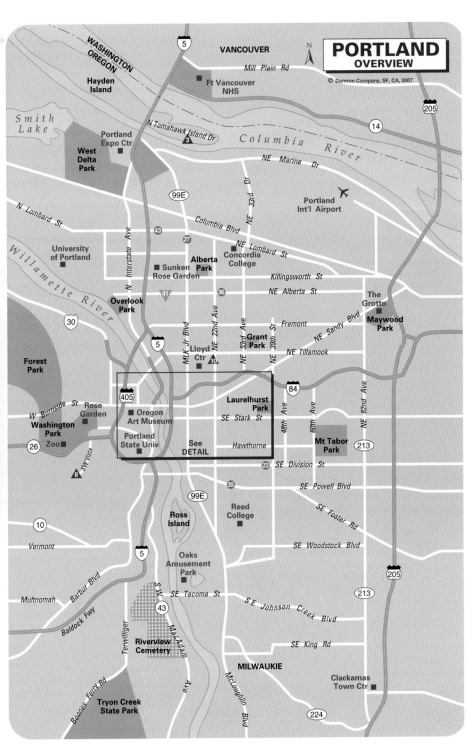

PORTLAND
OVERVIEW
© Damron Company, SF, CA, 2007

31 **Silverado** [★M,D,F,K,S,WC,GO] 503/224-4493 ■ 1217 SW Stark St (btwn SW 11th & 12th Aves) ■ *9am-2:30am, strippers* ■ www.silveradopdx.com

32 **Starky's** [★MW,NH,F,WC] 503/230-7980 ■ 2913 SE Stark St (at SE 29th Ave) ■ *11am-2am, patio, also restaurant, Sun brunch* ■ www.starkys.com

33 **Urban Wineworks** [GS] 503/226-9797 ■ 407 NW 16th Ave ■ *noon-8:30pm, till 6pm Sun, wine tasting & classes* ■ www.urbanwineworks.com

34 **Vault Martini Bar** [GS,F] 503/224-4909 ■ 226 NW 12th Ave ■ *4pm-1am, till 2am Fri-Sat, 1pm-10pm Sun, full menu* ■ www.vaultmartini.com

35 **Vino Vixens** [GS,NS] 503/231-8466 ■ 2929 SE Powell Blvd ■ *"Portland's first rock 'n' roll wine shop," retail & lounge* ■ www.badgirlwines.com

36 **Zaytoon** [GS,F,GO] 503/284-1168 ■ 2236 NE Alberta (at 23rd) ■ *5pm-1am, till 2:30am Fri-Sat, lesbian-owned* ■ www.zaytoonbar.com

Nightclubs

37 **Casey's** [MW,D] 503/241-0105 ■ 610 NW Couch (at 6th) ■ *3pm-2:30am* ■ www.myspace.com/caseyspdx

38 **Embers** [★M,D,F,DS,WC] 503/222-3082 ■ 110 NW Broadway (at NW Couch St) ■ *3pm-3am, also restaurant* ■ www.emberspdx.net

39 **Escape** [MW,D] 503/227-0830 ■ 333 SW Park (btwn SW Oak & SW Stark) ■ *10:30pm-close Fri-Sat only, Portland's only all-ages gay club*

40 **Holocene** [GS,D,E,DS] 503/239-7639 ■ 1001 SE Morrison (at E 10th) ■ *many lgbt theme nights, check local listings* ■ www.holocene.org

40 **Tart Monthly Queer Women's Dance Party** [W,D,MR,F] 503/239-7639 ■ 1001 SE Morrison (at SE 10th Ave, at Holocene) ■ *4pm-11pm 2nd Sun, check local listings* ■ www.tartparty.com

Cafes

Blend 503/234-8610 ■ 2327 E Burnside ■ *7am-6pm, from 8am Sun*

Bread & Ink Cafe [★BW,WC] 503/239-4756 ■ 3610 SE Hawthorne Blvd (at 36th) ■ *brkfst, lunch & dinner, packed for brunch on Sun*

Cafe Wonder [GS,TG,DS,NS,GO] 503/493-0371 ■ 128 NE Russell ■ *lunch & dinner, wknd brunch, full bar* ■ www.wonderballroom.com

Cup & Saucer Cafe [★F,NS] 503/236-6001 ■ 3566 SE Hawthorne Blvd (btwn 34th & 36th) ■ *7am-9pm, full menu, some veggie, very popular w/ lesbians*

Elephant's Delicatessen 503/299-6304 ■ 115 NW 22nd Ave ■ 7am-7:30pm, 9:30am-6:30pm Sun, deli, desserts, coffee ■ www.elephantsdeli.com

Haven Coffee [W,E,WI,WC,GO] 503/236-6890 ■ 3551 SE Division St ■ 7:30am-9pm, till 10pm wknds, shorter winter hours, lesbian-owned ■ www.havencoffee.com

Jackman Joe 503/222-0121 ■ 1111 NW 16th Ave (at Marshall) ■ 6:30am-5pm, 8:30am-2pm Sat, clsd Sun, dog-friendly

Marco's Cafe & Espresso Bar [F] 503/245-0199 ■ 7910 SW 35th (at Multnomah Blvd), Multnomah ■ 7am-9pm, from 8am Sat, 8am-2pm Sun ■ www.marcoscafe.com

The Pied Cow [WC] 503/230-4866 ■ 3244 SE Belmont (at 33rd Ave) ■ 4pm-midnight, till 1am Fri, noon-1am Sat, till midnight Sun, funky Victorian, great desserts, patio

Pix Pâtisserie 503/232-4407 ■ 3402 SE Division St ■ 10am-midnight, till 2am Fri-Sat, dessert ■ www.pixpatisserie.com

Three Friends Coffeehouse 503/236-6411 ■ 201 SE 12th Ave (at Ash) ■ 7am-10pm, from 8am Sun

Touchstone Coffee House [E,GO] 503/262-7613 ■ 7631 NE Glisan St ■ 6:30am-6:30pm, from 7am Sat, 8am-3pm Sun, also cards & gifts, outdoor garden, community resource room, lesbian-owned ■ www.touchstonecoffeehouse.com

Voodoo Doughnut 503/241-4704 ■ 22 SW 3rd Ave ■ 24hrs, clsd 2pm Sun-6am Mon ■ www.voodoodoughnut.com

RESTAURANTS

The Adobe Rose [BW] 503/235-9114 ■ 1634 SE Bybee Blvd (at Milwaukee) ■ lunch & dinner, clsd Sun-Mon, New Mexican cuisine

Andina 503/228-9535 ■ 1314 NW Glisan St ■ lunch, dinner & tapas, Peruvian, full bar ■ www.andinarestaurant.com

Assaggio [BW] 503/232-6151 ■ 7742 SE 13th (at Lambert) ■ 5pm-9:30pm, Italian, plenty veggie ■ www.assaggiorestaurant.com

Aura Restaurant & Lounge [D,WC] 503/597-2872 ■ 1022 W Burnside (btwn SW 10th & 11th) ■ 4:30pm-midnight, till 2:30am Fri-Sat, clsd Sun-Mon, also bar ■ www.auraportland.com

Bastas Trattoria 503/274-1572 ■ 410 NW 21st (at Flanders) ■ dinner nightly, northern Italian, full bar till late ■ www.bastastrattoria.com

Berbati's Pan [E] 503/226-2122 ■ 19 SW 2nd Ave (btwn Burnside & Ankeny) ■ 11am-2am, from 5pm Sun-Mon, Greek, full bar, live music venue ■ www.berbati.com

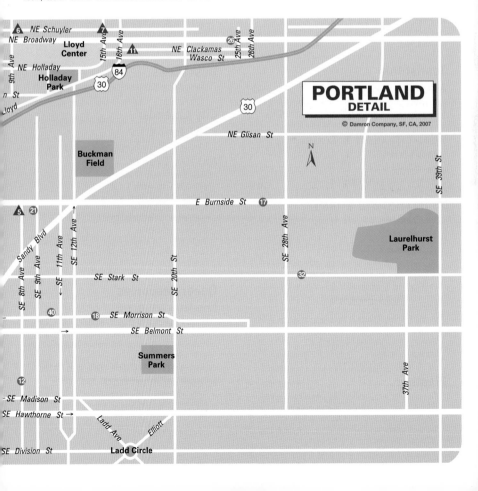

Bernie's [R] 503/282-9864 ■ 2904 NE Alberta St ■ 4pm-10pm, clsd Sun, Southern bistro, patio ■ www.bernies-bistro.com

Besaw's 503/228-2619 ■ 2301 NW Savier (at NW 23rd) ■ 7am-10pm, from 8am Sat, 8am-3pm Sun, clsd Mon, American ■ www.besaws.com

Bijou Cafe [★WC] 503/222-3187 ■ 132 SW 3rd Ave (at Pine St) ■ 7am-2pm, from 8am wknds, plenty veggie, "farm-fresh brkfst"

Bluehour [WC] 503/226-3394 ■ 250 NW 13th Ave (at NW Everett St) ■ lunch Sun-Fri, dinner nightly, Sun brunch, extensive wine list, upscale ■ www.bluehouronline.com

Chameleon [MW] 503/460-2682 ■ 2000 NE 40th Ave ■ 5:30pm-9:30pm, lounge open later Fri-Sat, clsd Sun-Mon, Asian fusion, patio ■ www.chameleonpdx.com

Daily Cafe in the Pearl 503/242-1916 ■ 902 NW 13th Ave (at Kearney St) ■ 7am-5pm, till 9pm Wed-Fri, 9am-9pm Sat, 9am-2pm Sun, Northwest cuisine ■ www.dailycafe.net

Delta [WC] 503/771-3101 ■ 4607 SE Woodstock (at 46th) ■ 5pm-midnight, bar till 1am Fri-Sat, Southern, plenty veggie

Dingo's Mexican Grill [★GO] 503/233-3996 ■ 4612 SE Hawthorne Blvd (at SE 39th) ■ noon-10pm, till 11pm Th, till 9pm Sun, popular Girls Night Out Th, lesbian-owned ■ www.dingosonline.com

Dot's Cafe [★WC] 503/235-0203 ■ 2521 SE Clinton (at 26th) ■ noon-2am, full bar, eclectic American, plenty veggie ■ www.eatatdotscafepdx.com

Equinox 503/460-3333 ■ 830 N Shaver St ■ dinner, brunch wknds, clsd Mon, int'l, patio ■ www.equinoxrestaurantpdx.com

Esparza's Tex-Mex Cafe [★] 503/234-7909 ■ 2725 SE Ankeny St (at 28th) ■ 11:30am-10pm, clsd Sun, funky

PORTLAND

Day Trips: Mt St Helens National Volcanic Monument (1 hour from downtown Portland)

Over 20 years ago, this now-famous volcano erupted due to an earthquake, causing the largest landslide in recorded history. A mushroom cloud of ash burst from the volcano, darkening the sky, and coating the landscape for miles. Mt St Helens lost 1300 vertical feet over 100 acres of mature forest. Nowadays, the monument is a lesson in rebirth and tenacity, as once devasted areas come back, and different species eke out an existence, creating a new environment.

Tourist Info

AIRPORT DIRECTIONS

Portland International. Take 205 South, then 84 West to City Center/Morrison Bridge exit. Cross the bridge, take Washington St into town.

PUBLIC TRANSIT & TAXIS

Radio Cab 503/227-1212.
Raz 503/684-3322.
Tri-Met System 503/238-7433, web: www.trimet.org.

TOURIST SPOTS & INFO

The Grotto 503/254-7371, web: www.thegrotto.org.
Microbreweries.
Old Town.
Pioneer Courthouse Square 503/223-1613, web: www.pioneercourthousesquare.org.
Portland Art Museum 503/226-2811, web: www.portlandartmuseum.org.
Washington Park.
World Forestry Center & Discovery Museum 503/228-1367, web: www.worldforestrycenter.org.
Visitor's Center: 877/678-5263, web: www.pova.com.
Travel Oregon 800/547-7842.

Weather

The wet and sometimes chilly winter rains give Portland a lush landscape that bursts into beautiful colors in the spring and fall. Summer brings sunnier days. (Temperatures can be in the 50's one day and the 90's the next.)

Best Views

International Rose Test Gardens at Washington Park.

City Calendar

LGBT PRIDE

June. 503/295-9788, web: www.pridenw.org.

ANNUAL EVENTS

May/ June - Rose Festival, web: www.rosefestival.org.
August - Mount Hood Jazz Festival, web: www.mthoodjazz.com.
September - AIDS Walk 503/223-5907, web: www.cascadeaids.org.
September - La Femme Magnifique International Pageant, web: www.darcellexv.com.
October - Portland LGBT Film Festival, web: www.plgff.org.

Queer Resources

COMMUNITY INFO

Lesbian Community Project, 503/227-0605, web: www.lesbiancommunityproject.org.
Portland Area Business Association 503/280-7222, web: www.paba.com.
Live & Let Live AA 503/238-6091, 1210 SE 7th.
Cascade AIDS Project 503/223-5907, web: www.cascadeaids.org.
AIDS and STD Hotline 503/223-2437.

Farm Cafe 503/736-3276 ■ 10 SE 7th Ave (at E Burnside St) ■ 5pm-midnight, till 11pm Sun, Northwest cuisine

Fish Grotto [★E,P,WC] 503/226-4171 ■ 1035 SW Stark (at SW 11th Ave, at Boxxes) ■ 5pm-10pm, till 9pm wknds, clsd Mon, some veggie, full bar ■ www.fishgrotto.com

Genies Cafe 503/445-9777 ■ 1101 SE Division St ■ 8am-3pm, brunch, house-infused vodkas

Genoa [BW,R] 503/238-1464 ■ 2832 SE Belmont St (at 29th) ■ dinner nightly from 5:30pm, Italian, 7-course prix-fixe ■ www.genoarestaurant.com

Gypsy Restaurant & Lounge [K,WC] 503/796-1859 ■ 625 NW 21st (btwn Hoyt & Irving) ■ 11:30am-2:30am, brunch wknds from 9am, full bar, inexpensive ■ www.conceptentertainmentgroup.com

Hurley's [WC] 503/295-6487 ■ 1987 NW Kearney (at 20th) ■ 5:30pm-10pm, clsd Sun-Mon, French, full bar ■ www.hurleys-restaurant.com

Le Happy 503/226-1258 ■ 1011 NW 16th Ave ■ 5pm-1am, till 2:30am Fri, 6pm-2:30am Sat, clsd Sun, crêpes ■ www.lehappy.com

Mama Mia Trattoria 503/295-6464 ■ 439 W 2nd Ave ■ 5pm-9pm, till 10pm Tue-Th, till midnight Fri-Sat ■ www.mamamiatrattoria.com

Masu [WI] 503/221-6278 ■ 406 SW 13th Ave ■ dinner only, sushi ■ www.masusushi.com

Mayas Taqueria 503/226-1946 ■ 1000 SW Morrison ■ 11am-10pm, till 8pm Sun

Mint 503/284-5518 ■ 816 N Russell St ■ 5pm-10pm, till 11pm Fri-Sat, clsd Sun, fusion food, also 820 Lounge ■ www.mintand820.com

Montage [★WC] 503/234-1324 ■ 301 SE Morrison ■ lunch Tue-Fri, dinner till 2am, till 4am Fri-Sat, Louisiana-style cookin', full bar ■ montagerestaurant@hotmail.com

Mother's Bistro & Bar 503/464-1122 ■ 212 SW Stark St (at 2nd Ave) ■ brkfst, lunch & dinner, clsd Mon, American ■ www.mothersbistro.com

Nicholas' 503/235-5123 ■ 318 SE Grand ■ 11am-9pm, from noon Sun, Middle Eastern ■ www.nicholasrestaurant.com

Old Town Pizza 503/222-9999 ■ 226 NW Davis ■ 11:30am-11pm, till midnight Fri-Sat, clsd Sun, above Shanghai Tunnels, supposedly home to 100-year-old ghost ■ www.oldtownpizza.com

Old Wives Tales [★BW,WC] 503/238-0470 ■ 1300 E Burnside St (at 13th) ■ 8am-9pm, till 10pm Fri-Sat, multi-ethnic vegetarian ■ www.oldwivestalesrestaurant.com

The Original Pancake House [★] 503/246-9007 ■ 8600 SW 24th Ave ■ brkfst & lunch, clsd Mon-Tue, crowded on wknds ■ www.originalpancakehouse.com

Paley's Place 503/243-2403 ■ 1204 NW 21st Ave (at NW Northrup St) ■ dinner nightly, Northwest cuisine

Papa Haydn [R] 503/228-7317 ■ 701 NW 23rd Ave (at NW Irving) ■ 11am-9:30pm, till midnight Fri-Sat, 10am-10pm Sun, bistro, full bar; also location at 5839 SE Milwaukie, 503/232-9440 ■ www.papahaydn.com

Paradox Palace Cafe [★] 503/232-7508 ■ 3439 SE Belmont ■ brkfst , lunch & dinner, vegetarian diner, killer Reuben

Pizzicato [★BW] 503/242-0023 ■ 505 NW 23rd (at Glisan) ■ 11:30am-9pm, till 10pm Fri-Sat, plenty veggie, many locations ■ www.pizzicatogourmetpizza.com

Pour 503/288-7687 ■ 2755 NE Broadway ■ 4:30pm-11pm, till midnight Fri-Sat, clsd Sun, wine bar & bistro ■ www.pourwinebar.com

The Roxy [★MW,WC] 503/223-9160 ■ 1121 SW Stark St ■ 24hrs, clsd Mon, retro American diner

Santa Fe Taqueria [★] 503/220-0406 ■ 831 NW 23rd (at Kearney) ■ 11am-midnight ■ www.santafetaqueria.com

Saucebox [MW,D,WC,GO] 503/241-3393 ■ 214 SW Broadway (at SW Oak) ■ 5pm-close, clsd Sun-Mon, pan-Asian, plenty veggie, full bar ■ www.saucebox.com

Vino Paradiso [NS,BW,GO] 503/295-9536 ■ 417 NW 10th Ave (btwn NW Glisan & Flanders) ■ 4pm-11pm, 3pm-9pm Sun, clsd Mon, wine bar & bistro, owned by Timothy Nishimoto of Pink Martini ■ www.vinoparadiso.com

Vista Spring Cafe [BW,WC] 503/222-2811 ■ 2440 SW Vista (at Spring) ■ 11am-9:30pm, from noon wknds, till 9pm Sun

Vita Cafe 503/335-8233 ■ 3024 NE Alberta St ■ brkfst, lunch & dinner, mostly vegetarian, some free-range meat ■ www.vita-cafe.com

Wildwood [★R] 503/248-9663 ■ 1221 NW 21st Ave (at Overton) ■ lunch & dinner Mon-Sat, full bar, upscale ■ www.wildwoodrestaurant.com

ENTERTAINMENT & RECREATION

Brian Marki Fine Art [GO] 503/249-5659 ■ 2236 NE Broadway ■ gallery ■ www.brianmarki.com

Froelick Gallery [GO] 503/222-1142 ■ 817 SW 2nd Ave ■ www.froelickgallery.com

Out Dancing [MW] 503/236-5129 ■ 975 SE Sandy Blvd (at SE Ankeny St & SE 9th Ave) ■ LGBT dance lessons ■ www.outdancing.info

Portland Gay Men's Chorus 503/226-2588 ■ 921 SW Morrison, Ste 220 (The Galleria) ■ www.pdxgmc.com

Rose City Rollers ■ Portland's female roller derby league, check web for upcoming events ■ www.rosecityrollers.com

Sauvie's Island Beach 25 miles NW (off US 30) ■ follow Reeder Rd to the Collins beach area, park at the farthest end of the road, then follow path to beach

Wonder Ballroom 503/284-8686 ■ 128 NE Russell St ■ live music venue ■ www.wonderballroom.com

BOOKSTORES

Countermedia 503/226-8141 ■ 927 SW Oak (btwn 9th & 10th) ■ 11am-7pm, noon-6pm Sun, alternative comics, vintage gay books/ periodicals

41   **In Other Words** [WC,E] 503/232-6003 ■ 8 NE Killingsworth (at Williams) ■ 10am-9pm, noon-5pm wknds, women's books, music & resource center ■ www.inotherwords.org

Laughing Horse Bookstore [WC] 503/236-2893 ■ 3652 SE Division St (at 37th) ■ 11am-7pm, clsd Sun, alternative/ progressive ■ www.geocities.com/laughinghorsebooks

Looking Glass Bookstore 503/227-4760 ■ 7983 SE 13th Ave (in Stellwood) ■ 8am-6pm, general, some LGBT titles ■ www.lookingglassbookstore.com

42   **Powell's Books** [★WC] 503/228-4651, 866/201-7601 ■ 1005 W Burnside (at 10th) ■ 9am-11pm, largest new & used bookstore in the world, cafe, readings ■ www.powells.com

Reading Frenzy [WC] 503/274-1449 ■ 921 SW Oak St (at 9th) ■ 11am-7pm, noon-6pm Sun, zines, comics, lgbt selection ■ www.readingfrenzy.com

Twenty-Third Ave Books [WC] 503/224-5097 ■ 1015 NW 23rd Ave (at Lovejoy) ■ *9:30am-7pm, from 10:30am wknds, general, LGBT section* ■ www.23rdavebooks.com

Retail Shops

Hip Chicks Do Wine 503/234-3790 ■ 4510 SE 23rd Ave (SE Holgate & 26th) ■ *11am-6pm* ■ www.hipchicks-dowine.com

It's My Pleasure 503/280-8080 ■ 3106 NE 64th Ave (at Sandy Blvd) ■ *noon-7pm, till 6pm Sun, books, erotica, toys, gifts,workshops*

The Jellybean [WC] 503/222-5888 ■ 721 SW 10th Ave (at Morrison) ■ *10am-6pm, noon-5pm Sun, cards, T-shirts, gifts* ■ www.thejellybean.com

Presents of Mind [WC] 503/230-7740 ■ 3633 SE Hawthorne (at 37th Ave) ■ *10am-7pm, jewelry, cards, unique gifts* ■ www.presentsofmind.tv

Under U 4 Men 503/274-2555 ■ 507 SW Broadway St (at Washington) ■ *10am-6pm, till 7pm Sat, noon-5pm Sun, designer underwear & in-store underwear models* ■ www.underu4men.com

Publications

Gertrude ■ www.gertrudepress.org

Just Out 503/236-1252 ■ *LGBT newspaper, extensive resource directory* ■ www.justout.com

Mary Magazine Northwest 323/874-8788 ■ *dish on Pacific Northwest's club scene* ■ www.odysseymagazine.net

Gyms & Health Clubs

Inner City Hot Tubs [GF,R] 503/238-1065 ■ 2927 NE Everett St (btwn 29th & 30th) ■ *9am-11pm, from 1pm Sun, wellness center* ■ www.cgwc.org

Men's Clubs

Club Portland [★18+,PC] 503/227-9992 ■ 303 SW 12th Ave (at Stark) ■ *24hrs, also hotel* ■ www.clubpdx.com

Steam Portland [MO,PC,GO] 503/736-9999 ■ 2885 NE Sandy Blvd ■ *24hrs* ■ www.steamportland.com

Erotica

Fantasy for Adults 503/239-6969 ■ 3137 NE Sandy Blvd (near NE 39th) ■ *24hrs* ■ www.fantasyforadultsonly.com

Fat Cobra Video 503/247-3425 ■ 5940 N Interstate Ave ■ *also 5501 NW St Helens Rd, 503/222-0180*

Spartacus Leathers 503/224-2604 ■ 302 SW 12th Ave (at Burnside) ■ www.spartacusleathers.com

Taboo Video 503/239-1678 ■ 237 SE MLK Blvd ■ www.taboovideo.com

---

PENNSYLVANIA

Philadelphia

Accommodations

1   **Alexander Inn** [GS,NS,WI,GO] 215/923-3535, 877/253-9466 ■ Spruce (at 12th St) ■ *restored hotel, fitness center* ■ www.alexanderinn.com

2   **Antique Row B&B** [GF] 215/592-7802 ■ 341 S 12th St (at Pine) ■ *1820s town house, full brkfst* ■ antiquerowbnb.com

3   **The Conwell Inn** [GS,SW,NS,WI,WC] 215/235-6200, 888/379-9737 ■ 1331 W Berks St (at Montgomery Ave) ■ *B&B on Temple University campus* ■ www.conwellinn.com

4   **Embassy Suites Center City** [GF] 215/561-1776, 800/362-2779 ■ 1776 Ben Franklin Pkwy (at 18th) ■ philadelphiacentercity.embsuites.com

5   **The Gables B&B** [GS,NS,WI,GO] 215/662-1918 ■ 4520 Chester Ave ■ *Victorian, garden* ■ www.gablesbb.com

6   **Hampton Inn Center City Philadelphia** [GS,SW,WI,WC] 215/665-9100, 800/426-7866 ■ 1301 Race St (13th St) ■ *jacuzzi, brkfst included* ■ www.hershahotels.com

7   **Holiday Inn Historic District** [GF,SW,NS,WI,WC] 215/923-8660, 800/972-2796 ■ 400 Arch St (at Market) ■ *kids ok* ■ www.holiday-inn.com/phlhistoric

  The Inn at Chester Springs [GF,SW,WI] 610/363-1100, 888/253-6119 ■ 815 N Pottstown Pike (Exit 312), Exton ■ *full-service hotel & conference center in Brandywine Valley (25 minutes from Philly)* ■ www.innatchestersprings.com

8   **Latham Hotel** [GF,WI,WC] 215/563-7474, 877/528-4261 ■ 135 S 17th St (at Walnut) ■ www.lathamhotel.com

9   **Morris House Hotel** [GF,NS,WI] 215/922-2446 ■ 225 S 8th St ■ *registered national historic landmark built in 1787, private garden, also M Restaurant* ■ www.morrishouseho-tel.com

10 **Philadelphia Marriott** [GF,SW,NS,WC] 215/625-2900, 800/320-5744 ■ 1201 Market St (btwn 12th & 13th) ■ *near the gay area in Philly* ■ www.marriott.com

11 **Rittenhouse Hotel** [GF,NS,WI] 215/546-9000, 800/635-1042 ■ 210 W Rittenhouse Square (at 19th) ■ *also restaurants & bar, kids/ pets ok* ■ www.rittenhouse-hotel.com

12 **Rodeway Inn** [GF,NS,WI] 215/546-7000, 877/424-6423 ■ 1208 Walnut St (btwn 12th & 13th) ■ *kids ok* ■ www.rodeway.com/hotel/pa271

13 **Shippen Way Inn** [GF] 215/627-7266, 800/245-4873 ■ 416-18 Bainbridge St (4th & 5th Sts) ■ *18th-c B&B, includes brkfst & afternoon tea* ■ shippenway.com

14 **Uncles Upstairs Inn** [M,NS,GO] 215/546-6660 ■ 1220 Locust St (at 12th) ■ *downtown town house B&B in center of gay district* ■ www.unclesphilly.com

Bars

15 **12th Air Command Headquarters for Men** [M,D,A,F,E,K,S] 215/545-8088 ■ 254 S 12th St (btwn Locust & Spruce) ■ *4pm-2am, from 2pm Sun, [17+] Sat* ■ www.12thair.com

16 **Bump** [MW,F,D] 215/732-1800 ■ 1234 Locust St (at 13th) ■ *5pm-2am, also dining, Sun brunch from 11am, "Austin-Powers chic"* ■ www.bumplounge.com

17 **L' Etage** [GS,D,F,C] 215/592-0656 ■ 624 S 6th St (at Bainbridge) ■ *7:30pm-1am, till 2am Fri-Sat, clsd Mon, [C] 1st Th, also restaurant downstairs, noon-11pm, from 10am wknds, crêperie* ■ www.creperie-beaumonde.com

18 **Key West** [MW,NH,D,F,P,WC] 215/545-1578 ■ 207-209 S Juniper (btwn Walnut & Locust) ■ *noon-2am, 4 bars, lunch served daily*

19 **The Khyber** [GF,E,WC] 215/238-5888 ■ 56 S 2nd St (btwn Market & Chestnut) ■ *noon-2am, from 4pm Sat, live bands* ■ www.thekhyber.com

20 **North Third** [GS,F] 215/413-3666 ■ 801 N 3rd (at Brown) ■ *4pm-2am, wknd brunch, also restaurant* ■ www.norththird.com

21 **Tavern on Camac** [MW,D,C,P] 215/545-0900 ■ 243 S Camac St (at Spruce) ■ *4pm-2am, 11:30am-3:30pm Sun brunch, also restaurant* ■ www.tavernoncamac.com

14 **Uncle's** [M,NH] 215/546-6660 ■ 1220 Locust St (at 12th) ■ *11am-2am*

22 **Venture Inn** [MW,NH,F] 215/545-8731 ■ 255 S Camac (at Spruce) ■ *11am-2am*

23 **The Westbury** [MW,NH,F,WC] 215/546-5170 ■ 261 S 13th (at Spruce) ■ *11am-2am, dinner till 10pm (till 11pm wknds)*

24 **Woody's** [★M,D,CW,F,K,S,V,YC,WC] 215/545–1893 ■ 202 S
    13th St (at Walnut) ■ 11am-2am, [18+] Wed, [K] Mon, Latin
    Th ■ www.woodysbar.com

NIGHTCLUBS

25 **Bike Stop** [★M,D,L] 215/627–1662 ■ 204-206 S Quince St
    (btwn 11th & 12th, Walnut & Locust) ■ 4pm-2am, from 2pm
    wknds, cruisy, 4 flrs, also The Gear Box custom leather shop ■
    www.thebikestop.com

PHILADELPHIA

Day Trips: Lancaster County & QVC Studios

About an hour west of Philadelphia lies Lancaster County, heart of Amish country. Sample the simple, hearty Pennsylvania Dutch fare, shop for beautiful handicrafts or antiques, and check out some of the historical sites in the area. Tour options abound, from air-conditioned buses to horse-drawn buggies to bicycles.

TV shop-a-holics shouldn't miss the QVC Studio Tour, located in the QVC Studios in West Chester, PA. It's no surprise that the tour winds up in the studio store; check out www.qvctours.com for all the details.

Local Food:

A Philly cheesesteak is required-eating while visiting the City of Brotherly Love. Wafer-thin sliced beef is sautéed with onions and green peppers, then stacked on a sliced Italian roll and blanketed with cheese: provolone, mozzarella, and Cheez Whiz are all acceptable.

The Reading Terminal Market provides rich shopping grounds for foodies of all stripes: local produce, fish, and fresh-baked goodies abound, as well as treats from nearby Amish country like homemade jams and shoofly pie. The soft pretzels are award-winning!

Tourist Info

AIRPORT DIRECTIONS
Philadelphia International. Take I-95 North to downtown. To go directly through downtown, take Hwy 611 from I-95 and follow through downtown area.

PUBLIC TRANSIT & TAXIS
Quaker City Cab 215/728-8000.
Transit Authority (SEPTA) 215/580-7800, web: www.septa.org.

TOURIST SPOTS & INFO
Academy of Natural Sciences 215/299-1000, web: www.acnatsci.org.
African American Museum 215/574-0380, web: www.aampmuseum.org.
Betsy Ross House 215/686-1252, web: www.betsyrosshouse.org.
Independence Hall 215/965-2305, web: www.nps.gov/inde.
Liberty Bell Pavilion.
National Museum Of American Jewish History 215/923-3811, web: www.nmajh.org.
Philadelphia Museum of Art 215/763-8100, web: www.philamuseum.org.
Reading Terminal Market, web: www.readingterminalmarket.org.
Rodin Museum 215/568-6026, web: www.rodinmuseum.org.
Visitor's Center: Philadelphia Convention & Visitors Bureau 215/636-3300, web: www.pcvb.org.

Weather
Winter temperatures hover in the 20°s. Summers are humid with temperatures in the 80°s and 90°s.

Best Views
Top of Center Square, 16th & Market.

City Calendar

LGBT PRIDE
June. 215/875-9288, web: www.phillypride.org.

ANNUAL EVENTS
April/May - Equality Forum 215/732-3378, web: www.equalityforum.com. Weekend of LGBT film, performances, literature, sports, seminars, parties & more.
June - Gay & Lesbian Theatre Festival 215/627-6483, web: www.philagaylesbiantheatrefest.org.
June - Womongathering 856/694-2037, web: www.womongathering.com. Women's spirituality fest.
July - Philadelphia International Gay & Lesbian Film Festival 267/765-9700, web: www.phillyfests.org.
October - OutFest 215/875-9288, web: www.phillypride.org.

Queer Resources

COMMUNITY INFO
William Way Gay, Lesbian, Bisexual & Transgendered Community Center 215/732-2220. 1315 Spruce St, 9am-10pm, 10am-7pm Sat, 10:30am-7pm Sun, web: www.waygay.org.
The Attic Youth Center 215/545-4331. 419 S 15th St, web: www.atticyouthcenter.org.
Women in Transition Hotline 215/751-1111, web: www.womenintransitioninc.org.
AA 215/923-7900, web: www.sepennaa.org.
Choice Hotline 215/985-3300, web: www.choice-phila.org.

26 **Bob & Barbara's Lounge** [GS,E,DS] 215/545-4511 ■ 1509 South St ■ *3pm-2am, clsd Sun, live jazz Fri-Sat & Mon, drag shows Th*

27 **Club Libations** [W,D,MR-AF,PC] 231 S Broad St (at Race St) ■ *Fri-Sat*

28 **Fabric** [MW,D] 1907 Chestnut St (at Devil's Alley) ■ *10pm 2nd Sat only* ■ www.thefabric.net

29 **Fluid** [GF,D,E,S,$] 215/629-3686 ■ 613 S 4th St (at Kater) ■ *10pm-2am, more gay wknds, theme nights* ■ www.fluid-nightclub.com

30 **girL** [W,D,E] 215/731-9930 ■ 200 S 12th St (at Sal's Restaurant) ■ *3rd Sat, live music, proceeds benefit a variety of good causes* ■ www.phillygirlparty.com

    Ladies 2000 856/869-0193 ■ *seasonal parties, call hotline or check website for details* ■ www.ladies2000.com

31 **Lounge 125** [GS,D,F,S,PC] 215/351-9026 ■ 125 S 2nd St (at Chestnut) ■ *midnight-3:20am, from 11pm Wed-Sat* ■ www.lounge125.com

32 **Luxx** [GS,D,S,A] 215/563-1038 ■ 121 S 19th St (at the Mansion at Rittenhouse) ■ *10pm-3:30am Tue only* ■ www.mansionatrittenhouse.com

33 **Pousse Cafe** [W,S] 215/849-7444 ■ 1734 Snyder Ave (at R Club) ■ *9pm-1am*

34 **Pure** [M,D,K,C,P,PC] 215/735-5772 ■ 1221 St James St (off 13th & Locust) ■ *9pm-3:30am Wed-Sun, also Pink Lounge nightly* ■ www.purephilly.com

34 **Pure Party Girl** [W,D,K] 856/869-0193, 215/735-5772 ■ 1221 St James St (at Pure) ■ *9pm-close 1st Sat* ■ www.ladies2000.com

35 **Shampoo** [GS,D,A] 215/922-7500 ■ 417 N 8th St (at Willow) ■ *9pm-2am, clsd Mon-Tue, more gay Fri* ■ www.shampooonline.com

36 **Sisters** [W,D,F,E,K,WC] 215/735-0735 ■ 1320 Chancellor St (at Juniper) ■ *5pm-2am, from noon Sun, from 8pm Mon, also restaurant [MW], dinner Wed-Sat, Sun brunch* ■ www.sistersnightclub.com

CAFES

10th Street Pour House [WC] 215/922-5626 ■ 262 S 10th St (at Spruce) ■ *7:30am-3pm, from 8:30am wknds, popular brunch wknds*

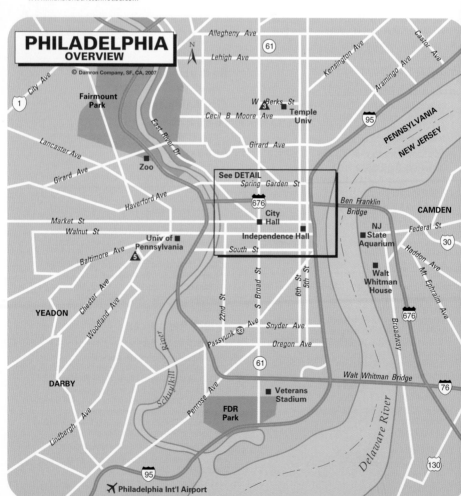

Brew HaHa! [WI] 215/893–5680 ■ 212 S 12th St (btwn Locust & Walnut) ■ *7am-8pm, from 8am Sat-Sun, also newsstand*

Capriccio 215/735–9797 ■ 1701 Locust St ■ *7am-11pm, till midnight Fri-Sat*

Green Line Cafe [F,E] 215/222–3431 ■ 4239 Baltimore Ave ■ *7am-11pm, 8am-7pm Sun* ■ www.greenlinecafe.com

Joe Coffee Bar [WI] 215/592–7384 ■ 1100 Walnut St ■ *6:30am-8pm, till 6:30pm Mon, from 8am Sat, clsd Sun* ■ www.joecoffeebar.com

Village Coffee House [★F,WI] 215/923–1992 ■ 1112 Locust St (at 12th) ■ *7am-10pm, 8am-11pm Fri-Sat, till 10pm Sun, soup, salad & sandwiches, patio* ■ www.thevillagecoffeehouse.com

RESTAURANTS

Abbraccio [WC] 215/727–8247 ■ 820 S 47th St (at 36th) ■ *lunch Sun-Fri, dinner nightly, bar till 1am* ■ abbracciorestaurant.com

The Adobe Cafe [E] 215/483–3947 ■ 4550 Mitchell St (at Greenleaf), Roxborough ■ *lunch Th-Sun & dinner nightly, plenty veggie* ■ adobebob@snip.net

Astral Plane Restaurant 215/546–6230 ■ 1708 Lombard St (btwn 17th & 18th) ■ *dinner nightly, Sun brunch, lots of veggie, full bar till 2am* ■ www.theastralplane.com

The Caboose Grille 215/721–1001 ■ 2 W Broad St, Souderton ■ *lunch & dinner Tue-Sat, brkfst wknds, clsd Mon*

Cafe Centraal 215/735–1880 ■ 1218 Pine St ■ *11am-9pm, Mexican/ Mediterranean, some veggie*

Cafe Habana [D,E] 102 S 21st St ■ *lunch & dinner, Sun brunch, bar till 2am Fri-Sat, Cuban* ■ www.cafehabana.com

The Continental 215/923–6069 ■ 138 Market St (at 2nd) ■ *lunch, dinner, wknd brunch, also bar until 2am, eclectic, some veggie* ■ www.continentalmartinibar.com

Cresheim Cottage Cafe [TG,NS,WC] 215/248–4365 ■ 7402 Germantown Ave (at Gowen Ave) ■ *lunch & dinner, Sun brunch, eclectic, full bar* ■ www.cresheimcottage.com

Deuce 1040 N 2nd St ■ *11:30am-1am, from 3pm Sat, American, also bar*

Figs [BYOB,WC] 215/978–8440 ■ 2501 Meredith St ■ *dinner nightly, wknd brunch, clsd Mon, eclectic Mediterranean* ■ www.figsrestaurant.com

A Full Plate Cafe [MR,TG,BYOB,GO] 215/627–4068 ■ 1009 Bodine St (at George St) ■ *11am-9pm, till 10pm Fri-Sat, from 10am wknds, till 3pm Sun, patio, lesbian-owned* ■ www.afullplate.net

The Happy Rooster [K] 215/963–9311 ■ 118 S 16th St (at Sansom St) ■ *11:30am-11pm, wknd brunch from 10:30am, cont'l, upscale, full bar till 1am* ■ www.thehappyrooster.com

L2 [E] 215/732–7878 ■ 2201 South St (at 22nd) ■ *dinner nightly, clsd Mon, Asian/ fusion, also bar* ■ www.L2restaurant.com

Liberties 215/238–0660 ■ 705 N 2nd St (at Fairmount) ■ *lunch & dinner, full bar till 2am* ■ www.libertiesrestaurant.com

Little Pete's 215/545–5508 ■ 219 S 17th St (at Locust) ■ *24hrs, diner*

Lolita [BYOB] 215/546–7100 ■ 106 S 13th St (at Sansom) ■ *5pm-10:30pm, till 11pm Fri-Sat, upscale Mexican* ■ www.lolitabyob.com

Mercato [BYOB] 215/985–2962 ■ 1216 Spruce St ■ *dinner, Italian* ■ www.mercatobyob.com

Mixto 215/592-0363 ■ 1141-43 Pine St ■ *brkfst, lunch & dinner, Latin American* ■ www.mixtophilly.com

More Than Just Ice Cream 215/574-0586 ■ 1119 Locust St (at 12th) ■ *11am-11pm, American*

My Thai 215/985-1878 ■ 2200 South St (at 22nd) ■ *5pm-10pm, till 11pm Fri-Sat, full bar*

New Harmony 215/627-4520 ■ 135 N 9th St (at Cherry) ■ *11am-11pm*

The Plough & the Stars [E] 215/733-0300 ■ 123 Chestnut St (at 2nd) ■ *lunch & dinner, popular brunch from 10:30am Sun, Irish pub fare, full bar, live music Sun* ■ www.ploughstars.com

Siam Lotus 215/769-2031 ■ 931 Spring Garden St ■ *lunch Tue-Fri, dinner nightly, clsd Mon, Thai* ■ www.siamlotuscuisine.com

Sisters [W] 215/735-0735 ■ 1320 Chancellor St (at Juniper) ■ *dinner 5pm-10pm Wed-Sat, Sun brunch from noon* ■ www.sistersnightclub.com

Striped Bass 215/732-4444 ■ 1500 Walnut St (at 15th) ■ *dinner nightly, upscale* ■ www.stripedbassrestaurant.com

Swanky Bubbles 215/928-1200 ■ 10 S Front St (at Market) ■ *5pm-1am, also bar till 2am, sushi & champagne* ■ www.swankybubbles.com

Valanni 215/790-9494 ■ 1229 Spruce St ■ *dinner nightly, Sun brunch, Mediterranean/ Latin, full bar* ■ www.valanni.com

El Vez 215/928-9800 ■ 121 S 13th St (at Sansom) ■ *lunch Mon-Sat, dinner nightly, Latin American/ Mexican, full bar* ■ www.elvezrestaurant.com

White Dog Cafe [E] 215/386-9224 ■ 3420 Sansom St (at Walnut) ■ *lunch & dinner, brunch Sun, full bar, eclectic American, cool Mon reading & Sun film series* ■ www.whitedog.com

Zócalo 215/895-0139 ■ 3600 Lancaster Ave (at 36th) ■ *lunch Mon-Fri, dinner nightly, clsd Sun, Mexican/ New Southwestern* ■ www.zocalophilly.com

ENTERTAINMENT & RECREATION

Amazon Country 215/898-6677 ■ WXPN-FM 88.5 ■ *11pm Sun, lesbian radio* ■ www.xpn.org

Philly Roller Girls ■ *Philly's female roller derby league, check web for upcoming events* ■ www.phillyrollergirls.com

Q Zine 215/898-6677 ■ WXPN-FM 88.5 ■ *11:30pm Sun, LGBT radio* ■ www.xpn.org

The Walt Whitman House 856/964-5383 ■ 328 Mickle Blvd (btwn S 3rd & S 4th Sts), Camden, NJ ■ *the last home of America's great & controversial poet, just across the Delaware River*

Wilma Theater 215/893-9456, 215/546-7824 (box office) ■ 265 S Broad St ■ *some LGBT-themed productions* ■ www.wilmatheater.org

BOOKSTORES

37 Giovanni's Room [★] 215/923-2960 ■ 345 S 12th St (at Pine) ■ *11:30am-7pm, from 1pm Sun, legendary LGBT bookstore* ■ www.giovannisroom.com

Robin's Bookstore 215/735-9600 ■ 108 S 13th St ■ *10am-8pm, from noon wknds, oldest independent bookstore in Philly* ■ www.robinsbookstore.com

RETAIL SHOPS

Amoeba Art Shop [GO] 215/242-4568 ■ 7174 Germantown Ave (at W Mt Airy Ave) ■ *art supplies & gifts* ■ www.amoebaartshop.com

Infinite Body Piercing 215/923-7335 ■ 626 S 4th St (at South) ■ *noon-10pm, till 11pm Fri-Sat, till 8pm Sun* ■ www.infinitebody.com

Jean-Jacques Gallery [GO] 215/242-5440 ■ 7118 Germantown Ave (at Mt Pleasant) ■ *noon-6pm, till 7pm Fri, 11am-6pm Sat, clsd Sun-Mon, functional art, gifts & jewelry* ■ www.jean-jacquesgallery.com

PHAG/ Philadelphia Home Art Garden 215/627-0461 ■ 1225 Walnut St ■ *11am-8pm, noon-6pm Sun, boutique* ■ www.thephagshop.com

PUBLICATIONS

EXP Magazine 302/227-5787, 877/397-6244 ■ *bi-weekly gay magazine for Mid-Atlantic* ■ www.expmagazine.com

HX Philadelphia 215/731-9010 ■ *complete weekly guide to gay Philly at night* ■ www.myspace.com/hxphilly

PGN (Philadelphia Gay News) 215/625-8501 ■ *LGBT newspaper w/ extensive listings* ■ www.epgn.com

Women's Yellow Pages of Greater Philadelphia 610/446-4747 ■ www.philawyp.com

GYMS & HEALTH CLUBS

12th St Gym 215/985-4092 ■ 204 S 12th St (btwn Locust & Walnut) ■ *5:30am-11pm, till 10pm Fri, 8am-8pm Sat, 8am-7pm Sun, day passes* ■ www.12streetgym.com

MEN'S CLUBS

Club Body Center [NS,WI,PC] 215/735-7671 ■ 1220 Chancellor St (at 12th) ■ *24hrs* ■ www.clubbodycenter.com

Philly Jacks [MO,18+,PC] 215/618-1519 ■ *3 sex parties per month, call for location* ■ www.philadelphiajacks.com

Sansom Street Gym [MO,V,PC] 267/330-0151 ■ 2020 Sansom St ■ *24hrs* ■ www.sansomstreetgym.com

EROTICA

Adonis Cinema Complex 215/557-9319 ■ 2026 Sansom St (at 20th) ■ *24hrs*

Condom Kingdom 215/829-1668 ■ 437 South St (at 5th) ■ *safer sex materials & toys*

Danny's New Adam & Eve Books 215/925-5041 ■ 133 S 13th St (at Walnut) ■ *24hrs* ■ www.shopdannys.com

The Gear Box 610/254-0055 ■ 206 S Quince St (downstairs at the Bikestop) ■ *10pm-close wknds, Philadelphia's gay leather shop* ■ www.thegearboxphilly.com

The Mood 215/413-1930 ■ 531 South St

Passional 215/829-4986, 877/826-7738 ■ 704 S 5th St (at Bainbridge) ■ *noon-10pm* ■ www.passional.net

The Pleasure Chest 215/561-7480 ■ 2039 Walnut (btwn 20th & 21st) ■ *11am-7pm, clsd Sun-Mon*

Spruce Street Video [M,GO] 215/985-2955 ■ 1201 Spruce St (at 12th) ■ *10am-midnight* ■ video@sprucestreet.com

Touch of Class 215/739-3348 ■ 3342 Kensington Ave ■ *10am-10pm, gay videos & toys*

Pittsburgh

ACCOMMODATIONS

1 **Arbors B&B** [MO,NS,WI,GO] 412/231-4643 ■ 745 Maginn St ■ *in restored farmhouse, hot tub* ■ **www.arborsbnb.com**

Camp Davis [MW,D,SW] 724/637-2402 ■ 311 Red Brush Rd, Boyers ■ *1 hour from Pittsburgh, cabins & campsites, variety of events* ■ campdaviscampground.com

2 **The Inn on the Mexican War Streets** [MW,F,NS,WI,GO] 412/231-6544 ■ 604 W North Ave ■ *located on the historic & gay-friendly North Side, in Boggs Mansion, also bar* ■ hometown.aol.com/innwarst/collect/index.htm

3 **The Inns on Negley** [GF,NS,WI,WC] 412/661-0631 ■ 703 S Negley Ave (at Elmer St) ■ *suite-style rooms, women-owned* ■ www.theinnsonnegley.com

PITTSBURGH

Day Trips: Fallingwater

This Frank Lloyd Wright masterpiece, is located about 90 miles southeast of Pittsburgh, outside Mill Run, in Fayette County. Named "Building of the Century" in 2000 by the American Institute of Architects, it is also a National Historic Landmark. The home is set within 5,000 acres of lush wilderness, and the surrounding environs, called Laurel Highlands, offer hiking, canoeing, and other outdoor pursuits to enjoy while you're in the area.

Local Food:

Another meat-loving town like Philadelphia, Pittsburgh is packed with substantial carnivorous treats. Chipped, or chopped, or chipped-chopped ham is paper-thin slices of processed ham, stacked in a sandwich of Italian or white bread. "Jumbo" is the local lingo for bologna, and sandwich-lovers shouldn't leave town without hoisting a hoagie, 'burgh-speak for the submarine sandwich. Whichever chow you choose, wash it all down with an Iron, short for Iron City Beer, the local brew.

Ice cream lovers: the Klondike bar was born here in 1929 to Samuel Isaly, the same man who brought us chipped-chopped ham.

Tourist Info

AIRPORT DIRECTIONS

Greater Pittsburgh International. To get to downtown, take Hwy 60 to I-279. Follow I-279 through Ft Pitt Tunnels and across Ft Bridge. Once across bridge, take exit for Liberty Ave.

PUBLIC TRANSIT & TAXIS

Yellow Cab 412/665-8100.
Airlines Transportation Co. 412/321-4990.
Port Authority Transit (PAT) 412/442-2000, web: www.portauthority.org.

TOURIST SPOTS & INFO

Andy Warhol Museum 412/237-8300, web: www.warhol.org.
Carnegie Museums of Pittsburgh 412/622-3131, web: www.carnegiemuseums.org.
Fallingwater (in Mill Run) 724/329-8501, web: www.paconserve.org.
Frick Art & Historical Center 412/371-0600, web: www.frickart.org.
Golden Triangle District.
Shopping & dining in the Strip District.
National Aviary 412/323-7235, web: www.aviary.org.
Phipps Conservatory 412/622-6914, web: www.phipps.conservatory.org.
Rachel Carson Homestead (in Springdale) 724/274-5459, web: www.rachelcarsonhomestead.org.
Station Square.
Visitor's Center: 412/281-7711 or 800/359-0758, web: www.visitpittsburgh.com.

City Calendar

LGBT PRIDE

June. 412/422-0114 (GLCC #), web: www.glccpgh.org.

ANNUAL EVENTS

June - Three Rivers Arts Festival 412/281-8723, web: www.artsfestival.net.
October - Pittsburgh International Lesbian & Gay Film Festival 412/422-6776, web: www.plgfs.org.

Queer Resources

COMMUNITY INFO

Gay/Lesbian Community Center 412/422-0114. 5808 Forward Ave, 2nd flr, 6pm-9pm, from noon wknds, till 6pm Sun, clsd Mon & Fri, web: www.glccpgh.org.
Lambda AA 412/471-7472, web: www.pghaa.org.
State HIV & AIDS Fact Line 800/662-6080.

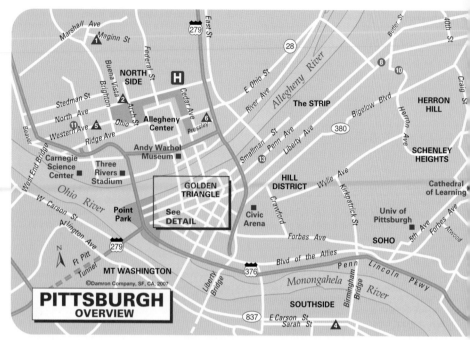

PITTSBURGH
OVERVIEW

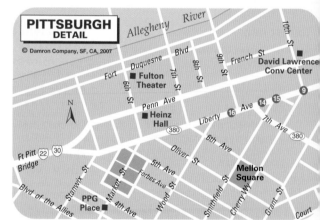

PITTSBURGH
DETAIL

© Damron Company, SF, CA, 2007

4 Morning Glory Inn B&B [GF,WI]
412/431-1707 ■ 2119 Sarah St
■ in 1862 Italianate-style Victorian
townhouse ■ www.morningglo-
rybedandbreakfast.com

5 The Parador Inn [GF,WI,GO]
412/231-4800, 888/540-1443
■ 939 Western Ave ■ Caribbean-
style B&B, fireplaces, gardens ■
www.theparadorinn.com

6 The Priory [GF,NS,WI,WC]
412/231-3338, 866/377-4679
■ 614 Pressley St (near Cedar Ave)
■ 24-rm Victorian, renovated 1888
monastery, fitness center ■
www.thepriory.com

BARS

7 5801 [★MW,F,V,WC]
412/661-5600 ■ 5801 Ellsworth
Ave (at Maryland) ■ 4pm-2am, also
restaurant Th-Sun only, deck ■ www.5801.us

Blue Moon Bar & Lounge [M,NH,TG,S] 412/781-1119
■ 5115 Butler St ■ noon-2am, 4pm-midnight Mon-Tue, 6pm-
midnight Sun ■ www.bluemoononbutler.com

8 Brewery Tavern [GF] 412/681-7991 ■ 3315 Liberty Ave (at
Herron Ave) ■ 10am-2am, from 11am Sun

9 Images [M,K,S,V] 412/391-9990 ■ 965 Liberty Ave (at 10th
St) ■ 2pm-2am, go-go boys

10 Leather Central [★M,D,L,F,V] 412/682-9869 ■ 1226
Herron Ave (at Liberty, in Donny's basement) ■ 9pm-2am Fri-
Sat, 5pm-midnight Sun

11 Nuance [GS,D,F,E] 900 Western Ave (at Galveston Ave)
■ 5pm-2am, from 8pm Sat

Pittsburgh Eagle [★M,D,L,WC] 412/766-7222 ■ 1740
Eckert St (near Beaver) ■ 9pm-2am, clsd Sun-Tue ■
www.pitteagle.com

12 PTown [MW,D] 412/621-0111 ■ 4740 Baum Blvd ■ 11am-
2am, from 6pm Sat, from 4pm Sun, till midnight Mon-Tue ■
www.ptownpgh.com

Ray's Marlin Beach Bar & Grill [GS,NH,MR]
412/781-6771 ■ 5121 Butler St, Lawrenceville ■ 11:30am-
2am, from 1pm Sun, also Caribbean restaurant on upper level
■ www.raysmarlinbeach.com

13 Real Luck Cafe [MW,NH,F,S,WC] 412/566-8988 ■ 1519
Penn Ave (at 16th) ■ 4pm-2am

14 There Video Lounge [MW,WC] 412/642-4435 ■ 931
Liberty Ave (at Smithfield) ■ 5:30pm-2am, from 8pm Sat-Sun

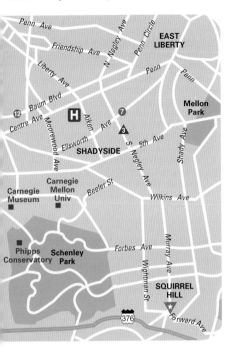

Zebra Lounge [MW,NH,D] 724/339-0298 ■ 910 Constitution Blvd (at 9th), New Kensington

NIGHTCLUBS

15 **941 Saloon** [★MW,D,K] 412/281-5222 ■ 941 Liberty Ave (at Smithfield St, 2nd flr) ■ 2pm-2am

10 **Donny's Place** [★MW,F] 412/682-9869 ■ 1226 Herron Ave (at Liberty) ■ 4pm-2am, from 3pm Sun, mostly women upstairs Fri-Sat, Leather Central [M] downstairs Fri-Sat

16 **Pegasus** [★MW,D,18+,YC] 412/281-2131 ■ 818 Liberty Ave (at 9th) ■ 9pm-2am, clsd Mon, Wed, Sun ■ www.pittpegasus.com

CAFES

Square Cafe [E,GO] 412/244-8002 ■ 1137 S Braddock Ave ■ 7am-3pm, from 8am Sun, live shows monthly, lesbian-owned ■ www.square-cafe.com

Tuscany Cafe 412/488-4475 ■ 1501 E Carson St (at 15th) ■ 8am-2am, full bar

ENTERTAINMENT & RECREATION

Andy Warhol Museum 412/237-8300 ■ 117 Sandusky St (at General Robinson) ■ 10am-5pm, till 10pm Fri, clsd Mon, is it soup or is it art?—see for yourself ■ www.warhol.org

BOOKSTORES

Jay's Bookstall 412/683-2644 ■ 3604 5th Ave (at Meyran) ■ 10am-5:45pm, till 4pm Sat, clsd Sun ■ www.angelfire.com/on2/jaysbookstall

RETAIL SHOPS

A Pleasant Present [WC] 412/421-7104, 877/421-7104 ■ 2301 Murray Ave (at Nicholson) ■ 10am-8pm, till 6pm Fri-Sat, clsd Sun ■ www.apleasantpresent.com

Slacker [WC] 412/381-3911 ■ 1321 E Carson St (btwn 13th & 14th) ■ 11am-9pm, till 11pm Fri-Sat, noon-6pm Sun, magazines, clothing, leather, piercing

PUBLICATIONS

Erie Gay News 814/456-9833 ■ www.eriegaynews.com

EXP Magazine 302/227-5787, 877/397-6244 ■ bi-weekly gay magazine for Mid-Atlantic ■ www.expmagazine.com

Out 412/381-3350 ■ LGBT newspaper ■ www.outpub.com

MEN'S CLUBS

Club Pittsburgh [PC] 412/471-6790 ■ 1139 Penn Ave (enter side) ■ 24hrs, 3 flrs, gym, steam/ sauna, rooftop tanning deck ■ www.clubpittsburgh.com

EROTICA

Adult Mart 412/765-2035 ■ 943 Liberty Ave ■ 24hrs; also at 346 Blvd of the Allies, 412/261-9119 ■ www.adultmart.com

RHODE ISLAND

Providence

ACCOMMODATIONS

1 **Courtyard by Marriott** [GF,NS] 401/272-1191, 888/887-7955 ■ 32 Exchange Terr (at Memorial Blvd) ■ www.marriott.com

Edgewood Manor [GF,NS,WI] 401/781-0099 ■ 232 Norwood Ave ■ 1905 Greek Revival mansion, some fireplaces & whirlpools ■ www.providence-lodging.com

BARS

2 **Alleycat** [MW,NH,V,GO] 401/273-0951 ■ 17 Snow St (at Washington) ■ 3pm-1am, till 2am Fri-Sat

3 **Club Gallery** [★MW,NH,D,WC] 401/751-7166 ■ 150 Point St ■ noon-1am, patio, fetish night Fri, mostly women Sat ■ www.clubgalleryri.com

4 **Mixx Lounge** [W,D] 401/421-4744 ■ 93 Clemence St ■ www.mixxlounge.net

5 **The Providence Eagle** [M,L,WC] 401/421-1447 ■ 198 Union St (at Weybosset) ■ 3pm-1am, till 2am Fri-Sat ■ www.providenceeagle.com

Sunset Bar & Grille [MW,D,F,E,K] 401/726-8889 ■ 888 Charles St ■ 6pm-1am, clsd Mon-Wed ■ www.sunset-barandgrille.com

5 **Union** [MW,K,P] 401/831-5366 ■ 200 Union St (next to the Providence Eagle) ■ 3pm-1am, 6pm-2am wknds

6 **Wheels** [MW,D,K,V,WC] 401/272-6950 ■ 125 Washington (at Mathewson) ■ noon-1am, till 2am Fri-Sat, DJ wknds

NIGHTCLUBS

7 **Dark Lady** [M,D,K,DS,V] 401/831-4297 ■ 124 Snow St (at Weybosset) ■ 9pm-1am, till 2am Fri-Sat ■ mrmounty@aol.com

7 **Entourage** [M,D,TG,18+] 401/831-3526 ■ 203 Westminster St (at DaVinci) ■ Sat only ■ www.chrisharrispresents.com

9 **Girl Spot** [W,D,K,S,18+,$] 401/751-7166 ■ 150 Point St ■ Sat only, women's party ■ www.girlspotri.com

10 **Mirabar** [M,D,S,WC] 401/331-6761 ■ 35 Richmond St (at Weybosset) ■ 3pm-1am, till 2am Fri-Sat, male dancers ■ www.mirabar.com

Therapy/ INSANE [GS,D,YC,WC] 401/490-7202 ■ 7 Dike St (at Troy) ■ 9pm-2am, till 4am Fri-Sat, clsd Sun-Mon, also gallery & cafe from 10am

11 **Trixx@XL** [MO,S,18+] 401/461-9522 ■ 257 Allens Ave (beside The Gay Mega-Plex) ■ 9pm-1am, till 2am Fri-Sat, 6pm-1am Sun, clsd Mon, nude male dancers ■ www.clubxlri.com

CAFES

Coffee Exchange 401/273-1198 ■ 207 Wickenden St ■ 6:30am-11pm, deck

Nicks on Broadway 401/421-0286 ■ 500 Broadway ■ dinner Wed-Sat, Sun brunch, clsd Mon-Tue

Reflections Cafe [F] 401/273-7278 ■ 8 Governor St (at Wickenden) ■ 7am-10pm, till 11pm Fri-Sat, fresh baked goods & specialty coffees, also sidewalk seating

White Electric 401/453-3007 ■ 711 Westminster ■ 7am-6:30pm, 8am-5:30pm Sat, 9am-4pm Sun

RESTAURANTS

Al Forno [★] 401/273-9760 ■ 577 S Main St ■ dinner only, clsd Sun-Mon, Little Rhody's best dining experience, patio

Camille's 401/751-4812 ■ 71 Bradford St (at Atwell's Ave) ■ lunch & dinner, clsd Sun, full bar ■ camillesonthehill.com

Haven Brothers Diner 401/861-7777 ■ 72 Spruce St (in a truck outside City Hall) ■ 5pm-3am, since the 1930s

Julian's 401/861-1770 ■ 318 Broadway (at Vinton) ■ 9am-11pm, gourmet, plenty veggie ■ www.juliansprovidence.com

Lot 401 401/490-3980 ■ 44 Hospital St ■ dinner, clsd Sun-Mon ■ www.lot401.com

Rue de l'Espoir [★WC] 401/751-8890 ■ 99 Hope St (at John) ■ brkfst, lunch & dinner, clsd Mon, full bar, Sun brunch, American Bistro ■ www.therue.com

Viola's 401/861-5766 ■ 58 DePasquale Plaza (on Federal Hill) ■ lunch Th-Sat, dinner nightly, clsd Mon-Tue, patio ■ www.violasitalianbistro.com

ENTERTAINMENT & RECREATION

Perishable Theatre 401/331-2695 ■ 95 Empire St ■ plays, also late-night comedy ■ www.perishable.org

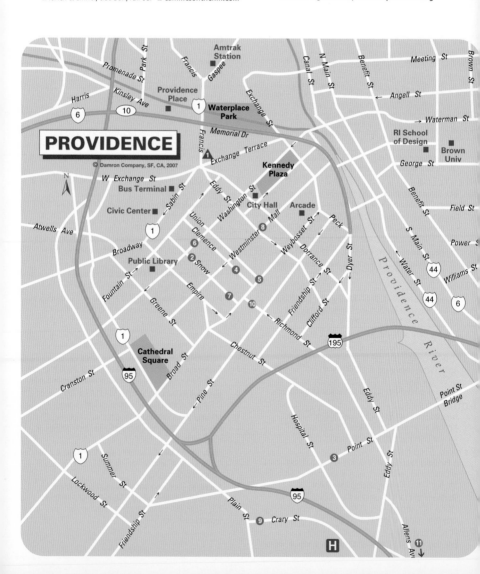

PROVIDENCE

Day Trips: Newport, RI (about 35 miles)

If you're in the mood for a jaunt out of town, number one on your list should be a trip to Newport. Enjoy the natural beauty of the New England coastline by walking the famous 3.5-mile Cliff Walk. Or take in the fabulous architecture and furnishings of the Gilded Age with a tour of the mansions once owned by the turn-of-the-century rich-and-famous who made Newport "America's First Resort Town." You can purchase ticket packages to see all the mansions, or just buy tickets to see the mansions of your choice at: www.newportmansions.org.

Tourist Info

AIRPORT DIRECTIONS
TF Green State Airport. To get downtown, take a right at the terminal exit. Then take US 95 North for approximately 15 minutes. To get to Providence from Boston's Logan Airport, take 93 South to 95 South for approximately 1 hour.

PUBLIC TRANSIT & TAXIS
Yellow Cab 401/941-1122.
RIPTA Bus Service 401/781-9400, web: www.ripta.com.

TOURIST SPOTS & INFO
Newport.
RISD Museum 401/454-6500, web: www.risd.edu.
Waterfire 401/272-3111, web: www.waterfire.com.
Visitor's Center: 401/456-0200 or 800/233-1636, web: www.goprovidence.com.

City Calendar

LGBT PRIDE
June. 401/467-2130, web: www.prideri.com.

ANNUAL EVENTS
May/ June - International Women's Playwriting Festival 401/621-6123, web: www.perishable.org.
Aug - Rhode Island Int'l Film Festival 401/861-4445, web: www.film-festival.org.

Queer Resources

COMMUNITY INFO
GLBT Helpline of Rhode Island 401/751-3322. 7pm-10pm Mon, Wed & Fri, web: www.glbthelpline.org.
AA 401/438-8860, web: www.rhodeisland-aa.org.
800/235-2331, web: www.aac.org.
AIDS Care Ocean State 401/521-3603, web: www.aidscareos.org.

Providence Roller Derby ■ *Providence's female roller derby league, check web for upcoming events* ■ www.providencerollerderby.com

WaterFire 401/272-3111 ■ Waterplace Park ■ *May-Oct only, bonfire installations along the Providence River at sunset, check local listings for dates* ■ www.waterfire.com

BOOKSTORES
Books on the Square 401/331-9097, 888/669-9660 ■ 471 Angell St (at Wayland) ■ *9am-9pm, noon-5pm Sun, some LGBT* ■ www.booksq.com

PUBLICATIONS
In Newsweekly 617/426-8246 ■ *New England's largest LGBT newspaper* ■ www.innewsweekly.com

Metroline 860/233-8334 ■ *regional newspaper & entertainment guide, covers CT, RI & MA* ■ www.metroline-online.com

MEN'S CLUBS
Club Body Center [NS,WI,PC] 401/274-0298 ■ 257 Weybosset St, 2nd flr (at Richmond) ■ *24hrs* ■ www.cbcresorts.com

The Gay Mega-Plex [PC,WC,GO] 401/780-8769 ■ 257 Allens Ave ■ *24hrs* ■ www.themega-plex.com

EROTICA
Amazing 401/274-4477 ■ 75 Empire St (at Weybosset) ■ www.amazing.net

Amazing Express 401/438-3070 ■ 155 Newport Ave/ Rte 1A (at New) ■ www.amazing.net

Amazing Super Store 401/467-7631 ■ 15 Thurbers Ave (at Rte 1A) ■ www.amazing.net

Miko 401/421-6646, 800/421-6646 ■ 653 N Main St (at Doyle) ■ *women-oriented, fetishwear, sex toys, classes* ■ www.mikoexoticwear.com

Romantix 401/785-1324 ■ 255 Allens Ave (at Point)

TENNESSEE

Memphis

ACCOMMODATIONS
1 **French Quarter Suites** [GF] 901/728-4000, 800/843-0353 ■ 2144 Madison ■ *also Bourbon St Cafe* ■ www.memphisfrenchquarter.com

2 **Madison Hotel** [GF,SW,NS] 901/333-1200 ■ 79 Madison Ave ■ www.madisonhotelmemphis.com

3 **Shellcrest Guesthouse** [GS,NS,WI,GO] 901/277-0223 ■ 671 Jefferson Ave (at N Orleans St) ■ *suites in Victorian* ■ www.shellcrest.com

4 **Talbot Heirs Guesthouse** [GF,NS] 901/527-9772, 800/955-3956 ■ 99 S 2nd St (btwn Union & Peabody Pl) ■ *suites w/ kitchens, funky decor* ■ www.talbotheirs.com

BARS
5 **The Jungle** [M,NH,L,F] 901/278-0521 ■ 1474 Madison (at McNeil) ■ *3pm-3am, from 2pm wknds, beer & set-ups only*

6 **Lorenz** [MW,D,E] 901/274-8272 ■ 1528 Madison Ave (at Avalon) ■ *24hrs, patio*

7 Madison Flame [W,NH,D] 901/278-0569 ■ 1588 Madison (at Avalon) ■ 7pm-3am Fri-Sat

8 The Metro [MW,D,F,K,WC] 901/274-8010 ■ 1349 Autumn St (at Cleveland) ■ 6pm-3am, from 4pm Sun ■ www.metromemphisclub.com

9 One More [GF,NH,MR,F] 901/278-6673 ■ 2117 Peabody Ave (at Cooper) ■ 11am-3am, from noon Sun, patio

10 The Paragon Lounge [M,D,F,E,K,C] 901/320-0026 ■ 2865 Walnut Grove Rd (at Tillman) ■ 8pm-close, [D] Fri ■ theparagonmemph@netscape.net

11 Pumping Station [M,D,WC] 901/272-7600 ■ 1382 Poplar (at Cleveland) ■ 4pm-3am, from 3pm wknds, courtyard ■ www.pumpingstationmemphis.com

12 RP Billiards [GF] 525 S Highland St ■ 5pm-3am

12 The Vault [GS,D,E,K] 901/452-6583 ■ 529 S Highland St ■ 5pm-3am, live jazz Wed

NIGHTCLUBS

13 Allusions [MW,D,MR-AF,DS,18+,BYOB] 901/357-8383 ■ 3204 N Thomas (in Northgate Shopping Center) ■ from 10pm Fri-Sat only, ladies night Fri ■ www.allusionsentertainmentcomplex.com

14 Backstreet [MW,D,K,C,18+,WC] 901/276-5522 ■ 2018 Court Ave (at Morrison) ■ 8pm-6am Wed-Sun only, beer & set-ups only ■ www.backstreetmemphis.com

15 Sessions [MW,NH,K,DS] 901/276-1882 ■ 1278 Jefferson (at Claybrook) ■ 4pm-midnight, till 3am wknds ■ www.sessionsmemphis.com

CAFES

Buns on the Run 901/278-2867 ■ 2150 Elzey Ave (at Cooper) ■ 7am-2pm, till 12:30pm Sat, clsd Sun-Mon

MEMPHIS

To most travelers, Memphis means one thing: Elvis. While no trip to Memphis would be complete without a visit to Graceland (800/238-2000), the city also boasts a number of other attractions. The Beale Street Historic District is the cradle of Mississippi Delta blues music, and nighttime still finds plenty of traditional blues, jazz, and rock 'n' roll in the area.

Tourist Info

AIRPORT DIRECTIONS

Memphis International. To get downtown, take US 240 West and head north to Union Ave exit. Follow Union Ave for approximately 20 minutes.

PUBLIC TRANSIT & TAXIS

Yellow Cab 901/577-7700.
MATA 901/274-6282, web: www.matatransit.com.

TOURIST SPOTS & INFO

Beale Street.
Graceland 800/238-2000, web: www.elvis.com/graceland.
Mud Island 800/507-6507, web: www.mudisland.com.
Nat'l Civil Rights Museum 901/521-9699, web: www.civilrightsmuseum.org.
Rock N Soul Museum 901/205-2533, web: www.memphisrocknsoul.org.
Overton Square.
Stax Museum 901/946-2535, web: www.staxmuseum.com.
Sun Studio 901/521-0664, web: www.sunstudio.com.
Visitor's Center: 901/543-5300, web: www.memphistravel.com.

Weather

Suth'n. H-O-T and humid in the summer, cold (30°s-40°s) in the winter, and a relatively nice (but still humid) spring and fall.

Best Views

A cruise on any of the boats that ply the river.

City Calendar

LGBT PRIDE

June. Mid-South Pride 901/382-6349, web: www.midsouthpride.org.

ANNUAL EVENTS

August - OutFlix International GLBT Film Festival 901/283-5935, web: www.outflixfestival.org.
September - The Cooper-Young Festival (arts, crafts & music) 901/276-7222, web: www.cooperyoungfestival.com.

Queer Resources

COMMUNITY INFO

Memphis Gay/ Lesbian Community Center 901/278-6422. 892 S Cooper, 6pm-9pm, 2pm-6pm wknds, web: www.mglcc.org.
Intergroup AA 901/454-1414, web: www.memphis-aa.org.
Friends For Life 901/272-0855, web: www.friendsforlifecorp.org.

MEMPHIS OVERVIEW
© Damron Company, SF, CA, 2007

MEMPHIS DETAIL
© Damron Company, SF, CA, 2007

Java Cabana [E] 901/272-7210 ■ 2170 Young Ave (at Cooper) ■ *6:30am-10pm, 8:30am-midnight Fri-Sat, noon-10pm Sun, clsd Mon, also art gallery* ■ javacabanacoffeehouse.com

Otherlands Coffee Bar [★F,E] 901/278-4994 ■ 641 S Cooper (at Central) ■ *7am-8pm, live music till 11pm Fri-Sat, also gift shop*

P&H Cafe [F,E,BW,WC] 901/726-0906 ■ 1532 Madison (at Adeline) ■ *3pm-3am, from 5pm Sat, clsd Sun* ■ www.pandhcafe.com

RESTAURANTS

Automatic Slim's Tonga Club [WC] 901/525-7948 ■ 83 S 2nd St (at Union) ■ *lunch Mon-Fri, dinner nightly, Caribbean & Southwestern, plenty veggie, full bar*

Cafe Society [WC] 901/722-2177 ■ 212 N Evergreen Ave (btwn McLean & Belvedere) ■ *lunch Mon-Fri, dinner nightly, full bar*

Dish 901/276-0002 ■ 948 S Cooper (at Young) ■ *dinner till 10pm, bar till 3am Wed-Sun, Mediterranean tapas* ■ www.dishmemphis.com

Leonard's Pit Barbeque 901/360-1963 ■ 5465 Fox Plaza Dr ■ *11am-9pm, Elvis ordered the pork sandwich at the original Leonard's (now closed), but the food is just as good here!*

Saigon Le 901/276-5326 ■ 51 N Cleveland ■ *11am-9pm, clsd Sun, pan-Asian*

ENTERTAINMENT & RECREATION

Center for Southern Folklore [F] 901/525-3655 ■ 119 S Main St (at Peabody Pl) ■ *11am-6pm, clsd Sun, open later for shows, live music, gallery, also cybercafe* ■ www.southernfolklore.com

Graceland 901/332-3322, 800/238-2000 ■ 3734 Elvis Presley Blvd ■ *no visit to Memphis would be complete w/out a trip to see The King* ■ www.elvis.com

Memphis Rock 'N Roll Tours 901/359-3102 ■ www.memphisrocktour.com

BOOKSTORES

Davis-Kidd Booksellers 901/683-9801 ■ 387 Perkins Rd Ext (at Poplar & Walnut Grove) ■ *9am-9pm, till 8pm Sun, some LGBT titles, also cafe* ■ www.daviskidd.com

RETAIL SHOPS

16 **Inz & Outz** [WC] 901/728-6535 ■ 553 S Cooper ■ *10am-7pm, till 8pm Fri-Sat, noon-5pm Sun, pride items, books & gifts*

EROTICA

Airport Book Mart 901/345-0657 ■ 2214 Brooks Rd E (at Airways)

Cherokee Books 901/744-7494 ■ 2947 Lamar

Getwell Books 901/454-7765 ■ 1275 Getwell (at Park)

Paris Theater 901/323-2665 ■ 2432 Summer Ave (at Hollywood)

Nashville

ACCOMMODATIONS

1 **The Big Bungalow B&B** [GF,E,NS] 615/256-8375 ■ 618 Fatherland St ■ *full brkfst, live music, massage available* ■ www.thebigbungalow.com

2 **Doubletree Nashville** [GF,WI] 615/244-8200 ■ 315 4th Ave N ■ *also restaurant & lounge, fitness center* ■ www.doubletreenashville.com

3 **Top O' Woodland Historic B&B Inn** [GF] 615/228-3868, 888/228-3868 ■ 1603 Woodland St (at 16th) ■ *full brkfst* ■ www.topofwoodland.com

BARS

4 **Blu** [MW,D,DS] 615/329-3838 ■ 1713 Church St (at 17th & 18th) ■ *Fri & Sat only, patio* ■ www.blunashville.com

4 **Blue Gene's** [M,B,K,WI] 615/329-3509 ■ 1715 Church St ■ *3pm-3am, from 11am Sun, clsd Mon* ■ www.bluegenes37203.com

5 **The Cabaret: Episode 2** [MW,D,C,DS] 615/367-1995 ■ 833 Murfreesboro Rd ■ *8pm-3am, clsd Sun-Tue* ■ www.cabaret2.4t.com

6 **DeVil's** [M,D,F,K] 615/256-9411 ■ 515 2nd Ave ■ *4pm-3am, from noon Sun* ■ www.angelicadevil.com/devils

7 **Illusions II** [M,D,TG,K,DS] 615/366-6696 ■ 339 Wilhagen Rd (at Murfeesboro) ■ *4pm-3am, cruise bar*

8 **Lucky's Garage** [MW,D,F,E,DS] 615/329-1383 ■ 207 14th Ave N ■ *5pm-close, clsd Mon, theme nights* ■ www.luckysnashville.com

15 **Purple Heys** [MW,NH,F,WC] 615/244-4433 ■ 1401 4th Ave S (btwn Lafayette & Chestnut) ■ *10:30am-1am, till 3am Fri-Sat*

9 **Trax** [M,NH,K,WI] 615/742-8856 ■ 1501 2nd Ave S (at Carney) ■ *noon-3am* ■ www.traxnashville.com

10 **Tribe/ Red** [MW,F,E,V,WC,GO] 615/329-2912 ■ 1517 Church St (at 15th Ave S) ■ *4pm-midnight, till 2am wknds, upscale, full restaurant* ■ www.TribeNashville.com

NIGHTCLUBS

11 **The Chute Complex** [★M,D,CW,L,K,DS,P,WC] 615/297-4571 ■ 2535 Franklin Pike (at Wedgewood) ■ *5pm-3am, 6 bars, patio, also restaurant w/ piano bar* ■ www.chutenashville.com

12 **Kiss After Hours** [GS,D] 270/469-0171 ■ 508 Lea Ave (at 6th) ■ *midnight-7am Fri-Sat night only* ■ kissafterhours.com

3 **Lipstick Lounge** [★W,D,E,K] 615/226-6343 ■ 1400 Woodland St (at 14th) ■ *4pm-close, from 7pm Fri, from 6pm wknds, live music* ■ www.thelipsticklounge.com

13 **Play Dance Bar** [M,D,MR,TG,E,DS,18+,WC] 615/322-9627 ■ 1519 Church St ■ *9pm-3am Wed-Sun* ■ www.playdancebar.com

CAFES

Bongo Java [E] 615/385-5282 ■ 2007 Belmont Blvd ■ *7am-11pm, from 8am wknds, coffeehouse, deck, also serves brkfst, lunch & dinner* ■ bongojava.com

Fido [F] 615/777-3436 ■ 1812 21st Ave S ■ *7am-11pm, till midnight Fri-Sat, from 8am wknds, also full menu* ■ www.bongojava.com

RESTAURANTS

Battered & Fried 615/226-9283 ■ 1008 Woodland St ■ *lunch & dinner, seafood, full bar, also Wave sushi bar* ■ www.batteredandfried.com

Beyond the Edge 615/226-3343 ■ 112 S 11th St ■ *11am-2am, pizza & sandwiches, full bar* ■ www.beyondtheedge.net

Cafe Coco [E,BW] 615/321-2626 ■ 210 Louise Ave ■ *24hrs, patio* ■ www.cafecoco.com

Calypso Cafe 615/321-3878 ■ 2424 Elliston Pl ■ *11am-9pm, 11:30am-8:30pm wknds, Caribbean* ■ calypsocafe.com

International Market 615/297-4453 ■ 2010 Belmont Blvd (at International) ■ *10:30am-9pm, Thai/ Chinese, plenty veggie*

The Mad Platter [R,WC] 615/242-2563 ■ 1239 6th Ave N (at Monroe) ■ *lunch Mon-Fri, dinner Wed-Sun* ■ madplatter.citysearch.com

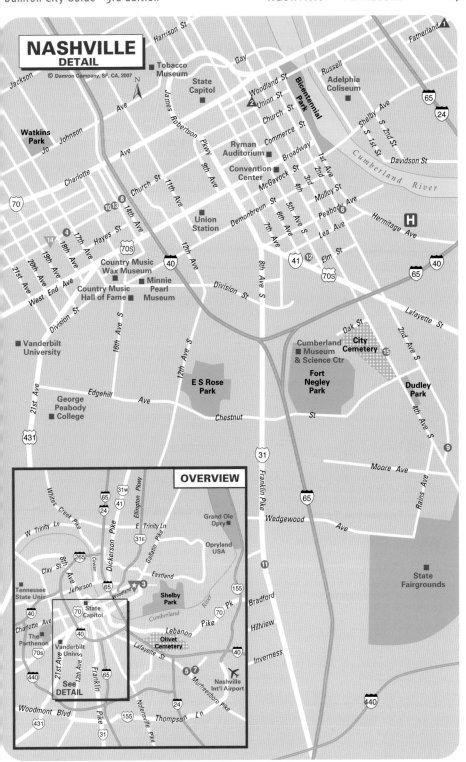

Mirror 615/383-8330 ■ 2317 12th Ave S (at Linden) ■ *dinner only, clsd Sun, also bar* ■ www.eatdrinkreflect.com

Rumba 615/321-1350 ■ 3009 W End Ave ■ *4pm-close, from 5pm Sun, Latin/ Asian, exotic drinks*

Rumours Wine & Art Bar 615/292-9400 ■ 2304 12th Ave S ■ *5pm-midnight, clsd Sun* ■ www.rumourswinebar.com

Sole Mio 615/256-4013 ■ 311 3rd Ave S ■ *11am-10pm, till midnight Fri-Sat, clsd Mon, Italian* ■ www.solemionash.com

The Standard at the Smith House 615/254-1277 ■ 167 8th Ave N (btwn Church & Commerce) ■ *11am-3pm, clsd wknds* ■ www.thestandardnashville.com

ENTERTAINMENT & RECREATION

NashTrash Tours [R] 615/226-7300, 800/342-2132 ■ *tours leave from the Farmers Market (900 8th Ave N)* ■ *campy tours of Nashville, ages 13+* ■ nashtrash.com

Tennessee Repertory Theater 615/244-4878 ■ 505 Deaderick St (at the Tennessee Performing Arts Center) ■ www.tnrep.org

BOOKSTORES

Davis-Kidd Booksellers 615/385-2645 ■ 4007 Hillsboro Rd (at Abbot-Martin) ■ *9am-9pm, till 10pm Fri-Sat, 10am-7pm Sun, LGBT section* ■ www.daviskidd.com

14   **Outloud Books & Gifts** [MW,GO] 615/340-0034 ■ 1703 Church St (btwn 17th & 18th Ave) ■ *10am-10pm, till 11pm Fri-Sat, LGBT* ■ www.outloudonline.com

PUBLICATIONS

Inside Out Nashville 615/831-1806 ■ *LGBT newspaper & bar guide* ■ www.insideOutNashville.com

Out & About Newspaper 615/596-6210 ■ *LGBT newspaper for Nashville, Knoxville, Chattanooga & Atlanta area, monthly* ■ www.outandaboutnewspaper.com

EROTICA

The Metro News [WI] 615/256-1310 ■ 822 5th Ave ■ *24hrs*

Purple Onion 615/259-9229 ■ 2807 Nolansville Rd (at SE Jeep Eagle) ■ *24hrs; also 2702 Dickerson Rd location, 615/227-8832*

NASHVILLE

Before Branson, before "new country," there was Nashville. Home of the Grand Ole Opry concert hall and the Country Music Hall of Fame, Nashville is still the mecca of country music. Kitsch lovers should stop by Bongo Java (see listing) home of the "Nun Bun," a cinnamon roll that bears a remarkable—some would say miraculous—resemblance to Mother Teresa. Sadly, the original Nun Bun was stolen in 2006, but you can still view a replica!

Tourist Info

AIRPORT DIRECTIONS

Nashville International. To get to most of the gay bars, take I-40 West and follow signs toward Memphis. Exit on Broadway.

PUBLIC TRANSIT & TAXIS

Yellow Cab 615/256-0101.
Gray Line Airport Shuttle 615/275-1180.
MTA 615/862-5969, web: www.nashvillemta.org.

TOURIST SPOTS & INFO

Country Music Hall of Fame 615/416-2001, web: www.countrymusichalloffame.com.
Grand Ole Opry & Opryland USA 615/871-OPRY, web: www.opry.com.
Jack Daniel's Distillery 615/279-4100, web: www.jackdaniels.com.
The Parthenon 615/862-8431, web: www.parthenon.org.
Ryman Auditorium 615/889-3060, web: www.ryman.com.
Tennessee Antebellum Trail 800/381-1865, web: www.antebellum.com.
Visitor's Center: 800/657-6910, web: www.nashvillecvb.com.

Weather

See Memphis.

Best Views

Try a walking tour of the city.

City Calendar

LGBT PRIDE

June. 615/650-6736, web: www.nashvillepride.org.
October. Black Pride 800/845-4266 x 269, web: www.brothersunited.com.

ANNUAL EVENTS

March - The Rainbow Ball, web: www.clarksvillepride.com.
October - AIDS Walk 615/259-4866, web: www.nashvillecares.org.
November - Artrageous 615/259-4866, web: www.nashvillecares.org.

Queer Resources

AA 615/831-1050, web: www.aanashville.org.
Nashville Cares 615/259-4866, web: www.nashvillecares.org.

TEXAS

Austin

ACCOMMODATIONS

1 **1888 Miller Crockett House** [★GF,WC,GO] 512/441-1600, 888/441-1641 ■ 112 Academy Dr (at Congress Ave) ■ *New Orleans-style estate, full brkfst, near outdoor recreation* ■ www.millercrockett.com

2 **Austin Folk House** [GS,NS,WC] 512/472-6700, 866/472-6700 ■ 506 W 22nd St (at San Antonio St) ■ *B&B in restored 1880 house* ■ www.austinfolkhouse.com

3 **Brava House** [GF,NS,WI] 512/478-5034, 866/892-5726 ■ 1108 Blanco St (at W 11th) ■ *1880s Victorian close to downtown & 6th Street* ■ www.bravahouse.com

4 **Carrington's Bluff** [GF,NS,WI] 512/479-0638, 888/290-6090 ■ 1900 David St (at W 22nd St) ■ *full brkfst* ■ www.carringtonsbluff.com

5 **Days Inn North** [GF,SW,WC] 512/835-4311, 866/835-4311 ■ 820 E Anderson Ln/ Hwy 183 (at I-35)

6 **Driskill Hotel** [GF,F,WC] 512/474-5911, 800/252-9367 ■ 604 Brazos St (at 6th) ■ *even if you don't stay in this landmark hotel, be sure to check out the lobby* ■ www.driskillhotel.com

---

AUSTIN

Day Trips: Bastrop State Park

Calling all country girls and boys! Point your hat southeast and head outta town about 30 miles for some great swimming, fishing, hiking, canoeing, biking, and more! Bastrop State Park is also home to the famed "Lost Pines," a somewhat mysteriously isolated patch of loblolly pines and hardwoods seperated from any other pine woodlands by close to a hundred miles. The park also boasts a golf course, picnic and camping sites, and swimming pools.

Tourist Info

AIRPORT DIRECTIONS

Austin-Bergstrom Int'l. To get to the State Capitol, take Bastrop Hwy north and exit on E 7th St. This will lead you deep into the heart of Austin.

PUBLIC TRANSIT & TAXIS

Yellow Cab 512/452-9999.

Various hotels have their own shuttles.

Capital Metro 512/474-1200, web: www.capmetro.org.

TOURIST SPOTS & INFO

Aqua Festival.
Austin Museum of Art at Laguna Gloria 512/458-8191, web: www.amoa.org.
Elisabet Ney Museum 512/458-2255, web: www.ci.austin.tx.us/elisabetney.
George Washington Carver Museum 512/974-4926, web: www.ci.austin.tx.us/carver.
Hamilton Pool 512/264-2740, web: www.texas-outside.com/hamiltonpool.htm.
LBJ Library & Museum 512/721-0200, web: www.lbjlib.utexas.edu.
McKinney Falls State Park 512/243-1643, web: www.tpwd.state.tx.us/park/mckinney.
Mount Bonnell.
Museo del Barrio de Austin 1402 E 1st St.
Zilker Park/Barton Springs, web: www.ci.austin.tx.us/zilker.
Visitor's Center: Austin Convention & Visitors Bureau 800/926-2282, web: www.austintexas.org.
Greater Austin Chamber of Commerce 512/478-9383, web: www.austin-chamber.org.

Weather

Summers are real scorchers (high 90°s-low 100°s) and last forever. Spring, fall, and winter are welcome reliefs.

Best Views

Texas State Capitol or the University of Texas Tower, web: www.utexas.edu/tower.

City Calendar

LGBT PRIDE

June. www.austinprideparade.org.

ANNUAL EVENTS

March - South by Southwest Music Festival, web: www.sxsw.com.
May & Labor Day - Splash Days. Weekend of parties in clothing-optional Hippie Hollow, web: www.houstonsplash.com.
September/October - Austin G/L Int'l Film Festival 512/302-9889, web: www.agliff.org.
October - Int'l Drag King Community Extravaganza, web: idkeaustin.com.

Queer Resources

COMMUNITY INFO

Austin Gay & Lesbian Chamber of Commerce 512/474-4422, web: www.aglcc.org.
Austin Queer People of Color Organization 512/472-2001, web: www.allgo.org.
Live & Let Live AA 512/444-0071, web: www.austinaa.org.
AIDS Services of Austin 512/458-2437, web: www.asaustin.org.

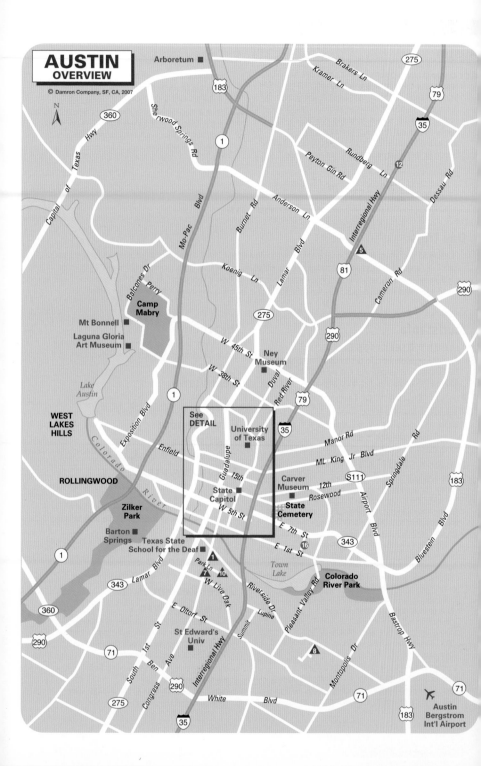

AUSTIN OVERVIEW

© Damron Company, SF, CA, 2007

N

Arboretum

Brakers Ln
Kramer Ln
275
79
183
35
360
1
Sherwood Springs Rd
12
Peyton Gin Rd
Rundberg Ln
Interregional Hwy
Dessau Rd
Anderson Ln
Burnet Rd
Mo-Pac Blvd
Lamar Blvd
5
Cameron Rd
290
81
Koenig Ln
Balcones Dr
Perry
Camp Mabry
275
290
Mt Bonnell
Laguna Gloria Art Museum
W 45th St
Ney Museum
W 38th St
Duval
Red River
79
Lake Austin
Exposition Blvd
1
WEST LAKES HILLS
See DETAIL
University of Texas
35
Manor Rd
Colorado River
Enfield
ML King Jr Blvd
Springdale Rd
ROLLINGWOOD
Guadalupe
15th
Carver Museum
S111
183
State Capitol
12th
Rosewood
Airport Blvd
Zilker Park
W 5th St
State Cemetery
Bluestein Blvd
1
Barton Springs
Texas State School for the Deaf
E 7th St
E 1st St
343
16
360
343
Town Lake
Colorado River Park
1
7
10
Park Ln
Pleasant Valley Rd
290
W Live Oak
Riverside Dr
Lupine
Lamar Blvd
E Oltorf St
St Edward's Univ
Summit
Bastrop Hwy
71
71
1st St
Ben
Congress Ave
South
Interregional Hwy
8
Montopolis Dr
275
290
White   Blvd
183
71
Austin Bergstrom Int'l Airport
35

7   **Hotel San Jose** [★GS,SW,NS,WC,GO] 512/444-7322, 800/574-8897 ■ 1316 S Congress Ave ■ *small boutique hotel* ■ www.sanjosehotel.com

8   **Mi Yard B&B** [GF,NS,WI] 512/789-3486 ■ 2307 Riverside Farms Rd (of I-35) ■ *minutes from downtown Austin, hot tub* ■ www.miyardbedandbreakfast.com

9   **Omni Austin Hotel Downtown** [GF,F,SW,WI,WC] 512/476-3700, 800/843-6664 ■ 700 San Jacinto (at 8th) ■ *4-diamond hotel, rooftop pool, also health club* ■ www.omnihotels.com

10 **Park Lane Guest House** [GS,SW,WC,GO] 512/447-7460, 800/492-8827 ■ 221 Park Ln (at Drake) ■ *full brkfst, also cottage, lesbian-owned* ■ parklaneguesthouse.com

    Robin's Nest [GF] 512/266-3413 ■ 1007 Stewart Cove ■ *B&B in 3 homes on Lake Travis* ■ www.robinsnestlake-travis.com

11 **Star of Texas Inn** [GF,NS] 512/472-6700, 866/472-6700 ■ 611 W 22nd St (at Rio Grande) ■ *neo-classical Victorian, full brkfst* ■ www.staroftexasinn.com

BARS

12 **'Bout Time** [★MW,NH,TG,K,DS,WI,WC] 512/832-5339 ■ 9601 N Ih 35 (at Rundberg) ■ *2pm-2am, volleyball court* ■ www.bouttimeaustin.com

13 **Casino El Camino** [GF,NH,F,WI,WC] 512/469-9330 ■ 517 E 6th St (at Red River) ■ *4pm-2am, psychedelic punk jazz lounge, great burgers* ■ www.casinoelcamino.net

14 **Chain Drive** [M,D,L,WC] 512/480-9017 ■ 504 Willow St (at Red River) ■ *4pm-2am, live music Wed, Bear Bust 2nd Sun, cruisy* ■ myspace.com/1chaindrive

15 **Charlie's Austin** [★M,D,DS,S,18+,YC,NS,WC] 512/474-6481 ■ 1301 Lavaca (at 13th) ■ *2pm-3am, smoking patio* ■ www.charliesaustin.com

16 **Peacock** [GF] 512/276-8979 ■ 515 Pedernales (1 mile E of I-35) ■ *4:30pm-2am, from 6:30pm Sat-Sun, retro-cool cocktail lounge that mixes vintage cocktails* ■ www.peacockaustin.com

17 **Rainbow Cattle Company** [MW,D,K,CW,WI] 512/472-5288 ■ 305 W 5th St (btwn Guadalupe & Lavaca) ■ *3pm-2am, from 8pm wknds, clsd Mon, CW dance classes Tue, Ladies night Th, Latino night Sun* ■ www.rainbowcattleco.com

NIGHTCLUBS

18 **Cock Pit** [M,D,S] 512/457-8010 ■ 113 San Jacinto Blvd (btwn 1st & 2nd) ■ *2pm-2am, from noon wknds, theme nights, patio* ■ www.cockpitaustin.com

19 **Oil Can Harry's** [★M,D,K,S,YC,WI,WC] 512/320-8823 ■ 211 W 4th St (btwn Lavaca & Colorado) ■ *2pm-close, patio, [18+] after 10pm Mon-Fri* ■ www.oilcanharrys.com

20 **Rain** [M,D,K] 512/494-1150 ■ 217-B W 4th St (at Colorado St) ■ *4pm-close, from 3pm Fri-Sun, upscale gay lounge* ■ www.rainon4th.com

    Sappho's Isle [W,D,A] 512/478-2979 ■ 705 Red River (at Elysium) ■ *9:30pm-2am Tue lesbian night, rest of the week popular gothic & industrial club* ■ www.elysiumonline.net/evt/sappho.html

CAFES

    Austin Java Cafe & Coffeehouse [F] 512/482-9450 ■ 1608 Barton Springs Rd (at Kinney Ave) ■ *7am-11pm, till midnight Fri, from 8am Saturday, till 11pm Sun; also 1206 Parkway (at 12th & Lamar), 512/476-1829 & 300 W 2nd St, Ste 100, 512/481-9400* ■ www.austinjava.com

Bouldin Creek Coffeehouse [F] 512/416-1601 ■ 1501 S 1st St (at Elizabeth) ■ *7am-midnight, from 9am wknds, completely vegetarian menu (brkfst all day); also hosts CampCamp "monthly queer performance hootenanny," 8pm 1st Th* ■ www.bouldincreek.com

Joe's Bakery & Coffee Shop 512/472-0017 ■ 2305 E 7th St (at Morelos & Northwestern) ■ *7am-3pm, clsd Mon, Tex-Mex* ■ www.joesbakery.com

Little City Espresso Bar & Cafe [F,BW,WI,WC] 512/476-2489 ■ 916 Congress Ave (at E 11th St) ■ *8am-midnight, from 9am wknds, till 10pm Sun, popular gay hangout* ■ www.littlecity.com

Spider House Patio Bar & Cafe [F,BW] 512/480-4562 ■ 2908 Fruth St (at West Dr) ■ *7am-2am, veggie menu, patio* ■ www.spiderhousecafe.com

RESTAURANTS

Castle Hill Cafe [WC] 512/476-0728 ■ 1101 W 5th St (at Baylor) ■ *lunch weekdays & dinner nightly, clsd Sun, romantic, some veggie* ■ www.castlehillcafe.com

Chuy's 512/474-4452 ■ 1728 Barton Springs Rd ■ *11am-10:30pm, till 11pm Fri-Sat, Tex-Mex, full bar* ■ chuys.com

Cosmic Cafe [BW] 512/482-0950 ■ 1110 W Lynn (at W 12th St) ■ *11am-10pm, till 10:30pm Fri-Sat, noon-9:30pm Sun, vegetarian* ■ www.cosmiccafeaustin.com

Eastside Cafe [BW,WC] 512/476-5858 ■ 2113 Manor Rd (at Coleto, by bright yellow gas station) ■ *11:30am-9:30pm, till 10pm Fri-Sat, wknd brunch from 10am, some veggie* ■ www.eastsidecafeaustin.com

El Sol y La Luna [★E,WC,GO] 512/444-7770 ■ 1224 S Congress Ave (at Academy) ■ *7am-10pm, till 3pm Sun-Tue, Latin American, great brkfst, live music Fri-Sat, lesbian-owned* ■ www.elsolylalunaaustin.com

Fonda San Miguel 512/459-4121 ■ 2330 W North Loop (at Hancock Rd) ■ *dinner only Mon-Sat, popular Sun brunch, interior & coastal Mexican, full bar* ■ www.fondasanmiguel.com

Jo's Hot Coffee & Good Food [WC,GO] 512/444-3800 ■ 1300 S Congress Ave (at James) ■ *7am-9pm, till 10pm Sat, "best lazy day outdoor dining scene," lesbian-owned; also 242 W 2nd St, 512/469-9003* ■ www.joscoffee.com

Katz's [WC] 512/472-2037 ■ 618 W 6th St (at Rio Grande) ■ *24hrs, NY-style deli, full bar*

Mother's Cafe & Garden [★] 512/451-3994 ■ 4215 Duval St (at 43rd) ■ *lunch, dinner, wknd brunch, vegetarian* ■ www.motherscafeaustin.com

Nueva Onda [GO] 512/447-5063 ■ 2218 College Ave (off S Congress & Oltorf) ■ *7:30am-3pm, from 8am Sun, Mexican, some veggie, patio* ■ www.nuevaaustin.com

Romeo's [E,WC] 512/476-1090 ■ 1500 Barton Springs Rd (near Lamar) ■ *11am-10pm, till 11pm Fri-Sat, Italian, some veggie, full bar, live music nightly* ■ www.austinromeos.com

Starlite [GO] 512/374-9012 ■ 407 Colorado St (at 4th St) ■ *5:30pm-10pm, till 11pm Th-Sat, 11am-3pm Sun, full bar, upscale hipster scene* ■ www.starliteaustin.net

Threadgill's [E] 512/451-5440 ■ 6416 N Lamar (at Koenig) ■ *11am-10pm, till 9pm Sun, great chicken-fried steak, live music Wed; also 301 W Riverside Dr, 512/472-9304, beer garden, live music* ■ www.threadgills.com

ENTERTAINMENT & RECREATION

Adventuring Outdoors 512/236-7176 ■ *Austin's group for LGBT outdoor enthusiasts* ■ www.main.org/adventuring

Barton Springs [N] Barton Springs Rd ■ *natural swimming hole*

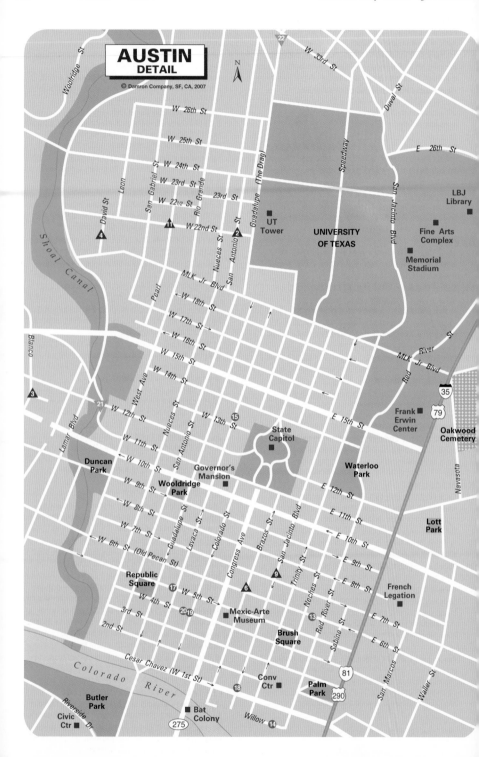

AUSTIN DETAIL

© Damron Company, SF, CA, 2007

Bat Colony Congress Ave Bridge (at Barton Springs Dr) ■ *everything's bigger in Texas—including the colony of bats that flies out from under this bridge every evening March-Oct*

Capital City Men's Chorus 512/477-7464 ■ *call or see website for events* ■ www.ccmcaustin.org

Historic Austin Tours 512/478-0098, 866/468-8784 ■ 209 E 6th St (in the Visitor Information Center, open 9am-5pm, till 6pm Sat-Sun) ■ *free guided & self-guided tours of the Capitol, Congress Ave & 6th St, Texas State Cemetery, Hyde Park* ■ www.austintexas.org/visitors/heritage/walking_tours

Kings N Things ■ *"Austin's premier drag king troupe,"* check web for events ■ www.kingsnthings.org

Queer Radio on KOOP 512/472-1369 ■ 91.7 FM ■ *"This Way Out"* 1:30pm-2pm Mon & *"Queer Waves"* (focusing on music) 3pm-4pm Sat ■ www.koop.org

Rainbow Rollerskating 512/258-8886 (rink info) ■ 9514 Anderson Mill Rd (at Skate World Austin) ■ *8pm-11pm 2nd Mon, $6* ■ www.main.org/rainbowskate

Texas Rollergirls ■ *Austin's female roller derby league,* check web for upcoming events ■ www.txrollergirls.com

Zachary Scott Theatre Center 512/476-0541 ■ 1510 Toomey Rd (off S Lamar Blvd) ■ *diverse theater* ■ www.zachscott.com

BOOKSTORES

Bookpeople 512/472-5050, 800/853-9757 ■ 603 N Lamar Blvd (at 6th) ■ *9am-11pm, clsd Thanksgiving Day, independent, readings* ■ www.bookpeople.com

21 **BookWoman** [WC] 512/472-2785 ■ 918 W 12th St (at Lamar) ■ *10am-9pm, noon-6pm Sun* ■ www.ebook-woman.com

22 **Lobo** [WC] 512/454-5406 ■ 3204-A Guadalupe (btwn 32nd & 33rd) ■ *10am-11pm, till midnight Fri-Sat, LGBT* ■ www.clickaustin.com

Resistencia Bookstore 512/416-8885 ■ 1801-A S 1st St (at W Annie) ■ *emphasis on Chicana/o, Latina/o & Native American titles, also some LGBT of color titles, readings* ■ www.resistenciabooks.com

RETAIL SHOPS

Celebration! 512/453-6207 ■ 3110 Guadalupe St, Ste 100 (at Speedway) ■ *10am-7pm, noon-5pm, artwork, crystals, psychic readings* ■ www.celebrationaustin.com

Tapelenders [GO] 512/472-0844 ■ 1114 W 5th St (at Baylor) ■ *10am-10pm, till midnight Fri-Sat, noon-10pm Sun, LGBT videos, novelties* ■ www.tapelenders.com

PUBLICATIONS

Ambush Mag 504/522-8049 ■ www.ambushmag.com

Austin Chronicle 512/454-5766 ■ PO Box 49066 78765 ■ *Austin's alternative weekly paper, has extensive online gay guide as well as events calendar* ■ www.austinchronicle.com

Shout Magazine 512/482-8252 ■ *1st & 3rd Th, LGBT arts, entertainment, lifestyle & leisure magazine for Texas* ■ www.shouttexas.com

GYMS & HEALTH CLUBS

Hyde Park Gym [GF] 512/459-9174 ■ 4125 Guadalupe (at 42nd St) ■ *5am-10pm, 7am-7pm Sat, 8am-6pm Sun, day passes $8* ■ www.hydeparkgym.com

MEN'S CLUBS

Midtowne Spa—Austin [PC] 512/302-9696 ■ 5815 Airport Blvd (at Koenig) ■ *24hrs, outdoor hot tub, sundeck* ■ www.midtowne-spa.com/austin/index.html

EROTICA

Adult Video Megaplexxx 512/442-5430 ■ 7111 S Ih 35 ■ *24hrs, also arcade*

Forbidden Fruit 512/478-8358 ■ 512 Neches (btwn 5th & 6th) ■ *woman-owned & operated* ■ www.forbiddenfruit.com

New Video 512/280-1142 ■ 7901 S Ih 35 ■ *24hrs, also arcade*

Dallas

ACCOMMODATIONS

1 **Amelia's Place** [GF,WI] 214/421-7427 ■ 1108 S Akard St #13 (at Griffin E) ■ *downtown apt, full brkfst* ■ www.ameliasplace.com

2 **Bailey's Uptown Inn** [GF,NS,WI] 214/720-2258 ■ 2505 Worthington St (at Hibernia) ■ www.baileysuptowninn.com

3 **Daisy Polk Inn** [GF] 214/522-4692 ■ 2917 Reagan St (at Dickason Ave) ■ *B&B in 1904 Arts & Crafts home* ■ www.daisypolkinn.com

4 **Holiday Inn Select Dallas Central** [GS,SW,WI,WC] 214/373-6000, 888/477-STAY ■ 10650 N Central Expwy (at Meadow) ■ www.sixcontinentshotels.com

5 **Melrose Hotel** [GF,P,SW,WC] 214/521-5151, 800/635-7673 ■ 3015 Oak Lawn Ave (at Cedar Springs) ■ *full brkfst, piano bar, lounge & 4 1/2-star restaurant, nonsmoking rooms available* ■ www.melrosehoteldallas.com

6 **Quality Inn Market Center** [GF,SW,WI,WC] 214/747-9551 ■ 1955 Market Center Blvd (at Turtle Creek Blvd) ■ www.qualityinndallas.com

7 **The Stoneleigh Hotel** [GF,WI,WC] 214/871-7111 ■ 2927 Maple Ave (at Randall St) ■ *landmark hotel, gym, also restaurant* ■ www.stoneleighhotel.com

BARS

8 **Barbara's Pavillion** [M,NH,WC] 214/941-2145 ■ 325 Centre St (1blk W of Zang) ■ *4pm-2am, from 6pm Sat, patio*

9 **Buddies II** [M,D,CW,K,SW] 214/526-0887 ■ 4025 Maple Ave (at Throckmorton) ■ *noon-2am, clsd Mon, volleyball court, [CW] wknds* ■ www.buddiesll.com

10 **Crews Inn** [★M,D,S,WC] 214/526-9510 ■ 3215 N Fitzhugh (at Travis) ■ *noon-2am, popular Tue nights, patio*

11 **Cross Bar** [M,NH,D,S] 214/443-8336 ■ 5334 Lemmon Ave (at Hudnall) ■ *noon-2am, male dancers Tue & Fri, patio* ■ www.crossbardallas.com

12 **Dallas Eagle** [M,B,L] 214/357-4375 ■ 2515 Inwood Rd #107 (at Maple, enter rear) ■ *4pm-2am, till 4am Fri-Sat* ■ www.dallaseagle.com

13 **The Hidden Door** [M,NH,L,WC] 214/526-0620 ■ 5025 Bowser Ave (at Mahanna) ■ *7am-2am, from noon Sun, patio* ■ www.hiddendoor-dallas.com

14 **Hideaway Club** [MW,C,P,OC,WC] 214/559-2966 ■ 4144 Buena Vista (at Fitzhugh) ■ *8am-2am, from noon Sun, upscale piano bar, also sports bar, patio*

15 **Illusions** [MW,NH,K,DS] 214/252-0552 ■ 4100 Maple Ave (at Throckmorton) ■ *noon-2am, [K] Th, [DS] Sat, potlucks Sun* ■ www.dallasillusions.com

16 **JR's Bar & Grill** [★MW,F,E,V,YC,WI,WC] 214/528-1004, 214/559-0650 (24hr info line) ■ 3923 Cedar Springs Rd (at Throckmorton) ■ *11am-2am, from noon Sun, upscale* ■ www.jrsdallas.com

17 **Mickey's** [M,K,C,V] 214/219-6425 ■ 3851 Cedar Springs Rd ■ *2pm-2am* ■ www.mickeysdallas.com

18 **Phases** [MW,NH,E,C,WC] 214/528-2026 ■ 2615 Oak Lawn Ave, Ste 101 (btwn Fairmount & Brown) ■ *9am-2am, from noon Sun* ■ www.phasesbar.com

19 **Pub Pegasus** [M,NH,WC] 214/559-4663 ■ 3326 N Fitzhugh (at Travis) ■ *10am-2am, from 1pm Sun, patio* ■ www.pubpegasus.com

20 **The Rocket Bar** [M,NH,D,DS] 469/855-8937 ■ 3903 Lemmon Ave (at Reagan) ■ *4pm-2am, from 2pm Sat, from noon Sun* ■ www.rocketbardallas.com

21 **Sue Ellen's** [★W,D,E,WC] 214/559-0707, 214/559-0650 (24hr info line) ■ 3903 Cedar Springs Rd (at Reagan) ■ *5pm-2am, from noon wknds, patio, Sun BBQ (summers)* ■ www.sueellensdallas.com

22 **Throckmorton Mining Co** [★M,D] 214/521-4205 ■ 3014 Throckmorton (at Cedar Springs) ■ *5pm-2am, till 4am Fri-Sun, clsd Mon-Tue* ■ www.caven.com

23 **Tin Room** [M,NH] 214/526-6365 ■ 2514 Hudnall St (at Maple Ave) ■ *10am-2am, from noon Sun*

24 **Woody's** [MW,K,V,WC] 214/520-6629 ■ 4011 Cedar Springs Rd (btwn Douglas & Throckmorton) ■ *2pm-2am, sports bar, patio* ■ www.dallaswoodys.com

19 **Zippers** [M,NH,S] 214/526-9519 ■ 3333 N Fitzhugh (at Travis) ■ *noon-2am*

NIGHTCLUBS

25 **Alexandre's** [GS,E] 214/559-0720 ■ 4026 Cedar Springs Rd (at Knight St) ■ *2pm-2am, live music* ■ www.alexandres.com

15 **The Brick** [MW,D,MR-AF,18+] 214/521-2024, 214/521-3154 ■ 4117 Maple Ave (at Throckmorton) ■ *9pm-4am Th-Sun* ■ www.brickdallas.com

24 **Havana Bar & Grill** [GS,D,MR-L,DS] 214/526-9494 ■ 4006 Cedar Springs Rd (at Throckmorton) ■ *grill 5pm-10pm Tue-Sun, lounge 10pm-2am Wed-Sun*

15 **Joe's Dallas** [MW,NH,D,F,K,S,WC,$] 214/219-5637 ■ 4125 Maple Ave (at Throckmorton) ■ *noon-2am, patio* ■ www.brickdallas.com

26 **Kaliente** [M,D,MR-L,K,DS] 214/520-6676 ■ 4350 Maple Ave (at Hondo) ■ *9pm-2am, clsd Tue, salsa & Tejano* ■ www.kaliente.cc

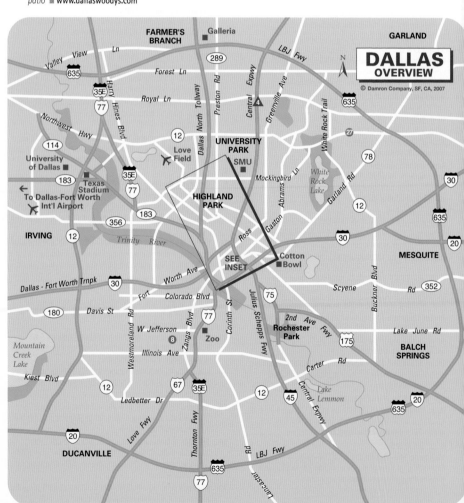

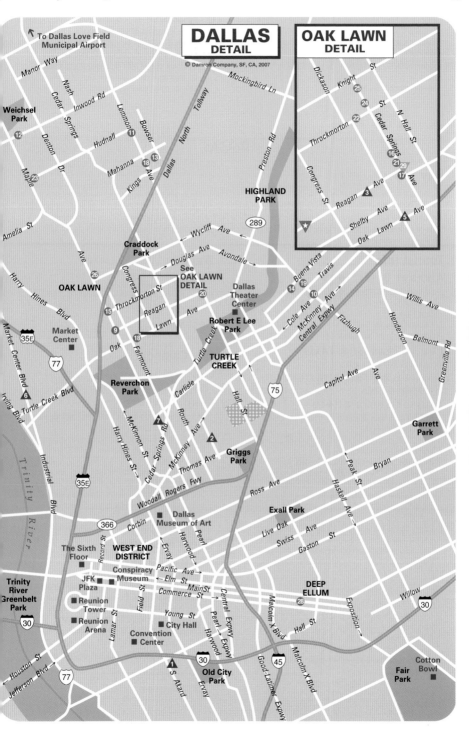

DALLAS
DETAIL

© Damron Company, SF, CA, 2007

OAK LAWN
DETAIL

27 **Once in a Blue Moon** [W,D,NS,BYOB] 972/237-0758
■ 10675 E Northwest Hwy, Ste 2600B (at DanceMasters
Ballroom) ■ 7pm-midnight 2nd Sat, women's dance ■
www.once-in-a-blue-moon.org
28 **One** [GS,D,A,18+,$] 214/741-1111 ■ 3025 Main St (in Deep
Ellum) ■ 10pm-4am Fri-Sat, till 2am Tue, more gay Fri ■
www.clubonedallas.com

17 **Round-Up Saloon** [★M,D,CW,K,WC] 214/522-9611 ■ 391:
Cedar Springs Rd (at Throckmorton) ■ 3pm-2am, from noon
wknds, [K] Sun-Th, 6 bars, patio ■ www.roundupsaloon.con
21 **Station 4** [★MW,D,C,DS,S,V,18+] 214/526-7171,
214/559-0650 (24hr info line) ■ 3911 Cedar Springs Rd
(at Throckmorton) ■ 9pm-4am Wed-Sun, also Rose Room
cabaret, patio ■ www.caven.com

DALLAS

Day Trips: Southfork Ranch
Located in Parker, TX, just about a 40-minute drive from downtown, is the filming location of the popular 1980s TV
drama *Dallas*. This is the ranch where the Ewings lived, loved, and fought for 13 unforgettable seasons. You can tour
the Ewing mansion and grounds, view *Dallas* memorabilia (including the gun that shot J.R.), and shop for series-
themed collectibles, clothing, home decor, and accessories in the two on-site giftshops. For more info, visit
www.southforkranch.com.

Tourist Info
AIRPORT DIRECTIONS
Dallas/Ft Worth International. To get to the heart
of Cedar Springs Rd, take Hwy 114 to Hwy 183.
Take Hwy 183 to I-35 E. Go south on I-35 and
exit on Oaklawn. Go north on Oaklawn to Cedar
Springs. Turn left on Cedar Springs.

PUBLIC TRANSIT & TAXIS
Yellow Cab 214/426-6262.
Dallas Area Rapid Transit (DART) 214/979-1111,
web: www.dart.org.

TOURIST SPOTS & INFO
African American Museum 214/565-9026, web:
www.aamdallas.org.
Crow Collection of Asian Art 214/979-6430, web:
www.crowcollection.com.
Dallas Arboretum & Botanical Garden
214/515-6500, web www.dallasarboretum.org.
Dallas Museum of Art 214/922-1200, web:
www.dallasmuseumofart.org.
Dallas Theater Center/ Frank Lloyd Wright
214/522-8499, web: www.dallastheatercenter.org.
Dallas World Aquarium 214/720-2224, web:
www.dwazoo.com.
Deep Ellum district, web: www.deepellumtx.com.
Fair Park, web: www.fairpark.org. 277-acre park
since 1880, home to Cotton Bowl, many
museums, and Texas State Fair.
Meadows Museum at SMU 214/768-2516, web:
www.meadowsmuseumdallas.org.
Modern Art Museum, Fort Worth 817/738-9215,
web: www.themodern.org.
Nasher Sculpture Center 214/242-5100, web:
www.nashersculpturecenter.org.
Sixth Floor Museum 214/747-6660, web:
www.jfk.org.
Texas State Fair & State Fair Park 214/565-9931,
web: www.bigtex.com.
The Women's Museum 214/915-0860, web:
www.thewomensmuseum.org.
Visitor's Center: 214/571-1000, web:
www.dallascvb.com.

Weather
Can be unpredictable. Hot summers (90°s–100°s)
with possible severe rain storms. Winter
temperatures hover in the 20°s through 40°s
range.

Best Views
Hyatt Regency Tower.

City Calendar
LGBT PRIDE
September. www.dallastavernguild.org.

ANNUAL EVENTS
March-April - AFI Dallas Int'l Film Festival, web:
www.afidallas.com.
March-April - Dallas Blooms at Dallas Arboretum
& Botanical Garden with over 400,000 spring-
blooming bulbs.
April – Deep Ellum Arts Festival, web: www.deep-
ellumartsfestival.com.
September-October - Texas State Fair, web:
www.bigtex.com. Largest in the country.
October - Out Takes Dallas 972/988-6333, web:
www.outtakesdallas.org. LGBT film festival.

Queer Resources
COMMUNITY INFO
Gay/Lesbian Switchboard 214/528-0022.
John Thomas Gay/Lesbian Community Center
214/528-9254, 2701 Reagan (at Brown), 9am-
9pm, 10am-6pm Sat, noon-6pm Sun, web:
www.resourcecenterdallas.org/glcc.html.
Lambda AA 214/267-0222. 2438 Butler, #106,
web: www.aadallas.org.
AIDS Services of Dallas 214/941-0523, web:
www.aidsdallas.org.
AIDS ARMS 214/521-5191, web:
www.aidsarms.org.

CAFES

Nodding Dog Coffee Company [F,E,WI] 214/941-1166 ■ 500 N Bishop Ave ■ 7am-10pm, till midnight Fri-Sat ■ www.noddingdogcoffee.com

Opening Bell Coffee [E,BW] 214/565-0383 ■ 1409 S Lamar St, Ste 012 ■ 7am-midnight, from 9am Sat, clsd Sun ■ www.openingbellcoffee.com

RESTAURANTS

Ali Baba Cafe 214/823-8235 ■ 1905 Greenville Ave (near Ross) ■ lunch & dinner, clsd Sun-Mon, Middle Eastern ■ www.alibabacafe.com

Black-Eyed Pea [WC] 214/521-4580 ■ 3857 Cedar Springs Rd (at Reagan) ■ 11am-10pm, Southern homecookin', some veggie ■ www.theblackeyedpea.com

Blue Mesa Grill 972/934-0165 ■ 5100 Beltline Rd (at Tollway), Addison ■ 11am-10pm, till 10:30pm Fri-Sat, 10am-9pm Sun, great fajitas, full bar ■ www.bluemesagrill.com

Bread Winners [GS,WC] 214/754-4940 ■ 3301 McKinney Ave ■ brkfst & lunch daily, dinner Tue-Sun, Sun brunch, int'l, full bar ■ www.breadwinnerscafe.com

The Bronx Restaurant & Bar [WC,GO] 214/521-5821 ■ 3835 Cedar Springs Rd (at Oak Lawn) ■ lunch Tue-Fri, dinner Tue-Sat, Sun brunch, clsd Mon, some veggie

Cosmic Cafe [F,E] 214/521-6157 ■ 2912 Oak Lawn Ave ■ 11am-11pm, noon-10pm Sun, veggie, also yoga & meditation ■ www.cosmiccafedallas.com

Cremona Bistro & Cafe 214/871-1115 ■ 3136 Routh St (at Cedar Springs) ■ lunch weekdays & dinner nightly, Italian, full bar, patio, live music Fri-Sat ■ www.cremonabistro.com

Dream Cafe [BW,WC] 214/954-0486 ■ 2800 Routh St (in the Quadrangle) ■ 7am-9pm, till 10pm Fri-Sat, brkfst served till 5pm, plenty veggie ■ www.thedreamcafe.com

Fitness Essentials [WC,GO] 214/528-5535 ■ 3878 Oak Lawn, Ste 100E (near Avondale) ■ 9am-7pm, till 6pm Sat, 11am-6pm Sun, organic, plenty veggie

Hunky's [★BW,WC,GO] 214/522-1212 ■ 4000 Cedar Springs Rd (at Throckmorton) ■ noon-10pm, till 11pm Fri-Sat, from 10am Sun, hamburgers & salads, patio

Lucky's Cafe 214/522-3500 ■ 3531 Oak Lawn ■ 7am-10pm, classic comfort food, great brkfsts

McCormick & Schmick's Seafood Restaurant 214/891-0100 ■ 307 NorthPark Center (at W Northwest Hwy) ■ lunch & dinner, fresh seafood, full bar ■ www.msnorthpark.com

Monica Aca y Alla [★TG,E,WC] 214/748-7140 ■ 2914 Main St (at Malcolm X) ■ lunch Mon-Fri, dinner Tue-Sun, brunch wknds, trendy, contemporary Mexican, full bar, live music wknds, Latin jazz/ salsa ■ www.monicas.com

Rocco's [WI] 214/871-9207, 214/871-9208 ■ 2916 McKinney Ave ■ 11am-2:30pm & 5pm-10pm, 11am-11pm Fri-Sat, 11:30am-10pm Sun, pizza & pasta ■ www.roccosuptown.com

Stephan Pyles 214/580-7000 ■ 1807 Ross Ave Ste 200 ■ lunch Mon-Fri, dinner Mon-Sat, clsd Sun, Southwestern cuisine ■ www.stephanpyles.com

Sushi on McKinney [WC] 214/521-0969 ■ 4500 McKinney Ave (at Armstrong) ■ lunch weekdays & dinner nightly, full bar

Thai Soon 972/234-6111 ■ 101 S Coit, Ste 401 (at Beltline) ■ lunch & dinner

Vitto [BW,WC,GO] 214/946-1212 ■ 316 W 7th St (at Bishop) ■ lunch & dinner, Italian ■ www.vittoitalian.com

Ziziki's [WC] 214/521-2233 ■ 4514 Travis St, #122 (in Travis Walk) ■ 11am-10pm, Sun brunch, Greek, full bar ■ www.zizikis.com

ENTERTAINMENT & RECREATION

Assassination City Derby 400 S Buckner Blvd (at What's Hot Fun World) ■ Dallas' female roller derby league, check web for upcoming events ■ www.acderby.com

Connecting Women Dallas 972/907-8804 (Bridal Blooms #) ■ connectingwomen@bridalbloom.com

Get Some Pride ■ social network for Dallas & Fort Worth ■ www.getsomepride.com

Lambda Weekly 972/263-5305 ■ KNON 89.3 FM ■ 1pm Sun, LGBT radio show for northern TX ■ www.geocities.com/lambdaweekly

Turtle Creek Chorale (TCC) 214/526-3214, 800/746-4412 ■ 3630 Harry Hines Blvd (at Sammons Center for the Arts) ■ world-famous male choir w/ several subscription concerts yearly & many CDs ■ www.turtle-creek.org

The Women's Chorus of Dallas (TWCD) 214/520-7828 ■ 3630 Harry Hines Blvd (at Sammons Center for the Arts) ■ several subscription & benefit concerts throughout year & many CDs ■ www.twcd.org

The Women's Museum 214/915-0860, 888/337-1167 ■ 3800 Parry Ave ■ noon-5pm, clsd Mon ■ www.thewomensmuseum.org

BOOKSTORES

29 **Crossroads Market Bookstore/ Cafe** [WC] 214/521-8919 ■ 3930 Cedar Springs Rd (at Throckmorton) ■ 9am-10pm, till 11pm Fri-Sat, LGBT ■ www.dallascrossroads.com

RETAIL SHOPS

An Occasional Piece 214/520-0868 ■ 3922 Cedar Springs Rd (at Throckmorton) ■ gifts, cards, collectibles

Obscurities 214/559-3706 ■ 4000-B Cedar Springs ■ noon-10pm, 2pm-8pm Sun, clsd Mon, tattoo & piercing ■ www.obscurities.com

29 **Tapelenders** [GO] 214/528-6344 ■ 3926 Cedar Springs Rd (at Throckmorton) ■ 9am-midnight, LGBT T-shirts, books, video rentals ■ www.tapelenders.com

Union Jack 214/528-9600 ■ 3920 Cedar Springs Rd ■ men's clothing & underwear ■ www.unionjackdallas.com

PUBLICATIONS

Dallas Voice 214/754-8710 ■ LGBT newspaper w/ extensive resource listings ■ www.dallasvoice.com

MEN'S CLUBS

Club Dallas [★SW,PC] 214/821-1990 ■ 2616 Swiss Ave (at Good Latimer) ■ 24hrs, full gym, steam room, sauna, sundeck ■ www.theclubs.com

Midtowne Spa—Dallas [★PC] 214/821-8989 ■ 2509 Pacific (at Hawkins) ■ 24hrs, 3 flrs, rooftop sundeck & hot tub, weekend cookouts ■ www.midtowne-spa.com

EROTICA

Alternatives 214/630-7071 ■ 1720 W Mockingbird Ln (at Hawes) ■ 24hrs ■ www.sexysite.com

Amazing Superstore 972/241-3944 ■ 11327 Reeder Rd (at Royal/ I-35) ■ 24hrs, bookstore w/ arcade

Leather Masters, Dallas 214/528-3865 ■ 3000 Main St ■ noon-10pm, till midnight Fri-Sat, clsd Sun-Mon, custom leather & more ■ www.leathermasters.com

Lido Theatre 214/630-7127 ■ 7035 John Carpenter Fwy (at Mockinbird Ln)

Mockingbird Video 214/631-3003 ■ 708 W Mockingbird Ln (at I-35 & Halifax) ■ 24hrs, bookstore w/ arcade

Odyssey Video 972/484-4999 ■ 11505 Anaheim Dr (at Forest Ln) ■ *24hrs*

Paris Adult Book & Video Store 972/263-0774 ■ 11118 Harry Hines Blvd ■ *24hrs, bookstore w/ arcade*

Shades of Grey Leather [WC] 214/521-4739 ■ 3930-A Cedar Springs Rd (at Throckmorton) ■ *11am-7pm, till midnight Fri-Sat, noon-6pm Sun*

Houston

ACCOMMODATIONS

1   **The Lovett Inn** [★GS,SW,NS,WI,GO] 713/522-5224, 800/779-5224 ■ 501 Lovett Blvd, Montrose (at Whitney) ■ *historic home of former Houston mayor & Federal Court judge, sundeck, hot tub* ■ www.lovettinn.com

2   **Robin's Nest B&B Inn** [GF,WI] 713/528-5821, 800/622-8343 ■ 4104 Greeley St ■ *Victorian & Craftsman in Montrose Museum District, lush gardens* ■ www.therobin.com

3   **Sycamore Heights B&B** [GF,NS,WI,GO] 713/861-4117 ■ 245 W 18th St ■ *circa 1905, garden* ■ www.sycamore-heights.com

BARS

4   **The 611 Club** [★M,NH] 713/526-7070 ■ 611 Hyde Park (at Stanford) ■ *11am-2am*

5   **Blur** [MW,D] 713/529-3447 ■ 710 Pacific St ■ *8pm-2am, from 6pm Sun, clsd Mon-Tue* ■ www.blurbar.com

6   **Brazos River Bottom (BRB)** [★M,D,CW] 713/528-9192 ■ 2400 Brazos (btwn Hadley & McIlhenny) ■ *noon-2am* ■ www.brbhouston.com

HOUSTON

Houston, the largest city in the bigger-than-life state of Texas, is home to the Astrodome, a fine collection of historical and fine arts museums, and the 570-ft San Jacinto Monument commemorating the independence of the Lone Star Republic.

Tourist Info

AIRPORT DIRECTIONS

Houston Intercontinental and Houston Hobby Airport. To get from Hobby to Montrose, take Broadway to I-45 North. Exit on the Allen Parkway and turn left. Take the Allen Parkway to Montrose and turn left.

To get from Houston International to Montrose, take the south exit on Hwy 59. Take Hwy 59 to I-45 South. Follow I-45 to the Allen Parkway. Take the Allen Parkway to Montrose and turn left.

PUBLIC TRANSIT & TAXIS

Yellow Cab 713/236-1111.

Metropolitan Transit Authority 713/635-4000, web: www.ridemetro.org.

TOURIST SPOTS & INFO

Contemporary Arts Museum 713/284-8250, web: www.camh.org.

The Galleria, 713/622-0663.

The Menil Collection 713/525-9400, web: www.menil.org.

Museum of Fine Arts 713/639-7300, web: www.mfah.org.

Rothko Chapel 713/524-9839, web: www.rothkochapel.org.

San Jacinto Monument 281/479-2421, web: www.sanjacinto-museum.org.

Six Flags SplashTown 281/355-3300, web: www.sixflags.com/splashtown.

Visitor's Center: 713/227-3100, web: www.visit-houstontexas.com.

Weather

Humid all year round—you're not that far from the Gulf. Mild winters, although there are a few days when the temperatures drop into the 30's. Winter also brings occasional rainy days. Summers are very hot.

Best Views

Spindletop, the revolving restaurant on top of the Hyatt Regency 713/654-1234.

City Calendar

LGBT PRIDE

June. 713/529-6979, web: www.pridehouston.org.

ANNUAL EVENTS

March - AIDS Walk 713/403-9255, web: www.aidswalkhouston.org.

Easter weekend - Jungle, web: www.junglehouston.com. Dance party benefiting HIV/AIDS education, research & care.

June - Juneteenth Freedom Festival, web: www.milleroutdoortheater.com.

Sept - Gay & Lesbian Film Festival, web: www.orbitweb.com/hglff.

Queer Resources

COMMUNITY INFO

Houston GLBT Center 713/524-3818. 3400 Montrose Blvd, Ste 207, noon-9pm, clsd wknds, web: www.houstonglbtcommunitycenter.org.

Gay/Lesbian Switchboard 713/529-3211. 24hrs, web: www.gayswitchboardhouston.org.

Women's Center Hotline 713/528-2121, 24hrs, web: www.hawc.org.

Lambda AA Center 713/521-1243. 1201 W Clay, web: www.lambdahouston.org.

Montrose Counseling Center 713/529-0037.

Chances [W,D,E,WC] 713/523-7217 ■ 1100 Westheimer (at Waugh) ■ *2pm-2am* ■ www.chancesbar.com

Club 1415 [MW,D,S] 713/522-7066 ■ 1415 California ■ *Wed-Th, special events wknds*

Cousins [MW,NH,DS] 713/528-9204 ■ 817 Fairview (at Converse) ■ *11am-2am, from noon Sun*

10 **Decades** [MW,NH] 713/521-2224 ■ 1205 Richmond (btwn Mandel & Montrose) ■ *11am-2am, from noon Sun*

1 **EJ's** [M,D,E,S] 713/527-9071 ■ 2517 Ralph (at Westheimer) ■ *7am-2am, from 10am Sun, 4 bars, patio* ■ www.ejsbar.com

2 **George** [M,NH,CW,GO] 713/528-8102 ■ 617 Fairview (at Stanford) ■ *7am-2am, from noon Sun, patio*

3 **Guava Lamp** [MW,K,V,WC] 713/524-3359 ■ 570 Waugh ■ *4pm-2am, from 2pm Sun, swanky lounge, [K] Wed & Sun* ■ www.guavalamphouston.com

4 **In and Out** [MW] 713/589-9780 ■ 1537 N Shepherd ■ *4pm-2am*

15 **JR's** [★M,K,DS,S,V,WC] 713/521-2519 ■ 808 Pacific (at Grant) ■ *noon-2am, patio* ■ www.jrsbarandgrill.com

16 **Mary's** [★MW,NH,L,S,WC] 713/527-9669 ■ 1022 Westheimer (at Waugh) ■ *7am-2am, from 10am Sun, also patio bar*

24 **Michael's Outpost** [M,NH,CW,E,DS,OC] 713/520-8446 ■ 1419 Richmond (at Mandell) ■ *3pm-2am, from noon Fri-Sun*

17 **Montrose Mining Co** [★M,CW,L] 713/529-7488 ■ 805 Pacific (at Grant) ■ *4pm-2am, till 3am Fri-Sat, patio*

7 **The New Barn Saloon** [W,D,CW] 713/523-7217 ■ 1100 Westheimer (at Waugh) ■ *8pm-2am, clsd Sun-Wed* ■ www.chancesbar.com/barn.htm

18 **Privé Lounge** [GS] 713/522-2542 ■ 910 Westheimer ■ *5pm-2am, from noon Wed-Sat, from 2pm Sun, rooftop patio* ■ www.privelounge.com

Rainbow Room [MW,D,E] 281/872-0215 ■ 527 Barren Springs Dr (at Ella Blvd) ■ *3pm-2am* ■ rainbowroom_1@msn.com

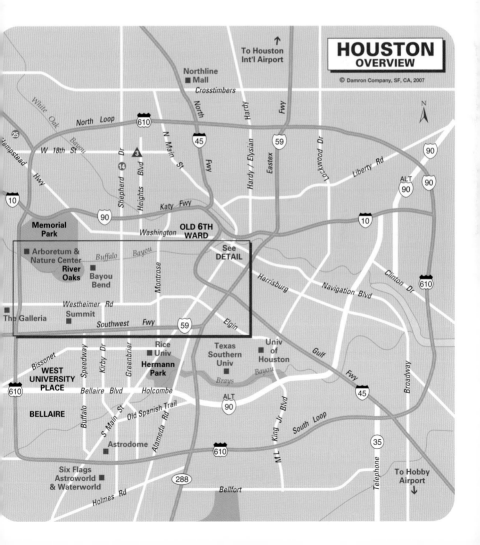

19 **Ripcord** [M,L,WC] 713/521-2792 ■ 715 Fairview (at Crocker)
    ■ *1pm-2am, till 4am Fri-Sat* ■ www.theripcord.com

20 **Tony's Corner Pocket** [MW,NH,K,S] 713/571-7870 ■ 817 W
    Dallas (btwn Arthur & Crosby) ■ *noon-2am, large 2-level deck*
    ■ www.tonyscornerpocket.com

Nightclubs

La Academia [M,D,MR-L,S,18+] 713/334-5422 ■ 5829 S
    Gessner (at Harwin) ■ *Th-Sun only* ■
    www.laacademiaclub.com

21 **Bartini** [MW,D,E,18+] 713/526-2271 ■ 1318 Westheimer Rd
    ■ *10pm-close Wed-Sun only, 2 levels* ■
    www.clubbartini.com

22 Club Dignity [W,D,MR-AF,F,K,S,OC,WC,GO] 713/395-6669
    ■ 1927 Scott St (off Hwy 45) ■ *sportsbar & restaurant,
    lesbian-owned*

7   G Spot [W,D,WC] 713/522-4065 ■ 1100 Westheimer (at
    Montrose) ■ *8pm-2am Th-Sat* ■
    www.chancesbar.com/gspot.htm

23 **Numbers** [GF,D,E,V,YC] 713/526-6551 ■ 300 Westheimer (at
    Taft) ■ *also live music venue* ■ www.numbersnightclub.com

    Ranch Hill Saloon [MW,NH,D,CW,K,WC,GO] 281/298-9035
    ■ 24704 I-45 N, Spring ■ *4pm-close, from 6pm Sat, clsd Sun,
    [K] Th, lesbian-owned* ■ www.ranchhill.com

15 **South Beach Nightclub** [★M,D,S] 713/529-7623 ■ 810
    Pacific ■ *9pm-5am, clsd Mon-Tue* ■ www.south-
    beachthenightclub.com

    Throb [W,D] 713/334-5422 ■ 5829 S Gessner (at La
    Academia) ■ *Fri only* ■ www.throbparties.info

25 **Viviana's Night Club** [M,D,MR-L] 713/681-4101 ■ 4624
    Dacoma St ■ *5pm-2am, clsd Mon, [S] Sun*

Cafes

Diedrich Coffee 713/526-1319 ■ 4005 Montrose (btwn
    Richmond & W Alabama) ■ *6am-11pm, till midnight Fri-Sat,
    7am-10pm Sun* ■ www.diedrich.com

Empire Cafe 713/528-5282 ■ 1732 Westheimer Rd
    ■ *7:30am-10pm, till 11pm Fri-Sat* ■ www.empirecafe.net

Restaurants

1308 Cantina 713/807-8996 ■ 1308 Montrose Blvd
    ■ *11am-9pm, till 10pm Wed-Th, till 11pm Fri-Sat, Mexican
    seafood* ■ www.1308cantina.com

Baba Yega's [★WC] 713/522-0042 ■ 2607 Grant (at
    Pacific) ■ *11am-10pm, till 11pm Fri-Sat, from 10am Sun, patio,
    full bar* ■ www.babayega.com

Barnaby's Cafe [★BW,WC] 713/522-0106 ■ 604 Fairview
    (btwn Stanford & Hopkins St) ■ *11am-10pm, till 11pm Fri-Sat,
    also 1701 S Shepherd, 713/520-5131* ■
    www.barnabyscafe.com

Black-Eyed Pea [★WC] 713/523-0200 ■ 2048 W Gray (at
    Shepherd) ■ *10:30am-10pm, from 11am wknds, Southern* ■
    www.theblackeyedpea.com

Bocado's [GS,D] 713/523-5230 ■ 1312 W Alabama,
    Hosuton ■ *lunch & dinner, clsd Sun-Mon, Mexican, full bar, [E]
    Wed*

Brasil [BW] 713/528-1993 ■ 2604 Dunlavy (at Westheimer)
    ■ *7:30am-2am, till midnight Sun, bistro, plenty veggie*

Cafe Annie 713/840-1111 ■ 1728 Post Oak Blvd (at San
    Felipe) ■ *lunch Tue-Fri, dinner Mon-Sat, clsd Sun, fine dining*
    ■ www.cafe-annie.com

Captain Benny's Half Shell [BW] 713/666-5469 ■ 8506
    Main ■ *11am-11pm*

Chapultepec [BW] 713/522-2365 ■ 813 Richmond (btwn
    Montrose & Main) ■ *24hrs, Mexican, some veggie*

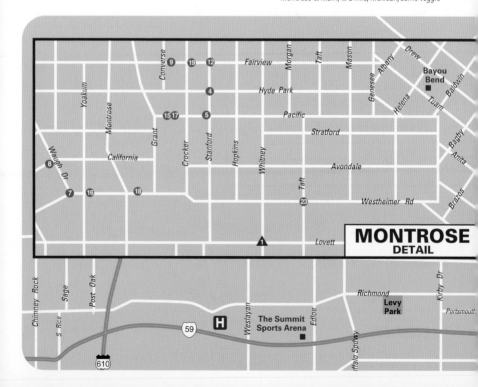

Hollywood Diner 713/523-8855 ■ 2409 Grant (at Fairview St) ■ *9am-2am, till 3am Fri-Sat* ■ www.hollywoodbistro.com

House of Pies [★] 713/528-3816 ■ 3112 Kirby Dr (at Richmond/ Alabama) ■ *24hrs* ■ www.houseofpies.com

Java Java Cafe [★] 713/880-5282 ■ 911 W 11th (at Shepherd) ■ *7:30am-3pm, from 8:30am wknds*

Julia's Bistro 713/807-0090 ■ 3722 Main St (at W Alabama) ■ *lunch Mon-Fri, dinner Mon-Sat, clsd Sun, Latin* ■ www.juliasbistro.com

Magnolia Bar & Grill [WC] 713/781-6207 ■ 6000 Richmond Ave (at Fountainview Dr) ■ *11am-10pm, till 11pm Fri-Sat, from 10:30am Sun, Cajun, full bar* ■ www.magnoliagrill.com

Ming's Cafe 713/529-7888 ■ 2703 Montrose (at Westheimer) ■ *11am-10pm, Chinese*

Mo Mong 713/524-5664 ■ 1201 Westheimer #B (at Montrose) ■ *11am-11pm, noon-10pm Sun, Vietnamese, full bar*

Ninfa's [★] 713/228-1175 ■ 2704 Navigation Blvd ■ *11am-10pm, till 11pm Fri-Sat, Mexican, full bar* ■ www.mamaninfas.com

Ninos 713/522-5120 ■ 2817 W Dallas (btwn Montrose & Waugh Dr) ■ *lunch Mon-Fri, dinner Mon-Sat, clsd Sun, Italian, some veggie, full bar* ■ www.ninos-vincents.com

Spanish Flower [BW] 713/869-1706 ■ 4701 N Main (at Airline) ■ *24hrs, till 10pm Tue, from 9am Wed, Mexican*

ENTERTAINMENT & RECREATION

After Hours 713/526-4000, 713/526-5738 (request line) ■ KPFT 90.1 FM (also 89.5 Galveston) ■ *1am-4am Sat, LGBT radio, also Queer Voices 8pm Mon* ■ www.kpft.org

DiverseWorks Art Space 713/223-8346, 713/335-3455 ■ 1117 East Fway (I-10 at N Main) ■ *gallery noon-6pm Wed-Sat, call or see website for events, some LGBT-themed art & performance* ■ www.diverseworks.org

Dominic Walsh Dance Theater 713/652-3938 ■ 2311 Dunlavy St, Ste 210 ■ *contemporary dance theater, annual Illumination Project benefits Baylor International Pediatric AIDS Initiative, call for events* ■ www.dwdt.org

Houston Comets 877/266-3879, 713/627-9622 ■ 1510 Polk St (at Toyota Center) ■ *check out the Women's National Basketball Association while you're in Houston* ■ www.wnba.com/comets

Houston Roller Derby ■ *Houston's female roller derby league, check web for upcoming events* ■ www.houstonrollerderby.com

Mukuru 713/623-6796 x226 ■ *arts for AIDS, see web for events* ■ www.mukuru.org

Queer Voices 713/526-5738, 713/529-6929 ■ *8pm Mon* ■ houston.kpft.org

Unhinged Productions ■ *GLBT theater company, see web for events* ■ www.u-p.org

RETAIL SHOPS

Black Hawk Leather 713/532-8437 ■ 711 Fairview ■ *noon-8pm, 2pm-7pm Sun; also inside Ripcord bar, 8pm-11pm, 11pm-3am Fri-Sat* ■ www.blackhawkleather.com

Hollywood Super Center 713/527-8510 ■ 807 Fairview St (at Crocker St) ■ *10am-2am, gifts, novelties*

Lucia's Garden 713/526-6494 ■ 2216 Portsmouth (at Greenbriar) ■ *10am-6pm, till 7pm Tue & Th, clsd Sun, spiritual herb center* ■ www.luciasgarden.com

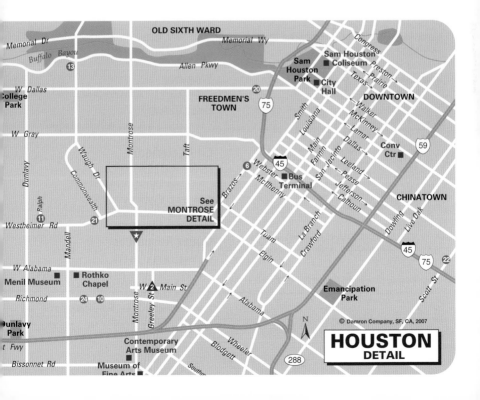
© Damron Company, SF, CA, 2007
HOUSTON DETAIL

PUBLICATIONS

OutSmart 713/520-7237 ■ *free monthly LGBT newsmagazine* ■ www.outsmartmagazine.com

Red Magazine 713/240-5508, 602/308-8310 ■ www.rednightlife.com

GYMS & HEALTH CLUBS

Fitness Exchange [GF] 713/524-9932 ■ 4040 Milam ■ *5am-10pm, 8am-8pm wknds* ■ www.fitnessexchange-houston.com

Houston Gym [GF,GO] 713/880-9191 ■ 1501 Durham Rd (at Washington & Shepherd) ■ *5am-10pm, 8am-6pm wknds* ■ www.houstongym.com

YMCA Downtown [GF,SW] 713/659-8501 ■ 1600 Louisiana St (btwn Pease & Bell) ■ *5am-10pm* ■ www.ymcahouston.org

MEN'S CLUBS

The Club Houston [★SW,PC] 713/659-4998 ■ 2200 Fannin St (at W Gray) ■ *24hrs* ■ www.the-clubs.com

Midtowne Spa—Houston [★SW,PC] 713/522-2379 ■ 3100 Fannin (at Elgin) ■ *24hrs* ■ www.midtowne-spa.com

EROTICA

BJ's 24 Hour News 713/649-9241 ■ 6314 Gulf Fwy ■ *24hrs*

Eros 1207 [GO] 713/944-6010 ■ 1207 Spencer Hwy (at Allen Genoa) ■ www.eros1207.com

Leather Forever 713/526-6940 ■ 604 Westheimer (at Stanford)

Q Video 713/522-4485 ■ 1415 California St

San Antonio

ACCOMMODATIONS

1   **Alamo Lodge** [GF,SW,WC] 210/518-1200, 210/222-9820 ■ 1126 E Elmira (at Wilmington) ■ *kids/ pets ok* ■ www.alamolodge.com

2   **Arbor House Suites B&B** [GS,NS,WC,GO] 210/472-2005, 888/272-6700 ■ 109 Arciniega (btwn S Alamo & S St Mary's) ■ *hot tub* ■ www.arborhouse.com

3   **Beauregard House B&B** [GF,NS,WI] 210/222-1198, 888/667-0555 ■ 215 Beauregard St ■ *Victorian in historic district* ■ www.beauregardhouse.com

4   **Beckman Inn** [GF,NS] 210/229-1449, 800/945-1449 ■ 222 E Guenther St ■ *B&B in King William historic district* ■ www.beckmaninn.com

5   **Brackenridge House** [GF,SW,WI] 210/271-3442, 800/221-1412 ■ 230 Madison ■ *B&B in historic King William district* ■ www.brackenridgehouse.com

6   **Das Liszt Ferienhaus** [GF] 210/422-8810 ■ 200 Loretta F ■ *3-bdrm rental near River Walk* ■ www.theplaceyous-tayinsa.com

SAN ANTONIO

Local Food:

Not surprisingly, Texas' southernmost city is also the one that boasts (and boast they DO!) the most culturally blended cuisine. In this, the Tex-Mex capital of the world, the best of North and South come together in some tantalizing and unforgettable unions.

Tourist Info

AIRPORT DIRECTIONS

San Antonio International. Take 281 S to the exits for downtown and The Alamo.

PUBLIC TRANSIT & TAXIS

Yellow-Checker 210/222-2222.
Via Info 210/362-2020, web: www.viainfo.net.

TOURIST SPOTS & INFO

The Alamo 210/225-1391, web: www.thealamo.org.
El Mercado.
Hemisfair Park.
The Majestic Theatre 210/226-5700, web: www.majesticempire.com.
Plaza de Armas.
River Walk.
San Antonio Museum of Art 210/978-8100, web: www.samuseum.org.
McNay Art Museum 210/824-5368, web: www.mcnayart.org.
Visitor's Center: 800/447-3372, web: www.sanantoniocvb.com.

Weather

60's-90's in the summer, 40's-60's in the winter.

Best Views

High in the Sky Lounge in the Tower of the Americas.

City Calendar

LGBT PRIDE

June. web: www.alamopridefest.org.

ANNUAL EVENTS

Late April - Fiesta San Antonio 877/723-4378, web: www.fiesta-sa.org.

Queer Resources

COMMUNITY INFO

Lesbian Information Line (LISA) 210/828-5472.
Lambda Club AA 210/979-5939. 319 E Camden St at Madison Sq Church.
San Antonio AIDS Foundation 210/225-4715, web: www.txsaaf.org.

Desert Hearts Cowgirl Club [WO,SW,NS,GO] 830/796-7001 ■ Bandera ■ 1-room cabin on 30-acre ranch, lesbian-owned ■ beaux2@indian-creek.net

7   Fiesta B&B [M,NS,WI,GO] 210/226-5548, 210/887-0074 ■ 1823 Saunders Ave (at Trinity) ■ full brkfst ■ www.fiestabandb.com

8   Grand Fleur de Lis [GF,NS,WI,GO] 210/271-7700 ■ 120 Cedar St ■ centrally located Victorian B&B ■ www.grand-fleurdelis.com

9   The Painted Lady Inn on Broadway [★MW,NS,WI,WC,GO] 210/220-1092 ■ 620 Broadway (at 6th) ■ full brkfst, private art deco suites, rooftop deck & spa ■ www.thepaintedladyinn.com

BARS

11   2015 Place [M,NH,K] 210/733-3365 ■ 2015 San Pedro (at Woodlawn) ■ 4pm-2am, patio, [K] Wed ■ 2015place.com

12   The Annex [M,NH,WC] 210/223-6957 ■ 330 San Pedro Ave (at Euclid) ■ 2pm-2am, patio ■ www.theannex-satx.com

13   Bermuda Triangle [W,NH,E,K,WC] 210/342-2276 ■ 119 El Mio (at San Pedro) ■ 7pm-2am, clsd Mon, DJ wknds, [K] Wed

14   Cobalt Club [MW,NH,WC] 210/734-2244 ■ 2022 McCullough (at Ashby) ■ 7am-2am, from noon Sun

15   Electric Company [MW,D,S,18+] 210/212-6635 ■ 820 San Pedro Ave (at W Laurel) ■ 9pm-3am Wed-Sun

16   Essence [M,NH] 210/223-5418 ■ 1010 N Main Ave (at E Euclid) ■ 2pm-2am, Sun BBQ benefits Garza Pharmacy ■ www.essence-satx.com

25   The Flying Saucer [GF] 210/647-7468 ■ 11255 Huebner Rd #212 (at I-10) ■ 11am-1am, till 2am Th-Sat, noon-midnight Sun, large beer selection ■ www.beerknurd.com

17   Gotham [GS,NH,WC] 210/527-1707 ■ 223 3rd St (at N Alamo) ■ noon-2am

18   One-Oh-Six Off Broadway [M,NH,F,OC] 210/820-0906 ■ 106 Pershing St (at Broadway) ■ noon-2am, from 7am Fri-Sat

19   Pegasus [M,S] 210/299-4222 ■ 1402 N Main (btwn Laurel & Evergreen) ■ 2pm-2am

20   Silver Dollar Saloon [MW,D,CW,K,S,WC] 210/227-2623 ■ 1418 N Main Ave (at Laurel) ■ 2pm-2am, patio bar

21   Sparks [M,E,S] 210/599-2335 ■ 8011 Webbles ■ 5pm-2am ■ www.sparks-sa.com

NIGHTCLUBS

22 **The Bonham Exchange** [★MW,D,V,18+,GO] 210/271–3811, 210/271–9219 ■ 411 Bonham St (at 3rd/ Houston) ■ 4pm–2am, from 8pm wknds, till 4am Fri-Sat, in 111-year-old mansion ■ www.bonhamexchange.net

23 **Heat** [M,D,S] 210/227–2600 ■ 1500 N Main Ave (at Evergreen) ■ 4pm–2am, after-hours Wed-Sun ■ www.heatsa.com

19 **The Saint** [M,D,DS,S,18+] 210/225–7330 ■ 1430 N Main (at Evergreen) ■ 4pm–2am ■ www.thesaint-satx.com

CAFES

Candlelight Coffeehouse & Wine Bar 210/738–0099 ■ 3011 N St Mary's (at Rte 281) ■ 4pm–midnight, Sun brunch 10am-2pm, clsd Mon-Tue ■ www.candlelightsa.com

Timo's Coffee House 210/733–8049 ■ 2021 San Pedro ■ 8am-10:30pm, 10am-4pm Sat, clsd Sun

RESTAURANTS

Chacho's [E,K] 210/366–2023 ■ 7870 Callaghan Rd (at I-10) ■ 24hrs, Mexican ■ www.chachos.com

Giovanni's Pizza & Italian Restaurant 210/212–6626 ■ 913 S Brazos (at Guadalupe) ■ 10am-6pm, till 9pm Fri-Sat, clsd Sun, some veggie

Lulu's Bakery & Cafe [WC] 210/222–9422 ■ 918 N Main (at W Elmira) ■ 24hrs, Tex-Mex ■ www.lulusbakeryand-cafe.com

Madhatter's Tea [BYOB,WC] 210/212–4832 ■ 320 Beauregard ■ 7am-10pm, till 11pm Fri, 8am-11pm Sat, 9am-9pm Sun, patio ■ www.madhatterstea.com

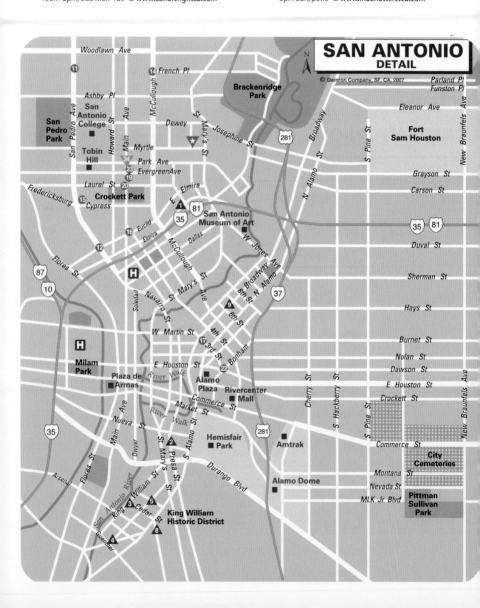

SAN ANTONIO DETAIL

© Damron Company, SF, CA, 2007

El Mirador [BW,WC] 210/225-9444 ■ 722 S St Mary's St (at Durango St) ■ 6:30am-9pm, till 3pm Mon, till 10pm Fri-Sat, 9am-2pm Sun, Tex-Mex, plenty veggie, patio

WD Deli 210/828-2322 ■ 3123 Broadway St ■ 10:30am-5pm, till 4pm Sat, clsd Sun

ENTERTAINMENT & RECREATION

Alamo City Roller Girls 223 Recoleta Rd (at the Rollercade) ■ San Antonio's female roller derby league, check web for upcoming events ■ www.alamocityrollergirls.com

San Antonio Silver Stars 210/444-5050 ■ SBC Center ■ check out the Women's National Basketball Association while you're in San Antonio ■ www.wnba.com/silverstars

RETAIL SHOPS

Black Hawk Leather 713/532-8437 ■ 1402 N Main (inside Pegasus) ■ 9pm-2am ■ www.blackhawkleather.com

On Main/ Off Main 210/737-2323 ■ 120 W Mistletoe Ave ■ 10am-6pm, till 5pm Sat, clsd Sun, gifts, cards & T-shirts ■ www.onmainoffmain.com

24 ZEBRAZ.com 210/472-2800, 800/788-4729 ■ 1608 N Main Ave (at E Park Ave) ■ 10am-10pm, LGBT dept store, also online version ■ www.zebraz.com

PUBLICATIONS

Shout Magazine 512/482-8252 ■ 1st & 3rd Th, LGBT arts, entertainment, lifestyle & leisure magazine for Texas ■ www.shouttexas.com

MEN'S CLUBS

Alternative Club Inc [SW,PC] 210/223-2177 ■ 827 E Elmira St (at St Mary's) ■ noon-9am, 24hrs wknds

Executive Health Club [PC] 210/299-1400 ■ 402 Austin St ■ 24hrs

EROTICA

Broadway News 210/223-2034 ■ 2202 Broadway (at Appler St)

Dreamers Apollo 210/653-3538 ■ 2376 Austin Hwy (at Walzem) ■ 24hrs ■ www.dreamersdvd.com

Encore Video 210/821-5345 ■ 1031 NE Loop 410

UTAH

Salt Lake City

ACCOMMODATIONS

1 Anton Boxrud B&B [GF,NS,WI] 801/363-8035, 800/524-5511 ■ 57 S 600 E (at S Temple) ■ full brkfst, hot tub, some shared baths ■ www.antonboxrud.com

2 Hotel Monaco Salt Lake City [GF,WC,WI] 801/595-0000, 877/294-9710 ■ 15 W 200 S ■ restaurant & bar, gym ■ www.monaco-saltlakecity.com

3 Parrish Place [GF,NS,WI] 801/832-0970, 888/832-0869 ■ 720 E Ashton Ave ■ Victorian mansion, hot tub ■ www.parrishplace.com

4 Peery Hotel [★GF,NS,WI,WC] 801/521-4300, 800/331-0073 ■ 110 W 300 S ■ full brkfst, also 2 restaurants & full bar ■ www.peeryhotel.com

5 Ric's Place [MO,NS,GO] 801/466-6747 ■ 1272 E 1300 S (at 13th E) ■ private home ■ texasstixx@aol.com

6 Under the Lindens [M,NS,GO] 801/355-9808 ■ 128 S 1000 E (downtown) ■ studios, hot tub, commitment ceremonies, mention Damron for discount ■ www.under-thelindens.com

BARS

7 Club Try-Angles [M,NH,D,F,PC,GO] 801/364-3203 ■ 251 W 900 S ■ 2pm-2am ■ www.clubtry-angles.com

8 MoDiggity's [W,D,E,V,PC] 801/832-9000 ■ 3424 S State St ■ 4pm-1am, till 12:30am Sun, sports bar, live DJs wknds ■ www.modiggitys.com

9 The Mynt Martini Lounge [GF,D,GO] 801/355-6968 ■ 63 W 100 South ■ 7pm-1am Wed-Sat ■ myspace.com/themynt

10 Paper Moon [W,D,F,E,K,PC,WC] 801/713-0678 ■ 3737 S State St ■ 3pm-1am

11 Radio City [M,WC] 801/532-9327 ■ 147 S State St (btwn 1st & 2nd) ■ 10am-2am, beer only

12 The Tavernacle [GF,K,P,NS,PC] 801/519-8900 ■ 201 E 300 South ■ "Duelin' Pianos" ■ www.tavernacle.com

13 The Trapp [MW,D,CW,PC,WC] 801/531-8727 ■ 102 S 600 W ■ 11am-2am, patio, food Sun ■ www.thetrapp.com

14 W Lounge [GS,D,NS,PC] 801/359-0637 ■ 358 SW Temple ■ 8pm-2am

NIGHTCLUBS

15 Club Manhattan [GF,D,E,WC] 801/364-7651 ■ 5 E 400 S (at Main) ■ 9pm-2am, more gay Sat for Latin salsa

16 Club Sound [★M,D] 801/328-0255 ■ 579 W 200 S (at 600 W) ■ gay 10pm-2am Fri only, live bands rest of the week

13 The Trapp Door [M,D,B,MR,TG,DS,PC,WC] 801/533-0173 ■ 615 W 100 S ■ 9pm-2am, clsd Mon-Tue ■ www.trapp-door.com

CAFES

Coffee Garden [WC] 801/355-3425 ■ 878 E 900 S ■ 6am-11pm, till midnight Fri-Sat, 7am-11pm Sun, light fare

Cup of Joe [E,WI] 801/363-8322 ■ 353 W 200 S (btwn 300 & 400 W) ■ 7am-midnight, 9am-8pm Sun, gallery

RESTAURANTS

Avenues Bakery & Bistro 801/322-4101 ■ 481 E South Temple ■ 7am-7pm, 7am-3pm wknds ■ www.avebakery.com

Bambara 801/363-5454 ■ 202 S Main St ■ lunch Mon-Fri, brkfst & dinner daily, upscale American ■ www.bambara-slc.com

Cafe Med 801/493-0100 ■ 420 E 3300 South ■ 11am-10pm, till 11pm Fri, 10am-11pm Sat, 10am-9pm Sun, Mediterranean

Cafe Trio Downtown 801/533-8746 ■ 680 S 900 E ■ 11am-9:30pm, till 10pm Fri-Sat, 10am-9pm Sun, Italian ■ www.triodining.com

Lambs Restaurant [E,WC] 801/364-7166 ■ 169 S Main St ■ 7am-9pm, from 8am Sat, clsd Sun ■ www.lambsgrill.com

Market St Grill [WC] 801/322-4668 ■ 48 W Market St ■ brkfst & lunch Mon-Sat, dinner nightly, Sun brunch, seafood/ steak, full bar ■ www.gastronomyinc.com

The Metropolitan [R] 801/364-3472 ■ 173 W Broadway ■ dinner only Mon-Sat, upscale New American ■ www.themetropolitan.com

New Yorker [WC] 801/328-1333 ■ 60 W Market St ■ lunch Mon-Fri, dinner nightly, clsd Sun, fine dining, steak ■ www.gastronomyinc.com

Nick-N-Willy's Pizza 801/273-8282 ■ 4536 S Highland Dr ■ 11am-9pm, noon-8pm

Panache 801/535-4311 ■ 299 S Main St, 2nd flr ■ lunch Mon-Fri, upscale American ■ www.panache.net

Rio Grande Cafe [★WC] 801/364-3302 ■ 270 S Rio Grande ■ lunch Mon-Sat & dinner nightly, Mexican, full bar

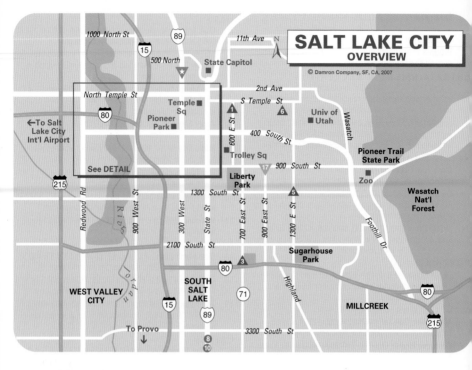

SALT LAKE CITY
OVERVIEW

© Damron Company, SF, CA, 2007

1000 North St

89

15

500 North

11th Ave

N

State Capitol

North Temple St

80

Temple Sq

Pioneer Park

←To Salt Lake City Int'l Airport

2nd Ave

S Temple St

600 E St

1

6

Univ of Utah

Wasatch

400 South St

Trolley Sq

900 South St

17

Pioneer Trail State Park

Zoo

See DETAIL

215

Liberty Park

1300 South St

5

Wasatch Nat'l Forest

River

West St

900 West St

300 West

State St

700 East St

900 East St

1300 E St

Foothill Dr

2100 South St

Sugarhouse Park

80

3

WEST VALLEY CITY

Jordan

SOUTH SALT LAKE

80

215

15

71

MILLCREEK

89

To Provo

3300 South St

8

10

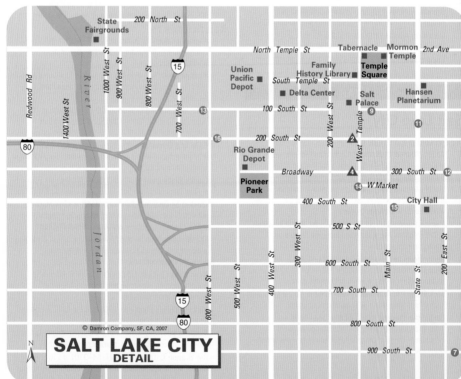

SALT LAKE CITY
DETAIL

N

© Damron Company, SF, CA, 2007

State Fairgrounds

200 North St

Redwood Rd

River

1400 West St

1000 West St

900 West St

800 West St

700 West St

15

North Temple St

Union Pacific Depot

South Temple St

Family History Library

Tabernacle

Temple Square

Mormon Temple

2nd Ave

Delta Center

100 South St

200 West St

West Temple

Salt Palace

9

Hansen Planetarium

11

13

16

200 South St

Rio Grande Depot

2

Pioneer Park

Broadway

4

14 W Market

300 South St

12

Jordan

300 West St

400 West St

500 West St

600 West St

15

80

400 South St

500 S St

600 South St

700 South St

800 South St

900 South St

Main St

State St

200 East St

15

City Hall

7

Sage's Cafe 801/322-3790 ■ 473 E 300 S ■ *lunch &
dinner, brkfst wknds, clsd Mon-Tue, vegan/ vegetarian* ■
www.sagescafe.com

Urban Bistro 801/322-4101 ■ 216 E 500 South ■ *lunch &
dinner, clsd Sun, eclectic American*

Entertainment & Recreation

Lambda Hiking Club 801/583-7064 ■ 700 E 200 S (meet
in parking lot btwn McDonald's & Chevron) ■ *activities 10am
every 1st & 3rd Sat* ■ www.gayhike.org

Plan-B Theatre Company 801/355-2787 ■ 138 W
Broadway (at Rose Wagner Performing Arts Center) ■ *at
least one LGBT-themed production each season* ■
www.planbtheatrecompany.org

Pygmalion Productions Theatre Company
801/355-2787, 888/451-2787 ■ 138 W Broadway (at
Rose Wagner Performing Arts Center) ■ *a "feminine
perspective" on theatre* ■ www.pygmalionproductions.org

Salt Lake Men's Choir 801/355-2787, 888/451-2787
■ www.saltlakemenschoir.org

Bookstores

Golden Braid Books 801/322-1162, 801/322-0404
(cafe) ■ 151 S 500 E ■ *10am-9pm, till 6pm Sun, also Oasis
Cafe, 8am-9pm, till 10pm wknds*

Retail Shops

17 **Cahoots** [WC,GO] 801/538-0606 ■ 878 E 900 S (at 900 E)
■ *9am-5pm, unique gift shop*

Gypsy Moon Emporium 801/521-9100 ■ 1011 E 900 S
■ *call for hours, Celtic & goddess-oriented gifts* ■
www.gypsymoonemporium.com

Publications

The Pillar 801/265-0066 ■ *LGBT monthly newspaper* ■
www.the-pillar.com

Q Salt Lake 801/649-6663, 800/806-7357 ■ *bi-weekly
LGBT newspaper* ■ www.qsaltlake.com

Men's Services

Dennis Massage [MO] 801/598-8344 ■ *full-body massage
for men* ■ www.dennismassage.com

Erotica

All For Love [TG,WC] 801/487-8358 ■ 3072 S Main St (at
33rd St S) ■ *clsd Sun, lingerie & S/M boutique* ■
www.allforlove.com

Blue Boutique 801/485-2072 ■ 2106 S 1100 E (at 2100 S)
■ *also piercing* ■ www.blueboutique.com

18 **Cahoots** [WC,GO] 801/538-0606 ■ 878 E 900 S (at 900 E)
■ *9am-5pm, gift store that also carries gay adult magazines,
cards, calendars & toys*

Mischievous 801/530-3100 ■ 559 S 300 W (at 6th St S)
■ *clsd Sun*

Sam's Magazines & Gifts 801/486-9925 ■ 1350 S State
St (at 13th St S)

Salt Lake City

Day Trips: There is no end to the beautiful scenery crowding the state of Utah. Home to five national parks,
Utah also boasts world-class skiing from November to April. Visit Park City, host to the 2002 Winter Olympics, and
check out the powder for yourself. The surrounding Wasatch Mountains offer hiking and fishing in the off-season,
and the scenic byways threading the Wasatch-Cache National Forest are a great way to see the area by car. To
experience the Great Salt Lake, visit Antelope Island State Park. Swimming, sailing, and bird-watching are popular
activities, and sunsets over the lake can be spectacular.

Tourist Info

Airport Directions
Salt Lake City International. To get to the area
covered by the detail map, take I-80 East to 15
North. Take the North Temple St exit.

Public Transit & Taxis
Yellow Cab 801/521-2100.
Utah Transit Authority (UTA) 801/743-3882, web:
www.utabus.com.

Tourist Spots & Info
Family History Library, one of the largest
genealogical research databases in the country
801/240-2584, web: www.familysearch.org.
Great Salt Lake.
Mormon Tabernacle Choir 801/240-4150, web:
www.mormontabernaclechoir.org.
Temple Square.
Skiing!
Trolley Square.
Visitor's Center: 801/521-2822, web: www.visit-
saltlake.com.

Weather
Home of "The Greatest Snow on Earth," the
Wasatch Mtns get an average of 535 inches of
powder, while the valley averages 59 inches.
Spring is mild with an average of 62°, while
summer temps average 88°, topping out at an
average of 92° in July.

City Calendar

LGBT Pride
June. 801/539-8800, web: www.utahpride.org.

Annual Events
Jan-Feb - Gay/ Lesbian Ski Week 877/429-6368,
web: www.gayskiing.org.

Queer Resources

Community Info
Utah Gay & Lesbian Center 801/539-8800 or
888/874-2743. 361 N 300 W, web:
www.glccu.com.
AA 801/484-7871, web: www.saltlakeaa.org.
801/487-2323, web: www.utahaids.org.

VIRGINIA

Norfolk

ACCOMMODATIONS

1   **Page House Inn** [GF,NS,WI] 757/625-5033, 800/599-7659 ■ 323 Fairfax Ave ■ B&B ■ www.pagehouseinn.com

2   **Tazewell Hotel & Suites** [GF,WI,WC] 757/623-6200 ■ 245 Granby St (at Tazewell St) ■ www.thetazewell.com

BARS

3   **The Garage** [M,NH,F,K,WC] 757/623-0303 ■ 731 Granby St (at Brambleton) ■ 9am-2am, from 11am Sat, from noon Sun ■ www.thegarage.co.nr

4   **Hershee Bar** [W,D,F,E,WC] 757/853-9842 ■ 6117 Sewells Pt Rd (at Norview) ■ 4pm-2am ■ www.hersheebar.com

5   **Nutty Buddy's** [M,D,MR,F,DS,WC] 757/588-6474 ■ 143 E Little Creek Rd ■ 4pm-2am Wed-Sun, more women Wed, also restaurant

6   **Skip's** [M,NH,F] 757/489-2345 ■ 3822 Hampton Blvd ■ 5pm-2am ■ www.skips.co.nr

7   **The Wave** [M,D,F,S,WC] 757/440-5911 ■ 4107 Colley Ave (at 41st St) ■ 4pm-2am, from 5pm Sat, clsd Sun, also restaurant

CAFES

Oasis Cafe [GO] 757/627-6161 ■ 142 W York St #101A (in York Center bldg) ■ 7:30am-4pm Mon-Fri

RESTAURANTS

Charlie's Cafe [BW] 757/625-0824 ■ 1800 Granby St (at 18th) ■ 7am-2pm, till 3pm wknds

Enrico's Ristorante [WC] 757/423-2700 ■ 4012 Colley Av ■ 11am-10pm, till 11pm Fri, 5pm-11pm Sat, clsd Sun, Greek & Italian ■ www.enricosristorante.com

BOOKSTORES

8   **Lambda Rising** [WC] 757/626-0969 ■ 322 W 21st St (in Palace Shops at Llewellyn Ave) ■ 10am-9pm, LGBT ■ www.lambdarising.com

EROTICA

Leather & Lace 757/583-4334 ■ 149 E Little Creek Rd (a Granby)

NORFOLK

Day Trips: Virginia Beach

Nearby Virginia Beach offers up sun and sand in the summer months, while whale-watching peaks in the winter. Colonial history buffs should visit First Landing Cross, a national monument marking the landing spot of the first English settlers, who arrived 13 years before the Pilgrims. Fast forward to the future with a visit to the Virginia Air and Space Center, where you can tour the original site of NASA, and check out the Apollo 12 Command Module.

City Calendar

LGBT PRIDE

September. 757/624-6886, web: www.hamptonroadspride.com.

ANNUAL EVENTS

September - Out Hampton Roads Film Festival 757/624-6886, web: www.outhamptonroadspride.com.

Queer Resources

AA, web: www.aavirginia.org.
AIDS Resource Center 757/446-6170, web: www.evms.edu/hivrsrc.

Tourist Info

AIRPORT DIRECTIONS

Norfolk International. To get to Civic Center, take a left on to Norview Ave. Take Norview Ave for about 4 miles and continue past Chesapeake Blvd. Once at Tidewater Dr, turn left and follow toward Civic Center.

PUBLIC TRANSIT & TAXIS

Checker Cab 757/855-3333, web: www.norfolkcheckertaxi.com.
Norfolk Airport Shuttle 757/857-5950, web: www.norfolkairportexpress.com.
Hampton Roads Transit 757/222-6100, web: www.hrtransit.org.

TOURIST SPOTS & INFO

Busch Gardens (in Williamsburg) 800/343-7946, web: www.buschgardens.com.
The Chrysler Museum of Art 757/664-6200, web: www.chrysler.org.
Douglas Macarthur Memorial 757/441-2965, web: www.macarthurmemorial.org.
The Ghent historic district.
Hermitage Foundation Museum 757/423-2052, web: www.hermitagefoundation.org.
Historic Williamsburg.
Norfolk Naval Base 757/322-2330, web: www.navstanorva.navy.mil.
St Paul's Episcopal Church 757/627-4353, web: www.saintpaulsnorfolk.org.
Waterside Festival Marketplace 757/627-3300, web: www.watersidemarketplace.com.
Visitor's Center: 757/664-6620 or 800/368-3097, web: www.norfolkcvb.com.

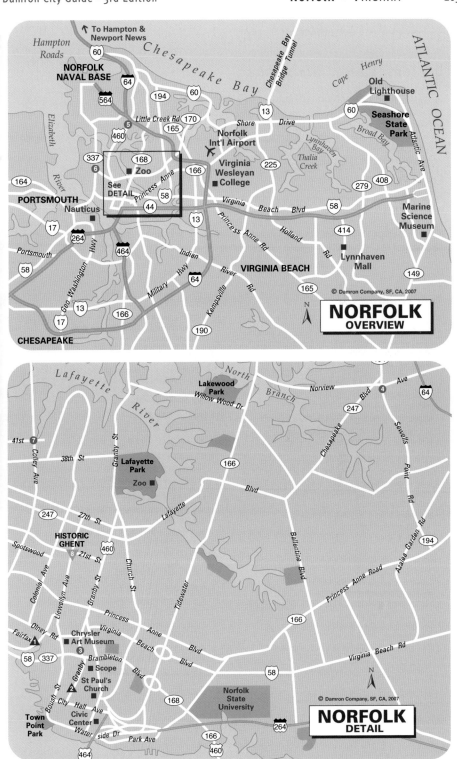

NORFOLK OVERVIEW

To Hampton & Newport News

Hampton Roads

Chesapeake Bay

60

NORFOLK NAVAL BASE

64

564

194

60

13

Chesapeake Bay Bridge Tunnel

Cape Henry

Old Lighthouse

60

Seashore State Park

ATLANTIC OCEAN

Little Creek Rd

5

170

165

Shore   Drive

Broad Bay

Atlantic Ave

460

337

6

168

Zoo

Norfolk Int'l Airport

Lynnhaven Bay

Thalia Creek

225

See DETAIL

166

Virginia Wesleyan College

279

408

Princess Anne

58

Virginia   Beach   Blvd

58

Marine Science Museum

44

414

13

Holland

Lynnhaven Mall

164

Elizabeth   River

PORTSMOUTH

Nauticus

17

264

464

Princess Anne Rd

Indian   River   Rd

Rd

149

Portsmouth

58

Geo Washington Hwy

Military   Hwy

64

VIRGINIA BEACH

165

13

166

17

Kempsville Rd

© Damron Company, SF, CA, 2007

CHESAPEAKE

190

N

NORFOLK OVERVIEW

NORFOLK DETAIL

Lafayette   River

North   Branch

Lakewood Park

Willow Wood Dr

Norview

Blvd

4

Ave

64

247

41st   7

Colley Ave

38th St

Granby St

Lafayette Park

Zoo

166

Blvd

Chesapeake   Blvd

Sewells   Point   Rd

247

27th St

HISTORIC GHENT

8   21st St

460

Church St

Lafayette

Ballentine   Blvd

194

Azalea Garden Rd

Spotswood

Colonial Ave

Llewellyn Ave

Granby St

Princess

Virginia

Anne

Tidewater

Princess Anne Road

166

Olney Rd

Fairfax   1

Chrysler Art Museum

3

Beach

Blvd

Blvd

Virginia Beach Rd

58   337

Brambleton

Scope

St Paul's Church

2

58

Bank St

Granby

City Hall Ave

Town Point Park

Civic Center

Water   side Dr

Park Ave

464

166

460

168

Norfolk State University

264

N

© Damron Company, SF, CA, 2007

NORFOLK DETAIL

SEATTLE

Day Trips: Mountains around the Emerald City

If you can tear yourself away from the lush Emerald City, you'll find even more natural beauty in the mountains surrounding Puget Sound. To the west is Olympic National Park, where you'll find snow-covered peaks, roaring surf, and a verdant rain forest. Be prepared: the Olympic peninsula has the highest annual rainfall in North America. Hikers and skiers will find year-round distraction in the Cascade Mountains. Mount St Helens National Volcanic Monument lies due south, and Route 2, northeast of the city, offers a breathtaking scenic drive over Stevens Pass. The crowning glory, of course, is majestic Mount Rainier. If you can't make it to the park for a hike, you can enjoy the postcard views from the city on a clear day.

Local Food:

Seattle's collective obsession with java gives a whole new meaning to "counter-culture." The original Starbucks (love 'em or hate 'em) is still going strong at Pike Place Market, but Seattle offers an endless array of cafes and coffeehouses for the more adventurous coffee drinker. Tame your caffeine buzz later with a dose of Seatte's other brew: rich, handcrafted beer. Redhook and Pyramid both hail from the Emerald City, and you'll find many breweries offering tours and free samples.

Tourist Info

AIRPORT DIRECTIONS

Seattle-Tacoma International (Sea-Tac). To get to the Capitol Hill District, take I-5 North and exit on Madison St. Take Madison St to Broadway. At Broadway, turn left.

PUBLIC TRANSIT & TAXIS

Farwest 206/622-1717.
Yellow Gray Top 206/282-8222.
Airport Shuttle Express 206/622-1424.
Metropolitan Transit 206/553-3000, web: www.metrokc.gov/tran.htm.

TOURIST SPOTS & INFO

Experience Music Project 206/367-5483, web: www.emplive.com.
Fremont, web: www.fremontseattle.com.
International District.
Museum of Flight 206/764-5720, web: www.museumofflight.org.
Pike Place Market.
Pioneer Square.
Seattle Art Museum 206/654-3100, web: www.seattleartmuseum.org.
Seattle Aquarium 206/386-4300, web: www.seattleaquarium.org.
Seattle Center Monorail 206/905-2620, web: www.seattlemonorail.com
Seattle Underground 206/682-4646, web: www.undergroundtour.com.
Space Needle 206/905-2100, web: www.space-needle.com.
Woodland Park Zoo 206/684-4800, web: www.zoo.org.
Visitor's Center: 206/461-5800, web: www.seattle.com.

Weather

Winter's average temperature is 50° while summer temperatures can climb up into the 90°s. Be prepared for rain at any time during the year.

Best Views

Top of the Space Needle, or from Admiral Way Park in West Seattle.

City Calendar

LGBT PRIDE

Last Sunday in June. 206/322-9561, web: www.seattlepride.org.

ENTERTAINMENT

Team Seattle 206/322-7769, web: www.teamseatle.org, a 35-team gay network.

ANNUAL EVENTS

September - Bumbershoot music & arts festival 206/281-7788, web: www.bumbershoot.org.
September - AIDS Walk 206/329-6923.
October - Seattle Gay & Lesbian Film Festival 206/323-4274, web: www.seattlequeerfilm.com.

Queer Resources

COMMUNITY INFO

Seattle LGBT Community Center 206/323-5428. 1115 E Pike St, web: www.SeattleLGBT.org.
Capitol Hill Alano Club 206/860-9560, web: www.capitolhillalanoclub.org. 1222 E Pine St 2nd fl, daily meetings.
Intergroup AA 206/587-2838.
HIV/STD hotline 206/205-7837.
Lifelong AIDS Alliance 206/328-8979, web: www.lifelongaidsalliance.org

WASHINGTON

Seattle

ACCOMMODATIONS

1 **11th Avenue Inn** [GF,NS,WI] 206/720-7161, 800/720-7161 ■ 121 11th Ave E ■ *full brkfst* ■ www.11thavenueinn.com

2 **The Ace Hotel** [GS,NS,WI,GO] 206/448-4721 ■ 2423 1st Ave (at Wall St) ■ *modern & stylish, some shared baths* ■ www.acehotel.com

3 **Alexis Hotel** [GF,WI,WC] 206/624-4844, 800/426-7033 ■ 1007 1st Ave (at Madison) ■ *luxury hotel w/ Aveda spa, kids/ pets ok* ■ www.alexishotel.com

Artist's Studio Loft B&B [GF,NS] 206/463-2583 ■ 16529 91st Ave SW, Vashon Island ■ *on 5 acres, garden, hot tub* ■ www.asl-bnb.com

4 **Bacon Mansion** [GS,NS,WI,WC] 206/329-1864, 800/240-1864 ■ 959 Broadway E (at E Prospect) ■ *Edwardian-style Tudor* ■ baconmansion.com

5 **Barclay Court East** [GS,NS,GO] 206/329-3914 ■ 1206 E Barclay Ct ■ *2 studios, private sunken garden patio* ■ www.barclaycourteast.com

6 **Bed & Breakfast on Broadway** [GF,NS,WI] 206/329-8933 ■ 722 Broadway Ave E (at Aloha) ■ *full brkfst* ■ www.bbonbroadway.com

7 **Chambered Nautilus B&B Inn** [GF,NS] 206/522-2536, 800/545-8459 ■ 5005 22nd Ave NE (at N 50th St) ■ *colonial home, full brkfst, sundecks* ■ www.chambered-nautilus.com

8 ➤**Gaslight Inn** [★GS,SW,NS,GO] 206/325-3654 ■ 1727 15th Ave (at E Howell St) ■ *B&B in Arts & Crafts home* ■ www.gaslight-inn.com

9 **Grand Hyatt Seattle** [GF,WI,WC] 206/774-1234 ■ 721 Pine St ■ *views of Puget Sound, Lake Union & the Olympic & Cascade Mtns* ■ grandseattle.hyatt.com

10 **Hill House B&B** [GF,NS] 206/323-4455, 866/417-4455 ■ 1113 E John St (at 12th Ave) ■ *full brkfst* ■ www.seattle-hillhouse.com

11 **Hotel Monaco** [GF,WI,WC] 206/621-1770, 800/945-2240 ■ 1101 4th Ave (at Spring St) ■ *gym, also Sazerac Cajun restaurant* ■ www.monaco-seattle.com

12 **Hotel Vintage Park** [GS,WI,WC] 206/624-8000, 800/853-3914 ■ 1100 5th Ave (at Spring) ■ *ultraluxe sleep in Seattle, also restaurant* ■ www.hotelvintagepark.com

13 **Inn at Queen Anne** [GS] 206/282-7357, 800/952-5043 ■ 505 1st Ave N (at Republican) ■ *kitchenettes* ■ www.innatqueenanne.com

14 **MarQueen Hotel** [GS] 206/282-7407, 888/445-3076 ■ 600 Queen Anne Ave N (btwn Roy & Mercer) ■ *in Theater District, kitchenettes* ■ www.marqueen.com

15 **Pioneer Square Hotel** [GF,NS,WI,WC] 206/340-1234, 800/800-5514 ■ 77 Yesler Wy (btwn 1st Ave & Alaskan Wy) ■ www.pioneersquare.com

16 **Salisbury House B&B** [GF,NS,WI] 206/328-8682 ■ 750 16th Ave E (at Aloha) ■ *full brkfst, jacuzzi, women-owned/ run* ■ www.salisburyhouse.com

Seahurst Garden Studio [WO,NS,WI,WC,GO] 206/551-7721 ■ 13713 16th Ave SW (at Ambaum Ave), Burien ■ *self-sufficient garden studio for 1 or 2 women, lesbian-owned* ■ www.seahurststudio.com

17 **Seattle Suites** [GS,NS,WI] 206/232-2799 ■ 1400 Hubbell Pl ■ *studio, 1 & 2-bdrm condos* ■ www.seattlesuite.com

11 **W Seattle** [GF,WI,WC] 206/264-6000, 877/WHOTELS (reservations only) ■ 1112 Fourth Ave ■ *also restaurant* ■ www.whotels.com/seattle

18 **Warwick Seattle Hotel** [GS,SW,WC] 206/443-4300 ■ 401 Lenora St (at 4th) ■ *full brkfst, jacuzzi* ■ res.seattle@warwickhotels.com

Wild Lily Ranch B&B [★GS,SW,NS,GO] 360/793-2103 ■ *cabins on Skykomish River, 1 hour from Seattle, cedar sauna* ■ www.wildlilyranch.com

BARS

19 **The Bad Juju Lounge** [GS,D,F,E] 206/709-9442, 206/709-9951 ■ 1425 10th Ave (at Pike) ■ *3pm-2am* ■ www.thebadjujulounge.com

20 **The Baltic Room** [GS,E] 206/625-4444 ■ 1207 Pine St (at Melrose) ■ *5pm-2am, 9pm-2am Sun, live music* ■ www.thebalticroom.com

21 **Beacon Pub** [GS,NH,K] 206/726-0238 ■ 3057 Beacon Ave S ■ *10am-close, from noon Sun*

22 **The Can Can** [GS,F,C] 206/652-0832 ■ 94 Pike St (in the Pike Place Market) ■ *4:30pm-2am, clsd Mon* ■ www.thecancan.com

23 **CC Attle's** [★M,NH,F,V,WC] 206/726-0565 ■ 1501 E Madison (at 15th Ave) ■ *noon-2am, patio, also Veranda Room & Men's Room*

24 **Changes** [M,NH,F,K,V,WC] 206/545-8363 ■ 2103 N 45th St (at Meridian) ■ *noon-2am* ■ www.changesinwallingford.com

25 **Chapel** [GS,D,F] 206/447-4180 ■ 1600 Melrose Ave (at E Pine) ■ *5pm-1am, till 2am Fri-Sat, upscale* ■ thechapelbar.com

26 **The Crescent Lounge** [GS,NH,K,WC] 206/720-8188 ■ 1413 E Olive Wy (at Bellevue) ■ *noon-2am, karaoke nightly*

27 **The Cuff** [★M,D,CW,B,WC] 206/323-1525 ■ 1533 13th Ave (at Pine) ■ *2pm-2am, after-hours wknds, T-dance Sun, levi crowd, patio* ■ www.cuffcomplex.com

28 **Double Header** [GS,NH] 206/464-9918 ■ 407 2nd Ave S Extension (at Washington) ■ *10am-midnight, till 2am Fri-Sat, "one of the oldest gay bars in the US"*

Gaslight Inn

Built in 1906, this grand Seattle landmark celebrated its centennial year in 2006 & 25th anniversary as a premier Seattle guesthouse. A stay at the Gaslight Inn will be the highlight of your Northwest visit.

This beautifully appointed Arts & Crafts inn boasts 8 comfortable and unique rooms. During the late spring, summer, and early fall, we encourage you to relax and unwind in our heated pool, on our numerous sundecks, or in our private garden.

1727 15th Ave, Seattle, WA 98122

www.gaslight-inn.com

PHONE **206/325-3654**

29 **Friends Martini Lounge** [MW] 206/324–5358 ■ 1509 Broadway (at Neighbours) ■ *8pm-close Th-Sat* ■ www.neighboursonline.com

30 **Hula Hula** [GF] 206/284–5003 ■ 106 1st Ave N (at Denny) ■ *4pm-close, tiki bar* ■ www.hulahula.org

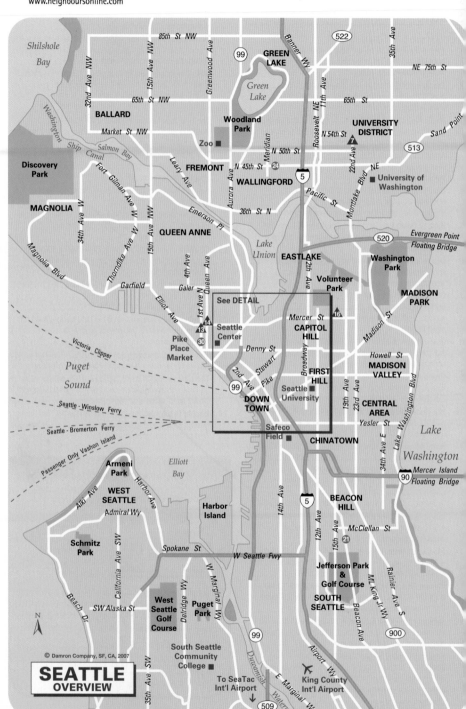

Shilshole Bay

85th St NW

GREEN LAKE

522

99

Green Lake

NE 75th St

35th Ave

BALLARD

65th St NW

Woodland Park

65th St

UNIVERSITY DISTRICT

Sand Point

Market St NW

Zoo

Meridian

N 54th St

7

513

Roosevelt NE

17th Ave

Discovery Park

Washington Ship Canal

Salmon Bay

FREMONT

N 45th St

N 50th St

24

University of Washington

32nd Ave NW

15th Ave NW

Greenwood Ave

Leary Ave

WALLINGFORD

5

Pacific St

Montlake Blvd NE

MAGNOLIA

Fort Gilman Ave W

Aurora Ave

36th St N

Emerson Pl

QUEEN ANNE

Lake Union

EASTLAKE

12th Ave

520

Evergreen Point Floating Bridge

Magnolia Blvd

34th Ave W

Thorndike Ave W

15th Ave W

Galer

4th Ave

Queen Ave

1st Ave

Volunteer Park

Washington Park

MADISON PARK

Garfield

Victoria Clipper

Elliot Ave

See DETAIL

13

14

Seattle Center

Mercer St

16

CAPITOL HILL

Madison St

Puget Sound

Pike Place Market

30

Denny St

Stewart

Pike

2nd Ave

Broadway

Howell St

MADISON VALLEY

Seattle - Winslow Ferry

99

DOWN TOWN

FIRST HILL

Seattle University

19th Ave

23rd Ave

CENTRAL AREA

Lake Washington Blvd

Seattle - Bremerton Ferry

Passenger Only Vashon Island

Elliott Bay

Safeco Field

Yesler St

CHINATOWN

34th Ave E

Lake Washington

Armeni Park

WEST SEATTLE

Harbor Ave

Harbor Island

14th Ave

5

BEACON HILL

90

Mercer Island Floating Bridge

Alki Ave

Admiral Wy

12th Ave

15th Ave

McClellan St

Schmitz Park

California Ave SW

Spokane St

W Seattle Fwy

21

Jefferson Park & Golf Course

ML King Jr Wy

Rainier Ave S

Beach Dr

SW Alaska St

West Seattle Golf Course

Delridge Wy

W Marginal Wy

Puget Park

SOUTH SEATTLE

Beacon Ave

900

35th Ave SW

South Seattle Community College

99

To SeaTac Int'l Airport

Duwamish

E Marginal Wy

Waterway

Airport Wy

King County Int'l Airport

N

© Damron Company, SF, CA, 2007

509

SEATTLE OVERVIEW

31 **Madison Pub** [★M,NH,F,WC] 206/325-6537 ■ 1315 E Madison St (at 13th) ■ *noon-2am* ■ www.madisonpub.com

32 **Manray** [M,F,K,DS,V] 206/568-0750 ■ 514 E Pine (at Belmont) ■ *4pm-2am* ■ www.manrayvideo.com

33 **Martin's Off Madison** [M,NH,F,P,WC] 206/325-7000 ■ 1413 14th Ave (at Madison) ■ *11am-2am, from 9am wknds* ■ www.martinsoffmadison.com

34 **R Place** [M,NH,D,F,K,S,V,WI] 206/322-8828 ■ 619 E Pine (at Boylston) ■ *4pm-2am, from 2pm wknds, 3 flrs, video sports bar* ■ www.rplaceseattle.com

35 **Rendezvous** [GF,C,E] 206/441-5823 ■ 2322 2nd Ave (at Battery) ■ *4pm-2am, live shows, also restaurant* ■ www.jewelboxtheater.com

36 **The Seattle Eagle** [M,L,WC] 206/621-7591 ■ 314 E Pike St (at Bellevue) ■ *2pm-2am, patio, rock 'n' roll, theme nights including Vibrator 9pm 3rd Tue [W]* ■ www.SeattleEagle.com

37 **Sonya's Bar & Grill** [M,NH,F] 206/441-7996 ■ 1919 1st Ave (btwn Virginia & Stewart) ■ *1:30pm-2am*

38 **Temple Billiards** [GF,F] 206/682-3242 ■ 126 S Jackson ■ *11am-2am, from 3pm wknds* ■ www.templebilliards.com

39 **Wildrose Bar & Restaurant** [W,NH,D,F,E,K,WC] 206/324-9210 ■ 1021 E Pike St (at 11th) ■ *3pm-2am, till 1am Sun & Mon* ■ www.thewildrosebar.com

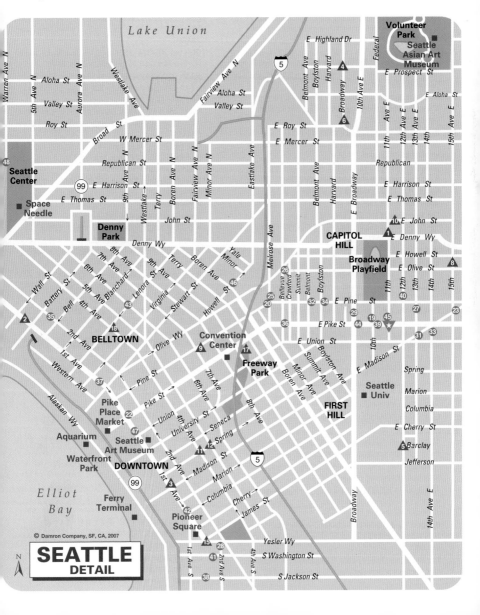

NIGHTCLUBS

40 **The Blacklight** [GS,D,A,DS] 206/388-0569 ■ 1621 12th Ave (at E Pine) ■ 10:30pm-2am Fri-Sun, fetish Fri ■ www.vogue-seattle.com

41 **Club Heaven** [GS,D,F,$] 206/622-1863 ■ 172 S Washington St (at 2nd) ■ 6pm-2am, call for events ■ www.theheavensnightclub.com

42 **Contour** [GF,D,F,E] 206/447-7704 ■ 807 1st Ave (at Columbia) ■ 11:30am-2am, till 4:30am Th, till 6am Fri, 2pm-6am Sat, till 2am Sun, 3pm-2am Mon, fire performances ■ www.clubcontour.com

43 **Dimitriou's Jazz Alley** [GF,F,E,NS,$] 206/441-9729 ■ 2033 6th Ave (at Lenora) ■ call for events & reservations ■ www.jazzalley.com

44 **Girl4Girl Productions** [W,D,E,S] 925 E Pike St (at Neumos) ■ 3rd Sat only, Seattle's largest all-women dance event ■ www.girl4girlseattle.com

29 **Neighbours Dance Club** [★MW,D,YC,WC] 206/324-5358 ■ 1509 Broadway (at Pike & Pine) ■ 9pm-2am, till 3am Th, till 4am Fri-Sat, 2 flrs, also [18+] room Th-Sat ■ www.neigh-boursnightclub.com

45 **Purr** [M,F] 206/325-3112 ■ 1518 11th Ave (at Pike St) ■ 3pm-2am, cocktail lounge, Mexican-inspired food ■ www.purrseattle.com

46 **Re-bar** [★GS,D,E,C] 206/233-9873 ■ 1114 Howell (at Boren Ave) ■ 6pm-2am, clsd Mon, DJ Th-Sun, more women Sat ■ www.rebarseattle.com

47 **Showbox** [GF,E,$] 206/628-3151 ■ 1426 1st Ave (at Pike) ■ live music venue ■ www.showboxonline.com

44 **Sugar** [M,D] 206/323-7428 ■ 916 E Pike St ■ www.sugarseattle.com

48 **The Vera Project** [GF] 206/956-8372 ■ corner of Warren Ave N & Republican St (in Seattle Center) ■ all-ages music venue ■ www.theveraproject.org

CAFES

The Allegro [WI] 206/633-3030 ■ 4214 University Wy NE (entrance on 15th) ■ 6am-10:30pm

Animals [WI] 206/726-9600 ■ 550 12th Ave ■ 6:30am-5pm, 8:30am-3:30pm Sat, clsd Sun

Cafe Besalu 206/789-1463 ■ 5909 24th Ave NW ■ 7am-3pm, clsd Mon-Tue, great pastries

Espresso Vivace 206/860-5869 ■ 901 E Denny Wy #100 ■ 6:30am-11pm ■ www.espressovivace.com

Fuel Coffee 206/329-4700 ■ 610 19th Ave E ■ 6am-9pm, pastries, internet access ■ www.fuelcoffeeseattle.com

Insomniax Coffee & Juice [WI] 206/322-6477 ■ 102 15th Ave E ■ 6:30am-6:30pm, 8:30am-6pm Sat, 9am-3pm Sun ■ www.insomniaxcoffee.com

Louisa's 206/325-0081 ■ 2379 Eastlake Ave E

RESTAURANTS

1200 Bistro & Lounge [★GO] 206/320-1200 ■ 1200 E Pike St (at 12th Ave) ■ dinner nightly, brunch Sun

Addis Cafe [★] 206/325-7805 ■ 1224 E Jefferson (at 13th) ■ lunch & dinner, Ethiopian

Al Boccalino 206/622-7688 ■ 1 Yesler Wy (at Alaskan) ■ lunch Tue-Fri, dinner nightly, classy southern Italian ■ alboccalino@aol.com

Bamboo Garden 206/282-6616 ■ 364 Roy St (at 3rd Ave N) ■ 11am-10pm, Chinese vegetarian ■ www.bamboogar-den.net

The Broadway Grill [★] 206/328-7000 ■ 314 Broadway E (at E Harrison) ■ 9am-2am, 8am-3am wknds, full bar

Cafe Flora [BW,NS,WC] 206/325-9100 ■ 2901 E Madison St ■ lunch, dinner, wknd brunch ■ www.cafeflora.com

Cafe Septieme [★MW] 206/860-8858 ■ 214 Broadway Ave E (at Thomas & John) ■ 9am-11pm, till midnight Fri-Sat, also bar

Campagne [R] 206/728-2800 ■ 86 Pine St (at 1st) ■ dinner only, French, also full bar, also Cafe Campagne 206/728-2233 ■ www.campagnerestaurant.com

Dahlia Lounge 206/682-4142 ■ 2001 4th Ave (at Virginia) ■ lunch Mon-Fri, dinner nightly, New American, full bar ■ tomdouglas.com

Dick's Drive In 206/302-1300 ■ 115 Broadway E (at Denny) ■ 10:30am-2am, excellent fries & shakes ■ www.ddir.com

Flying Fish 206/728-8595 ■ 2234 1st Ave (at Bell) ■ lunch Mon-Fri, dinner nightly, bar till 2am ■ www.flyingfishseat-tle.com

Glo's [★] 206/324-2577 ■ 1621 E Olive Wy (at Summit Ave E) ■ 7am-3pm, till 4pm wknds, brkfst only

Julia's [E] 206/860-1818 ■ 300 Broadway E (at Thomas) ■ 8am-11pm, till midnight Fri-Sat, full bar, [DS] Sat ■ www.eatatjulias.com

Kabul 206/545-9000 ■ 2301 N 45th St ■ 5pm-9:30pm, till 10pm Fri-Sat, Afghan, some veggie ■ www.kabulrestau-rant.com

Mae's Phinney Ridge Cafe [★WC] 206/782-1222 ■ 6412 Phinney Ridge N (at 65th) ■ 7am-3pm, brkfst menu, some veggie ■ www.maescafe.com

Mama's Mexican Kitchen 206/728-6262 ■ 2234 2nd Ave (in Belltown) ■ lunch & dinner, cheap & funky ■ www.mamas.com

Paseo 206/545-7440 ■ 4225 Fremont Ave N (at N 43rd St) ■ 11:30am-9pm, from noon Sun, clsd Mon, Cuban

Queen City Grill [★WC] 206/443-0975 ■ 2201 1st Ave (at Blanchard) ■ dinner only, fresh seafood, full bar ■ www.queencitygrill.com

Rosebud Restaurant & Bar [NS] 206/323-6636 ■ 719 E Pike St (at Harvard Ave) ■ dinner nightly, wknd brunch ■ rosebud-restaurant.com

Snappy Dragon 206/528-5575 ■ 8917 Roosevelt Wy NE ■ 11am-9:30pm, 4pm-9pm Sun, Chinese, plenty veggie ■ www.snappydragon.com

Sunlight Cafe [BW,WC] 206/522-9060 ■ 6403 Roosevelt Wy NE (at 64th) ■ 8am-9pm, vegetarian

Szmania's 206/284-7305 ■ 3321 W McGraw St (in Magnolia Bluff) ■ lunch Tue-Fri, dinner nightly, clsd Mon, full bar ■ szmanias.com

Teapot Vegetarian House 206/325-1010 ■ 345 15th Ave E ■ 11:30am-10pm, vegan ■ www.teapotvegetarianhouse.com

Thaiger Room 206/632-9299 ■ 4228 University Wy NE ■ 11am-10pm, from noon wknds

Wild Ginger Asian Restaurant & Triple Bar [★] 206/623-4450 ■ 1401 3rd Ave (at Union) ■ lunch Mon-Sat, dinner nightly, bar till 1am ■ www.wildginger.net

Wild Mountain 206/297-9453 ■ 1408 NW 85th St ■ 8:30am-9:30pm, clsd Tue ■ www.wildmtncafe.com

ENTERTAINMENT & RECREATION

Alki Beach Park 1702 Alki Ave SW, West Seattle ■ popular on warm days

43 **Century Ballroom** [MW,D,F] 206/324-7263 ■ 915 E Pine, 2nd flr ■ Outdancing 9:30pm 4th Fri, lessons at 8:30pm, also restaurant ■ www.centuryballroom.com

Garage [★F,21+] 206/322-2296 ■ 1130 Broadway ■ *3pm-2am, way-cool pool hall, full bar, also bowling alley* ■ www.garagebilliards.com

Gay Bingo 206/323-0069, 206/328-8979 ■ 860 Terry Ave N (at S Lake Union Naval Reserve Bldg) ■ *2nd Sat only, Oct-June* ■ www.llaa.org

Harvard Exit 206/781-5755 ■ 807 E Roy St (at Harvard) ■ *rep film theater* ■ www.landmarktheatres.com

Northwest Lesbian & Gay History Museum Project 206/903-9517 ■ *exhibits & publication* ■ www.lgbthistorynw.org

The Paramount Theatre [E] 206/467-5510 ■ 911 Pine St ■ *historic Beaux Arts-style theater, tours 10am 1st Sat* ■ www.theparamount.com

Rat City Roller Girls ■ *Seattle's female roller derby league, check web for upcoming events* ■ www.ratcityrollergirls.com

Richard Hugo House [C,WC] 206/322-7030 ■ 1634 11th Ave ■ *1pm-5pm, till 9pm Mon-Tue, clsd Sun; houses the Zine Archive & Publishing Project; open later for frequent workshops, readings & other events; also cafe* ■ www.hugohouse.org

Seattle Men's Chorus 206/323-0750 ■ *world's largest & most successful gay men's chorus* ■ www.seattlemenschorus.org

Seattle Storm 206/217-9622 ■ 305 Harrison St (Key Arena) ■ *check out the Women's National Basketball Association while you're in Seattle* ■ www.wnba.com/storm

Tacky Tourist Clubs 800/807-5214 ■ *fabulous social events* ■ www.ttca.org

BOOKSTORES

Bailey/ Coy Books [WC] 206/323-8842 ■ 414 Broadway Ave E (at Harrison) ■ *10am-10pm, till 8pm Sun*

Edge of the Circle 206/726-1999 ■ 701 E Pike (at Boylston) ■ *noon-9pm, alternative spirituality store* ■ www.edgeofthecircle.com

Elliott Bay Book Company 206/624-6600, 800/962-5311 ■ 101 S Main St ■ *9:30am-10pm, 11am-7pm Sun, in historic Globe building* ■ www.elliottbaybook.com

Fremont Place Book Company 206/547-5970 ■ 621 N 35th (at Fremont Ave N) ■ *10am-8pm, noon-6pm Sun* ■ www.fremontplacebooks.com

Left Bank Books 206/622-0195 ■ 92 Pike St (at 1st Ave) ■ *10am-7pm, 11am-6pm Sun, new & used books, LGBT section, worker-owned* ■ www.leftbankbooks.com

Twice Sold Tales 206/324-2421 ■ 905 E John (at Broadway E)

RETAIL SHOPS

Archie McPhee 206/297-0240 ■ 2428 NW Market St (in Ballard) ■ *10am-7pm, till 6pm Sun, weird & wonderful toys & trinkets* ■ www.mcphee.com

Broadway Market [★] 401 Broadway E (at Harrison & Republican) ■ *mall full of funky, hip stores*

Metropolis 206/782-7002 ■ 7220 Greenwood Ave N (at 73rd) ■ *10am-7pm, till 6pm Sat, noon-5pm Sun, cards & gifts*

PUBLICATIONS

Mary Magazine 323/874-8788 ■ *dish on Pacific Northwest's club scene* ■ www.odysseymagazine.net

SGN (Seattle Gay News) 206/324-4297 ■ *weekly LGBT newspaper* ■ www.sgn.org

The Stranger 206/323-7101 ■ *queer-positive alternative weekly* ■ www.thestranger.com

GYMS & HEALTH CLUBS

Gold's Gym [GF] 206/583-0640 ■ 825 Pike St (at Washington Sate Convention Center) ■ goldsgym.com/seattledowntownwa

Hothouse Spa & Sauna [WO] 206/568-3240 ■ 1019 E Pike St (at 11th, 2 blocks E of Broadway) ■ *noon-midnight, clsd Tue, baths, hot tub, massage* ■ www.hothousespa.com

MEN'S CLUBS

Basic Plumbing [PC] 206/323-2799 ■ 1505 10th Ave (btwn Pike & Pine) ■ *4pm-9am, 24hrs wknds; HIV testing 6pm-9pm Tue & Th* ■ www.bpseattle.com

Club Seattle [★WI,PC] 206/329-2334 ■ 1520 Summit Ave (btwn Pine & Pike) ■ *24hrs* ■ clubsea.com

➤ **Club Z** [PC] 206/622-9958 ■ 1117 Pike St (at Boren) ■ *4pm-9am, 24hrs wknds, discounts for out-of-towners* ■ www.thezclub.com

EROTICA

Babeland [WC,GO] 206/328-2914 ■ 707 E- Pike (btwn Harvard & Boylston) ■ 11am-10pm, noon-7pm Sun, lesbian-owned ■ www.babeland.com

Castle Superstore 206/621-7236 ■ 206 Broadway Ave E ■ www.castlemegastore.com

The Crypt Off Broadway 206/325-3882 ■ 1113 10th Ave E (at Denny)

Deja Vu Adult Superstore 206/624-1784 ■ 1510 1st Ave (at Pike) ■ 24hrs

Fantasy Unlimited 206/682-0167 ■ 2027 Westlake Ave (at 7th) ■ 24hrs

Hollywood Erotic Boutique 206/363-0056 ■ 12706 Lake City Wy NE ■ 24hrs, theater, toys, lingerie

Taboo Video 206/622-7399 ■ 1012 1st Ave ■ 24hrs ■ www.taboovideo.com

WISCONSIN

Milwaukee

ACCOMMODATIONS

1   Acanthus Inn B&B [GF,NS] 414/342-9788, 800/361-3698 ■ 3009 W Highland Blvd ■ in 1897 mansion, some shared baths ■ milwaukee-bed-and-breakfast.com

2   The Brumder Mansion [GF,NS,WI] 414/342-9767, 866/793-3676 ■ 3046 W Wisconsin Ave ■ B&B, fireplaces, some whirlpools, 3 dogs on premises ■ www.brumdermansion.com

3   Comfort Inn & Suites [GF,WI,WC] 414/276-8800, 800/328-7275 ■ 916 E State St (at Marshall) ■ also restaurant ■ www.parkeasthotel.com

1   Kilbourn Guesthouse [GS,NS,WI,GO] 414/344-3167 ■ 2825 W Kilbourn Ave (at N 28th St) ■ www.kilbournguesthouse.com

4   The Milwaukee Hilton [GF,F,SW] 414/271-7250, 800/445-8667 ■ 509 W Wisconsin Ave (at 5th St) ■ also indoor waterpark ■ www.hiltonmilwaukee.com

BARS

5   Art Bar [GS,E,GO] 414/372-7880 ■ 722 E Burleigh St (at Fratney) ■ 4pm-1am, till 2:30am Fri-Sat, boys' night Th, also gallery ■ www.artbar-riverwest.com

6   Ballgame [M,NH] 414/273-7474 ■ 196 S 2nd St (at Pittsburgh) ■ 2pm-2am, from 11am wknds

7   Boom/ The Room [MW,NH,F,V] 414/277-5040 ■ 625 S 2nd (at W Bruce) ■ 5pm-2am, from 11am Sun, patio, also martini bar ■ www.boommke.com

8   Boot Camp Saloon [M,NH,L] 414/643-6900 ■ 209 E National Ave (at Barclay) ■ 3pm-2am, from 9pm Sat ■ www.bootcampsaloon.com

9   City Lights Chill & Grill [MW,NH,F] 414/481-1441 ■ 111 W Howard Ave ■ 3pm-close, from noon wknds ■ www.citylightschillmilwaukee.com

10 Fluid [M,NH] 414/643-5843 ■ 819 S 2nd St (at W National) ■ 5pm-close, from 2pm wknds ■ fluid.gaymke.com

11 Harbor Room [M,L] 414/672-7988 ■ 117 E Greenfield Ave ■ 7am-2am, till 2:30am Fri-Sat ■ www.harbor-room.com

12 Kruz [M,L] 414/272-5789 ■ 354 E National Ave (at S Water St) ■ 3pm-close, patio, cruisy

13 M's [MW,TG,E] 414/383-8900 ■ 1101 S 2nd St (at W Washington St) ■ 4pm-close, from 11am Sat-Sun, clsd Mon

14 Milwaukee Pumphouse [GS,NH] 414/744-7008 ■ 2011 S 1st St ■ 10am-2am, till 2:30am Fri-Sat ■ www.milwaukee-pumphouse.com

15 The Nomad [GF,E] 414/224-8111 ■ 1403 E Brady St (at Warren) ■ 2pm-close, from noon wknds, soccer pub ■ www.nomadworldpub.com

16 Nut Hut [W,NH] 414/647-2673 ■ 1500 W Scott (at 15th St) ■ 2pm-2am, from noon Fri-Sun

17 Redroom Cocktail Lounge [GF,D,WC] 414/224-7666 ■ 1875 N Humboldt (at Kane) ■ 5pm-close, from 8pm wknds, also coffee bar, patio

18 Switch [MW,D,NH,K] 414/220-4340 ■ 124 W National Ave (at 1st) ■ 7pm-2am, from 5pm Fri, till 2:30am Fri-Sat, clsd Mon, [S] Fri, patio ■ www.switch.gaymke.com

19 Taylor's [GS,NH,WC,GO] 414/271-2855 ■ 795 N Jefferson St (at Wells) ■ 4pm-close, from 5pm wknds, patio ■ www.taylorsmilwaukee.com

20 The Tazzbah Bar & Grill [M,F] 414/672-8466 ■ 1712 W Pierce ■ 11am-2am, till 2:30am Fri-Sat, from 4pm Mon ■ www.tazzbah.com

21 This Is It [★M,OC] 414/278-9192 ■ 418 E Wells St (at Jefferson) ■ 3pm-2am, till 2:30am Fri-Sat

22 Triangle Bar [M,NH,WC] 414/383-9412 ■ 135 E National Ave (at Barclay) ■ noon-close, from 6am wknds ■ triangle.gaymke.com

10 Walker's Pint [W,NH,D,E,K,GO] 414/643-7468 ■ 818 S 2nd St (at National Ave) ■ 4:30pm-2am, till 2:30am Fri-Sat, till midnight Sun, lesbian-owned ■ www.walkerspintmilwaukee.com

23 Woody's [M,NH] 414/672-0806 ■ 1579 S 2nd St (at Lapham St) ■ 4pm-close, from 2pm wknds, sports bar ■ www.woodys-mke.com

NIGHTCLUBS

24 Cage [★M,D,S,V,YC,WC] 414/383-8330 ■ 801 S 2nd St (at National) ■ 10pm-close Wed-Sat, also martini bar 6pm-close nightly

25 Club Anything [GS,D,A,E] 414/383-5680 ■ 807 S 5th St (at National) ■ 9pm-close, from 7pm wknds, gothic/ industrial ■ www.geocities.com/clubanything

26 Mad Planet [GF,D,A,E] 414/263-4555 ■ 533 E Center St ■ retro dance Fri, live rock venue ■ www.mad-planet.net

27 MO'NA'S [MW,F,GO] 414/643-0377 ■ 1407 S 1st St (at Greenfield) ■ 4pm-close, from 6pm Sat-Mon, also restaurant, lesbian-owned ■ www.m-o-n-a-s.com

CAFES

Alterra Coffee Roasters 414/273-3753 ■ 2211 N Prospect Ave (at North) ■ 6:30am-10pm, till 11pm Fri, 7am-11pm Sat, 7am-10pm Sun ■ www.alterracoffee.com

Bella Caffe 414/273-5620 ■ 189 N Milwaukee St ■ 6:30am-9pm, till 11pm Fri-Sat, till 5pm Sun ■ www.bellacaffe.com

Fuel Cafe 414/374-3835 ■ 818 E Center St ■ 7am-10pm, till 11pm Fri-Sat, infamous for their strong coffee ■ www.fuelcafe.com

RESTAURANTS

Annona Bistro 414/744-2224 ■ 2643 S Kinnickinnic Ave ■ 11am-9pm, till 10pm Fri, 9am-10pm Sat, 9am-2pm Sun, Italian ■ www.annonabistro.com

Barossa [★BW,WC] 414/272-8466 ■ 235 S 2nd St (at Oregon) ■ dinner, Sun brunch, organic, plenty veggie ■ www.barossawinebar.com

Beans & Barley 414/278-7878 ■ 1901 E North Ave ■ *8am-9pm, vegetarian cafe & deli* ■ www.beansandbarley.com

Cafe Vecchio Mondo 414/273-5700 ■ 1137 N Old World 3rd St (at Juneau) ■ *dinner, Sun brunch, full bar* ■ www.cafevecchio.com

Chip & Py's [E] 262/241-9589 ■ 1340 W Towne Sq Rd, Mequon ■ *lunch Mon-Fri, dinner nightly, clsd Mon, American, live jazz Fri-Sat* ■ www.chipandpys.com

Coquette Cafe 414/291-2655 ■ 316 N Milwaukee St (btwn Buffalo & St Paul) ■ *11am-10pm, till 11pm Fri, 5pm-11pm Sat, clsd Sun, bistro fare* ■ www.coquettecafe.com

The Knick [★WC] 414/272-0011 ■ 1030 E Juneau Ave (at Waverly) ■ *11am-midnight, from 9am wknds, some veggie, full bar* ■ www.theknickrestaurant.com

La Perla 414/645-9888 ■ 734 S 5th St (at National) ■ *11am-10pm, till 11:30pm Fri-Sat, Mexican, also bar* ■ www.laperlahot.com

Range Line Inn [R] 262/242-0530 ■ 2635 W Mequon Rd, Mequon ■ *4:30pm-9:30pm, till 10:30pm Fri-Sat, clsd Sun-Mon, American*

Sanford Restaurant 414/276-9608 ■ 1547 N Jackson St ■ *dinner only, clsd Sun, Milwaukee fine dining Euro-style* ■ www.sanfordrestaurant.com

ENTERTAINMENT & RECREATION

Boerner Botanical Gardens 414/525-5600 ■ 9400 Boerner Dr (in Whitnall Park), Hales Corners ■ *8am-dusk, 40-acre garden & arboretum, garden clsd in winter* ■ www.boernerbotanicalgardens.org

Hotcakes Gallery 414/961-7714 ■ 3379 N Pierce St ■ *noon-5pm Fri-Sat only* ■ www.hotcakesgallery.com

Mitchell Park Domes 414/649-9800 ■ 524 S Layton Blvd (at 27th St & Pierce) ■ *9am-5pm, botanical gardens*

Rosebud Cinema & Drafthouse 414/607-9446 ■ 6823 W North Ave, Wauwatosa ■ *mainstream & art house films, food served, full bar* ■ www.rosebudcinemadrafthouse.com

Uncommon Theatre 800/595-4849 ■ 703 S 2nd St (Milwaukee Gay Arts Center) ■ *LGBT theater* ■ www.uncommontheatre.net

BOOKSTORES

28   <u>Broad Vocabulary</u> [★] 414/744-8384 ■ 2241 S Kinnickinnic Ave (at Lincoln) ■ *10am-8pm, 11am-5pm Sun, feminist, also gifts, magazines & more, also hosts readings, events, live music, workshops* ■ www.broadvocabulary.com

Harry W. Schwartz Bookshop 414/332-1181 ■ 2559 N Downer Ave ■ *9am-10pm, till 9pm Sun* ■ www.schwartzbooks.com

29 **OutWords Books, Gifts & Coffee** [WC] 414/963-9089 ■ 2710 N Murray Ave (at Park) ■ *11am-9pm, till 6pm Sun-Tue, LGBT, pride items, DVDs, CDs & more* ■ www.outwordsbooks.com

Peoples' Books 414/962-0575 ■ 2122 E Locust St (at Maryland) ■ *noon-6pm, clsd Sun*

Woodland Pattern 414/263-5001 ■ 720 E Locust St ■ www.woodlandpattern.org

RETAIL SHOPS

Adambomb Gallerie 414/276-2662 ■ 2028 N Martin Luther King Dr ■ *11am-8pm, from noon Sun, clsd Mon, tattoo studio* ■ adambombgallerie.com

Miss Groove [GO] 414/298-9185 ■ 1225 E Brady St (btwn Arlington & Franklin) ■ *11am-7pm, 10am-6pm Sat, noon-5pm Sun, accessories & gifts* ■ www.missgroove.com

Out of Solitude [GO] 414/223-3101 ■ 918 E Brady St (at Astor) ■ *11am-6pm, till 4pm Sat, clsd Sun, jewelry & gifts* ■ www.outofsolitude.com

Yellow Jacket 414/372-4744 ■ 1237 E Brady (at North Ave) ■ *noon-7pm, till 5pm Sun, vintage clothes* ■ www.yellowjacketvintageclothing.com

PUBLICATIONS

Queer Life News 414/383-8200 ■ *monthly LGBT newspaper* ■ www.queerlifenews.com

Quest 920/655-0611, 800/578-3785 ■ *good bar list* ■ www.quest-online.com

MEN'S CLUBS

Midtowne Spa—Milwaukee [PC,WC] 414/278-8989 ■ 315 S Water ■ *24hrs, sauna, whirlpool* ■ www.midtowne-spa.com/milwaukee/

EROTICA

Booked Solid 414/774-7210 ■ 7035 Greenfield Ave (at 70th), West Allis

MILWAUKEE

Day Trips: Kohler Design Center

Interior-design mavens should make a pilgrimage to the Kohler Design Center, in the town of Kohler, about an hour north on I-43. Take the factory tour, and leave time to linger in the Designer Showcase, where famous designers display inventive kitchen and bath ideas using Kohler fixtures. Afterward, bring your home-spa fantasy to life with some pampering at the Kohler Water Spa, located across the way in the American Club.

Local Food:

Don't leave the Dairy State without sampling the cheese. Milwaukee has plenty of farmers' markets during the warmer months, great places to pick up locally made cheeses and fresh produce. Wisconsin is part of the "fruit belt" that surrounds Lake Michigan, so summer and fall yield bushels of apples, pears, grapes, strawberries, and cherries. Check locally for a pick-your-own orchard.

Tourist Info

AIRPORT DIRECTIONS

General Mitchell Int'l. To get to many of the gay bars take I-49 North to the W National Ave exit. Head east on W National to either S 2nd or S 1st.

PUBLIC TRANSIT & TAXIS

Yellow Cab 414/271-1800.
Milwaukee Transit 414/344-6711, web: www.ridemcts.com.

TOURIST SPOTS & INFO

Annunciation Greek Orthodox Church 414/461-9400, web: www.annunciationwi.com.
Breweries.
Grand Avenue.
Milwaukee Art Museum, web: www.mam.org.
Mitchell Park Horticultural Conservatory, 414/649-9800.
Pabst Theatre 414/286-3663, web: www.pabsttheater.org.
Visitor's Center: 414/273-7222 or 800/231-0903, web: www.visitmilwaukee.org.

Weather

Summer temperatures can get up into 90°s. Spring and fall are pleasantly moderate but too short. Winter brings snow, cold temperatures, and even colder wind chills.

Best Views

Hyatt's revolving rooftop restaurant, Polaris 414/276-1234.

City Calendar

LGBT PRIDE

June. 414/272-3378, web: www.pridefest.com.

ANNUAL EVENTS

June-July - Summerfest, web: www.summerfest.com.
August - Wisconsin State Fair 414/266-7000, web: wistatefair.com
September - AIDS Walk 800/348-WALK, web: www.aidswalkwis.org.

Queer Resources

COMMUNITY INFO

Milwaukee LGBT Community Center 414/271-2656. 315 W Court St #101, 10am-10pm, from 6pm Sat, clsd Sun, web: www.mkelgbt.org.
Gay People's Union Hotline 414/645-0585.
AA Galano Club 414/276-6936. 315 W Court St #201, web: www.galanoclub.org.
Aids Resource Center of Wisconsin (ARCW) 414/273-1991, web: www.arcw.org.

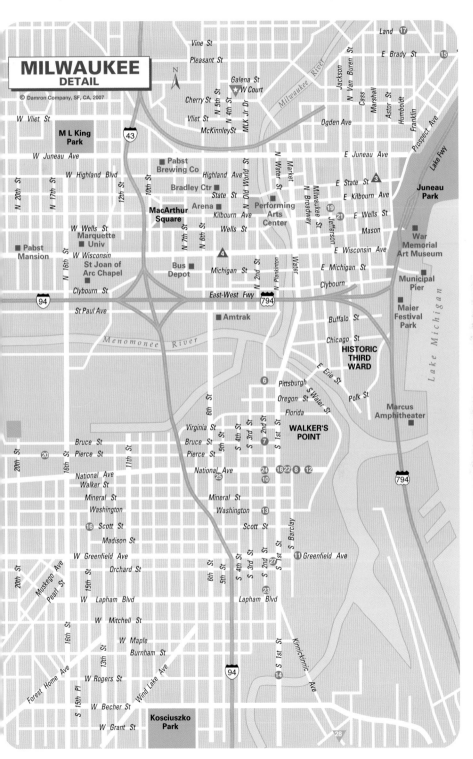

BRITISH COLUMBIA

Vancouver

ACCOMMODATIONS

1 **A Place at Penny's** [GF,NS,WC] 604/254-2229 ■ 810 Commercial Dr (at Venables) ■ *antique-decorated B&B, kitchens* ■ www.pennysplacevancouver.com

2 **Aberdeen Mansion** [GF] 604/254-2229 ■ 1110 Victoria Dr ■ *B&B* ■ www.aberdeenmansion.com

3 **Barclay House B&B** [GS,NS,GO] 604/605-1351, 800/971-1351 ■ 1351 Barclay St (at Jervis) ■ *restored Victorian, full brkfst* ■ www.barclayhouse.com

4 **The Buchan Hotel** [GF,NS] 604/685-5354, 800/668-6654 ■ 1906 Haro St (btwn Denman & Gilford) ■ *some shared baths* ■ www.buchanhotel.com

5 **Columbia Cottage B&B** [GF,NS] 604/874-7787 ■ 205 W 14th Ave (at Manitoba) ■ *1920s Tudor, full brkfst* ■ www.columbiacottage.com

6 **Comfort Inn Downtown** [GS,F] 604/605-4333, 888/605-5333 ■ 654 Nelson St (at Granville St) ■ *boutique-style hotel, also Doolin's Irish Pub & Restaurant* ■ www.comfortinndowntown.com

7 **Hawks Ave B&B** [WO,NS] 604/728-9441, 604/253-0989 ■ 734 Hawks Ave ■ *town house, near downtown* ■ louiseonhawks@604net.ca

8 **Hostelling International–Vancouver Central** [GF,WC] 604/685-5335, 888/203-8333 ■ 1025 Granville St ■ *hostel right on Granville St, kids ok, bar on-site* ■ www.hihostels.ca/vancouvercentral

9 **Hostelling International–Vancouver Downtown** [GS,WC] 604/684-4565, 888/203-4302 ■ 1114 Burnaby St ■ *hostel located in West End, kids ok, travel agent in lobby* ■ www.hihostels.ca/vancouverdowntown

10 **Inn Penzance** [GF,NS,WI,GO] 604/681-2889, 888/546-3327 ■ 1388 Terrace Ave (at Capilano Rd), North Vancouver ■ *cottage, suite, or room; gay weddings performed* ■ www.innpenzance.com

11 **The Langtry** [GS,NS,GO] 604/687-7892, 800/699-7892 ■ 968 Nicola St ■ *B&B apts in West End, full brkfst* ■ www.thelangtry.com

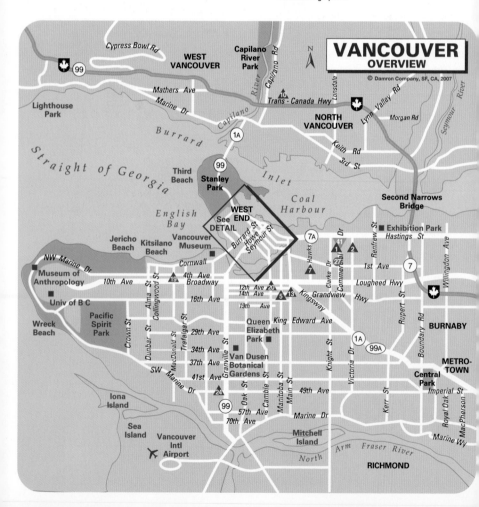

12➤ **The Listel Hotel** [GS,F,SW] 604/684-8461, 800/663-5491 ■ 1300 Robson St (at Jervis) ■ *boutique hotel, restaurant & bar, gym, hot tub* ■ www.thelistelhotel.com

13 **The Manor Guest House** [GF,NS,WI] 604/876-8494 ■ 345 W 13th Ave (at Cambie) ■ *full brkfst, hot tub, some shared baths* ■ www.manorguesthouse.com

14 **Moda Hotel** [GS] 604/683-4251, 877/683-5522 ■ 900 Seymour St (at Smithe) ■ *also 3 bars [M]* ■ www.modahotel.ca

VANCOUVER

Day Trips: Grouse Mountain Skyride

San Francisco may have a song about cable cars that climb halfway to the stars, but Vancouver easily beats that with the Grouse Mountain Skyride. It's a one-mile ride on North America's largest aerial tramway. When you reach the summit, you can see Vancouver, the Gulf Islands, and the endless Pacific far below. There's even The Observatory restaurant where you can savor the breathtaking view with a delicious meal. For more information, check out: www.grousemountain-skyride.cfm.

Tourist Info

AIRPORT DIRECTIONS

Vancouver International. To get to Gastown or the West End, take Hwy 99 north and exit at Seymour St.

PUBLIC TRANSIT & TAXIS

Yellow Cab 604/681-1111, web: www.yellowcabvancouver.ca.

Vancouver Airporter 604/946-8866, 800/668-3141, web: www.yvrairporter.com.

TransLink 604/953-3333, web: www.translink.bc.ca.

A Visitors' Map of all bus lines is available through the tourist office.

TOURIST SPOTS & INFO

Capilano Suspension Bridge, web: www.capbridge.com.
Chinatown.
Dr Sun Yat-Sen Chinese Garden 604/662-3207, web: vancouverchinesegarden.com
Gastown.
Granville Island, web: www.granvilleisland.com.
Grouse Mountain, web: www.grousemountain.com.
Museum of Anthropology 604/822-5087, web: www.moa.ubc.ca.
Science World 604/443-7443, web: www.scienceworld.bc.ca.
Stanley Park.
Vancouver Aquarium 604/659-3474, web: www.vanaqua.org.
Vancouver Lookout 604/689-0421, web: www.vancouverlookout.com.
Vancouver Museum 604/736-4431 web: www.vanmuseum.bc.ca.
Van Dusen Botanical Gardens 604/878-9274, web: www.vandusengarden.org.
Visitor's Center: 604/683-2000, web: www.tourismvancouver.com.

Weather

It's cold and wet in the winter (32-45°F), but it's absolutely gorgeous in the summer (52-75°F)!

Best Views

Biking in Stanley Park, or on a ferry between peninsulas and islands. Atop one of the surrounding mountains.

City Calendar

LGBT PRIDE

August. 604/687-0955, web: www.vanpride.bc.ca.

ENTERTAINMENT

Wreck Beach (great gay beach).

ANNUAL EVENTS

January-February - Gay & Lesbian Ski Week, web: www.gaywhistler.com.
May - Vancouver International Marathon 604/872-2928, web: www.adidasvanmarathon.ca.
June - Dragon Boat Festival 604/688-2382, web: www.adbf.com.
June-July - Vancouver Int'l Jazz Festival 604/872-5200, web: www.coastaljazz.ca.
July - Folk Music Festival 604/602-9798, web: www.thefestival.bc.ca.
August - Queer Film & Video Festival 604/844-1615, web: www.outonscreen.com
September/October - International Film Festival 604/685-0260, web: www.viff.org.

Queer Resources

COMMUNITY INFO

The Vancouver Gay/Lesbian Centre 604/684-5307. 1170 Bute St (between Davie & Pendrell), 9am-10pm, web: www.lgtbcentrevancouver.com.
The Greater Vancouver Pride Line 800/566-1170, 7pm-10pm.
AA 604/434-3933.
AIDS Vancouver 604/893-2222, web: www.aidsvancouver.org.couver Pride Line 800/566-1170, 7pm-10pm.

15 **Nelson House B&B** [MW,WI,GO] 604/684–9793, 866/684–9793 ■ 977 Broughton St (btwn Nelson & Barclay) ■ *Edwardian mansion, full brkfst* ■ www.downtownbandb.com

16 **"O Canada" House B&B** [GS,WI,GO] 604/688–0555, 877/688–1114 ■ 1114 Barclay St (at Thurlow) ■ *restored 1897 Victorian home, full brkfst* ■ www.ocanadahouse.com

17 **Opus Hotel** [GF,WC] 604/642–6787, 866/642–6787 ■ 322 Davie St (Yaletown) ■ *hip luxury boutique hotel, also bar & Elixer French brasserie* ■ www.opushotel.com

18 **Pacific Palisades Hotel** [GF,SW] 604/688–0461, 800/663–1815 ■ 1277 Robson St (at Jervis) ■ *suites, hot tub* ■ www.pacificpalisadeshotel.com

19 **Penny Farthing Inn** [GF,NS] 604/739–9002, 866/739–9002 ■ 2855 W 6th Ave (at MacDonald) ■ *1910 heritage house in Kitsilano, full brkfst* ■ www.pennyfarthinginn.com

20 **Plaza 500 Hotel** [GF] 604/873–1811, 800/473–1811 ■ 500 W 12th Ave (at Cambie St) ■ *full brkfst, gym, kids ok* ■ www.plaza500.com

River Run Cottages [GF,WC] 604/946–7778 ■ 4551 River Rd W, Ladner ■ *on the Fraser River, full brkfst* ■ www.riverruncottages.com

21 **Rosedale on Robson** [GF,SW,WI] 604/689–8033, 800/661–8870 ■ 838 Hamilton St (at Robson) ■ www.rosedaleonrobson.com

22 **Sandman Suites on Davie** [GS,SW,NS,WC] 604/681–7263, 800/726–3626 ■ 1160 Davie St (at Thurlow St) ■ *West End suites* ■ www.sandmansuites.com

23 Stay 'n Touch Guesthouse [WO,SW,GO] 604/681–2446 ■ 1060 Alberni St, Apt 408 (at Burrard St) ■ *apt, jacuzzi, lesbian-owned* ■ stayntouchwanda@direct.ca

24 **Treehouse B&B** [GF] 604/266–2962, 877/266–2960 ■ 2490 W 49th Ave (btwn Larch & Balsam) ■ *full brkfst, jacuzzi* ■ www.treehousebb.com

25 **The West End Guest House** [GS,NS,GO] 604/681–2889, 888/546–3327 ■ 1362 Haro St (at Broughton) ■ *1906 Victorian, full brkfst* ■ www.westendguesthouse.com

BARS

26 **1181** [M] 604/687–3991 ■ 1181 Davie St ■ *4pm-close, upscale cocktail lounge*

27 Avanti's Pub [GF,F] 604/254–5466 ■ 1601 Commercial Dr ■ *11am-midnight, till 1am Fri-Sat, sports bar, popular w/ local lesbian ball teams*

14 **The Duff** [MW,E,DS,S] 604/683–4251 ■ 900 Seymour St (at Moda Hotel) ■ *noon-2am, till midnight Sun, 3 bars (tavern, pub & lounge)* ■ www.the-duff.com

28 **The Fountainhead Pub** [MW,NH,TG] 604/687–2222 ■ 1025 Davie St ■ *11am-midnight, till 2am Fri-Sat, wknd brunch, patio* ■ www.thefountainheadpub.com

29 **Gerard Lounge** [GF,F] 604/682–5511 ■ 845 Burrard St (in Sutton Place Hotel) ■ *11:30am-1am, 4:30pm-midnight Sun, great martinis*

30 **Lotus Lounge/ Honey** [GS,D,F] 604/685–7777 (hotel #) ■ 455 Abbott St (at Pender, in The Lotus Hotel) ■ www.lotussoundlounge.com

31 **The Oasis** [M,NH,F,E,P] 604/685–1724 ■ 1240 Thurlow (at Davie) ■ *5pm-midnight, 3:30pm-1am Fri-Sat, martini bar, tapas* ■ www.oasisvancouver.com

32 **The PumpJack Pub** [M,NH,L,WC] 604/685–3417 ■ 1167 Davie St (off Bute) ■ *1pm-1am, till 2am Fri-Sat* ■ www.pumpjackpub.com

33 **Sugar Daddy's** [MW,F,V] 604/632–1646 ■ 1262 Davie St (at Jervis St) ■ *11am-11pm, till 1am Fri-Sat, from 10am wknds for brunch, patio* ■ emenus.ca/sugardaddys

NIGHTCLUBS

34 **816 Granville/ The World** [M,D] 816 Granville ■ *midnight-6am Fri-Sun* ■ www.816.ca

35 **Celebrities** [M,D] 604/681–6180 ■ 1022 Davie St (at Burrard St) ■ *theme nights* ■ www.celebritiesnightclub.com

36 **Club 23 West** [MW,D] 604/662–3277 ■ 23 W Cordova (at Carrall) ■ *10pm-4am Fri-Sat, call for events*

36 Drag King Vancouver [W,DS] 604/662–3277 ■ 23 W Cordova (at Club 23 West) ■ *from 9pm 4th Sat* ■ www.dragkingvancouver.com

Flygirl Productions [W,D] 604/839–9819 ■ *dance parties & events, check local listings for info* ■ www.flygirlproductions.com

30 Lick/ The Mix [W,D] 604/685–7777 (hotel #) ■ 455 Abbott St (at Pender, in The Lotus Hotel) ■ *theme nights, check calendar for schedule* ■ myspace.com/themixclub

37 **Numbers** [★M,D,K,V] 604/685–4077 ■ 1042 Davie (btwn Thurlow & Burrard) ■ *9pm-2am, till 4am Fri-Sat, 8pm-2am Sun* ■ www.numbers.ca

38 **The Odyssey** [★M,D,DS,S,YC] 604/689–5256 ■ 1251 Howe St (at Davie) ■ *9pm-2am, till 3am Fri-Sat, patio, theme nights* ■ www.theodysseynightclub.com

39 **Shine** [GF,D] 604/408–4321 ■ 364 Water St ■ www.shinenightclub.com

CAFES

Coffee A Go-Go [F] 604/687–2909 ■ 829 Davie St ■ *7am-9pm, 9am-6pm wknds, WiFi, local art* ■ members.shaw.ca/coffeeagogo

Coming Home [GO] 604/288–9850 ■ 753 6th St (at 8th Ave), New Westminster ■ *11am-8pm, till 5pm Sun & Tue, clsd Mon*

Delaney's 604/662–3344 ■ 1105 Denman St ■ *6am-11pm, from 6:30am wknds, coffee shop*

JJ Bean 604/254–3723 ■ 2206 Commercial Dr ■ *lesbian Meet & Greet 2nd Wed* ■ www.jjbeancoffee.com

Melriches Coffeehouse 604/689–5282 ■ 1244 Davie St ■ *6am-11pm, from 7am wknds*

Sweet Revenge [GO] 604/879–7933 ■ 4160 Main St (at 26th) ■ *7pm-midnight, till 1am Fri-Sat, 2pm-midnight Sun, patisserie* ■ www.sweet-revenge.ca

Turk's Coffee Exchange [MW] 604/255–5805 ■ 1276 Commercial Dr ■ *6:30am-11pm*

RESTAURANTS

Accents Restaurant [GO] 604/734–6660 ■ 1967 W Broadway (at Arbutus) ■ *lunch Tue-Fri, dinner Tue-Sun, clsd Mon, European/ int'l fine-dining* ■ www.accentsrestaurant.com

Bin 941 [★] 604/683–1246 ■ 941 Davie St ■ *5pm-2am, till midnight Sun, tiny tapas parlor; also 1521 W Broadway, 604/734–9421* ■ www.bin941.com

Brioche 604/682–4037 ■ 401 W Cordova (at Homer, in Gastown) ■ *7am-7pm, 9am-6pm wknds, Italian restaurant & bakery* ■ www.brioche.ca

Cafe Deux Soleils [MW,E] 604/254–1195 ■ 2096 Commercial Dr ■ *8am-midnight, till 5pm Sun, lots of veggie* ■ www.cafedeuxsoleils.com

Cafe Luxy [E,WC] 604/669–5899 ■ 1235 Davie St (btwn Bute & Jervis) ■ *11am-10:30pm, wknd brunch 9am-3pm, some veggie, full bar* ■ www.cafeluxy.com

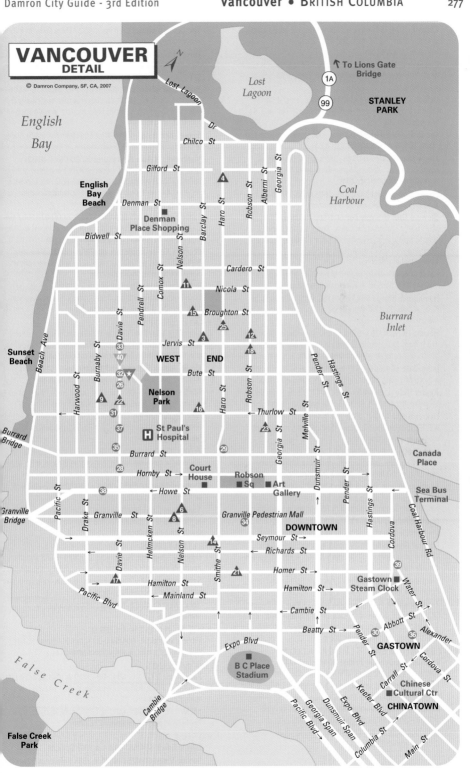

VANCOUVER DETAIL

© Damron Company, SF, CA, 2007

To Lions Gate Bridge
1A
99
STANLEY PARK

English Bay

Lost Lagoon
Lost Lagoon
Dr
Chilco St
Gilford St
Georgia St
Alberni St
Robson St
Haro St
Barclay St
Nelson St
Comox St
Pendrell St
Davie St
Burnaby St
Harwood St

Coal Harbour

Burrard Inlet

English Bay Beach
Denman St
Denman Place Shopping
Bidwell St

Cardero St
Nicola St
Broughton St
Jervis St
WEST END
Bute St
Haro St
Robson St
Thurlow St
Georgia St
Melville St
Pender St
Hastings St

Sunset Beach
Beach Ave

Nelson Park

St Paul's Hospital
H

Burrard St
Burrard Bridge
Hornby St →
Court House
Robson Sq
Art Gallery
Howe St ←
Granville Pedestrian Mall
DOWNTOWN
Dunsmuir St
Pender St
Hastings St
Cordova St
Coal Harbour Rd
Canada Place
Sea Bus Terminal

Granville Bridge
Pacific St
Drake St
Granville St
Helmcken St
Nelson St
Smithe St
Davie St
Granville
Seymour St →
Richards St
Homer St
Hamilton St →
Gastown Steam Clock
Gastown ■
39
Water St
Alexander St
Cordova St
GASTOWN
Abbott St
Carrall St
Pender St
30
36

Pacific Blvd
Hamilton St
Mainland St ←
Cambie St
Beatty St →
Expo Blvd
B C Place Stadium

Chinese Cultural Ctr ■
CHINATOWN
Keefer Blvd
Expo Blvd
Columbia St
Main St.

Cambie Bridge
Georgia Span
Dunsmuir Span
Pacific Blvd →

False Creek

False Creek Park

Granville Bridge

Markers: 4, 11, 15, 25, 3, 12, 18, 33, 40, 32★, 26, 22, 9, 31, 37, 35, 28, 38, 6, 8, 34, 14, 21, 17, 23, 29, 30, 36, 39

Chianti's 604/738-8411 ■ 1850 W 4th Ave (at Burrard) ■ *11am-10pm, till 11pm Fri-Sat, from 3pm Sun* ■ www.chianticafe.com

Cincin 604/688-7338 ■ 1154 Robson St (off Bute) ■ *lunch Mon-Fri, dinner nightly, Italian/ Mediterranean, full bar* ■ ww.cincin.net

Delilah's [WC] 604/687-3424 ■ 1789 Comox St (at Denman) ■ *5:30pm-11pm, prix-fixe menu, full bar* ■ www.delilahs.ca

The Dish [GO] 604/689-0208 ■ 1068 Davie St ■ *7am-10pm, 9am-9pm Sun, veggie fast food*

Elbow Room Cafe 604/685-3628 ■ 560 Davie St (at Seymour) ■ *8am-4pm, till 5pm wknds, great brkfst* ■ www.theelbowroomcafe.com

Foundation Lounge 604/708-0881 ■ 2301 Main St ■ *noon-1am, till 2am wknds, vegetarian*

Glowbal Grill & Satay Bar 604/602-0835 ■ 1079 Mainland St (Yaletown) ■ *lunch, dinner, brunch wknds, eclectic menu, martinis, extensive wine list; also check out Afterglow next door, nightly 6pm-late* ■ www.glowbalgrill.com

Habit 604/877-8582 ■ 2610 Main St (at 10th) ■ *5pm-1:30am, till 11pm Sun* ■ www.habitlounge.ca

Hamburger Mary's 604/687-1293 ■ 1202 Davie St (at Bute) ■ *8am-3am, till 4am Fri-Sat, till 2am Sun, some veggie, full bar*

Havana [★] 604/253-9119 ■ 1212 Commercial Dr ■ *11am-11pm, from 10am wknds, Cuban fusion, full bar, patio, also gallery & theater* ■ www.havana-art.com

India Gate 604/684-4617 ■ 616 Robson St (at Granville) ■ *lunch Mon-Sat, dinner nightly* ■ www.indiagatefood.com

Jupiter Cafe [E] 604/609-6665 ■ 1216 Bute St (at Davie St) ■ *live jazz Wed-Th, DJs Fri-Sat* ■ www.jupitercafe.com

Lickerish 604/696-0725 ■ 903 Davie St (at Hornby) ■ *5:30pm-midnight, till 1am Th-Sun, global cuisine, cocktail lounge* ■ www.lickerish.ca

Lolita's 604/696-9996 ■ 1326 Davie St (at Jervis) ■ *4:30pm till late, wknd brunch, innovative Mexican, tiny space but worth the wait* ■ www.lolitasrestaurant.com

Martini's Whole Wheat Pizza 604/873-0021 ■ 151 W Broadway (btwn Cambie & Main) ■ *11am-2am, from 2pm Sat, till 1am Sun, great pizza & full bar* ■ www.martinis.ca

Naam [E,WC] 604/738-7151 ■ 2724 W 4th St (at MacDonald) ■ *24hrs, vegetarian* ■ www.thenaam.com

Natural Garden 604/875-0233 ■ 3432 Cambie St (at 18th) ■ *noon-9pm Wed-Sun, macrobiotic* ■ naturalgarden-canada.com

Tanpopo Sushi 604/681-7777 ■ 1122 Denman (at Pendrell) ■ *excellent, affordable sushi*

Zin Restaurant & Lounge 604/408-1700 ■ 1277 Robson St (at Jervis St, in Pacific Palisades Hotel) ■ *7am-midnight, till 1am Fri-Sat, from 8am wknds, contemporary int'l, trendy crowd* ■ www.zin-restaurant.com

ENTERTAINMENT & RECREATION

Capilano Suspension Bridge 604/985-7474 ■ 3735 Capilano Rd, N Vancouver ■ www.capbridge.com

Cruisey T [MW,D,F,E,$] 604/551-2628 ■ *leaves from N foot of Denman St (at Harbor Cruises)* ■ *Sun (seasonal), 4-hour party cruise around Vancouver Harbour, tickets at Little Sister's, 1238 Davie St* ■ www.cruiseyt.com

Laff Riot Girls [$] 604/291-0291 ■ *stand-up comedienne group* ■ www.laffriotgirls.com

The Lesbian Show Co-op Radio 102.7 FM ■ *8pm-9pm Th* ■ www.coopradio.org

Queer FM 604/822-1242 ■ CITR 101.9 FM ■ *6pm-8pm Sun, political & social issues in queer community* ■ geocities.com/iwantmyqueerfm

Rockwood Adventures 604/980-7749, 888/236-6606 ■ 839 W 1st St #C, North Vancouver ■ *rain forest walks & city tours for all levels w/ free hotel pick-up* ■ www.rockwoodadventures.com

Sunset Beach right in the West End (near Burrard St Bridge) ■ *home of Vancouver AIDS memorial*

Vancouver Nature Adventures [$] 604/684-4922, 800/528-3531 ■ 1251 Cardero St #2005 ■ *orca-watching safari, guided kayaking day trip & beach BBQ, no experience required, free hotel pickup* ■ www.lotuslandtours.com

BOOKSTORES

40 **Little Sister's** [★WC] 604/669-1753, 800/567-1662 (in Canada only) ■ 1238 Davie St (btwn Bute & Jervis) ■ *10am-11pm, LGBT* ■ www.littlesistersbookstore.com

People's Co-op Bookstore 604/253-6442, 888/511-5556 ■ 1391 Commercial Dr ■ *LGBT section* ■ www.peoplescoopbookstore.com

Spartacus Books 604/688-6138 ■ 319 W Hastings (at Hamilton) ■ *10am-8:30pm, 11am-7pm Sat, noon-7pm Sun, LGBT section* ■ www.spartacusbooks.org

RETAIL SHOPS

Cupcakes 604/974-1300 ■ 1116 Denman St (at Pendrell) ■ *10am-9pm, till 10pm Fri-Sat, women-owned cupcake shop; also at 2887 W Broadway* ■ www.cupcakesonline.com

Liquid Amber Tattoo 604/738-3667 ■ 1252 Burrard St #100 (at Burnaby) ■ www.liquidambertattoo.com

Mintage 604/871-0022 ■ 1714 Commercial Dr ■ *vintage & future fashions* ■ www.mintagevintage.com

Next Body Piercing 604/684-6398 ■ 1068 Granville St (at Nelson) ■ *noon-6pm, 11am-7pm Fri-Sat, also tattooing* ■ www.nextbody.com

Priape 604/630-2330 ■ 1148 Davie St (btwn Bute & Thurlow) ■ *clubwear, leather, books, toys & more* ■ www.priape.com

State of Mind 604/682-7116 ■ 1100 Davie St (at Thurlow) ■ *10am-6pm, designer queer clothes*

TopDrawers [WC] 604/684-4861 ■ 1030 Denman St #115 ■ *10am-7pm, till 9pm Th-Sat, men's clothing & underwear* ■ www.topdrawers.com

PUBLICATIONS

Odyssey Magazine Northwest 323/874-8788 ■ *dish on Pacific Northwest's club scene* ■ www.odysseymagazine.net

Sapphic Sentinal ■ *queer women's- & trans-inclusive paper* ■ www.geocities.com/sapphicsentinal

Xtra! West 604/684-9696 ■ *LGBT newspaper* ■ www.xtra.ca

GYMS & HEALTH CLUBS

Fitness World [GF] 604/681-3232 ■ 1214 Howe St (at Davie) ■ *day passes* ■ www.fitnessworld.ca

MEN'S CLUBS

Fahrenheit 212° [PC] 604/689-9719 ■ 1048 Davie St (at Burrard) ■ *24hrs; also 430 Columbia St, 604/540-2117* ■ www.F212.com

M2M [L,PC] 604/684-6011 ■ 1210 Granville, downstairs (S of Davie) ■ *24hrs* ■ www.F212.com

EROTICA

Love's Touch 604/681-7024 ■ 1069 Davie St

Source Video 604/251-9191 ■ 2838 E Hastings St ■ *24hrs*

thelistelhotel.com

604 684.8461

1 800 663.5491

1300 Robson Street

Vancouver BC Canada

"Art is much less important than life,
but what a poor life without it."

Robert Motherwell

THE LISTEL HOTEL

Whether you're a cultural explorer
or a weekend wanderer, The Listel Hotel's
art-infused atmosphere and perfect
location on the city's most vibrant street
guarantees a memorable visit. High design,
original art, live jazz and exceptional food
and wine all complete the scene.

Tom's Video 604/433-1722 ■ 2887 Granview Hwy (at Renfew) ■ *24hrs*

41　**Womyn's Ware** [GO] 604/254-2543, 888/WYM-WARE (orders only) ■ 896 Commercial Dr (at Venables) ■ *11am-6pm, till 7pm Th-Fri, till 5:30pm Sun, toys for men too, lesbian-owned* ■ www.womynsware.com

ONTARIO

Toronto

ACCOMMODATIONS

1　**1871 Historic House B&B** [GF,NS] 416/923-6950 ■ 65 Huntley St (at Bloor) ■ *1871 historic house, full brkfst* ■ www.1871bnb.com

2　**213 Carlton Street—Toronto Townhouse** [GS,NS,WI,GO] 416/323-8898, 877/500-0466 ■ *upscale town house, full brkfst, some shared baths* ■ www.toronto-townhouse.com

3　**312 Seaton** [GF,NS,GO] 416/968-0775, 866/968-0775 ■ 312 Seaton ■ *B&B, also rental apt, dog on premises* ■ www.312seaton.com

4　**A Seaton Dream** [GS,NS,GO] 416/929-3363, 866/878-8898 ■ 243 Seaton St (at Sherbourne & Gerrard) ■ *B&B, full brkfst, garden patio* ■ www.aseatondream.ca

5　**Allenby B&B** [GF,NS] 416/461-7095 ■ 351 Wolverleigh (near Danforth & Woodbine) ■ *shared bath* ■ www.theallenby.ca

6　**Banting House Inn** [MW,NS,WI,GO] 416/924-1458, 800/823-8856 ■ 73 Homewood Ave (at Wellesley) ■ *Edwardian home, garden* ■ www.bantinghouse.com

7　**The Bearfoot Inn** [MO,B,N,WI] 416/922-1658, 888/871-2327 ■ 30-A Dundonald St ■ www.bearfootinn.com

8　**Bent Inn** [M,L,WI,GO] 416/925-4499 ■ 107 Gloucester St ■ *B&B w/ well-equipped cellar dungeon* ■ www.bentinn.com

9　**Bonnevue Manor B&B** [GS,NS,WI] 416/536-1455 ■ 33 Beaty Ave (at Queen St & Roncesvalles) ■ *B&B, full brkfst, kids ok* ■ bonne@interlog.com

10　**Cawthra Square Bed & Breakfast Inns** [MW,NS,GO] 416/966-3074, 800/259-5474 ■ *multiple Heritage homes, some shared baths, meeting rooms, spa* ■ www.sleepwithfriends.com

11　**Drake Hotel** [GF,NS] 416/531-5042, 866/372-5386 ■ 1150 Queen St W ■ *boutique hotel* ■ www.thedrakehotel.ca

12　**Dundonald House** [M,NS,GO] 416/961-9888, 800/260-7227 ■ 35 Dundonald St (at Church) ■ *full brkfst, hot tub, sauna, gym, bicycles, shared baths* ■ www.dundonaldhouse.com

13　**The Gladstone Hotel** [GS,NS] 416/531-4635 ■ 1214 Queen St W ■ *artistic, also Melody bar* ■ www.gladstonehotel.com

14　**The Grange Hotel** [GF] 416/603-7700, 888/232-0002 ■ 165 Grange Ave (at Queen) ■ *kitchenettes* ■ www.grangehotel.com

15　**Hotel Victoria** [GF,WC] 416/363-1666, 800/363-8228 ■ 56 Yonge St ■ www.hotelvictoria-toronto.com

16　**House on McGill** [GS,NS,GO] 416/351-1503, 877/580-5015 ■ 110 McGill St (at Church & Carlton) ■ *Victorian town house, shared baths, garden w/ deck, cat on premises* ■ www.mcgillbb.ca

17　**Pimblett's Rest B&B** [GS,NS,GO] 416/929-9525, 416/921-6896 ■ 242 Gerrard St E ■ *Victorian, full brkfst, hot tub, theme rooms* ■ pimblett.ca

Toronto B&B Reservation Service [GF,NS] 705/738-9449, 877/922-6522 ■ *reservation service* ■ torontobandb.com

18　**Toronto Downtown Bed & Breakfast**® [GS,NS,GO] 416/921-3533, 877/950-6200 ■ 57 Chicora Ave ■ *luxurious, full brkfst* ■ www.tdbab.com

50　**Two Aberdeen B&B** [MW,NS] 416/944-1426 ■ 2 Aberdeen Ave ■ *circa 1883 Victorian in historic Cabbagetown, full brkfst* ■ www.twoaberdeen.com

19　**Victoria's Mansion Guest House** [GF,NS,WI] 416/921-4625 ■ 68 Gloucester St ■ *converted mansion* ■ www.victoriasmansion.com

BARS

20　**Alibi** [★M,NH,D] 416/964-9869 ■ 529 Yonge St (at Maitland) ■ *3pm-close, [CW] Tue, underwear party Sun, 2 floors, 3 bars, "cruise maze," patio* ■ www.alibitoronto.com

21　**Andy Poolhall** [GS] 416/923-5300 ■ 489 College St (at Markham) ■ *6pm-2am, from 7pm Tue-Fri, clsd Sun, Pop Art pool hall* ■ andypoolhall.com

22　**Beaver Cafe** [MW,D,F,GO] 416/537-2768 ■ 1192 Queen St W ■ *10am-2am, patio*

23　**The Black Eagle** [M,B,L,F] 416/413-1219 ■ 457 Church St (btwn Maitland & Alexander) ■ *2pm-2am, 3 bars, theme nights, heated rooftop patio* ■ www.blackeagletoronto.com

24　**The Cameron House** [GS,E] 416/703-0811 ■ 408 Queen St ■ *4pm-close, also theater* ■ www.thecameron.com

25　**The Cellblock/ Yard** [M,D,DS] 416/921-0066 ■ 72 Carlton St (behind Zipperz) ■ *10pm-2am, from 9pm Sun, clsd Mon-Tue* ■ www.zipperz-cellblock.ca

26　**The Churchmouse & Firkin** [MW,NH] 416/927-1735 ■ 475 Church St (at Maitland) ■ *11am-2am, English pub, leather brunch 3rd Sun* ■ churchmouse.firkinpubs.com

21　**Ciao Edie** [GS,F,E] 416/927-7774 ■ 489 College St (at Markham) ■ *8pm-2am, clsd Mon-Tue, Here Kitty Kitty women's night 9pm Sun, cocktail lounge w/ DJ, live music* ■ www.ciaoedie.com

27　**Crews/ Tango** [M,NH,D,K,DS] 416/972-1662 ■ 508 Church ■ *4pm-2am, deck overlooking Church St, also Tango [W] from 10:30pm Th-Sat, popular Sat* ■ www.crews-tango.com

21　**George's Play** [M,MR-L] 416/963-8251 ■ 504 Church St (at Alexander) ■ *11am-2am, bingo nightly* ■ www.playonchurch.com

28　**The Hair of the Dog** [MW,NH,F] 416/964-2708 ■ 425 Church St (at Wood) ■ *10am-2am, pub & restaurant, patio*

29　**The House on Parliament Pub** [GS,NH,F] 416/925-4074 ■ 456 Parliament St ■ *11:30am-2am, patio*

30　**Lo'la** [M,D] 416/920-0946 ■ 7 Maitland (at Yonge) ■ *7pm-2am, clsd Sun-Tue, martini lounge* ■ www.lolamartinis.com

13　**Melody Bar** [GS,E,K] 416/531-4635 ■ 1214 Queen St W (at Gladstone Hotel) ■ *more gay Wed for Hump Day Bump* ■ www.gladstonehotel.com

21　**Midtown** [GF,NH,F] 416/920-4533 ■ 552 College St (W of Euclid) ■ *5pm-2am, from 3pm Fri-Sun, pool bar, tapas served*

27　**O'Grady's** [GS] 416/323-2822 ■ 518 Church St (at Maitland) ■ *11am-2am, till 3am Fri-Sat, casual dining, huge patio, also lounge upstairs, [B] Fri*

31　**Pegasus on Church** [MW,NH] 416/927-8832 ■ 489-B Church St (at Wellesley, upstairs) ■ *11am-2am* ■ www.pegasusonchurch.com

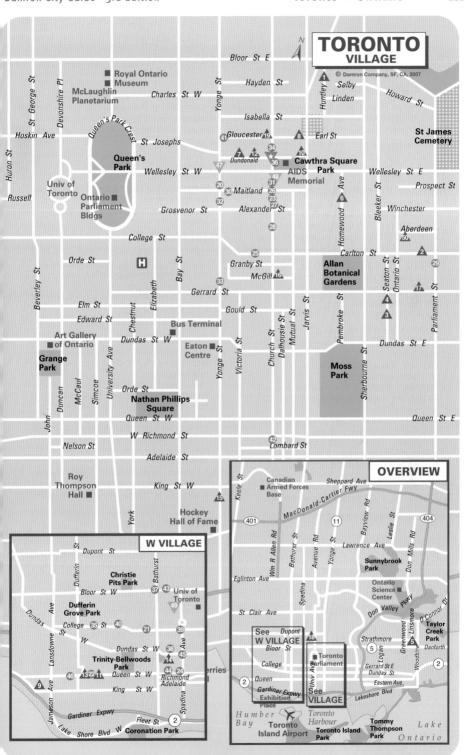

TORONTO VILLAGE

© Damron Company, SF, CA, 2007

Bloor St E

Royal Ontario Museum
McLaughlin Planetarium
Charles St W
Hayden St
Selby
Linden
Howard St
St George St
Devonshire Pl
Yonge St
Huntley St

Isabella St

Hoskin Ave
Queen's Park Crest
St Josephs
Gloucester 19
Earl St
St James Cemetery

Huron St
Queen's Park
7 12
Dundonald
34
36
10
Cawthra Square Park

Univ of Toronto
Wellesley St W
47
48
AIDS Memorial
Wellesley St E
St

Russell
Ontario Parliament Bldgs
20
30 Maitland
31
25
23
27
6
Prospect St
Bleeker St
Winchester St

Grosvenor St
32
Alexander St
Homewood Ave
Aberdeen

College St
28
Carlton St
50 2

Orde St
H
25
Granby St
McGill 16
Allan Botanical Gardens
Carlton St
Seaton St
Ontario St
29

Beverley St
Bay St
33
Gerrard St
17

Elm St
Chestnut
Elizabeth
Gould St
Pembroke St
4
3
Parliament St

Edward St

Art Gallery of Ontario
Dundas St W
Bus Terminal
Eaton Centre
Victoria St
Church St
Dalhousie St
Mutual St
Jarvis St
Dundas St E

Grange Park
Orde St
Yonge St
Moss Park
Sherbourne St

Duncan
McCaul
Simcoe
University Ave
Nathan Phillips Square
Queen St W
Queen St E

John
W Richmond St

Nelson St
Adelaide St
Lombard St 42

Roy Thompson Hall
King St W
York
15
Hockey Hall of Fame
Keele St
OVERVIEW

Canadian Armed Forces Base
Sheppard Ave
MacDonald-Cartier Fwy
401
11
Bayview Rd
Leslie St
404

Wm R Allen Rd
Bathurst St
Avenue Rd
Yonge St
Lawrence Ave

Sunnybrook Park
Don Mills Rd

W VILLAGE

Dupont St
St
Christie Pits Park
37 43
Univ of Toronto
49
Eglinton Ave
St Clair Ave
Spadina
Ontario Science Center
Don Valley Pkwy
O'Connor Dr
Taylor Creek Park
Danforth

Dufferin
Bathurst
Bloor St W
Dufferin Grove Park

Dundas Ave
College 35 St 40
21
39
See Dupont
W VILLAGE
Bloor St
18
Strathmore
5
Logan
Greenwood
Woodbine
Linsmore
2

Lansdowne
Dundas St W
38
14
45
Trinity-Bellwoods Park
44 22
Queen St W
Richmond
Adelaide
College
Toronto Parliament
Gerrard St E
Dundas St
Eastern Ave

Jameson Ave
9
46
13 22 11
King St W
erries
Queen
Univ Ave
See VILLAGE
Lakeshore Blvd

Gardiner Expwy
Lake Shore Blvd
Fleet St
2
Coronation Park
Humber Bay
Toronto Island Airport
Gardiner Expwy
Exhibition Place
2
Toronto Harbour
Toronto Island Park
Tommy Thompson Park
Lake Ontario

TORONTO

Day Trips: Niagara Falls

Just over an hour out of town, you simply can't pass up a visit to the falls! As if the amazingly beautiful waterfalls weren't enough, the area is also full of other wonderful sites and activities, including a butterfly conservatory, botanical gardens, heritage sites, a casino, wineries, and much more. For more info, please visit www.niagaraparks.com.

Tourist Info

AIRPORT DIRECTIONS

Lester B Pearson International. To get to many of the gay bars, take 427 South to Queen Elizabeth Way (QEW) East. QEW becomes Gardiner Expressway. From Gardiner, exit on York St or Bay St.

PUBLIC TRANSIT & TAXIS

Co-op Taxi 416/504-2667.
Grey Coach 416/393-7911.
TTC 416/393-4636, web: www.city.toronto.on.ca/ttc.

TOURIST SPOTS & INFO

Art Gallery of Ontario 416/979-6648, web: www.ago.net.
Bata Shoe Museum 416/979-7799, web: www.batashoemuseum.ca.
CN Tower 416/868-6937, web: www.cntower.ca.
Dr Flea's International Flea Market 416/745-3532, web: www.drfleas.com.
Gardiner Museum of Ceramic Art, 416/586-8080, web: www.gardinermuseum.on.ca.
Harbourfront Centre 416/973-4000, web: www.harbourfront.on.ca.
Hockey Hall of Fame 416/360-7765, web: www.hhof.com.
Kensington Market.
Ontario Place 416/314-9900, web: www.ontarioplace.com.
Rogers Centre 416/341-1707, web: www.rogerscentre.com.
Royal Ontario Museum 416/586-8000, web: www.rom.on.ca.
Underground City.
Visitor's Center: 800/499-2514, web: www.torontotourism.com.

Weather

Summers are hot (upper 80°s–90°s) and humid. Spring is gorgeous. Fall brings cool, crisp days. Winters are cold and snowy, just as you'd imagined they would be in Canada!

Best Views

The top of one of the world's tallest buildings, of course: the CN Tower. Or try a sight-seeing air tour or a three-masted sailing ship tour.

City Calendar

LGBT PRIDE

June. 416/927-7433, web: www.pridetoronto.com.

ANNUAL EVENTS

April - International Gay & Lesbian Comedy and Music Festival 416/907-9099, web: www.werefunnythatway.com.
May - Inside Out: Lesbian & Gay Film and Video Festival 416/977-6847, web: insideout.on.ca.
June - Downtown Jazz Festival 416/928-2033, web: www.tojazz.com.
International Dragon Boat Race Festival 416/595-1739, web: www.dragonboats.com.
July - Folsom Fair North, web: www.folsomfairnorth.com.
September - International Film Festival 416/968-3456, web: www.e.bell.ca/filmfest.
November - Mr Leatherman Toronto Competition, web: www.mrlt.com.

Queer Resources

COMMUNITY INFO

Community Centre 416/392-6874. 519 Church St (on Cawthra Park), 9am-10pm, till 5pm wknds, web: www.the519.org.
Xtra! Gay/Lesbian Info Line 416/925-9872 (touchtone info).
AA Gay/Lesbian 416/487-5591, web: www.aatoronto.org.
AIDS Action Now 416/340-2437, web: www.actoronto.org.
Hassle Free Clinic 416/922-0566 (women's), 416/922-0603 (men's), web: www.hasslefreeclinic.org.

32 Pinocchio [M,NH,TG,DS,S] 416/961-5808 ■ 502-A Yonge St (at Alexander) ■ *11am-2am, cruisy* ■ www.pinocchiobar.com

23 Queer Indian Mela [MW,D,MR] 416/648-8310 ■ 518 Church St (at O'Grady's) ■ *3rd Sat, South Asian party* ■ www.queerindianmela.com

33 Remington's Men of Steel [MO,S,WC,GO] 416/977-2160 ■ 379 Yonge St (at Gerrard) ■ *5pm-2am, strip bar, women welcome Fri & Sun only* ■ www.remingtons.com

34 Slack's Restaurant & Bar [★W,NH,D,F,V] 416/928-2151 ■ 562 Church St (at Wellesley) ■ *4pm-midnight, till 2am Wed-Sat, also restaurant, upscale pub fare, brunch wknds, lesbian-owned* ■ www.slacks.ca

35 Smiling Buddha [GS,F,K,C,YC] 416/516-2531 ■ 961 College St ■ *4pm-2am* ■ www.smilingbuddhabar.com

26 Statlers [M,E,P,OC] 416/925-0341 ■ 471 Church St (at Maitland) ■ *2pm-2am* ■ www.statlers.ca

36 Voglie [MW,D,F] 416/929-9108 ■ 582 Church St ■ *11am-close, from 2pm Fri-Sat, clsd Mon, martini bar, also restaurant, patio* ■ www.voglieristobar.com

26 Woody's/ Sailor [★M,NH,E,DS,V,18+,WC] 416/972-0887 ■ 465-467 Church (at Maitland) ■ *1pm-2am, Bad Boy's Night Out Tue, Best Chest Contest Th, cruisy* ■ www.woodystoronto.com

25 Zipperz [M,P] 416/921-0066 ■ 72 Carlton St (at Church) ■ *noon-2am, patio* ■ www.zipperz-cellblock.ca

NIGHTCLUBS

37 The Annex Wreck Room [GS,D,A,E] 416/536-0346 ■ 794 Bathurst St ■ *10pm-close Fri-Sat only, alternative music venue* ■ www.theannexwreckroom.com

AsianXpress (AX) [M,D,MR-A] 416/318-8950 ■ *last Sat, call or check web for more info* ■ www.aznxp.com

38 The Boat [GS,D] 416/593-9218 ■ 158 Augusta ■ *9pm-2am, priate theme*

39 The Comfort Zone [GS,D] 416/763-9139 ■ 480 Spadina Ave (N of College) ■ *after-hours Th-Sun only* ■ comfortzoneto.com

40 El Convento Rico [★GS,D,MR-L,TG,DS] 416/588-7800 ■ 750 College St (at Crawford) ■ *9pm-4am, 7pm-3am Sun, clsd Mon-Th, [DS] Fri-Sat* ■ www.elconventorico.com

41 Fly Nightclub [★M,D,$] 416/410-5426, 416/925-6222 ■ 8 Gloucester St (2 streets N of Yonge & Wellesley) ■ *10pm-5am, clsd Mon-Wed, circuit crowd (you may recognize this club as Babylon from the 1st season of Queer As Folk!)* ■ www.flynightclub.com

Girl Toronto [W,D,MR] 416/593-0311, 416/915-9493 ■ *sexy women's dance parties & events* ■ girltoronto.com

42 Goodhandy's [M,TG,S] 416/760-6556, 416/760-6514 ■ 120 Church St, 2nd flr (at Richmond) ■ *9pm-close, clsd Sun-Tue, [M] Wed, transwomen Th, transmen Fri, pansexual Sat* ■ www.goodhandys.com

43 Lee's Palace/ Dance Cave [GS,D,E] 416/532-1598 ■ 529 Bloor St ■ *live bands, dance club upstairs* ■ www.leespalace.com

44 Savage Garden [GF] 416/504-2178 ■ 550 Queen St W (at Bathurst) ■ *Fri-Sat only, gothic/ industrial cyber punk bar* ■ www.savagegarden.ca

21 Savour [W,D] 416/923-5300 (club#) ■ 489 College St (at Markham, at Andy Poolhall) ■ *10pm 4th Sat only, monthly women's dance party* ■ www.denisebenson.com

45 Sonic [GF,D] 416/599-5550 ■ 270 Spadina Ave (at Dundas) ■ *more gay wknds* ■ www.sonicnightclub.com

46 Stones Place [GS,D,E] 416/536-4242 ■ 1255 Queen St W ■ *9pm-2am, Rolling Stones-themed bar, more gay 1st Sat for Big Primpin (gay hip-hop night)* ■ www.stonesplace.ca

CAFES

Alternative Grounds 416/534-5543 ■ 333 Roncesvalles Ave ■ *7am-7pm, till 8pm Fri-Sat, from 8am wknds* ■ www.alternativegrounds.com

Cafe Diplomatico [★] 416/534-4637 ■ 594 College (at Clinton, in Little Italy) ■ *9am-midnight, patio*

Croissant Tree 416/925-8379 ■ 625 Church St ■ *7am-8pm, 8am-6pm wknds*

JetFuel 416/968-9982 ■ 519 Parliament St ■ *7am-8pm* ■ www.jetfuelcoffee.com

RESTAURANTS

Allen's Restaurant [E] 416/463-3086 ■ 143 Danforth Ave (at Broadview) ■ *lunch & dinner, great scotch selection, patio* ■ www.allens.to

Big Mammas Boy 416/927-1593, 416/927-7777 ■ 554 Parliament St ■ *4:30pm-1am, 11am-midnight Sun, pizza* ■ www.bigmammasboy.ca

Bistro 422 416/963-9416 ■ 422 College St ■ *4pm-2am, full bar*

Byzantium [M,GO] 416/922-3859 ■ 499 Church St (S of Wellesley) ■ *5:30pm-11pm, Sun brunch 11am-3pm, chic, cont'l/ global, also martini bar till 2am, patio* ■ www.byz.ca

Cafe 668 416/703-0668 ■ 668 Dundas ■ *lunch & dinner, clsd Mon, vegetarian* ■ cafe668.com

Easy Restaurant 416/537-4893 ■ 1645 Queen St W ■ *9am-5pm* ■ www.easyrestaurant.ca

Fire on the East Side [MW] 416/960-3473 ■ 6 Gloucester St (at Yonge) ■ *noon-1am, 10am-midnight wknds, clsd Mon, Southern comfort food, patio* ■ www.fireontheeastside.ca

Flo's Diner [GO] 416/961-4333 ■ 70 Yorkville Ave (near Bay St) ■ *7:30am-10pm, till 9pm Mon, from 8:30am Sat, 9am-9pm Sun* ■ flosdiner.com

Fresh 416/599-4442 ■ 147 Spadina (at Queen St W) ■ *lunch & dinner, vegetarian, patio; also at 894 Queen St W, 416/ 913-2720* ■ www.juiceforlife.com

Fuzion 416/944-9888 ■ 580 Church St ■ *5pm-11pm, till midnight Fri-Sat, clsd Sun-Mon, also martini bar* ■ www.fuzionexperience.com

Golden Thai 416/868-6668 ■ 105 Church St (at Richmond) ■ *10:30am-9pm, 5pm-10pm Sat, 5pm-9pm Sun*

Il Fornello 416/920-7347 ■ 1560 Yonge St (1 block N of St Clair) ■ *lunch Mon-Fri, dinner nightly, Sun brunch, Italian, plenty veggie; also 214 King W (at Simcoe), 416/977-2855 & 576 Danforth Ave (at Carlaw), 416/466-2931* ■ www.ilfornello.com

Jamie Kennedy Wine Bar 416/362-1957 ■ 9 Church St ■ *11:30am-11pm, tapas-style dishes* ■ www.jkkitchens.com

Joy Bistro [NS] 416/465-8855 ■ 884 Queen St E ■ *8am-10pm, patio; also Over Joy lounge upstairs 6pm-2am Th-Sat*

Kalendar 416/923-4138 ■ 546 College St ■ *11am-midnight, till 1am Th, till 2am Fri-Sat, wknd brunch from 10:30am, eclectic, patio* ■ www.kalendar.com

La Hacienda 416/703-3377 ■ 640 Queen St W (near Bathurst) ■ *noon-11pm, from 11am wknds, sleazy, loud & fun Mexican restaurant*

Laurentian Room 416/925-8680 ■ 51A Winchester St ■ *dinner Tue-Sat, full bar, upscale*

The Living Well Restaurant & Bar [MW] 416/922-6770 ■ 692 Yonge St (at Isabella) ■ *11:30am-1am, plenty veggie, also bar, open 6pm-2am, live DJ, 2 patios* ■ www.livingwellcafe.ca

Mitzi's Sister [★GO] 416/532-2570 ■ 1554 Queen St W ■ *4pm-2am, popular wknd brunch from 10am, upscale pub eats, full bar*

River 416/535-3422 ■ 413 Roncesvalles Ave ■ *lunch Th-Fri, dinner Tue-Sat, wknd brunch, also lounge Tue-Sun, upscale, supports homeless & at-risk youth* ■ www.river314.ca

Savannah Room [E] 416/975-0845 ■ 294 College St (at Spadina) ■ *6pm-2am, live music venue, eclectic tapas, also bar* ■ bookingssavannah@gmail.com

Splendido [WC] 416/929-7788 ■ 88 Harbord St (at Spadina) ■ *5pm-10pm, great decor & gnocchi, full bar* ■ www.splendido.ca

The Superior Restaurant [WC] 416/214-0416 ■ 253 Yonge St (across from Eaton Centre) ■ *11:30am-10pm, till 8pm Mon, clsd Sun, oysters, full bar* ■ www.superiorrestaurant.com

The Village Rainbow 416/961-0616 ■ 477 Church St (at Maitland) ■ *7am-midnight, till 1am Th-Sat, from 8am Sun, full bar, big patio*

Zelda's [★MW,DS] 416/922-2526 ■ 542 Church St ■ *11am-11:30pm, till 12:30am Fri-Sat, 10am-10:30pm Sun, full bar, big patio* ■ www.zeldas.ca

ENTERTAINMENT & RECREATION

AIDS Memorial in Cawthra Park

The Bata Shoe Museum 416/979-7799 ■ 327 Bloor St W ■ *10,000 shoes from over 4,500 years—including the platforms of Elton John and the pumps of Marilyn Monroe* ■ www.batashoemuseum.ca

Buddies in Bad Times Theatre 416/975-8555 ■ 12 Alexander St (at Yonge) ■ *LGBT theater; also Tallulah's cabaret Fri-Sat [D]* ■ www.buddiesinbadtimestheatre.com

BOOKSTORES

47 **Glad Day Bookshop** [★] 416/961-4161, 877/783-3725 ■ 598-A Yonge St (at Wellesley) ■ *10am-6:30pm, till 9pm Th-Fri, noon-7pm Sat, noon-6pm Sun, great selection of LGBT books, mags & videos* ■ www.gladdaybookshop.com

48 **This Ain't The Rosedale Library** [★] 416/929-9912 ■ 483 Church St (at Wellesley) ■ *11am-10pm, till 11pm Fri-Sat, 1pm-9pm Sun, LGBT books & magazines*

49 Toronto Women's Bookstore 416/922-8744, 800/861-8233 ■ 73 Harbord St (at Spadina) ■ *10:30am-6pm, till 8pm Th-Fri, noon-5pm Sun* ■ www.womensbookstore.com

WonderWorks 416/323-3131 ■ 79-A Harbord St (at Spadina) ■ *10:30am-6pm, till 8pm Th-Fri, noon-5pm Sun, books & gifts* ■ www.gowonderworks.com

RETAIL SHOPS

Out on the Street 416/967-2759, 800/263-5747 ■ 551 Church St ■ *10am-8pm, till 9pm Th-Fri, 11am-6pm Sun, LGBT accessories*

Passage Tattoo 416/929-7330 ■ 473 Church St, 2nd flr ■ *noon-7pm, clsd Sun-Mon* ■ passage.ws

Secrets From Your Sister [WC] 416/538-1234 ■ 476 Bloor St W ■ *11am-7pm, 10am-6pm Sat, noon-6pm Sun, "beautiful lingerie in realistic sizes for the modern woman"* ■ www.secretsfromyoursister.com

Take a Walk on the Wild Side [TG] 416/921-6112, 800/260-0102 ■ 161 Gerrard St E (at Jarvis) ■ *"hotel, boutique & club for crossdressers, transvestites, transsexuals & other persons of gender"* ■ www.wildside.org

Vixon 416/960-6464 ■ 620 Yonge St (at St Joseph) ■ *11am-8pm, clubwear*

PUBLICATIONS

The Pink Pages 416/926-9588 ■ *annual LGBT directory* ■ www.thepinkpages.info

Xtra! 416/925-6665 ■ *LGBT newspaper* ■ www.xtra.ca

GYMS & HEALTH CLUBS

Body Blitz [WO] 416/364-0400 ■ 471 Adelaide St W (at Spadina) ■ *10am-8pm, till 9pm Fri, till 6pm Sun, water spa* ■ www.bodyblitzspa.com

MEN'S CLUBS

Cellar 416/975-1799 ■ 78 Wellesley St E (at Church) ■ *24hrs, no sign, enter through black door*

Central Spa 416/588-6191 ■ 1610 Dundas St W ■ *11am-midnight, till 3am Fri-Sat* ■ www.centralspa.ca

Club Toronto Baths & Health Club [SW,PC] 416/977-4629 ■ 231 Mutual St (at Carlton) ■ *24hrs, gym equipment* ■ www.clubtoronto.com

GI Joe [★WC] 416/927-0210 ■ 543 Yonge St, 4th flr (at Wellesley) ■ *24hrs*

Spa Excess [★] 416/260-2363, 877/867-3301 ■ 105 Carlton St ■ *24hrs, 4 flrs* ■ www.spaexcess.com

Steamworks [WI] 416/925-1571 ■ 540 Church St (level 2) ■ *24hrs* ■ www.steamworks.ca

EROTICA

ASLANLeather.com 416/306-0462 ■ 135 Tecumseth St, Unit 6 (rear) ■ *leather, rubber & vinyl dildo harnesses, fine bondage gear, by appointment only* ■ www.ASLANleather.com

Come As You Are 416/504-7934 ■ 701 Queen St W (at Bathurst) ■ *co-op-owned sex store* ■ www.comeasyouare.com

Good For Her 416/588-0900, 877/588-0900 ■ 175 Harbord St (near Bathurst) ■ *11am-7pm, till 8pm Fri, till 6pm Sat, noon-5pm Sun (women- & trans-only, also 11am-2pm Th), women's sexuality products* ■ www.goodforher.com

Lovecraft 416/923-7331 ■ 27 Yorkville Ave (btwn Bay & Yonge) ■ *toys, lingerie, videos, books* ■ www.lovecraftsexshop.com

North Bound Leather [WC] 416/972-1037 ■ 586 Yonge (W of Wellesley St) ■ *toys & clothing* ■ www.northbound.com

Priape [★] 416/586-9914, 800/461-6969 ■ 465 Church St (at Wellesley, above Woody's) ■ *clubwear, leather, books, toys & more* ■ www.priape.com

Seduction 416/966-6969 ■ 577 Yonge St ■ www.seduction.ca

Stag Shop 416/368-3507 ■ 239 Yonge St ■ *also 449 Church St, 416/323-0772* ■ www.stagshop.com

Montréal

Note: M°=Metro station

ACCOMMODATIONS

1   **Abri du Voyageur Hotel** [GF] 514/849-2922, 888/302-2922 ■ 9 rue Ste-Catherine Ouest ■ *charming, good-value hotel in downtown Montréal, 15-minute walk to the Village* ■ www.abri-voyageur.ca

2   **Absolument Montréal B&B** [GS,NS,WI,GO] 514/223-0017, 866/360-1351 ■ 1790 Amherst (at Maisonneuve) ■ www.absolumentmontreal.com

3   **Accommodations International B&B** [MO,WI,GO] 514/596-2317, 888/334-0348 ■ 2002 Champlain #1 (at Ontario, above Citibar) ■ *"quiet, clean, inexpensive,"* outside terrace ■ www.gaybed.ca

4   **Alcazar B&B** [M,NS,GO] 514/223-2622, 866/589-8964 ■ 1589 Alexandre de Sève (at Maisonneuve) ■ *in heart of gay Village* ■ www.alcazarmontreal.com

5   **Alexandre Logan** [GF] 514/598-0555, 866/895-0555 ■ 1631 rue Alexandre de Sève ■ www.alexandrelogan.com

6   **Alexandrie-Montréal** [GF,NS,WI,GO] 514/525-9420 ■ 1750 Amherst (at Robin) ■ *rooms & apts in the Village* ■ www.alexandrie-montreal.com

7   **Angelica Blue B&B** [GS,NS,WI] 514/844-5048, 800/878-5048 ■ 1213 Ste-Elisabeth (at Ste-Catherine) ■ *theme rooms, full brkfst, some shared baths* ■ www.angelicablue.com

    Au Bellerive B&B [M,NS,GO] 514/355-4636 (9am-noon EST) ■ aubellerivebb@hotmail.com

8   **Auberge Belles Vues B&B** 514/521-9998 ■ 1407 Panet #2 ■ *located in the Gay Village* ■ www.bellesvues.com

9   **Auberge Cosy** [★MO,GO] 514/525-2151 ■ 1274 Ste-Catherine Est (at de la Visitation) ■ *in the heart of the Village, hot tub, shared baths* ■ www.aubergecosy.com

10 **Auberge de la Fontaine** [GS,WI,WC] 514/597-0166, 800/597-0597 ■ 1301 rue Rachel Est (at Chambord) ■ www.aubergedelafontaine.com

11 **Auberge le Pomerol** [GF,NS,WI] 514/526-5511, 800/361-6896 ■ 819 boul de Maisonneuve E ■ *many rooms w/ whirlpools* ■ www.aubergelepomerol.com

12► **Aubergell B&B** [MO,F,NS,WI,GO] 514/597-0878, 514/525-7744 ■ 1641 Amherst (at de Maisonneuve) ■ *also full bar, rooftop terrace* ■ www.aubergell.com

13 **Aux Studios Montcalm—Guesthouse** [M,GO] 514/815-6195 ■ 1303 Montcalm St (at Ste-Catherine St) ■ www.auxstudiosmontcalm.com

14 **B&B L'escogriffe** [MO,WI,GO] 514/523-4800, 877/523-6105 ■ 1264 rue Wolfe (at rue Ste-Catherine E) ■ www.lescogriffe.com

15 **B&B Le Cartier** [GS,NS,WI,GO] 514/917-1829, 877/524-0495 ■ 1219 rue Cartier (at Ste-Catherine Est) ■ *newly renovated 100-year-old stone house in Gay Village* ■ www.bblecartier.com

16 **B&B Le Terra Nostra** [GF,NS,WI] 514/762-1223, 866/550-5235 ■ 277 Beatty (at Lasalle) ■ www.leterra-nostra.com

13 **BBV (B&B du Village)** [M] 514/522-4771, 888/228-8455 ■ 1279 rue Montcalm (at Ste-Catherine) ■ *jacuzzi* ■ www.bbv.qc.ca

17 **Big Boys Guesthouse** [MO,WI,GO] 514/525-4222, 866/889-2697 ■ 1478 de Maisonneuve Est (at Alexandre de Sève) ■ www.bigboysguesthouse.com

71 **Le Bliss** [GS,NS,GO] 514/277-0170 ■ 1282 rue Panêt (at Ste-Catherine) ■ *rental apt, short- or long-term stays* ■ www.lebliss.com

18 **Le Café au Lit** [GF,NS] 514/523-3733 ■ 1479 rue Amherst ■ *Victorian B&B* ■ www.lecafeaulit.com

19 **Le Chasseur B&B** [GS,GO] 514/521-2238, 800/451-2238 ■ 1567 rue St-André (at Maisonneuve) ■ *Victorian row house, summer terrace* ■ www.lechasseur.com

20 **Chateau Cherrier** [MW,NS,GO] 514/844-0055, 800/816-0055 ■ 550 rue Cherrier (at St-Hubert) ■ *seasonal, full brkfst* ■ www.chateaucherrier.com

21 **Chez Philippe** [GS,NS,WI,GO] 514/890-1666, 877/890-1666 ■ 2457 rue Ste-Catherine Est (at Fullum) ■ *B&B w/in walking distance of Gay Village, vegan brkfst, large terrace* ■ www.chezphilippe.info

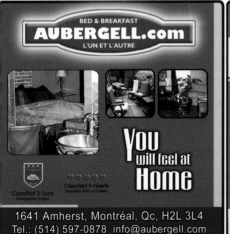

MONTRÉAL

Local Food:

Taking a cue from their French ancestors, Québecois cheesemakers are creating award-winning cheeses on small farms across the province. Many of the cheeseries are located in quaint villages in the Eastern Townships (think of New England, only en français). Artisan cheese and food shops along the way will provide you with the *fromage* and *paté*; stop at the local *boulangerie* for a loaf of crusty bread; and enjoy a picnic in the countryside. Because they are not pasteurized, many of Québec's cheeses can't be exported to the US, so enjoy them while you can.

Tourist Info

AIRPORT DIRECTIONS

Dorval International. To get to downtown, take Hwy 20 North and use the downtown exit.

PUBLIC TRANSIT & TAXIS

Diamond Cab 514/273-6331.
Montréal Urban Transit 514/786-4636, web: www.stcum.qc.ca.

TOURIST SPOTS & INFO

Bonsecours Market 514/872-7730, web: www.marchebonsecours.qc.ca.
Latin Quarter.
Montréal Biodome 514/868-3000, web: www2.ville.montreal.qc.ca/biodome.
Montréal Botanical Garden & Insectarium 514/872-1400, web: www2.ville.montreal.qc.ca/jardin.
Montréal Museum of Fine Arts 514/285-2000, web: www.mmfa.qc.ca.
Old Montréal & Old Port.
Olympic Park.
Underground City.
Visitor's Center: 514/873-2015, web: www.tourism-montreal.org.

Weather

It's north of New England so winters are for real. Beautiful spring and fall colors. Summers get hot and humid.

Best Views

From a caleche ride (horse-drawn carriage) or from the top of the Montréal Tower or from the patio of the old hunting lodge atop Mont Royal.

City Calendar

LGBT PRIDE

July/August. 514/285-4011, web: www.diverscite.org.

ENTERTAINMENT

Info Gay Events Hotline 514/252-4429.
Tourisme Québec www.bonjourquebec.com/gay.

ANNUAL EVENTS

February/March - Festival Montréal en Lumière (Montréal High Lights Festival) 514/288-9955, web: www.montrealenlumiere.com.
June/July - L'International des Feux Loto-Québec (fireworks competition) 514/397-2000, web: www.internationaldesfeux.com.
Festival International de Jazz de Montréal 514/523-3378, www.montrealjazzfest.com.
Festival International Montréal en Arts 514/522-4646, web: www.festivaldesarts.org.
July - Just For Laughs Comedy Festival 888/244-3155, web: www.hahaha.com.
August/September - Montréal World Film Festival 514/848-3883, web: www.ffm-montreal.org.
October - Black & Blue Party 514/875-7026, web: www.bbcm.org. AIDS benefit dance & circuit party.
November - International Gay/ Lesbian Film Festival, web: www.image-nation.org.
Harvest Theatre Festival: A cornucopia of diversity in the performance arts, web: www.villagescene.com.

Queer Resources

COMMUNITY INFO

Centre Communitaire des Gais et Lesbiennes 514/528-8424. 2075 rue Plessis, 10am-noon & 1pm-5pm, clsd wknds; library 1pm-8pm Wed & Fri, web: www.ccglm.org.
Women's Centre of Montréal 514/842-4780. 9am-noon & 1pm-5pm Mon-Fri, web: www.centredes-femmesdemtl.org.
Gay Info Line 514/866-5090 (English), 514/866-0103 (French).
Gay Chamber of Commerce 514/522-1885, web: www.ccgq.ca.
AA 514/376-9230 web: www.alcoholicsanony-mousmontreal.com.
ACCM 514/527-0928, web: www.accmontreal.org.

2 **Chez Roger Bontemps** [GS] 514/598-9587, 888/634-9090 ■ 1441 rue Wolfe (at Ste-Catherine) ■ *B&B & furnished apts in two 1873 homes* ■ www.bbcanada.com/2058.html

3 **La Claire Fontaine** [GF] 514/528-9862 ■ 1652 rue la Fontaine ■ *B&B in quiet neighborhood* ■ www.laclaire-fontaine.com

4► **La Conciergerie Guest House** [★M,N,NS,WI,GO] 514/289-9297 ■ 1019 rue St-Hubert (at Viger) ■ *hot tub, gym & sundeck* ■ www.laconciergerie.ca

5 **Delta Montréal** [GF,SW,WC] 514/286-1986, 877/286-1986 ■ 475 Ave President Kennedy (at City Councilor) ■ *hot tub, kids/ pets ok, restaurant, bar, garden terrace* ■ www.deltahotels.com

6 **Four Points by Sheraton** [GF,WI,WC] 514/842-3961 ■ 475 Sherbrooke St W ■ *complimentary pool & fitness center across the street; also restaurant, bar & cafe* ■ www.four-pointsmontreal.com

7 **Gingerbread House B&B** [MW,NS,WI,GO] 514/597-2804 ■ 1628 St-Christophe (at Maisonneuve) ■ *full brkfst, shared bath* ■ www.gbhouse.ca

8 **Hôtel Dorion** [GS] 514/523-2427, 877/523-5908 ■ 1477 rue Dorion ■ *in the Gay Village* ■ www.hoteldorion.com

9 **Hotel du Fort** [GS,WC] 514/938-8333, 800/565-6333 ■ 1390 rue du Fort (at Ste-Catherine) ■ www.hoteldufort.com

10 **Hotel Dynastie** [GS,NS,GO] 514/529-5210, 877/529-5210 ■ 1723 St-Hubert ■ www.hoteldynastie.com

11 **Hôtel Gouverneur Montréal Place Dupuis** [GF,SW] 888/910-1111 ■ 1415 rue St-Hubert ■ www.gouverneur.com

12 **Hotel le St-André** [GS,WI] 514/849-7070, 800/265-7071 ■ 1285 rue St-André (at Ste-Catherine) ■ *B&B inn, on edge of Gay Village* ■ www.hotelsaintandre.ca

13 **Hotel Lord Berri** [GF,WC] 514/845-9236, 888/363-0363 ■ 1199 rue Berri (at Ste-Catherine) ■ *nonsmoking rooms available, also Italian resto-bar* ■ www.lordberri.com

12 **Hotel Manoir des Alpes** [GF] 514/845-9803, 800/465-2929 ■ 1245 rue St-André (at Ste-Catherine) ■ www.hotelmanoirdesalpes.qc.ca

34 **Hotel XIXe Siècle** [GF,WI] 514/985-0019, 877/553-0019 ■ 262 rue St-Jacques ■ *large, modern rooms* ■ www.hotelxixsiecle.com

35 **Le Houseboy B&B** [MO,NS,WI,GO] 514/525-1459, 866/525-1459 ■ 1281 rue Beaudry (at Ste-Catherine Est) ■ *full brkfst, shared baths, garden & patio, in the Gay Village* ■ www.lehouseboy.com

7 **Jade Blue B&B** [GS,NS,WI] 514/878-9843, 800/878-5048 ■ 1225 de Bullion ■ *theme rooms, full brkfst* ■ www.jadeblue.net

36 **Lindsey's B&B for Women** [★WO,NS,WI,GO] 514/843-4869, 888/655-8655 ■ 3974 Laval Ave (near Duluth) ■ *charming town house near Square St-Louis & rue Prince Arthur, full brkfst, lesbian-owned* ■ lindseys.ca

37 **Loews Hotel Vogue** [GF,WC] 514/285-5555, 800/465-6654 ■ 1425 rue de la Montagne (near Ste-Catherine) ■ *full-service 5-star hotel* ■ www.loewshotels.com

38 **Les Lofts de L'Apothicaire** [M,NS,WI,GO] 514/998-2056 ■ 1625 rue Amherst (at de Maisonneuve) ■ *luxurious loft in the heart of the Gay Village, private entrance* ■ www.lesloftsdelapothicaire.com

39 **Maison Chablis** [MO,GO] 514/527-8346 ■ 1643 rue St-Hubert (at Maisonneuve) ■ *some shared baths*

   Le Matou Noir Guesthouse [MO,B,L,GO] 514/354-2999 ■ *near Gay Village* ■ matounoirgh@yahoo.ca

40 **Montréal Boutique Suite Guesthouse** [MW,NS,WI,GO] 514/521-9436, 514/521-3523 ■ 1269 rue de Champlain (at Ste-Catherine) ■ www.montrealboutiquesuite.com

41 **Montréal Gay** [M,WI,GO] 514/524-8789 ■ 1607 rue Montcalm (at Maisonneuve) ■ *located in heart of Gay Village* ■ www.accommodationmontrealgay.com

30 **Nuzone B&B** [M,N,WI,GO] 514/524-5292 ■ 1729 rue St-Hubert ■ *in Victorian house, full brkfst* ■ www.nuzone.ca

42 **Plaza Hotel** [GF,SW,WI,WC] 514/842-8581, 800/561-4644 ■ 505 rue Sherbrooke Est (at Berri) ■ *breathtaking views, full brkfst, hot tub, also restaurant & full bar* ■ www.cpmontreal.com

37 **Le Roy d'Carreau Guest House** [MW,NS,WI,GO] 514/524-2493, 877/527-7975 ■ 1637 rue Amherst (at Maisonneuve) ■ *in Gay Village, sundeck, also apts, no unregistered guests* ■ www.leroydcarreau.com

8 **Ruta Bagage** [GS] 514/598-1586 ■ 1345 rue Ste-Rose (at Panêt) ■ *Victorian B&B, full brkfst, shared baths* ■ **www.rutabagage.qc.ca**

43►**Sir Montcalm** [M,NS,WI,GO] 514/522-7747 ■ 1455 Montcalm (at Ste Catherine St) ■ *B&B* ■ **www.sirmontcalm.com**

44 **Le St-Christophe** [MO,N,NS,GO] 514/527-7836, 888/521-7836 ■ 1597 rue St-Christophe (at Maisonneuve) ■ *full brkfst, sundeck & hot tub* ■ **www.stchristophe.com**

45 **St-Lawrence Apartments** [GS,WI] 514/998-0047 ■ 65 René-Lévèsque Est (at St-Laurent) ■ *fully furnished apts, near Gay Village* ■ **www.apartments-montreal.com**

4 **Turquoise B&B** [M,GO] 514/523-9943, 877/707-1576 ■ 1576 rue Alexandre de Sève (at Maisonneuve) ■ *Victorian B&B, shared baths* ■ **www.turquoisebb.com**

46 **W Montréal** [GF,WI,WC] 514/395-3100, 877/WHOTELS (reservations only) ■ 901 Square Victoria ■ *also spa, restaurant & 3 bars* ■ **www.whotels.com/montreal**

BARS

47 **L' Adonis** [MO,S] 514/521-1355 ■ 1680 rue Ste-Catherine Est (at Papineau) ■ *3pm-3am, nude dancers*

48 **Bar Rocky** [M,V,OC] 514/521-7865 ■ 1673 rue Ste-Catherine Est (at Papineau) ■ *8am-3am, [E] wknds*

49 **Black Eagle Bar (Aigle Noir)** [M,L,PC] 514/529-0040 ■ 1315 Ste-Catherine Est (at Visitation) ■ *8am-3am, theme nights* ■ **www.aiglenoir.com**

50 **Cabaret Mado** [★MW,D,K,C,DS,WC] 514/525-7566 ■ 1115 rue Ste-Catherine Est (at Amherst, below Le Campus) ■ *1pm-3am, clsd Th, theme nights, owned by the fabulous Mado!* ■ **www.mado.qc.ca**

50 **Le Campus** [M,S] 514/526-3616 ■ 1111 rue Ste-Catherine Est, 2nd flr (at Amherst) ■ *3pm-3am, nude dancers, ladies night Sun* ■ **www.campusmtl.com**

3 **Citibar** [GS,NH] 514/525-4251 ■ 1603 Ontario Est (at Champlain) ■ *10am-3am*

51 **Club Bolo** [MW,D,CW,$] 514/849-4777 ■ 960 rue Amherst (at Viger) ■ *10pm-2am Fri, special events Sat, T-dance from 4pm-9pm Sun, also lessons* ■ **www.clubbolo.com**

52 **Club Date** [MW,NH,K,P,S] 514/521-1242 ■ 1218 rue Ste-Catherine Est (at Beaudry) ■ *8am-3am, karaoke nightly*

53 **Cocktail** [MW,NH] 514/597-0814 ■ 1669 Ste-Catherine Est ■ *8am-3am*

54 **Le Drugstore** [★MW,F] 514/524-1960 ■ 1366 rue Ste-Catherine Est (at Panêt) ■ *8am-3am, many bars, boutiques, restaurant & many flrs overlooking the Village's main drag*

55 **Foufounes Electriques** [GF,D,E] 514/844-5539 ■ 87 Ste-Catherine Est (at St-Laurent) ■ *4pm-3am, patio* ■ **www.foufounes.qc.ca**

56 **Fun Spot** [MW,NH,D,TG,K,DS] 514/522-0416 ■ 1151 rue Ontario Est (at Wolfe) ■ *11am-3am, poker machines* ■ **funspot@arobas.net**

12 **Le Gotha** [M,NH,E] 514/597-0878 ■ 1641 Amherst (at Maisonneuve) ■ *4pm-3am* ■ **www.aubergell.com/en/gotha/**

Lady Loft [MW,D,F] 514/585-1393 ■ 990 rue St-Antoine Ouest (at Mansfield) ■ *9pm-3am, clsd Mon-Th, also full restaurant 5pm-9pm*

53 **Météor** [MW,D,F,K,DS,OC] 514/523-1481 ■ 1661 rue Ste-Catherine Est (at Champlain) ■ *9am-3am, '60s-themed bar, ballroom dancing, square dancing*

57 **Le Mystique** [MW,NH] 514/844-5711 ■ 1424 rue Stanley (at Maisonneuve) ■ *4pm-3am, English underground pub, poker machines*

58 **Normandie** [MW,NH,V] 514/522-2766 ■ 1295 Amherst (at Ste-Catherine) ■ *10am-2am, terrace, one of Montréal's oldest taverns, popular happy hour*

49 **La Relaxe** [M,NH] 514/523-0578 ■ 1309 rue Ste-Catherine Est, 2nd flr ■ *noon-2am, open to the street—as the name implies, a good place to relax & people-watch*

59 **St-Sulpice** [GS] 514/844-9458 ■ 1680 rue St-Denis (at Ontario) ■ *noon-3am, 3 flrs, large terrace*

50 **Stock Bar** [MO,S] 514/842-1336 ■ 1171 Ste-Catherine ■ *shows start at 8pm nightly, nude dancers* ■ **www.stockbar.ca**

60 **Le Stud** [MO,D,B,L,K] 514/598-8243 ■ 1812 rue Ste-Catherine Est (at Papineau) ■ *10am-3am, theme nights* ■ **www.studbar.com**

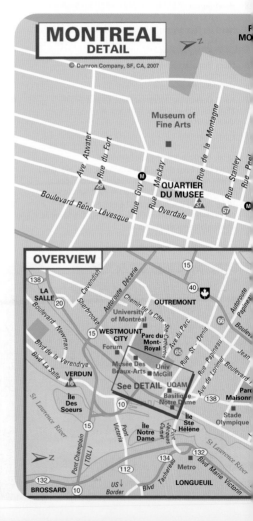

51 Taboo [MO,S] 514/597-0010 ■ 1950 boul de Maisonneuve Est (at Dorion) ■ *7pm-2am, nude dancers* ■ www.taboomontreal.com

NIGHTCLUBS

52 Cabaret Cafe Cleopatra [M,D,TG,K,DS] 514/871-8065 ■ 1230 boul St-Laurent (at Ste-Catherine) ■ *8pm-3am* ■ www.cleopatramontreal.com

53 Circus After Hours [GS,D] 514/844-0188 ■ 915 rue Ste-Catherine Est ■ *2am-10am Th-Sat only* ■ www.circusafter-hours.com

58 Club Parking [★M,D,L,YC] 514/282-1199 ■ 1296 rue Amherst ■ *10pm-3am, 2 flrs, [MO] Fri-Sat* ■ www.parking-bar.com

64 Club Tools [★M,D] 514/523-4679 (hotel) ■ 1592 Ste-Catherine Est ■ *9pm-close Fri-Sun only, '70s, '80s & '90s club disco, 3 flrs w/ large back patio, sex club* ■ www.club-tools.com

58 Lips [W,D] 514/282-1199 (Club Parking) ■ 1294 rue Amherst (at rue Ste-Catherine) ■ *[WO] Fri-Sat, MW Wed-Th, clsd Sun-Tue*

65 Meow Mix [W,D] 514/284-0122 ■ 4848 boul St-Laurent (at La Sala Rossa) ■ *monthly party, check local listings for dates* ■ www.casadelpopolo.com

66 Red Lite (After Hours) [★GF,D,$] 450/967-3057 ■ 1755 rue de Lierre, Laval ■ *Fri-Sun only, after-hours club* ■ www.red-lite.net

67 Sky Complex [★MW,D,A,L,F,C,DS,S] 514/529-6969, 514/529-8989 ■ 1474 rue Ste-Catherine Est ■ *11am-3am, 3 levels, cabaret & dance club Fri-Sat, T-dance Sun* ■ www.complexesky.com

68 Stéréo [★GS,$] 514/286-0325 ■ 858 rue Ste-Catherine Est ■ *after-hours Fri-Sun only* ■ www.stereo-nightclub.com

69 Unity [★MW,D,S,YC] 514/523-2777 ■ 1171 rue Ste-Catherine Est ■ *10pm-close, clsd Sun-Tue, 4 flrs & great rooftop terrace* ■ www.clubunitymontreal.com

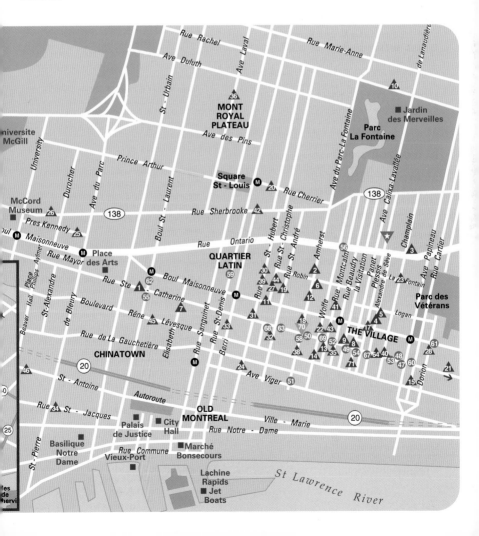

CAFES

Cafe Titanic [★WI] 514/849-0894 ■ 445 St-Pierre (in Old Montréal) ■ 7am-4:30pm, clsd wknds, salads & soups ■ www.titanic-mtl.ca

Kilo 514/596-3933 ■ 1495 rue Ste-Catherine Est ■ 11am-11pm, till midnight Fri-Sat, cakes, coffee & light meals ■ www.kilo.ca

The Second Cup [NS] 514/598-7727 ■ 1351 rue Ste-Catherine Est ■ 24hrs, très gay coffee shop

RESTAURANTS

L' Anecdote [MW] 514/526-7967 ■ 801 rue Rachel Est (at St-Hubert) ■ 9am-10pm, burgers, veggie

Après le Jour [MW,BYOB,WC] 514/527-4141 ■ 901 rue Rachel Est (at St-Andre) ■ 5pm-9pm, till 9:30pm Fri-Sat, Italian/ French, seafood

Area [R] 514/890-6691 ■ 1429 rue Amherst ■ 6pm-10pm, French/ Italian/ Asian fusion ■ www.rest-area.qc.ca

Bato Thai [★MW,BW] 514/524-6705 ■ 1310 rue Ste-Catherine Est ■ lunch weekdays & dinner nightly

Beauty's [★] 514/849-8883 ■ 93 Mont-Royal Ouest ■ diner, worth the wait ■ www.beautys.ca

La Binerie 514/285-9078 ■ 367 Mt-Royal ■ brkfst, lunch & dinner, Québecois ■ www.labineriemontroyal.com

Chu Chai [★] 514/843-4194 ■ 4088 rue St-Denis (at Rachel) ■ lunch & dinner, vegetarian Thai, full bar

Cluny Art Bar 514/866-1213 ■ 257 rue Prince ■ 8am-5pm, till 10pm Th, Mediterranean ■ www.cluny.info

La Colombe [BYOB] 514/849-8844 ■ 554 Duluth Est ■ 5:30pm-10pm, clsd Sun-Mon, French

Commensal [BW,WC] 514/845-2627 ■ 1720 rue St-Denis (at Ontario) ■ 11am-10:30pm, till 11pm Fri-Sat, vegetarian, other locations ■ www.commensal.com

L' Exception 514/282-1282 ■ 1200 rue St-Hubert (at Réné-Lévèsque) ■ 11am-9pm, clsd wknds, burgers & sandwiches, plenty veggie, terrace

L' Express [★R,WC] 514/845-5333 ■ 3927 rue St-Denis (at Duluth) ■ 8am-2am, from 10am Sat, 10am-1am Sun, French bistro & bar, great pâté

Fantasie [GO] 514/523-3466 ■ 1355 rue Ste-Catherine Est ■ lunch & dinner, sushi

La Strega [WC] 514/523-6000 ■ 1477 rue Ste-Catherine Est ■ 10am-midnight, from 4:30pm wknds, inexpensive Italian, some veggie

La Paryse [MW,GO] 514/842-2040 ■ 302 rue Ontario Est (near Sanguinet) ■ lunch & dinner, clsd Mon, '50s-style diner, lesbian-owned

Piccolo Diavolo [★WC] 514/526-1336 ■ 1336 rue Ste-Catherine Est (at Panêt) ■ 5pm-11pm, also lunch Th-Fri, Italian, charming waiters ■ www.piccolodiavolo.com

Le Planète [YC,BW] 514/528-6953 ■ 1451 rue Ste-Catherine Est (at Plessis) ■ lunch weekdays & dinner nightly, brunch only Sun, global cuisine

Resto du Village 1310 rue Wolfe ■ 24hrs, "cuisine canadienne"

Saloon Cafe [★] 514/522-1333 ■ 1333 rue Ste-Catherine Est (at Panêt) ■ 7:30am-11pm, till midnight wknds, int'l cuisine, plenty veggie, big dishes & even bigger drinks

Schwartz's Deli 514/842-4813 ■ 1895 boul St-Laurent ■ 8am-12:30am, till 1:30am Fri, till 2:30am Sat, smoked meat ■ www.schwartzsdeli.com

Taro [GS,D] 514/289-9888 ■ 862 rue Ste-Catherine Est ■ lunch & dinner, till 3am Fri-Sat, full bar, DJ Fri-Sat ■ www.tarosushi.com

Thai Grill 514/270-5566 ■ 5101 boul St-Laurent (at Laurier) ■ lunch Sun-Th & dinner nightly, one of Montréal's best Thai eateries ■ www.thaigrill.ca

ENTERTAINMENT & RECREATION

Ça Roule 514/866-0633, 877/866-0633 ■ 27 rue de la Commune Est ■ join the beautiful people skating up & down Ste-Catherine ■ www.caroulemontreal.com

Cinéma du Parc 514/281-1900 ■ 3575 Parc (btwn Milton & Prince Arthur) ■ repertory film theater ■ www.cinemadu-parc.com

Prince Arthur Est at boul St-Laurent, not far from Sherbrooke Métro station ■ closed-off street w/ tons of outdoor restaurants & cafés—it's touristy but oh-so-European

BOOKSTORES

70 **Serge et Real** 514/527-7759 ■ 1455 rue Amherst ■ 11am-6pm, till 9pm Th-Fri, 10am-5pm Sat, noon-5pm Sun, LGBT bookstore ■ www.sergetreal.com

RETAIL SHOPS

Cuir Mont-Royal 514/527-0238, 888/338-8283 ■ 826-A Mont Royal Est (at St-Hubert) ■ leather, fetish ■ www.cuirmontroyal.com

Mad-Âme 514/396-7000 ■ 1276 rue Amherst ■ 11am-6pm, till 9pm Th-Fri, till 5pm wknds, clothes that define "le look lesbien" ■ www.mad-ame.ca

Priape [★] 514 /521-8451, 800/461-6969 ■ 1311 Ste-Catherine Est (at Visitation) ■ 10am-9pm, noon-9pm Sun, clubwear, leather, books, toys & more ■ www.priape.com

Screaming Eagle 514/849-2843 ■ 1424 boul St-Laurent ■ leather shop

PUBLICATIONS

Fugues 514/848-1854, 888/848-1854 ■ glossy LGBT bar/entertainment guide ■ www.fugues.com

The Mirror 514/393-1010 ■ free queer-positive weekly, reviews, event listings & more in English ■ www.montrealmirror.com

RG 514/523-9463 ■ monthly newsmagazine ■ www.rgmag.com

La Voix 514/522-8204, 888/244-5429 ■ monthly magazine for men ■ www.lavoixduvillage.com

MEN'S CLUBS

5018 Sauna [V] 514/277-3555 ■ 5018 boul St-Laurent (at St-Joseph) ■ 24hrs, hot tub ■ www.le5018.com

Backroom [★MO] 1452 rue Ste-Catherine E ■ 4pm-10am, 24hrs wknds ■ www.backroommontreal.com

Colonial Bath 514/285-0132 ■ 3963 av Colonial (at Napoléon) ■ noon-midnight, till 2am Fri-Sat, from 7am Sun ■ www.colonialbath.com

GI Joe [★L,E,V,PC] 514/528-3326 ■ 1166 Ste-Catherine Est ■ 24hrs, hot tub, specials for leather crowd

L' Oasis [★V,PC] 514/521-0785 ■ 1390 Ste-Catherine Est ■ 24hrs, hot tub

Sauna 1286 [V] 450/677-1286 ■ 1286 chemin Chambly (at Breggs), Longueuil

Sauna 456 [★SW,PC] 514/871-8341 ■ 456 rue de la Gauchetière Ouest (at Metro Square) ■ 24hrs, 3 flrs, hot tub, also gym ■ www.le456.ca

Sauna Centre-Ville 514/524-3486 ■ 1465 rue Ste-Catherine Est (at Plessis) ■ 24hrs ■ www.saunacentreville.com

Sauna du Plateau 514/528-1679 ■ 961 rue Rachel Est (at Boyer) ■ *24hrs* ■ www.saunaduplateau.com

Sauna Pont-Viau [V] 450/663-3386 ■ 15-A boul des Laurentides, Laval

Sauna St-Hubert [V] 514/277-0176 ■ 6527 rue St-Hubert (at Beaubien) ■ *24hrs Th-Sun*

Sauna Ste-Catherine 514/523-5355 ■ 1836 rue Ste-Catherine Est ■ *24hrs* ■ www.saunastecath.com

EROTICA

La Capoterie 514/845-0027 ■ 2061 St-Denis ■ *adult novelties, condoms* ■ www.lacapoterie.com

Il Bolero 514/270-6065 ■ 6842-46 St-Hubert (btwn St-Zotique & Bélanger) ■ *fetish & clubwear emporium, ask about monthly fetish party* ■ www.ilbolero.com

Québec City

ACCOMMODATIONS

1   **Le 727 Guest House (Chambres et Pension)** [M,GO] 418/523-7705, 866/523-7705 ■ 727 rue d'Aiguillon (btwn St-Augustin & Côte Ste-Geneviève) ■ *B&B in private home, full brkfst, terrace* ■ www.le-national.com/727

2   **L' Auberge du Quartier** [GS,NS] 418/525-9726, 800/782-9441 ■ 170 Grande Allée Ouest (at av Cartier) ■ *cont'l brkfst* ■ www.aubergeduquartier.com

3   **Auberge Place D'Armes** [GF,NS,WI] 418/694-9485, 866/333-9485 ■ 24 rue Ste-Anne ■ www.auberge-placedarmes.com

QUÉBEC CITY

Day Trips:

Visit a sugar shack to see for yourself how Québec's cavity-inducing maple treats are made. Spring is sugaring-off time in the province, and many maple syrup operations around Québec City welcome visitors—picturesque Île d'Orléans is a good place to start. If you're here during the summer, the island comes alive with farmers markets, where you'll find local wares like fruit jams, fresh produce, and Québec's world-class artisan cheese.

Local Food:

Savory French Canadian cuisine brings the best of two worlds to the table. Traditional French recipes blended with the hearty game and vegetables found in Québec make for local faves like *tourtière* (meat pie), *cretons* (pork paté) and *fevres au lard* (baked beans). Satisfy your sweet tooth with one of the maple desserts the region is famous for: *le sucre a la crème* is a type of maple fudge, and *tarte au sucre* is maple syrup pie.

Tourist Info

AIRPORT DIRECTIONS

Québec City Aéroport. To get downtown, follow Boulevard Aéroport to Hwy Charest 440 East. Take Hwy Charest 440 East to downtown.

PUBLIC TRANSIT & TAXIS

Taxi Québec 418/525-8123.
Autobus La Quebecoise 888/872-5525, web: www.autobus.qc.ca
RTC (bus service) 418/627-2511, web: www.rtcquebec.ca.

TOURIST SPOTS & INFO

Change of Guards at the Citadel.
Château Frontenac 418/692-3861, web: www.fairmont.com/frontenac.
Grand Allée.
Hôtel du Parlement.
Notre-Dame-de-Québec Basilica.
Old Québec.
Quartier du Petit-Champlain 418/692-2613, web: www.quartierpetitchamplain.com.
Visitor's Center: 877/266-5687 and 514/873-2015, web: www.bonjourquebec.com.

City Calendar

LGBT PRIDE

September. 418/809-3383, web: www.fetearcenciel.qc.ca.

ENTERTAINMENT

Tourisme Québec web: www.bonjourquebec.com/gay.

ANNUAL EVENTS

January/February - Carnaval (Winter Celebration) 866/422-7628, web: www.carnaval.qc.ca.
July - Summer Festival 888/992-5200, web: www.infofestival.com.

Queer Resources

Le Reseau (CATIE) 800/263-1638, web: www.catie.ca.

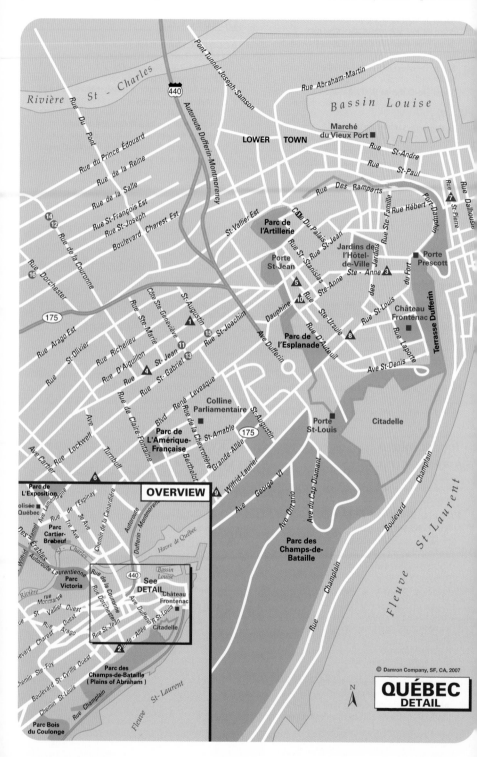

Le Château du Faubourg [GF,NS,GO] 418/524-2902 ■ 429 rue St-Jean ■ B&B in château w/ 2nd French Empire Napoleon III architecture, also beauty salon, also rental cottage 50 minutes from the city ■ www.lechateaudu-faubourg.com

Le Coureur des Bois Guest House [MW,NS,GO] 418/692-1117, 800/269-6414 ■ 15 rue Ste-Ursule (at St-Jean, in Old Québec) ■ also apts, shared baths ■ gayquebec.net/hebergement.html

Dans les Bras de Morphée [GF,SW] 418/829-3792 ■ 225 chemin Royal, St-Jean-De-L'Ile d'Orléans ■ full brkfst, near beach, shared baths, animals on premises, lesbian-owned ■ www.danslesbrasdemorphee.ca

Gîte aux Deux Lions [GF,WI] 418/780-8100, 877/777-9444 ■ 25 boul René-Lévesque Est ■ cozy B&B in refined 1909 home ■ www.giteauxdeuxlions.com

Hôtel Dominion 1912 [GF,WI,WC] 418/692-2224, 888/833-5253 ■ 126 rue St-Pierre ■ boutique hotel in city's 1st skyscraper ■ www.hoteldominion.com

Hôtel Germain Des Prés [GF,WC] 418/658-1224, 800/463-5253 ■ 1200 av Germain des Prés (at Laurier Blvd), Sainte-Foy ■ modern & elegant hotel, restaurant ■ www.germaindespres.com

Hotel Le Clos Saint-Louis [GS,NS,WI] 418/694-1311, 800/461-1311 ■ 69 St-Louis (at St-Ursule) ■ small Victorian-style boutique hotel located in historic district near shops & restaurants ■ www.clossaintlouis.com

Hôtel-Motel Le Voyageur [GS,SW] 418/661-7701, 800/463-5568 ■ 2250 boul Ste-Anne (at Estimauville) ■ kids ok, restaurant, 2 bars ■ www.motel-voyageur.com

Loews Le Concorde [GF,SW,WC] 418/647-2222, 800/463-5256 ■ 1225 cours du Général De Montcalm ■ 4-stars, located on Grand Allée, w/ revolving restaurant ■ www.loewsleconcorde.com

Maison du Cocher [GF,WI] 418/261-6610 ■ 31 rue Dauphine ■ www.maisonducocher.com

Le Moulin de St-Laurent Chalets [GS,SW,NS] 418/829-3888, 888/629-3888 ■ 754 chemin Royal, St Laurent, Ile d' Orleans ■ cottages, kids/ pets ok, also restaurant ■ www.moulinstlaurent.qc.ca

BARS

L' Amour Sorcier [★W,NH,F,V] 418/523-3395 ■ 789 côte Ste-Geneviève (at St-Jean) ■ 2pm-3am, till 8pm Sun & Wed, clsd Mon, cafe-bar, terrace ■ amoursorcier@videotron.ca

Bar 321 [M,NH,TG,S] 418/525-5107 ■ 321 de la Couronne (at La Salle) ■ 11am-3am

Bar 889 [MW,NH] 418/524-5000 ■ 889 côte Ste-Geneviève ■ 11am-3am, patio

Bar de la Couronne [★M,S] 418/525-6593 ■ 310 rue de la Couronne (btwn rues de la Reine & de la Salle) ■ 9pm-3am, nude dancers, [MO] Th-Sat

Bar Le Drague [★M,NH,D,F,K,C,DS,WC] 418/649-7212 ■ 815 rue St-Augustin (at St-Joachim) ■ 10am-3am, DJ Fri-Sun, terrace ■ www.ledrague.com

Pub L'Echouerie [W,D,E] 290 rue St-Joseph ■ lounge, DJ wknds

NIGHTCLUBS

Le Gai Serpentin [M,S] 418/831-4055 ■ 101 boul du Pont (on Hwy 132), St-Nicolas ■ 2pm-3am Th-Sat

RESTAURANTS

Le Commensal 418/647-3733 ■ 860 rue St-Jean ■ 11am-10pm, vegetarian/ vegan ■ www.commensal.com

Le Hobbit 418/647-2677 ■ 700 rue St-Jean (at Ste-Geneviève) ■ 9am-10pm, some veggie

Le Moulin de St-Laurent Restaurant 418/829-3888 ■ 754 chemin Royal, St Laurent, Ile d' Orleans ■ lunch & dinner, May-Oct only, live music Sun ■ www.moulinstlaurent.qc.ca

La Piazzetta 418/529-7489 ■ 707 rue St-Jean

Le Poisson d'Avril 418/692-1010, 877/692-1010 ■ 115 quai St-André (at St-Thomas) ■ 5pm-close, from 11:30am Fri, name is French for "April Fools" ■ www.poissondavril.net

Restaurant Diana [★] 418/524-5794 ■ 849 rue St-Jean (at St-Augustine) ■ 8am-1am, till 2am Fri-Sat, Italian & Greek

ENTERTAINMENT & RECREATION

Fairmont Le Château Frontenac [GF,SW] 418/692-3861, 800/257-7544 ■ 1 rue des Carrières ■ this hotel disguised as a castle remains the symbol of Québec—even if you can't afford the princess' ransom to stay the night, come & enjoy the view from outside ■ www.chateaufrontenac.com

Ice Hotel [GF] 418/875-4522, 877/505-0423 ■ Sainte-Catherine-de-la-Jacques-Cartier ■ sometimes getting put on ice isn't a bad thing—check it out before it melts away, 9 km E of Québec City in Montmorency Falls Park (Jan-March only) ■ www.icehotel-canada.com

MEN'S CLUBS

Bloc 225 [PC] 418/523-2562, 877/523-2562 ■ 225 St-Jean (at Turnbull) ■ 24hrs, also Capital Gym ■ gayquebec.net/sauna.html

Sauna Backboys [V] 418/521-6686, 877/523-6686 ■ 264 rue de la Couronne (at Prince Edward) ■ 24hrs during week

Sauna/ Hotel Hippocampe [★V] 418/692-1521, 888/388-1521 ■ 31 rue McMahon ■ 24hrs, bar, also small hotel (www.hotelhippocampe.com) ■ www.saunahip-pocampe.com

EROTICA

Empire Lyon 418/648-2301 ■ 225A rue St-Jean (at Turnbull) ■ DVDs, toys, lubes, magazines, underwear & more ■ wegavideo.ca

Importation André Dubois [TG,WC] 418/692-0264 ■ 46 côte de la Montagne (at Frontenac Castle)

PUERTO RICO

San Juan

ACCOMMODATIONS

1 Acacia Seaside Inn [GF,SW] 787/727-0626, 800/946-3244 ■ 8 Taft St (at McLeary) ■ www.acaciaseasideinn.com

2 Andalucia Guesthouse & Vacation Rentals [M,GO] 787/309-3373 ■ 2011 McLeary St (at San Miguel St, Ocean Park) ■ guesthouse ■ www.andalucia-puertorico.com

3 At Wind Chimes Inn [GF,SW,NS,WC] 787/727-4153, 800/946-3244 ■ 1750 McLeary Ave, Condado ■ restored Spanish villa, 1 block from Condado beach ■ www.atwindchimesinn.com

Caribe Mountain Villas [GF,SW,GO] 787/769-0860 ■ Carr 857, km 6.0, Carolina ■ resort in Carolina rain forest (25 miles from San Juan) ■ www.caribevillas.com

4   **Casa del Caribe Guest House** [GF,NS] 787/722-7139, 877/722-7139 ■ Calle Caribe 57, Condado ■ B&B in heart of Condado ■ www.casadelcaribe.net

5   **Condado Inn** [MW,GO] 787/724-7145 ■ Av Condado 6 (at Av Ashford) ■ also bar ■ canadianpet@yahoo.com

     Embassy Suites Hotel & Casino [GF,SW,WC] 787/791-0505, 888/791-0505 ■ 8000 Tartak St (at Isla Verde Blvd), Carolina ■ www.embassysuitessanjuan.com

6   **Hotel El Convento** [★GF,SW] 787/723-9020, 800/468-2779 ■ Calle Cristo 100, Old San Juan (btwn Caleta de las Monjas & Calle Sol) ■ 17th-c former Carmelite convent, gym ■ www.elconvento.com

7   **L' Habitation Beach Guesthouse** [MW,GO] 787/727-2499 ■ Calle Italia 1957, Ocean Park (near Santa Ana) ■ also restaurant & bar ■ www.habitationbeach.com

     Miramar Hotel [GF,WI] 787/977-1000, 877/647-2627 ■ Ponce de León 606 ■ www.miramarhotelpr.com

8   **Numero Uno on the Beach** [GS,SW,WC] 787/726-5010, 866/726-5010 ■ Calle Santa Ana 1, Ocean Park (near Calle Italia) ■ also Pamela's restaurant & bar ■ www.numero1guesthouse.com

9   **The San Juan Water & Beach Club Hotel** [GF,SW,NS,WI,WC] 787/728-3666, 888/265-6699 ■ 2 Tartak St (Isla Verde), Carolina ■ boutique hotel on beach, restaurant & lounge ■ www.waterbeachclubhotel.com

Bars

6   **Cafe Bohemio** [GF,E] 787/723-9202, 787/723-9200 ■ Calle Cristo 100, Old San Juan (in Gran Hotel El Convento) ■ 11am-2am, clsd Wed, more gay Tue, also restaurant, food till 11pm, professional crowd, live music Th-Sat ■ www.elconvento.com

10   **Cups** [★W,D,E] 787/268-3570 ■ Calle San Mateo 1708 (btwn Calles Barbe & San Jorge), Santurce ■ 7pm-close, from 8pm Sat, clsd Sun-Tue, live music Wed & Fri

5   **Downstairs Cafe** [M] 787/724-7145 ■ Av Condado 6 (at Condado Inn) ■ 1pm-close, near beach, hustlers

11   **Junior's** [★MW,NH,DS,S] 787/723-9477 ■ Calle Condado 613 (btwn Calle del Carmen & Av Ponce de León), Santurce ■ 8pm-close, local crowd, two locations

12   **Nuestro Ambiente** [W,D,E] 787/724-9093 ■ Av Ponce de León 1412 (across from Central High School), Santurce ■ 8pm-close, clsd Mon-Tue, live music wknds, comedy ■ nuestroambiente@yahoo.com

     El Quenepo [M] 787/721-7420 ■ Calle de Parque 411, Parada 23, Santurce ■ 5pm-close, popular happy hour

13   **Starz** [MW,D,TG,DS,S] 787/721-8645 ■ 1507 Ponce de Leon Ave (at Diego) ■ www.starzclub.com

14   **Tia Maria's** [★MW,NH] 787/724-4011 ■ Av Jose de Diego, Stop 22 (at Ponce de León), Santurce ■ noon-2am, professional crowd, also liquor shop

Nightclubs

15   **Club Lazer** [GF,D] 787/725-7581 ■ Calle Cruz 251, Old San Juan ■ 8pm-close, popular w/ gay cruises ■ www.clublazer.com

     HIM The Club [M,D,DS,S] 787/751-9067, 787/942-1534 ■ 898 Ave Munoz Rivera, Rio Piedras ■ www.himtheclub.com

16   **Krash Klub** [★MW,D,DS,S,V,GO] 787/722-1131 ■ Av Ponce de León 1257 (btwn Calles Villamil & Labra), Santurce ■ 9pm-4am, clsd Mon, theme nights ■ www.krashpr.com

     Medusa [GS,D] 787/764-9230 ■ Av Roosevelt 7 (at America), Hato Rey ■ more gay wknds ■ www.medusatheclub.com

Cafes

17   **Cafe Berlin** [★] 787/722-5205 ■ Calle San Francisco 407, Plaza Colón, Old San Juan (btwn Calles Norzagary & O'Donnel) ■ 9am-11pm, plenty veggie

Restaurants

     Aguaviva 787/722-0665 ■ 364 Calle La Fortaleza, Old San Juan ■ dinner nightly, fresh seafood & ceviche ■ www.oofrestaurants.com/aguaviva

     Al Dente 787/723-7303 ■ 309 Calle Recinto S, Old San Juan ■ lunch & dinner, clsd Sun, Italian, also wine bar ■ www.aldentepr.com

     Amadeus Cafe [★GO] 787/722-8635 ■ Calle San Sebastián 106, Old San Juan (btwn Calles San José & del Cristo) ■ lunch & dinner, also bar

     La Bombonera [★] 787/722-0658 ■ Calle San Francisco 259, Old San Juan ■ 7:30am-8pm, come for the strong coffee & pastries, since 1903!

     Buyé Bistro Criollo [E] 787/725-4826 ■ Calle Canals 202, Parada 19 1/2, Santurce ■ lunch & dinner, Sun brunch, outdoor dining

     Dragonfly 787/977-3886 ■ 364 S Fortaleza St, Old San Juan (across from Parrot Club) ■ 6pm-11pm, till midnight Th Sat, full bar, Latin/ Asian fusion ■ www.oofrestaurants.com/dragonfly

     Fleria 787/268-0010 ■ 1754 Calle Loiza, Santurce ■ lunch & dinner, clsd Sun-Mon, Greek, some veggie

     Mona's [E] 787/282-0207 ■ 510 Ponce de León, Hato Rey ■ Mexican

     The Parrot Club [E] 787/725-7370 ■ Calle Fortaleza 363, Old San Juan (btwn Plaza Colón & Callejón de la Capilla) ■ lunch & dinner, chic Nuevo Latino bistro & bar, live music ■ www.oofrestaurants.com/parrotclub

     Transylvania Restaurant [E] 787/977-2328 ■ Recinto S 317, Old San Juan ■ lunch Tue-Sat & dinner nightly, Romanian, also bar & gallery, live music

Entertainment & Recreation

     Saliendo del Closet 787/607-3939 ■ WIAC 740AM ■ 7:30pm-9pm Th ■ www.radiopr740.com

Retail Shops

12   **The Rainbow Shop** 787/721-0401, 787/721-2982 ■ Av Ponce de León 1412 (inside Nuestro Ambiente), Santurce ■ 11am-6pm Wed, gay items, flags, stickers, etc ■ www.rainbowshoppr.com

Gyms & Health Clubs

     International Fitness [GS] 787/721-0717 ■ Av Ashford 1131, Condado (btwn Avs Cervantes & Caribe) ■ 5am-10pm, till 9pm Fri, call for wknd hours

Erotica

     Condom World 787/751-0997 ■ 311 Roosevelt Ave, Hato Rey ■ condoms, toys, videos & more—21 locations in Puerto Rico

     Pleasure Paradise 787/706-0855 ■ Av Roosevelt 1367 (in Plazoleta Julio Garriga), Hato Rey

     Red Zone 787/723-9099 ■ 1199 Calle Condado ■ www.redzonepr.com

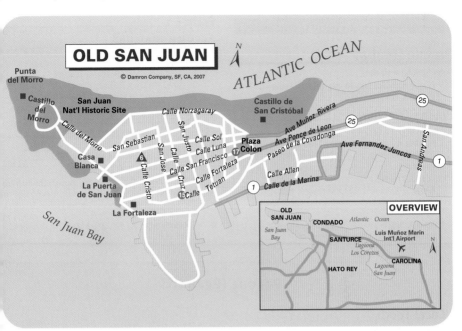

OLD SAN JUAN

© Damron Company, SF, CA, 2007

ATLANTIC OCEAN

Punta
del Morro

Castillo
del
Morro

San Juan
Nat'l Historic Site

Calle del Morro

San Sebastian

Casa
Blanca

La Puerta
de San Juan

La Fortaleza

San Juan Bay

Calle Norzagaray

San Justo

Calle Sol

Calle Luna

Calle San Francisco

Calle Fortaleza

Calle Tetuan

Calle Cruz

San Jose

Calle Cristo

Castillo de
San Cristóbal

Plaza
Colon

17

Ave Muñoz Rivera

25

Ave Ponce de Leon

Paseo de la Covadonga

Calle Allen

Calle de la Marina

1

25

Ave Fernandez Juncos

San Andreas

1

25

OVERVIEW

OLD
SAN JUAN

San Juan
Bay

SANTURCE

HATO REY

CONDADO   Atlantic Ocean

Luis Muñoz Marin
Int'l Airport

Lagoona
Los Corozos

Lagoona
San Juan

CAROLINA

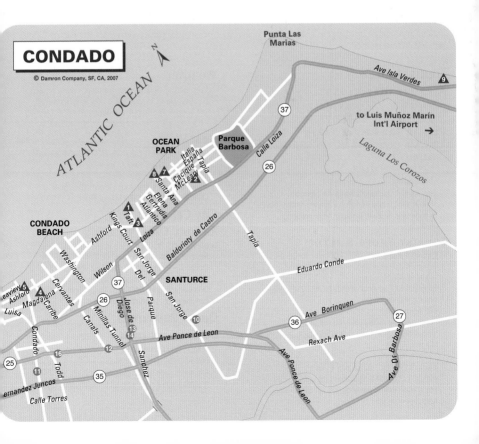

CONDADO

© Damron Company, SF, CA, 2007

ATLANTIC OCEAN

Punta Las
Marias

Ave Isla Verdes

9

37

to Luis Muñoz Marín
Int'l Airport →

OCEAN
PARK

Parque
Barbosa

Calle Loiza

Laguna Los Corozos

Italia

España

Cacique

Tapia

McLeary

Santa Ana

Elena

Gertrudis

Atlantico

Loiza

Taft

Kings Court

Ashford

Wilson

Washington

Cervantes

Magdalena

Caribe

Canals

Minillas Tunnel

San Jorge

Del

Parque

Jose de
Diego

Baldorioty de Castro

Tapia

Eduardo Conde

Sanchez

San Jorge

SANTURCE

Ave Ponce de Leon

Ave Borinquen

Rexach Ave

Ave Ponce de Leon

Ave Dr Barbosa

27

36

CONDADO
BEACH

eaview

Ashford

Luisa

Condado

25

fernandez Juncos

Calle Torres

Todd

37

26

26

10

13

14

12

35

16

11

5

4

8

7

3

1

2

37

Prague (Praha)

Note: M°=Metro station
Prague is divided into 10 city districts: Praha—1,
Praha—2, etc.

Praha—Overview

ACCOMMODATIONS
Apartments in Prague [GF,WI,WC] 420/251-512-502,
303/800-0858 ■ apt rental service ■ apartments-in-
prague.org

PUBLICATIONS
Amigo 420/602-641-274 ■ bi-monthly magazine w/ guide
to gay scene in Czech Republic & Slovakia, personals ■
www.amigo.cz
Maxx 420/222-210-595 ■ monthly erotica magazine,
classified ads (in Czech) ■ www.amigo.cz

Praha—1

ACCOMMODATIONS
1   Old Town Apartments [M,GO] 36/309-323-334 ■ apts ■
     www.gaystay.net/OldTown
2   Prague Center Guest Residence [MW,GO]
     36-309/323-334 ■ Stepanska Street (at Zitna) ■ apt, near
     Wenceslas Square ■ gaystay.net/PragueCenter
3   Vodickova Apartments [GF,WI,WC] 420/222-242-431
     ■ Vodickova 38 (at Wenceslas Square) ■ fully equipped flats
     w/ kitchen ■ www.pragueapartment.cz

BARS
4   Friends Bar [★M,NH,D,V] 420/226-211-920
     ■ Bartolomejská 11 ■ 6pm-4am, DJ Wed-Sat, internet access
     ■ www.friends-prague.cz
5   Tingl Tangl [MW,D,F,C,DS] 420/224-238-278 ■ Karolíny
     Svetlé 12 ■ 11am-10pm, [C] 9pm-5am Wed & Fri-Sat, full
     restaurant ■ www.tingltangl.cz
6   U Rudolfa [M,BW,OC] 420/605-872-492 ■ Mezibranská 3
     ■ 4pm-2am

PRAGUE (PRAHA)

Local Food:

In this increasingly international city, it can be easy to eat like you're back home. As tempting as it may be to
reach for a burger or a slice of pizza, try a restaurant such as Staromestska Restaurace for authentic (if touristy) Czech
fare. Czech midday and evening meals are decidedly meat-centric, and many dishes are fried and served in rich sauces.
If dumplings, goulash, fried cheese, and saurkraut are not your idea of good eating, you will at least want to try the
wonderful Czech pastries!

Tourist Info

AIRPORT DIRECTIONS
Ruzyne is about 12 miles west of the city center,
and is easily accessible by public transit.

PUBLIC TRANSIT & TAXIS
Taxi AAA 420/222-333-222, web: www.radiotaxi-
aaa.cz.
Profi Taxi 420/261-314-151.
CSA shuttle.
There are 6 Transportation Info Centers
throughout city with info on metro, trams, buses
& funicular, Ruzyne Airport, web: www.dp-
praha.cz.

TOURIST SPOTS & INFO
Charles Bridge.
Jewish Museum 420/221-711-511, web:
www.jewishmuseum.cz.
Museum of Fine Arts 420/222-220-218, web:
www.cmvu.cz.
Old Jewish Quarter.
Prague Castle 420/224-373-368, web:
www.hrad.cz/en/prazsky_hrad/navesta_hradu.sht
m.
Wenceslas Square.
Visitor's Center: Tourist Info Center
420/221-714-444. Staromestské radnice, Old
Town Hall, 9am-6pm Mon-Fri, till 5pm wknds,
web: www.pis.cz.

Weather
Continental climate. Late spring or early fall are
the best times to visit, especially in June before
the tourist season is in full swing. Winters can get
very cold with average daytime highs of 34° F.

Best Views
For a great view of the whole of Prague, head for
the Observation Tower (a mini version of the
Eiffel Tower) on Petrin Hill. The Old Town Bridge
Tower affords a fabulous view of Old Town, the
Charles Bridge, and the Vltava River.

City Calendar

ANNUAL EVENTS
May/June - Prague Spring International Music
Festival, web: www.festival.cz.
October - International Jazz Festival 420/224-
235-340, web: www.jazzfestivalpraha.cz.
October - Mezipatra, Czech Gay & Lesbian Film
Festival, web: www.mezipatra.cz.

Queer Resources

COMMUNITY INFO
Prague Gay Guide, web:
www.prague.gayguide.net.
AA, web: www.sweb.cz/aacesko.
CSAP 420/224-814-284, web: aids-pomoc.cz.

NIGHTCLUBS

Escape Club [MO,D,F,S,$] 420/602-403-744, 420/606-111-177 ■ V Jame 8 (off Wenceslas Square) ■ *9pm-4am, disco from 10pm, go-go boys, also restaurant, hustlers* ■ www.volny.cz/escapeclub

Roxy [GS,D,V,YC] 420/224-826-296 ■ Dlouhá 33 (M° Námestí Republiky) ■ *9pm-6am, cool events* ■ www.roxy.cz

CAFES

Cafe Cafe 420/224-210-597 ■ Rytirská 10 (at Perlová, near Oldtown Square) ■ *10am-11pm, from 10am wknds* ■ www.cafe-cafe.cz

Cafe Érra [GS,F] 420/222-220-569 ■ Konviktská 11 ■ *9am-midnight, from 11am wknds, salads, sandwiches & entrées* ■ www.sweb.cz/erra.cafe

Cafe Louvre [GS,F,NS] 420/224-930-912 ■ Národni 20 (M° Narodni Trida) ■ *8am-11:30pm, from 9am wknds, billiard tables* ■ www.cafelouvre.cz

Downtown Cafe [GO] 420/724-111-276 ■ Ujezd 19 ■ *9am-11pm, till 11:30pm Th, till midnight Fri-Sat* ■ www.downtowncafe.cz

Kafirna U Ceského Pána [★M] 420/222-328-283 ■ Kozí 13, Stare Mesto ■ *noon-11pm, from 3pm wknds, small bar popular w/ locals*

RESTAURANTS

Credo 420/222-324-634 ■ Petrska 11 ■ *9am-midnight, from 10:30am Sat, clsd Sun, full bar [GF]* ■ www.credo-restaurace.cz

La Provence [GO] 420/296-826-155 ■ Stupartska 9 (near Old Town Square) ■ *noon-11pm, French* ■ www.kampa-group.com/en

Staromestska Restaurace 420/224-213-015 ■ Staromestske namesti 19 ■ *11am-midnight, local Czech specialties* ■ www.staromestskarestaurace.cz

MEN'S CLUBS

Sauna Babylonia [★V] 420/224-232-304 ■ Martinská 6 ■ *popular w/ tourists, gym equipment, bar* ■ www.amigo.cz/babylonia

EROTICA

Amigo Shop 420/222-233-250 ■ U Pujcovna 6 ■ *clsd Sun-Mon, videos, DVDs, magazines* ■ www.pinkshop.cz

Praha—2

ACCOMMODATIONS

9 **Balbin Penzion** [GF,WI] 420/222-250-660 ■ Balbinova 26 (near Wenceslas Square) ■ www.balbin.cz

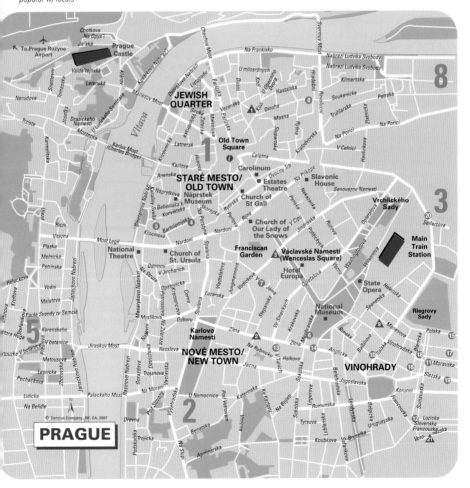

PRAGUE

Prague Saints [MW,GO] 420/775-152-041, 420/775-152-042 ■ Polska 32 (office location) (at Trebizkeho, at Saints Bar) ■ apts in gay Vinohrady district ■ www.praguesaints.cz

Bars

10 **Bar 21** [MW,F,YC] 420/724-254-048 ■ Rimska 21 ■ 4pm-4am, cellar bar, mostly Czechs

11 **Fajn Bar** [M,F,DS,S] 420/602-350-413 ■ Moravska 21 ■ 2pm-4am, cafe-bar, occasional drag or strip shows

12 **Gay Club Stella** [MW,F] 420/224-257-869 ■ Luzická 10 (in Vinohrady) ■ 8pm-5am, cozy bar/ cafe, terrace ■ stellaclub.webpark.cz

13 JampaDampa [★W,D,K] 420/737-105-193, 420/739-592-099 ■ V Tunich 10 ■ 1pm-3am, till 6am Fri, 6pm-6am Sat, 6pm-1am Sun ■ www.jampadampa.cz

14 **Klub Streclec** [GF,BW] 420/224-941-446 ■ Zitna 51 ■ 5pm-2am, till midnight Sun

15 **Saints** [MW] 420/222-250-326 ■ Polska 32 (at Trebizkeho) ■ 7pm-4am ■ www.praguesaints.cz

16 Street Cafe [GS,D,F] 420/222-013-116 ■ Blanická 28 ■ 4pm-close, from 7pm Fri-Sat, clsd Sun-Mon ■ www.street-cafe.cz

Nightclubs

17 **Termix** [★MW,D] 420/222-710-462 ■ Trebizkeho 4 ■ 8pm-5am ■ www.club-termix.cz

18 **Valentino** [MW,D,V] 420/222-513-491, 420/776-360-698 (cell) ■ Vinohradska 40 ■ 2pm-5am, 3 levels, darkroom ■ www.club-valentino.cz

Restaurants

Celebrity Cafe [GS] 420/222-511-343 ■ Vinohradska 40 (in Vinohrady) ■ 8am-2am, noon-3am Sat, noon-midnight Sun, also bar ■ www.celebritycafe.cz

Radost FX [GS] 420/224-254-776, 420/603-193-711 ■ Belehradska 120, Vinohrady ■ fabulous wknd brunch, vegetarian cafe, also nightclub [GF] w/ popular monthly gay party ■ www.radostfx.cz

Sahara Cafe 420/222-514-987 ■ Namesti Miru 6 ■ lunch & dinner; salad, pasta & meat ■ www.saharacafe.com

Vinny Senk U Primátora [GO] 420/224-916-557 ■ Trojanova 16 ■ noon-10pm, clsd wknds, Bavarian ■ vinnysenkuprimatora.sweb.cz

Men's Clubs

Marco [★V] 420/224-262-833 ■ Lublanská 1916/17, Vinohrady ■ 2pm-3am, also bar, booths, small but popular ■ www.saunamarco.cz

Praha—3

Accommodations

Studio Henri [M,GO] 420/271-773-837, 420/271-773-847 ■ Jeseniova 52/1196 ■ apt, jacuzzi, great view of Old Town Prague ■ www.studiohenri.cz

Bars

Eclipse [WO,D] 420/731-702-094 ■ Milicova 25 ■ 8pm-4am Fri-Sat only ■ www.eclipse-klub.ic.cz

Gulliver [MW,GO] 420/721-031-965 ■ Milicova 6 ■ noon-10pm, from 5pm wknds, wine bar, lesbian-owned

19 **Latimerie Club Cafe** [MW] 420/224-252-049 ■ Slezska 74 ■ 4pm-close ■ www.latimerieclub.cz

Piano Bar [★MW,F] 420/22-969-888, 420/775-727-796 (cell) ■ Milesovská 10 ■ 5pm-close, mostly Czech ■ sweb.cz/pianobar

20 **Pinocchio** [★M,D,DS,S,V,AYOR] 420/602-969-374 ■ Seifertova 3 ■ 6pm-3am, till 5am Fri-Sat, rent boys, also se shop, pension (see overview map)

Cafes

Galerie Cafe [GS] 420/222-730-056, 420/605-108-29 ■ Jagellonska 20, Vinohrady ■ 10am-10pm, from 5pm Sun, clsd Sat, works by gay artists ■ www.galerie-cafe.info

Entertainment & Recreation

TV Tower 420/242-418-778, 420/242-418-766 ■ Mahlerovy sady 1 ■ get a bird's-eye view of the city from the top of this tower, also restaurant 10am-11pm ■ www.tower.cz

Gyms & Health Clubs

Bravo Fitness [MW,GO] 420/271-731-412 ■ Srobarova 9, Zizkov (at Pisecká) ■ 9am-10pm, 2pm-9pm wknds

Men's Clubs

Alcatraz [MO,L,V,S] 420/222-711-458 ■ Borivojova 58 (of Seifertova, in Zizhkov) ■ 10pm-5am, S/M club, theme nights ■ www.alcatraz.cz

Real Club [MO] 420/775-674-672 ■ Ondrickova 15 ■ 5pm-7am, cruisy, darkroom ■ www.realclub.cz

Erotica

City Fox 420/222-540-358 ■ Pribenicka 12, Zizkov ■ clse Sun-Mon, small video store, Czech & US titles, cabins ■ www.foxpress.cz/city.html

Praha—4

Gyms & Health Clubs

Plavecky Stadion Podoli [GS,F] 420/241-433-952 ■ Podolská 74 ■ 6am-9:45 pm, public baths, restaurants, women's sauna Th-Fri & Sun ■ www.pspodoli.cz

Praha—5

Men's Clubs

Drake's [MO,F,S,V,$] 420/257-326-828 ■ Zborovska 50 (a Petrinska) ■ 24hrs, darkroom, maze, sex shop, free Sun buffe from 8pm ■ www.drakes.cz

Praha—8

Accommodations

Hotel Villa Mansland Prague [M,SW,GO] 420/286-884-405, 420/777-839-733 ■ Stepnicná 9, Liben ■ sauna, also restaurant ■ www.villa-mansland.com

Men's Clubs

Sauna David [V] 420/222-317-869 ■ Sokolovská 44, Karlin ■ 9am-11pm, from 11am wknds, oldest sauna in Prague, gym ■ www.gaysauna.cz

Praha—10

Accommodations

21 **Arco Guest House** [M,GO] 36-309/323-334 (English & German) ■ Voronézská 24 (in Vinohrady) ■ internet access ■ www.gaystay.net/Arco/

Gay Guesthouse Nouvum Garden [MO,SW,WI,GO] Zernovská 1195/2 ■ steam bath, massage, ful brkfst ■ www.nouvum.com

Ron's Rainbow Guest House [GS,GO] 420/271-725-664, 420/731-165-022 (cell) ■ Bulharska 4 (at Finská) ■ jacuza ■ www.gay-prague.com

ENGLAND

London

London is divided into 6 regions:
London—Overview
London—Central
London—West
London—North
London—East
London—South

London—Overview

ACCOMMODATIONS
London First Choice Apartments [GF]
44–(0)20/8990–9033 ■ *short-term apt rentals, also hotel reservations* ■ www.lfca.co.uk

ENTERTAINMENT & RECREATION
London Gay Symphony Orchestra 44–(0)79/6385–3099 ■ www.lgso.org.uk

LONDON

Day Trips: Brighton

Fans of the original *Queer As Folk* will know all about the wild times in Manchester, London's rival to the north for a wild (k)night on the town. But we recommend you make like a Londoner and head south to Brighton and Hove. Once the pleasure-playground for George IV, one of England's most funloving kings, Brighton today offers great nightlife for commoners and royalty alike, fabulous restaurants, a sizeable gay and lesbian community, and of course the seaside. All of this makes for a wonderful year-round escape from the big city. For more info, visit www.tourism.brighton.co.uk.

Tourist Info

AIRPORT DIRECTIONS
London has 4 airports: Heathrow, Gatwick, Stansted and London City. All are well connected to Central London by rail and bus; Heathrow's Terminal 4 has its own Underground station (Piccadilly line).

PUBLIC TRANSIT & TAXIS
Freedom Cars 44–(0)20-7734-1313.
Ladycabs 44–(0)20/7254-3501.
London Travel Information (Tube & buses) 44–(0)20/7222-1234, 24hr info, web: www.tfl.gov.uk.

TOURIST SPOTS & INFO
British Museum 44–(0)20/7323-8299, web: www.thebritishmuseum.ac.uk.
Buckingham Palace 44–(0)20/7766-7300.
Globe Theatre 44–(0)20/7902-1400, web: www.shakespeares-globe.org.
Kensington Palace 44–(0)87/0751-5170.
Madame Tussaud's 44–(0)87/0999-0046, web: www.madame-tussauds.co.uk.
National Gallery 44–(0)20/7747-2885, web: www.nationalgallery.org.uk.
Oscar Wilde's house (34 Tite Street).
St Paul's Cathedral 44–(0)20/7236-4128, web: www.stpauls.co.uk.
Tate Gallery 44–(0)20/7887-8008, web: www.tate.org.uk.
Tower of London 44–(0)87/0756-6060.
Westminster Abbey 44–(0)20/7654-4900, web: www.westminster-abbey.org.
Visitor's Center: 44–(0)20/7292-2333, web: www.visitlondon.com, www.londoninformation.org.

Weather

London is warmer and less rainy than you may have heard. Summer temperatures reach the 70's and the average annual rainfall is about half of that of Atlanta, GA or Hartford, CT.

Best Views

London Eye, 44–(0)87/0990-8883, web: www.londoneye.com

City Calendar

LGBT PRIDE
June-July. www.pridelondon.org.

ANNUAL EVENTS
March-April - Lesbian & Gay Film Festival 44–(0)20/7928-3232, web: www.llgff.org.uk.
June-July - Pride Festival Fortnight 44–(0)20-7164-2182, web: www.pridelondon.org.
August - Mr Gay UK Contest, web: www.mrgayuk.co.uk.

Queer Resources

COMMUNITY INFO
London Lesbian & Gay Switchboard 44–(0)20/7837-7324, web: www.llgs.org.uk.
AA 44–(0)84/5769-7555, web: www.aa-uk.org.uk.
National AIDS Helpline 0800/567-123, web: www.playingsafely.co.uk.

<u>The Women's Library, London Metropolitan University</u>
[NS] 44–(0)20/7320-2222 ■ Old Castle St ■ clsd Sun, also
cafe, museum, cultural center, call for events ■
www.londonmet.ac.uk/thewomenslibrary

PUBLICATIONS

<u>Boyz</u> 44–(0)20/7025-6100 ■ free weekly scene guide for
boys ■ www.boyz.co.uk

<u>Diva</u> 44–(0)20/7424-7400 ■ monthly lesbian magazine ■
www.divamag.co.uk

<u>Gay Times</u> 44–(0)20/7424-7400 ■ gay glossy ■
www.gaytimes.co.uk

<u>The Pink Paper</u> 44–(0)20/7424-7414 ■ free LGBT
newspaper ■ www.pinkpaper.com

<u>QX International</u> 44–(0)20/7379-7887 ■ weekly, covers
London's lgbt party/ music scene ■ www.qxmagazine.com

<u>Time Out</u> 44–(0)20/7813-3000 ■ weekly city scene guide
w/ gay section ■ www.timeout.com

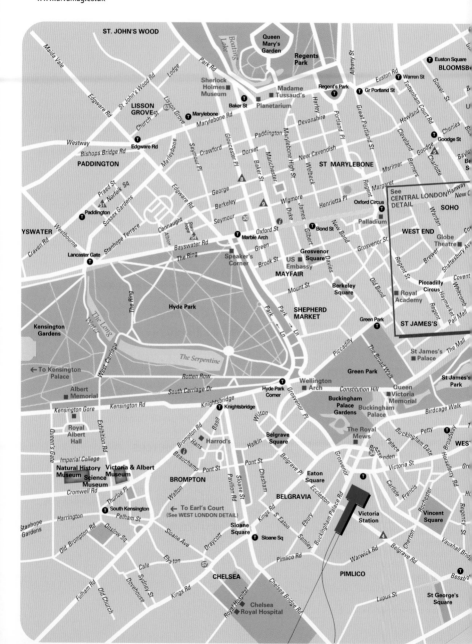

London—Central

London—Central includes Soho, Covent Garden, Bloomsbury, Mayfair, Westminster, Pimlico & Belgravia

ACCOMMODATIONS

1   **Central London Guestrooms & Apartments** [MW,NS,GO]
44-(0)20/8743-5577 ■ 33-34 Warple Wy (Acton)
■ *superior accommodations in Soho, Covent Garden, West End* ■ www.apartment-centre.co.uk

2   **Checkin Accommodation London** [GS,NS,WI,GO]
44-(0)79/0983-6487 ■ 20 Trentishoe Mansions, 90 Charing Cross Rd (at Cambridge Circus) ■ *3-bdrm flat in the heart of London's West End, rent a room or the whole apt, kids ok* ■ www.checkin.se/london

3   **Clone Zone Luxury Apartments** [MW,GO]
44-(0)20/7287-3530 ■ 64 Old Compton St (at Whitcomb) ■ *fully equipped apts above Clone Zone retail store* ■ www.clonezone.co.uk

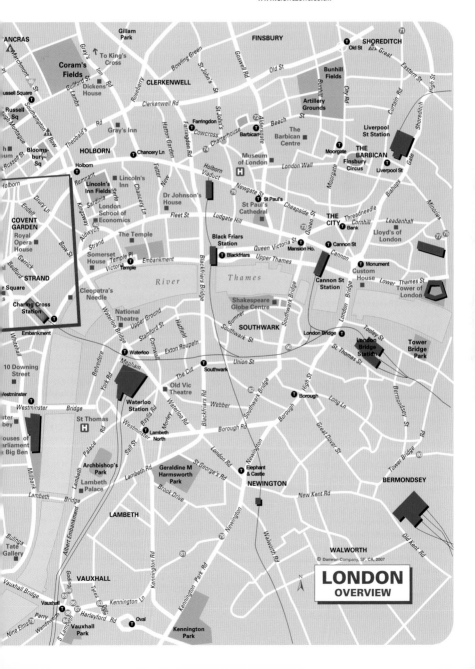

© Damron Company, SF, CA, 2007

LONDON
OVERVIEW

4 **Dover Hotel** [GF,WI] 44–(0)20/7821–9085 ■ 42/44 Belgrave Rd ■ www.dover-hotel.co.uk

5 **Fitz B&B** [MW,NS,WI,GO] 44–(0)78/3437–2866 ■ Colville Place (btwn Charlotte St & Whitfield St) ■ *18th-century townhouse, 3-night minimum* ■ www.fitzbb.me.uk

6 **George Hotel** [GF] 44–(0)20/7387–8777 ■ 58–60 Cartwright Gardens (N of Russell Square) ■ *full brkfst, some shared baths* ■ www.georgehotel.com

7 **Hazlitt's** [GF,WI] 44–(0)20/7434–1771 ■ 6 Frith St (Soho Sq) ■ *3 historic Georgian buildings furnished w/ antiques* ■ www.hazlitts.co.uk

8 **Lincoln House Hotel** [GS,WI,WC] 44–20/7486–7630 ■ 33 Gloucester Pl, Marble Arch (at Baker St) ■ *B&B, full brkfst (see overview map)* ■ www.lincoln-house-hotel.co.uk

   London Gay Accommodation [MW,NS,GO] 44–(0)20/7486–0855 ■ *room in private apt, shared bath, hot tub* ■ www.londongay.co.uk

9 **Manors & Co** [GF,WC] 44–(0)20/7486–5982, 800/454–4385 ■ 1 Baker St ■ *luxury apts in the heart of London (see overview map)* ■ www.londonapartment.co.uk

10 **Soho B&B** [GF,NS,GO] 44–(0)78/3437–2866 ■ Old Compton St (at Charing Cross Rd) ■ *2-bdrm apt w/ shared bathroom & kitchenette, rent room or whole apt, 3-night minimum* ■ www.sohobb.me.uk

11 **Waverley House Hotel** [GF,F] 44–(0)20/7833–3691, 44–(0)20/7833–2579 ■ 130-134 Southampton Row (Bloomsbury) ■ *full brkfst, restaurant, bar (see overview map)* ■ www.waverleyhousehotel.co.uk/waverley

Bars

Note: "Pub hours" usually means 11am-11pm Mon-Sat and noon-3pm & 7pm-10:30pm Sun

12 **79 CXR** [★M,D,WC] 44–(0)20/7734–0769 ■ 79 Charing Cross Rd (Soho) ■ *1pm-3am, till 10:30pm Sun, 2 flrs, cruisy* ■ www.79cxr.co.uk

13 **The Admiral Duncan** [★MW,NH,TG] 44–(0)20/7437–5300 ■ 54 Old Compton St (Soho) ■ *pub hours*

14 **Bar Aquda** [★MW] 44–(0)20/7557–9891 ■ 13–14 Maiden Ln (btwn Bedford & Southampton, Covent Garden) ■ *2pm-11pm, till 10:30pm Sun, cafe-bar*

15 **Bar Code** [MW,D,E,YC] 44–(0)20/7734–3342 ■ 3-4 Archer St (btwn Windmill & Rupert, off Shaftesbury, Soho) ■ *4pm-1am, till 11pm Sun, Comedy Camp Tue* ■ www.bar-code.co.uk

16 **Bar Saaqi** [GF,MR-A,F] 44–(0)20/7734–5525 ■ 21-22 Poland St ■ *Indian, more gay Fri for Pink Rupee* ■ www.saaqi.co.uk

17 **The Box** [★M,D,F,V,WC] 44–(0)20/7240–5828 ■ 32–34 Monmouth St (near Shaftesbury Ave, Covent Garden) ■ *11am-11pm, noon-10:30pm Sun, cafe-bar* ■ www.boxbar.com

18 **The Candy Bar** [★W,D,F,K,S] 44–(0)20/7494–4041 ■ 4 Carlisle St, S (at Dean) ■ *5pm-11:30pm, till 2am Fri-Sat, men welcome as guests; also a location in Brighton* ■ www.candybarsoho.com

19 **Compton's of Soho** [★M,L,F,WC] 44–(0)20/7479–7961 ■ 51-53 Old Compton St ■ *noon-11pm, till 10:30pm Sun, cruisy* ■ www.comptons-of-soho.co.uk

20 **Duke of Wellington** [MW,F] 44–(0)20/7439–1274 ■ 77 Wardour (Soho) ■ *pub hours*

21 **The Edge** [★MW,D,F,WC] 44–(0)20/7439–1313 ■ 11 Soho Square ■ *noon-1am, till 10:30pm Sun, 4 flrs, cafe-bar, live music, outdoor seating* ■ www.edgesoho.co.uk

22 **The Escape** [★M,D,V] 44–(0)20/7734–2626 ■ 10 Brewer St (near Regent St) ■ *5pm-3am, clsd Sun* ■ www.kudos-group.com

23 **Freedom Cafe-Bar** [MW,D,F,YC] 44–(0)20/7437–3490 ■ 66 Wardour St (off Old Compton St) ■ *5pm-3am, from 2pm Fri-Sat, 2pm-11:30pm Sun* ■ www.freedombarsoho.com

20 **Friendly Society** [MW,YC] 44–(0)20/7434–3805 ■ 79 Wardour St (the basement at Old Compton, enter Tisbury Ct) ■ *4pm-11pm, from 2pm Sat, 2pm-10:30pm Sun*

24 **The G.A.Y Bar** [MW,F,V] 44–(0)20/7494–2756 ■ 30 Old Compton St ■ *noon-midnight, till 10:30pm Sun, basement women's bar (men as guests), soap operas & videos shown* ■ www.g-a-y.co.uk/bar.asp

25 **Glass Bar** [WO,F,E,PC] 44–(0)20/7387–6184, 44–(0)20/7387–4153 ■ *5pm-11:30pm, clsd wknds, 2 flrs, Slap & Tickle comedy night 2nd Fri, theme nights & events (see overview map)* ■ www.glassbar.ndo.co.uk

26 **Halfway to Heaven** [★M,NH,K,C,OC,GO] 44–(0)20/7321–2791, 44–(0)70/9042–1969 ■ 7 Duncannon St (at Charing Cross, West End) ■ *noon-11pm, till 10:30pm Sun*

27 **King's Arms** [M,NH,B,F,K,V] 44–(0)20/7734–5907 ■ 23 Poland St (Soho) ■ *noon-11pm, till 1am Fri-Sat, 1pm-midnight Sun, popular bear hangout, 2 flrs* ■ www.kingsarms-london.com

12 **Ku Bar** [MW,K,YC,WI] 44–(0)20/7437–4303 ■ 30 Lisle St (Leicester Sq) ■ *noon-11pm, till 10pm Sun, trendy cafe-bar, T-dance Sun* ■ www.ku-bar.co.uk

28 **Kudos** [★MW,MR,F,V,WC,GO] 44–(0)20/7379–4573 ■ 10 Adelaide St (off the Strand) ■ *noon-midnight, till 11pm Sun, trendy cafe-bar, basement video bar open from 4pm* ■ www.kudosgroup.co.uk

29 **Profile** [MW] 44–(0)20/7734–8300 ■ 56 Frith St ■ *4pm-close, from noon wknds* ■ www.profilesoho.com

30 **The Quebec** [M,NH,OC] 44–(0)20/7629–6159 ■ 12 Old Quebec St (at Marble Arch) ■ *pub hours, live DJs Fri-Sat, [C] Sun (overview map)* ■ www.thequebec.co.uk

31 **The Retro Bar** [★MW,NH,D,A,K] 44–(0)20/7321–2811 ■ 2 George Ct ■ *pub hours*

32 **Rupert Street** [★MW,F,WC] 44–(0)87/1223–0842, 44–(0)20/7734–5614 ■ 50 Rupert St (off Brewer) ■ *pub hours, upscale "fashiony-types"*

33 **The Soho Revue Bar** [M,D,E] 44–(0)20/7734–0377 ■ 11-12 Walkers Ct (off Brewer St, Soho) ■ *[TG] Wed for Trannyshack, popular Sat for Shampoo* ■ www.sohorevue-bar.com

34 **The Stag** [M,F,C] 44–(0)20/7828–7287 ■ 15 Bressenden Pl (near Victoria Stn) ■ *noon-midnight, till 2am Fri, from 5pm Sat, till 10pm Sun, terrace (see overview map)*

35 **Star at Night** [MW,D,F,E] 44–(0)20/7494–2488 ■ 22 Great Chapel St ■ *Italian restaurant during day, 6pm-midnight, clsd Sun-Mon, relaxed cafe/ bar* ■ www.thestaratnight.com

20 **The Village Soho** [★M,F,V,YC] 44–(0)20/7434–2124 ■ 81 Wardour St (at Old Compton) ■ *3pm-1am, till 11:30pm Sun, 3 flrs, trendy, more women Wed for Girls on Girls downstairs* ■ www.village-soho.co.uk

36 **The Yard** [★MW,F,E,YC,WC] 44–(0)20/7437–2652, 871/426–2243 ■ 57 Rupert St (off Brewer) ■ *pub hours, 2 levels* ■ www.yardbar.co.uk

NIGHTCLUBS

37 <u>Club Wotever</u> [W,D,TG] 44–(0)20/7734–4243 ■ 12 Denman St (at Masters Club) ■ *9pm-3am, genderqueers & their admirers* ■ www.woteverworld.com

38 **Discotec** [M,D,$] 44–(0)20/7419–9199 ■ 18 W Central St (at The End) ■ *10pm-4am Th only, 2 rooms* ■ www.discotec-club.com

39 **Electrogogo** [GS,E] 44–(0)20/7734–8932, 44–(0)20/7734–3040 ■ 8 Brewer St (at Madame JoJo's, Soho) ■ *8pm-3am 1st Th, live music* ■ www.electrogogo.com

40 **Exilio** [MW,D,MR-L] 44–(0)79/3137–4391 ■ Houghton St (at London School of Economics Underground) ■ *10pm-3am Sat* ■ www.exilio.co.uk

41 **G.A.Y.** [★M,D,E,YC,$] 44–(0)20/7734–6963 ■ 157 Charing Cross Rd (at Oxford St, in London Astoria theatre complex) ■ *10:30pm-4am Mon & Th-Sat only, this is a HUGE club* ■ www.g-a-y.co.uk

42 <u>The Ghetto</u> [MW,D,A] 44–(0)20/7287–3726 ■ 5-6 Falconberg Court (off Charing Cross, behind the Astoria) ■ *10:30pm-3am, till 5am Fri-Sat, more women for Rockstarz Mon, Miss-Shapes Th, Wig Out Sat* ■ www.ghetto-london.co.uk

43 **Heaven** [★M,D] 44–(0)20/7930–2020 ■ The Arches (off Villiers St) ■ *Mon, Wed, Fri-Sat, the mother of all London gay clubs, call for hours/ events* ■ www.heaven-london.com

44 <u>Lounge</u> [W] 44–(0)79/0620–5014 ■ 93-107 Shaftesbury Ave (at Teatro) ■ *8pm-3am 1st & 3rd Th, visit website for schedule, men welcome as guests* ■ www.lounge.uk.net

45 **Rush** [GS,TG,D] 44–(0)20/7734–9992 ■ 25 Frith St (Soho) ■ *4pm-1am, from noon wknds, till 12:30am Sun* ■ www.rush-soho.com

46 **Salvation** [GS,$] 44–(0)20/7287–3834 (venue), 44–(0)87/1474–6002 (tickets) ■ Bloomsbury Ballrooms (Victoria House, Bloomsbury Sq) ■ www.salvation-london.com

33 **Shadow Lounge** [MW,D] 44–(0)20/7287–7988 ■ 5 Brewer St (Soho) ■ *10pm-3am, from 9pm Th-Sat, clsd Sun* ■ www.shadowlounge.co.uk

47 **Shaun & Joe** [M,D,F,E,C] 44–(0)20/7734–9858 ■ 5 Gosslett Yard (off Charing Cross Rd, Covent Garden) ■ *6pm-3am, sophisticated cocktail bar & nightclub* ■ www.shaun-nandjoe.com

48 **Trash Palace** [MW,D,A,E] 44–(0)20/7734–0522 ■ 11 Wardour St (Leceister Sq end) ■ *5pm-midnight, till 3am Fri-Sat, till 11pm Sun* ■ www.trashpalace.co.uk

CAFES

Balans Cafe [★MW] 44–(0)20/7439–3309 ■ 34 Old Compton St ■ *8am-5am, till 6am Fri-Sat, till 2am Sun, all-day brkfst, salads & sandwiches, terrace* ■ www.balans.co.uk

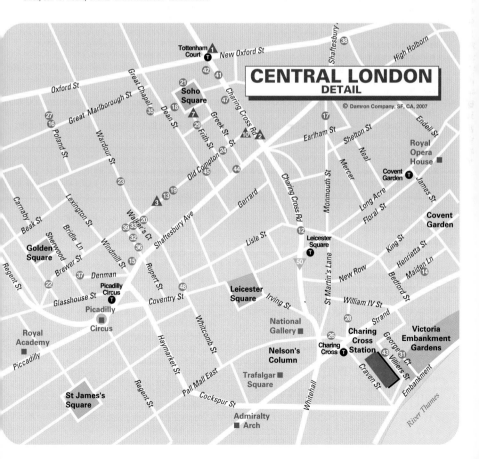

First Out [MW,F] 44-(0)20/7240-8042 ■ 52 St Giles High St (btwn Charing Cross & Shaftesbury) ■ 10am-11pm, 11am-10:30pm Sun, cont'l cafe, some veggie, full bar

RESTAURANTS

Asia de Cuba [R] 44-(0)20/7300-5588 ■ 45 St Martin's Ln (near Leicester Square) ■ noon-midnight, till 10:30pm Sun, Cuban/ Asian, chic scene ■ asiadecuba-restaurant.com

Balans [★TG,S,WC] 44-(0)20/7439-2183 ■ 60 Old Compton St ■ 8am-5am, till 6am Fri-Sat, till 2am Sun, cafe-bar, all-day/ night brunch ■ www.balans.co.uk

Food for Thought [BYOB] 44-(0)20/7836-0239 ■ 31 Neal St, downstairs (Covent Garden) ■ 9:30am-8:30pm, noon-5pm Sun, vegetarian, inexpensive hole-in-the-wall

The Gay Hussar [WC] 44-(0)20/7437-0973 ■ 2 Greek St (on Soho Square) ■ lunch & dinner, clsd Sun, Hungarian ■ www.gayhussar.co.uk

Just Falafs 44-(0)20/7734-1914 ■ 155 Wardour St ■ 8am-11pm, organic falafel ■ www.justfalafs.com

Mildred's [★] 44-(0)20/7494-1634 ■ 45 Lexington ■ noon-11pm, clsd Sun, vegetarian, plenty vegan ■ www.mildreds.co.uk

Nusa Dua 44-(0)20/7437-3559, 44-(0)87/1332-7468 ■ 11-12 Dean St (Oxford Circus) ■ Indonesian

Steph's [MW] 44-(0)20/7734-5976 ■ 39 Dean St (btwn Old Compton & Bateman) ■ lunch Mon-Fri & dinner Mon-Sat, clsd Sun, British ■ www.stephs-restaurant.com

Wagamama Noodle Bar [NS] 44-(0)20/7292-0990 ■ 10-A Lexington St ■ noon-11pm, till midnight Fri-Sat, till 10pm Sun, Japanese; many locations throughout city ■ www.wagamama.com

ENTERTAINMENT & RECREATION

Comedy Camp [★GS,$] 44-(0)20/7483-2960, 08-700/600-100 (TicketWeb) ■ 3-4 Archer St (at Barcode, btwn Windmill & Rupert, off Shaftesbury, Soho) ■ 8:30pm Tue, amateur & established comedy acts ■ www.comedy-camp.co.uk

Drill Hall [GS,NS,WC] 44-(0)20/7307-5060 (box office), 44-(0)20/7307-5061 (admin) ■ 16 Chenies St (btwn Alfred Pl & Ridgmount, Bloomsbury) ■ theatre company, many lesbian-themed performances ■ www.drillhall.co.uk

Prince Charles Cinema [GF] 44-(0)87/0811-2559 ■ 7 Leicester Pl (off Leicester Square) ■ sing-alongs, often show LGBT & alternative films ■ www.princecharlescinema.com

Queer Council [MW,TG] 44-(0)78/1640-5791 ■ 12 Denman St (at Masters Club) ■ 10pm-3am last Sat ■ www.queercouncil.com

BOOKSTORES

49 Gay's the Word 44-(0)20/7278-7654 ■ 66 Marchmont St (near Russell Square) ■ 10am-6:30pm, 2pm-6pm Sun, LGBT ■ www.gaystheword.co.uk

50 Silver Moon Women's Bookshop at Foyles [WC] 44-(0)20/7440-1562 ■ 113-119 Charing Cross Rd, 3rd flr ■ lesbian/ feminist, also videos & DVDs ■ www.silvermoon-bookshop.co.uk

RETAIL SHOPS

Prowler Soho [★] 44-(0)20/7734-4031 ■ 5-7 Brewer St (behind Village Soho bar) ■ 11am-10pm, from 10am Sat, noon-8pm Sun, large gay department store ■ www.prowler-stores.co.uk

GYMS & HEALTH CLUBS

London Central YMCA [GF,SW] 44-(0)20/7343-1844 ■ 112 Great Russell St ■ www.centralymca.org.uk

Soho Athletic Club [★M] 44-(0)20/7242-1290 ■ 12 Macklin St (at Drury Ln, Covent Garden) ■ www.sohogyms.com

MEN'S CLUBS

Chariots Waterloo 44-(0)20/7401-8484 ■ 101 Lower Marsh ■ 24hrs, sauna cabin, steam room, internet cafe, video room ■ www.gaysauna.co.uk

Pleasuredrome [F,V,NS] 44-(0)20/7633-9194 ■ Arch 124, Alaska St (at Alaska St, Waterloo) ■ 24hrs, day passes ■ www.pleasuredrome.com

EROTICA

Femme Boudoir 44-(0)20/7637-5794 ■ 17b Riding House St ■ lingerie, corsets, leather, rubber, toys, woman-owned/ run ■ www.femmeboudoir.com

RoB London [WC] 44-(0)20/7735-7893 ■ 24 Wells St (near Berwick St) ■ leather/ fetish shop ■ www.rob.nl

Soho Cinemas [V] 44-070/9042-2274 ■ 7-12 Walkers Court (off Brewer St, Soho) ■ 10:30am-11pm, till 1am Fri-Sat, 1pm-10pm Sun ■ www.sohogaycinemas.co.uk

London—West

London—West includes Earl's Court, Kensington, Chelsea & Bayswater

ACCOMMODATIONS

51 Cardiff Hotel [GF,WI] 44-(0)20/7723-3513, 44-(0)20/7723-9068 ■ 5, 7, 9 Norfolk Sq (Hyde Park) ■ B&B hotel in 3 Victorian townhouses, some share bathrooms ■ www.cardiff-hotel.com

52 Comfort Inn Kensington [GF,F,WI] 44-(0)20/7373-3300 ■ 22-32 W Cromwell Rd (Earl's Court) ■ also bar ■ www.hotels-kensington.com

53 Kensington International Inn [GF] 44-(0)20/7370-4333 ■ 4 Templeton Pl ■ www.kensingtoninternationalinn.com

Millennium Bailey's Hotel [GF] 44-(0)20/7373-6000, 44-(0)20/7331-6331 ■ 140 Gloucester Rd (at Old Brompton Rd, Kensington) ■ 4-star hotel, also restaurant & bar ■ www.mill-cop.com

54 Parkwood Hotel [GF,NS] 44-(0)20/7402-2241 ■ 4 Stanhope Pl (Marble Arch) ■ full brkfst ■ www.parkwood-hotel.com

BARS

55 Brompton's [★M,D,F,C,S] 44-(0)20/7370-1344 ■ 294 Old Brompton Rd (at Warwick Rd) ■ 4pm-2am, 5pm-12:30am Sun ■ BromptonCL@aol.com

56 The Coleherne [★M,NH,L,OC,WC] 44-(0)20/7244-5951 ■ 261 Old Brompton Rd (at Coleherne Rd) ■ pub hours, cruisy

The Culvert [M,NH,F,C,DS] 44-(0)70/9042-1416 ■ 54 Cowley Mill Rd (Uxbridge) ■ 11am-close

57 Queen's Head [M,NH,F,OC] 44-(0)20/7589-0262 ■ 27 Tryon St (btwn King's Rd & Sloane Ave, Chelsea) ■ pub hours, professional crowd (see overview map)

Richmond Arms [MW,D,K,C,DS] 44-(0)20/8940-2118 ■ 20 The Square (at Princes, Richmond) ■ pub hours, professional crowd

Ted's Place [M,D,TG,K,DS,V,PC] 44-(0)20/7385-9359 ■ 305-A North End Rd (at Lillie Rd, Earl's Ct) ■ 7pm-11pm, clsd Mon, cruisy

West Five (W5) [MW,F,C,P] 44-(0)20/8579-3266 ■ 5 Popes Ln (South Ealing) ■ 7pm-11pm, till midnight Wed-Th & Sun, open later Fri-Sat, lunch Sun, lounge & cabaret, garden

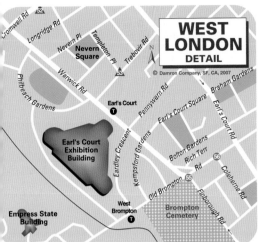

WEST LONDON DETAIL
© Damron Company, SF, CA, 2007

NIGHTCLUBS

She Chic [W,OC] 44-(0)20/8741-9173 (Hit Bar), 44-(0)79/3084-0781 ■ 14 Hammersmith Broadway (at the Hit Bar) ■ *8pm-1am every other 2nd Sat, women over age 25 only* ■ www.shechic.co.uk

RESTAURANTS

Balans West [MW] 44-(0)20/7244-8838 ■ 239 Old Brompton Rd ■ *8am-1am, till 2am Th-Sat, English* ■ www.balans.co.uk

The Churchill Arms 44-(0)20/7727-4242 ■ 119 Kensington Church St ■ *inexpensive, fantastic Thai, also pub*

Star of India 44-(0)20/737-2901 ■ 154 Old Brompton Rd ■ *lunch & dinner, upscale*

Thai Princess [MW,TG,WC] 44-(0)20/7373-1244 ■ 30-31 Philbeach Gardens (at the Philbeach Hotel) ■ *6pm-11:30pm* ■ www.philbeachhotel.co.uk

ENTERTAINMENT & RECREATION

Walking Tour of Gay SOHO 44-(0)20/7437-6063 ■ 56 Old Compton St (at Admiral Duncan Pub) ■ *2pm Sun, £5* ■ www.kairosinsoho.org.uk

RETAIL SHOPS

Adonis Art Gallery 44-(0)20/7460 3888 ■ 1b Coleherne Rd ■ *gay art* ■ www.adonis-art.com

Clone Zone [GO] 44-(0)20/7373-0598 ■ 266 Old Brompton Rd (Earl's Court) ■ *10am-8pm, noon-6pm Sun, magazines, videos, toys, solarium, tattooing; also Soho location, 64 Old Compton St, 44-(0)20/7287-3530* ■ www.clonezone.co.uk

GYMS & HEALTH CLUBS

Soho Athletic Club [GF] 44-(0)20/7370-1402 ■ 254 Earls Ct Rd ■ *also at 193 Camden High St, 44-(0)20/7482-4524* ■ www.sohogyms.com

London—North

London—North includes Paddington, Regents Park, Camden, St Pancras & Islington

ACCOMMODATIONS

Ossian Guesthouse [GF] 44-(0)20/8340-4331 ■ 20 Ossian Rd ■ *Victorian house in quiet suburb* ■ www.ossianguesthouse.co.uk

The Town House [M,GO] 44-(0)20/7609-9082 ■ Caledonian Rd (Islington) ■ www.sbr22.dircon.co.uk

BARS

58 The Black Cap [★MW,D,TG,F,K,C] 44-(0)20/7428-2721 ■ 171 Camden High St (Camden Town) ■ *noon-1am, till-2am Fri-Sat, till 10:30pm Sun, London's leading cabaret, roof garden* ■ www.theblack-cap.com

59 Blush [W,NH,F,E,K] 44-(0)20/7923-9202 ■ 8 Cazenove Rd (Stoke Newington) ■ *5pm-midnight, 1pm-midnight Sun, clsd Mon, friendly cafe-bar, [K] Fri, Bedroom 1st Sat [W], woman-owned* ■ www.blushbar.co.uk

Catch 22 [MW,NH,K] 44-(0)20/8881-1900 ■ 1a Wellington Ter, 679 Green Lanes (at Falkland Rd, Harringay) ■ *4pm-12:30am, till 1am Th, till 3am Fri-Sat*

The George Music Bar [M,TG,C,GO] 44-(0)20/8560-1456 ■ 114 Twickenham Rd (Isleworth) ■ *5pm-close, from noon wknds, George Cabaret every Fri-Sat & every other Sun, patio garden* ■ www.georgemusicbar.com

The Golden Lion [M,D,K,E,DS] 44-(0)20/7837-4734 ■ 2 Britannia St ■ *noon-12:30am, till 2:30am Th-Sat* ■ www.goldenlionlondon.co.uk

60 The Green [MW,F] 44-(0)20/7226-8895 ■ 74 Upper St (Islington) ■ *4pm-midnight, till 1am Th, noon-2am Fri, 11am-2am Sat, 11am-midnight Sun, full menu* ■ www.the-green.co.uk

61 King Edward VI/ Sunroom Cafe [★MW,NH,F,WC] 44-(0)20/7704-0745 ■ 25 Bromfield St (at Parkfield St, Islington) ■ *noon-midnight, cafe-bar, beer garden* ■ edwardvi.8m.com

62 King William IV [★MW,F] 44-(0)20/7435-5747 ■ 77 Hampstead High St ■ *pub hours, beer garden* ■ www.kw4.co.uk

63 Kings Head [MW,DS] 44-(0)20/8534-0197 ■ 11 Church St (Stratford)

64 Klub Fukk [MW,D,TG] 44-(0)20/7278-3294 ■ 37 Wharfdale Rd (at Central Station, King's Cross) ■ *7pm-midnight 2nd Fri only* ■ www.woteverworld.com

65 The Oak Bar [W,D,F,K,S,V] 44-(0)20/7354-2791 ■ 79 Green Lanes (Stoke Newington) ■ *5pm-midnight, till 2am Fri-Sat, from 1pm Sun, Lower the Tone last Fri, theme nights* ■ www.oakbar.co.uk

64 Wotever World [W,D,TG] 44-(0)20/7278-3294 ■ 37 Wharfdale Rd (at Central Station, King's Cross) ■ *6pm-midnight Tue (Bar Wotever) & Wed (Film Wotever), genderqueers & their admirers* ■ www.woteverworld.com

NIGHTCLUBS

64 Central Station [★MW,D,TG,F,C,DS,S,V] 44-(0)20/7278-3294 ■ 37 Wharfdale Rd (King's Cross) ■ *5pm-close, from 1pm wknds, complex includes Sports Bar, Cabaret & The Underground [M], theme nights, terrace* ■ www.centralstation.co.uk

66 Club Kali [★MW,D,MR-A,TG,E,$] 44-(0)20/7272-8153 (Dome #) ■ 1 Dartmouth Park Hill (at The Dome) ■ *10pm-3am 1st & 3rd Fri, South Asian music* ■ www.clubkali.com

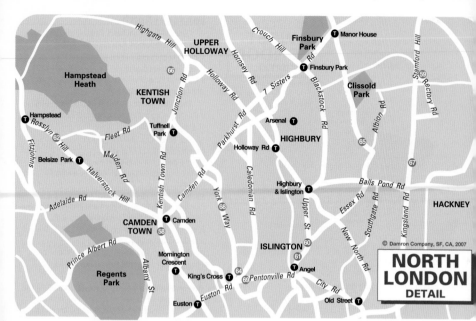

© Damron Company, SF, CA, 2007

NORTH LONDON
DETAIL

67 **Club Motherfu*ker** [MW,D,E] 44–(0)20/7249-9557 ■ 38-44 Stoke Newington Rd (at Bardens Boudoir) ■ *8pm-2am 2nd Sat* ■ www.clubmotherfucker.com

68 **Egg** [GS,D] 44–(0)20/7609-8364 ■ 200 York Way (Kings Cross) ■ *10pm Fri-10am Sat, 10pm Sat until late afternoon Sun, 3 flrs, theme nights* ■ www.egglondon.net

69 **Popstarz** [★MW,D,$] 44–(0)20/7833-2022 (Scala) ■ 275 Pentonville Rd (at The Scala, Kings Cross) ■ *10pm-4am Fri, 4 rooms* ■ www.popstarz.org

RESTAURANTS

Providores/ Tapa Room 44–(0)20/7935-6175 ■ 109 Marylebone High St (at New Cavendish St) ■ *lunch & dinner, Asian fusion; more casual Tapa room downstairs open for brkfst, lunch & dinner, tapas* ■ www.theprovidores.co.uk

Sauce 44–(0)20/7482-0777 ■ 214 Camden High St ■ *noon-11pm, till 4pm Sun, organic, lots of veggie*

ENTERTAINMENT & RECREATION

Rosemary Branch Theatre [GS,F] 44–020/7704-2730 (bar), 44–020/7704-6665 (theatre) ■ 2 Shepperton Rd ■ *also restaurant & bar, many gay-themed plays* ■ www.rosemarybranch.co.uk

Waltzing With Hilda [WO,D,$] 44–(0)79/3907-2958, 44–(0)20/8340-5226 ■ 269a Archway Rd (Jacksons Ln Art Centre, Highgate) ■ *7:45pm-midnight 2nd & last Sat, Latin & ballroom dancing, also lessons* ■ www.hildas.org.uk

RETAIL SHOPS

Fettered Pleasures 44–(0)20/7619-9333 ■ 90 Holloway Rd ■ *S/M & fetish gear* ■ www.fetteredpleasures.com

MEN'S CLUBS

Chariots Farringdon [F,V] 44–(0)20/7251-5553 ■ 57 Cowcross St (across from Farringdon tube) ■ *11am-11pm* ■ www.gaysauna.co.uk

MA1 Club [M] 44–(0)20/7278-3294 ■ 37 Wharfdale Rd (at Central Station, King's Cross) ■ *9pm-1am Fri-Sat, 7pm-midnight Sun, Spurt! (J/O party) Fri-Sun* ■ www.ma1club.com

Play Pit [BYOB] 44–(0)77/7063-1385 ■ 76 Caledonian Rd (at Kings Cross Cruising Club) ■ *9pm-2am Th, till 3am Fri-Sat, 3pm-7pm Sun* ■ www.londonplaypit.co.uk

EROTICA

Regulation 44–(0)20/7226-0665 ■ 17a St Albans Pl (Islington Green) ■ *fetish gear & toys "made to measure"* ■ www.regulation-london.co.uk

London—East

London—East includes City, Tower, Clerkenwell & Shoreditch
See London Overview map on page 300

ACCOMMODATIONS

70 **The Hoxton** [GF,NS,WI] 44–020/7550-1000 ■ 81 Great Eastern St ■ *also restaurant; free mineral water & milk in fridge; Pret Lite brkfst; reasonably priced phone calls* ■ www.hoxtonhotels.com

BARS

71 **Bar Music Hall** [GF,D,E] 44–(0)20/7613-5951, 44–(0)20/7729-7216 ■ 134 Curtain Rd (Shoreditch) ■ *11am-midnight, till 2am Fri-Sat, more gay Sat for Antisocial (DIY fashion party)* ■ www.hellshoreditch.com

BJ's White Swan [M,D,TG,F,WC] 44–(0)20/7780-9870 ■ 556 Commercial Rd (near Bromley St) ■ *9pm-close, from 6pm Sun, clsd Mon, [K] Tue, [S] Wed, talent show Th, [C] Fri, [D] Sat-Sun* ■ www.bjswhiteswan.com

Charlie's Bar [MW,NH] 44–(0)20/7790-1007 ■ 124 Globe Rd (Stepney) ■ *pub hours* ■ www.haveadrink.net

E One Club [M,NH,D,TG,E,K,C,DS,S,V,WC] 44–(0)20/7790-1684 ■ 168 Mile End Rd (across from the Globe Centre, Stepney Green) ■ *7pm-close*

72 **Essence** [GS,D,F] 44-(0)20/7253-6009 ■ 2-5 Carthusian St (Clerkenwell) ■ noon-11pm, till midnight Th, till 2am Fri, 7pm-2am Sat, clsd Sun, tapas bar & restaurant, also various queer nights ■ www.essence-bar.com

The Old Ship [MW,NH,C,DS,YC,WC] 44-(0)20/7790-4082 ■ 17 Barnes St (Stepney) ■ 6pm-11pm, from 7:30pm Sat, 1pm-10:30pm Sun

NIGHTCLUBS

Backstreet [MO,L,PC] 44-(0)20/8980-8557, 44-(0)20/8980-7880 ■ Wentworth Mews, Burdett Rd (at Mile End Rd, Bow) ■ 10pm-2am, till 3am Fri-Sat, 11pm-1am Sun, clsd Mon-Wed, strict leather/ rubber dress code ■ www.thebackstreet.com

Central Station-Walthamstow [MW,D,C] 44-(0)20/8520-4836 ■ 80 Brunner Rd (Walthamstow) ■ 5:30pm-1am, till 2am Th-Sat, 1pm-midnight Sun ■ www.centralstation.co.uk

73 Curves [WO,D,$] 44-(0)79/4731-0967, 44-(0)79/0758-1412 ■ 10-15 Queen St (at Apt) ■ 9pm-3am 1st Sat only, upscale nightclub & lounge ■ www.bluecube.net

74 **DTPM** [★MW,D,YC,$] 44-(0)20/7749-1199 ■ 77-A Charterhouse St, Smithfield Mkt (at Fabric) ■ 10pm-5am Sun, huge, stylish techno club ■ www.dtpm.net

Pleasure Unit [MW,D,E] 44-(0)20/7729-0167 ■ 359 Bethnal Green Rd (Bethnal Green) ■ 6pm-midnight, till 2am Fri-Sat, Unskinny Bop [W] 3rd Sat ■ www.pleasureunitbar.com

75 Rumours [★WO,D] 44-(0)79/4947-7804 ■ 64-73 Minories (at The Minories) ■ call for events, 2 bars ■ www.girl-rumours.co.uk

Stunners [TG,D,PC] 44-(0)77/1022-2549 ■ Cable St Studios (at Butcher Row, Limehouse) ■ 10pm-6am Fri, till 10am Sat, clsd Sun-Th ■ www.stunners.tv

76 **Vision** [GS,D] 18 Old Bailey (at Firefly, near St Paul's) ■ 10pm-4am 1st Sat, house

77 **Way Out Club** [MW,D,TG,S,PC,$] 44-(0)77/7815-7290 ■ 9 Crosswall (at Charlie's) ■ 9pm-4am Sat only, TV/TS & their friends ■ www.thewayoutclub.com

RESTAURANTS

Bonds Restaurant & Bar 44-(0)20/7657-8088 ■ 5 Threadneedle St ■ hours vary Mon-Th, clsd wknds, formerly a bank lobby, tapas served ■ www.theetoncollection.com

Cafe Spice Namaste 44-(0)20/7488-9242 ■ 16 Prescott St ■ lunch Mon-Fri, dinner nightly, clsd Sun, Indian ■ www.cafespice.co.uk

Cantaloupe [★] 44-(0)20/7729-5566 ■ 35-42 Charlotte Rd (Shoreditch) ■ 11am-midnight, from noon weekends, till 11:30pm Sun, also bar ■ www.alphabetbar.com

Les Trois Garçons [R] 44-(0)20/7613-1924 ■ 1 Club Row (at Bethnal, Shoreditch) ■ 7pm-midnight, clsd Sun, French, eclectic decor ■ www.lestroisgarcons.com

SoSho [★] 44-(0)20/7920-0701 ■ 2 Tabernacle St ■ noon-midnight, till 1am Wed-Th, till 3am Fri, 7pm-4am Sat, 9pm-6am Sun, clsd Mon, also bar ■ www.sosho3am.com

MEN'S CLUBS

Chariots Limehouse [F,V] 44-(0)20/7791-2808 ■ 574 Commercial Rd (near Limehouse tube) ■ 24hrs, sauna, steam, tanning & jacuzzi, roof-garden, 4 flrs ■ www.gaysauna.co.uk

Chariots Shoreditch [★SW,F,V] 44-(0)20/7247-5333 ■ 1 Fairchild St (Shoreditch) ■ noon-9am, sauna, steam, jacuzzi, gym equipment; also Chariots Café-Bar ■ www.gaysauna.co.uk

E15 Club 44-(0)20/8555-5455 ■ 6 Leytonstone Rd ■ noon-midnight, jacuzzi, steamroom, garden, also bar ■ www.londonnoise.com/e15

EROTICA

Expectations 44-(0)20/7739-0292 ■ 75 Great Eastern St (Shoreditch) ■ London's premier leather/ rubber store, also mail order ■ www.expectations.co.uk

Sh! Women's Erotic Emporium 44-(0)20/7613-5458 ■ 39 Coronet St (off Old St, Shoreditch) ■ noon-8pm, men very welcome when accompanied by a woman; also mail order ■ www.sh-womenstore.com

London—South

London—South includes Southwark, Lambeth, Kennington, Vauxhall, Battersea, Lewisham & Greenwich
See London Overview map on page 300

ACCOMMODATIONS

Griffin House [MW,WI,GO] 44-(0)20/7096-3332 ■ 22 Stockwell Green ■ 2 rental apts near Vauxhall Gay Village & West End, kitchens ■ www.griffinhouse.info

BARS

Bar Lava [MW,E,V] 44-(0)20/8771-9777 ■ 8 Westow St (Crystal Palace)

78 **Battersea Barge** [GF,F,E,C,GO] 44-(0)20/7498-0004 ■ Riverside Walk Nine Elms Ln (Vauxhall) ■ 11:30am-late, clsd Mon, cabaret, comedy on the Thames River! ■ www.batterseabarge.com

79 The Chocolate Lounge [W,D,F,E,PC] 44-(0)20/7735-5306 ■ 146-148 Newington Butts (Kennington) ■ 5pm-midnight, 7pm-2am Fri, 7pm-4am Sat, noon-10:30pm Sun, clsd Mon, women-only basement, [K] Wed ■ www.thechocolateloungelondon.com

Escape Bar & Art [GF,D] 44-(0)20/7737-0333 ■ 214-216 Railton Rd (Herne Hill) ■ 10am-late, till 11:30pm Sun, features local & international artists, more gay Th for Fat Nancy's disco ■ www.escapebarandart.com

80 **The Fort** [M,L] 44-(0)20/7237-7742, 44-(0)70/9042-1746 ■ 131 Grange Rd (off Tower Bridge Rd, Bermondsey) ■ pub hours, darkroom, theme nights, strict dress code, cruisy

George & Dragon [MW,C] 44-(0)20/8691-3764 ■ 2 Blackheath Hill (Greenwich) ■ 6pm-2am, till 4am Fri-Sat, [K] Th ■ www.georgedragon.com

Kazbar [MW,TG,V] 44-(0)20/7622-0070 ■ 50 Clapham High St (Clapham) ■ 4pm-midnight, till 1am Fri-Sat, from noon wknds, cafe-bar ■ www.kudosgroup.com

81 **The Little Apple** [MW,D,TG,F,WC] 44-(0)20/7735-2039 ■ 98 Kennington Ln ■ noon-midnight, till 10:30pm Sun, terrace

82 **Man Bar** [★MO,D] 44-(0)20/7928-3223 ■ 82 Great Suffolk St ■ 8pm-1am, 2pm-midnight Sun, boots only Mon & Th, underwear only Wed & Sun, cruisy ■ www.manbar.info

83 **South Central** [M,D,E,C] 44-(0)20/7793-0903 ■ 349 Kennington Ln (Vauxhall) ■ 8pm-1am, 9pm-2am Wed-Sat, 2pm-10:30pm Sun

The Star and Garter [MW,NH] 44-(0)20/8464-4979 ■ 227 High St (Bromley) ■ pub hours ■ www.gaybromley.co.uk/star_and_garter.html

The Two Brewers [MW,D,K,C,V] 44-(0)20/7498-4971 ■ 114 Clapham High St (Clapham) ■ 5pm-2am, till 3am Fri-Sat, 2pm-12:30am Sun ■ www.the2brewers.com

NIGHTCLUBS

84 **A:M** [MW,D,$] 44-(0)79/0503-5682 ■ S Lambeth Rd (at Fire, Vauxhall) ■ after-hours, 11pm Fri-11am Sat ■ www.fireclub.co.uk

Afterglow [W,D] 44-(0)77/3179-9530 ■ 6 Cavendish Parade (Clapham Common S Side) ■ 2nd Th ■ www.after-glowgirls.com

85 **Area** [M,D] 67-68 Albert Embankment ■ frequent one-off parties, see website for info ■ www.areaclub.info

Blessence [W,D,$] 44-(0)79/5045-7930 ■ occasional parties, call or see website for info ■ www.blessence.com

Club Camp [MW,D,C] 44-(0)20/8680-2233 ■ 68 High St (at Black Sheep Bar, Croydon) ■ 8pm-late Wed only ■ www.blacksheepbar.com

86 **Crash** [★MW,D,V,$] 44-(0)20/7278-0995 ■ 66 Goding St, Albert Embankment (Vauxhall) ■ see web for event location & details ■ www.crashlondon.co.uk

87 **Duckie** [★MW,D,C] 44-(0)20/7737-4043 ■ 372 Kennington Ln (at Royal Vauxhall Tavern) ■ 10pm-2am every Sat, retro indie ■ www.duckie.co.uk

Ego [M,D,K] 44-(0)20/8761-5200 ■ 82 Norwood High St ■ 8pm-close, [MO] 1st Tue for Nanti ■ www.egolondon.com

84 **Gravity** [M,D] 44-(0)20/7434-1113, 44-(0)20/7582-9890 ■ S Lambeth Rd (at Fire, Vauxhall) ■ 11pm-10am Th ■ www.fireclub.co.uk

Hard On [M,PC] 44-020/7820-1702 (Hidden) ■ 100 Tinworth St (at Hidden, in Vauxhall) ■ monthly parties, strict dress code, cruisy ■ www.hardonclub.co.uk

88 **The Hoist** [M,L] 44-(0)20/7735-9972 ■ Railway Arch 47b&tc, S Lambeth Rd (Vauxhall) ■ 8:30pm-midnight Th, from 10pm Th-Sun, till 3am Fri, till 4am Sat, till 2am Sun, clsd Mon-Wed, S/M club w/ strict dress code ■ www.thehoist.co.uk

84 **Juicy** [M,D] 44-(0)79/0503-5682 ■ S Lambeth Rd (at Fire, Vauxhall) ■ 11pm-close Sat only ■ www.juicyclub.net

Reflex [M,D] 44-(0)20/8549-9911 ■ 184 London Rd ■ 10pm-3am Fri-Sat only ■ www.reflexnightclub.com

87 **Royal Vauxhall Tavern** [M,NH,D,TG,F,WC] 44-(0)20/7820-1222 ■ 372 Kennington Ln (Vauxhall) ■ 7pm-midnight, 9pm-2am Fri-Sat, 2pm-midnight Sun, comedy Wed, [C] Th, popular wknds, more women Sat for Duckie ■ www.theroyalvauxhalltavern.co.uk

84 **Rude Boyz** [MO,D,S] 44-(0)79/0503-5682 ■ S Lambeth Rd (at Fire, Vauxhall) ■ 10:30pm-close Th, sporty lad dress code, cruisy ■ www.fireclub.co.uk

89 **Starkers** [GS,D,N] 44-(0)77/9656-1331 ■ 65 Goding St (at The Factory) ■ 10pm-close 3rd Fri, naked club, not sex club, footwear required ■ www.starkersclub.co.uk

Urban Desi [MW,D,MR-A] 44-(0)79/5568-3144, 44-(0)79/5568-3134 ■ 65 Goding St (at Factory) ■ 11pm-5am 1st Sat, South Asian ■ www.urban-desi.co.uk

90 **XXL** [MO,D,B] 44-(0)78/1204-8574 ■ 51-53 Southwark St (at London Bridge Arches) ■ 10pm-6am Sat, till 3am Wed, "one club fits all" ■ www.xxl-london.com

ENTERTAINMENT & RECREATION

Oval Theatre Cafe Bar [F] 44-(0)20/7582-0080 ■ 52-54 Kennington Oval ■ 6pm-11pm Tue-Sat (cafe), call to inquire about current theatre & art ■ www.ovalhouse.com

RETAIL SHOPS

The Host 44-(0)20/7793-1551 ■ 44a Parry St ■ 11am-7pm, clsd Sun, rubber & fetish gear ■ www.the-host.co.uk

GYMS & HEALTH CLUBS

Paris Gymnasium [MO] 44-(0)20/7735-8989 ■ 73 Godin St (behind Vauxhall Tavern, Vauxhall) ■ 6:30am-11pm, 10am-10pm Sat, 10am-8pm Sun, £10 day pass ■ www.parisgym.com

MEN'S CLUBS

Chariots Streatham 44-(0)20/8696-0929 ■ 292 Streatham High Rd (at Babington Rd, enter rear) ■ 24hrs wknds ■ www.gaysauna.co.uk

The Locker Room [V] 44-(0)20/7582-6288 ■ 8 Cleaver S (Kennington) ■ 24hrs wknds

Star Steam [V] 44-(0)20/7924-2269 ■ 38 Lavender Hill (Battersea) ■ 11am-late, seasonal terrace

FRANCE

Paris

Note: M°=Métro station

Paris is divided by arrondissements (city districts); 01=1st arrondissement, 02=2nd arrondissement, etc ■ the detail maps have been designed around region names that include several arrondissements

Paris—Overview

Note: When phoning Paris from the US, dial the country code + the city code + the local phone number

ACCOMMODATIONS

Gay Accommodation Paris [GO] 33-1/4348-1382 ■ 271, rue du Faubourg Saint Antoine ■ studios for rent in central Paris ■ www.gayaccommodationparis.com

Insightful Travelers [GF] 617/859-0720 (US#) ■ short-term apt rentals, 3-day minimum stay ■ www.latoile.com

Marais Flats/ Studios [GO] 33-1/4039-9297 (European daytime only) ■ 8 rue Marie Stuart ■ several spacious apts available for weekly or monthly rental in different Paris locations, close by to gay districts ■ www.maraisflat.com

RentParis.com LLC [GS,NS,GO] 33-6/6703-5471 ■ fully furnished studios & apts, kids ok ■ www.RentParis.com

ENTERTAINMENT & RECREATION

Cour et Jardin 33-1/3975-1908 ■ amateur lgbt theater group, call for performance times & locations ■ www.couretjardinparis.free.fr

PUBLICATIONS

Lesbia ■ monthly glossy magazine ■ www.lesbiamag.com

PREF Mag 33-1/4087-1070 ■ bimonthly magazine ■ www.prefmag.com

Têtu 33-1/5680-2080 ■ stylish & intelligent LGBT monthly (en français) ■ www.tetu.com

Paris—01

See Louvre & Les Halles map or Marais & Quartier Latin map

ACCOMMODATIONS

1 **Hotel Louvre Richelieu** [GS] 33-1/4297-4620 ■ 51 rue de Richelieu (M° Palais-Royal) ■ www.louvre-richelieu.com

2 **Hotel Louvre Saint-Honoré** [GS,WI,WC] 33-1/4296-2323 ■ 141 rue Saint-Honoré (at rue du Louvre) ■ *3-star* ■ www.regetel.com

BARS

3 **Le Banana Cafe** [★MW,D,E,P,S,YC,WC] 33-1/4233-3531 ■ 13-15 rue de la Ferronnerie (near rue St-Denis, M° Châtelet) ■ *6pm-dawn, tropical decor, theme nights, Latina/o night Sun, terrace* ■ www.bananacafeparis.com

4 **Le Tropic Cafe** [MW,D,TG,F,YC,WC] 33-1/4013-9262 ■ 66 rue des Lombards (M° Châtelet) ■ *4pm-5am, tapas, terrace*

5 **Le Vagabond** [M,F,OC] 33-1/4296-2723 ■ 14 rue Thérèse (at av de l'Opera, M° Pyramides) ■ *6pm-close, clsd Mon, oldest gay bar & restaurant in Paris*

NIGHTCLUBS

6 **Le Club 18** [★M,D,YC,PC,$] 33-1/4297-5213 ■ 18 rue du Beaujolais (at rue Vivienne, M° Palais-Royal) ■ *clsd Mon-Tue* ■ www.club18.fr

7 **L' Insolite** [★M,D,$] 33-1/4020-9859 ■ 33 rue des Petits-Champs (at rue du Beaujolais, enter through back courtyard, M° Pyramides) ■ *11pm-5am, till 6am Fri-Sat*

8 **Le London** [M,D,F,$] 33-1/4233-4145 ■ 33 bis rue des Lombards, in basement (look for red door) ■ *11pm-5am, till 7am Fri-Sat, clsd Mon, theme nights, Asian night Tue, also restaurant/ bar upstairs (open from 8:30pm)*

Rexy Club [GF,D] 33-1/4026-5105 ■ 9 rue de la Grande Truanderie (M° Etienne Marcel)

PARIS

Who doesn't adore Paris? The most romantic city in the world, Paris is a capricious lover. Beautiful and witty, dignified and grand, flirtatious and coy, Paris is worthy of life-long devotion. It's hardly surprising, then, that so many artists and thinkers have made Paris their home. Whether it's the museums, the couture, the cafes, the history, the churches, the people...Paris seduces at every turn.

Tourist Info

AIRPORT DIRECTIONS

Parisian drivers make Bostonians look tame. Damron recommends the many excellent public transit options from both Orly (Orlyrail/Orlybus) and Charles de Gaulle (Roissyrail/Roissybus) airports into Paris. Air France also provides bus service.

PUBLIC TRANSIT & TAXIS

Alpha Taxi 33-1/4585-8585.
Taxi Bleu 33-8/9170-1010.
RATP (bus and Métro) 33-8/9268-7714, web: www.ratp.fr.

TOURIST SPOTS & INFO

Arc de Triomphe 33-1/5537-7377, web: www.monuments-nationaux.fr.
Notre Dame Cathedral 33-1/5310-0700.
Eiffel Tower (up in lights for 10 minutes each hour from sunset till past midnight!) 33-1/4411-2323, web: www.tour-eiffel.fr.
Louvre 33-1/4020-5050, web: www.louvre.fr.
Musée d'Orsay 33-1/4049-4814, web: www.musee-orsay.fr.
Picasso Museum 33-1/4271-2521, web: www.musee-picasso.fr.
Rodin Musuem 33-1/4418-6110, web: www.musee-rodin.fr.
Sacre-Coeur Basilica 33-1/5341-8900, web: www.sacre-coeur-montmarte.com.
Sainte-Chapelle 33-1/5340-6096, web: www.monuments-nationaux.fr.
Visitor's Center: Carrousel du Louvre 33-8/9268-3000. 99 rue de Rivoli, web: www.parisinfo.com.
Also www.paris.org.

Weather

Paris really *is* beautiful in the springtime. Chilly in the winter, the temperatures reach the 70's during the summer.

Best Views

Eiffel Tower (but of course!) and Sacre Coeur.

City Calendar

LGBT PRIDE

June. web: www.gaypride.fr.

ANNUAL EVENTS

May-June - French Open tennis championship 33-1/4743-5252 (tickets), 33-1/4743-4800 (Roland Garros), web: www.rolandgarros.com.
June - One Mighty Party benefit for the Elton John AIDS Foundation at the Disneyland Resort Paris, web: www.onemightyweekend.com.
July - Tour de France, web: www.letour.fr.
July 14 - Bastille Day.
November-December - Paris Gay & Lesbian Film Festival, web: www.ffglp.net.

Queer Resources

COMMUNITY INFO

Centre Gai et Lesbien de Paris 33-1/4357-2147. 3 rue Keller (11e, see Marais map), drop-in 4pm-8pm Mon-Sat, web: www.cglparis.org.
Ecoute Gaie 33-8/1081-1057 (helpline). 6pm-10pm Mon-Fri, web: www.ecoute-gaie.france.qrd.
English-speaking AA 33-1/4634-5965, web: www.aaparis.org.
SIDA Info Service, 0800/84.08.00, web: www.sida-info-service.org.

PARIS
OVERVIEW

© Damron Company, SF, CA, 2007

17e

8e

16e

7e

15e

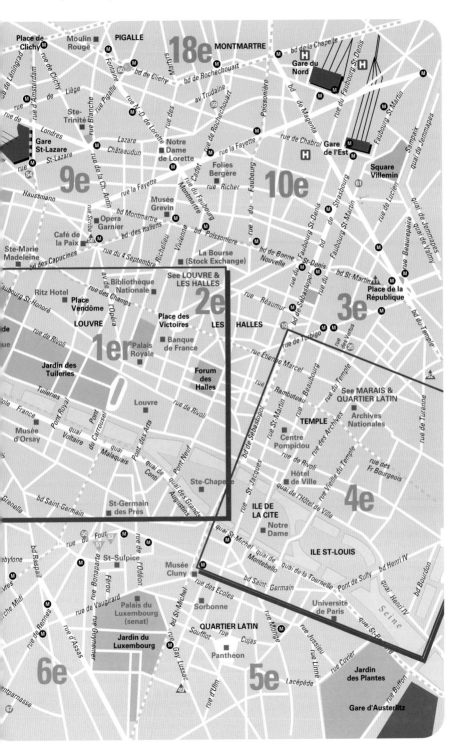

RESTAURANTS

L' Amazonial [MW,C,DS,WC] 33-1/4233-5313 ■ 3 rue Ste-Opportune (at rue Ferronnerie, M° Châtelet) ■ *lunch & dinner, brunch wknds, Brazilian/ int'l, heated terrace*

Au Diable des Lombards 33-1/4233-8184 ■ 64 rue des Lombards (at rue St-Denis, M° Châtelet) ■ *8am-1am, American, full bar, terrace* ■ www.diable.com

Au Rendez-Vous des Camionneurs [M] 33-1/4354-8874 ■ 72 quai des Orfèvres (M° Pont Neuf) ■ *lunch & dinner, traditional bistro*

Chez Max 33-1/4508-8013 ■ 47 rue Saint Honoré (M° Louvre) ■ *lunch & dinner, traditional French*

Jet Lag [D] 33-1/4488-2230 ■ 4 rue Montmartre (M° Etienne Marcel) ■ *7am-1:30am, 2 patios* ■ www.jet-lag.fr

Marc Mitonne 33-1/4261-5316 ■ 60 rue de l'Arabe-Sec (M° Les Halles) ■ *6pm-2am, clsd Sun, theme nights [GF,E,C,S]* ■ www.marc-mitonne.com

La Poule au Pot 33-1/4236-3296 ■ 9 rue Vauvilliers (M° Les Halles) ■ *7pm-5am, clsd Mon, clsd Aug, traditional French* ■ www.lapouleaupot.fr

ENTERTAINMENT & RECREATION

Forum des Halles 33-1/4476-9556 ■ 101 Porte Berger (M° Châtelet-Les Halles) ■ *underground sports/ entertainment complex w/ museums, theater, shops, clubs, cafes & more* ■ www.forum-des-halles.com

GYMS & HEALTH CLUBS

Club Med Gym [GS] 33-1/4020-0303 ■ 147 bis rue St-Honoré (M° Louvre) ■ *day passes available, many locations throughout city* ■ www.clubmedgym.com

MEN'S CLUBS

Gym Louvre [★MO,F,V,WI] 7 bis rue de Louvre ■ *9am-2am, from noon Sun, also gym & sauna* ■ www.gymlouvre.com

Til't [V] 33-1/4296-0743 ■ 41 rue Ste-Anne (near av de l'Opera, M° Pyramides) ■ *24hrs, bar*

EROTICA

Boxxman 33-1/4221-4702 ■ 2 rue de la Cossonnerie (M° Châtelet) ■ *videos, toys & fetish gear, also sex club, internet access* ■ www.boxxman.fr

IEM Les Halles 33-1/4296-0574 ■ 43 rue de l'Arbre Sec (near rue de Rivoli, M° Louvre) ■ www.iem.fr

Paris—02

See Louvre & Les Halles map

BARS

9 **La Champmeslé** [★W,C,OC,WC] 33-1/4296-8520 ■ 4 rue Chabanais (at rue des Petits Champs, M° Pyramides) ■ *3pm-3am, till 7am Fri-Sat, Sun, [C] Th, theme nights*

10 **L' Impact** [MO,N,V] 33-1/4221-9424 ■ 18 rue Greneta (M° Châtelet) ■ *8pm-3am, 10pm-6am Fri-Sat, from 3pm Sun, cruise bar, 100% naked, backroom, theme nights, free brkfst wknds (see overview map)* ■ www.impact-bar.com

RESTAURANTS

Aux Trois Petits Cochons [★MW,R,GO] 33-1/4233-3969 ■ 31 rue Tiquetonne (at rue St-Denis, M° Etienne-Marcel) ■ *8pm-1am, gourmet French* ■ www.auxtroispetitsco-chons.fr

Le César [MW] 33-1/4296-8113 ■ 4 rue Chabanais (M° Pyramides) ■ *6pm-5am, also bar* ■ lecesar.ifrance.com

Le Dénicheur 33-1/4221-3101 ■ 4 rue Tiquetonne (M° Etienne-Marcel) ■ *noon-midnight, clsd Mon, sandwiches, quiche, salads*

Le Loup Blanc [★MW] 33-1/4013-0835 ■ 42 rue Tiquetonne (M° Etienne-Marcel) ■ *7:30pm-midnight, till 1am Sat, also brunch 11am-4:30pm Sun, French/ int'l* ■ www.loup-blanc.com

Pig'z [M] 33-1/4233-0589 ■ 5 rue Marie-Stuart (M° Etienne Marcel) ■ *8pm-midnight, clsd Sun-Mon* ■ www.pigz.fr

RETAIL SHOPS

Galerie au Bonheur du Jour 33-1/4296-5864 ■ 11 rue Chabanais ■ *2:30pm-7:30pm, clsd wknds, gay art* ■ www.curiostel.tm.fr/aubonheurdujour

MEN'S CLUBS

Euro Men's Club [V,SW,OC] 33-1/4233-9263 ■ 8-10 rue St-Marc (M° Bourse) ■ *run-down* ■ www.e-m-c.fr

Paris—03

See Marais & Quartier Latin map

ACCOMMODATIONS

11 **A B&B Gay Paris Center** [M, GO] 33-6/6453-6450 ■ place de la République ■ *in a historical area on the edge of Le Marais* ■ bnbparis.free.fr

12 **Absolu Living** [MW,GO] 33-1/4454-9700 ■ 236 rue St Martin ■ *fully furnished apts in central Paris, short & long-term stays* ■ www.absoluliving.com

Adorable Apartment in Paris [★GF,NS,GO] 415/397-6454 (US#) ■ (M° Rambuteau) ■ www.adorableapartmentin-paris.com

13 **Hôtel du Vieux Saule** [GF] 33-1/4272-0114 ■ 6 rue de Picardie ■ www.hotelvieuxsaule.com

BARS

14 **Boobsbourg** [W,F,GO] 26 rue Montmorency ■ *5:30pm-2am, clsd Mon, restaurant 6pm-11pm*

15 **Le CUD Club** [M,D,B] 33-1/4271-5660 ■ 12 rue des Haudriettes ■ *4pm-8am* ■ www.cud-bar.com

16 **Le Dépôt** [MO,D,S,YC,$] 33-1/4454-9696 ■ 10 rue aux Ours (btwn bd de Sébastopol & rue St-Martin, M° Rambuteau) ■ *2pm-8am, huge cruise bar on 3 flrs, backroom, T-dance 5pm Sun, go-go boys* ■ www.ledepot.com

17 **Le Duplex** [MW,NH,S] 33-1/4272-8086 ■ 25 rue Michel-le-Comte (at rue Beaubourg, M° Rambuteau) ■ *8pm-2am, till 4am Fri-Sat, friendly bar w/ internet access* ■ www.duplex-bar.com

18 **One Way** [M,NH,B,L,F,V,OC] 33-1/4887-4610 ■ 28 rue Charlot (at rue des 4 Fils, M° République) ■ *5pm-2am, cruisy, darkroom, tapas*

19 **Snax Kfé** [M,F] 33-1/4027-8933 ■ 182 rue Saint Martin (M° Rambuteau) ■ *10am-2am, from 3:30pm Sat, clsd Sun* ■ www.snaxkfe.fr

20 **Le Tango/ La Boite à Frissons** [★MW,F] 33-1/4272-1778 ■ 11 rue au Marie (M° Arts-et-Metiers) ■ *10:30pm-5am, clsd Mon, T-dance Sun (see overview map)* ■ www.boite-a-frissons.fr

21 **Unity Bar** [W,NH,YC] 33-1/4272-7059 ■ 176-178 rue St-Martin (near rue Réaumur, M° Rambuteau) ■ *4pm-2am, men welcome as guests* ■ unity.bar.free.fr

22 **Villa Keops** [MW,D,F] 33-1/4027-9992 ■ 58 blvd Sébastopol (M° Etienne Marcel) ■ *noon-2am, till 5am Fri-Sat, till 3am Sun (clsd in Aug), also restaurant*

NIGHTCLUBS

23 **Les Bains Douches** [★GF,D,F,$] 7 rue du Bourg-l'Abbé (at bd de Sébastopol, M° Etienne-Marcel) ■ *11pm-close, gay Sun-Mon* ■ www.lesbainsdouches.net

RESTAURANTS

Les Epicuriens du Marais [WC] 33-1/4027-0083 ■ 19 rue Commines (M° Filles-du-Calvaire) ■ noon-2am, traditional French ■ www.lesepicuriens.fr

La Fontaine Gourmande 33-1/4278-7240 ■ 11 rue Charlot ■ lunch Tue-Fri & dinner Tue-Sun, French

ENTERTAINMENT & RECREATION

Musée Picasso [WC] 33-1/4271-2521 ■ 5 rue de Thorigny (in the Hôtel Salé, M° St-Paul) ■ 9:30am-5:30pm, clsd Tue ■ www.musee-picasso.fr

MEN'S CLUBS

The Glove [L] 33-1/4887-3136 ■ 34 rue Charlot (M° St-Sebastien-Froissard) ■ 10:30pm-close, 4:30pm-9pm Sun, clsd Mon-Wed, strict dress code, leather/ rubber/ uniform, theme nights, also bar, brkfst wknds ■ www.th-glove.com

Sun City [★MO] 33-1/4274-3141 ■ 62 blvd Sébastopol ■ noon-6am, huge spaces

EROTICA

Rexx 33-1/4277-5857 ■ 42 rue de Poitou (at rue Charlot, M° St-Sébastien-Froissard) ■ clsd Sun, new, custom & secondhand leather & S/M accessories ■ www.rexfetish.com

Paris—04

See Marais & Quartier Latin map

ACCOMMODATIONS

24   **Big Ruby's La Villa Mazarin Paris** [GS,NS,WI,GO] 33-1/5301-9090 ■ 6 rue des Archives ■ in the heart of the Marais district ■ www.villamalraux.com

     Chambres D'Hôte Rivoli [MW,WI,GO] 33-1/7711-3832 ■ B&B ■ mapage.noos.fr/roominparis

     Historic Rentals [GF,NS,WI] 800/537-5408 (US#) ■ 100 W Kennedy Blvd #260, Tampa, FL 33602 ■ 1-bdrm apt, in the heart of the Marais ■ www.historicrentals.com

25   **Hôtel Beaubourg** [GS,WI] 33-1/4274-3424 ■ 11 rue Simon le Franc (btwn rue Beaubourg & rue du Temple, M° Hôtel-de-Ville) ■ next to Centre Pompidou ■ www.hotel-beaubourg.com

26   **Hôtel Central Marais** [M,WI,GO] 33-1/4887-5608 ■ 2 rue Ste-Croix-de-la-Bretonnerie ■ central location, some shared baths, also gay bar ■ www.hotelcentralmarais.com

27   **Hôtel de la Bretonnerie** [GF] 33-1/4887-7763 ■ 22 rue Ste-Croix-de-la-Bretonnerie (M° Hôtel-de-Ville) ■ 17th-c hotel w/ Louis XIII decor ■ www.hotelbretonnerie.com

28   **Hôtel du Vieux Marais** [GF] 33-1/4278-4722 ■ 8 rue du Plâtre (M° Hôtel-de-Ville) ■ centrally located ■ www.hotelduvieuxmarais.com

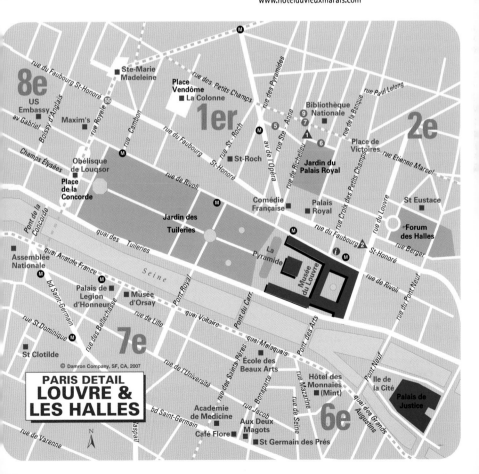

PARIS DETAIL
**LOUVRE &
LES HALLES**

© Damron Company, SF, CA, 2007

29 **Paris-Apart** [GS,NS,GO] 14 rue François Miron ■ *loft in old Le Marais, kids ok* ■ www.paris-apart.com

Bars

30 **3W Kafe** [W,D,S,V] 33-1/4887-3926 ■ 8 rue des Ecouffes (M° St Paul) ■ *5:30pm-2am, men welcome* ■ www.3w-kafe.com

31 **Le 49** [MW,P,NS] 33-1/4027-9742 ■ 49 rue des Blancs-Manteaux (at rue du Temple, M° Rambuteau) ■ *5pm-2am, T-dance Sun*

27 **Akhenaton Cafe** [MW,NH] 33-1/488-70-259 ■ 12 rue de Plâtre (btwn rue du Temple & rue des Archives, M° Hôtel-de-Ville) ■ *5pm-2am, from 6pm Sun, cafe-bar*

32 **L' Amnésia Café** [★MW,D,F] 33-1/4272-1694 ■ 42 rue Vieille du Temple (at rue des Blancs-Manteaux, M° Hôtel-de-Ville) ■ *6pm-close* ■ www.amnesia-cafe.com

33 **Le Bar du Palmier** [MW,F] 33-1/4278-5353 ■ 16 rue des Lombards (at bd de Sébastopol, M° Châtelet) ■ *5pm-5am, terrace* ■ www.paris-zoom.com

34 **Bears' Den** [MO,D,B,V] 33-1/4271-0820 ■ 6 rue des Lombards (at rue St-Martin, M° Hôtel-de-Ville) ■ *4pm-2am, till 4am Fri-Sat, theme nights, T-dance Sun, darkroom, terrace* ■ www.bearsden.fr

35 **Bliss Kfé** [MW,D,GO] 33-1/4278-4936 ■ 30 rue du Roi de Sicile (M° Hôtel-de-Ville) ■ *5pm-2am, stylish new bar* ■ www.bliss-kfe.com

36 **Le Carré** [MW,F] 33-1/4459-3857 ■ 18 rue du Temple (M° Hôtel-de-Ville) ■ *10am-4am, Sun brunch, lounge & restaurant, terrace*

26 **Le Central** [★M] 33-1/4887-5608 ■ 33 rue Vieille du Temple (below Hôtel Central Marais) ■ *4pm-2am, from 2pm Fri-Sun, int'l crowd, a Marais landmark* ■ www.hotelcentralmarais.com

37 **Cox** [★M] 33-1/4272-0800 ■ 15 rue des Archives (at rue Ste-Croix-de-la-Bretonnerie, M° Hôtel-de-Ville) ■ *noon-2am, cruisy, terrace* ■ www.cox.fr

69 **L' Enchanteur** [MW,P] 33-1/4804-0238 ■ 15 rue Michel Lecomte (M° Rambuteau) ■ *4pm-2am*

38 **Le Feeling** [MW,NH,YC] 33-1/4804-7003 ■ 43 rue Ste-Croix-de-la-Bretonnerie (M° Hôtel-de-Ville) ■ *3pm-2am*

39 **Full Metal** [M,L] 33-1/4272-3005 ■ 40 rue des Blancs-Manteaux (M° Rambuteau) ■ *5pm-4am, till 6am Fri-Sat, well-stocked "hard backroom bar," theme parties, dress code* ■ www.fullmetal.fr

70 **Les Jacasses** [MW] 33-1/4271-7551 ■ 5 rue des Ecouffes (M° St Paul) ■ *5pm-2am*

40 **Le Mic-Man** [M,NH,V] 33-1/4274-3980 ■ 24 rue Geoffroy-l'Angevin (at rue du Renard, M° Rambuteau) ■ *noon-2am, open later wknds, friendly bar w/ cruisy cave downstairs*

41 **Le Mixer Bar** [★MW,D,YC] 33-1/4887-5544 ■ 23 rue Ste-Croix-de-la-Bretonnerie (at rue des Archives, M° Hôtel-de-Ville) ■ *4pm-2am, 3-flr techno/ house bar, theme nights* ■ www.mixerbar.com

42 **Oh! Fada** [MW] 33-1/4029-4440 ■ 35 rue Ste-Croix-de-la-Bretonnerie (at rue du Temple, M° Hôtel-de-Ville) ■ *5pm-2am Th-Sun only*

43 **L' Oiseau Bariolé** [MW] 33-6/1038-4651, 33-1/4272-3712 ■ 16 rue Saint-Croix-de-la-Bretonnerie (M° Hotel de Ville) ■ *5pm-close, quiet*

44 **Okawa** [★GS,F,C,P,YC] 33-1/4804-3069 ■ 40 rue Vieille du Temple (at rue Ste-Croix-de-la-Bretonnerie, M° Hôtel-de-Ville) ■ *9am-2am, trendy cafe-bar in 12th- & 13th-c caves, theme nights, [P] Tue-Wed, also restaurant*

37 **L' Open Cafe** [★MW,F,YC] 33-1/4887-8025 ■ 17 rue des Archives (at rue Ste-Croix-de-la-Bretonnerie, M° Hôtel-de-Ville) ■ *10am-2am, till 4am Fri-Sat, sidewalk cafe-bar; also L'Open Coffee Shop, 23 rue du Temple, 33-1/4887-8025, salads & sandwiches* ■ opencafe@caramail.com

45 **Le QG** [MO,L,V] 33-1/4887-7418 ■ 12 rue Simon Lefranc (at rue du Renard, M° Rambuteau) ■ *4pm-8am, theme parties Fri, dress code, sex bar* ■ www.qgbar.com

46 **Quetzal** [★M,NH,S] 33-1/4887-9907 ■ 10 rue de la Verrerie (at rue des Archives, M° Hôtel-de-Ville) ■ *5pm-5am, cruise bar, internet access, Latino night Mon, go-go boys/ shows Tue & Th, darkroom, terrace* ■ www.quetzalbar.com

47 **Le Raidd** [M,D,S] 23 rue du Temple (M° Hotel de ville) ■ *5:30pm-close* ■ www.raiddbar.com

Cafes

Le 3 [M] 33-1/4274-7152 ■ 3 rue Ste-Croix-de-la-Bretonnerie (at rue Vieille du Temple, M° Hôtel-de-Ville) ■ *8pm-midnight, full bar, patio*

Restaurants

Au P'tit Canaillou 33-1/4277-2545 ■ 4 rue St-Merri ■ *lunch & dinner, French/ Asian fusion* ■ www.auptitcanaillou.com

Le Chant des Voyelles 33-1/4277-7707 ■ 4 rue des Lombards (M° Châtelet) ■ *lunch & dinner, traditional French, terrace*

Le Crocman [M] 33-1/4277-6002 ■ 6 rue Geoffroy l'Angevin (M° Rambuteau) ■ *7pm-close, clsd Tue-Wed*

Curieux Spaghetti Bar 33-1/4272-7597 ■ 14 rue Saint Merri (M° Rambuteau) ■ *noon-2am, till 4am Th-Sat, brunch wknds, home of scented vodka "Chup" shots* ■ www.curieuxspag.com

Le Dos de la Baleine 33-1/4272-3898 ■ 40 rue des Blancs-Manteaux (M° Rambuteau) ■ *lunch Tue-Fri, dinner Tue-Sat, clsd Sun-Mon (also clsd Aug), gourmet seafood* ■ www.ledosdelabaleine.com

Equinox [DS,P] 33-1/4271-9241 ■ 33 rue des Rosiers (M° St-Paul) ■ *7pm-midnight, Québecois/ French, full bar*

L' Exotikal [M,C,S] 33-1/4271-4057 ■ 20 rue de la Reynie (M° Les Halles) ■ *noon-midnight* ■ www.lexotikal.com

Le Gai Moulin [MW] 33-1/4887-0600 ■ 10 rue St-Merri (at rue du Temple, M° Hôtel-de-Ville) ■ *dinner, French/ int'l* ■ www.le-gai-moulin.com

Le Kofi du Marais [MW] 33-1/4887-4871 ■ 54 rue Ste-Croix-de-la-Bretonnerie (M° Hôtel de Ville) ■ *coffee & light meals*

Le Petit Picard [MW] 33-1/4278-5403 ■ 42 rue Ste-Croix-de-la-Bretonnerie (M° Hôtel-de-Ville) ■ *lunch & dinner, clsd Mon*

Les Piétons [GS] 33-1/4887-8287 ■ 8 rue des Lombards (M° Châtelet) ■ *noon-2am, brunch noon-6pm Sun, Spanish/ tapas, also bar, [D] Wed* ■ www.lespietons.com

Entertainment & Recreation

Gay Beach E end of Ile St-Louis ■ *sunbathing*

Bookstores

48 **Blue Book Paris** [★] 33-1/4887-0304 ■ 61 rue Quincampoix (at Rambuteau) ■ *11am-11pm, from 1pm Sun-Mon, LGBT, also cafe & gallery* ■ www.bluebookparis.com

43 **Les Mots à la Bouche** 33-1/4278-8830 ■ 6 rue Ste-Croix-de-la-Bretonnerie (near rue du Vieille du Temple, M° Hôtel-de-Ville) ■ *11am-11pm, 1pm-9pm Sun, LGBT, English titles* ■ www.motsbouche.com

RETAIL SHOPS

Abraxas 33-1/4804-3355 ■ 9 rue St-Merri ■ *tattoos, piercing, large selection of body jewelry* ■ www.abraxas.fr

Boy's Bazaar Collections 33-1/4887-2910 ■ 3 rue Ste-Croix-de-la-Bretonnerie (M° Hôtel-de-Ville) ■ *noon-8pm, till 10pm Fri-Sat, from 2pm Sun, clothing & accessories*

Boy's Bazaar Collections 33-1/4271-3400 ■ 5 rue Ste-Croix-de-la-Bretonnerie (at rue Vieille du Temple, M° Hôtel-de-Ville) ■ *2pm-10pm, 1pm-11pm Fri-Sat, clubwear to drag to leather; also Boy'z Bazaar Videostore, 38 rue Ste-Croix-de-la-Bretonnerie, 33-1/4271-8023*

Sweetman 33-8/9270-5550 ■ 17 blvd de Raspail ■ *10:30am-7pm, clsd Sun, outrageous underwear store* ■ www.sweetman.tm.fr

EROTICA

BMC Store 33-1/4027-9809 ■ 21 rue des Lombards ■ *videos, DVDs, toys* ■ www.bmc-video.com

IEM Marais 33-1/4274-0161 ■ 16 rue Ste-Croix-de-la-Bretonnerie (M° Hôtel-de-Ville) ■ *leather, latex, uniforms & fetish gear* ■ www.iem.fr

Paris—05

ACCOMMODATIONS

Historic Rentals [GF,NS,WI] 800/537-5408 (US#) ■ 100 W Kennedy Blvd #260, Tampa, FL 33602 ■ *1-bdrm apts, steps to Notre Dame & Luxembourg Gardens* ■ www.historicrentals.com

49 **Paris Latin Quarters** [MW,NS,WI,GO] 33-1/4325-2903 ■ rue des Ursulines (at rue St-Jacques) ■ *luxury apts* ■ www.parislatinquarters.com

RESTAURANTS

Le Petit Prince [★] 33-1/4354-7726 ■ 12 rue de Lanneau (M° Maubert-Mutualité) ■ *2:30pm-midnight, French*

ENTERTAINMENT & RECREATION

Open-Air Sculpture Museum 33-1/4326-9190 ■ Quai Saint-Bernard ■ *along the Seine between the Jardin des Plantes & the Institut du Monde Arabe*

Paris—06

NIGHTCLUBS

50 **Le Rive-Gauche** [W,D,$] 33-1/4020-4323 ■ 1 rue du Sabot (M° St-Sulpice) ■ *11pm-dawn Fri-Sat only* ■ www.lerivegauche.com

BOOKSTORES
51 **Les Amazones** 33-1/4046-0837 ■ 68 rue Bonaparte ■ *specializes in antique, lesbian & feminist books* ■ www.galaxidion.fr/amazones
52 **The Village Voice** 33-1/4633-3647 ■ 6 rue Princesse (M° Mabillon) ■ *10am-7:30pm, from 2pm Mon, 1pm-6pm Sun, English-language bookshop* ■ www.villagevoicebookshop.com

Paris—08

ACCOMMODATIONS
53 **François 1er** [GF,WI] 33-1/4723-4404 ■ 7 rue Magellan French West Indies ■ *boutique hotel near les Champs-Elysées, also bar* ■ www.the-paris-hotel.com

BARS
54 **Le Day Off** [W,NH,F] 33-1/4522-8790 ■ 10 rue de l'Isly (M° Gare-St-Lazare) ■ *5pm-3am Mon-Fri only, cocktail bar*

NIGHTCLUBS
55 **K-liente** [M,D] 33-1/4265-2794 ■ 3 rue Royale (at Maxim's) ■ *11pm-6am 2nd Sat only* ■ www.spiritofstar.com
56 **Le Queen** [★M,D,TG,DS,YC,$] 33-8/9270-7330 ■ 102 av des Champs-Élysées (btwn rue Washington & rue de Berri, M° Georges-V) ■ *midnight-dawn, more women Wed, very trendy, selective door, theme nights, drag shows, go-go boys* ■ www.queen.fr
57 **Under** [M,D] 33-1/4723-6917 ■ 22 rue Quentin Bauchart (at ave des Champs-Elysées, in Club 79) ■ *6am-noon Sun only* ■ www.fluidparty.com

MEN'S CLUBS
Banque Club [S,V] 33-1/4256-4926 ■ 23 rue de Penthièvre (off Champs d'Élysées, M° Miromesnil) ■ *3pm-dawn, 3 levels, maze, theme nights, also bar* ■ www.banque-club.fr

EROTICA
French Art [V] 33-1/4522-5735 ■ 64 rue de Rome (M° Europe) ■ *clsd Sun* ■ www.cadinot-films-france.com/store
Vidéovision 33-1/4293-6604 ■ 62 rue de Rome (M° Europe) ■ *clsd Sun* ■ www.cadinot.fr

Paris—09

ACCOMMODATIONS
58 **The Grand** [GF] 33-1/4007-3232, 800/327-0200 (US#) ■ 2 rue Scribe ■ *ultraluxe art deco hotel* ■ www.paris-le-grand.intercontinental.com

BARS
59 **Mec Zone** [M,L,V] 33-1/4082-9418 ■ 27 rue Turgot (M° Anvers) ■ *9pm-5am, cruisy, theme nights, darkroom*

NIGHTCLUBS
60 **Folies Pigalle** [GS,D,MR,$] 33-1/4878-5525, 33-1/4280-1203 (BBB info line) ■ 11 place Pigalle (M° Pigalle) ■ *midnight-dawn Tue-Sat, more gay at popular Black, Blanc, Beur T-dance 6pm-midnight Sun & Escualita [MR-L,TG] from midnight Sun* ■ www.folies-pigalle.com

MEN'S CLUBS
IDM [★V] 33-1/4523-1003 ■ 4 rue du Faubourg-Montmartre (at bd St-Martin, M° Grand-Blvds) ■ *3 levels, full gym, jacuzzi, bar* ■ www.idm-sauna.com

EROTICA
Yanko 33-1/4526-7119 ■ 10 place de Clichy (M° place de Clichy) ■ *videos & cinema*

Paris—10

BARS
61 **Cafe Moustache** [M,NH,B,V] 33-1/4607-7270 ■ 138 rue du Faubourg St-Martin (at bd de Magenta, M° Gare-de-l'Est) ■ *5pm-2am, darkroom, patio* ■ cafe.moustache.free.fr
O' Kubi [W,D] 33-1/4201-3508 ■ 219 rue St-Maur (M° Goncourt) ■ *6pm-2am, clsd Sun* ■ www.okubicaffe.com

MEN'S CLUBS
Key West Sauna [★V,SW] 33-1/4526-3174 ■ 141 rue Lafayette (M° Gare-du-Nord) ■ *noon-1am, till 2am Fri-Sat, 3 levels, gym equipment, jacuzzi*

EROTICA
IEM St-Maur 33-1/4018-5151 ■ 208 rue St-Maur (M° Goncourt) ■ *clsd Sun, huge sex shop, whole flr of leather/ latex items* ■ www.iem.fr

Paris—11

ACCOMMODATIONS
62 **Hôtel Beaumarchais** [GS] 33-1/5336-8686 ■ 3 rue Oberkampf (btwn bd Beaumarchais & bd Voltaire, M° Filles-du-Calvaire) ■ www.hotelbeaumarchais.com

BARS
Le Bataclan [GF,E] 33-1/4314-0030 ■ 50 blvd Voltaire (M° Saint Ambroise) ■ *live music venue, more gay for the Follyvores & Crazyvores, call for events* ■ www.le-bataclan.com
63 **Interface** [M] 33-1/4700-6715 ■ 34 rue Keller (rue de La Roquette) ■ *5pm-2am, till 4am wknds, art exhibitions (see Marais & Quartier Latin map)* ■ interface.keller@free.fr
64 **Keller's** [MO,L,$] 33-1/4700-0539 ■ 14 rue Keller (M° Bastille) ■ *10:30pm-2am, till 4am Th-Sat, raunchy cruise bar, theme parties, strict dress code, darkroom (see Marais & Quartier Latin map)* ■ www.kellers.fr

NIGHTCLUBS
65 **La Scène-Bastille** [GF,F,E] 33-1/4806-5070 (club), 33-1/4806-1213 (restaurant) ■ 2 bis rue des Taillandiers (M° Bastille) ■ *more gay Fri, also restaurant* ■ www.la-scene.com

RESTAURANTS
L' ArtiShow [C] 33-1/4348-5604 ■ 3 cite Souzy ■ *lunch & dinner, French/ Thai, cabaret Sat* ■ www.artishowlive.com
Le Sofa 33-1/4314-0746 ■ 21 rue St-Sabin (M° Bastille) ■ *6pm-midnight, till 2am Th-Sat, clsd Sun, also bar* ■ www.lesofa.com
Le Tabarin [MW,P] 33-1/4807-1522 ■ 3 rue du Pasteur-Wagner (M° Bastille) ■ *lunch Sun-Fri, dinner Sun-Sat, full bar*

ENTERTAINMENT & RECREATION
O Chateau, Wine Tasting in Paris [GF,TG] 33-1/4473-9780 ■ 100 rue de la Folie Mericourt ■ www.o-chateau.com

BOOKSTORES
Violette & Co [GO] 33-1/4372-1607 ■ 102 rue de Charonne (at boulevard Voltaire) ■ www.violetteandco.com

MEN'S CLUBS
Bastille Sauna [MR,V] 33-1/4338-0702 ■ 4 passage St-Antoine (near rue Keller, M° Ledru-Rollin) ■ *gym equipment, bar*
Bunker [V] 33-1/5336-0116 ■ 150 rue St-Maur (M° Goncourt) ■ *4pm-2am, till 3:30am Fri, till 4:30am Sat, till 1am Sun, backroom, theme nights* ■ www.docks-cruising.com

EROTICA
Démonia 33-1/4314-8270 ■ 10 Cité Joly (M° Pere-Lachaise) ■ *clsd Sun, huge BDSM shop* ■ www.demonia.com

Paris—12

GYMS & HEALTH CLUBS
Alantide [GS] 33-1/4342-2243 ■ 13 rue Parrot (M° Gare de Lyon) ■ *noon-close, Turkish bath, cabins, tanning, women welcome* ■ www.atlantide-sauna.com

Paris—14

ENTERTAINMENT & RECREATION
Catacombes 33-1/4322-4763 ■ 1 place Denfert Rochereau (M° Denfert-Rochereau) ■ *a ghoulish yet intriguing tourist destination, these burial tunnels were the headquarters of the Résistance during World War II*

Paris—15

BARS
Mix Tea Dance [M,D] 33-1/5680-3737 ■ 24 rue de l'Arrivée ■ *7pm-2am Sun* ■ www.mixclub.fr

NIGHTCLUBS
Le Red Light [M,D,DS] 33-1/4279-9453 ■ 34 rue du Depart (M° Montparnasse-Bienvenue) ■ *midnight-5am* ■ www.enfer.fr

ENTERTAINMENT & RECREATION
Friday Night Fever [GS] Plaza Dautry (near Montparnasse Rail Station) ■ *10pm-1am Fri (weather permitting), meet 9:30pm, rollerblade through the city* ■ www.pari-roller.com

MEN'S CLUBS
Le Steamer [MO] 33-1/4250-3649 ■ 5 rue du Dr Jacquemarie Clemenceau ■ *2pm-10pm, also bar*

Paris—16

ACCOMMODATIONS
Keppler [GF,WI] 33-1/4720-6505 ■ 12 rue Keppler ■ *near major tourist stops, also bar* ■ www.hotelkeppler.com

Paris—17

MEN'S CLUBS
King Sauna [V] 33-1/4294-1910 ■ 21 rue Bridaine (near place de Clichy, M° Rome) ■ *1pm-7am, bar*

Paris—18

BARS
Le Tagada Bar [M,F] 33-1/4255-9556 ■ 40 rue Trois-Frères (M° Abesses) ■ *6:30pm-2am, clsd Sun, upscale food* ■ tagadabar.free.fr/tagada.html

Paris—20

ENTERTAINMENT & RECREATION
Père Lachaise Cemetery bd de Ménilmontant (M° Père-Lachaise) ■ *perhaps the world's most famous resting place, where lie such notables as Chopin, Gertrude Stein, Oscar Wilde, Sarah Bernhardt, Isadora Duncan & Jim Morrison*

MEN'S CLUBS
Le Riad [SW,V] 33-1/4797-2552 ■ 184 rue des Pyrénnées (M° Gambetta) ■ *Middle Eastern-themed sauna, bar* ■ www.le-riad.com

---

GERMANY

Berlin

Berlin is divided into 5 regions:
Berlin—Overview
Berlin—Kreuzberg
Berlin—Prenzlauer Berg-Mitte
Berlin—Schöneberg-Tiergarten
Berlin—Outer

Berlin—Overview

ACCOMMODATIONS
Berlin Vacation Rental [GS,GO] 49-30/2196-9595 ■ www.apartment_berlin.info

NIGHTCLUBS
MegaDyke Productions [★W,D] 49-30/7870-3094 ■ *popular parties & events for lesbians, including L-Tunes at SchwuZ & annual pride events for lesbians in other locations* ■ www.megadyke.de

ENTERTAINMENT & RECREATION
The Jewish Museum Berlin 49-30/3087-85681 ■ Lindenstr 9-14 ■ *10am-8pm, till 10pm Mon, German-Jewish history & culture* ■ www.jmberlin.de
Schwules (Gay) Museum 49-30/6959-9050 ■ U6/U7 Mehringdamm ■ *2pm-6pm, till 7pm Sat, clsd Tue, guided tours 5pm Sat (in German)* ■ www.schwulesmuseum.de

PUBLICATIONS
Sergej 49-30/443-1980 ■ *free monthly gay magazine* ■ www.sergej.de
Siegessäule 49-30/235-5390, 49-30/2355-3932 ■ *free monthly LGBT city magazine (in German), awesome maps* ■ www.siegessaeule.de

Berlin—Kreuzberg

BARS
1 **Barbie Bar** [MW] 49-30/6956-8610 ■ Mehringdamm 77 ■ *4pm-close, lounge, terrace* ■ www.barbiebar.de
2 **Bierhimmel** [GS,YC] 49-30/615-3122 ■ Oranienstr 183 (U-Kottbusser Tor) ■ *1pm-3am*
3 **Club Trommel** [M,D,TG] 49-30/686-7345 ■ Thomasstr 53 ■ *7pm-close*
4 **Ficken 3000** [M,D,L,V,YC] 49-30/6950-7335 ■ Urbanstr 70 (at Hermannplatz) ■ *10pm-close, cruisy, large darkroom (see overview map)*
4 **Frauen 3000** [W,D] 49-30/6950-7335 ■ Urbanstr 70 (at Hermannplatz, in Ficken 3000) ■ *8pm-close 1st Mon only, large darkroom (see overview map)* ■ www.frauen3000.de
5 **Mobel Olfe** [★MW] Kottbusser Tor/ Dresden Str (U-Kottbusser Tor) ■ *6pm-close Tue-Sun (see overview map)*
6 **Rauschgold** [MW] 49-30/7889-9299 ■ Mehringdamm 62 (U-Mehringdamm) ■ *8pm-close*
7 **Roses** [★MW,TG,YC] 49-30/615-6570 ■ Oranienstr 187 (at Kottbusser Tor) ■ *10pm-close (see overview map)*
8 **Triebwerk** [M,L,V,WC] 49-30/6950-5203 ■ Urbanstr 64 (at Leinestr, U-Hermannplatz) ■ *10pm-close, cruise bar w/ darkroom (see overview map)*

NIGHTCLUBS
9 **Böse Buben** [MO] 49-30/6270-5610 ■ Lichtenrader Str 32 (at Kienitzer Str) ■ *darkroom (see overview map)*
10 **Club Culture Houze** [MW] 49-30/6170-9669 ■ Görlitzer Str 71 (off Skalitzer Str) ■ *also darkroom*

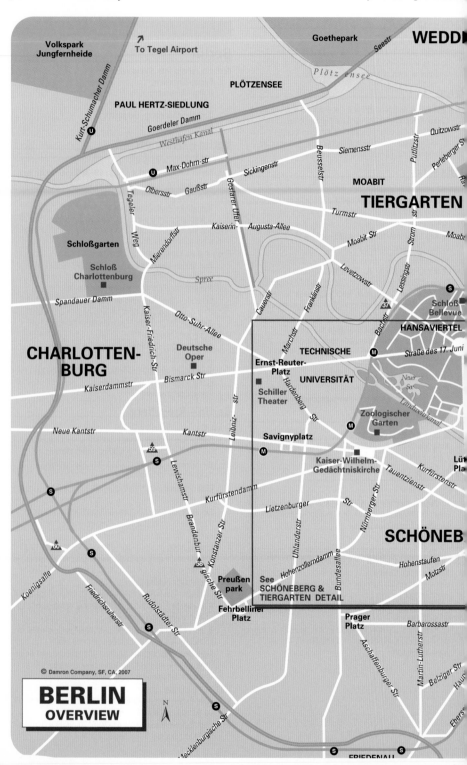

BERLIN
OVERVIEW

© Damron Company, SF, CA, 2007

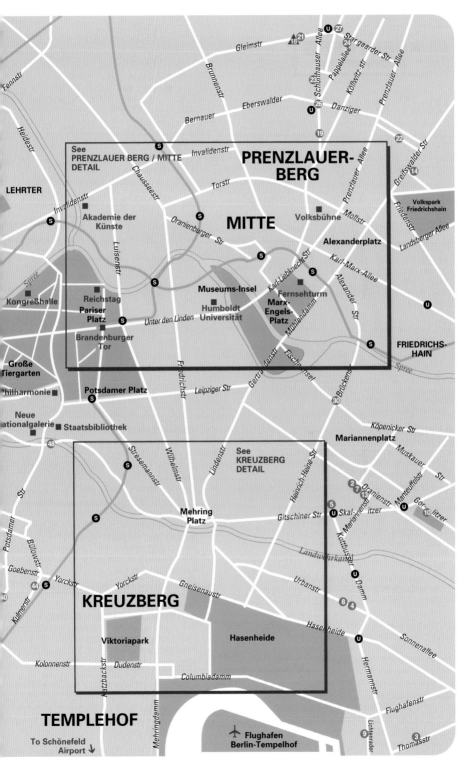

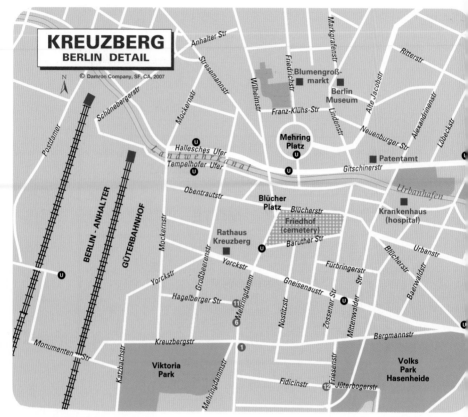

11 SchwuZ (SchwulenZentrum) [★M,D,S,YC,$]
49-30/693-7025 ■ Mehringdamm 61 (enter through Café
Sundstroem) ■ *from 11pm Fri-Sat, theme nights include
PopStaRrZ (pop, indie, electronic), Bump (retro) & Subterra [W]
2nd Fri* ■ www.schwuz.de

12 Serene Bar [MW,D] 49-30/6904-1580 ■ Schwiebusser Str
2 ■ *popular Girls Bar Th, also Girls Dance 2nd & 4th Sat* ■
www.serenebar.de

13 SO 36 [★GS,D,TG,S,V,YC,WC] 49-30/6140-13067,
49-30/6140-1307 ■ Oranienstr 190 (at Kottbusser Tor)
■ *theme nights, also live music venue (see overview map)* ■
www.so36.de

CAFES

Melitta Sundström [MW,WC] 49-30/692-4414
■ Mehringdamm 61 (at Gneisenaustr, U-Mehringdamm)
■ *10am-8pm, till 4pm Sat, clsd Sun, terrace, also lgbt
bookstore*

Muvuca [F] 49-30/6390-1756 ■ Gneisenaustr 2a (at
Mehringdamm) ■ *4pm-close, radical/ political int'l cafe*

Schoko-Café [WO,D,E] 49-30/615-1561,
49-30/694-1077 ■ Mariannenstr 6 (at Kottbusser Tor)
■ *5pm-close, cafe, bar & community center, also steam bath*
■ www.schokofabrik.de/schokofabrik

RESTAURANTS

Amrit 49-30/612-5550 ■ Oranienstr 200 ■ *Indian*

Kaiserstein 49-30/7889-5887 ■ Mehringdamm 80 ■ *int'l*

Locus [★MW] 49-30/691-5637 ■ Marheinekeplatz 4
■ *10am-2am, Mexican, full bar, lesbian-owned*

SUMO 49-30/6900-4963 ■ Bergmanstr 89 ■ *trendy
Japanese* ■ www.s-u-m-o.com

EROTICA

Altelier Dos Santos [GO] 49-30/6823-7115
■ Mehringdamm 119 (U Platz der Luftbrucke) ■ *lesbian-
owned custom leather & fetish wear*

Playstixx 49-30/6165-9500 ■ Waldemarstrasse 24
■ *makers & sellers of silicone toys for women & lovers* ■
www.playstixx.de

Sexclusivitäten 49-30/693-6666 ■ Fürbringer Str 2
■ *lesbian sex shop, toys, leather, videos, Open Salon sex party
noon-8pm Fri, also escort service* ■
www.sexclusivitaeten.de

Berlin—Prenzlauer Berg-Mitte

ACCOMMODATIONS

14 Hotel Transit Loft [GF] 49-30/4849-3773 ■ Greifswalde
Str 219 (enter at Immanuelkirchstrasse 14) ■ *hotel in restore
19th-c factory, brkfst included (see overview map)* ■
www.hotel-transit.de

15 Intermezzo Hotel for Women [WO,WC]
49-30/2248-9096 ■ Gertrud-Kolmar Str 5 (at
Brandenburger Tor) ■ *(see overview map)* ■ www.hotelin-
termezzo.de

16 Kunstlerheim Luise [GF] 49-30/284-480 ■ Luisenstr 19
(Mitte) ■ *former palace w/ rooms re-imagined by local artists
near River Spree*

7   Le Moustache [M] 49-30/281-7277 ■ Gartenstr 4 (at Rosenthaler Platz, U-Oranienburger Tor) ■ *also Moustache Bar [M,L,F], open 8pm-close, clsd Mon-Tue* ■ www.lemoustache.de

8   Schall & Rauch Pension [MW] 49-30/443-3970, 49-30/448-0770 ■ Gleimstr 23 (at Schönhauser Allee) ■ *also bar & restaurant (see overview map)* ■ www.schall-und-rauch-berlin.de

BARS

9   Bärenhöhle [M,B,BW] 49-30/4473-6553 ■ Schönhauser Allee 90 ■ *4pm-6am, beer bar (see overview map)* ■ www.baerenhoehle-berlin.de

0   Besenkammer Bar [MW] 49-30/242-4083 ■ Rathausstr 1 (at Alexanderplatz, under the S-Bahn bridge) ■ *24hrs, tiny "beer bar" (see detail map)*

1   Cafe Amsterdam [GS,TG,F,YC,WC] 49-30/448-0792, 49-30/231-6796 ■ Gleimstr 24 (at Schönhauser Allee) ■ *9am-3am, till 5am Fri-Sat, cafe-bar, terrace, also pension (see overview map)* ■ www.pension-amsterdam.de

    DarkRoom [MO,L] 49-30/444-9321 ■ Rodenbergstr 23 (at Schönhauser Allee) ■ *10pm-6am, uniform bar, darkroom, theme parties wknds* ■ www.darkroom-berlin.de

2   Flax [M,F] 49-30/4404-6988, 49-30/441-9856 ■ Chodowieckistr 41 (off Greifswalder Str) ■ *5pm-3am, 3pm-5am Sat, brunch from 10am Sun (see overview map)*

3   Freizeitheim [MW] 49-30/17440-26444 ■ Schönhauser Allee 57 ■ *more women Th (see overview map)*

    Greifbar [MO,L,V] 49-30/444-0828 ■ Wichertstr 10 (at Greifenhagener Str, S/U-Schönhauser Allee) ■ *10pm-6am, darkroom*

Grosse Freiheit 114 [MO] Boxhagener Str 114 (in Friedrichshain) ■ *darkroom, cruisy*

24 Marietta [MW] 49-30/4372-0646 ■ Stargarder Str 13 ■ *popular gay night Wed (see overview map)*

    The Midnight Sun [MO,D,V,PC] 49-30/4471-6395 ■ Paul Robeson Str 50 (at Schönhauser Allee) ■ *10pm-close, 24hr wknds, darkroom, cruising*

25 Reingold [GS,GO] 49-30/2838-7676 ■ Novalisstr 11 (U-Oranienburger Str) ■ *lesbian-owned cocktail lounge, more gay Th*

26 Schoppenstube [M,D] 49-30/442-8204 ■ Schönhauser Allee 44 (at Eberswalder Str) ■ *8pm-close, from 10pm Fri-Sun, theme nights, terrace, cruisy (see overview map)* ■ www.schoppenstube.com

27 Stahlrohr [MO] 49-30/4473-2747 ■ Greifenhagener Str 54 (off Wicherts Str, U-Schonhauser Allee) ■ *10pm-close, sex parties (see overview map)* ■ www.stahlrohr.com

    Stiller Don [★M,NH,L,F] 49-17/2182-0168 ■ Erich-Weinert-Str 67 (at Schönhauser Allee) ■ *8pm-close, terrace*

NIGHTCLUBS

    Berghain [MW,D] Am Wrietzener (near Ostbahnhof station)

28 Cafe Moskau (GMF) [M,D] Karl-Marx-Allee 34 (U-Schillingstr) ■ *Sun T-dance* ■ www.barlounge808.de

29 Klub International [M,D,$] 49-30/2475-6011 ■ Karl-Marx-Allee 33 (at Kino International, U-Schillingstr) ■ *11pm-close 1st Sat, largest gay club in Berlin*

30 Sage Club [GS,D,TG] 49-30/278-9830 ■ Köpenicker Str 76 (at Brückenstr) ■ *11pm-7am Th-Sun, more gay on wknds (see overview map)* ■ www.sagegroup.de

PRENZLAUER BERG & MITTE
BERLIN DETAIL

© Damron Company, SF, CA, 2007

CAFES

Cafe Seidenfaden [WO,NS] 49-30/283-2783 ■ Dircksenstr 47 (U-Alexanderplatz) ■ noon-9pm, clsd Sun, drug- & alcohol-free women's cafe, info board ■ ■ www.frausuchtzukunft.de

November [MW] 49-30/442-8425 ■ Husemannstr 15 (at Sredzkistr) ■ 9am-2am, cafe-bar, terrace, brkfst buffet wknds

RESTAURANTS

Drei 49-30/4473-8471 ■ Lychener Str 30 (U-Eberswalder Str) ■ pan-Asian

Rice Queen 49-30/4404-5800 ■ Danziger Str 13 (U-Eberswalder Str) ■ Asian

Schall & Rauch Wirtshaus [MW,BW] 49-30/443-3970, 49-30/448-0770 ■ Gleimstr 23 (at Schönhauser Allee) ■ 10am-close ■ www.schall-und-rauch-berlin.de

Thüringer Stuben 49-30/4463-3391 ■ Stargarder Str 2? (at Dunckerstr, S/U-Schönhauser Allee) ■ 4pm-1am, from noon wknds, full bar

BOOKSTORES

31 Ana Koluth [GO] 49-30/2472-6903 ■ Karl Liebknecht St? 13 (at Rosa Luxemburg Str, U-Alexanderplatz) ■ 10am-8pm, till 4pm Sat, clsd Sun, lesbian-owned ■ christiane@anako luth.de

MEN'S CLUBS

Gate Sauna [F,V] 49-30/229-9430 ■ Wilhelmstr 81 (nea? Brandenburger Tor, U-Mohrenstr) ■ 24hrs wknds, also bar, theme nights ■ www.gate-sauna.de

Treibhaus Sauna [F,V,YC] 49-30/448-4503 ■ Schönhaus? Allee 132 (U-Eberswalder Str) ■ 24hrs wknds, also bar, student discount ■ www.treibhaussauna.de

BERLIN

In the last century, Berlin has seen just about everything: the outrageous art and cabaret of the Weimar era; the ravages of world war; ideological standoffs that physically divided families, lovers, and the city itself; and a largely peaceful revolution that brought Germany and the world together. Through it all, the Berliners have retained their own brand of cheeky humor—Berliner Schnauze, it's called—and a fierce loyalty to their city. While Berlin's museums and monuments are world-class, the city's real charm is in its art cafes and countercultural milieu.

Tourist Info

AIRPORT DIRECTIONS

Tempelhof, Tegel, and Schönefeld.

PUBLIC TRANSIT & TAXIS

Taxifunk Berlin 49-800/443-322, web: www.taxifunkberlin.de.

Jet Express-Bus X9 from Tegel Airport to central Berlin 49-30/19449.

U-Bahn (subway) and bus 49-30/19449, web: www.bvg.de.

S-Bahn (elevated train) 49-30/2974-3333, web: www.s-bahn-berlin.de.

TOURIST SPOTS & INFO

Bauhaus Design Museum 49-30/254-0020, web: www.bauhaus.de.

Brandenburg Gate.

Charlottenburg Palace 49-30/320-911.

Egyptian Museum 49-30/2090-5577.

Gay Museum 49-30/6959-9050, web: www.schwulesmuseum.de.

Homo Memorial (at Nollendorfplatz station).

The Jewish Museum Berlin 49-30/2599-3300, web: www.juedisches-museum-berlin.de.

Kaiser Wilhelm Memorial Church.

Käthe-Kollwitz Museum 49-30/882-5210, web: www.kaethe-kollwitz.de.

Museuminsel (Museum Island) 49-30/266-2987, web: www.smb.spk-berlin.de.

New National Gallery 49-30/266-2651, web: www.neue-nationalgalerie.de.

Reichstag 49-30/2273-2152.

Visitor's Center: Berlin-Tourism 49-30/250-025, web: www.btm.de.

Europa Center 49-30/190-016-316, web: www.europa-center-berlin.de.

Weather

Berlin is on the same parallel as Newfoundland, so if you're visiting in the winter, prepare for snow and bitter cold. Summer is balmy while spring and fall are beautiful, if sometimes rainy.

City Calendar

LGBT PRIDE

Christopher Street Day, 3rd or 4th Saturday in June, web: www.csd-berlin.de.

ANNUAL EVENTS

February - Berlinale: Berlin Int'l Film Festival w/ Queer Teddy Award 49-30/259-200, web: www.berlinale.de.

April - Berlin Queer Festival, web: www.berlin-queerfestival.net.

June - Lesbian & Gay City Festival, web: www.regenbogenfonds.de.

October - Lesbian Film Festival 49-30/852-2305, web: www.lesbenfilmfestival.de.

November - Jazz Fest Berlin, www.berlinerfest-spiele.de.

November/ December - Verzaubert Int'l Queer Film Festival, web: www.verzaubertfilmfest.com.

Queer Resources

COMMUNITY INFO

Mann-O-Meter (Gay Center), 49-30/216-8008. Bülostr 106, 5pm-10pm, from 4pm wknds, web: www.mann-o-meter.de.

Lesbenberatung (lesbian line) 49-30/215-2000, web: www.lesbenberatung-berlin.de.

AA 49-30/216-8008. Meets at Mann-O-Meter 8pm Th.

Berliner AIDS-Hilfe 49-30/885-6400, web: www.berlin.aidshilfe.de.

ROTICA

Bad Boy'z [V] 49-30/440-8165 ■ Schliemannstr 38 (U-Eberswalder Str) ■ *toys, videos, cruising, safer sex party 3rd Sat (dress code)* ■ www.badboyz.de

Blackstyle 49-30/4468-8595 ■ Seelower Str 5 (S/U-Schönhauser Allee) ■ *clsd Sun, latex & rubber wear, also mail order* ■ www.blackstyle.de

Duplexx 49-30/4849-4200 ■ Schönhauser Allee 131 (U-Eberswalder Str) ■ *videos, cruisy*

Berlin—Schöneberg-Tiergarten

ACCOMMODATIONS

2 Arco Hotel [GS,WC,GO] 49-30/235-1480 ■ Geisbergstr 30 (at Ansbacherstr, U-Wittenbergplatz) ■ *B&B inn, centrally located, kids/ pets ok* ■ www.arco-hotel.de

3 Art-Hotel Connection [MO,L,WI,WC,GO] 49-30/2102-18800 ■ Fuggerstr 33 (corner Welser Str, near U-Wittenbergplatz) ■ *also special "fantasy" apt for kink & S/M types, some shared baths* ■ www.arthotel-connection.de

4 Berlin B&B [MW,WI,GO] 49-30/2648-4756 ■ *full brkfst* ■ www.k37.de

5 Gaybed.de [GS,GO] 49-30/8185-1988 ■ Perleberger Str (at Stephan Str) ■ *B&B, hot tub, shared bath, pets ok (see overview map)* ■ www.gaybed.de

36 Hotel California [GF] 49-30/880-120 ■ Kurfürstendamm 35 (at Knesebeckstr, U-Uhlandstr) ■ *full brkfst* ■ www.hotel-california.de

37 Hotel Hansablick [GF] 49-30/390-4800 ■ Flotowstr 6 (at Bachstr, off Str des 17 Juni) ■ *full brkfst (see overview map)* ■ www.hotel-hansablick.de

38 Hotel Sachsenhof [GS] 49-30/216-2074 ■ Motzstr 7 (at Nollendorfplatz) ■ www.hotel-sachsenhof-berlin.de

39 Pension Niebuhr [GS,GO] 49-30/324-9595, 49-30/324-9596 ■ Niebuhrstr 74 (at Savignyplatz) ■ *some shared baths* ■ www.pension-niebuhr.de

40 RoB Play 'n Stay Leather Apartments [MO,GO] 49-30/2196-7400 ■ Fuggerstr 19 (behind RoB Berlin shop) ■ *in the heart of Berlin's gay scene, playroom* ■ www.rob.nl/html/berlin_apartments.html

BARS

41 Ajpnia eV [MO] 49-30/425-5241 ■ Eisenacher Str 23 (U-Eisenacher Str) ■ *sex parties*

42 Blue Boy Bar [M,V] 49-30/218-7498 ■ Eisenacher Str 3a (at Fuggerstr, U-Nollendorfplatz) ■ *24hrs, ring bell, hustlers; also Fugger-Eck [GS,NH], 49-30/218-3506, 1pm-6am, clsd Sun, termed*

43 Chez Nous [GS,DS,$] 49-30/213-1810 ■ Marburger Str 14 (at Tauentzienstr, U-Wittenbergplatz) ■ *famous drag revue, shows 8:30pm & 11pm nightly, pricey 1-drink minimum* ■ www.cabaret-chez-nous.de

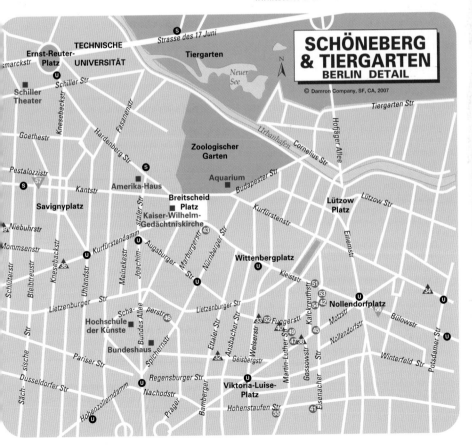

44 **Flipflop** [M,F] 49-30/216-2825 ■ Kulmer Str 20a (at Yorckstr) ■ *7pm-close, from 11am Sun (see overview map)*

45 **Hafen** [★M,TG,S,YC] 49-30/211-4118 ■ Motzstr 19 (at Eisenacher Str, U-Nollendorfplatz) ■ *8pm-close*

46 **Harlekin** [M,NH,F] 49-30/218-2579 ■ Schaperstr 12-13 (at Lietzenburger Str, U9-Spichernstr, in Wilmersdorf) ■ *4pm-close, from 2pm Sun, terrace*

47 **Heile Welt** [MW,F] 49-30/2191-7507 ■ Motzstr 5 ■ *6pm-close* ■ www.heile-welt-berlin.de

48 **Kumpelnest 3000** [GF,D,TG,YC] 49-30/261-6918 ■ Lützowstr 23 (at Potsdamer Str, U-Kurfürstenstr) ■ *5pm-5am, till 8am Fri-Sat, cocktail bar (see overview map)*

49 **Mutschmann's** [MO,L] 49-30/2191-9640 ■ Martin-Luther-Str 19 (at Motzstr, U-Nollendorfplatz) ■ *10pm-close, from 11pm Fri-Sat, clsd Sun-Mon, also bar, darkroom*

50 **Neues Ufer** [MW,OC] 49-30/784-1578 ■ Haupstrasse 157 (U-Bahn Kleistpark) ■ *9am-2am, clsd wknds, city's oldest gay bar (see overview map)*

51 **New Action** [★MO,L,V] 49-30/211-8256 ■ Kleiststr 35 (at Eisenacherstr, U-Nollendorfplatz) ■ *8pm-close, from 1pm Sun, uniform bar, darkroom, very cruisy*

52 **Prinz Knecht** [★M] 49-30/236-27444 ■ Fuggerstr 33 (U-Nollendorfplatz) ■ *6pm-close, theme nights*

45 **Scheune** [★MO,L,V] 49-30/213-8580 ■ Motzstr 25 (at Nollendorfplatz) ■ *9pm-7am, till 9am Fri-Sat, uniform bar, theme nights, darkroom*

53 **Spot** [M,NH,F] 49-30/213-2267 ■ Eisenacher Str 2 (at Nollendorfplatz) ■ *4pm-4am, open later wknds, from 6pm in winter, terrace*

54 **Tabasco** [M,F,AYOR] 49-30/214-2636 ■ Fuggerstr 3 (at Schönhauser Allee, U-Nollendorfplatz) ■ *6pm-6am, 24hrs wknds, hustlers*

55 **Together** [MW] 49-30/2191-6300 ■ Hohenstauffenstr 53 (off Luther Str, U-Viktoria Luise Platz)

45 **Tom's Bar** [★MO,L,V] 49-30/213-4570 ■ Motzstr 19 (at Eisenacherstr, U-Nollendorfplatz) ■ *10pm-6am, open later Fri-Sat, very cruisy, downstairs maze* ■ www.tomsbar.de

NIGHTCLUBS

33 **Connection** [★MO,D,L,V,$] 49-30/218-1432 ■ Fuggerstr 33 (at Art-Hotel Connection) ■ *11pm-close Fri-Sat only, cruisy, darkroom; also sex shop & cinema* ■ www.connection-berlin.com

KitKat Club [GS,D] 49-30/2173-6841 ■ 2 Bessemerstr ■ *8pm-close Th, 11pm-6am Fri-Sat, call for gay theme nights [M], also S/M club* ■ www.kitkatclub.de

CAFES

Cafe Berio [★WC] 49-30/216-1946 ■ Maaßenstr 7 (at Winterfeldtstr, U-Nollendorfplatz) ■ *8am-1am, int'l, brkfst all day, seasonal terrace, also bar* ■ www.berio.de

Cafe Savigny 49-30/312-8195 ■ Grolmanstr 53-54 (at Savignyplatz) ■ *9am-1am, artsy crowd, full bar, terrace*

Windows [MW] 49-30/214-2384 ■ Martin-Luther-Str 22 (at Motzstr, U-Wittenbergplatz) ■ *4pm-4am, from 3pm Sun, full bar, terrace*

RESTAURANTS

Art [MW,WC] 49-30/313-2625 ■ Fasanenstr 81a (at Kantstr, in S-Bahn arches, Charlottenburg, S/U-Zoologischer Garten) ■ *noon-2am, from 10:30am wknds, also bar, internet access* ■ www.art-restaurant.com

Gnadenbrot Martin-Luther-Str 20a ■ *cheap & good*

ENTERTAINMENT & RECREATION

Xenon Kino 49-30/792-8850 ■ Kolonnenstr 5-6 ■ *gay & lesbian cinema* ■ www.xenon-kino.de

BOOKSTORES

56 **Bruno's** [GO] 49-30/6150-0385 ■ Bülowstr 106 (U-Nollendorfplatz) ■ *10am-10pm, clsd Sun, many art photography books, also video/ DVD rentals; also Schönhaus Allee 131, 49-(0)30/6150-0387* ■ www.brunos.de

57 **Prinz Eisenherz Buchladen** [WC] 49-30/313-9936 ■ Lietzenburger Str 9 A (in Schoeneberg) ■ *10am-8pm, clsd Sun, LGBT books, magazines, DVDs "in all languages"* ■ www.prinz-eisenherz.com

RETAIL SHOPS

Galerie Janssen 49-30/881-1590 ■ Pariser Str 45 (at Nollendorfplatz, U1/9-Spichernstr) ■ *clsd Sun, books & artwork for men* ■ www.galerie-janssen.de

MEN'S CLUBS

Apollo City Sauna [F,V] 49-30/213-2424 ■ Kurfürstenstr 101 (in Charlottenburg, U-Wittenbergplatz) ■ *gym equipment, tanning booths, also bar* ■ www.gay-weit.de/sauna1.htm

Steam Sauna Club [L,F,V] 49-30/218-4060 ■ Kurfürstenstr 113 (U-Wittenbergplatz) ■ *24hrs wknds, jacuzzi, also bar* ■ www.steam-sauna.de

EROTICA

Beate Uhse International Joachimstaler Str 4 (at Kantstr, at Erotic Museum) ■ *cinema, video cabins & bar*

City Men 49-30/218-2959 ■ Fuggerstr 26 ■ *videos, magazines, toys*

The Jaxx Club [V] 49-30/213-8103 ■ Motzstr 19 (U-Nollendorfplatz) ■ *movies, mags & toys*

Mazeworld Kurfürstenstr 79 (at Keithstr)

Mister B 49-30/2199-7704 ■ Nollendorfstrasse 23 ■ *clsd Sun, leather, rubber, toys* ■ www.misterb.com

Pool Berlin [V] 49-30/214-1989 ■ Schaperstr 11 (at Joachimsthaler Str, in Wilmersdorf, U-Kurfürstendamm) ■ *clsd Sun, gay emporium*

RoB Berlin 49-30/2196-7400 ■ Fuggerstr 19 ■ www.rob.nl

Berlin—Outer

ACCOMMODATIONS

58 **Artemisia Women's Hotel** [WO] 49-30/873-8905, 49-30/869-9320 ■ Brandenburgischestr 18 (at Konstanzerstr) ■ *the only hotel for women in Berlin, sundeck, some shared baths* ■ www.frauenhotel-berlin.de

59 **Charlottenburger Hof** [GF,F] 49-30/329-070 ■ Stuttgarter Platz 14 (at Wilmersdorfer Str) ■ *also bar* ■ www.charlottenburger-hof.de

60 **Hotel Kronprinz Berlin** [GF,WC] 49-30/896-030 ■ Kronprinzendamm 1 (at Kurfürstendamm, in Halensee) ■ www.kronprinz-hotel.de

BARS

Himmelreich [MW] 49-30/2936-9292 ■ Simon Dach Str 36 (off Warschauer Str, in Friedrichshain, U-Frankfurter Tor) ■ *from 6pm Mon-Fri, 2pm-close wknds, women's night Tue* ■ Himmelreich@partyworks.de

NIGHTCLUBS

Haus B [★MW,D,S,$] 49-30/296-0800 ■ Warschauer Platz 18 ■ *9:30pm-5am Wed & Sun, 10pm-6am Fri-Sat, terrace* ■ www.dashausb.de

CAFES

Schrader's [GO] 49-30/4508-2663 ■ Malplaquetstr 16b (at Utrechter Str, Wedding) ■ *also bar* ■ www.schraders-berlin.de

RESTAURANTS

Cafe Rix 49-30/686-9020 ■ Karl-Marx-Str 141 (in Neükolln) ■ *10am-5pm, Mediterranean, plenty veggie, also bar, open till 1am*

ICELAND

Reykjavik

ACCOMMODATIONS

1 **101 Hotel** [GS,WI] 354/580-0101, 354/861-4710 (cell) ■ *design hotel, hot tub, also restaurant & bar* ■ www.101hotel.is

2 **Arctic Sun** [GS,WI] 354/587-2292 ■ Ingolfsstraeti 12 ■ *centrally located* ■ www.arcticsunguesthouse.com

3 **Hotel Fron** [GS] 354/511-4666 ■ Laugavegi 22A ■ www.hotelfron.is

4 **Luna Hotel Apartments & Guesthouse** [GO] 354/511-2800 ■ Spitalastigur 1 ■ home.islandia.is/luna

5 **Room with a View** [★M,WI,GO] 354/896-2559, 354 /552-7262 ■ Laugavegur 18 (on the 6th flr) ■ www.roomwithaview.is

6 **Tower Guesthouse** [GS] 354/896-6694 ■ Grettisgata 6 ■ *view of city & bay* ■ www.tower.is

BARS

7 **Barinn** [GF,D,F] 354/578-7800 ■ Laugavegur 22 (at Klapparstigur) ■ *popular DJs, also restaurant early*

8 **Cafe Cozy** [M,NH] 354/511-1033 ■ Austurstraeti 3

9 **Oliver** [GF,D,E,F] 354/552-2300 ■ Laugavegur 20A (at Klapparstigur) ■ *DJs, live bands, also restaurant, popular for brunch* ■ www.cafeoliver.is

10 **Prikid** [GF,D,F] 354/551-2866 ■ Bankastraeti 12 ■ *8am-1am, till 5:30am Fri-Sat, from noon Sat-Sun, hipster dive bar, DJs, also restaurant* ■ www.prikid.is

11 **Qbar** [MW] 354/550-9660 ■ Ingolfsstraeti 3 ■ *upscale lounge* ■ www.qbar.is

NIGHTCLUBS

12 **MSC Club** [MO,L] Bankastraeti 11 (enter on Ingolfsstraeti, ring bell at iron gate) ■ *11pm-3am Sat only, dress code* ■ www.msc.is

13 **NASA** [GF,D,E] 354/511-1313 ■ Asturvollur ■ *dance club featuring famous DJs, also live bands* ■ www.nasa.is

14 **Sirkus** [★GF,D,YC] Klapparstigur (at Laugavegur) ■ *divey dance bar w/ guest DJs, young hipster crowd, check out the 2nd flr*

CAFES

Kaffi Hljomalind [E,F,NS] 354/517-1980 ■ Laugavegur 21 (at Klapparstigur) ■ *organic cafe* ■ www.kaffihljomalind.org

Kaffitar 354/511-4540 ■ Bankastraeti 8 ■ *7:30am-6pm, 10am-5pm Sun, excellent coffee* ■ www.kaffitar.is

Mokka 354/552-1174 ■ Skolavordustig 3a ■ *9:30am-11:30pm, from noon Sun, Reykjavik's oldest cafe* ■ www.mokka.is

RESTAURANTS

101 Hotel 354/580-0101, 354/861-4710 (cell) ■ Hverfisgata 10 ■ *7am-11pm, popular upscale restaurant* ■ www.101hotel.is

A Naestu Grosum 354/552-8410 ■ Laugavegur 20B ■ *11:30am-10pm, from noon Sat, from 5pm Sun, vegetarian*

Apotek 354/575-7900 ■ Austurstraeti 16 ■ *lunch Mon-Fri, dinner nightly, chic restaurant in former pharmacy* ■ www.veitingar.is

Baejarins Beztu [★] 354/894-4515 ■ Tryggvagata (at Posthusstraeti) ■ *10am-3am, Icelandic hot dog stand*

Graenn Kostur 354/552-2028 ■ Skolavordustigur 8 ■ *11:30am-9pm, from 1pm Sun, vegetarian* ■ www.graennkostur.is

Hressingarskalinn/ Hresso 354/561-2240 ■ Austurstraeti 20 ■ *popular for brunch, patio* ■ www.hresso.is

Humarhusid/ Lobster House 354/561-3303 ■ Amtmannsstig 1 ■ *traditional Icelandic cuisine, upscale* ■ www.humarhusid.is

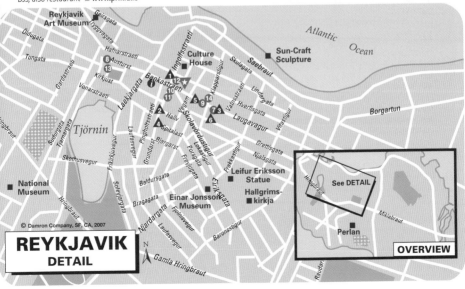

REYKJAVIK

Day Trips:

Reykjavik is charming, but you need to get outside the city to understand why Iceland is called the land of fire and ice. "Iceland" is a complete misnomer, by the way, a clever ruse by the Vikings to divert traffic away from this lush oasis in the Atlantic. Reykjavik Excursions (www.re.is) offers an endless array of trips for curious tourists, all highlighting the diverse landscape, flora, and fauna of this tiny, verdant island country.

The absolute minimum requirement is a jaunt around the Golden Circle, where you'll see Gullfoss waterfall, Geysir hot spring, Pingvellir Nat'l Park, and the Kerid volcanic crater (Bjork performed from inside it!). Along the way you'll be amazed by the grassy countryside and volcanic cliffs, which give a visual history of the creation of the island from hot lava.

If you're looking for a little more excitement, book a trip to the glacier, where you can either hike or snowmobile around on the Myrdalsjökull ice cap. Visiting in wintertime? Take advantage of the long nights by checking out the Northern Lights.

Local Food:

Fishing is an anchor of Iceland's economy, and you'll find the seafood here excellent: fresh, plentiful and innovatively prepared. And although cultural taboos make the following Icelandic traditions sound unappealing or downright cruel to some, you might be pleasantly surprised by the flavor of whale meat or horse meat, puffin or reindeer.

Brave hearts shouldn't leave the island without tossing back a shot of *Brennivin*, locally made schnapps flavored with carraway seeds. Finally, your trip to Reykjavik will not be complete until you wolf down a couple of *pylsur*, the Icelandic incarnation of the humble hot dog that is best eaten while standing on the sidewalk. Order "eina med ollu," or "one with everything."

Tourist Info

AIRPORT DIRECTIONS

Keflavik Int'l Airport, web: www.keflavikairport.com.

PUBLIC TRANSIT & TAXIS

BSR Taxi 354/561-0000, web: www.bsr.is.
BSH Taxi 354/555-0888.
Flybus 354/562-1011.
Straeto Bus 354/540-2700, web: www.bus.is.

TOURIST SPOTS & INFO

Blue Lagoon 354/420-8800, web: www.bluelagoon.com.
Einar Jonsson Museum 354/551-3797, web: www.skulptur.is.
Geothermal swimming pools.
The Golden Circle.
Hallgrimskirkja, web: www.hallgrimskirkja.is.
Icelandic Institute of Natural History 354/590-0500, web: www.ni.is.
National Gallery of Iceland 354/515-9600, web: www.listasafn.is.
National Museum of Iceland 354/530-2200, web: www.natmus.is.
Northern Lights.
Reykjavik City Museum Settlement Exhibition 354/411-6370, web: www.reykjavik871.is.
Saga Museum 354/511-1517, web: www.sagamuseum.is.
Tjornin Lake.
Waterfront/ Sun Voyager sculpture.
Visitor's Center: The Centre 354/590-1550.
Adalstraeti 2 , web: www.visitreykjavik.is.

Weather

Because of its location in the Gulf Stream, weather in Iceland remains fairly mild year round. In summer, expect highs in the mid-60°s, with lows in the mid-30°s in winter. Not quite cold enough for snow, but be prepared for rain and high winds any time of year. Iceland's proximity to the Arctic Circle means 24 hours of daylight during the summer.

Best Views

From the tower of Hallgrimskirkja church, or from the rotating restaurant atop Perlan.

City Calendar

LGBT PRIDE

August, web: www.gaypride.is.

ANNUAL EVENTS

February - Winter Lights Festival, web: www.visitreykjavik.is.
May - Reykjavik Art Festival, web: www.artfest.is.
September - Reykjavik Int'l Film Festival, web: www.filmfest.is.
October - Iceland Airwaves. Huge alternative music festival. 354/0380, web: www.icelandairwaves.com.

Queer Resources

COMMUNITY INFO

Samtokin 78, 354/552-7878, web: www.samtokin78.is. Laugavegur 3, 4th flr, 1pm-5pm Mon-Fri.
Women with Women, web: www.kmk.is.
Gay AA noon Sun (English-speaking) 354/552-7878.
AIDS Iceland 354/552-8586, web: www.aids.is.

Jomfruin 354/551-0100 ■ Laekjargata 4 ■ *Danish-style open-face sandwiches*

Mathur Lifandi 354/585-8700 ■ Haetharsmara 6 ■ *10am-10pm, till 5pm Sat, clsd Sun, vegetarian health food store, also cafe & salad bar* ■ www.madurlifandi.is

Osushi [GO] 354/561-0562 ■ Laekjargotu 2A (upstairs from bookstore) ■ *noon-10pm, sushi* ■ www.osushi.is

Perlan 354/562-0200 ■ *dinner nightly, upscale revolving restaurant, great views, full bar, also cafeteria from 10am* ■ www.perlan.is

Prir Frakkar 354/552-3939 ■ Baldursgata 14 ■ *fresh seafood* ■ www.3frakkar.com

Reykjavik Pizza Company [★] 354/561-3838 ■ Laugavegur 81 ■ www.rpco.is

Vegamot [★] 354/511-3040 ■ Vegamotastig 4 ■ *11am-1am, till 5am Fri-Sat, int'l menu, also popular bar with DJs* ■ www.vegamot.is

ENTERTAINMENT & RECREATION

Blue Lagoon 354/420-8800 ■ *geothermal pool, spa, also restaurant & cafe* ■ www.bluelagoon.com

Hallgrimskirkja 354/510-1000 ■ Skolavordustigur (at Frakkastigur) ■ *9am-5pm, amazing view from top of tower* ■ www.hallgrimskirkja.is

Kolaportid Tryggvagata (btwn Naustin & Saebraut) ■ *11am-5pm Sat-Sun, flea market w/ fish & local food vendors*

Nautholsvik Thermal Beach [GF] 354/551-6630 ■ *off Hildarfotur at Nautholsvegur (south of Perlan, behind Reykjavik airport)* ■ *open May-Sept only, man-made thermal beach with hot pots*

Rainbow Cafe 354/552-7878 ■ Laugavegur 3, 4th flr ■ *8pm-11:30pm Mon & Th, LGBT community center open house* ■ www.samtokin78.is

Reykjavik Excursions 354/562-1011 ■ *top-notch tour company providing excursions to all parts of Iceland* ■ www.re.is

Vesturbaejarlaug Hofsvallagata (in West Town) ■ *thermal pool, sauna, kids ok*

BOOKSTORES

Bokabudin Borg Laekjargotu 2 ■ *some English-language books, good souvenir selection*

RETAIL SHOPS

Bonus 354/562-8200 ■ Laugavegur 59 (at Vitastigur) ■ www.nat.is/bonus_store_iceland.htm

Tiger Laugavegur 13 ■ *Danish dollar-style store*

PUBLICATIONS

Grapevine 354/540-3601 ■ Vesturgata 5 ■ *indispensable English-language weekly* ■ www.grapevine.is

Nightlife Guide 354/822-6600 ■ *bi-weekly guide to Reykjavik bars & clubs, in English* ■ www.nightlifefriend.is

NETHERLANDS

Amsterdam

Amsterdam is divided into 5 regions:
Amsterdam—Overview
Amsterdam—Centrum
Amsterdam—Jordaan
Amsterdam—Rembrandtplein
Amsterdam—Outer

Amsterdam—Overview

ACCOMMODATIONS

Country & Lake [GS,NS,WI] 31-299/372-190 ■ IJsselmeerdijk 26, Warder ■ *3 beautiful apts in countryside 15 miles outside Amsterdam, one lakeview apt* ■ www.countryandlake.nl

Flatmates Amsterdam [★MW,SW,NS,WC,GO] 31-20/620-1545 ■ *apts, studios, house boats & B&Bs* ■ www.flatmates.nl

Rembrandt Park Guesthouse [GS,NS,GO] 31-62/502-0858 ■ www.rembrandtparkhouse.com

Simply Amsterdam Apartments [GF,GO] 31-20/620-6608 ■ *apts, studios, canal houses & houseboat* ■ www.simplyamsterdam-apartments.nl

NIGHTCLUBS

Venus Freaks ■ *"men-friendly women's dance parties"; check site & papers for locations* ■ www.venusfreaks.nl

ENTERTAINMENT & RECREATION

The Anne Frank House 31-20/556-7100, 31-20/556-7105 (info tape) ■ Prinsengracht 267 (in the Jordaan) ■ *the final hiding place of Amsterdam's most famous resident* ■ www.annefrank.org

Boom Chicago 31-20/423-0101 (tickets) ■ Leidseplein 12 (Leidseplein Theater) ■ *English-language improv comedy; also dinner & drinks; distributes free Boom! magazine; € 18-20 (not including food/ drink)* ■ www.boomchicago.nl

Homomonument Westermarkt (in the Jordaan) ■ *moving sculptural tribute to lesbians & gays killed by Nazis* ■ www.homomonument.nl

MacBike 31-20/620-0985 ■ Stationsplein 12 (next to Centraal Station) ■ *rental bikes & map for self-guided tour of Amsterdam's gay points of interest* ■ www.macbike.nl

De Pijp near Albert Cuypmarkt ■ *gay-friendly neighborhood teeming w/ lots of interesting shops & restaurants*

The van Gogh Museum [WC] 31-20/570-5200 ■ Paulus Potterstr 7 (on the Museumplein) ■ *10am-6pm, till 10pm Fri, a must-see museum dedicated to this Dutch master painter* ■ www.vangoghmuseum.nl

PUBLICATIONS

COC Update 31-20/623-4596 ■ *news & events calendar for COC* ■ www.coc.nl

Expreszo 31–20/359–0713 ■ *for LGBT youth (in Dutch)* ■ www.expreszo.nl

Gay News Amsterdam 31–20/679–1556 ■ *bilingual paper, extensive listings* ■ www.gay-news.com

Gay & Night 31–20/788–1360 ■ *free monthly bilingual entertainment paper w/ club listings* ■ www.gay-night.nl

GK Magazine 31–499/39–10–00 ■ *nat'l LGBT newspaper in Dutch w/ English summaries* ■ www.gk.nl

Squeeze 31–09/684–1234 ■ *glossy for boys, in Dutch* ■ www.squeeze.nl

Amsterdam—Centrum

ACCOMMODATIONS

1 **Aaron B&B Amsterdam** [GS,NS] 31–62/817–2817 ■ Singel 401 ■ www.aaron-bedandbreakfast.com

2 **Amsterdam 37** [GS,WI,GO] 31–20/620–2403 ■ Beursstraat 37 (at Oudebrugstraat) ■ *"the best in kinky accommodation"* ■ www.etxeaerasmus.com

3 **Amsterdam Canal Apartments** [M,WI,GO] 31–20/471–0272, 31–6/4748–4046 (cell) ■ Kloveniersburgwal 55 ■ *close to museums & nightlife* ■ www.amsterdamcanalapartments.com

4 **Amsterdam Central B&B** [MW,WI,GO] 31–62/445–7593 ■ Oudebrugsteeg 6-II (Warmoesstraat) ■ *near main gay area (Warmoesstraat) & train station, in 16th-c guesthouse, also apartments, full brkfst* ■ www.amsterdamcentralbedand-breakfast.nl

5 **Amsterdam Escape** [GS] 800/216–7295 (reservations), 31–20/320–6402 ■ Geldersekade 106 (at Centrum) ■ *luxury apts & canal houses* ■ www.amsterdamescape.com

6 **Anco Hotel-Bar** [MO,L,N,WI,GO] 31–20/624–1126 ■ OZ Voorburgwal 55 (across from the Oude Kerk) ■ *1640 canal house, some shared baths, also bar (open 9am–10pm)* ■ www.ancohotel.nl

7 **The Black Tulip Hotel** [★MO,L,R,WI,GO] 31–20/427–0933 ■ Geldersekade 16 ■ *luxury leather & S/M hotel* ■ www.blacktulip.nl

8 **Bob's Youth Hostel** [GF,YC] 31–20/623–0063 ■ Nieuwezijds Voorburgwal 92 ■ *women's, men's & mixed dorms, brkfst included, 3am curfew*

9 **Bulldog** [GF,18+] 31–20/620–3822 ■ Oudezijds Voorburgwal 220 ■ *hostel in Red Light District, dorms & private rooms, brkfst included, coffeeshop & lounge/bar, no lockout or curfew* ■ www.bulldoghotel.nl

10 **Centre Apartments Amsterdam** [GS,GO] 31–20/627–2503, 31–65/371–3452 (cell) ■ Heintje Hoeksteeg 27 ■ *self-catering studios & apts* ■ www.centre-apartments-amsterdam.nl

11 **Cosmos Hostel** [GF,NS] 31–20/625–2438 ■ Nieuwe nieuwstraat 17-1 ■ *hostel in 17th-c hotel, dorms, no curfew, ages 18-35 only* ■ www.hostelcosmos.com

12 **Crowne Plaza Amsterdam City Centre** [GF,SW,WC] 31–20/620–0500, 877/227–6963 (US#) ■ NZ Voorburgwal 5 ■ www.amsterdam-citycentre.crowne-plaza.com

13 **Friendzz** [MW,GO] 31–6/4140–4820 ■ Oudezijds Achterburgwal 34 ■ www.friendzz.com

14 **The Grand Sofitel Demeure Amsterdam** [GF,SW] 31–20/555–3111, 31–20/555–3555 ■ OZ Voorburgwal 197 ■ *5-star deluxe hotel located in the former City Hall—all rooms w/ canal or courtyard views* ■ www.thegrand.nl

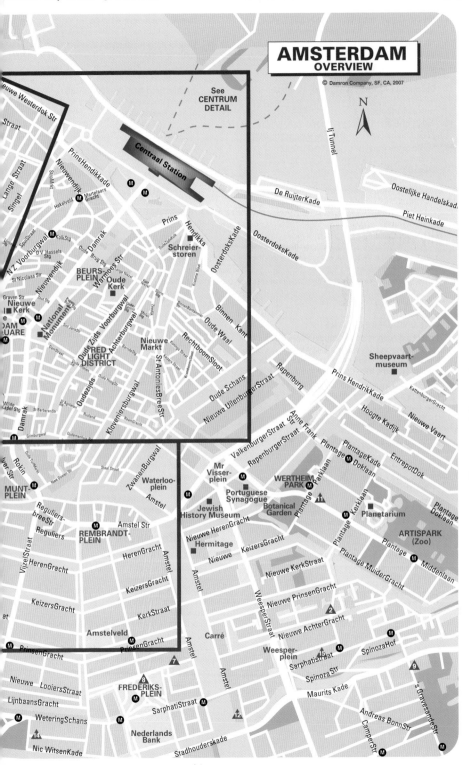

AMSTERDAM
OVERVIEW

© Damron Company, SF, CA, 2007

N

See
CENTRUM
DETAIL

Centraal Station

Nieuwe Westerdok Str

Straat

Lange Straat

Singel

PrinsHendikkade

StraMkt

Nieuwendijk

Hekelveld   Martelaars
             Gracht

NZ Voorburgwal

SpuiStraat

KolkStd

D V Hassels
Stg

Oude Damrak

Oude Brug Stg

Nieuwendijk

St Nicolaas

Zout Stg

BEURS-
PLEIN

Warmoes Str

Oude Kerk

Oude Zijds Voorburgwal

Achterburgwal

Graven Str

Nieuwe
Kerk

National
Monument

RED
LIGHT
DISTRICT

Oudezijds

Oude Hoog Str

St Agnieten

Wijde
kapel Stg

St Barberen Str

Grimburgwal

Oudemanhuis Pr

Kloveniersburgwal

Rusland

Raamgracht

Nieuwe
Markt

St AntoniesBreeStr

Prins

Hendikka

Schreier-
storen

OostderdoksKade

Binnen Kant

Oude Waal

Rechtboomsloot

Oude Schans

Nieuwe Uilenburger Straat

Ij Tunnel

De RuijterKade

Oostelijke Handelskad

Piet Heinkade

OosterdoksKade

Sheepvaart-
museum

Prins HendrikKade

Hoogte Kadijk

Nieuwe Vaart

Kattenburgergracht

Rokin

Oude Turfmarkt

Nieuwe Doelen Str

Steel Straat

ZwanenBurgwal

Waterloo-
plein

Amstel

MUNT-
PLEIN

Reguliers-
breeStr

Reguliers

VijzelStraat

HerenGracht

KeizersGracht

Amstelveld

PrinsenGracht

Nieuwe
LooiersStraat

LijnbaansGracht

WeteringSchans

Nic WitsenKade

REMBRANDT-
PLEIN

Amstel Str

HerenGracht

KeizersGracht

KerkStraat

Amstel

Mr
Visser-
plein

Jewish
History Museum

Portuguese
Synagogue

Nieuwe HerenGracht

Hermitage

Nieuwe

KeizersGracht

Botanical
Garden

WERTHEIM
PARK

Plantage
Parklaan

Plantage

Plantage Kade

Plantage
Kerklaan

Planetarium

ARTISPARK
(Zoo)

Plantage

Plantage MuiderGracht

Middenlaan

EntrepotDok

Plantage
Doklaan

DokLaan

Valkenburgerstraat
Str

RapenburgerStraat

Rapenburg

Anne Frank

Nieuwe KerkStraat

Nieuwe PrinsenGracht

Weesperstraat

Nieuwe AchterGracht

Carré

Weesper-
plein

Sarphatistraat

Spinoza Str

Maurits Kade

Andreas BonnStr

Camper Str

s GravesandeStr

SpinozaHof

Nederlands
Bank

SarphatiStraat

Stadhouderskade

FREDERIKS-
PLEIN

PrinsenGracht

Amstel

Amstel

2

7

8

12

14

15

9

15 **NH City Centre Hotel** [GF,WI,WC] 31-20/420-4545 ■ Spuistraat 288-292 ■ kids/pets ok ■ www.nh-hotels.nl

16 **NH Grand Hotel Krasnapolsky** [GF,WI,WC] 31-20/554-9111 ■ Dam 9 ■ full-service hotel in the city center opposite Royal Palace, jacuzzi, includes business center & 5 restaurants ■ www.nh-hotels.com

17 **Old Harbour Apartments** [GS,NS,GO] 31-20/428-5758 ■ Prins Hendrikkade 125-1 ■ private entrances & patio ■ www.oldharbour.nl

18 **Palace B&B** [GS,NS,WI,GO] 31-6/4260-8847 ■ Spuistraat 224 ■ 1794 bldg w/ indoor garden ■ www.palace-bb.nl

19 **Stablemaster Hotel** [MO,L] 31-20/625-0148 ■ Warmoesstraat 23 ■ shared baths, also bar ■ www.stablemaster.nl

20 **Stayokay Amsterdam Stadsdoelen** [GF] 31-20/624-683 ■ Kloveniersburgwal 97 ■ www.stayokay.com

21 **Victoria Hotel Amsterdam** [GF,SW,WC] 31-20/623-4255 800/814-70000 ■ Damrak 1-5 (opposite Centraal Station) ■ 4-star hotel, gym, restaurants, bar ■ www.parkplazaeurope.com

22 **Winston Hotel** [GF,A] 31-20/623-1380 ■ Warmoesstraat 129 ■ hipster hotel w/ alt-rock bar & decor, some shared baths ■ www.winston.nl

AMSTERDAM

Day Trips: The Hague

Just about 40 minutes out of Amsterdam lies the political hub of The Netherlands. Take a guided tour of the Parliament buildings, or visit some of the amazing castles and cemeteries. The Hague also boasts many museums (including a brand-new museum devoted entirely to Dutch artist MC Escher).

Tourist Info

AIRPORT DIRECTIONS

Direct rail connection to Centraal Station (about a 20-minute ride). Driving and parking in Amsterdam are hellish and pricey; take advantage of the excellent transit system instead, or rent a bicycle.

PUBLIC TRANSIT & TAXIS

31-20/677-7777.
Can also be found at taxi stands on the main squares.
KLM Bus 31-20/653-4975.
GVB 0900-8011 (€.50 per minute), web: www.gvb.nl, or visit their office across from the Centraal Station (Stationsplein 10). Trams, buses & subway.

TOURIST SPOTS & INFO

Anne Frank House 31-20/556-7105, web: www.annefrank.org.
Hermitage Amsterdam 31-20/530-8755, web: www.hermitage.nl.
Homomonument, web: www.homomonument.nl.
Jewish Historical Museum 31-20/531-0310, web: www.jhm.nl.
Rembrandt House 31-20/520-0400, web: www.rembrandthuis.nl.
Rijksmuseum 31-20/674-7000, web: www.rijksmuseum.nl.
Stedelijk Museum of Modern Art 31-20/573-2911, web: www.stedelijk.nl.
Vincent van Gogh Museum 31-20/570-5200, web: www.vangoghmuseum.nl.
Visitor's Center: Amsterdam Tourism & Convention Board 31-20/551-2525, web: www.amsterdamtourist.nl. Visit their office directly opposite Centraal Station. Netherlands Board of Tourism, web: www.holland.com.

Weather

Temperatures hover around freezing in the winter and rise to the mid-60°s in the summer. Rain is possible year-round.

City Calendar

LGBT PRIDE

1st wknd in August, web: www.amsterdampride.nl.

ANNUAL EVENTS

April 30 - Queen's Birthday/ Roze Wester Festival, web: www.gala-amsterdam.nl.
May - Memorial Day & Liberation Day.
May/ June - Holland Festival, web: www.holland-festival.nl.
August - Heart's Day. Drag festival in the Red Light District, web: www.hartjesdagen.nl.
October - Leather Pride, web: www.leatherpride.nl.

Queer Resources

COMMUNITY INFO

COC 31-20/626-3087. Rozenstraat 14, web: www.cocamsterdam.nl.
Gay & Lesbian Switchboard 31-20/623-6565, 10am-10pm (English spoken), web: www.switchboard.nl.
Pink Point, LGBT info kiosk & gift shop by Homomonument, web: www.pinkpoint.org.
AA 31-20/625-6057, web: www.aa-netherlands.org & www.aa-nederland.nl.
Stop AIDS Now 31-20/528-7828, web: www.aids.nl.

BARS

3   **Argos** [★MO,L] 31-20/622-6595 ■ Warmoesstraat 95
■ 10pm-3am, till 4am Fri-Sat, the oldest leather bar in Europe,
popular darkroom, strict dress code, very popular SOS (Sex on
Sunday) last of month (dress code: nude) ■
www.argosbar.com

4   **De Barderij** [M,NH,OC] 31-20/420-5132 ■ Zeedijk 14
■ noon-1am, till 3am Fri-Sat, large brown café

5   **Boys Club 21** [MO,S] 31-20/622-8828 ■ Spuistraat 21
■ noon-2am, boys' house (escorts) w/ full bar & live strip
shows

26   **The Cuckoo's Nest** [MO,L,V,18+] 31-20/627-1752 ■ NZ
Kolk 6 ■ 1pm-1am, till 2am Fri-Sat, cruisy, large play cellar ■
www.cuckoosnest.nl

27   **Dirty Dick's (The Sleaze Pit)** [MO,L] 31-20/627-8634
■ Warmoesstraat 86 ■ 10am-4am Fri-Sat, till 3am Sun, very
cruisy, darkroom ■ theeagle@xs4all.nl

28   **The Eagle Amsterdam** [MO,L] 31-20/627-8634
■ Warmoesstraat 90 ■ 10pm-4am, till 5am Fri-Sat, darkroom,
FF Party 1st Sun 3pm-9pm ■ theeagle@xs4all.nl

29   **De Engel van Amsterdam** [M] Zeedijk 21 ■ 1pm-1am, till
2am Fri-Sat, patio

30   **Getto** [★MW,F,K] 31-20/421-5151 ■ Warmoesstraat 51
■ 4pm-1am, from 7pm Tue, 1pm-midnight Sun, clsd Mon,
also restaurant, some veggie, live DJs, Sun brunch ■
www.getto.nl

31   **Prik** [MW,F] 31-20/320-0002 ■ Spuistraat 109 ■ 4pm-
1am, till 3am Fri-Sat, clsd Mon, patio ■ www.prikamster-
dam.nl

32   **Queen's Head** [M,DS,S] 31-20/420-2475 ■ Zeedijk 20 (off
Nieuwmarkt) ■ 4pm-1am, till 3am Fri-Sat, bingo Tue ■
www.queenshead.nl

19   **Stablemaster Bar** [MO,L] 31-20/625-0148
■ Warmoesstraat 23 ■ 9pm-1am, till 3am Fri-Sat, clsd Tue-
Wed, very cruisy, nightly jack-off parties ■ www.stablemas-
ter.nl

33   **Vrankrijk** [GS,A] Spuistraat 216 ■ rowdy, friendly squat bar,
more gay Mon ■ www.vrankrijk.org

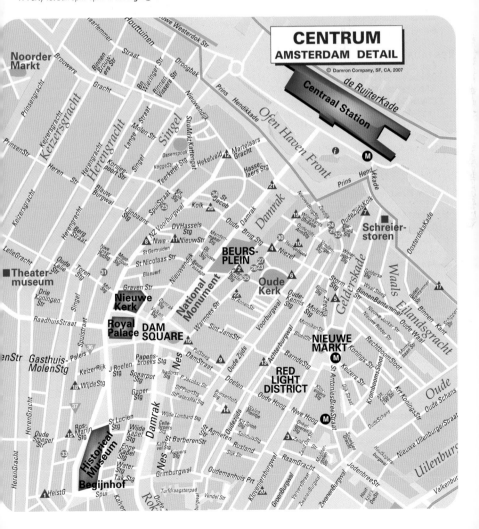

34 **The Web** [★MO,B,L,V] 31–20/623–6758 ■ St Jacobsstraat 6 (btwn Nieuwendijk & NZ Voorburgwal) ■ 2pm-1am, till 2am Fri-Sat, darkroom, rooftop patio, [B] Sat

NIGHTCLUBS

35 **Cockring** [★MO,D,S,V] 31–20/623–9604 ■ Warmoesstraat 96 ■ 11pm-4am, till 5am Fri-Sat, cruisy darkroom, strippers/ sex shows Th, wknds ■ www.clubcockring.com

CAFES

Custom Cafe Sugar [W] Hazenstraat 19 ■ 6pm-1am, till 3am Fri-Sat, clsd Tue-Wed ■ www.les-bi-friends.com

Dampkring 31–20/638–0705 ■ Handboogstr 29 (at Heiligeweg) ■ smoking coffeeshop, friendly & funky ■ www.xs4all.nl/~dampweb/

easyEverything 31–20/320–6294 ■ Damrak 33 ■ 9am-10pm, internet cafe, hundreds of terminals ■ www.easyeverything.com

Gary's Late Night [★] 31–20/637–3643 ■ Witbolstraat 13 ■ noon-3am, till 4am Fri-Sat, fresh muffins & bagels ■ www.garys-muffins.com

Puccini Bomboni [★] 31–(0)20/626–5474 ■ Staalstraat 17 ■ If you love chocolate, do we have a cafe for you! ■ www.puccinibomboni.com

Rokerij 31–20/422–6643 ■ Singel 8 ■ smoking coffeeshop, 3 other locations ■ www.rokerij.net

RESTAURANTS

Cafe de Jaren [GS,YC] 31–20/625–5771 ■ Nieuwe Doelenstraat 20-22 ■ 10am-11pm, till midnight Fri-Sat, int'l, full bar, terrace, cash only ■ www.cafedejaren.nl

Cafe de Schutter 31–20/622–4608 ■ Voetboogstraat 13-15 (upstairs) ■ noon-1am, till 3am Fri-Sat, popular local hangout, plenty veggie, full bar, terrace ■ www.cafedeschutter.nl

Cafe Latei [WI] 31–20/625–7485 ■ Zeedijk 143 (in Red Light District) ■ 8am-5pm, from 9am Sat, from 11am Sun, brkfst & lunch, great coffee hangout, everything you see you can buy, too

Green Planet [★] 31–20/625–8280 ■ Spuistraat 122 ■ 5:30pm-midnight (kitchen till 10:30pm), clsd Sun, vegetarian/ vegan ■ www.greenplanet.nl

Greenwoods 31–20/623–7071 ■ Singel 103 (near Dam Square) ■ English-style brkfst & tea snacks

Hemelse Modder [★WC,GO] 31–20/624–3203 ■ Oude Waal 11 ■ 6pm-10pm, clsd Mon, French/ int'l, popular w/ lesbians & gay men, full bar ■ www.hemelsemodder.nl

Krua Thai [WC] 31–20/622–9533 ■ Staalstraat 22 ■ 6pm-10:30pm, clsd Sun-Mon, Thai, terrace; also at Spuistraat 90a, 620-0623, full bar ■ www.kruathai.nl

La Strada [★] 31–20/625–0276 ■ NZ Voorburgwal 93-95 ■ 4pm-1am, till 2am wknds, food served till 10pm, Mediterranean, plenty veggie, full bar, terrace, lesbian-owned

Het Land van Walem [WC,GO] 31–20/625–3544 ■ Keizersgracht 449 ■ lunch & dinner, int'l, local crowd, canalside terrace, lesbian-owned ■ www.cafewalem.nl

Maoz 31–20/420–7435 ■ Muntplein 1 ■ vegetarian/ falafel ■ www.maoz.nl

Old Highlander 31–20/420–8321 ■ Sint Jacobsstraat 8 ■ 9am-8pm, Scottish food, brkfst all day

Pygma-lion [R,NS,GO] 31–20/420–7022 ■ Nieuwe Spiegelstraat 5a (in Spiegelhof Arcade) ■ 5:30pm-11pm, clsd Mon, South African cuisine, exotic meats & several veggie dishes ■ www.pygma-lion.com

't Sluisje [★MW,TG,DS] 31–20/624–0813 ■ Torensteeg 1 ■ 6pm-close, clsd Mon-Tue, steak house, full bar (open later), drag shows nightly, cash only ■ www.sluisje.nl

Song Kwae 31–20/624–2568 ■ Kloveniersburgwal 14 (near Nieuwmarkt & Chinatown) ■ 1pm-10:30pm, Thai, full bar, terrace ■ www.songkwae.nl

BOOKSTORES

The American Book Center [WC] 31–20/625–5537 ■ Spul 12 ■ 10am-8pm, till 9pm Th, 11am-6:30pm Sun, books & magazines in English imported from US & UK, large LGBT section ■ www.abc.nl

36 **Boekhandel Vrolijk Gay & Lesbian Bookshop** [★] 31–20/623–5142 ■ Paleisstraat 135 (near Dam Square) ■ 10am-6pm, 11am-6pm Mon, 10am-5pm Sat, from 1pm Sun, LGBT books, videos & gadgets, also mail order ■ www.vrolijk.nu

37 **Intermale Gay Bookstore** 31–20/625–0009 ■ Spuistraat 251 ■ 11am-6pm Mon, from 10am Tue-Sat, till 9pm Th, noon-5pm Sun, wide selection of gay men's titles in English & Dutch ■ www.intermale.nl

RETAIL SHOPS

Conscious Dreams Kokopelli [★] 31–20/421–7000 ■ Warmoesstr 12 ■ 11am-10pm, "smart-warehouse," internet ■ www.consciousdreams.nl

Gays & Gadgets 31–20/330–1461 ■ Spuistraat 44 ■ cards, gifts & art gallery ■ www.gaysandgadgets.com

Magic Mushroom 31–20/427–5765 ■ Spuistraat 249 ■ 11am-7pm, till 8pm Fri-Sat, "smartshop": magic mushroom & more; also Singel 524, 31–20/422-7845 ■ magicmushroom.com

Sissy Boy 31–20/638–9305 ■ Kalverstraat 199 ■ French & Dutch designers duke it out on the racks here ■ www.sissyboy.nl

GYMS & HEALTH CLUBS

The Fitness & Health Garden [GS] 31–20/320–0233 ■ Jodenbreestraat 158 ■ health club ■ www.healthgarden.nl

Splash 31–20/624–8404 ■ Looiersgracht 26-30 ■ gym & wellness center ■ www.splashhealthclubs.nl

MEN'S CLUBS

Boomerang 31–20/622–6162 ■ Heintje Hoeksteeg 8 ■ gay sauna & suntanning studio

EROTICA

4men 31–20/625–8797 ■ Spuistraat 21 ■ cinema, darkroom, all-day ticket, private cabin, large sexshop ■ www.adonis-4men.info

Absolute Danny 31–20/421–0915 ■ Oudezijds Achterburgwal 78 (in the Red Light District) ■ 11am-9pm, from noon wknds, upscale erotica, woman-owned ■ www.absolutedanny.com

Adonis [V] 31–20/627–2959 ■ Warmoesstraat 92 ■ 10am-1am, till 3am wknds, cinema, darkroom, large sexshop ■ www.adonis-4men.info

Alfa Blue 31–20/627–1664 ■ Nieuwendijk 26 ■ porn store & video theater

Christine Le Duc 31–20/624–8265 ■ Spui 6 ■ video shop w/ private cabins ■ www.christineleduc.nl

Condomerie Het Gulden Vlies 31–20/627–4174 ■ Warmoesstraat 141 ■ 11am-6pm, clsd Sun, condoms in every size or color or configuration & the lube to go w/ them ■ www.condomerie.com

DeMask 31-20/620-5603 ■ Zeedijk 64 ■ *11am-7pm, till 9pm Th, noon-5pm Sun, rubber & leather clothing* ■ www.demask.com

Drake's of LA [★] 31-20/627-9544 ■ Damrak 61 ■ *videos & magazines, video cabins, cinema* ■ www.drakes.nl

Female & Partners 31-20/620-9152 ■ Spuistraat 100 ■ *fashions & toys for women, also mail order* ■ www.femaleandpartners.nl

Mr B [WC] 31-20/422-0003 ■ Warmoesstraat 89 ■ *leather & rubber, also tattoo & piercing* ■ www.misterb.com

RoB Accessories 31-20/620-7719 ■ Warmoesstraat 32 ■ *leather, rubber, toys* ■ www.rob.eu

Robin & Rik 31-20/627-8924 ■ Runstraat 30 (at Prinsengracht) ■ *by appointment only, custom leatherwear*

Le Salon 31-20/622-6565 ■ Nieuwendijk 20-22 (near the Spui) ■ *sex supermarket, cinema*

Wooden Shoe 31-20/624-9355 ■ Warmoesstraat 61

Amsterdam—Jordaan

ACCOMMODATIONS

1   Amsterdam B&B Barangay [★GS,NS,WI,GO] 31-6/2504-5432 ■ *1777 town house near tourist attractions, full brkfst* ■ www.barangay.nl

2   Budget Hotel Clemens Amsterdam [GF] 31-20/624-6089 ■ Raadhuisstraat 39 (at Herengracht) ■ *small hotel in Amsterdam's center, some shared baths* ■ www.clemenshotel.com

3   Canal Apartments [GF] 31-20/626-4532, 877/283-7540 (US#) ■ *studio, 1-bdrm & 2-bdrm apts, close to city center* ■ www.canalapartments.com

4   The Dylan [GF] 31-20/530-2010 ■ Keizersgracht 384 ■ *also restaurant* ■ www.dylanamsterdam.com

5   En Suite Apartment [GF] 31-20/421-1887, 31-6/5234-3256 (cell) ■ Keizersgracht 320 ■ *apt in historic 1675 canal house* ■ www.ensuite-logies.nl

6   Hotel Acacia [GF] 31-20/622-1460 ■ Lindengracht 251 ■ *"homey hotel in heart of Jordaan"; also self-catering studios & houseboat* ■ www.hotelacacia.nl

7   Hotel Brian [GF] 31-20/624-4661 ■ Singel 69 ■ *cheap, no frills, but friendly, shared baths, no curfew* ■ www.hotelbrian.com

8   Hotel New Amsterdam [GF,NS,WI] 31-20/522-2345 ■ Herengracht 13-19 ■ *"the quiet hotel," full brkfst* ■ www.hotelnewamsterdam.com

9   Hotel Pulitzer [GF] 31-20/523-5235 ■ Prinsengracht 315-331 ■ *occupies 24 17th-c bldgs facing the Prinsengracht & Keizersgracht—2 of Amsterdam's most picturesque canals* ■ www.luxurycollection.com/pulitzer

10   Maes B&B [★GS,NS,GO] 31-20/427-5165 ■ Herenstraat 26 hs ■ *renovated 18th-c home between 2 canals* ■ www.bedandbreakfastamsterdam.com

11   Marnixkade Canalview Apartments [★MW,NS,WI,GO] 31-6/1012-1296 ■ *fully furnished apts in 19th-c canal house on a quiet canal in heart of Jordaan* ■ www.marnixkade.nl

12   Rembrandt Residence Hotel [GS] 31-20/622-1727, 31-20/623-6638 ■ Herengracht 255 ■ *canalside hotel near Dam Square* ■ www.rembrandtresidence.nl

13   Sunhead of 1617 [★GS,NS,WI,GO] 31-20/626-1809 ■ Herengracht 152 (at Leliegracht & Raadshuisstraat) ■ *B&B, full brkfst* ■ www.sunhead.com

BARS

6   Cafe de Gijs [GF,TG] 31-20/638-0740, 31-6/2537-3674 ■ Lindengracht 249 ■ *4pm-1am, 1st Wed of month hosts T&T, social gathering for transvestites & transsexuals, from 10pm (trans-friendly rest of the time, too)* ■ www.t-en-t.nl/cafe_gijs.htm

14   Saarein 2 [W,NH,F] 31-20/623-4901 ■ Elandsstraat 119 ■ *noon-1am, till 2am Fri-Sat, clsd Mon, brown cafe, men welcome* ■ www.saarein.nl

NIGHTCLUBS

de Trut [★MW,D,A,YC] 31-20/612-3524 ■ Bilderdijkstraat 165 ■ *11pm-4am Sun only, hip underground party in legalized squat, doors close when it's full (between 11:30pm-midnight) so come early*

CAFES

Cafe Legendz 31-20/772-3456 ■ Nicolas Berchemstraat 4 ■ *7:30am-midnight, till 2am Fri-Sat, noon-8pm Sun, students by day, goths by night* ■ www.legendz.nl

Cafe 't Smalle 31-20/344-4560 ■ Egelantiersgracht 12 ■ *10am-1pm, brown cafe, full bar, outdoor seating*

Rokerij 31-20/422-6643 ■ Singel 8 ■ *smoking coffeeshop, 3 other locations* ■ www.rokerij.net

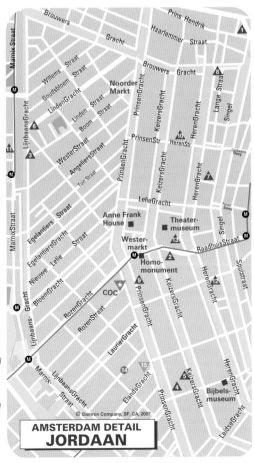

AMSTERDAM DETAIL
JORDAAN

© Damron Company, SF, CA, 2007

Tops 31–20/627–3436 ■ Prinsengracht 480 ■ smoking coffeeshop & internet cafe ■ members.tripod.com/~cafetops

RESTAURANTS

Bojo [★] 31–20/622–7434 ■ Lange Leidsedwarsstraat 49–51 (near Leidseplein) ■ 4pm-2am, till 4am Fri-Sat, from noon wknds, Indonesian ■ www.bojo.nl

De Bolhoed 31–20/626–1803 ■ Prinsengracht 60 (at Tuinstr) ■ noon-11pm, from 11am Sat, vegetarian/ vegan

Burger's Patio 31–20/623–6854 ■ 2e Tuindwarsstr 12 ■ l6pm-1am, talian, plenty veggie

Foodism 31–20/427–5103 ■ Oude Leliestraat 8 ■ 11:30am-11pm, till 6pm wknds, great soups & sandwiches, funky & fun ■ www.foodism.nl

Granada [E] 31–20/625–1073 ■ Leidsekruisstraat 13 ■ 5pm-close, clsd Tue, Spanish, tapas, also bar, live music wknds ■ www.granadarestaurant.nl

't Swarte Schaep [★R] 31–20/622–3021 ■ Korte Leidsedwarsstraat 24 (near Leidseplein) ■ noon-11pm, French

Vijf [MW] 31–20/428–2455 ■ Prinsenstraat 10 ■ 6pm-10pm, piano wknds

De Vliegende Schotel 31–20/625–2041 ■ Nieuwe Leliestraat 162 ■ 4pm-11:30pm, kitchen till 10:45pm, vegetarian & fish, some vegan ■ www.vliegendeschotel.com

ENTERTAINMENT & RECREATION

De Looier Art & Antiques Market 31–20/624–9038, 31–20/427–4990 ■ Elandsgracht 109 ■ 11am-5pm, clsd Fri ■ www.looier.nl

BOOKSTORES

15 Xantippe Unlimited [GO] 31–20/623–5854 ■ Prinsengracht 290 ■ 10am-7pm, till 6pm Sat, noon-5pm Sun, 1pm-7pm Mon, women's, lesbian section, English titles, lesbian-owned ■ www.xantippe.nl

RETAIL SHOPS

Dare to Wear 31–20/686–8679 ■ Buiten Oranjestraat 15 ■ noon-7pm, 1pm-6pm Sun, 1pm-7pm Mon, piercing, jewelry & accessories ■ www.dare2wear.info

House of Tattoos 31–20/330–9046 ■ Haarlemmerdijk 130c ■ 11am-6pm, from noon Sun, great tattoos, great people ■ www.houseoftattoos.nl

Lust for Leather 31–6/5573–4047 ■ Lindengracht 220 ■ 2pm-6pm 1st Sat or by appointment, hip showroom, day & fetish wear ■ www.lustforleather.nl

MEN'S CLUBS

Thermos Day [★SW,F] 31–20/623–9158 ■ Raamstraat 33 ■ noon-11pm, till 10pm wknds, cruisy sauna on 5 flrs, also bar & cafe ■ www.thermos.nl

SEX CLUBS

Sameplace [GS,TG,D] 31–20/475–1981 ■ Nassaukade 120 ■ [MO] Mon, theme nights, darkroom ■ www.sameplace.nl

EROTICA

Black Body [WC] 31–20/626–2553 ■ Lijnbaansgracht 292 (across from Rijksmuseum) ■ clsd Sun, rubber clothing specialists, also leather, toys, DVDs & more ■ www.blackbody.nl

Amsterdam—Rembrandtplein

ACCOMMODATIONS

1 Amsterdam House [GF] 31–20/626–2577 & 624–6607 (hotel), 800/618–1008 (US#) ■ 's Gravelandseveer 7 ■ hotel, apts & houseboats ■ www.amsterdamhouse.com

2 Best Western Eden Hotel [GF,WI,WC] 31–20/530–7878 ■ Amstel 144 ■ 3-star hotel overlooking Amstel River, brasserie ■ www.edenhotelgroup.com

3 Dikker & Thijs Fenice Hotel [GF] 31–20/620–1212 ■ Prinsengracht 444 (at Leidsestraat) ■ 4-star hotel overlooking canal, restaurant & bar ■ www.dtfh.nl

4 Hotel Amistad [★M,WC,GO] 31–20/624–8074 ■ Kerkstraa 42 (at Leidsestraat) ■ friendly staff, some shared baths, internet lounge ■ www.amistad.nl

5 Hotel de l'Europe [GF,SW] 31–20/531–1777 ■ Nieuwe Doelenstraat 2-8 ■ grand hotel on the River Amstel ■ www.leurope.nl

6 Hotel Monopole [GF] 31–20/624–6271 ■ Amstel 60 ■ centrally located, kids ok, also apts; also Cafe Rouge ■ www.hotel-monopole.nl

7 Hotel Orlando [GF,GO] 31–20/638–6915 ■ Prinsengracht 1099 (at Amstel River) ■ beautifully restored 17th-c canalhouse ■ www.hotelorlando.nl

8 Hotel The Golden Bear [★MW,B,OC,WI,GO] 31–20/624–4785 ■ Kerkstraat 37 (at Leidsestraat) ■ formerly the Hotel Unique, the oldest gay hotel in Amsterdam (since 1948) w/ friendly multilingual staff, some shared baths ■ www.goldenbear.nl

9 Hotel Waterfront [GF] 31–20/421–6621 ■ Singel 458 ■ located in city's center ■ www.hotelwaterfront.nl

10 ITC Hotel [★MW,GO] 31–20/623–0230, 31–20/623–1711 ■ Prinsengracht 1051 (at Utrechtsestraat) ■ 18th-c canal house, great location, also bar & lounge ■ www.itc-hotel.com

11 Jolly Hotel Carlton [GF,WI] 31–20/521–6810 ■ Vijzelstraat 4 ■ 4-star overlooking the famous flower market & Munt Tower ■ www.jollycarlton.nl

12 The Orfeo Hotel [M] 31–20/623–1347 ■ Leidsekruisstraat 14 (at Prinsengracht) ■ exclusively gay (since 1969!), some shared baths, also bar & restaurant ■ www.hotelorfeo.com

13 Seven Bridges [★GF] 31–20/623–1329 ■ Reguliersgracht 31 ■ small & so elegant, canalside, view of 7 bridges (surprise!), brkfst brought to you ■ www.sevenbridgeshotel.nl

BARS

14 Amstel Taveerne [M,NH] 31–20/623–4254 ■ Amstel 54 (at Rembrandtplein) ■ 4pm-1am, till 3am Fri-Sat, classic brown café gone gay

15 April [★M,V] 31–20/625–9572 ■ Reguliersdwarsstraat 37 (at Rembrandtplein) ■ 2pm-1am, till 3am Fri-Sat, 3 bars, 1 revolving

16 ARC [★GS,D,F,YC] 31–20/689–7070 ■ Reguliersdwarsstraat 44 ■ 4pm-1am, till 3am Fri-Sat, trendy & fun 20-something crowd, also restaurant ■ www.bararc.com

6 Cafe Rouge [M,NH] 31–20/420–9881 ■ Amstel 60 ■ 4pm-1am, till 3am wknds ■ www.caferouge.nl

17 Cafe Sappho [W,E] 31–6/1714–0296 ■ Vijzelstraat 103 ■ 11am-1am, till 3am Fri-Sat, women's pub but men welcome, [WO] Fri, DJs Fri-Sat ■ www.sappho.nl

18 Entre-Nous [MW,NH] 31–20/623–1700 ■ Halvemaansteeg 14 (at Rembrandtplein) ■ 8pm-3am, till 4am Fri-Sat

19 Exit Cafe [M] 31–20/625–8788 ■ Reguliersdwarsstraat 42 ■ 11am-4am, till 5am Fri-Sat, upscale, part of 4-bar Exit complex ■ www.exitcafe.nl

19 Garbo [W,D] Reguliersdwarsstraat 42 (at Exit) ■ 4pm-10pm 4th Sun only ■ www.garboinexit.nl

20 **Habibi Ana** [MW,MR,E] 31-06/620-1788 ■ Lange Leidsedwarsstraat 4-6 ■ 7pm-1am, till 3am Fri-Sat, Arabian clientele, Arabian & int'l music, bellydancing shows wknds ■ www.habibiana.nl

21 **Hot Spot Cafe** [M,NH] 31-20/622-8335 ■ Amstel 102 ■ 8pm-3am, 4pm-4am Fri-Sat, 4pm-3am Sun

22 **de Krokodil** [M,NH,OC] 31-20/626-2243 ■ Amstelstraat 34 ■ 4pm-1am, till 2am Fri-Sat

23 **Het Leeuwtje Cafe** [M,NH] 31-20/528-5485 ■ Reguliersdwarsstraat 105 ■ 3pm-1am, till 3am Fri-Sat

24 **Lellebel** [★M,NH,TG,F,K,DS] 31-20/427-5139 ■ Utrechtsestraat 4 ■ 9pm-3am, from 10pm Fri-Sun, till 4am Fri-Sat, drag bar, very trans-friendly ■ www.lellebel.nl

Mankind [M,F] 31-20/638-4755 ■ Weteringstraat 60 ■ noon-10pm, clsd Sun, cafe-bar, canalside terrace ■ www.mankind.nl

25 **Mix Cafe** [★MW] 31-20/420-3388 ■ Amstel 50 ■ 8pm-3am, 6pm-4am Fri, 8pm-4am Sat ■ www.mixcafe.nl

26 **Le Montmartre** [★M,NH,YC] 31-20/620-7622 ■ Halvemaansteeg 17 ■ 4pm-1am, till 3am Fri-Sat, very Dutch

27 **Music Box** [M,AYOR] 31-20/620-4110 ■ Paardenstraat 9 (near Rembrandtplein) ■ 8pm-2am, till 3am Fri-Sat, hustlers

28 **Reality** [M,NH,MR-L] 31-20/639-3012 ■ Reguliersdwarsstraat 129 ■ 8pm-3am, till 4am Fri-Sat, Surinamese ■ www.barreality.freehomepage.com

29 **Soho** [★MW,D,YC] 31-20/422-3312 ■ Reguliersdwarsstraat 36 ■ 8pm-3am, till 4am Fri-Sat, British pub 1st flr, lounge upstairs, happy hour 10pm-11pm ■ www.pubsoho.eu

30 **Spijker** [★MO,NH,L,V] 31-20/620-5919 ■ Kerkstraat 4 ■ 1pm-1am, till 2am Fri-Sat, darkroom, TVs showing hardcore porn & cartoons

31 **Vivelavie** [W] 31-20/624-0114 ■ Amstelstraat 7 (at Rembrandtplein) ■ 3pm-1am, till 3am Fri-Sat ■ www.vivelavie.net

32 **Het Wapen van Londen** [★M,YC] 31-6/1539-5317 ■ Amstel 14 ■ 4pm-1am, till 2am Fri-Sat, clsd Mon, cafe-bar, terrace

NIGHTCLUBS

19 **Exit** [★MO,D,$] 31-20/625-8788 ■ Reguliersdwarsstraat 42 ■ midnight-4am, till 5am Fri-Sat, clsd Mon-Wed, 4 bars, 4 kinds of music, darkroom ■ www.clubexit.eu

33 **Studio 80** [GS,D] 31-20/521-8333 ■ Rembrandtplein 17 ■ www.studio-80.nl

34 **You II** [MW,D] 31-20/421-0900 ■ Amstel 178 (at Wagenstraat) ■ 10pm-4am, till 5am Fri-Sat, 4pm-1am Sun, clsd Mon-Wed, ladies night Sat ■ www.youii.nl

CAFES

Downtown Coffeeshop [★M,GO] 31-20/622-9958 ■ Reguliersdwarsstr 31 (at Koningsplein) ■ 10am-8pm, till 10pm Fri-Sat, terrace open in summer ■ www.coffeeshop-downtown.nl

Global Chillage 31-20/777-9777 ■ Kerkstr 51 ■ 11am-midnight, till 1am Fri-Sat, smoking coffeeshop, publisher's choice ■ www.globalchillage.nl

The Other Side [M,GO] 31-20/421-1014 ■ Reguliersdwarsstr 6 (at Koningsplein) ■ 11am-1am, gay smoking coffeeshop

RESTAURANTS

Barney's Breakfast Bar [★YC] 31-20/625-9761 ■ Haarlemmerstraat 102 ■ 7am-midnight, brkfst all day, lunch & dinner menu, plenty veggie ■ www.barneys.biz

Garlic Queen [R] 31-20/422-6426 ■ Reguliersdwarsstr 27 ■ 6pm-close, clsd Mon-Tue, even the desserts are made w/ garlic! ■ www.garlicqueen.nl

Golden Temple [NS] 31-20/626-8560 ■ Utrechtsestr 126 ■ brkfst, lunch & dinner, mix of Indian, Mexican & Mediterranean, vegetarian & vegan ■ www.restaurantgoldentemple.com

De Huyschkaemer 31-20/627-0575 ■ Utrechtsestraat 137 ■ 4pm-1am, till 3am wknds ■ www.huyschkaemer.nl

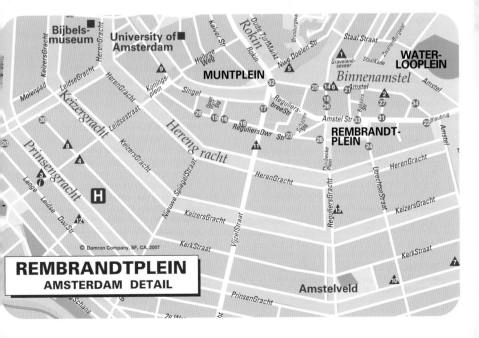

REMBRANDTPLEIN
AMSTERDAM DETAIL

Le Monde [MW,GO] 31-20/626-9922 ■ Rembrandtplein 6 ■ *8am-11pm, brkfst till 4pm (open 4pm-10pm Mon-Fri in winter), plenty veggie, terrace dining*

Rose's Cantina [★] 31-20/625-9797 ■ Reguliersdwarsstr 38-40 (near Rembrandtplein) ■ *5pm-11pm, Tex-Mex, full bar* ■ www.rosescantina.com

Saturnino [MW] 31-20/639-0102 ■ Reguliersdwarsstr 5 ■ *noon-midnight, Italian, full bar*

RETAIL SHOPS

Conscious Dreams Dreamlounge 31-20/626-6907 ■ Kerkstr 113 ■ *11am-9pm, noon-6pm Sun-Mon, "psychedelicatessen," internet access* ■ www.conscious-dreams.nl

MEN'S CLUBS

Thermos Night 31-20/623-4936 ■ Kerkstraat 58-60 (near Leidseplein) ■ *11pm-8am, till 10am Sun, sauna on 3 flrs, also bar* ■ www.thermos.nl

EROTICA

B1 Cinema 31-20/623-9546 ■ Reguliersbreestraat 4 ■ www.b1sex.nl

The Bronx 31-20/623-1548 ■ Kerkstraat 53-55 (near Leidseplein) ■ *huge gay shop for sex supplies, videos, magazines & toys, also cinema* ■ www.bronx.nl

Der Stringslip 31-20/638-1143 ■ Reguliersdwarsstr 59 ■ *underwear, clothing, leather, rubber, accessories*

Xarina 31-20/624-6383 ■ singel 416 ■ *latex clothing & accessories* ■ www.xarina.nl

Amsterdam—Outer

see overview map

ACCOMMODATIONS

1   **Abba Budget Hotel** [GF] 31-20/618-3058 ■ Overtoom 122 (1st Constantyn Huygenstraat) ■ *"smoker"-friendly* ■ www.abbabudgethotel.com

2   **Amsterdam B&B** [GF,NS,WI,GO] 31-20/624-0174 ■ Roeterstraat 18 ■ *powered by green energy* ■ www.amsterdambedandbreakfast.com

    Amsterdam Room Service [GS,GO] 31-20/679-4941 ■ 2e van der Helststraat 26 III ■ *apt & B&B rooms in Amsterdam, cash only* ■ members.chello.nl/r.loose

    Between Art & Kitsch [GF,WI] 31-20/679-0485, 31-6/4744-2072 (cell) ■ Ruysdaelkade 75-2 ■ *near museum* ■ www.between-art-and-kitsch.com

3   **Blue Moon B&B** [GS,WI,GO] 31-20/428-8800 ■ Weteringschans 123A ■ www.bluemoon-amsterdam.nl

    Chico's Guesthouse [GF] 31-20/675-4241 ■ Sint Willibrordusstraat 77 (at Van Woustraat & Ceintuurbaan, near Sarphatipark) ■ *in De Pijp* ■ www.chicosguesthouse.tk

    The Collector B&B [GF,GO] 31-6/1101-0105 (cell), 31-20/673-6779 ■ De Lairessestr 46 hs (in museum area) ■ *full brkfst* ■ www.the-collector.nl

4   **The Flying Pig** [GF] 31-20/400-4187 ■ Vossiusstraat 46-47 (at Leidseplein) ■ *hostel, dorms, no curfew, kitchen facilities, also Centrum location* ■ www.flyingpig.nl

5   **Flynt B&B Amsterdam** [MW,WI,GO] 31-20/618-4614, 31-(0)6/5260-1160 (cell) ■ Eerste Helmersstraat 34 ■ *250 meters from Vondelpark* ■ www.flynt.nl

6   **Freeland Hotel** [GF,GO] 31-20/622-7511 ■ Marnixstraat 386 ■ *2-star hotel, full brkfst* ■ www.hotelfreeland.com

7   **The Friendship B&B** [GS,GO] 31-20/620-9103 ■ Achtergracht 17G ■ *houseboat sleeps up to 4* ■ www.friendshipbnb.nl

8   **Hemp Hotel** 31-20/625-4425 ■ Frederiksplein 15 ■ *only in Amsterdam: sleep on a hemp mattress, eat a hemp roll (THC-free) for brkfst or drink hemp beer in the downstairs Hemp Temple bar* ■ www.hemp-hotel.com

    Hotel Aadam Wilhelmina [GF] 31-20/662-5467 ■ Koninginneweg 169 ■ *charming, full brkfst buffet, some shared baths* ■ www.hotel-aadam-wilhelmina.nl

9   **Hotel Arena** [★GF,WI] 31-20/850-2400 ■ Gravesandestraat 51 ■ *hotel in former orphanage, popular nightclub in restored chapel* ■ www.hotelarena.nl

10 **Hotel Fita** [NS] 31-20/679-0976 ■ Jan Luykenstraat 37 ■ *small family-owned hotel* ■ www.fita.nl

11 **Hotel Rembrandt** [GF,NS] 31-20/627-2714 ■ Plantage Middenlaan 17 ■ *beautiful brkfst rm w/ 17th-c art, near Rembrandtplein* ■ www.hotelrembrandt.nl

    Hotel Sander [GF] 31-20/662-7574 ■ Jacob Obrechtstraat 69 ■ *also 24hr bar & coffee lounge* ■ www.hotel-sander.nl

12 **InterContinental Amstel Amsterdam** [WI] 31-20/622-6060 ■ Professor Tulpplein 1 ■ *5 stars (ultraluxe since it opened in 1867); for the queen (the royal kind) w/ money to burn: €500+* ■ www.amsterdam.intercontinental.com

13 **International Budget Hostel** [GF] 31-20/624-2784 ■ Leidsegracht 76 (at Leidseplein) ■ *in 17th-c warehouse on canal, lounge w/ internet, clean 4-person dorms* ■ www.internationalbudgethostel.com

14 **Kap Hotel** [GS,GO] 31-20/624-5908 ■ Den Texstraat 5 ■ *bikes available to rent, also self-catering apt* ■ www.kaphotel.nl

    Kerstin's B&B [GF,NS] 31-20/612-6969 ■ Kwakerstraat 2 ■ *B&B & self-catering apt overlooking new canal, kids ok* ■ www.bed-and-breakfast-in-amsterdam.nl

15 **Lilianne's Home** [WO,NS] 31-20/627-4006 ■ Sarphatistraat 119 (at Weesperplein Station) ■ *full brkfst, shared bath, also apt*

    Lloyd Hotel [★GF,F,WI] 31-20/561-3636, 31-20/561-3604 ■ Oostelijke Handelskade 34 ■ *hip hotel for all budgets in cool Eastern Harbor area* ■ www.lloydhotel.com

16 **NL Hotel** [GS,WI] 31-20/689-0030 ■ Nassaukade 368 ■ www.nl-hotel.com

17 **Prinsen Hotel** [GF] 31-20/616-2323 ■ Vondelstraat 36-38 (near Leidseplein) ■ www.prinsenhotel.nl

18 **Stayokay Amsterdam Vondelpark** [GF,WI,WC] 31-20/589-8996 ■ Zandpad 5 ■ *dorms & rms, inside Vondelpark, also bar & restaurant* ■ www.stayokay.com

NIGHTCLUBS

    Flirtation [W,D] Oostelijke Handelskade 4 (at Club Panama) ■ *bi-monthly women's dance party, check web or local listing for next event* ■ www.letsbeopen.nl

19 **Melkweg** [GS,E] 31-20/531-8181 ■ Lijnbaansgracht 234 (at Leidseplein) ■ *popular live-music venue, also restaurant, cinema, theater* ■ www.melkweg.nl

9   **ToNight @ Arena** [★GF,D] 31-20/850-2451 ■ Gravesandestraat 51 (at Hotel Arena) ■ *theme nights; come to see the club itself—a restored chapel from an orphanage* ■ www.hotelarena.nl

RESTAURANTS

    An 31-20/624-4672 ■ Weteringschans 76 (in Museum Quarter) ■ *6pm-11:30pm (kitchen till 10pm), Japanese, patio*

    Boom Chicago 31-20/423-0101 ■ Leidseplein 12 (Leidseplein Theater) ■ *lunch & dinner, patio, comedy/improv show at 8:30pm (tickets not included in price)* ■ www.boomchicago.nl

De Waaghals 31-20/679-9609 ■ Frans Halsstraat 29 ■ *5pm-11pm, kitchen open till 9:30pm, clsd Mon, vegetarian* ■ www.waaghals.nl

RETAIL SHOPS

Gallery Faubourg 31-20/676-1918 ■ Overtoom 426 ■ *clsd Mon, gay art & antique gallery* ■ www.faubourg.nl

EROTICA

RoB 31-20/428-3000 ■ Weteringschans 253 (at Reguliersgracht) ■ *clsd Sun, Amsterdam's first leathershop* ■ www.rob.eu

SPAIN

Madrid

Note: M°=Metro station

See Chueca map

ACCOMMODATIONS

1   **Chueca Pension** [MW] 34/91-523-1473 ■ Gravina 4, 2nd flr (at Calle Hortaleza) ■ *hostel, free Internet access* ■ www.chuecapension.com

2   **Hostal CasaChueca** [MW,GO] 34/91-523-8127, 34/63-589-2805 ■ San Bartolomé 4, 2nd flr ■ www.casachueca.com

3   **Hostal Hispano** [GF] 34/91-531-4871, 34/91-531-2898 ■ Hortaleza 38, 2nd flr (at Perez Galdos, M° Chueca) ■ www.hostalhispano.com

4   **Hostal La Fontana** [MW] 34/91-521-8449, 34/91-523-1561 ■ Valverde 6, 1° (M° Gran Vía) ■ www.hostallafontana.com

5   **Hostal la Zona** [M,GO] 34/91-521-9904 ■ Calle Valverde 7, 1 & 2 (at Gran Vía) ■ *full bkfst* ■ www.hostallazona.com

3   **Hostal Odesa** [★M] 34/91-521-0338, 34/91-521-5901 ■ Hortaleza 38, 3rd flr (at Perez Galdos) ■ www.hostalsonsodesa.com/odesa.htm

6   **Hostal Oporto** [GF] 34/91-429-7856 ■ Calle Zorilla 9, 1st flr (M° Sol) ■ *10-minute walk to gay scene* ■ www.hostaloporto.com

7   **Hostal Puerta del Sol** [M,WC,GO] 34/91-522-5126 ■ Plaza Puerta del Sol 14, 4° (at Calle de Alcalá, M° Sol) ■ *centrally located* ■ www.hostalpuertadelsol.com

8   **Hostal Sonsoles** [M] 34/91-532-7523 ■ Fuencarral 18, 2nd flr (M° Chueca) ■ www.hostalsonsodesa.com/sonsoles.html

9   **Hotel A Gaudí** 34/91-531-2222 ■ Gran Vía 7-9 (at Alcalá) ■ *4-star hotel in the heart of the city* ■ www.hoteles-catalonia.es

MADRID

Local Food:

Tapas! Perhaps the secret to the nonstop party that is Madrid? For those not yet aquainted with this Spanish tradition, tapas are small portions of appetizers or savory entreés that are served in most bars, and which headline in tapas bars. Though tasty meals in their own right, tapas are also great for tiding you over until lunch or dinner, and help keep you going late into the night if you are drinking!

Tourist Info

AIRPORT DIRECTIONS

Barajas Airport is a short bus ride or cab ride to the city center.

PUBLIC TRANSIT & TAXIS

Metro 34/90-244-4403, web: www.metromadrid.es.

TOURIST SPOTS & INFO

Chueca.
El Rastro (flea market).
Museo del Prado 34/91-330-2800, web: museoprado.mcu.es.
Museo Thyssen-Bornemisza 34/91-369-0151, web: www.museothyssen.org.
Museo de Reina Sofia (home of Picasso's *Guernica*) 34/91-774-1000, web: museoreina-sofia.mcu.es.
El Retiro (park).
Royal Palace 34/91-454-8700.
Visitor's Center: Oficina Municipale de Turismo 34/91-308-0400, web: www.descubremadrid.com.

Weather

Winter temps average in the 40°s (and maybe even a little snow!). Summer days in Madrid are hot, with highs well into the 80°s.

Best Views

From the funicular in the Parque des Atracciones.

City Calendar

LGBT PRIDE

June, web: www.orgullogay.org.

ANNUAL EVENTS

October/November - International Gay & Lesbian Film Festival, web: www.lesgaicinemad.com.

Queer Resources

COMMUNITY INFO

COGAM (Colectivo de Lesbianas, Gays, Transexuales y Bisexuales de Madrid) 34/91-522-4517. Calle de La Puebla 9, web: www.cogam.org
Gai Inform (helpline) 34/91-523-0070.

10 **Hotel Suecia** [GF] 34/91-531-6900, 800/448-8355
■ Marqués de Casa Riera 4 (M° Banco de España) ■ *jacuzzis*
■ www.hotelsuecia.com

11 **Hotel Urban Madrid** [GF,SW] 34/91-787-7770 ■ Carrera
de San Jerónimo 34 ■ *upscale hotel w/ 3 restaurants &
rooftop pool* ■ www.derbyhotels.com

12 **Hotel Villa Real** [GS,WI] 34/91-420-3767 ■ Plaza de Las
Cortes, 10 ■ *located in the cultural, political & financial center
of Madrid, full brkfst* ■ www.derbyhotels.com

12 **The Westin Palace** [GF] 34/91-360-8000,
800/325-3589 ■ Plaza de Las Cortes 7 ■ *grand hotel* ■
www.westinpalacemadrid.com

BARS

13 **A Noite** [M,D,DS,S,V] 34/91-531-0715 ■ Hortaleza 43 (M°
Chueca)

14 **The Angel** [M,D] 34/68-779-1452 ■ Campoamor 11
■ *noon-5:30am, till 6am Fri-Sat, clsd Mon-Tue* ■
www.theangelmadrid.com

15 **Bajo Cuerda** [★M,NH,S,V,OC] Benito Pérez Galdós 8 (M°
Chueca) ■ *9pm-3am, darkroom*

16 **Bear's Bar** [★MO,B,L,V] 34/91-521-7358 ■ Pelayo 4 (M°
Chueca, ring to enter) ■ *6pm-2:30am, till 3:30am wknds, clsd
Mon, 3 bars, darkroom, cruisy* ■ www.bearsbar.net

17 **Black & White (Blanco y Negro)** [★M,D,S]
34/91-531-1141 ■ Libertad 34 (at Gravina, M° Chueca)
■ *8pm-5am, till 6am Fri-Sat, disco downstairs* ■
www.discoblack-white.net

18 <u>**La Bohemia**</u> [W,NH,D,F] Plaza de Chueca 10 (M° Chueca)
■ *8pm-close, from 9pm wknds* ■ labohemia@interocio.es

18 <u>**Chueca's Friends**</u> [W] Plaza de Chueca 9 ■ *5pm-4am*

19 **Clip** [M] 34/91-521-5143 ■ Gravina 8 (M° Chueca) ■ *8pm-
2am*

20 **Copper** [MO,D,L,N] San Vincente Ferrer 34 (M° Tribunal)
■ *2pm-3am, till 3:30am Fri-Sat, theme nights, dress code,
sling, darkroom* ■ www.copperbar.net

15 **Cruising** [★M,D,L,V,YC] 34/91-521-5143 ■ c/ Benito Pérez
Galdós 5 (M° Chueca) ■ *8pm-close, till 3:30am Fri-Sat, cruise
bar, darkroom*

21 **Dumbarton** [M,NH,OC] 34/91-429-8191 ■ Zorrilla 7
(behind Congress bldg, M° Sevilla, ring to enter) ■ *7pm-2am*

22 **Eagle Madrid** [M,L,F,V,N,PC] 34/91-524-1627 ■ Pelayo 30
(M° Chueca) ■ *2pm-close, from 5pm wknds, leather/ uniform
bar, theme nights, darkroom* ■ www.eaglespain.com

23 **Enfrente** [M,B,L] 34/68-779-1462 ■ Infantas 12 (M° Gran
Vía) ■ *8pm-3am, DJs Th & Sun* ■
www.theangelmadrid.com/enfrente.html

24 **Hot Bar** [M,B,L,V] Infantas 9 (M° Chueca, ring to enter)
■ *6pm-close, cruise bar, darkroom, [B] 1st Sat* ■
www.barhot.com

25 **Leather** [MO,D,L,S,V,OC] 34/91-308-1462 ■ Pelayo 42 (at
Gravina, M° Chueca) ■ *7pm-3pm, from 8pm Sat, till 3:30am
Fri-Sat, [S] Th-Sat, darkroom* ■ leather@leathermadrid.com

26 **Liquid** [M,D,V] 34/91-532-7428 ■ Barquillo 8 (M° Banco)
■ *9pm-close, trendy bar* ■ www.liquid.es

27 **LL** [★M,D,S,V] 34/91-523-3121 ■ Pelayo 11 (M° Chueca)
■ *6pm-close, darkroom, cruisy*

28 **La Lupe de Lavapies** [MW,C] 34/91-527-5019 ■ Torrecilla
del Leal 12 (M° Antón Martín) ■ *5pm-2:30am, flea market
Sun (see overview map)*

29 **El Mojito** [MW,NH] 34/91-539-4617 ■ Olmo 6 (M° Antón
Martín) ■ *10pm-3am, till 3:30am Fri-Sat, cocktail bar, great
music, (see overview map)*

O'Clock [M,B] Calle de San Marcos (M° Chueca) ■ *5:30pm-
close, cruisy*

30 **The Paso** [M,V] 34/91-522-0888 ■ Costanilla de
Capuchinos 1 (M° Gran Vía) ■ thepaso1@yahoo.es

31 **Priscilla** [GS,D] San Bartolomé 6 (M° Gran Vía) ■ *9pm-3am,
till 5am Fri-Sat, trendy dance bar*

32 **Querelle** [M,V] 34/91-528-3860 ■ Lavapiés 12 (M° Tirso de
Molina) ■ *10pm-2am, 11pm-close Fri-Sat, sex club, darkroom,
(see overview map)*

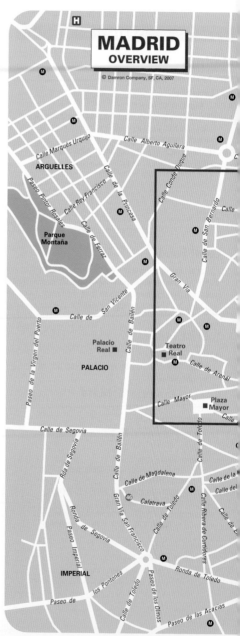

33 Refugio [★M,D] 34/91–369–4038, 34/91–523–4689 ■ Doctor Cortezo 1 (M° Tribunal) ■ midnight-6am, clsd Sun, hottest on Fri night, (see overview map)

34 Rick's [★M,D,YC] 34/91–531–9186 ■ Clavel 8 (at Infantas, M° Gran Vía, ring to enter) ■ 11pm-6am, open later Fri-Sat, 9pm-2am Sun, open later Fri-Sat, "see-and-be-scene"

35 Rimmel [M,NH,V,YC] Luis de Góngora 2 (M° Chueca) ■ 7pm-3am, darkroom, hustlers

36 Sunrise [MW,D,S] 34/91–523–2808, 34/91–522–4317 ■ Barbieri 7 (btwn San Marcos & Infantas, M° Chueca) ■ midnight-close, clsd Mon-Tue

37 Truco [★W,D] 34/91–532–8921 ■ Gravina 10 (at Plaza de Chueca) ■ 8pm-close, clsd Mon-Tue, dance bar, seasonal terrace

38 Why Not? [★GF,$] 34/91–523–0581, 34/91–521–8034 ■ San Bartolomé 6 (M° Gran Vía) ■ 10pm-close, fun dance bar

NIGHTCLUBS

39 **Bangalá** [M,MR,V,YC,N] Escuadra 1 (M° Antón Martin/Lavapiés) ■ 9pm-2:30am, till 3am Fri-Sat, darkroom, (see overview map) ■ www.bangalamadrid.com

40 **Delirio** [M,D,S] 34/91-531-1870 ■ Libertad 28 ■ www.deliriochueca.com

37 **Escape** [W,D,DS] Gravina 13 (at Plaza de Chueca) ■ 10pm-5am Wed-Sun, drag shows

41 **Griffin's** [M,D,DS,E] 34/91-522-2079 ■ Marqués de Valdeiglesias 6 (M° Banco de España) ■ midnight-5am, till 6am Fri-Sat, theme nights ■ www.griffinsmadrid.com

Heaven @ Sala But [★GF] Barceló 11 (M° Tribunal) ■ 12:30am-6am Sun only, mixed metrosexual party ■ www.heavenmadrid.com

42 **Joy Eslava** [★GS,D,DS,S] 34/91-366-3733 ■ arenal 11 (M° Sol) ■ 11:30pm-6pm, fabulous crowd ■ www.joy-eslava.com

43 **Medea** [★WO,D,C,YC,$] Cabeza 33 (M° Antón Martin) ■ 11pm-7am Th-Sat only, dance bar, men welcome as guests (see overview map)

44 **Mito** [MW,NH,D,DS] 34/91-531-8996 ■ Augusto Figueroa 3 (M° Chueca) ■ 11pm-6:30pm ■ www.discomito.com

45 **Ohm** [★M,D,S] 34/91-531-0132 ■ Plaza de Callao 4 (at Sala Bash, M° Callao) ■ midnight-close Fri-Sat ■ www.tripfamily.com

46 **The Paw** [M,N] 34/91-366-6093 ■ Calatrava 29 (M° La Latina) ■ 9pm-5am, 11pm-close Wed-Sat, 5pm-close Sun, sex club, darkroom, slings, (see overview map)

47 **Polana** [MW,D,C] 34/91-532-3305 ■ Barbieri 10 (M° Chueca) ■ 10pm-5am, trendy

48 **Royal Dance Coolture** [GS,D] 34/91-542-3439 ■ Isabel la Católica 6 (M° Santo Domingo) ■ sleek 2-flr ballroom, more gay Sat for "Bunker Bears Club" ■ www.fsmgroup.es/productosymarcas/royaldance

18 **Sachas** [MW,D,DS] Plaza de Chueca 1 (M° Chueca) ■ 8pm-5am Th-Sun, bar open 8pm-3am nightly, terrace

Space of Sound [MW,D] 34/90-249-9994 ■ Macumba (at Estación de Chamartin) ■ 10pm-close Sun only ■ www.comunidadspaceofsound.com

49 **Strong Center** [M,D,L,S,V,$] 34/91-541-5415 ■ Trujillos 7 (M° Santo Domingo) ■ midnight-close, cruisy, huge darkroom ■ www.strongcenter-disco.com

50 **Tábata** [MW,D,YC,$] 34/91-547-9735 ■ Vergara 12 (next to Teatro Real, M° Opera) ■ 11:30pm-late Th-Sat ■ www.pubtabata.com

45 **Week-end** [★MW,D,A,$] 34/91-531-0139 ■ Plaza de Callao 4 (at Sala Bash, M° Callao) ■ midnight-6am Sun ■ www.tripfamily.com

CAFES

BAires Cafe [MW] 34/91-532-9879 ■ Gravina 4 (M° Chueca) ■ 4pm-2am, also bar, hip crowd ■ www.interocio.es/baires

Cafe Acuarela [MW] 34/91–532–8735, 34/91–570–6907 ■ Gravina 10 (M° Chueca) ■ *3pm-3am, from 11am Sat-Sun, bohemian cafe-bar*

Cafe Figueroa [★MW] 34/91–521–1673 ■ Augusto Figueroa 17 (at Hortaleza, M° Chueca) ■ *also bar, theme parties*

Cafe la Troje [★MW] 34/91–531–0535 ■ Pelayo 26 (at Figueroa, M° Chueca) ■ *2pm-2am, till 2:30am wknds, full bar*

Color [M] 34/91–522–4820 ■ Augusto Figueroa 11 (M° Chueca) ■ *3pm-midnight, from 5pm wknds, tapas & desserts, full bar*

D'Mystic [★GS,F] 34/91–308–2460 ■ Gravina 5 (M° Chueca) ■ *9:30am-close, hip cafe-bar in Chueca area* ■ www.dmystic.net/dmystic3d.html

El Jardin [MW] 34/91–521–9045, 34/91–523–1218 ■ Infantas 9 (M° Gran Via)

Mama Inés [★GS] 34/91–523–2333 ■ Hortaleza 22 (M° Chueca) ■ *10am-2am, sandwiches, pies* ■ www.mamaines.com

La Sastrería [★MW] 34/91–532–0771 ■ Hortaleza 74 (at Gravina, M° Chueca) ■ *10am-2am, till 3am Fri-Sat, from 11am wknds, trendy, internet access* ■ lasastreria@eresmas.com

Star's [MW,D] 34/91–522–2712 ■ Marqués de Valdeiglesias 5 (at Infantas, M° Banco) ■ *9am-6pm & 11pm-close, clsd Sun, cafe-bar, DJ Th-Sat*

XXX Cafe [M,F,C] 34/91–532–8415 ■ Clavel 4 (M° Gran Vía) ■ *10am-close, cafe-bar, [C] wknds*

RESTAURANTS

A Brasileira 34/91–308–3625 ■ Pelayo 49 (M° Chueca) ■ *lunch & dinner, Brazilian*

Al Natural 34/91–369–4709 ■ Zorrilla 11 (M° Sevilla) ■ *lunch & dinner, vegetarian*

El Armario [MW,S] 34/91–532–8377 ■ San Bartolomé 7 (btwn Figueroa & San Marcos, M° Chueca) ■ *lunch & dinner, Mediterranean* ■ www.elarmariorestaurante.com

Artemisa [MW] 34/91–429–5092 ■ Ventura de la Vega 4 (at Zorrilla) ■ *vegetarian; also Tres Cruces 4 location, 34/91–521-8721*

Botin 34/91–366–4217 ■ Cuchilleros 17 ■ *one of the oldest restaurants in the world (open since 1725) & an old Hemingway haunt* ■ www.botin.es

Chez Pomme 34/91–532–1646 ■ Pelayo 4 (M° Chueca) ■ *lunch & dinner, clsd Sun, int'l/ vegetarian*

Colby 34/91–521–2554 ■ Fuencarral 52 (M° Chueca) ■ *9:30am-close, from 11:30am Sun* ■ www.restaurantecolby.com

La Coqueta [MW] 34/91–523–0647 ■ Libertad 3 ■ *clsd Sun, lunch & dinner, Mediterranean* ■ www.elarmariorestaurante.com

Divina La Cocina [MW] 34/91–531–3765 ■ Colmenares 13 (at San Marcos, M° Chueca) ■ *lunch & dinner, clsd Sun, elegant & trendy* ■ www.divinalacocina.com

Ecocentro 34/91–553–5502, 34/91–532–3346 ■ Esquilache 2, 4, y 6 (at Pablo Iglesias, M° Rios Rosas) ■ *open till midnight, vegetarian, natural foods, also shop, herbalist school* ■ www.ecocentro.es

Los Girasoles 34/91–308–4494 ■ Hortaleza 106 ■ *clsd Sun, creative Spanish, tapas*

Gula Gula [★MW,E,DS,R] 34/91–522–8764 ■ Gran Via 1 (M° Gran Via) ■ *lunch & dinner, buffet/ salad bar, full bar* ■ www.gulagula.net

Lombok 34/91–531–3566 ■ Augusto Figueroa 32 (M° Chueca) ■ *lunch & dinner, clsd Sun, int'l*

Marsot [MW] 34/91–531–0726 ■ Pelayo 6 (M° Chueca) ■ *lunch & dinner, clsd Sun*

Momo [NS,GO] 34/91–532–7162 ■ Augusto Figueroa 41 (M° Chueca) ■ *lunch & dinner*

Moskada 34/91–563–0630 ■ Francisco Silvela 71 (at General Oraa) ■ *lunch Mon-Fri, dinner Mon-Sat, clsd Sun*

Nina 34/91–591–0046 ■ Manuel Malasana 10 (M° Bilbao) ■ *contemporary Spanish food, open every day* ■ ninarestaurant@telefonica.net

Pink Pollo 34/91–531–1675 ■ Infantas 18 (near Plaza Vazquez de Mella) ■ *12:30pm-12:30am, till 2:30am Fri-Sat, open daily for light meals/ snacks, cute & casual* ■ pinkpollo@pinkpollo.com

Restaurante Miau 34/91–429–2272 ■ Plaza Santa Ana 6 ■ *Madrileño cuisine & tapas*

El Rincón de Pelayo [★MW] 34/91–521–8407 ■ Pelayo 19 (M° Chueca) ■ *lunch & dinner* ■ www.interocio.es/elrincondepelayo

Sama-Sama 34/91–521–5547 ■ San Bartolomé 23 (M° Chueca) ■ *lunch & dinner, clsd Sun, Balinese decor, also Infante 5 location, 34/91–389-6890* ■ www.restaurantesamasama.com

BOOKSTORES

22 **A Different Life** 34/91–532–9652 ■ Pelayo 30 (M° Chueca) ■ *11am-10pm, LGBT, books, magazines, music, videos, sex shop downstairs* ■ www.lifegay.com

51 **Berkana Bookstore** [WC] 34/91–522–5599 ■ Hortaleza 64 ■ *10:30am-9pm, from 11:30am Sat, from noon Sun, LGBT, Spanish & English titles, ask for free gay map of Madrid* ■ www.libreriaberkana.com

RETAIL SHOPS

AKM 34/91–531–1388 ■ Pelayo 14 (M° Chueca) ■ *clsd Sun, military-style fashion & fetish store*

La Catedral [L] 34/91–319–2874 ■ San Gregorio 3 (M° Chueca) ■ *custom-made leather clothing, repairs, objects, fetish*

Ovlas 34/92–522–7327 ■ Augusto Figueroa 1 (M° Chueca) ■ *10:30am-9:30pm, men's clothing, clubwear* ■ www.ovlas.com

PUBLICATIONS

Odisea 34/91–523–2154 ■ Espiritu Santo 33 ■ *free monthly magazine (en español)* ■ www.odiseaeditorial.com

Shangay Express 34/91–445–1741 ■ *free bi-weekly gay paper, also publishes Shanguide* ■ www.shangay.com

Zero 34/91–701–0089 ■ *stylish & intelligent LGBT monthly (en español)* ■ www.zeropress.com

GYMS & HEALTH CLUBS

Energy Gym [★GF] 34/91–531–1029, 34/91–522–3073 ■ Hortaleza 19 (M° Gran Vía, Chueca) ■ *8:30am-11:30pm, 10am-6pm Sun, crowded after 6pm, wet area is cruisy*

Gimnasio V35 [M] 34/91–523–9352 ■ Valverde 35 (M° Gran Via) ■ *8:30am-11pm, 10am-10pm Sat, clsd Sun*

Holiday Gym [GF] 34/91–547–4033 ■ Serrano Jover 3 (M° Argüelles) ■ *central location* ■ www.holidaygym.com

MEN'S CLUBS

Adán [V,SW] 34/91–532–9138 ■ San Bernardo 38 (M° Noviciado) ■ *24hrs wknds, 3 flrs, darkroom, also bar, hustlers* ■ www.saunasmadrid.com

Alameda [SW] 34/91–429–8745 ■ Alameda 20 (M° Atocha) ■ *darkroom, also bar, no steam room* ■ www.saunasmadrid.com

Caldea's [YC,V] 34/91–522–9956 ■ Valverde 32 (at Gran Vía, M° Chueca) ■ *24hrs, gym equipment, bar*

Comendadoras [★OC,V] 34/91–532–8892 ■ Plaza Comendadoras 9 (M° Noviciado) ■ *24hrs, also bar* ■ www.saunasmadrid.com

Cristal [V,SW] 34/91–531–4489 ■ Augusto Figueroa 17 (M° Tribunal y Gran Vía) ■ *3pm-3am, also bar* ■ www.saunas-madrid.com

Hell [MO,L] Buenavista 14 (M° Antón Martín) ■ *10:30pm-3am, 11:30am-3:30am Fri-Sat, clsd Mon, rubber/ leather/ uniforms welcome, selective entry policy* ■ www.hellsex-club.com

Into the Tank [MO,D,L] 34/91–521–7734 ■ *12:30pm-6am, theme nights, basement, dress code, darkroom* ■ www.intothetank.org

Men [V] 34/91–531–2583 ■ Pelayo 25 (M° Chueca) ■ *3pm-8am, 24hrs wknds, bar*

Octopus [M,V,SW] 34/91–183–2832 ■ Churruca 10 (M° Tribunal/ Chueca) ■ *3pm-midnight, darkroom, bar* ■ www.mundoplacer.com/octopus.html

Odarko [MO] 34/91–522–9251 ■ Loreto & Chicote 7 (M° Callao) ■ *10pm-close, from 6pm Sun, "pervy & fetish sex club in Madrid"* ■ www.odarko.com

Paraíso [★V] 34/91–522–4232, 34/91–531–9891 ■ Norte 15 (at San Vicente F, M° Noviciado) ■ *2pm-midnight, 24hrs wknds, gym equipment, also bar, darkroom*

Sauna Plaza [V] 34/91–548–3741 ■ Gran Vía 88 (in Edificio España, M° Sevilla) ■ *10am-10pm, gym equipment, bar*

Sauna Príncipe [F,V] 34/91–559–5353, 34/91–548–2218 ■ Travesía de las Beatas 3 (M° Opera) ■ *2pm-midnight, also bar, darkroom*

Sauna Puerta de Toledo Cuesta de las Descargas 6 (M° Puerta de Toledo) ■ *2pm-11pm* ■ www.saunapuertadetoledo.es/index2.html

EROTICA

Amantis 34/91–702–0510 ■ Pelayo 46

California [V] Valverde 20 (at Gran Vía) ■ *10am-10pm*

City Sex Store 34/91–181–2723 ■ c/ Hortaleza, next to #18 (in Chueca) ■ *open every day* ■ www.citydvd.biz

Happy Sex [V] 34/91–448–6902 ■ Fuencarral 101, downstairs (M° Tribunal) ■ *videos*

Los Placeres de Lola [TG] 34/91–468–6178 ■ Doctor Fourquet, 34 ■ *noon-10pm, clsd Sun, toys, leather, books & videos for women, also cafe* ■ www.losplaceresdelola.net

Play 34/91–523–0841 ■ Pelayo 31 (M° Chueca) ■ *sex shop, open daily*

SR [GO] 34/91–523–1964 ■ Pelayo 7 (M° Chueca) ■ *clsd Sun, fetish, military, leather* ■ www.sr-shop.com

---

Cape Town

ACCOMMODATIONS

1　**18 on Crox** [GS,SW,WI] 27–21/433–2318, 27–82/576–3000 ■ 18 Croxteth Rd (Green Point) ■ www.18oncrox.com

2　**30 Fiskaal Rd Guest House** [GF,SW,WI,GO] 27–(0)21/438–1206 ■ 30 Fiskaal Rd (Camps Bay) ■ *4-star, in Mediterranean-style villa overlooking Camps Bay & Table Mtn, full brkfst* ■ www.30fiskaal.com

3　**4 on Varneys** [GS,SW,WI,GO] 27–(0)21/434–7167 ■ 4 Varneys Rd, Green Point (Green Point) ■ *full brkfst, "in heart of Cape Town's most vibrant quarter"* ■ www.4onvarneys.co.za

2　**65 Kloof Guest House** [MO,SW] 27–(0)21/434–0815, 27–(0)82/962–1828 ■ 65 Kloof Rd (at Fresnaye, Sea Point) ■ *large pool & secluded garden* ■ www.65kloof.co.za

4　**An African Villa** [GS,SW,WI] 19 Carsterns St (Tamboerskloof) ■ *19th-c terrace houses, full brkfst* ■ www.capetowncity.co.za/villa

5　**Amsterdam Guest House** [★MO,SW,N,GO] 27–(0)21/461–8236 ■ 19 Forest Rd ■ *full brkfst, sauna, also Sea Point location* ■ www.amsterdam.co.za

6　**Blackheath Lodge** [GF,SW,GO] 27–(0)21/439–2541 ■ 6 Blackheath Rd (Sea Point) ■ www.blackheathlodge.co.za

　Buçaco Sud & Buçaco Sea Guest Houses [GF,F,SW,WC,GO] 27–(0)28/272–9750 ■ 2609 Clarence Dr (Main Rd), Betty's Bay ■ *guesthouse, full brkfst, set w/in a world biosphere reserve, restaurant* ■ www.bucacosud.co.za

7　**Cactus House** [MO,GO] 27–(0)21/422–5966 ■ 4 Molteno Rd (City Bowl) ■ *also apt in Sea Point* ■ www.cactushouse.co.za

　Camps Bay Beach Village [GS] 27–(0)21/438–4444, 27–(0)21/438–3972 ■ 59 Victoria Rd (Camps Bay) ■ *self-catering rentals* ■ www.campsbayvillage.com

　Capsol Property & Tourism Solutions [GS,SW,WC] 27–(0)21/422–3521 ■ *rentals, full brkfst, jacuzzi, kids ok* ■ www.capsol.co.za

　Clarence House [MW,SW] 27–(0)21/683–0307 ■ 6 Obelisk Rd (Claremont) ■ *4-star guesthouse in "Beverly Hills of Cape Town"* ■ www.chchouse.co.za

8　**De Waterkant House** [GS] 27–(0)21/438–3972 ■ 35 Loader St (Waterfront), Dewaterkant ■ *self-catering, kids ok, pool* ■ www.dewaterkant.com

9　**The Decks** [M,SW,WI] 27–21/434–0471, 27–73/299–4306 (cell) ■ 3 Friars Rd (Sea Point) ■ *centrally located, jacuzzi* ■ www.gaycapetown.net

　Drop Anchor [GF,SW,GO] 27–(0)22/714–1207 ■ 7 Flamingo St (Camp Rd), Saldanha ■ *beachfront B&B & self-catering unit, w/in driving distance of Cape Town* ■ www.dropan-chor.co.za

10　**Four Seasons Guest House** [GS] 27–21/439–0803, 27–21/439–1059 ■ 9 Oldfield Rd (Sea Point) ■ *full brkfst, garden court w/ jacuzzi* ■ www.fourseasonsguesthouse.co.za

11　**The Glen Boutique Hotel** [M,SW,GO] 27–(0)21/439–0086 ■ 3 The Glen (off High Level Rd, Sea Point) ■ www.glenho-tel.co.za

12　**Guest House One Belvedere** [MO,SW,WI,GO] 27–(0)21/461–2442 ■ 1 Belvedere Ave (Oranjezicht) ■ *full bkrfst, jacuzzi* ■ www.onebelvedere.co.za

13 **Huijs Haerlem** [GS,SW,GO] 27-(0)21/434-6434 ■ 25 Main Dr (Sea Point) ■ *guesthouse, full brkfst* ■ www.huijshaerlem.co.za

14 **Kingslyn Guesthouse** [GF] 27-(0)21/439-9305 ■ 8 Hill Rd (Green Point) ■ *full brkfst* ■ www.kingslyn.co.za

15 **Kinneret** [GF,SW] 27-21/439-9237 ■ 11 Arthurs Rd (Sea Point) ■ *near beach* ■ www.kinneret.co.za

16 **Little Lemon Tree** [GS,SW] 27-21/439-1990, 27-82/338-2888 (cell) ■ 9 Antrim Rd (Green Point) ■ *garden w/ fish pond, no credit cards* ■ www.little-lemon.com

17 **Maison Chablis** [GS,SW] 27-21/876-2366, 27-72/170-8409 (cell) ■ 15 Berg Ln (Franschhoek) ■ *B&B, garden* ■ www.maisonchablis.co.za

18 **Mediterranean Villa** [GF,SW] 27-(0)21/423-2188 ■ 21 Brownlow Rd (Tamboerskloof) ■ www.medvilla.co.za

19 **Metropole Luxury Boutique Hotel** [GF] 27-(0)21/424-7247 ■ 38 Long St ■ *luxury boutique hotel, also M-Bar lounge & Veranda restaurant* ■ www.metropolehotel.co.za

20 **Nelson's Spa & Guesthouse** [GS,SW] 27-21/433-2602 ■ 209 High Level Rd (Sea Point) ■ *on Signal Hill, views of Atlantic Ocean* ■ www.nelsons.co.za

CAPE TOWN

Day Trips: The Winelands
You owe it to yourself to take at least a day to visit the beautiful wineries and lovely towns of the winelands, only about 45 minutes east of Cape Town. Though the region is the world's 7th largest wine-producer, the area remains relatively unspoiled. Take a train from Cape Town to Stellenbosch, one of the prettiest and most culturally rich of the wineland towns, where you can get in on one of the local wine tours. Or explore the town on foot either with a group, or using one of the Discover Stellenbosch on Foot flyers, which you can get free at the tourist information bureau at 36 Market St (www.stellenbosch.org.za.).

You will soon discover that the winelands also boast some of South Africa's best cuisine. In Stellenbosch, try Decameron at 50 Plein St for great Italian food or Volkskombius & De Oewer for Cape cuisine.

Local Food: Try Cape originals such as *waterblommetjiebredie*, a stew made using water hyacinths.

Tourist Info

AIRPORT DIRECTIONS
Cape Town Int'l Airport 27-(0)21/937-1200, web: www.airports.co.za, is about a 30-minute cab ride from City Bowl.

PUBLIC TRANSIT & TAXIS
Hire from taxi ranks around town, or call Marine Taxi Hire 27 (0)21/ 434-0434.

TOURIST SPOTS & INFO
Castle of Good Hope 27-(0)21/787-1249, web: www.castleofgoodhope.co.za.
Company's Gardens.
District Six Museum 27-(0)21/466-7200, web: www.districtsix.co.za.
Greenmarket Square.
Nelson Mandela Gateway & Robben Island Museum 27-(0)21/409-5100, web: www.robben-island.org.za.
Slave Lodge 27-(0)21/460-8240, web: www.iziko.org.za/slavelodge.
South African National Gallery 27-(0)21/467-4660, web: www.iziko.org.za/sang.
Table Mountain.
Tokai Forest.
Two Oceans Aquarium 27-(0)21/418-3823, web: www.aquarium.co.za.
World of Birds 27-(0)21/290-2730, web: www.worldofbirds.org.za.

Weather
Mediterranean-like climate with mild winters, pleasant summers. Beware the "Cape Doctor" however, the (in)famous South-Easter that cools the cape's otherwise warm and dry summers. Watch for heavy showers in winter (May-August), particularly in July and August.

City Calendar

LGBT PRIDE
February. 27-(0)83/919-2525, web: capetown-pride.co.za.

ENTERTAINMENT
December - Mother City Queer Project (costume party), web: www.mcqp.co.za.

ANNUAL EVENTS
March - Out in Africa LGBT film festival, web: www.oia.co.za.
July-December - Whale migrations.
December - Mother City Queer Project, web: www.mcqp.co.za. Celebrate the beginning of summer.

Queer Resources

COMMUNITY INFO
Gay, Lesbian & Bisexual Helpline 27-(0)21/422-2500.
Life Line AIDS (0)800/0123-22.

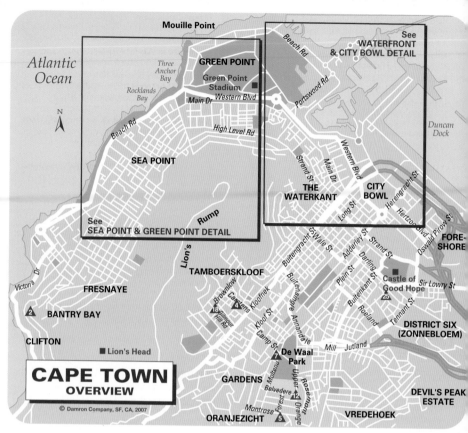

CAPE TOWN
OVERVIEW

© Damron Company, SF, CA, 2007

Atlantic Ocean

Mouille Point

GREEN POINT

Green Point Stadium

Main Dr   Western Blvd

High Level Rd

Three Anchor Bay

Rocklands Bay

Beach Rd

SEA POINT

See
SEA POINT & GREEN POINT DETAIL

Rump

Lion's

TAMBOERSKLOOF

FRESNAYE

BANTRY BAY

CLIFTON

Lion's Head

Victori's

GARDENS

ORANJEZICHT

See
WATERFRONT & CITY BOWL DETAIL

Beach Rd

Portswood Rd

Western Blvd

Duncan Dock

THE WATERKANT   CITY BOWL

Strand St   Main Dr   Western Blvd

Long St   Herengracht St

Hertzog Blvd   Oswald Pirow St

FORE-SHORE

Buitengracht St   Wale St

Adderley St   Strand St

Plein St   Darling St

Buitensingle   Annandale

Brownlow   Carstens   Kloofnek

Fillmour   Kloof St

Buitenkant St   Roeland

Camp St

Castle of Good Hope   Sir Lowry St

Tennant St

DISTRICT SIX
(ZONNEBLOEM)

De Waal Park

Molteno

Belvedere   Upper Orange

Rosemont

Mill   Jutland

VREDEHOEK

DEVIL'S PEAK ESTATE

Montrose   Forest

Newlands Guest House [GS,SW,NS,GO]
27–(0)21/686–0013,
27–(0)83/251–7274 (cell) ■ 4 Alcis Rd,
Newlands ■ in old Cape homestead, full
brkfst ■ www.newlandsguest.co.za

2 O on Kloof [GS,SW,WI]
27–21/439–2081 ■ 92 Kloof Rd (Bantry
Bay) ■ boutique hotel ■
www.oonkloof.co.za

21 Oceantide Apartments [GS,SW,GO]
27–(0)21/433–0303,
27–(0)82/670–4317 ■ 38 London Rd
(Sea Point) ■ self-catering apts ■
www.oceantide.co.za

4 Parker Cottage [GF,GO]
27–(0)21/424–6445,
27–(0)83/702–5743 (cell) ■ 3 Carstens
St (Tamboerskloof) ■ B&B in restored
Victorian ■ www.parkercottage.co.za

22 Romney Park Luxury Suites &
Wellness Centre [GF,SW,WC]
27–(0)21/439–4555 ■ corner of Hill Rd
& Romney Rd (at Highlevel Rd, Green
Point) ■ sea-facing suites, private
terraces, kids ok, also wellness center ■
www.romneypark.co.za

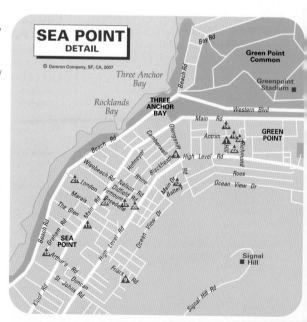

SEA POINT
DETAIL

© Damron Company, SF, CA, 2007

Bay Rd

Green Point Common

Greenpoint Stadium

Three Anchor Bay

Rocklands Bay

THREE ANCHOR BAY

Beach Rd

Western Blvd

GREEN POINT

Main Rd

Antrim

Hill

Richmond

Roos

Ocean View Dr

Glengariff   Camberwell

Holmeyer   High Level Rd

Blackheath   Rhine

Beach Rd

Wisebeach Rd   Nelson Rd

London   Oldfield

Finmount

Rosedene

Main Dr   Battery

Marais

The Glen   Main Rd

Graham Rd

SEA POINT

Arthur's Rd

Kloof Rd

St Johns Rd

Duncan

Friars Rd

Ocean View Dr

Signal Hill

Signal Hill Rd

23 **Rosedene Lodge** [GS,SW,WI] 27–21/439-7037 ■ 3 Rosedene Rd (Sea Point) ■ *full brkfst* ■ www.rosedenelodge.com
Seamount Cottages [GS] 27–21/782-4040 ■ 304 Main Rd (Clovelly Rd), Kalk Bay ■ *2-bdrm fully equipped self-catering seaside cottages, 40 minutes to Cape Town* ■ www.seamountcottages.co.za

24 **Sir Francis** [GS,SW] 27–21/439-3434 ■ 34 High Level Rd (Green Point) ■ *near gay area* ■ www.sirfrancis.co.za
Steenberg Hotel [GF,SW,NS,WI,WC] 27–21/713-2222 ■ Steenberg Estate (corner of Steenberg & Tokai) ■ *five star hotel on historic wine farm in foothills of Stone Mtns* ■ www.steenberghotel.com

25 **Sunset House Greyton** [GS,WC,GO] 27–28/254-9895, 27–82/778-0070 (cell) ■ 19 Caledon St (Greyton) ■ *self-catering cottage w/ outdoor French kitchen, private courtyard & spectacular mountain views, fully equipped* ■ www.sunsethousegreyton.co.za
The Twelve Apostles Hotel [GS,SW,WC,GO] 27–(0)21/437-9000 ■ Victoria Rd, Camps Bay ■ *5-star hotel* ■ www.12apostleshotel.com

26 **Verona Lodge** [GF] 27–(0)21/434-9477 ■ 11 Richmond Rd (Three Anchor Bay) ■ *guesthouse close to Clifton, beaches & Table Rock, full brkfst* ■ www.veronalodge.co.za
Villa Exner [GF,SW,NS] 27–(0)21/859-3596, 27–(0)21/859-7440 ■ 11 Essenhout Ave, Grabouw ■ *close to Cape Town, 5-star comforts* ■ www.villaexner.com

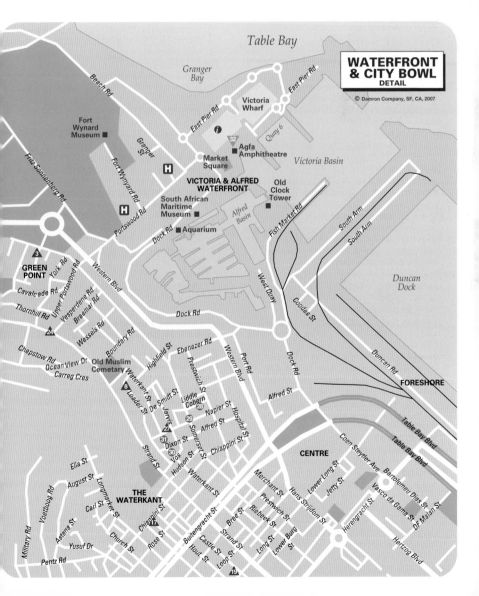

27 **Village Lodge** [GS,SW,WI] 27–21/421–1106 ■ 49 Napier ■ *upscale accommodations in the Village* ■ www.thevil-lagelodge.com

BARS

28 **Bar Code** [★MO,L,V] 27–(0)21/421–5305 ■ 18 Cobern Rd (at Somerset Rd, Green Point) ■ *9pm-1am, 10pm-3am Fri-Sat, darkroom* ■ info@leatherbar.co.za

29 **Bronx Action Bar** [★M,D,K] 27–(0)21/419–9216 ■ 35 Somerset Rd (Napier St, Green Point) ■ *8pm-late, cruisy, [K] Mon* ■ www.bronx.co.za

30 **Cafe Manhattan** [★MW,F,C,GO] 27–(0)21/421–6666 ■ 74 Waterkant St (at Napier) ■ *mixed crowd in daytime, mostly men at night, longest standing gay-owned/ run venue in Cape Town* ■ www.manhattan.co.za

29 **Cruz** [M,D,E,C] 27–21/425–4010 ■ 21 Somerset Rd (Green Point) ■ *8pm-4am* ■ www.cruzcapetown.co.za

19 **M-Bar & Lounge** [GS,D] 27–21/424–7247 ■ 38 Long St (at Metropole Hotel) ■ *noon-late* ■ www.metropolehotel.co.za

22 **Rosie's** [M,NH,B] 27–21/421–6666 ■ 125-A Waterkant St (Green Point) ■ *small pool bar*

31 **Spartacus** [MO,V] 27–21/447–0982 ■ 89 Roodebloem Rd ■ *from 6pm Tue-Sun, dark room, hustlers*

Stargayzer [MW] 27–83/269–3236 ■ 12 Caxton St (Parow) ■ *9pm-close Wed & Fri-Sat only*

NIGHTCLUBS

Aqua [M,D] 27–82/732–2199 ■ corner of York Rd & Prince Alfred St (Port Elizabeth) ■ *8pm-late Wed & Fri-Sat* ■ www.clubaqua.co.za

Brenda's Bash [W,D] 083/250–1195 ■ Koeberg Rd (Theo Marais Park) ■ *monthly women's dance parties*

29 **Lush** [W,D] 082/565–6174 ■ 27 Somerset Rd (at Sliver Upstairs, off Naiper St) ■ *women's dance party every other Sat* ■ www.lushcapetown.co.za

29 **Sliver** [MW,D] 27–(0)72/400–3183, 083/444–4441 ■ 27 Somerset Rd (at Napier St, Green Point) ■ *10pm-4am Fri, midnight-6am Sat, lounge, patio*

RESTAURANTS

Andiamo 27–21/421–3687, 27–21/421–3688 ■ Cape Quater, 72 Waterkant St ■ *9am-10:30pm, till 11pm Wed-Sat, Italian* ■ nicci@capequater.co.za

Balducci's 27–21/421–6002 ■ V&A Waterfront #6162 ■ *9am-11pm, Italian & sushi, also full bar* ■ www.balduccis.co.za

Beluga 27–21/418–2948 ■ The Foundry, Prestwich St (Green Point) ■ *seafood & grill* ■ www.beluga.co.za

Cafe Bardeli 27–21/423–4444 ■ Longkloof Studios, Darters Rd ■ *deli & cocktails*

Cafe Erte [★GO] 27–(0)21/434–6624 ■ 265-a Main Rd (Sea Point) ■ *10am-4am nightly, restaurant & coffee bar, vegetarian, internet access, lesbian-run* ■ www.cafeerte.com

Cafe Paradiso 27–21/423–8653 ■ 110 Kloof St ■ *9:30am-11pm, from noon Mon, Mediterranean* ■ www.cafeparadiso.co.za

Don Pedro's 27–(0)21/447–0482 ■ 113 Roodebloem Rd (Woodstock) ■ *7:30pm till late nightly, Mediterranean, full bar*

Five Flies 27–21/424–4442 ■ 14-16 Keerom St ■ *upscale dining, also cigar lounge & wine bar* ■ www.fiveflies.co.za

Lola's [GO] 27–(0)21/423–0885 ■ 228 Long St (at Buiten St) ■ *vegetarian retro diner*

Madame Zingara 27–(0)21/426–2458 ■ 192 Loop St ■ *dinner only, clsd Sun, Italian/ Mediterranean, glamorous bohemian atmosphere*

L' Orient [GO] 27–(0)21/439–6572 ■ 50 Main Rd (Three Anchor Bay) ■ *6:30pm-10:30pm, clsd Sun, Malaysian & Indonesian* ■ lorient@mweb.co.za

Tank 27–(0)21/419–0007 ■ 72 Waterkant St (Cape Quarter) ■ *trendy retro joint w/ bar, int'l* ■ www.the-tank.co.za

Veranda 27–21/424–7247 ■ 38 Long St (at Metropole Hotel) ■ *stylish, modern South African* ■ www.metropolehotel.co.za

ENTERTAINMENT & RECREATION
Clifton 3rd Beach ■ *popular gay beach*

Mother City Queer Project 27–(0)21/426–5709 ■ *huge costume party, December* ■ www.mcqp.co.za

On Broadway [★F,DS,R,WC] 27–(0)21/424–1194 ■ 88 Shortmarket St, Green Point ■ *7pm-close, dinner cabaret* ■ www.onbroadway.co.za

BOOKSTORES
32 **Exclusive Books** 27–(0)21/419–0905 ■ V&A Waterfront #6160 ■ *9am-10:30pm, till 9pm Sun, general bookstore, gay/ lesbian section, many locations throughout South Africa* ■ www.exclusivebooks.com

PUBLICATIONS
Exit Newspaper 27–(0)21/622–2275 ■ *South Africa's monthly lgbt newspaper* ■ www.exit.co.za

GYMS & HEALTH CLUBS
Virgin Active [★] 27–(0)21/434–0750 ■ Bill Peters Dr (Green Point) ■ *many locations throughout South Africa* ■ www.virginactive.co.za

MEN'S CLUBS
The Hot House [F,V] 27–(0)21/418–3888 ■ 18 Jarvis St (at Napier St, Green Point) ■ *24hrs wknds, maze, darkrooms, 2 bars & restaurant* ■ www.hothouse.co.za

The Pumphouse/ GHC [MO] 27–21/683–3493 ■ 91-93 Main Rd (at Vineyard)

EROTICA
Wet Warehouse 27–(0)21/419–0458 ■ 1 Sea St ■ *clsd Sun* ■ inn@telkomsa.net

Sydney

See Sydney detail map

ACCOMMODATIONS
1 **Altamont Boutique Hotel** [GF] 61–2/9360–6000 ■ 207 Darlinghurst Rd ■ www.altamont.com.au

2 **Apartment Hotel East Sydney** [GS,NS] 61/404–793–159 ■ 150 Liverpool St, E Sydney (at Oxford St) ■ *terrace & gourmet kitchen* ■ www.apartmenthotel.com.au

3 **Brickfield Hill B&B Inn** [GS,WI,GO] 61–2/9211–4886 ■ 403 Riley Street (at Foveaux), Surry Hills ■ *beautifully & carefully restored Victorian terrace-house in the gay Oxford St District, near beaches & downtown* ■ www.brickfieldhill.com.au

4 **Chelsea Guest House** [GS,NS,GO] 61–2/9380–5994 ■ 49 Womerah Ave (at Oswald Ln), Darlinghurst ■ *Victorian w/ Italianate courtyard* ■ www.chelsea.citysearch.com.au

5 **Citigate Sebel Sydney** [GF,SW,WC] 61-2/9213-3820, 800/024-231 ■ 28 Albion St (at Elizabeth, Surry Hills) ■ *4-star hotel near Oxford St, full brkfst, jacuzzi, kids ok* ■ www.mirvachotels.com.au

Echo Point Holiday Accommodation [GF,NS] 61-2/4782-3275 ■ 36 Echo Point Rd (at Cliff Drive), Katoomba ■ *rental villas & cottages (2-night minimum)* ■ www.echopointvillas.com.au

6 **Footprints Westend** [GF,NS,WC] 61-2/9211-4588, 1800/013-186 ■ 412 Pitt St ■ *budget/ backpacker's accommodations, activity programs, cafe (see overview map)* ■ www.footprintswestend.com.au

7 **Governors on Fitzroy B&B** [M,GO] 61-2/9331-4652 ■ 64 Fitzroy St, Surry Hills ■ *Victorian B&B, 3 blocks from Oxford St, full brkfst, hot tub, shared baths, garden* ■ www.governors.com.au

8 **Hotel Stellar** [MW,WI] 61-2/9264-9754 ■ 4 Wentworth Ave ■ *kitchenette in each room* ■ www.hotelstellar.com

SYDNEY

Sydney is one of the most popular LGBT travel destinations in the world—and with good reason. Its diversity of cultures and subcultures, great food, tolerant atmosphere, friendly people, and lovely weather draw visitors from all over the world. You'll find most of the lesbians and gay men in Darlinghurst and Kings Cross, especially along the main artery of Oxford Street. Women will also enjoy the cafes of Newtown and the dyke scene in Leichhardt.

And everyone will love the fact that Sydney is home to the biggest annual LGBT party in the Southern Hemisphere—Mardi Gras.

Tourist Info

AIRPORT DIRECTIONS

Sydney Airport. Served by Airport Link train and Airport Express bus. By car, take Rte 64 (South Dowling St) to Victoria St, Darlinghurst, and Kings Cross.

PUBLIC TRANSIT & TAXIS

Airport Express 61-2/131-500.
State Transit Authority 61-2/131-500, web: www.sta.nsw.gov.au.
Monorail 61-2/9285-5600, web: www.metrolightrail.com.au.

TOURIST SPOTS & INFO

Art Gallery of New South Wales 61-2/9225-1700.
Australian Museum 61-2/9320-6000, web: www.austmus.gov.au.
Bondi Beach.
Chinatown.
Darling Harbour.
Featherdale Wildlife Park 61-2/9622-1644, web: www.featherdale.com.au.
Manly beaches.
Museum of Contemporary Art 61-2/9245-2400, web: www.mca.com.au.
Queen Victoria Building 61-2/9264-9209, web: www.qvb.com.au.
The Rocks.
Royal Botanical Gardens 61-2/9231-8111, web: www.rbgsyd.gov.au.
Sydney Harbour Bridge.
Sydney Jewish Museum 61-2/9360-7999, web: sydneyjewishmuseum.com.au.
Sydney Opera House 61-2/9250-7111, web: www.sydneyoperahouse.com.
Visitor's Center: Sydney Tourist Information, web: www.discoversydney.com.au.
Sydney Visitors Centre, 61-2/9240-8788, web: www.sydneyvisitorscentre.com.

Weather

Temperate—in the 50°s-70°s year-round. The summer months (January-March) can get hot and humid. Spring (September-December) sees the least rain. It's sunny most of the year. Bring a hat and lots of sunscreen!

Best Views

From the AMP Centrepoint Tower or Mrs Macquarie's Chair.

City Calendar

LGBT PRIDE

June - Sydney Gay & Lesbian Pride. 61-2/9550-6188, web: www.pridecentre.com.au.

ANNUAL EVENTS

January - Sydney Festival, web: www.sydneyfestival.org.au.
February/March - Sydney Gay & Lesbian Mardi Gras Festival. Nearly a month of events and parties. 61-2/9568-8600, web: www.mardigras.org.au.
April - Sydney Leather Pride Week, web: www.sydneyleatherpride.org.
September - Manly Jazz Festival 61-2/9976-1500, web: www.manly.nsw.gov.au/manlyjazz.
October - Sleaze Ball 61-2/9568-8600.

Queer Resources

COMMUNITY INFO

Sydney PRIDE Centre 61-2/9550-6188. 104 Erskineville Rd, Erskineville, web: www.pridecentre.com.au.
Sydney Lesbian & Gay Line 61-2/9207-2800.

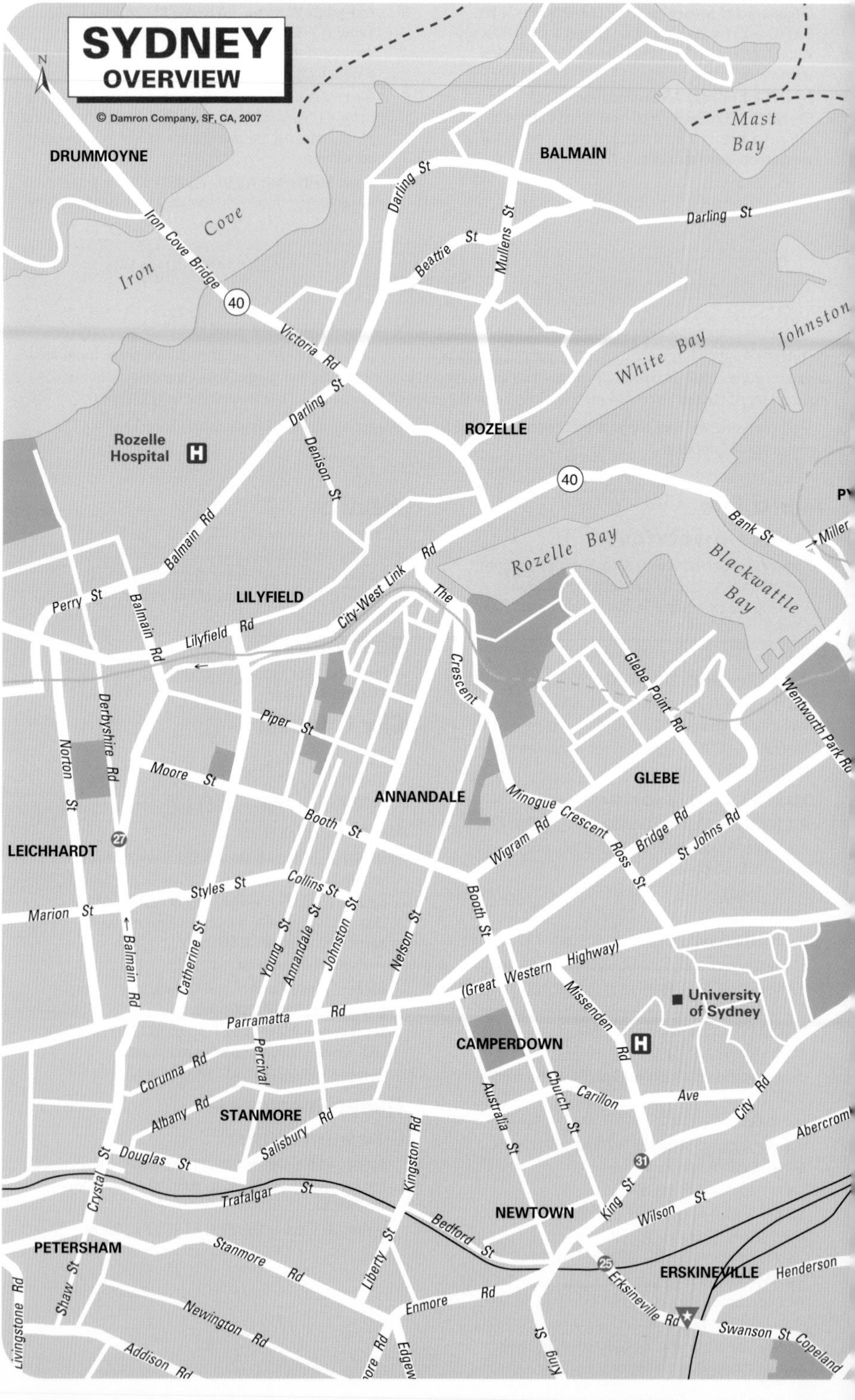

SYDNEY
OVERVIEW

© Damron Company, SF, CA, 2007

N

DRUMMOYNE

BALMAIN

Mast Bay

Iron Cove

Darling St

Beattie St

Mullens St

Darling St

Iron

Iron Cove Bridge

40

Victoria Rd

White Bay

Johnston

Darling St

Rozelle Hospital H

ROZELLE

Balmain Rd

Denison St

40

Rozelle Bay

Bank St

Miller

P

Blackwattle Bay

Perry St

Balmain Rd

LILYFIELD

City West Link Rd

The

Lilyfield Rd

Crescent

Glebe Point Rd

Wentworth Park Rd

Derbyshire Rd

Piper St

Moore St

ANNANDALE

GLEBE

Minogue Crescent

Wigram Rd

Ross St

Bridge Rd

St Johns Rd

Norton St

27

Booth St

LEICHHARDT

Styles St

Collins St

Booth St

Marion St

Catherine St

Young St

Annandale St

Johnston St

Nelson St

Baina Rd

(Great Western Highway)

Missenden

University of Sydney

Parramatta Rd

Corunna Rd

Percival Rd

CAMPERDOWN

H

Ave

City Rd

Albany Rd

STANMORE

Salisbury Rd

Kingston Rd

Australia St

Church St

Carillon

Abercrom

Douglas St

Crystal St

Trafalgar St

Bedford St

NEWTOWN

King St

Wilson St

31

PETERSHAM

Stanmore Rd

Liberty St

Enmore Rd

25

Erskineville Rd

ERSKINEVILLE

Henderson

Livingstone Rd

Shaw St

Newington Rd

Addison Rd

Edgew

Swanson St Copeland

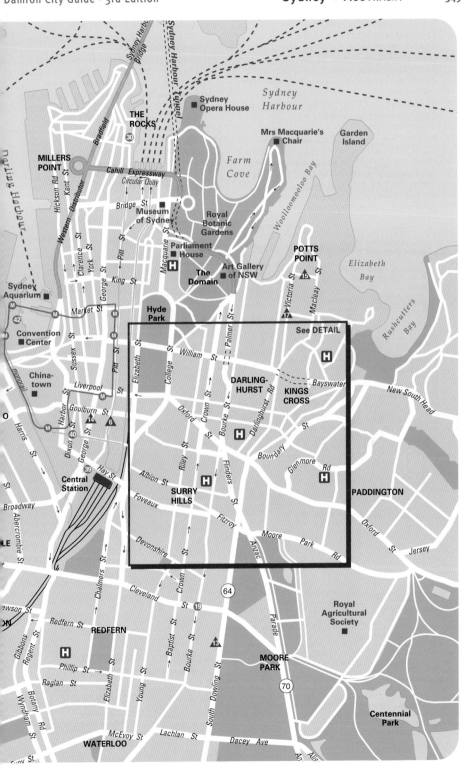

Sydney Harbour Bridge

Sydney Harbour Tunnel

Bradfield

THE ROCKS

Sydney Opera House

Sydney Harbour

Mrs Macquarie's Chair

Garden Island

MILLERS POINT

Hickson Rd
Kent St

Western Distributor

Cahill Expressway
Circular Quay

Farm Cove

Woolloomooloo Bay

Darling Harbour

Bridge St

Museum of Sydney

Royal Botanic Gardens

Clarence St
York St
George St
Pitt St
King St

Macquarie St

Parliament House

The Domain

Art Gallery of NSW

POTTS POINT

Victoria St
Macleay St

Elizabeth Bay

Rushcutters Bay

Sydney Aquarium

Market St

Hyde Park

See DETAIL

Convention Center

Sussex St
Pitt St

Elizabeth St

College St

William St

Palmer St

DARLING-HURST

KINGS CROSS

Bayswater

Darlinghurst Rd

New South Head

China-town

Liverpool St

Harris St

Harbor St

Goulburn St

Dixon St
George St

Oxford St
Crown St
Riley St
Bourke St

Flinders St

Boundary St

Glenmore Rd

PADDINGTON

Central Station

Hay St

Albion St

SURRY HILLS

Foveaux St

Fitzroy St

Moore Park Rd

Oxford St
Jersey

Broadway

Abercrombie St

Devonshire St

Anzac Pde

64

19

Royal Agricultural Society

Cleveland St

Crown St

Chalmers St

Baptist St

Bourke St

South Dowling St

Parade

MOORE PARK

70

REDFERN

Redfern St

Gibbons St
Regent St
Phillip St
Raglan St

Elizabeth St

Young St

Centennial Park

Botany Rd
Wyndham St

McEvoy St

Lachlan St

Dacey Ave

WATERLOO

9   **Kirketon Boutique Hotel** [GF,WI] 61-2/9332-2011 ◼ 229 Darlinghurst Rd ◼ *also restaurant & bars, kids ok* ◼ www.kirketon.com.au

10   **Manor House Boutique Hotel** [GS,F,SW,NS,WI] 61-2/9380-6633 ◼ 86 Flinders St, Darlinghurst ◼ *terrace mansion, also Lush restaurant & cocktail bar* ◼ www.manor-house.com.au

11   **Medusa** [GF,WI] 61-2/9331-1000 ◼ 267 Darlinghurst Rd, Darlinghurst ◼ *modern boutique hotel* ◼ www.medusa.com.au

12   **Oasis on Flinders** [MO,N,GO] 61-2/9331-8791 ◼ 106 Flinders St, Darlinghurst ◼ *B&B in 3-story Victorian for gay naturist men, hot tub, gym* ◼ www.oasisonflinders.com.au

13   **Park Lodge Hotel** [MW,GO] 61-2/9318-2393 ◼ 747 S Dowling St (near Cleveland St), Moore Park ◼ *"Sydney's friendliest gay-owned & operated 3-star boutique hotel" (see overview map)* ◼ www.parklodgesydney.com

14   **Pensione Hotel** [GF] 61-2/9265-8888, 800/885-886 ◼ 631-635 George St ◼ *also restaurant & bar* ◼ www.pensione.com.au

15   **Simpsons of Potts Point** [GS] 61-2/9356-2199 ◼ 8 Challis Ave, Potts Point ◼ *circa 1892 restored mansion (see overview map)* ◼ www.simpsonshotel.com

16   **Sydney Star Accommodation** [GS] 61-2/9358-1445 ◼ 273-275 Darlinghurst Rd (at Liverpool), Darlinghurst ◼ *stylish & private, in heart of colorful Darlinghurst* ◼ www.sydneystar.com.au

17   **Victoria Court Hotel Sydney** [GF] 61-2/9357-3200, 1800/630-505 (in Australia) ◼ 122 Victoria St (at Orwell) ◼ *historic boutique hotel in elegant Victorian, full brkfst (see overview map)* ◼ www.victoriacourt.com.au

18   **Wattle Hotel** [GF] 61-2/9332-4118 ◼ 108 Oxford St (at Palmer St, Darlinghurst) ◼ *boutique hotel in heart of Oxford St, also restaurant & bar* ◼ www.sydneywattle.com

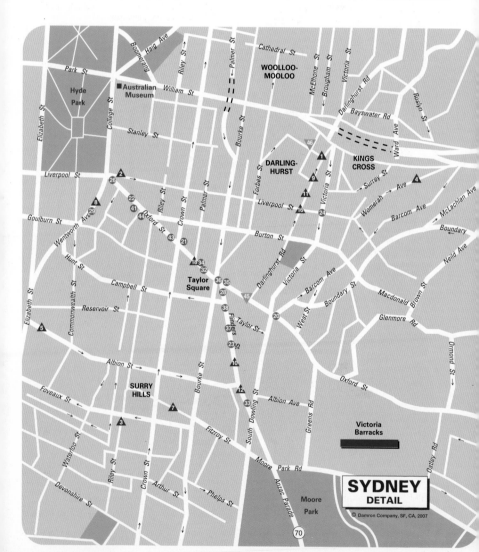

SYDNEY DETAIL

© Damron Company, SF, CA, 2007

BARS

19   **Bar Cleveland/ Hershey Bar** [GS,A,YC] 61-2/9698-1908 ■ 443 Cleveland St (at Bourke), Surry Hills ■ *11am-4am, noon-midnight Sun, cocktail lounge, DJ (see overview map)*

20   **The Beauchamp** [★GS,NH,GO] 61-2/9331-2575 ■ 267 Oxford St, Darlinghurst ■ *noon-midnight, till 2am wknds; pronounced "Bee-chum"*

21   **The Colombian** [★MW,D] 61-2/9360-2151 ■ 117 Oxford St (Darlinghurst) ■ *10am-4am, till 5am Fri, till 6am Sat, trendy pub & cocktail bar*

22   The Exchange/ Phoenix [MW,D,DS] 61-2/9331-2956 ■ 34 Oxford St, Darlinghurst ■ *10am-5am, till 7am Fri-Sun, clsd Mon-Tue, 3 bars: main bar [GS]; Lizard Lounge upstairs, cocktails; more gay downstairs in Phoenix [D,$], cruisy*

23   **Flinders** [MW,D,S,YC] 61-2/9360-4929 ■ 63-65 Flinders St, Darlinghurst ■ *popular late, strippers, more women 1st Fri for Les-Deluxe* ■ www.flindershotel.com

24   **Green Park Hotel** [GS] 61-2/9380-5311 ■ 360 Victoria St (at Liverpool), Darlinghurst ■ *10am-2am, noon-midnight Sun, very gay Sun, stylish bar*

25   **The Imperial Hotel** [MW,D,F,DS,S] 61-2/9519-9899 ■ 35 Erskineville Rd, Newtown ■ *open late, 3 bars: main bar popular w/ women; cruisy dance bar downstairs [M]; back bar [GS,D] is the home of "Priscilla" (see overview map)* ■ www.theimperialhotel.com.au

26   Lava Bar [★GS,S] 61-2/9331-3066 ■ 2 Oxford St (top flr of Burdekin Hotel), Darlinghurst ■ *popular w/ lesbians Fri*

27   Leichhardt Hotel [W,NH,F] 61-2/9569-1217 ■ Balmain Road (at Short St, Leichhardt) ■ *10am-midnight, noon-10pm Sun-Mon (see overview map)*

28   **Manacle** [M,B,L] 61-2/9331-2950 ■ 1 Patterson Ln (at Taylor Square Hotel, enter on Patterson), Darlinghurst ■ *8pm-late Th-Sun, 7am-4pm Sun-Mon for Bent, big, cruisy butch bar* ■ www.manacle.com.au

29   **Mars Lounge** [GS,D,F] 61-2/9267-6440 ■ 16 Wentworth Ave ■ *5pm-midnight, till 3am Th-Fri, 7pm-3am Sat, 7pm-1am Sun, clsd Mon-Tue, more gay Sun for Flash* ■ www.marslounge.com.au

30   **Mr. Mary's** [MW,D,DS] 61-2/9690-0610 ■ 106-110 George St (at Redfern St)

31   **The Newtown Hotel** [MW,NH,F,DS,P] 61-2/9557-1329 ■ 174 King St (near Missenden, Newtown) ■ *10am-midnight, till 10pm Sun, also restaurant (see overview map)*

32   **The Oxford** [★MW,L,TG,OC] 61-2/9331-3467 ■ 134 Oxford St (at Taylor Square), Darlinghurst ■ *24hrs, 3 bars: main bar cruise bar & gaming lounge w/ DJ; Gilligans, 5pm-late daily, [B] Fri; Ginger's lounge, trendy cocktail bar w/ DJ*

33   **The Palace Hotel** [GS,D,YC] 61-2/9361-5170 ■ 122 Flinders St (at S Dowling St) ■ *4pm-1am*

34   **The Palms On Oxford** [DS,P] 61-2/9357-4166 ■ 124 Oxford St, Darlinghurst ■ *8pm-late, clsd Mon-Tue, piano lounge & drag shows*

35   **Sol's Deck Bar** [GS,D,F,E] 61-2/9360-8868 ■ 191 Oxford St (at Flinders St) ■ *live music Sun-Th, more women Fri for Bitch* ■ www.solsdeckbar.net.au

36   **The Stonewall** [★M,D,K,DS,S] 61-2/9360-1963 ■ 175 Oxford St, Darlinghurst ■ *11am-6am, pub downstairs, cocktail lounge 2nd flr, dance club 3rd flr, [K] Tue, male dancers, patio* ■ www.stonewallhotel.com

37   **The Taxi Club** [M,D,TG,F,K,DS,PC,$] 61-2/9331-4256 ■ 40-42 Flinders St (at Grosvenor Club), Darlinghurst ■ *24hrs, [K] Th, [DS] Sun* ■ taxiclub.citysearch.com.au

NIGHTCLUBS

38   ARQ [★M,D,F,DS,$] 61-2/9380-8700 ■ 16 Flinders St (at Taylor Square), Darlinghurst ■ *11pm-6am, 9pm-late Th-Sun, [DS] Th* ■ www.arqsydney.com.au

    Diamonds & Pearls [MW,D,DS,$] 61-4/3323-2425 (cell), 61-2/9825-3300 (Moorebank Sports Club) ■ Heathcote Rd (at Moorebank Sports Club), Hammondville ■ *8pm-2am, monthly dance party* ■ www.diamondsandpearls1.zoomshare.com

39   **Gas Nightclub/ Bohem Lounge** [GS,D] 61-2/9211-3038 ■ 477 Pitt St, Haymarket ■ *3 bars, 4 lounges, stylish (see overview map)*

40   **Golden Palace Hotel** [GS,D,K,DS] 61-2/9281-0821 ■ 68 Dixon St, Haymarket ■ *9am-4am, more gay Sun for Gaymarket* ■ www.goldenpalacehotel.com.au

41   **Hellfire** [GS,D,A,L,E,S,$] 61-2/9380-9244 ■ 16-18 Oxford Square (on corner of Riley, at Rogues), Darlinghurst ■ *9:30pm-late 3rd Fri, fetish party, live shows (see overview map)* ■ www.hellfiresydney.com

42   **Home** [★GF,D,$] 61-2/9266-0600 ■ Cockle Bay Wharf (Darling Harbour) ■ *open Fri-Sun, hosts Homesexual (see overview map)* ■ www.homesydney.com

43   **The Midnight Shift** [★M,D,V] 61-2/9360-4319 ■ 85 Oxford St, Darlinghurst ■ *10pm-late Fri-Sat, video bar downstairs, dance bar upstairs* ■ www.themidnightshift.com

44   **Slide** [MW,D,F,E,C] 41 Oxford St ■ *6pm-3am, 5pm-4am Fri, 7pm-4am Sat-Sun, clsd Mon-Tue* ■ www.slide.com.au

CAFES

    Cafe Sopra [★] 61-2/9699-3174 ■ 7 Danks St ■ *10am-3pm, from 8am Sat, clsd Sun-Mon, Italian vegetarian*

    Coffee, Tea or Me? 61-2/9331-3452 ■ 536 Crown St

    Numero Uno Coffee 61-2/8399-0111 ■ 63 Nickson St ■ *bean roaster* ■ www.numerouno.com.au

    Victoire 61-2/9818-5529 ■ 285 Darling St ■ *great bread*

    Vinyl Lounge Cafe [MW,F] 61-2/9326-9224 ■ 17 Elizabeth Bay Rd, Elizabeth Bay ■ *7am-4pm, from 8am wknds, clsd Mon, light menu, plenty veggie, cash only*

RESTAURANTS

    Bentley Restaurant & Bar 61-2/9332-2344 ■ 320 Crown St ■ *tapas & small plates, excellent wine*

    Bertoni Casalinga 61-2/9818-5845 ■ 281 Darling St ■ *6:30am-7:30pm, till 7pm Sat, 7:30am-6:30pm Sun, Italian*

    Betty's Soup Kitchen [MW] 61-2/9360-9698 ■ 84 Oxford St, Darlinghurst ■ *noon-11pm, till midnight Fri-Sat, healthy homecooking, plenty veggie*

    Bills Surry Hills 61-2/9360-4762 ■ 359 Crown St ■ *7am-10pm, great ricotta pancakes* ■ www.bills.com.au

    Billy Kwong [★R,WC] 61-2/9332-3300 ■ 3/355 Crown St ■ *Chinese*

    Bird Cow Fish 61-2/9380-4090 ■ 500 Crown St ■ *8am-10pm, till 5pm Sun, bistro & espresso bar* ■ www.birdcow-fish.com.au

    The Boathouse on Blackwattle Bay [R] 61-2/9518-9011 ■ End of Ferry Road (Glebe) ■ *lunch & dinner Tue-Sun, gourmet seafood, some veggie, great view* ■ www.boathouse.net.au

    Cafe Comity [GO] 61-2/9331-2424 ■ 139 Oxford St (at Crown) ■ *10am-late, Mediterranean, full bar* ■ comity@ozemail.com.au

    Chu Bay 61-2/9331-3386 ■ 312a Bourke St, Darlinghurst ■ *5:30pm-11pm, Vietnamese, some veggie*

Danks Street Depot 61-2/9698-2201 ▪ 2 Danks St ▪ *great brkfst*

Fu Manchu [NS] 61-2/9360-9424 ▪ 249 Victoria St, Darlinghurst ▪ *lunch & dinner, chic noodle bar, plenty veggie, cash only*

Iku Wholefood Kitchen [NS] 61-2/9692-8720 ▪ 25a Glebe Point Rd, Glebe ▪ *lunch & dinner, creative vegan/ macrobiotic fare, outdoor seating*

Lo Studio 61-2/9212-4118 ▪ 53-55 Brisbane St (upper ground flr) ▪ *noon-3pm Mon-Fri & 6pm-11pm Mon-Sat, clsd Sun, Italian* ▪ www.lostudio.com.au

Pink Peppercorn [GO] 61-2/9360-9922 ▪ 122 Oxford St (near Taylor Square, Darlinghurst) ▪ *6pm-10:30pm, Laotian & Thai*

Ristorante Riva [NS] 61-2/9380-5318 ▪ 379 Liverpool St, Darlinghurst ▪ *lunch & dinner, northern Italian, seafood, some veggie, full bar*

Sean's Panorama 61-2/9365-4924 ▪ 270 Campbell Parade, Bondi Beach Austria ▪ *lunch Sat-Sun, dinner Wed-Sat, clsd Mon-Tue* ▪ www.seanspanaroma.com.au

Sojourn 61-2/9555-9764 ▪ 79 Darling St ▪ *European*

Thai Kanteen [★GO] 61-2/9960-3282 ▪ 541 Military Rd, Mosman ▪ *lunch Th-Fri, dinner Tue-Sun, clsd Mon, modern Thai* ▪ www.thaikanteen.com.au

Thai Pothong 61-2/9550-6277 ▪ 294 King St (Newtown) ▪ *lunch Tue-Sun, dinner nightly* ▪ www.thaipothong.com.au

Yipiyiyo [MW,C,GO] 61-2/9332-3114 ▪ 209 Crown St, Darlinghurst ▪ *6:30pm-10pm, till 11pm Fri-Sat, Tex-Mex/ Mediterranean* ▪ www.yipiyiyo.com.au

ENTERTAINMENT & RECREATION

Sydney by Diva 61-2/9360-5557 ▪ departs from Oxford Hotel (in Taylor Square, Darlinghurst) ▪ *5pm-8pm Sun, tour Sydney w/ drag queen host* ▪ www.sydneybydiva.com

Sydney Gay/ Lesbian Mardi Gras 61-2/9568-8600 ▪ 297-299 Trafalgar St, Petersham 2049 ▪ *the wildest party under the rainbow on this planet* ▪ www.mardigras.org.au

BOOKSTORES

45 **The Bookshop Darlinghurst** 61-2/9331-1103 ▪ 207 Oxford St (near Darlinghurst Rd), Darlinghurst ▪ *10am-10pm, till 11pm Th, till midnight Fri-Sat, 11am-11pm Sun, Australia's oldest LGBT magazine, videos, DVDs, staff happy to help w/ tourist info* ▪ www.thebookshop.com.au

Gertrude & Alice 61-2/9130-5155 ▪ 40 Hall St (Bondi Beach) ▪ *second-hand books, also coffee shop*

46 **LOTL** 61-2/9332-2725 ▪ 24A Rosebank St, Darlinghurst ▪ *7am-6pm, 8am-1pm Sat, clsd Sun, LGBT cafe & bookstore*

PUBLICATIONS

DNA 61-2/9764-0200, 888/263-2624 (US #) ▪ *monthly gay men's magazine* ▪ www.dnamagazine.com.au

LOTL Magazine 61-2/9332-2725 ▪ *LOTL stands for Lesbians on the Loose, monthly magazine* ▪ www.lotl.com

SX Weekly 61-2/9360-8934 ▪ *free gay/ lesbian weekly* ▪ www.sxnews.com.au

Sydney Star Observer 61-2/8263-0500 ▪ *weekly newspaper w/ club & event listings* ▪ www.ssonet.com.au

GYMS & HEALTH CLUBS

Bayswater Fitness 61-2/9356-2555 ▪ 33 Bayswater Rd, Kings Cross ▪ *6am-midnight, till 11pm Fri, 7am-10pm Sat, 7am-9pm Sun* ▪ www.bayswaterfitness.com.au

City Gym 61-2/9360-6247 ▪ 107-113 Crown St ▪ *day passes available* ▪ www.citygym.com.au

MEN'S CLUBS

Bodyline Spa & Sauna [★V] 61-2/9360-1006 ▪ 10 Taylo St (off Flinders), Darlinghurst ▪ *24hrs wknds, jacuzzi, sauna, steam, cabins, sundeck* ▪ www.bodylinesydney.com

Headquarters [V] 61-2/9331-6217 ▪ 273 Crown St (near Oxford), Darlinghurst ▪ *24hrs, theme rooms, theme nights* ▪ www.headquarters.com.au

Ken's at Kensington [SW,18+] 61-2/9662-1359 ▪ 83 Anzac Parade, Kensington ▪ *24hrs wknds, steam, sauna, spa & gym*

Kingsteam 61-2/9360-3431, 61-2/8250-1818 (info line) ▪ 38-42 Oxford St (next to Exchange Hotel), Darlinghurst ▪ *24hrs wknds, small sauna, spa, steam & gym* ▪ www.kingsteam.com

Newtown Basement 61-2/9516-3997 ▪ 304 King St (Newtown)

Signal [V] 61-2/9331-8830 ▪ at Riley & Arnold Sts (upstairs), Darlinghurst ▪ *theme nights* ▪ www.signal-house.com.au

Sydney City Steam 61-2/9267-6766 ▪ 357 Sussex (Darling Harbour) ▪ *10am-6pm, 24hrs wknds* ▪ www.sydneycitysteam.com.au

Urge [F,V,PC] 61-2/9332-3402 ▪ 97 Oxford St (at Crown), Darlinghurst ▪ *24hrs wknds*

SEX CLUBS

Aarows [MW,TG,18+,N] 61-2/9638-0553 ▪ 17 Bridge St, Rydalmere ▪ *24hrs* ▪ www.aarows.com.au

EROTICA

Numbers [GO] 61-2/9331-6099 ▪ 95 Oxford St (next to Midnight Shift) ▪ *24hrs, leather, videos, books, toys, cruisy*

Pleasure Chest 61-2/9356-3640 ▪ 161 Oxford St, Darlinghurst ▪ *24hrs; also 56 Darlinghurst Rd, Kings Cross* ▪ www.pleasurechest.com.au

The Probe [S] 61-2/9361-5924 ▪ 159 Oxford St, upstairs, Darlinghurst ▪ *2-flr sauna, also shop*

Sax Fetish [GO] 61-2/9331-6105 ▪ 110a Oxford St (Taylor Square) ▪ *leather & fetish, clothing, accessories, toys* ▪ saxfetish.com

Toolshed 61-2/9332-2792 ▪ 81 Oxford St, Darlinghurst ▪ *clothing, fetishgear, toys, pride items & more; 191 Oxford St, Taylor Square (61-2/9360-1100)* ▪ www.toolshed.com.au